COP 1

A 11701 621520

D1034435

THE OXFORD CONCISE CONCORDANCE

TO THE REVISED STANDARD VERSION OF THE

HOLY BIBLE

. . .

COMPILED BY

BRUCE M. METZGER AND ISOBEL M. METZGER

Kern County Free Library
Bakersfield, California

R 220. 2

NEW YORK

OXFORD UNIVERSITY PRESS

1962

COP 1

© 1962, BY OXFORD UNIVERSITY PRESS, INC.

Excerpts from the REVISED STANDARD VERSION OF THE BIBLE, Old Testament
Section copyright 1952, New Testament Section copyright 1946,
by Division of Christian Education of the National Council of
the Churches of Christ in the United States of America.

PRINTED IN THE UNITED STATES OF AMERICA

FOREWORD

THIS CONCORDANCE is intended to meet the needs of the general reader of the Bible. Within the limits of the space available, those nouns, verbs, adjectives, and adverbs were chosen for inclusion which will be of interest to a variety of users. In the selection of context lines containing these words, preference was given to passages which are intrinsically significant or which, for some other reason, can be regarded as noteworthy. Proper names, instead of standing in a separate list, are included in alphabetical order within the concordance itself, thus facilitating their consultation. References to many of the more important persons and places mentioned in the Bible are set forth in the form of brief digests of salient biographical or geographical details.

ABBREVIATIONS

Acts	The Acts of the Apostles	Jude	Jude
Am.	Amos	1 Kg.	1 Kings
1 Chr.	1 Chronicles	2 Kg.	2 Kings
2 Chr.	2 Chronicles	Lam.	Lamentations
Col.	Colossians	Lev.	Leviticus
1 Cor.	1 Corinthians	Lk.	Luke
2 Cor.	2 Corinthians	Mal.	Malachi
Dan.	Daniel	Mic.	Micah
Dt.	Deuteronomy	Mk.	Mark
Ec.	Ecclesiastes	Mt.	Matthew
Eph.	Ephesians	Nah.	Nahum
Est.	Esther	Neh.	Nehemiah
Ex.	Exodus	Num.	Numbers
Ezek.	Ezekiel	Ob.	Obadiah
Ezra	Ezra	1 Pet.	1 Peter
Gal.	Galatians	2 Pet.	2 Peter
Gen.	Genesis	Phil.	Philippians
Hab.	Habakkuk	Philem.	Philemon
Hag.	Haggai	Pr.	Proverbs
Heb.	Hebrews	Ps.	Psalms
Hos.	Hosea	Rev.	Revelation
Is.	Isaiah	Rom.	Romans
Jas.	James	Ru.	Ruth
Jer.	Jeremiah	1 Sam.	1 Samuel
Jg.	Judges	2 Sam.	2 Samuel
Jl.	Joel	S. of S.	Song of Solomon
Jn.	John	1 Th.	1 Thessalonians
1 Jn.	1 John	2 Th.	2 Thessalonians
2 Jn.	2 John	1 Tim.	1 Timothy
3 Jn.	3 John	2 Tim.	2 Timothy
Job	Job	Tit.	Titus
Jon.	Jonah	Zech.	Zechariah
Jos.	Joshua	Zeph.	Zephaniah

CONCORDANCE

AARON

appointed to be Moses' spokesman, Ex.4.14–16, 27; appeals to Pharaoh, Ex.5.1,4; his rod becomes a serpent, Ex.7.10; changes water into blood, Ex.7.20; causes the plagues of frogs, lice, flies, Ex.8.5, 17, 24; with Hur holds up Moses' hands, Ex.17.12; set apart for priest's office, Ex.28; makes the golden calf, Ex.32.4; his excuse to Moses, Ex.32.22; consecration, Ex.29; Lev.8; speaks against Moses, Num.12.1; his rod sprouted, and is kept in ark for a token, Num.17.8; Heb.9.4; for unbelief excluded from the promised land, Num.20.12; dies on Mount Hor, Num.20.28

ABASE

God *a*. the proud, but he saves	Job 22.29
a. that which is high	Ezek.21.26
who walk in pride he is able to *a*.	Dan.4.37
I know how to be *a*., and I	Phil.4.12

ABEDNEGO

Dan.1.7; 2.49; 3.12–30

ABEL

second son of Adam, Gen.4.2; his offering accepted, Gen.4.4; slain by Cain, Gen.4.8; righteous, Mt.23.35; 1 Jn.3.12; blood of, Lk. 11.51; Heb.12.24; faith of, Heb.11.4

ABHOR

All my intimate friends *a*. me	Job 19.19
I hate and *a*. falsehood	Ps.119.163
who *a*. justice and pervert all	Mic.3.9
You who *a*. idols, do you rob . . . ?	Rom.2.22

ABIDE

shall not *a*. in man for ever	Gen.6.3
their heritage will *a*. for ever	Ps.37.18
my hand shall ever *a*. with him	Ps.89.21
who *a*. in the shadow of the Almighty	Ps.91.1
admonition will *a*. among the wise	Pr.15.31
the arrogant man shall not *a*.	Hab.2.5
A. in me, and I in you	Jn.15.4
If you *a*. in me, and my words *a*.	Jn.15.7
So faith, hope, love *a*.	1 Cor.13.13
the word of the Lord *a*. for ever	1 Pet.1.25
how does God's love *a*. in him?	1 Jn.3.17
if we love . . . God *a*. in us	1 Jn.4.12
and he who *a*. in love *a*. in God	1 Jn.4.16

ABILITY

I have given to all able men *a*.	Ex.31.6
LORD has put *a*. and intelligence	Ex.36.1
men of *a*., had the oversight	1 Chr.26.30
to each according to his *a*.	Mt.25.15
every one according to his *a*.	Acts 11.29

ABIMELECH

(1) king of Gerar; reproved by God about Abraham's wife, Gen.20.2–3; rebukes Abraham and restores Sarah, Gen.20.9,14; healed at Abraham's prayer, Gen.20.17; (2) king of the Philistines, Gen.26.1; Isaac rebuked by, Gen.26.9–10; covenants with Isaac, Gen.26.28; (3) king at Shechem; son of the judge Gideon, Jg.8.31; murders his brethren, Jg.9.5; his death, Jg.9.54

ABLE

every man shall give as he is *a*.	Dt.16.17
no man has been *a*. to withstand	Jos.23.9
a. to stand before the LORD	1 Sam.6.20
so that none is *a*. to withstand	2 Chr.20.6
The LORD is *a*. to give you much	2 Chr.25.9
believe that I am *a*. to do this?	Mt.9.28
Are you *a*. to drink the cup that I	Mt.20.22
God is *a*. from these stones to raise	Lk.3.8
that God was *a*. to do what he had	Rom.4.21
will be *a*. to separate us from	Rom.8.39
that you may be *a*. to endure it	1 Cor.10.13
within us is *a*. to do far more	Eph.3.20
that God was *a*. to raise men even	Heb.11.19
Now to him who is *a*. to keep you	Jude 24

ABNER

cousin of Saul, commander of his army, 1 Sam. 14.50; reproved by David, 1 Sam.26.5,14; makes Ish-bosheth king, 2 Sam.2.8–9; comes to David, 2 Sam.3.20; slain by Joab, 2 Sam.3.27; mourned by David, 2 Sam.3.31

ABODE (noun)

I will make my *a*. among you	Lev.26.11
His *a*. has been established	Ps.76.2
From thy lofty *a*. thou waterest	Ps.104.13
he blesses the *a*. of the righteous	Pr.3.33

ABOMINABLE

You shall not eat any *a*. thing	Dt.14.3
she had an *a*. image made	1 Kg.15.13
put away the *a*. idols from all	2 Chr.15.8
less one who is *a*. and corrupt	Job 15.16
they do *a*. deeds, there is none that	Ps.14.1
are corrupt, doing *a*. iniquity	Ps.53.1
they made their *a*. images	Ezek.7.20

ABOMINATION

that is an *a*. to the Egyptians	Gen.43.32
for it is an *a*. to the LORD	Dt.7.25
are an *a*. to the LORD your God	Dt.25.16
perverse man is an *a*. to the LORD	Pr.3.32
Lying lips are an *a*. to the LORD	Pr.12.22
sacrifice of the wicked is an *a*.	Pr.21.27

incense is an *a.* to me	Is.1.13
ashamed when they committed *a.*?	Jer.6.15
is an *a.* in the sight of God	Lk.16.15

ABOUND

faithful man will *a.* with blessings	Pr.28.20
continue in sin that grace may *a.*?	Rom.6.1
so that . . . you may *a.* in hope	Rom.15.13
always *a.* in the work of the Lord	1 Cor.15.58
be abased, and I know how to *a.*	Phil.4.12
increase and *a.* in love to one	1 Th.3.12

ABRAHAM

blessed by God, and sent to Canaan, Gen.12.2–5; goes down to Egypt, Gen.12.10; causes his wife to pass as his sister, Gen.12.13; 20.2; strife between him and Lot, Gen.13.7; separates from Lot, Gen.13.11; delivers Lot from captivity, and refuses the spoil, Gen.14.16–23; blessed by Melchizedek, king of Salem, Gen. 14.19; Heb.7.4; his faith counted for righteousness, Gen.15.6; God's covenant with, Gen. 15.18; Ps.105.9; he and house circumcised, Gen.17; entertains angels, Gen.18; pleads for Sodom, Gen.18.23; sends away Hagar and Ishmael, Gen.21.14; his faith in offering Isaac, Gen.22; sends for a wife for his son, Gen.24; gives his goods to Isaac, Gen.25.5; dies, Gen.25.8; his faith and works, Is.51.2; Jn.8.33; Acts 7.2; Rom.4; Gal.3.6; Heb.11.8; Jas.2.21

ABSALOM

David's son, 2 Sam.3.3; slays Ammon, 2 Sam. 13.28; conspires against David, 2 Sam.15; caught by head in an oak, 2 Sam.18.9; slain by Joab, 2 Sam.18.14; mourned by David, 2 Sam.18.33; 19.1

ABSENT

when we are *a.* one from the other	Gen.31.49
For though *a.* in body I am present	1 Cor.5.3
For though I am *a.* in body	Col.2.5

ABSTAIN

to them to *a.* from the pollutions	Acts 15.20
let not him who *a.* pass judgment	Rom.14.3
that you *a.* from immorality	1 Th.4.3
a. from every form of evil	1 Th.5.22

ABUNDANCE

but in an *a.* of counselors there is	Pr.11.14
a. of salvation, wisdom, and knowledge	Is.33.6
For out of the *a.* of the heart	Mt.12.34
all contributed out of their *a.*	Lk.21.4
those who receive the *a.* of grace	Rom.5.17
you with every blessing in *a.*	2 Cor.9.8
elated by the *a.* of revelations	2 Cor.12.7
plenty and hunger, *a.* and want	Phil.4.12

ABUNDANT

O how *a.* is thy goodness, which	Ps.31.19
according to thy *a.* mercy blot out	Ps.51.1
Great is our LORD, and *a.* in power	Ps.147.5
you know the *a.* love that I have	2 Cor.2.4

ABUNDANTLY

to our God, for he will *a.* pardon	Is.55.7
they may have life, and have it *a.*	Jn.10.10
For as we share *a.* in Christ's	2 Cor.1.5
is able to do far more *a.* than all	Eph.3.20

ACCEPT

A., I pray you, my gift that is	Gen.33.11
to be *a.* it must be perfect	Lev.22.21
the LORD *a.* Job's prayer	Job 42.9

A. my offerings of praise, O LORD	Ps.119.108
therefore the LORD does not *a.* them	Jer.14.10

ACCEPTABLE

the meditation of my heart be *a.*	Ps.19.14
sacrifice *a.* to God is a broken	Ps.51.17
justice is more *a.* to the LORD	Pr.21.3
Your burnt offerings are not *a.*	Jer.6.20
to proclaim the *a.* year of the Lord	Lk.4.19
Behold, now is the *a.* time	2 Cor.6.2
offered to God a more *a.* sacrifice	Heb.11.4
let us offer to God *a.* worship	Heb.12.28
sacrifices *a.* to God through Jesus	1 Pet.2.5

ACCOMPLISH

the LORD of hosts will *a.* this	Is.37.32
it shall *a.* that which I purpose	Is.55.11
his departure, which he was to *a.*	Lk.9.31
if only I may *a.* my course	Acts 20.24
which he *a.* in Christ when he	Eph.1.20

ACCORD

Yea, they conspire with one *a.*	Ps.83.5
the LORD and serve him with one *a.*	Zeph.3.9
But I have not come of my own *a.*	Jn.7.28
All these with one *a.* devoted	Acts 1.14
with one *a.* gave heed to what was	Acts 8.6
in *a.* with Christ Jesus	Rom.15.5
What *a.* has Christ with Belial?	2 Cor.6.15
being in full *a.* and of one mind	Phil.2.2

ACCOUNT (noun)

Behold, I am of small *a.*	Job 40.4
men will render *a.* for every	Mt.12.36
persecution . . . on *a.* of the word	Mk.4.17
Turn in the *a.* of your stewardship	Lk.16.2
shall give *a.* of himself to God	Rom.14.12
as men who will have to give *a.*	Heb.13.17

ACCURSED

who do not know the law, are *a.*	Jn.7.49
I myself were *a.* and cut off from	Rom.9.3
has no love . . . let him be *a.*	1 Cor.16.22
There shall no more be anything *a.*	Rev.22.3

ACCUSE

In return for my love they *a.* me	Ps.109.4
so that they might *a.* him	Mt.12.10
Do not think that I shall *a.* you	Jn.5.45
their conflicting thoughts *a.*	Rom.2.15

ACCUSER

I must appeal for mercy to my *a.*	Job 9.15
May my *a.* be put to shame	Ps.71.13
I am an object of scorn to my *a.*	Ps.109.25
Make friends quickly with your *a.*	Mt.5.25
accused met the *a.* face to face	Acts 25.16
for the *a.* of our brethren has been	Rev.12.10

ACKNOWLEDGE

In all your ways *a.* him	Pr.3.6
We *a.* our wickedness, O LORD	Jer.14.20
I also will *a.* before my Father	Mt.10.32
they did not see fit to *a.* God	Rom.1.28
fruit of lips that *a.* his name	Heb.13.15

ACT (verb)

all who *a.* dishonestly, are an	Dt.25.16
trust in him, and he will *a.*	Ps.37.5
a prudent man *a.* with knowledge	Pr.13.16
A man of quick temper *a.* foolishly	Pr.14.17
I know that you *a.* in ignorance	Acts 3.17
Did we . . . *a.* in the same spirit?	2 Cor.12.18
that forgets but a doer that *a.*	Jas.1.25
a. as those who are to be judged	Jas.2.12

ADAM

(1) created, Gen.1; called the son of God, Lk.3.38; blessed, Gen.1.28; placed in Eden, Gen.2.8; first called Adam, Gen.2.19; creatures named by, Gen.2.19; calls his wife Eve, Gen.3.20; his fall and punishment, Gen.3; hides from God, Gen.3.8; ground cursed for his sake, Gen.3.17; his death, Gen.5.5; his transgression, Rom.5.14; the first Adam, 1 Cor.15.22,45; 1 Tim.2.13; the last Adam, 1 Cor.15.45; (2) a place, Jos.3.16

ADDER

like the deaf *a*. that stops its ear	Ps.58.4
tread on the lion and the *a*.	Ps.91.13
a serpent, and stings like an *a*.	Pr.23.32

ADJURE

I *a*. you by the living God, tell	Mt.26.63
I *a*. you by God, do not torment me	Mk.5.7
I *a*. you by the Jesus whom Paul	Acts 19.13
I *a*. you by the Lord that this	1 Th.5.27

ADMONISH

Hear, O my people, while I *a*. you	Ps.81.8
to *a*. you as my beloved children	1 Cor.4.14
you teach and *a*. one another	Col.3.16
a. the idle, encourage	1 Th.5.14

ADORN

how it was *a*. with noble stones	Lk.21.5
women . . . *a*. themselves modestly	1 Tim.2.9
they may *a*. the doctrine of God	Tit.2.10
holy women . . . used to *a*. themselves	1 Pet.3.5
as a bride *a*. for her husband	Rev.21.2

ADULLAM

Jos.12.15; 1 Sam.22.1; 2 Sam.23.13; Mic.1.15

ADULTERY

You shall not commit *a*.	Ex.20.14
If a man commits *a*. with the wife	Lev.20.10
Neither shall you commit *a*.	Dt.5.18
was said, 'You shall not commit *a*.'	Mt.5.27
committed *a*. with her in his heart	Mt.5.28
and marries another, commits *a*.	Mt.19.9
and marries another commits *a*.	Lk.16.18
woman who had been caught in *a*.	Jn.8.3
You shall not commit *a*.	Rom.13.9
They have eyes full of *a*.	2 Pet.2.14
who commit *a*. with her I will	Rev.2.22

ADVANTAGE

It is to your *a*. that I go away, for	Jn.16.7
Then what *a*. has the Jew? Or what	Rom.3.1
not seeking my own *a*., but that	1 Cor.10.33
Christ will be of no *a*. to you	Gal.5.2

ADVERSARY

my *a*. sharpens his eyes against me	Job 16.9
Vindicate me against my *a*.	Lk.18.3
none of your *a*. will be able to	Lk.21.15
of fire which will consume the *a*.	Heb.10.27
Your *a*. the devil prowls around	1 Pet.5.8

ADVERSITY

redeemed my soul out of every *a*.	1 Kg.1.29
He thinks . . . I shall not meet *a*.	Ps.10.6
thou hast taken heed of my *a*.	Ps.31.7
and a brother is born for *a*.	Pr.17.17
and in the day of *a*. consider	Ec.7.14
the bread of *a*. and the water of	Is.30.20

AFFECTION

| love one another with brotherly *a*. | Rom.12.10 |

| all with the *a*. of Christ Jesus | Phil.1.8 |
| and godliness with brotherly *a*. | 2 Pet.1.7 |

AFFLICT

But the LORD *a*. Pharaoh and his	Gen.12.17
You shall not *a*. any widow or	Ex.22.22
the LORD has *a*. me and the Almighty	Ru.1.21
does not forget the cry of the *a*.	Ps.9.12
for I am lonely and *a*.	Ps.25.16
right of the *a*. and the destitute	Ps.82.3
It is good for me that I was *a*.	Ps.119.71
LORD maintains the cause of the *a*.	Ps.140.12
stricken, smitten by God, and *a*.	Is.53.4
he was *a*., yet he opened not	Is.53.7
to bring good tidings to the *a*.	Is.61.1
In all their affliction he was *a*.	Is.63.9
We are *a*. in every way, but not	2 Cor.4.8
relieved the *a*., and devoted	1 Tim.5.10
destitute, *a*., ill-treated	Heb.11.37

AFFLICTION

the LORD has looked upon my *a*.	Gen.29.32
I have seen the *a*. of my people	Ex.3.7
the bread of *a*. – for you came out	Dt.16.3
For *a*. does not come from the dust	Job 5.6
caught in the cords of *a*.	Job 36.8
Consider my *a*. and my trouble	Ps.25.18
he raises up the needy out of *a*.	Ps.107.41
Look on my *a*. and deliver me	Ps.119.153
this is vanity; it is a sore *a*.	Ec.6.2
tried you in the furnace of *a*.	Is.48.10
Remember my *a*. and my bitterness	Lam.3.19
who comforts us in all our *a*.	2 Cor.1.4
I wrote you out of much *a*.	2 Cor.2.4
what is lacking in Christ's *a*.	Col.1.24
publicly exposed to abuse and *a*.	Heb.10.33

AFRAID

I was *a*., because I was naked	Gen.3.10
Then Moses was *a*., and thought	Ex.2.14
I become *a*. of all my suffering	Job 9.28
of whom shall I be *a*.?	Ps.27.1
When I am *a*., I put my trust in thee	Ps.56.3
heart is steady, he will not be *a*.	Ps.112.8
I will trust, and will not be *a*.	Is.12.2
Fear not, nor be *a*.; have I not told	Is.44.8
Be not *a*. of them, for I am with you	Jer.1.8
Why are you *a*., O men of little	Mt.8.26
they were *a*., and they glorified God	Mt.9.8
so I was *a*., and I went and hid	Mt.25.25
said to the women, "Do not be *a*.	Mt.28.5
the angel said to them, "Be not *a*.	Lk.2.10
troubled, neither let them be *a*.	Jn.14.27
Lord is my helper, I will not be *a*.	Heb.13.6

AGE

have borne him a son in his old *a*.	Gen.21.7
the harvest is the close of the *a*.	Mt.13.39
So it will be at the close of the *a*.	Mt.13.49
in the *a*. to come eternal life	Mk.10.30
she was of a great *a*., having lived	Lk.2.36
Jesus . . . was about thirty years of *a*.	Lk.3.23
that in the coming *a*. he might show	Eph.2.7
hidden for *a*. and generations but	Col.1.26
the powers of the *a*. to come	Heb.6.5
the end of the *a*. to put away sin	Heb.9.26
are thy ways, O King of the *a*.	Rev.15.3

AGREE

| *A*. with God, and be at peace | Job 22.21 |
| if two of you *a*. on earth about | Mt.18.19 |

a. with one another . . . in peace 2 Cor.13.11
entreat Syntyche to *a.* in the Lord Phil.4.2
three witnesses . . . and these three *a.* 1 Jn.5.8

AHAB
king of Israel, 1 Kg.16.29; marries Jezebel; his
idolatry, 1 Kg.16.31; meets Elijah, 1 Kg.18.17;
defeats the Syrians, 1 Kg.20; punished for
sparing Ben-hadad, 1 Kg.20.42; takes Naboth's
vineyard, 1 Kg.21.16; his repentance, 1 Kg.
21.27; trusts false prophets, and is mortally
wounded at Ramoth-gilead, 1 Kg.22.6,34;
2 Chr.18

AHASUERUS
reigns from India to Ethiopia, Est.1.1; Vashti's
disobedience to, and divorce, Est.1.12; 2.4;
makes Esther queen, Est.2.17; promotes
Haman, Est.3.1; his decree to destroy the Jews,
Est.3.12; rewards Mordecai's loyalty, Est.6;
hangs Haman, Est.7.9; 8.7; advances Mordecai,
Est.10

AHAZ
king of Judah, 2 Kg.15.38; 16; spoils the temple,
2 Kg.16.17; his idolatry, 2 Chr.28.2; afflicted by
Syrians, 2 Chr.28.5; comforted by Isaiah, Is.7;
will not ask a sign, Is.7.12

AHAZIAH
(1) king of Israel, 1 Kg.22.40,49; his sickness
and idolatry, 2 Kg.1; his judgment by Elijah,
2 Kg.1; (2) king of Judah, his wicked reign,
2 Kg.8.25; goes with Joram to meet Jehu, 2
Kg.9.21; smitten by Jehu, 2 Kg.9.27; 2 Chr.22.9

AIM (noun)
Make love your *a.*, and earnestly 1 Cor.14.1
we make it our *a.* to please him 2 Cor.5.9
since his *a.* is to satisfy the one 2 Tim.2.4
you have observed . . . my *a.* in life 2 Tim.3.10

AIR
sea, and over the birds of the *a.* Gen.1.26
another that no *a.* can come Job 41.16
birds of the *a.* have . . . habitation Ps.104.12
and birds of the *a.* have nests Mt.8.20
I do not box as one beating the *a.* 1 Cor.9.26
you will be speaking into the *a.* 1 Cor.14.9
the prince of the power of the *a.* Eph.2.2
clouds to meet the Lord in the *a.* 1 Th.4.17

ALEXANDER
(1) Mk.15.21; (2) a member of the Sanhedrin,
Acts 4.6; (3) an Ephesian Jew, Acts 19.33;
(4) a coppersmith, 1 Tim.1.20; 2 Tim.4.14

ALIVE
Joseph my son is still *a.* Gen.45.28
but you . . . are all *a.* this day Dt.4.4
I kill and I make *a.* Dt.32.39
behold, the Lord has kept me *a.* Jos.14.10
He does not keep the wicked *a.* Job 36.6
my son was dead, and is *a.* again Lk.15.24
presented himself *a.* after his Acts 1.3
dead to sin and *a.* to God in Rom.6.11
in Christ shall all be made *a.* 1 Cor.15.22
of the Lord, that we who are *a.* 1 Th.4.15
flesh but made *a.* in the spirit 1 Pet.3.18
and behold I am *a.* for evermore Rev.1.18

ALLEGORY
speak an *a.* to the house of Israel Ezek.17.2
Is he not a maker of *a.*? Ezek.20.49

utter an *a.* to the rebellious house Ezek.24.3
Now this is an *a.*: these women are Gal.4.24

ALLOW
he *a.* no one to oppress them 1 Chr.16.21
Am I not *a.* to do what I choose Mt.20.15
nor *a.* those who would enter to go Mt.23.13
Spirit of Jesus did not *a.* them Acts 16.7

ALMIGHTY
who sees the vision of the *A.* Num.24.4
for the *A.* has dealt very bitterly Ru.1.20
despise not the chastening of the *A.* Job 5.17
Can you find out the limit of the *A.*? Job 11.7
when the *A.* was yet with me Job 29.5
a faultfinder contend with the *A.*? Job 40.2
who abides in the shadow of the *A.* Ps.91.1
destruction from the *A.* . . . will come Is.13.6
like the thunder of the *A.* Ezek.1.24
the voice of God *A.* when he speaks Ezek.10.5
who was and who is to come, the *A.* Rev.1.8
Holy, holy, holy, is the Lord God *A.* Rev.4.8
Lord God *A.*, who art and who wast Rev.11.17
For the Lord our God the *A.* reigns Rev.19.6

ALMS
when you give *a.*, sound no trumpet Mt.6.2
But give for *a.* those things which Lk.11.41
Sell your possessions, and give *a.* Lk.12.33
gave *a.* liberally to the people Acts 10.2

ALONE
not good that the man should be *a.* Gen.2.18
that man does not live by bread *a.* Dt.8.3
and I *a.* have escaped to tell you Job 1.15
to him who *a.* does great wonders Ps.136.4
Man shall not live by bread *a.* Mt.4.4
Who can forgive sins but God *a.*? Mk.2.7
No one is good but God *a.* Lk.18.19
yet I am not *a.*, for the Father is Jn.16.32
by works and not by faith *a.* Jas.2.24
For thou *a.* art holy Rev.15.4

ALPHA
I am the *A.* and the Omega Rev.1.8; 21.6; 22.13

ALTAR
Then Noah built an *a.* to the Lord Gen.8.20
Abraham built an *a.* there Gen.22.9
Moses built an *a.* and called Ex.17.15
An *a.* of earth you shall make for Ex.20.24
Joshua built an *a.* in Mount Ebal Jos.8.30
built there an *a.* by the Jordan Jos.22.10
Saul built an *a.* to the Lord 1 Sam.14.35
he repaired the *a.* of the Lord 1 Kg.18.30
He made an *a.* of bronze, twenty 2 Chr.4.1
at thy *a.*, O Lord of hosts, my King Ps.84.3
are offering your gift at the *a.* Mt.5.23
We have an *a.* from which those who Heb.13.10

ALWAYS
I keep the Lord *a.* before me Ps.16.8
He will not *a.* chide, nor will he Ps.103.9
I am with you *a.*, to the close of Mt.28.20
For you *a.* have the poor with you Mk.14.7
Rejoice in the Lord *a.* Phil.4.4
Let your speech *a.* be gracious Col.4.6
We give thanks to God *a.* for you all 1 Th.1.2
To this end we *a.* pray for you, that 2 Th.1.11
I thank my God *a.* when I remember Philem. 4

AMAZIAH
(1) king of Judah, his good reign, 2 Kg.14.1;
2 Chr.25.1; defeats Edom, 2 Chr.25.11; defeated

by Joash king of Israel, 2 Chr.25.21–23; slain at Lachish, 2 Kg.14.19; (2) priest of Bethel, Am.7.10

AMAZED

all the people were *a*.	Mt.12.23
they were all *a*. and glorified God	Mk.2.12
in a white robe; and they were *a*.	Mk.16.5
he said to them, "Do not be *a*.	Mk.16.6
they were *a*. and wondered	Acts 2.7
all who heard him were *a*.	Acts 9.21

AMBASSADOR

So we are *a*. for Christ	2 Cor.5.20
for which I am an *a*. in chains	Eph.6.20
Paul, an *a*. and now a prisoner also	Philem. 9

AMEN

all the people shall say, '*A*.'	Dt.27.16
"*A*., *A*.," lifting up their hands	Neh.8.6
let all the people say, "*A*.!"	Ps.106.48
power and the glory, for ever. *A*.	Mt.6.13
Jesus Christ be with you all. *A*.	Rom.16.24
say the "*A*." to your thanksgiving	1 Cor.14.16
write: 'The words of the *A*.	Rev.3.14

ANANIAS

(1) (and Sapphira), their lie and death, Acts 5.1–10; (2) (disciple), sent to Paul at Damascus, Acts 9.10; 22.12; (3) (high priest), Paul brought before, Acts 22.30; rebuked by Paul, Acts 23.3

ANDREW

the Apostle, Mt.4.18; Mk.1.29; 13.3; Jn.1.40; 6.8; 12.22; Acts 1.13

ANEW

I say to you, unless one is born *a*.	Jn.3.3
I said to you, 'You must be born *a*.'	Jn.3.7
have been born *a*. to a living hope	1 Pet.1.3
You have been born *a*.	1 Pet.1.23

ANGEL

The *a*. of the Lord found her by a	Gen.16.7
the ass saw the *a*. of the Lord	Num.22.25
God sent the *a*. to Jerusalem to	1 Chr.21.15
The *a*. of the Lord encamps around	Ps.34.7
the *a*. of his presence saved	Is.63.9
God sent his *a*. and shut the lions'	Dan.6.22
He strove with the *a*. and prevailed	Hos.12.4
He will give his *a*. charge of you	Mt.4.6
the reapers are *a*.	Mt.13.39
more than twelve legions of *a*.?	Mt.26.53
the *a*. said to the women, "Do not be	Mt.28.5
And Mary said to the *a*.	Lk.1.34
an *a*. of the Lord appeared to them	Lk.2.9
suddenly there was with the *a*.	Lk.2.13
a. of God ascending and descending	Jn.1.51
But at night an *a*. of the Lord	Acts 5.19
his face was like the face of an *a*.	Acts 6.15
nor *a*., nor principalities	Rom.8.38
not know that we are to judge *a*.?	1 Cor.6.3
in the tongues of men and of *a*.	1 Cor.13.1
Satan disguises himself as an *a*.	2 Cor.11.14
but received me as an *a*. of God	Gal.4.14
some have entertained *a*. unawares	Heb.13.2
the *a*. that did not keep their own	Jude 6
To the *a*. of the church in Ephesus	Rev.2.1
sent his *a*. to show his servants	Rev.22.6

ANGER

Cursed be their *a*., for it is fierce	Gen.49.7
Then the *a*. of the Lord was kindled	Ex.4.14

The Lord is slow to *a*.	Num.14.18
thou art a God . . . slow to *a*.	Neh.9.17
O Lord, rebuke me not in thy *a*.	Ps.6.1
Turn not thy servant away in *a*.	Ps.27.9
For his *a*. is but for a moment	Ps.30.5
For we are consumed by thy *a*.	Ps.90.7
The Lord is . . . slow to *a*.	Ps.145.8
but a harsh word stirs up *a*.	Pr.15.1
Be not quick to *a*.	Ec.7.9
not in thy *a*., lest thou bring me	Jer.10.24
repent and turn from his fierce *a*.	Jon.3.9
not let the sun go down on your *a*.	Eph.4.26
do not provoke your children to *a*.	Eph.6.4
slow to speak, slow to *a*.	Jas.1.19

ANGRY

Be *a*., but sin not; commune with your	Ps.4.4
Wilt thou be *a*. with us for ever?	Ps.85.5
one who is *a*. with his brother	Mt.5.22
Now Herod was *a*. with the people	Acts 12.20
Be *a*. but do not sin; do not let	Eph.4.26

ANGUISH

will speak in the *a*. of my spirit	Job 7.11
Trouble and *a*. have come upon me	Ps.119.143
when distress and *a*. come upon you	Pr.1.27
When *a*. comes, they will seek peace	Ezek.7.25
for I am in *a*. in this flame	Lk.16.24
and unceasing *a*. in my heart	Rom.9.2
men gnawed their tongues in *a*.	Rev.16.10

ANIMAL

seven pairs of all clean *a*.	Gen.7.2
Noah . . . took of every clean *a*.	Gen.8.20
When you offer blind *a*. in sacrifice	Mal.1.8
all kinds of *a*. and reptiles and	Acts 10.12
the bodies of those *a*. whose blood	Heb.13.11
But these, like irrational *a*.	2 Pet.2.12
know by instinct as irrational *a*.	Jude 10

ANOINT

you shall *a*. Aaron and his sons	Ex.30.30
you shall not *a*. yourself with the	Dt.28.40
Wash therefore and *a*. yourself	Ru.3.3
thou *a*. my head with oil, my cup	Ps.23.5
look upon the face of thine *a*.	Ps.84.9
the Lord has *a*. me to bring good	Is.61.1
a. themselves with the finest oils	Am.6.6
a. your head and wash your face	Mt.6.17
You did not *a*. my head with oil	Lk.7.46
servant Jesus, whom thou didst *a*.	Acts 4.27
has *a*. thee with the oil of gladness	Heb.1.9

ANSWER (noun)

A soft *a*. turns away wrath, but a	Pr.15.1
a. of the tongue is from the Lord	Pr.16.1
If one gives *a*. before he hears, it	Pr.18.13
for there is no *a*. from God	Mic.3.7
were amazed at . . . his *a*.	Lk.2.47
granted us in *a*. to many prayers	2 Cor.1.11

ANSWER (verb)

he will *a*. him from his holy heaven	Ps.20.6
I cry by day, but thou dost not *a*.	Ps.22.2
When he calls to me, I will *a*. him	Ps.91.15
the Lord *a*. me and set me free	Ps.118.5
A. not a fool according to his folly	Pr.26.4
no one was able to *a*. him a word	Mt.22.46
Then the righteous will *a*. him	Mt.25.37
what you are to *a*. or what you are	Lk.12.11
to meditate beforehand how to *a*.	Lk.21.14
who are you . . . to *a*. back to God?	Rom.9.20

ANT

may be able to *a.* those who pride 2 Cor.5.12
know how you ought to *a.* every one Col.4.6

ANT

Go to the *a.*, O sluggard Pr.6.6
the *a.* are a people not strong Pr.30.25

ANTICHRIST

you have heard that *a.* is coming 1 Jn.2.18
This is the *a.*, he who denies the 1 Jn.2.22
This is the spirit of *a.* 1 Jn.4.3
such a one is the deceiver and the *a.* 2 Jn.7

ANTIOCH

(1) capital of Syria; disciples first called Christians at, Acts 11.26; Barnabas and Saul called to apostleship at, Acts 13.1–3; Paul withstands Cephas (Peter) at, Gal.2.11; (2) (Pisidia) Paul's first address at, Acts 13.14–41; Paul and Barnabas persecuted at, Acts 13.50

ANXIETY

A. in a man's heart weighs him down Pr.12.25
in this tent, we sigh with *a.* 2 Cor.5.4
of my *a.* for all the churches 2 Cor.11.28
Have no *a.* about anything, but in Phil.4.6

ANXIOUS

eating the bread of *a.* toil Ps.127.2
do not be *a.* about your life Mt.6.25
do not be *a.* about tomorrow Mt.6.34
do not be *a.* beforehand what you Mk.13.11
which of you by being *a.* can add a Lk.12.25
the married man is *a.* about worldly 1 Cor.7.33
be genuinely *a.* for your welfare Phil.2.20

APART

LORD has set *a.* the godly for himself Ps.4.3
I have no good *a.* from thee Ps.16.2
set them *a.* for the day of slaughter Jer.12.3
led them up a high mountain *a.* Mt.17.1
for *a.* from me you can do nothing Jn.15.5
set *a.* for the gospel of God Rom.1.1
A. from the law sin lies dead Rom.7.8
so faith *a.* from works is dead Jas.2.26

APOLLOS

eloquent and well versed in the Scriptures, Acts 18.24; 19.1; 1 Cor.1.12; 3.4

APOSTLE

The names of the twelve *a.* are these Mt.10.2
he was enrolled with the eleven *a.* Acts 1.26
they arrested the *a.* and put them Acts 5.18
The *a.* and the elders were gathered Acts 15.6
they are men of note among the *a.* Rom.16.7
For I am the least of the *a.* 1 Cor.15.9
have made demands as *a.* of Christ 1 Th.2.6
a. and high priest of our confession Heb.3.1
O saints and *a.* and prophets Rev.18.20
names of the twelve *a.* of the Lamb Rev.21.14

APPEAR

one place, and let the dry land *a.* Gen.1.9
I *a.* to Abraham, to Isaac, and to Ex.6.3
None shall *a.* before me empty-handed Ex.23.15
and who can stand when he *a.*? Mal.3.2
outwardly *a.* righteous to men Mt.23.28
then will *a.* the sign of the Son of Mt.24.30
those in which I will *a.* to you Acts 26.16
must all *a.* before the judgment 2 Cor.5.10
you also will *a.* with him in glory Col.3.4
Christ . . . will *a.* a second time, not Heb.9.28
it does not yet *a.* what we shall be 1 Jn.3.2

APPLY

A. your mind to instruction Pr.23.12
When I *a.* my mind to know wisdom Ec.8.16
be careful to *a.* themselves to good Tit.3.8

APPOINT

to *a.* me as prince over Israel 2 Sam.6.21
time which I *a.* I will judge Ps.75.2
place which thou didst *a.* for them Ps.104.8
And he *a.* twelve, to be with him Mk.3.14
Collect no more than is *a.* you Lk.3.13
I chose you and *a.* you that you Jn.15.16
when they had *a.* elders for Acts 14.23
the *a.* time has grown very short 1 Cor.7.29
God has *a.* in the church first 1 Cor.12.28
For this I was *a.* a preacher and 1 Tim.2.7
whom he *a.* the heir of all things Heb.1.2
the law *a.* men in their weakness Heb.7.28

APPROVE

they not only do them but *a.* those Rom.1.32
a. what is excellent Rom.2.18
acceptable to God and *a.* by men Rom.14.18
as we have been *a.* by God to be 1 Th.2.4
present yourself to God as one *a.* 2 Tim.2.15

AQUILA

(and Priscilla) go with Paul from Corinth to Ephesus, Acts 18.2,19; their constancy, Rom. 16.3–4; 1 Cor.16.19; Apollos instructed by, Acts 18.26

ARARAT

Gen.8.4; Is.37.38; Jer.51.27

ARIMATHEA

Mt.27.57; Mk.15.43; Lk.23.50; Jn.19.38

ARISE

though war *a.* against me, yet I will Ps.27.3
A., O God, judge the earth Ps.82.8
A., shine; for your light Is.60.1
A., go to Nineveh, that great city Jon.1.2
of Nineveh will *a.* at the judgment Mt.12.41
or persecution *a.* on account of Mt.13.21
Little girl, I say to you, *a.* Mk.5.41
A great prophet has *a.* among us Lk.7.16
I will *a.* and go to my father Lk.15.18
a. from the dead, and Christ shall Eph.5.14
priest to *a.* after . . . Melchizedek Heb.7.11

ARK

Make yourself an *a.* of gopher wood Gen.6.14
shall make an *a.* of acacia wood Ex.25.10
bearing the *a.* of the covenant Jos.3.14
he caused the *a.* of the LORD Jos.6.11
And the *a.* of God was captured 1 Sam.4.11
the priests took up the *a.* 1 Kg.8.3
put out his hand to hold the *a.* 1 Chr.13.9
the Levites took up the *a.* 2 Chr.5.4
Put the holy *a.* in the house 2 Chr.35.3
incense and the *a.* of the covenant Heb.9.4
constructed an *a.* for the saving Heb.11.7
during the building of the *a.* 1 Pet.3.20

ARM (noun)

because of the greatness of thy *a.* Ex.15.16
underneath are the everlasting *a.* Dt.33.27
Have you an *a.* like God, and can Job 40.9
Break thou the *a.* of the wicked Ps.10.15
Thou didst with thy *a.* redeem thy Ps.77.15
he will gather the lambs in his *a.* Is.40.11
and his *a.* shall be against the Is.48.14
to whom has the *a.* of the LORD been Is.53.1

Let his *a.* be wholly withered	Zech.11.17
he took them in his *a.* and blessed	Mk.10.16
to whom has the *a.* of the Lord been	Jn.12.38
with uplifted *a.* he led them out	Acts 13.17

ARMAGEDDON

They assembled them at . . . *A.*	Rev.16.16

ARMOR

Saul clothed David with his *a.*	1 Sam.17.38
They put his *a.* in the temple of	1 Sam.31.10
put on the *a.* of light	Rom.13.12
Put on the whole *a.* of God	Eph.6.11
take the whole *a.* of God	Eph.6.13

ARMY

the God of the *a.* of Israel	1 Sam.17.45
Is there any number to his *a.?*	Job 25.3
A king is not saved by his great *a.*	Ps.33.16
not go forth, O God, with our *a.*	Ps.108.11
you see Jerusalem surrounded by *a.*	Lk.21.20
in war, put foreign *a.* to flight	Heb.11.34
the *a.* of heaven, arrayed in fine	Rev.19.14

ARRAY

Worship the LORD in holy *a.*	1 Chr.16.29
worship the LORD in holy *a.*	Ps.29.2
was not *a.* like one of these	Mt.6.29
a. him in a purple robe	Jn.19.2
The kings . . . set themselves in *a.*	Acts 4.26

ARREST (verb)

he heard that John had been *a.*	Mt.4.12
But when they tried to *a.* him	Mt.21.46
in order to *a.* Jesus by stealth	Mt.26.4
but no one *a.* him, because his hour	Jn.8.20
they *a.* the apostles and put them	Acts 5.18
he proceeded to *a.* Peter also	Acts 12.3

ARROGANT

a. heart I will not endure	Ps.101.5
one who is *a.* is an abomination	Pr.16.5
he will punish the *a.* boasting of	Is.10.12
the *a.* man shall not abide	Hab.2.5
Some are *a.*, as though I were not	1 Cor.4.18
love . . . is not *a.* or rude	1 Cor.13.5
he must not be *a.* or quick-tempered	Tit.1.7

ARTAXERXES

(1) (king of Persia), oppresses the Jews, Ezra 4; (2) (Longimanus), permits Ezra to restore the temple, Ezra 7; and Nehemiah to rebuild Jerusalem, Neh.2

ASA

begins his reign, 1 Kg.15.8; wars with Baasha, 1 Kg.15.16; his prayer against the Ethiopians, 2 Chr.14.11; his zeal, 2 Chr.15; seeks aid of the Syrians, 2 Chr.16.2–4; reproved by Hanani the seer, 2 Chr.16.7; reigns forty years, and dies much honored, 2 Chr.16.13

ASAPH

(1) a Levite, musical composer, and leader of David's choir, 1 Chr.6.39; 2 Chr.5.12; 29.30; 35.15; Neh.12.46; Psalms 50 and 73 to 83 are ascribed to him; (2) 2 Kg.18.18

ASCEND

Who shall *a.* the hill of the LORD?	Ps.24.3
If I *a.* to heaven, thou art there	Ps.139.8
Who has *a.* to heaven and come down?	Pr.30.4
angels of God *a.* and descending	Jn.1.51
No one has *a.* into heaven but he	Jn.3.13
I have not yet *a.* to the Father	Jn.20.17
When he *a.* on high he led a host	Eph.4.8

ASHAMED

were both naked, and were not *a.*	Gen.2.25
are you not *a.* to wrong me?	Job 19.3
let them be *a.* who are wantonly	Ps.25.3
so your faces shall never be *a.*	Ps.34.5
Fear not, for you will not be *a.*	Is.54.4
For whoever is *a.* of me and of my	Lk.9.26
For I am not *a.* of the gospel	Rom.1.16
I do not write this to make you *a.*	1 Cor.4.14
Do not be *a.* then of testifying to	2 Tim.1.8
I am not *a.*, for I know whom I	2 Tim.1.12
workman who has no need to be *a.*	2 Tim.2.15
God is not *a.* to be called their	Heb.11.16
as a Christian, let him not be *a.*	1 Pet.4.16

ASHDOD

Jos.15.46; city of Philistines; the ark carried there; men of, smitten, 1 Sam.5; subdued by Uzziah, 2 Chr.26.6; predictions concerning, Jer.25.20; Am.1.8; Zeph.2.4; Zech.9.6

ASHER

(1) son of Jacob, Gen.30.13; his descendants, Num.1.40; 26.44; 1 Chr.7.30; their inheritance, Jos.19.24; Jg.5.17; see Ezek.48.34; Rev.7.6; Anna, prophetess, descended from, Lk.2.36; (2) a town, Jos.17.7

ASHES

I who am but dust and *a.*	Gen.18.27
and sat among the *a.*	Job 2.8
Your maxims are proverbs of *a.*	Job 13.12
I have become like dust and *a.*	Job 30.19
For I eat *a.* like bread, and mingle	Ps.102.9
He feeds on *a.*	Is.44.20
give them a garland instead of *a.*	Is.61.3
with fasting and sackcloth and *a.*	Dan.9.3
with sackcloth, and sat in *a.*	Jon.3.6
the *a.* of a heifer sanctifies	Heb.9.13

ASIA

in the New Testament not the continent, but a Roman province in the western part of Asia Minor (including the cities Ephesus, Smyrna, Pergamum, Thyatira, Sardis, Philadelphia, and Laodicea Rev.2–3), Acts 2.9; 16.6; 19.26; Rom.16.5

ASLEEP

Your shepherds are *a.*, O king	Nah.3.18
in the stern, *a.* on the cushion	Mk.4.38
said to Peter, "Simon, are you *a.?*	Mk.14.37
and as they sailed he fell *a.*	Lk.8.23
Our friend Lazarus has fallen *a.*	Jn.11.11
though some have fallen *a.*	1 Cor.15.6
precede those who have fallen *a.*	1 Th.4.15
For ever since the fathers fell *a.*	2 Pet.3.4

ASS

enemy's ox or his *a.* going astray	Ex.23.4
When the *a.* saw the angel	Num.22.27
plow with an ox and an *a.* together	Dt.22.10
he found a fresh jawbone of an *a.*	Jg.15.15
the wild *a.* quench their thirst	Ps.104.11
whip for the horse, a bridle for the *a.*	Pr.26.3
and the *a.* its master's crib	Is.1.3
Be like a wild *a.* in the desert	Jer.48.6
he, humble and riding on an *a.*	Zech.9.9
having an *a.* or an ox that has	Lk.14.5
found a young *a.* and sat upon it	Jn.12.14

ASSEMBLE

A. the people, men, women, and   Dt.31.12
A., all of you, and hear   Is.48.14
I will *a.* the lame and gather   Mic.4.6
when you *a.* as a church, I hear   1 Cor.11.18
to *a.* them for battle on the great   Rev.16.14

ASSEMBLY

when the whole *a.* of the congregation   Ex.12.6
Sanctify a solemn *a.* for Baal   2 Kg.10.20
Solomon and the *a.* sought the LORD   2 Chr.1.5
And all the *a.* said "Amen"   Neh.5.13
praise him in the *a.* of the elders   Ps.107.32
Sanctify a fast, call a solemn *a.*   Jl.1.14
I take no delight in your solemn *a.*   Am.5.21
it has seemed good to us in *a.* to   Acts 15.25
to the *a.* of the first-born who   Heb.12.23
in fine clothing comes into your *a.*   Jas.2.2

ASSURANCE

he has given *a.* to all men by   Acts 17.31
the full *a.* of hope until the end   Heb.6.11
a true heart in full *a.* of faith   Heb.10.22
Now faith is the *a.* of things hoped   Heb.11.1

ASTONISHED

As many were *a.* at him   Is.52.14
the crowds were *a.* at his teaching   Mt.7.28
And they were *a.* beyond measure   Mk.7.37
all were *a.* at the majesty of God   Lk.9.43
for he was *a.* at the teaching of   Acts 13.12
I am *a.* that you are so quickly   Gal.1.6

ASTRAY

They have all gone *a.*, they are   Ps.14.3
The wicked go *a.* from the womb   Ps.58.3
I have gone *a.* like a lost sheep   Ps.119.176
and your knowledge led you *a.*   Is.47.10
All we like sheep have gone *a.*   Is.53.6
their shepherds have led them *a.*   Jer.50.6
going *a.* from me after their idols   Ezek.44.10
sheep, and one of them has gone *a.*   Mt.18.12
Take heed that no one leads you *a.*   Mk.13.5
to lead *a.*, if possible, the elect   Mk.13.22
No, he is leading the people *a.*   Jn.7.12
led *a.*, slaves to various passions   Tit.3.3
They always go *a.* in their hearts   Heb.3.10

ASUNDER

I was at ease, and he broke me *a.*   Job 16.12
Let us burst their bonds *a.*   Ps.2.3
joined together, let no man put *a.*   Mt.19.6

ATHENS

Acts 17.15,16,22; 18.1; 1 Th.3.1

ATONEMENT

Aaron shall make *a.* upon its horns   Ex.30.10
the priest shall make *a.* for them   Lev.4.20
make *a.* for him before the LORD   Lev.14.29
seventh month is the day of *a.*   Lev.23.27
shall they make *a.* for the altar   Ezek.43.26
make *a.* for the house of Israel   Ezek.45.17

ATTACK (verb)

those who *a.* me with lies   Ps.69.4
the king of the south shall *a.*   Dan.11.40
a worm which *a.* the plant   Jon.4.7
no man shall *a.* you to harm you   Acts 18.10

ATTAIN

it is high, I cannot *a.* it   Ps.139.6
until we all *a.* to the unity of the   Eph.4.13
if possible . . . *a.* the resurrection   Phil.3.11
hold true to what we have *a.*   Phil.3.16

ATTENTION

O foolish men, pay *a.*   Pr.8.5
Gallio paid no *a.* to this   Acts 18.17
pay the closer *a.* to what we have   Heb.2.1
do well to pay *a.* to this as to   2 Pet.1.19

AUTHORITY

When the wicked are in *a.*   Pr.29.16
he taught them as one who had *a.*   Mt.7.29
All *a.* in heaven and on earth has   Mt.28.18
the Son of man has *a.* . . . to forgive sins   Mk.2.10
For I am a man set under *a.*   Lk.7.8
Tell us by what *a.* you do these   Lk.20.2
I can do nothing on my own *a.*   Jn.5.30
For I have not spoken on my own *a.*   Jn.12.49
let the men of *a.* among you go   Acts 25.5
For there is no *a.* except from God   Rom.13.1
Do I say this on human *a.*?   1 Cor.9.8
exhort and reprove with all *a.*   Tit.2.15
our God and the *a.* of his Christ   Rev.12.10

AVENGE

If Cain is *a.* sevenfold, truly   Gen.4.24
for he *a.* the blood of his servants   Dt.32.43
said, "May the LORD see and *a.*!"   2 Chr.24.22
he . . . *a.* him by striking the Egyptian   Acts 7.24
Beloved, never *a.* yourselves, but   Rom.12.19
thou wilt judge and *a.* our blood   Rev.6.10

AVOID

not only to *a.* God's wrath but also   Rom.13.5
A. the godless chatter and   1 Tim.6.20
A. such people   2 Tim.3.5
to *a.* quarreling, to be gentle   Tit.3.2
But *a.* stupid controversies, genealogies   Tit.3.9

AWAKE

a., O my God; thou hast appointed   Ps.7.6
A., my soul! *A.*, O harp and lyre   Ps.57.8
When I *a.*, I am still with thee   Ps.139.18
I slept, but my heart was *a.*   S.of S.5.2
A., *a.*, put on strength, O arm of   Is.51.9
who says to a wooden thing, *A.*   Hab.2.19
A., O sleeper, and arise from the   Eph.5.14
but let us keep *a.* and be sober   1 Th.5.6
A., and strengthen what remains   Rev.3.2
Blessed is he who is *a.*, keeping   Rev.16.15

AWE

as they had stood in *a.* of Moses   Jos.4.14
stand in *a.* of him, all you sons   Ps.22.23
let . . . the world stand in *a.* of him   Ps.33.8
stand in *a.* of the God of Israel   Is.29.23
the disciples . . . were filled with *a.*   Mt.17.6
not become proud, but stand in *a.*   Rom.11.20
worship, with reverence and *a.*   Heb.12.28

AXE

Abimelech took an *a.* in his hand   Jg.9.48
his *a.* head fell into the water   2 Kg.6.5
Shall the *a.* vaunt itself over him   Is.10.15
Even now the *a.* is laid to the root   Lk.3.9

AZARIAH

(1) (also called Uzziah) king of Judah, his good reign, 2 Kg.14.21; 2 Chr.26.4; his wars, 2 Chr.26.6; stricken with leprosy, 2 Kg.15.5; 2 Chr.26.20; (2) prophet, exhorts Asa, 2 Chr. 15; (3) a priest, 2 Chr. 26.17

BAAL

Israel yoked himself to *B.* of Peor   Num.25.3
the altar of *B.* which your father   Jg.6.25

saying, "O *B*., answer us!" 1 Kg.18.26
Sanctify a solemn assembly for *B*. 2 Kg.10.20
no longer will you call me, 'My *B*.' Hos.2.16
who have not bowed the knee to *B*. Rom.11.4
BABE
by the mouth of *b*. and infants Ps.8.2
understanding and revealed them to *b*. Mt.11.25
the *b*. in my womb leaped for joy Lk.1.44
you will find a *b*. wrapped in Lk.2.12
men of the flesh, as *b*. in Christ 1 Cor.3.1
be *b*. in evil, but in thinking 1 Cor.14.20
Like newborn *b*., long for the pure 1 Pet.2.2
BABEL
Nimrod king of, Gen.10.10; confusion of tongues at tower of, Gen.11.9
BABYLON
(1) the capital of the Babylonian Empire; ambassadors from, to Hezekiah, 2 Kg.20.12; 2 Chr.32.31; Is.39; Jewish captivity there, 2 Kg.25; 2 Chr.36; Jer.39; 52; return from, Ezra 1; Neh.2; greatness of, Dan.4.30; taken by the Medes, Dan.5.30; fall of, Is.13.14; 21.2; 47; Jer.25.12; 50; 51; church in, 1 Pet.5.13; (2) the great, Rev.14.8; 17.1–18.24
BAD
It is *b*., it is *b*.," says the buyer Pr.20.14
and the *b*. figs very *b*., so *b*. that Jer.24.3
make the tree *b*., and its fruit *b*. Mt.12.33
For no good tree bears *b*. fruit Lk.6.43
B. company ruins good morals 1 Cor.15.33
will go on from *b*. to worse 2 Tim.3.13
BALAAM
requested by Balak to curse Israel, is forbidden, Num.22.5,13; his anger, Num.22.27; blesses Israel, Num.23.19; 24; his prophecies, Num. 23.9,24; 24.17; his wicked counsel, Num. 31.16; Dt.23.4; *see* Jos.24.9; Jg.11.25; Mic. 6.5; 2 Pet.2.15; Jude 11; Rev.2.14; slain, Num.31.8; Jos.13.22
BALANCE
A false *b*. is an abomination to the Pr.11.1
A just *b*. and scales are the LORD's Pr.16.11
weighed . . . the hills in a *b*.? Is.40.12
weighed in the *b*. and found wanting Dan.5.27
and its rider had a *b*. in his hand Rev.6.5
BALM
a little *b*. and a little honey Gen.43.11
Is there no *b*. in Gilead? Jer.8.22
Take *b*. for their pain; perhaps Jer.51.8
early figs, honey, oil, and *b*. Ezek.27.17
BANQUET
it was Esther's *b*. Est.2.18
Herod on his birthday gave a *b*. Mk.6.21
When you give a dinner or a *b*. Lk.14.12
none . . . invited shall taste my *b*. Lk.14.24
BAPTISM
he saw many . . . coming for *b*. Mt.3.7
The *b*. of John, whence was it? Mt.21.25
preaching a *b*. of repentance for Mk.1.4
the *b*. with which I am baptized Mk.10.38
Was the *b*. of John from heaven or Lk.20.4
beginning from the *b*. of John Acts 1.22
preached a *b*. of repentance to Acts 13.24
They said, "Into John's *b*." Acts 19.3
baptized with the *b*. of repentance Acts 19.4
buried therefore with him by *b*. Rom.6.4

one Lord, one faith, one *b*. Eph.4.5
you were buried with him in *b*. Col.2.12
B., which corresponds to this 1 Pet.3.21
BAPTIZE
I *b*. you with water for repentance Mt.3.11
b. them in the name of the Father Mt.28.19
able . . . to be *b*. with the baptism Mk.10.38
he will *b*. you with the Holy Spirit Lk.3.16
who sent me to *b*. with water Jn.1.33
although Jesus himself did not *b*. Jn.4.2
be *b*. every one of you in the Acts 2.38
they were *b*., both men and women Acts 8.12
had only been *b*. in the name of Acts 8.16
hearing Paul believed and were *b*. Acts 18.8
Rise and be *b*., and wash away Acts 22.16
who have been *b*. into Christ Jesus Rom.6.3
not send me to *b*. but to preach 1 Cor.1.17
all were *b*. into Moses in the 1 Cor.10.2
we were all *b*. into one body 1 Cor.12.13
b. on behalf of the dead? 1 Cor.15.29
BARABBAS
a robber, released instead of Jesus, Mt.27.16; Mk.15.6,7; Lk.23.18; Jn.18.40
BARAK
Jg.4.6–5.15; Heb.11.32
BARE
foundations . . . were laid *b*. Ps.18.15
LORD will lay *b*. their secret parts Is.3.17
I will make you a *b*. rock Ezek.26.14
a *b*. kernel, perhaps of wheat or 1 Cor.15.37
BARN
Is the seed yet in the *b*.? Hag.2.19
but gather the wheat into my *b*. Mt.13.30
I will pull down my *b*. Lk.12.18
have neither storehouse nor *b*. Lk.12.24
BARNABAS
Levite of Cyprus, Acts 4.36; preaches at Antioch, Acts 11.22; accompanies Paul, Acts 11.30; 12.25; 13; 14; 15; 1 Cor.9.6; disagrees with Paul about John Mark, Acts 15.36–40; is misled at Antioch by Judaizing emissaries from Jerusalem, Gal.2.13
BARREN
Now Sarai was *b*.; she had no child Gen.11.30
The *b*. has borne seven, but she 1 Sam.2.5
He gives the *b*. woman a home Ps.113.9
Sing, O *b*. one, who did not bear Is.54.1
no child, because Elizabeth was *b*. Lk.1.7
they will say, 'Blessed are the *b*. Lk.23.26
O *b*. one that dost not bear Gal.4.27
that faith apart from works is *b*.? Jas.2.20
BARTHOLOMEW
Mt.10.3; Mk.3.18; Lk.6.14; Acts 1.13
BARUCH
receives Jeremiah's evidence, Jer.32.12–13; 36; discredited by Azariah, and carried into Egypt, Jer.43.2–6; God's message to, Jer.45
BASE (adjective)
b. fellows, beset the house round Jg.19.22
the wicked and *b*. fellows among 1 Sam.30.22
before my eyes anything that is *b*. Ps.101.3
the *b*. fellow to the honorable Is.3.5
God gave them up to a *b*. mind Rom.1.28
dissension, slander, *b*. suspicions 1 Tim.6.4
by teaching for *b*. gain what they Tit.1.11

BASKET
eating it out of the *b.* on my head	Gen.40.17
took for him a *b.* made of bulrushes	Ex.2.3
One *b.* had very good figs	Jer.24.2
A *b.* of summer fruit	Am.8.2
they took up twelve *b.* full of the	Mt.14.20
pieces left over, seven *b.* full	Mk.8.8
the wall, lowering him in a *b.*	Acts 9.25
let down in a *b.* through a window	2 Cor.11.33

BATHSHEBA
wife of Uriah, taken by David, 2 Sam.11; 12;
appeals to David for Solomon against Adonijah,
1 Kg.1.15; intercedes with Solomon for Adonijah, 1 Kg.2.19

BATTLE (noun)
for the *b.* is the LORD's and he	1 Sam.17.47
the *b.* is not yours but God's	2 Chr.20.15
He smells the *b.* from afar	Job 39.25
gird me with strength for the *b.*	Ps.18.39
in safety from the *b.* that I wage	Ps.55.18
covered my head in the day of *b.*	Ps.140.7
nor the *b.* to the strong, nor bread	Ec.9.11
The noise of *b.* is in the land	Jer.50.22
locusts were like horses arrayed for *b.*	Rev.9.7

BEACH
the whole crowd stood on the *b.*	Mt.13.2
Jesus stood on the *b.*	Jn.21.4
kneeling down on the *b.* we prayed	Acts 21.5
they noticed a bay with a *b.*	Acts 27.39

BEAR (noun)
lion and from the paw of the *b.*	1 Sam.17.37
two she-*b.* came out of the woods	2 Kg.2.24
who made the *B.* and Orion	Job 9.9
Let a man meet a she-*b.* robbed	Pr.17.12
The cow and the *b.* shall feed	Is.11.7
fled from a lion, and a *b.* met him	Am.5.19

BEAR (verb)
punishment is greater than I can *b.*	Gen.4.13
then let me *b.* the blame for ever	Gen.43.9
You shall not *b.* false witness	Ex.20.16
curses his God shall *b.* his sin	Lev.24.15
I am not able alone to *b.* you	Dt.1.9
Blessed be the Lord, who daily *b.* us up	Ps.68.19
On their hands they will *b.* you up	Ps.91.12
you who *b.* the vessels of the LORD	Is.52.11
he shall *b.* their iniquities	Is.53.11
good . . . that he *b.* the yoke in his	Lam.3.27
On their hands they will *b.* you up	Mt.4.6
You shall not *b.* false witness	Mt.19.18
How long am I to *b.* with you?	Mk.9.19
B. fruits that befit repentance	Lk.3.8
but came to *b.* witness to the light	Jn.1.8
Even if I do *b.* witness to myself	Jn.8.14
Every branch of mine that *b.* no fruit	Jn.15.2
that we may *b.* fruit for God	Rom.7.4
Spirit himself *b.* witness with our	Rom.8.16
strong ought to *b.* with the failings	Rom.15.1
Love *b.* all things, believes all	1 Cor.13.7
B. one another's burdens, and so	Gal.6.2
each man will have to *b.* his own load	Gal.6.5
I *b.* on my body the marks of Jesus	Gal.6.17
offered once to *b.* the sins of many	Heb.9.28

BEAST
And God made the *b.* of the earth	Gen.1.25
formed every *b.* of the field and	Gen.2.19
the likeness of any *b.* that is on	Dt.4.17

For every *b.* of the forest is mine	Ps.50.10
has regard for the life of his *b.*	Pr.12.10
the spirit of the *b.* goes down to	Ec.3.21
four great *b.* came up out of	Dan.7.3
I fought with *b.* at Ephesus?	1 Cor.15.32
every kind of *b.* . . . . can be tamed	Jas.3.7
I saw a *b.* rising out of the sea	Rev.13.1

BEAT
B. your plowshares into swords	Jl.3.10
shall *b.* their swords into plowshares	Mic.4.3
winds blew and *b.* upon that house	Mt.7.25
the waves *b.* into the boat	Mk.4.37
some they *b.* and some they killed	Mk.12.5
who stripped him and *b.* him	Lk.10.30
but *b.* his breast, saying, 'God, be	Lk.18.13
have *b.* us publicly, uncondemned	Acts 16.37
I do not box as one *b.* the air	1 Cor.9.26
Three times . . . *b.* with rods	2 Cor.11.25
wrong and are *b.* for it you take	1 Pet.2.20

BEAUTIFUL
but Rachel was *b.* and lovely	Gen.29.17
Let *b.* young virgins be sought out	Est.2.2
b. in elevation, is the joy of all	Ps.48.2
a *b.* woman without discretion	Pr.11.22
has made everything *b.* in its time	Ec.3.11
the branch of the LORD shall be *b.*	Is.4.2
How *b.* upon the mountains are the	Is.52.7
tombs, which outwardly appear *b.*	Mt.23.27
alms at the *B.* Gate of the temple	Acts 3.10
How *b.* are the feet of those who	Rom.10.15

BEAUTY
to behold the *b.* of the LORD, and to	Ps.27.4
Out of Zion, the perfection of *b.*	Ps.50.2
strength and *b.* are in his sanctuary	Ps.96.6
Charm is deceitful and *b.* is vain	Pr.31.30
Your eyes will see the king in his *b.*	Is.33.17
and no *b.* that we should desire him	Is.53.2
to make . . . one vessel for *b.*	Rom.9.21
flower falls, and its *b.* perishes	Jas.1.11

BED
My *b.* will comfort me, my couch	Job 7.13
chastened with pain upon his *b.*	Job 33.19
every night I flood my *b.* with tears	Ps.6.6
when I think of thee upon my *b.*	Ps.63.6
If I make my *b.* in Sheol, thou art	Ps.139.8
so does a sluggard on his *b.*	Pr.26.14
For the *b.* is too short to stretch	Is.28.20
Woe to those who lie upon *b.* of ivory	Am.6.4
Rise, take up your *b.* and go home	Mt.9.6
a vessel, or puts it under a *b.*	Lk.8.16
there will be two men in one *b.*	Lk.17.34
let the marriage *b.* be undefiled	Heb.13.4

BEELZEBUL
called the master of the house *B.*	Mt.10.25
said, "He is possessed by *B.*	Mk.3.22
And if I cast out demons by *B.*	Lk.11.19

BEFALL
Does not calamity *b.* the unrighteous	Job 31.3
no evil shall *b.* you	Ps.91.10
that nothing worse *b.* you	Jn.5.14
knowing all that was to *b.* him	Jn.18.4
not knowing what shall *b.* me	Acts 20.22

BEFIT
Praise *b.* the upright	Ps.33.1
Bear fruits that *b.* repentance	Lk.3.8
as *b.* women who profess religion	1 Tim.2.10

teach what *b*. sound doctrine Tit.2.1
their journey as *b*. God's service 3 Jn.6
BEG
May his children wander . . . and *b*. Ps.109.10
the children *b*. for food, but no one Lam.4.4
Give to him who *b*. from you Mt.5.42
I am ashamed to *b*. Lk.16.3
the man who used to sit and *b*.? Jn.9.8
So I *b*. you to reaffirm your love 2 Cor.2.8
I . . . *b*. you to lead a life worthy of Eph.4.1
BEGINNING (noun)
In the *b*. God created the heavens Gen.1.1
And though your *b*. was small Job 8.7
fear of the LORD . . . *b*. of wisdom Ps.111.10
fear of the LORD is the *b*. of knowledge Pr.1.7
The *b*. of wisdom is this: Get wisdom Pr.4.7
Better is the end of a thing than its *b*. Ec.7.8
but from the *b*. it was not so Mt.19.8
The *b*. of the gospel of Jesus Christ Mk.1.1
In the *b*. was the Word, and the Word Jn.1.1
He was a murderer from the *b*. Jn.8.44
he is the *b*., the first-born from Col.1.18
neither *b*. of days nor end of life Heb.7.3
That which was from the *b*. 1 Jn.1.1
the devil has sinned from the *b*. 1 Jn.3.8
the Amen . . . the *b*. of God's creation Rev.3.14
I am . . . the *b*. and the end Rev.21.6
BEHAVIOR
who were ashamed of your lewd *b*. Ezek.16.27
how . . . blameless was our *b*. to you 1 Th.2.10
women likewise to be reverent in *b*. Tit.2.3
your good *b*. in Christ may be put 1 Pet.3.16
BEHEADED
they . . . slew him, and *b*. him 2 Sam.4.7
He went and *b*. him in the prison Mk.6.27
who had been *b*. for their testimony Rev.20.4
BEHELD
they *b*. God, and ate and drank Ex.24.11
Thy eyes *b*. my unformed substance Ps.139.16
Then I *b*., and, lo, a form that had Ezek.8.2
whenever the unclean spirits *b*. him Mk.3.11
we have *b*. his glory, glory as of Jn.1.14
BEHIND
But Lot's wife *b*. him looked back Gen.19.26
b. him was a ram, caught in a Gen.22.13
Thou dost beset me *b*. and before Ps.139.5
I heard *b*. me the sound of a great Ezek.3.12
said to Peter, "Get *b*. me, Satan Mt.16.23
came up *b*. him, and touched the Lk.8.44
the cross, to carry it *b*. Jesus Lk.23.26
forgetting what lies *b*. Phil.3.13
I heard *b*. me a loud voice like Rev.1.10
BEING (noun)
and man became a living *b*. Gen.2.7
desirest truth in the inward *b*. Ps.51.6
praises to my God while I have *b*. Ps.146.2
so that no human *b*. might boast 1 Cor.1.29
in bondage to *b*. that by nature are Gal.4.8
but no human *b*. can tame the tongue Jas.3.8
BELIEVE
they will not *b*. me or listen to my Ex.4.1
If they will not *b*. you Ex.4.8
I *b*. that I shall see the goodness Ps.27.13
Who has *b*. what we have heard? Is.53.1
Do you *b*. that I am able to do this? Mt.9.28
repent, and *b*. in the gospel Mk.1.15

synagogue, "Do not fear, only *b*." Mk.5.36
All things are possible to him who *b*. Mk.9.23
b. that you receive it, and you will Mk.11.24
the cross, that we may see and *b*. Mk.15.32
that they may not *b*. and be saved Lk.8.12
that all might *b*. through him Jn.1.7
that whoever *b*. in him should not Jn.3.16
He who *b*. in the Son has eternal Jn.3.36
Unless you see . . . you will not *b*. Jn.4.48
The Jews did not *b*. that he had Jn.9.18
shall never die. Do you *b*. this? Jn.11.26
b. in the light, that you may become Jn.12.36
b. in God, *b*. also in me Jn.14.1
B. me that I am in the Father and Jn.14.11
we *b*. that you came from God Jn.16.30
hear the word of the gospel and *b*. Acts 15.7
B. in the Lord Jesus, and you Acts 16.31
to us who *b*. in him that raised Rom.4.24
we preach to save those who *b*. 1 Cor.1.21
Love bears all things, *b*. all things 1 Cor.13.7
since we *b*. that Jesus died and 1 Th.4.14
to God must *b*. that he exists and Heb.11.6
Even the demons *b*.–and shudder Jas.2.19
Abraham *b*. God, and it was reckoned Jas.2.23
BELLY
upon your *b*. you shall go, and dust Gen.3.14
was in the *b*. of the fish three Jon.1.17
out of the *b*. of Sheol I cried Jon.2.2
nights in the *b*. of the whale Mt.12.40
destruction, their god is the *b*. Phil.3.19
BELONG
I heard this: that power *b*. to God Ps.62.11
for to thee *b*. all the nations Ps.82.8
but the victory *b*. to the LORD Pr.21.31
to the Lord our God *b*. mercy and Dan.9.9
Deliverance *b*. to the LORD Jon.2.9
are called to *b*. to Jesus Christ Rom.1.6
of Christ does not *b*. to him Rom.8.9
"I *b*. to Paul," or "I *b*. to Apollos 1 Cor.1.12
I do not *b*. to the body," that 1 Cor.12.15
To him *b*. glory and dominion for 1 Pet.4.11
and glory and power *b*. to our God Rev.19.1
BELOVED
for he gives to his *b*. sleep Ps.127.2
This is my *b*. Son, with whom I am Mt.17.5
from heaven, "Thou art my *b*. Son Mk.1.11
I will send my *b*. son; it may be Lk.20.13
he freely bestowed on us in the *B*. Eph.1.6
Luke the *b*. physician and Demas Col.4.14
This is my *b*. Son, with whom I am 2 Pet.1.17
B., I am writing you no new 1 Jn.2.7
B., let us love one another 1 Jn.4.7
BELSHAZZAR
Dan.5.1,22,30; 7.1; 8.1
BELTESHAZZAR
Dan.1.7; 4.9,19; 5.12; 10.1
BENEFIT
soul, and forget not all his *b*. Ps.103.2
A man who is kind *b*. himself Pr.11.17
I say this for your own *b*. 1 Cor.7.35
since those who *b*. by their 1 Tim.6.2
want some *b*. from you in the Lord Philem. 20
BENHADAD
Kings of Syria: (1) in league with Asa against
Baasha, 1 Kg.15.18; (2) wars with Ahab, 1
Kg.20; baffled by Elisha, 2 Kg.6.8–10; besieges

Samaria, 2 Kg.6.24; 7; slain by Hazael, 2 Kg.8.7–15; (3) son of Hazael, wars with Israel, 2 Kg.13.3,25

BENJAMIN
Patriarch, youngest son of Jacob, his birth at Bethlehem, Gen.35.16,18; goes into Egypt, Gen.43.15; Joseph's stratagem to detain, Gen. 44; Jacob's prophecy concerning, Gen.49.27; his descendants, Gen.46.21; 1 Chr.7.6; twice numbered, Num.1.36; 26.38; blessed by Moses, Dt.33.12; their inheritance, Jos.18.11; their wickedness chastised, Jg.20; 21; the first king chosen from, 1 Sam.9; 10; support the house of Saul, 2 Sam.2.9; afterwards adhere to that of David, 1 Kg.12.21; 1 Chr.11; the tribe of Paul, Phil.3.5

BEREFT
the woman was *b.* of her two sons   Ru.1.5
my soul is *b.* of peace   Lam.3.17
But since we were *b.* of you   1 Th.2.17
depraved . . . and *b.* of the truth   1 Tim.6.5

BESEECH
Save us, we *b.* thee, O Lord   Ps.118.25
O Lord GOD, forgive, I *b.* thee   Am.7.2
I *b.* you, do not torment me   Lk.8.28
We *b.* you on behalf of Christ   2 Cor.5.20
I *b.* you as aliens and exiles   1 Pet.2.11

BESTOW
that he may *b.* a blessing upon you   Ex.32.29
majesty thou dost *b.* upon him   Ps.21.5
the LORD God . . . *b.* favor and honor   Ps.84.11
the gifts *b.* on us by God   1 Cor.2.12
he freely *b.* on us in the Beloved   Eph.1.6
exalted him and *b.* on him the name   Phil.2.9

BETHANY
lies on the eastern shoulder of the Mount of Olives, little more than a mile east of Jerusalem; visited by Christ, Mt.21.17; 26.6; Mk.11.1; Lk.19.29; Jn.12.1; raising of Lazarus at, Jn.11.18; ascension of Christ at, Lk.24.50

BETHEL
city of Palestine, formerly Luz, named Bethel by Jacob, Gen.28.19; 31.13; eight miles north of Jerusalem; altar built by Jacob at, Gen.35.1; occupied by the house of Joseph, Jg.1.22; sons of prophets resident there, 2 Kg.2.2,3; 17.28; the king's sanctuary, Am.7.13; idolatry of Jeroboam at, 1 Kg.12.28–33; 13.1–32; reformation by Josiah at, 2 Kg.23.15–25

BETHLEHEM
about five miles south of Jerusalem; it is also called Ephrath (Gen.35.19) and Ephrathah (Mic.5.2) to distinguish it from the northern city of the same name (Jos.19.15); Naomi and Ruth return to, Ru.1–4; David anointed at, 1 Sam. 16.13; 20.6; well of, 2 Sam.23.15; 1 Chr.11.17; Christ's birth at, Mt.2.1; Lk.2.4; Jn.7.42; predicted, Mic.5.2; male children of, slain, Mt.2.16

BETHSAIDA
native place of Philip, Peter, and Andrew, Mk.6.45; Jn.1.44; 12.21; blind man cured at, Mk.8.22; condemned for unbelief, Mt.11.21; Christ feeds the five thousand at, Lk.9.10–17

BETRAY
b. one another, and hate one   Mt.24.10

of them, for your accent *b.* you   Mt.26.73
I have sinned in *b.* innocent blood   Mt.27.4
I say to you, one of you will *b.* me   Mk.14.18
you *b.* the Son of man with a kiss?   Lk.22.48
For he knew who was to *b.* him   Jn.13.11
whom you have now *b.* and murdered   Acts 7.52
on the night when he was *b.*   1 Cor.11.23

BETTER
to obey is *b.* than sacrifice   1 Sam.15.22
B. is a little that the righteous has   Ps.37.16
a day in thy courts is *b.* than   Ps.84.10
It is *b.* to take refuge in the LORD   Ps.118.9
for wisdom is *b.* than jewels   Pr.8.11
B. is a little with righteousness   Pr.16.8
It is *b.* to be of a lowly spirit   Pr.16.19
B. is a dry morsel with quiet than   Pr.17.1
There is nothing *b.* for a man than   Ec.2.24
B. is the end of a thing than its   Ec.7.8
how much *b.* is your love than   S. of S.4.10
is *b.* for you to enter life maimed   Mk.9.43
would be *b.* for him if a millstone   Lk.17.2
is *b.* to marry than to be aflame   1 Cor.7.9
count others *b.* than yourselves   Phil.2.3
as the covenant he mediates is *b.*   Heb.8.6
is *b.* to suffer for doing right   1 Pet.3.17

BEWARE
B. of practicing your piety before   Mt.6.1
B. of the leaven of the Pharisees   Mt.16.11
B. of the scribes, who like to go   Mk.12.38
b. of all covetousness   Lk.12.15
b. lest you be carried away with   2 Pet.3.17

BIND
B. them upon your heart always   Pr.6.21
B. up the testimony, seal the   Is.8.16
sent me to *b.* up the brokenhearted   Is.61.1
whatever you *b.* on earth shall be   Mt.16.19
love, which *b.* everything together   Col.3.14

BIRD
every winged *b.* according to its   Gen.1.21
every *b.* according to its kind   Gen.7.14
Flee like a *b.* to the mountains   Ps.11.1
In them the *b.* build their nests   Ps.104.17
net spread in the sight of any *b.*   Pr.1.17
Look at the *b.* of the air   Mt.6.26
the *b.* of the air devoured it   Lk.8.5
more value are you than the *b.*   Lk.12.24

BIRTH
you forgot the God who gave you *b.*   Dt.32.18
Job . . . cursed the day of his *b.*   Job 3.1
better . . . death, than the day of *b.*   Ec.7.1
Now the *b.* of Jesus Christ took   Mt.1.18
many will rejoice at his *b.*   Lk.1.14
she gave *b.* to a son   Lk.1.57
she gave *b.* to her first-born   Lk.2.7
Then desire . . . gives *b.* to sin   Jas.1.15

BIRTHRIGHT
Jacob said, "First sell me your *b.*"   Gen.25.31
Thus Esau despised his *b.*   Gen.25.34
who sold his *b.* for a single meal   Heb.12.16

BISHOP
Philippi, with the *b.* and deacons   Phil.1.1
one aspires to the office of *b.*   1 Tim.3.1
Now a *b.* must be above reproach   1 Tim.3.2
For a *b.*, as God's steward, must be   Tit.1.7

BITTER
they made life *b.* for Isaac and   Gen.26.35

why . . . life to the *b*. in soul	Job 3.20
For thou writest *b*. things against	Job 13.26
Today also my complaint is *b*.	Job 23.2
for they made his spirit *b*.	Ps.106.33
strong drink is *b*. to those who	Is.24.9
And he went out and wept *b*.	Lk.22.62
But if you have *b*. jealousy	Jas.3.14

BITTERNESS

Surely the *b*. of death is past.	1 Sam.15.32
will complain in the *b*. of my soul	Job 7.11
The heart knows its own *b*.	Pr.14.10
Remember my affliction and my *b*.	Lam.3.19
Their mouth is full of curses and *b*.	Rom.3.14
Let all *b*. and wrath and anger	Eph.4.31
that no "root of *b*." spring up	Heb.12.15

BLAMELESS

walk before me, and be *b*.	Gen.17.1
a *b*. and upright man, who fears God	Job 1.8
Then I shall be *b*., and innocent	Ps.19.13
The LORD knows the days of the *b*.	Ps.37.18
give heed to the way that is *b*.	Ps.101.2
Blessed are those whose way is *b*.	Ps.119.1
those of *b*. ways are his delight	Pr.11.20
Bloodthirsty men hate one who is *b*.	Pr.29.10
should be holy and *b*. before him	Eph.1.4
to present you holy and *b*.	Col.1.22
righteous and *b*. was our behavior	1 Th.2.10
For a bishop . . . must be *b*.	Tit.1.7

BLASPHEME

He who *b*. the name of the LORD	Lev.24.16
but he who *b*. against the Holy	Lk.12.10
tried to make them *b*.	Acts 26.11
I formerly *b*. and persecuted	1 Tim.1.13
Is it not they who *b*. that honorable	Jas.2.7

BLASPHEMY

the *b*. against the Spirit will not	Mt.12.31
It is *b*.! Who can forgive sins	Mk.2.7
We stone you . . . for *b*.	Jn.10.33
its mouth to utter *b*. against God	Rev.13.6

BLEMISH (noun)

Your lamb shall be without *b*.	Ex.12.5
See that they are without *b*.	Num.28.31
offered himself without *b*. to God	Heb.9.14
that of a lamb without *b*. or spot	1 Pet.1.19
without spot or *b*., and at peace	2 Pet.3.14
to present you without *b*. before	Jude 24

BLESS

The LORD *b*. you and keep you	Num.6.24
May the LORD *b*. his people with	Ps.29.11
I will *b*. the LORD at all times	Ps.34.1
B. the LORD, O my soul; and all	Ps.103.1
The LORD *b*. you from Zion	Ps.128.5
Come, *b*. the LORD, all you servants	Ps.134.1
Every day I will *b*. thee	Ps.145.2
shall *b*. himself by the God of truth	Is.65.16
B. are the poor in spirit, for	Mt.5.3
b. those who curse you, pray for	Lk.6.28
It is more *b*. to give than to	Acts 20.35
B. those who persecute you	Rom.12.14
When reviled, we *b*.; when	1 Cor.4.12
awaiting our *b*. hope, the appearing	Tit.2.13
With it we *b*. the Lord and Father	Jas.3.9
B. are the dead who die in the Lord	Rev.14.13

BLESSING (noun)

turned the curse into a *b*. for you	Dt.23.5
This is the *b*. with which Moses the	Dt.33.1

He will receive *b*. from the LORD	Ps.24.5
By his *b*. they multiply greatly	Ps.107.38
The *b*. of the LORD be upon you	Ps.129.8
The *b*. of the LORD makes rich	Pr.10.22
they shall be showers of *b*.	Ezek.34.26
down for you an overflowing *b*.	Mal.3.10
of service to them in material *b*.	Rom.15.27
The cup of *b*. which we bless	1 Cor.10.16
you with every *b*. in abundance	2 Cor.9.8
the same mouth come *b*. and cursing	Jas.3.10
B. and glory and wisdom	Rev.7.12

BLIND

the LORD opens the eyes of the *b*.	Ps.146.8
Then the eyes of the *b*. shall be	Is.35.5
the *b*. receive their sight and the	Mt.11.5
Let them alone; they are *b*. guides	Mt.15.14
Can a *b*. man lead a *b*. man?	Lk.6.39
the maimed, the lame, the *b*.	Lk.14.13
that though I was *b*., now I see	Jn.9.25
that you are a guide to the *b*.	Rom.2.19

BLOOD

your brother's *b*. is crying to me	Gen.4.10
Whoever sheds the *b*. of man	Gen.9.6
dipped the robe in the *b*.	Gen.37.31
that was in the Nile turned to *b*.	Ex.7.20
The *b*. shall be a sign for you	Ex.12.13
Behold the *b*. of the covenant	Ex.24.8
Moreover you shall eat no *b*. whatever	Lev.7.26
precious is their *b*. in his sight	Ps.72.14
for this is my *b*. of the covenant	Mt.26.28
I am innocent of this man's *b*.	Mt.27.24
had a flow of *b*. for twelve years	Mk.5.25
and drinks my *b*. has eternal life	Jn.6.54
cup is the new covenant in my *b*.	1 Cor.11.25
we have redemption through his *b*.	Eph.1.7
peace by the *b*. of his cross	Col.1.20
more shall the *b*. of Christ	Heb.9.14
with the precious *b*. of Christ	1 Pet.1.19
the *b*. of Jesus his Son cleanses	1 Jn.1.7
by thy *b*. didst ransom men for God	Rev.5.9
them white in the *b*. of the Lamb	Rev.7.14
drunk with the *b*. of the saints	Rev.17.6

BLOT (verb)

I will *b*. out man whom I have	Gen.6.7
thy . . . mercy *b*. out my transgressions	Ps.51.1
b. out all my iniquities	Ps.51.9
be *b*. out of the book of the living	Ps.69.28
He who *b*. out your transgressions	Is.43.25
nor *b*. out their sin from thy sight	Jer.18.23
When I *b*. you out, I will cover the	Ezek.32.7
that your sins may be *b*. out	Acts 3.19
will not *b*. his name out of the book	Rev.3.5

BLOW

God made a wind *b*. over the earth	Gen.8.1
the breath of the LORD *b*. upon it	Is.40.7
b. the trumpet among the nations	Jer.51.27
B. the trumpet in Zion; sanctify a	Jl.2.15
The wind *b*. where it wills, and you	Jn.3.8

BOAST

Do not *b*. about tomorrow, for you do	Pr.27.1
Let him who *b*., of the Lord	1 Cor.1.31
lest any man should *b*.	Eph.2.9
do not *b*. and be false to the truth	Jas.3.14
As it is, you *b*. in your arrogance	Jas.4.16

BOAT

Immediately they left the *b*.	Mt.4.22

so that the *b*. was being swamped by	Mt.8.24
got into the *b*. with his disciples	Mk.8.10
he saw two *b*. by the lake	Lk.5.2
saw Jesus . . . drawing near to the *b*.	Jn.6.19
had lowered the *b*. into the sea	Acts 27.30

BOAZ
Ru.2.1; 3.2; 4.1; 1 Chr.2.12; Mt.1.5; Lk.3.32

BODY

my *b*. wasted away through my	Ps.32.3
destroy both soul and *b*. in hell	Mt.10.28
Take, eat; this is my *b*.	Mt.26.26
do not fear those who kill the *b*.	Lk.12.4
But he spoke of the temple of his *b*.	Jn.2.21
deliver me from this *b*. of death?	Rom.7.24
to present your *b*. as a living	Rom.12.1
so we . . . are one *b*. in Christ	Rom.12.5
absent in *b*. I am present in spirit	1 Cor.5.3
b. is not meant for immorality	1 Cor.6.13
your *b*. is a temple of the Holy	1 Cor.6.19
but I pommel my *b*. and subdue it	1 Cor.9.27
This is my *b*. which is for you	1 Cor.11.24
just as the *b*. is one and has	1 Cor.12.12
there are many parts, yet one *b*.	1 Cor.12.20
Now you are the *b*. of Christ	1 Cor.12.27
it is raised a spiritual *b*.	1 Cor.15.44
away from the *b*. and at home with	2 Cor.5.8
I bear on my *b*. the marks of Jesus	Gal.6.17
There is one *b*. and one Spirit	Eph.4.4
He is the head of the *b*., the church	Col.1.18
soul and *b*. be kept sound	1 Th.5.23
offering of the *b*. of Jesus Christ	Heb.10.10
For as the *b*. apart from the spirit	Jas.2.26

BOLD

A wicked man puts on a *b*. face	Pr.21.29
but the righteous are *b*. as a lion	Pr.28.1
he had preached *b*. in the name of	Acts 9.27
He began to speak *b*. in the synagogue	Acts 18.26
though I am *b*. enough in Christ to	Philem.8

BOND

broke your yoke and burst your *b*.	Jer.2.20
will burst your *b*. asunder	Nah.1.13
you are . . . in the *b*. of iniquity	Acts 8.23
unity of the Spirit in the *b*. of peace	Eph.4.3
having canceled the *b*. which stood	Col.2.14

BONDAGE

the people . . . groaned under their *b*.	Ex.2.23
from Egypt, out of the house of *b*.	Ex.13.3
God has not forsaken us in our *b*.	Ezra 9.9
We . . . have never been in *b*. to any one	Jn.8.33
that they might bring us into *b*.	Gal.2.4
were subject to lifelong *b*.	Heb.2.15

BONE

This at last is *b*. of my *b*. and	Gen.2.23
Surely you are my *b*. and my flesh	Gen.29.14
a soft tongue will break a *b*.	Pr.25.15
came together, *b*. to its *b*.	Ezek.37.7
they are full of dead men's *b*.	Mt.23.27
a spirit has not flesh and *b*.	Lk.24.39
Not a *b*. of him shall be broken	Jn.19.36

BOOK

blot me . . . out of thy *b*. which	Ex.32.32
Take this *b*. of the law, and put it	Dt.31.26
Ezra opened the *b*. in the sight	Neh.8.5
that they were inscribed in a *b*.	Job 19.23
Of making many *b*. there is no end	Ec.12.12
read from the *b*. of the LORD	Is.34.16

is inscribed in the *b*. of truth	Dan.10.21
a *b*. of remembrance was written	Mal.3.16
not contain the *b*. that would be	Jn.21.25
whose names are in the *b*. of life	Phil.4.3
blot his name out of the *b*. of life	Rev.3.5
another *b*. was opened, which is	Rev.20.12

BORN

man is *b*. to trouble as the sparks	Job 5.7
Man that is *b*. of a woman is of few	Job 14.1
peoples, "This one was *b*. there."	Ps.87.6
a time to be *b*., and a time to die	Ec.3.2
Cursed be the day on which I was *b*.	Jer.20.14
Now when Jesus was *b*. in Bethlehem	Mt.2.1
to you is *b*. this day in the city	Lk.2.11
unless one is *b*. anew, he cannot see	Jn.3.3
That which is *b*. of the flesh is	Jn.3.6
opened the eyes of a man *b*. blind	Jn.9.32
You were *b*. in utter sin, and would	Jn.9.34
we have been *b*. anew to a living	1 Pet.1.3
No one *b*. of God commits sin	1 Jn.3.9
For whatever is *b*. of God overcomes	1 Jn.5.4

BOSOM

by hiding my iniquity in my *b*.	Job 31.33
I bear in my *b*. the insults of the	Ps.89.50
anger lodges in the *b*. of fools	Ec.7.9
by the angels to Abraham's *b*.	Lk.16.22
who is in the *b*. of the Father, he	Jn.1.18

BOUGHT

And I *b*. the field at Anathoth	Jer.32.9
all who sold and *b*. in the temple	Mt.21.12
b. with them the potter's field	Mt.27.7
(Now this man *b*. a field with the	Acts 1.18
I *b*. this citizenship for a large	Acts 22.28
you were *b*. with a price	1 Cor.6.20
denying the Master who *b*. them	2 Pet.2.1

BOUND

Folly is *b*. up in the heart of a	Pr.22.15
cast three men *b*. into the fire?	Dan.3.24
on earth shall be *b*. in heaven	Mt.16.19
whom Satan *b*. for eighteen years	Lk.13.16
woman is *b*. by law to her husband	Rom.7.2
we are *b*. to give thanks to God	2 Th.2.13
b. him for a thousand years	Rev.20.2

BOW (noun)

I set my *b*. in the cloud, and it	Gen.9.13
for lo, the wicked bend the *b*.	Ps.11.2
he breaks the *b*., and shatters the	Ps.46.9
the *b*. that is in the cloud	Ezek.1.28
horse, and its rider had a *b*.	Rev.6.2

BOW (verb)

you shall not *b*. down to their gods	Ex.23.24
you shall not *b*. down to them	Dt.5.9
Mordecai did not *b*. down or do	Est.3.2
shall come and *b*. down before thee	Ps.86.9
O come, let us worship and *b*. down	Ps.95.6
The evil *b*. down before the good	Pr.14.19
To me every knee shall *b*.	Is.45.23
he *b*. his head and gave up his	Jn.19.30
who have not *b*. the knee to Baal	Rom.11.4
every knee shall *b*. to me	Rom.14.11
name of Jesus every knee should *b*.	Phil.2.10

BOY

the *b*. Samuel continued to grow	1 Sam.2.26
be full of *b*. and girls playing in	Zech.8.5
the *b*. was cured instantly	Mt.17.18
immediately it convulsed the *b*.	Mk.9.20

BRANCH

a *b*. shall grow out of his roots	Is.11.1
raise up for David a righteous *B*.	Jer.23.5
a righteous *B*. to spring forth	Jer.33.15
I will bring my servant the *B*.	Zech.3.8
Every *b*. of mine that bears no fruit	Jn.15.2
the *b*. cannot bear fruit by itself	Jn.15.4
if the root is holy, so are the *b*.	Rom.11.16

BREAD

Seven days . . . eat unleavened *b*.	Ex.12.15
I will rain *b*. from heaven for you	Ex.16.4
eat up my people as they eat *b*.	Ps.53.4
Man ate of the *b*. of the angels	Ps.78.25
gave them *b*. from heaven	Ps.105.40
I will satisfy her poor with *b*.	Ps.132.15
b. eaten in secret is pleasant	Pr.9.17
B. gained by deceit is sweet	Pr.20.17
Cast your *b*. upon the waters	Ec.11.1
Man shall not live by *b*. alone	Mt.4.4
Give us this day our daily *b*.	Mt.6.11
Jesus took *b*., and blessed	Mt.26.26
command this stone to become *b*.	Lk.4.3
he took the *b*. and blessed	Lk.24.30
Jesus said . . . "I am the *b*. of life	Jn.6.35
I am the living *b*. which came down	Jn.6.51
who eats this *b*. will live for ever	Jn.6.58
The *b*. which we break, is it not a	1 Cor.10.16
as you eat this *b*. and drink the	1 Cor.11.26

BREAST

it is melted within my *b*.	Ps.22.14
a child quieted at its mother's *b*.	Ps.131.2
beat his *b*., saying, 'God, be	Lk.18.13
returned home beating their *b*.	Lk.23.48
close to the *b*. of Jesus	Jn.13.23
with a golden girdle round his *b*.	Rev.1.13

BREASTPLATE

He put on righteousness as a *b*.	Is.59.17
put on the *b*. of righteousness	Eph.6.14
put on the *b*. of faith and love	1 Th.5.8
they had scales like iron *b*.	Rev.9.9

BREATH

everything that has the *b*. of life	Gen.1.30
By the *b*. of God they perish	Job 4.9
By the *b*. of God ice is given	Job 37.10
surely every man is a mere *b*.	Ps.39.11
Man is like a *b*., his days are like	Ps.144.4
who gives *b*. to the people upon it	Is.42.5

BREATHE

they *b*. out violence	Ps.27.12
Let everything that *b*. praise the	Ps.150.6
a loud cry, and *b*. his last	Mk.15.37
he *b*. on them, and said to them	Jn.20.22

BRETHREN

one teacher, and you are all *b*.	Mt.23.8
to one of the least of these my *b*.	Mt.25.40
turned again, strengthen your *b*.	Lk.22.32
you are *b*., why do you wrong each	Acts 7.26
they gave great joy to all the *b*.	Acts 15.3
be the first-born among many *b*.	Rom.8.29
Peace be to the *b*., and love	Eph.6.23
he is not ashamed to call them *b*.	Heb.2.11
made like his *b*. in every respect	Heb.2.17
to lay down our lives for the *b*.	1 Jn.3.16

BRIBE

you shall take no *b*.	Ex.23.8
a *b*. blinds the eyes of the wise	Dt.16.19

does not take a *b*. against the	Ps.15.5
he who hates *b*. will live	Pr.15.27
take a *b*., and turn aside the needy	Am.5.12

BRIDE

my *b*., you have ravished my heart	S.of S.4.9
He who has the *b*. is the bridegroom	Jn.3.29
to present you as a pure *b*.	2 Cor.11.2
prepared as a *b*. adorned for her	Rev.21.2
The Spirit and the *B*. say, "Come."	Rev.22.17

BRIDEGROOM

like a *b*. leaving his chamber	Ps.19.5
when the *b*. is taken away from them	Mt.9.15
As the *b*. was delayed, they all	Mt.25.5
Can . . . guests fast while the *b*. is with	Mk.2.19
He who has the bride is the *b*.	Jn.3.29

BRIGHT

thee, the night is *b*. as the day	Ps.139.12
b. as the sun, terrible as an army	S.of S.6.10
a *b*. cloud overshadowed them	Mt.17.5
angels . . . robed in pure *b*. linen	Rev.15.6
b. as crystal, flowing from the	Rev.22.1

BRIMSTONE

the LORD rained . . . *b*. and fire	Gen.19.24
he will rain coals of fire and *b*.	Ps.11.6
tormented with fire and *b*.	Rev.14.10
lake that burns with fire and *b*.	Rev.21.8

BROKENHEARTED

The LORD is near to the *b*.	Ps.34.18
needy and the *b*. to their death	Ps.109.16
He heals the *b*., and binds up their	Ps.147.3
he has sent me to bind up the *b*.	Is.61.1

BROOD

he said to them, "You *b*. of vipers	Mt.3.7
You *b*. of vipers! how can you	Mt.12.34
hen gathers her *b*. under her wings	Lk.13.34

BROTHER

Cain rose up against his *b*. Abel	Gen.4.8
it is when *b*. dwell in unity	Ps.133.1
a *b*. is born for adversity	Pr.17.17
friend who sticks closer than a *b*.	Pr.18.24
first be reconciled to your *b*.	Mt.5.24
B. will deliver up *b*. to death	Mt.10.21
If your *b*. sins against you, go and	Mt.18.15
Whoever does the will of God is my *b*.	Mk.3.35
if your *b*. sins, rebuke him, and if	Lk.17.3
to her, "Your *b*. will rise again."	Jn.11.23
do you pass judgment on your *b*.?	Rom.14.10
that makes your *b*. stumble	Rom.14.21
lest I cause my *b*. to fall	1 Cor.8.13
apostles except James the Lord's *b*.	Gal.1.19
as an enemy, but warn him as a *b*.	2 Th.3.15
treat younger men like *b*.	1 Tim.5.1
who hates his *b*. is in the darkness	1 Jn.2.11
one who hates his *b*. is a murderer	1 Jn.3.15

BRUISE (verb)

he shall *b*. your head, and you shall	Gen.3.15
a *b*. reed he will not break, and a	Is.42.3
he was *b*. for our iniquities	Is.53.5
was the will of the LORD to *b*. him	Is.53.10
he will not break a *b*. reed	Mt.12.20

BUILD

let us *b*. ourselves a city, and a	Gen.11.4
For the LORD will *b*. up Zion	Ps.102.16
Unless the LORD *b*. the house	Ps.127.1
those who *b*. it labor in vain	Ps.127.1
I will *b*. them up, and not tear them	Jer.24.6

on this rock I will *b.* my church — Mt.16.18
lest I *b.* on another . . . foundation — Rom.15.20
"Knowledge" puffs up, but love *b.* up — 1 Cor.8.1
b. yourselves up on your most holy — Jude 20

BUILDER
the stone which the *b.* rejected — Mt.21.42
like a skilled master *b.* I laid — 1 Cor.3.10
Moses as the *b.* of a house has — Heb.3.3
whose *b.* and maker is God — Heb.11.10

BUILDING (noun)
The *b.* that was facing the temple — Ezek.41.12
to him, "Do you see these great *b.*? — Mk.13.2
you are God's field, God's *b.* — 1 Cor.3.9
we have a *b.* from God, a house not — 2 Cor.5.1

BUILT
Then Noah *b.* an altar to the LORD — Gen.8.20
Moses *b.* an altar and called — Ex.17.15
Joshua *b.* an altar in Mount Ebal — Jos.8.30
David *b.* there an altar to the — 2 Sam.24.25
Wisdom has *b.* her house, she has set — Pr.9.1
foolish man who *b.* his house upon — Mt.7.26
and he *b.* us our synagogue — Lk.7.5
b. upon the foundation of the — Eph.2.20
b. up in him and established — Col.2.7

BURDEN (noun)
Cast your *b.* on the LORD, and he — Ps.55.22
yoke is easy, and my *b.* is light — Mt.11.30
you load men with *b.* hard to bear — Lk.11.46
Bear one another's *b.*, and so — Gal.6.2
I do not lay upon you any other *b.* — Rev.2.24

BURN
And Aaron shall *b.* fragrant incense — Ex.30.7
Let not thy anger *b.* against me — Jg.6.39
he *b.* the chariots with fire — Ps.46.9
long will thy wrath *b.* like fire? — Ps.89.46
altars to *b.* incense to Baal — Jer.11.13
chaff he will *b.* with unquenchable — Mt.3.12
Did not our hearts *b.* within us — Lk.24.32
If any man's work is *b.* up — 1 Cor.3.15
if I deliver my body to be *b.* — 1 Cor.13.3
the lake that *b.* with fire and — Rev.21.8

BURNT
Your *b.* offerings are not acceptable — Jer.6.20
of God, rather than *b.* offerings — Hos.6.6
more than all whole *b.* offerings — Mk.12.33
in *b.* offerings and sin offerings — Heb.10.6

BURST
fountains of the great deep *b.* forth — Gen.7.11
Let us *b.* their bonds asunder — Ps.2.3
new wine will *b.* the skins and it — Lk.5.37
falling headlong he *b.* open in — Acts 1.18

BURY
So Joseph went up to *b.* his father — Gen.50.7
the Egyptians were *b.* all their — Num.33.4
leave the dead to *b.* their own dead — Mt.8.22
potter's field, to *b.* strangers in — Mt.27.7
anointed my body beforehand for *b.* — Mk.14.8
The rich man also died and was *b.* — Lk.16.22
Devout men *b.* Stephen, and made — Acts 8.2
We were *b.* therefore with him by — Rom.6.4
that he was *b.*, that he was raised — 1 Cor.15.4
and you were *b.* with him in baptism — Col.2.12

BUSH
fire out of the midst of a *b.* — Ex.3.2
Moses, in the passage about the *b.* — Mk.12.26

grapes picked from a bramble *b.* — Lk.6.44
Sinai, in a flame of fire in a *b.* — Acts 7.30

BUSHEL
light a lamp and put it under a *b.* — Mt.5.15
brought in to be put under a *b.* — Mk.4.21
puts it in a cellar or under a *b.* — Lk.11.33

BUSINESS
doing *b.* on the great waters — Ps.107.23
I have seen the *b.* that God has — Ec.3.10
also is vanity and an unhappy *b.* — Ec.4.8
to his farm, another to his *b.* — Mt.22.5

BUY
to Egypt to Joseph to *b.* grain — Gen.41.57
B. truth, and do not sell it — Pr.23.23
b. wisdom . . . and understanding — Pr.23.23
Come, *b.* wine and milk without money — Is.55.1
B. my field which is at Anathoth — Jer.32.8
no sword sell his mantle and *b.* one — Lk.22.36
those who *b.* as though they had — 1 Cor.7.30
counsel you to *b.* from me gold — Rev.3.18
so that no one can *b.* or sell — Rev.13.17

CAESAR
Mt.22.17; Lk.2.1; Jn.19.12; Acts 25.12; 28.19

CAESAREA
Mt.16.13; Acts 8.40; 12.19; 21.16; 25.4

CAIN
Gen.4.1; his anger, Gen.4.5; murders Abel,
Gen.4.8; 1 Jn.3.12; his punishment, Gen.4.11–
12; Jude 11

CALAMITY
and all my *c.* laid in the balances — Job 6.2
Does not *c.* befall the unrighteous — Job 31.3
They came upon me in the day of my *c.* — Ps.18.18
I also will laugh at your *c.* — Pr.1.26
He who sows injustice will reap *c.* — Pr.22.8
in afflictions, hardships, *c.* — 2 Cor.6.4
hardships, persecutions, and *c.* — 2 Cor.12.10

CALEB
(1) faith of, Num.13.30; 14.6–10; permitted to
enter Canaan, Num.26.65; 32.12; Dt.1.36; his
request, Jos.14.6; his possessions, Jos.15.13;
gives his daughter to Othniel as wife, Jg.1.13;
(2) 1 Chr.2.18; (3) 1 Chr.2.42–50

CALF
graving tool, and made a molten *c.* — Ex.32.4
made a *c.* in Horeb and worshiped — Ps.106.19
you killed for him the fatted *c.* — Lk.15.30
And they made a *c.* in those days — Acts 7.41

CALL (noun)
his angels with a loud trumpet *c.* — Mt.24.31
gifts and the *c.* of God are — Rom.11.29
For consider your *c.*, brethren — 1 Cor.1.26
of the upward *c.* of God in Christ — Phil.3.14
command, with the archangel's *c.* — 1 Th.4.16
God may make you worthy of his *c.* — 2 Th.1.11
brethren, who share in a heavenly *c.* — Heb.3.1
to confirm your *c.* and election — 2 Pet.1.10
Here is a *c.* for the endurance — Rev.13.10

CALL (verb)
Every day I *c.* upon thee, O LORD — Ps.88.9
c. upon him while he is near — Is.55.6
Before they *c.* I will answer — Is.65.24
you shall *c.* his name Jesus — Mt.1.21
for they shall be *c.* sons of God — Mt.5.9
For I came not to *c.* the righteous — Mt.9.13

all generations will *c.* me blessed   Lk.1.48
I have not come to *c.* the righteous   Lk.5.32
Why do you *c.* me 'Lord, Lord,' and   Lk.6.46
he *c.* his own sheep by name and   Jn.10.3
whoever *c.* on the name of the Lord   Acts 2.21
whom he predestined he also *c.*   Rom.8.30
every one who *c.* upon the name   Rom.10.13
For God has *c.* us to peace   1 Cor.7.15
had *c.* me through his grace   Gal.1.15

CAMEL
Now John wore a garment of *c.* hair   Mt.3.4
is easier for a *c.* to go through   Mt.19.24
out a gnat and swallowing a *c.*   Mt.23.24

CANA
Jn.2.1; 4.46; 21.2

CANAAN
land of, Ex.23.31; Jos.1.4; Zeph.2.5; promised
to Abraham, Gen.12.7; 13.14–15; 17.8; inhabitants of, Ex.15.15; their wickedness at Sodom
and Gomorrah, Gen.13.13; 19; Israelites not to
walk in the ways of, Lev.18.3,24,30; 20.23;
language of, Is.19.18; kingdoms of, Ps.135.11;
king of, Jg.4.2,23,24; 5.19; wars of, Jg.3.1;
dwelling of Abraham in, Gen.12.6–9; Isaac
and Jacob, Gen.28; Esau, Gen.36; Joseph,
Gen.37; allotted to children of Israel, Jos.14;
the spies visit, and their report, Num.13; Moses
sees, from Pisgah, Num.27.12; Dt.3.27; 34.1–4

CAPERNAUM
on the northwest shore of the sea of Galilee;
Christ dwells at, Mt.4.13; Jn.2.12; preaches
at, Mt.4.13–17; Mk.1.21; miracles at, Mt.8.5–34;
Jn.6.17; parables at, Mk.4; condemned for im-
penitence, Mt.11.23; Lk.10.15

CAPTIVE
carried the people *c.* to Assyria   2 Kg.15.29
had carried *c.* to Babylonia   Ezra 2.1
by all those who held them *c.*   Ps.106.46
to proclaim liberty to the *c.*   Is.61.1
the LORD's flock has been taken *c.*   Jer.13.17
be led *c.* among all nations   Lk.21.24
dead to that which held us *c.*   Rom.7.6
making me *c.* to the law of sin   Rom.7.23
every thought *c.* to obey Christ   2 Cor.10.5

CAPTIVITY
for they shall go into *c.*   Dt.28.41
he took into *c.* from Jerusalem   2 Kg.24.15
my young men have gone into *c.*   Lam.1.18
went into *c.* for their iniquity   Ezek.39.23

CAPTURED
the ark of God has been *c.*   1 Sam.4.17
Then they *c.* the king, and brought   Jer.52.9
being *c.* by him to do his will   2 Tim.2.26
And the beast was *c.*, and with   Rev.19.20

CARE (noun)
but the *c.* of the world and the   Mt.13.22
him to an inn, and took *c.* of him   Lk.10.34
each man take *c.* how he builds   1 Cor.3.10
take *c.* lest this liberty of yours   1 Cor.8.9
have the same *c.* for one another   1 Cor.12.25
Take *c.*, brethren, lest there be   Heb.3.12

CARE (verb)
I will *c.* for all your wants   Jg.19.20
son of man that thou dost *c.* for him?   Ps.8.4
the shepherds who *c.* for my people   Jer.23.2
you are true . . . and *c.* for no man   Mt.22.16

Teacher, do you not *c.* if we perish?   Mk.4.38
do you not *c.* that my sister has   Lk.10.40
not that he *c.* for the poor but   Jn.12.6
how can he *c.* for God's church?   1 Tim.3.5
cast . . . anxieties on him, for he *c.*   1 Pet.5.7

CARMEL
1 Sam.15.12; 1 Kg.18.19; S.of S.7.5; Am.1.2

CARRY
you shall *c.* up my bones from   Gen.50.25
C. them in your bosom, as a nurse   Num.11.12
be thou their shepherd, and *c.* them   Ps.28.9
when he dies he will *c.* nothing   Ps.49.17
Can a man *c.* fire in his bosom and   Pr.6.27
he will *c.* them in his bosom   Is.40.11
whose sandals I am not worthy to *c.*   Mt.3.11
man they compelled to *c.* his cross   Mt.27.32
C. no purse, no bag, no sandals   Lk.10.4
died and was *c.* by the angels to   Lk.16.22
if you have *c.* him away, tell me   Jn.20.15
a man lame from birth was being *c.*   Acts 3.2
they *c.* her out and buried her   Acts 5.10
he *c.* me away in the Spirit   Rev.17.3

CASE
Moses brought their *c.* before the   Num.27.5
will you plead the *c.* for God?   Job 13.8
Argue your *c.* with your neighbor   Pr.25.9
Set forth your *c.*, says the LORD   Is.41.21
I would plead my *c.* before thee   Jer.12.1
laid Paul's *c.* before the king   Acts 25.14
you incompetent to try trivial *c.*?   1 Cor.6.2

CAST
Aaron *c.* down his rod before   Ex.7.10
C. the lot between me and my son   1 Sam.14.42
c. lots, just as their brethren   1 Chr.24.31
God had *c.* me into the mire, and I   Job 30.19
for my raiment they *c.* lots   Ps.22.18
C. me not off, forsake me not, O God   Ps.27.9
Why are you *c.* down, O my soul   Ps.42.5
Yet thou hast *c.* us off and abased us   Ps.44.9
Do not *c.* us off for ever   Ps.44.23
C. me not away from thy presence   Ps.51.11
C. your burden on the LORD   Ps.55.22
C. your bread upon the waters   Ec.11.1
And if I *c.* out demons by Beelzebul   Mt.12.27
Be taken up and *c.* into the sea   Mt.21.21
How can Satan *c.* out Satan?   Mk.3.23
Why could we not *c.* it out?   Mk.9.28
I came to *c.* fire upon the earth   Lk.12.49
who comes to me I will not *c.* out   Jn.6.37
for my clothing they *c.* lots   Jn.19.24
then *c.* off the works of darkness   Rom.13.12
C. all your anxieties on him   1 Pet.5.7
but perfect love *c.* out fear   1 Jn.4.18
c. their crowns before the throne   Rev.4.10

CATCH (verb)
A slothful man will not *c.* his prey   Pr.12.27
They set a trap; they *c.* men   Jer.5.26
henceforth you will be *c.* men   Lk.5.10
He *c.* the wise in their craftiness   1 Cor.3.19

CAUSE (noun)
multiplies my wounds without *c.*   Job 9.17
For thou hast maintained my just *c.*   Ps.9.4
He committed his *c.* to the LORD   Ps.22.8
and defend my *c.* against an ungodly   Ps.43.1
Plead my *c.* and redeem me   Ps.119.154
Who has wounds without *c.*?   Pr.23.29

to divorce one's wife for any *c.*?   Mt.19.3
They hated me without a *c.*   Jn.15.25
CAUSE (verb)
The LORD will *c.* you to be defeated   Dt.28.25
Thou dost *c.* the grass to grow for   Ps.104.14
He has *c.* his wonderful works to be   Ps.111.4
Lord GOD will *c.* righteousness and   Is.61.11
If your right eye *c.* you to sin   Mt.5.29
Whoever *c.* one of these little ones   Mk.9.42
What *c.* wars, and what *c.* fightings   Jas.4.1
CAVE
he may give me the *c.* of Machpelah   Gen.23.9
to David at the *c.* of Adullam   2 Sam.23.13
it was a *c.*, and a stone lay upon   Jn.11.38
in dens and *c.* of the earth   Heb.11.38
hid in the *c.* and among the rocks   Rev.6.15
CEASE
day and night, shall not *c.*   Gen.8.22
He makes wars *c.* to the end of the   Ps.46.9
grinders *c.* because they are few   Ec.12.3
steadfast love of the LORD never *c.*   Lam.3.22
the wind *c.*, and there was a . . . calm   Mk.4.39
she has not *c.* to kiss my feet   Lk.7.45
as for tongues, they will *c.*   1 Cor.13.8
day and night they never *c.* to sing   Rev.4.8
CEDAR
See now, I dwell in a house of *c.*   2 Sam.7.2
from the *c.* that is in Lebanon to   1 Kg.4.33
the LORD breaks the *c.* of Lebanon   Ps.29.5
grow like a *c.* in Lebanon   Ps.92.12
will liken you to a *c.* in Lebanon   Ezek.31.3
Wail. . . for the *c.* has fallen   Zech.11.2
CENSUS
When you take the *c.* of the people   Ex.30.12
Take a *c.* of all the congregation   Num.1.2
Then Solomon took a *c.* of all the   2 Chr.2.17
Judas . . . arose in the days of the *c.*   Acts 5.37
CENTURION
And to the *c.* Jesus said, "Go   Mt.8.13
the *c.* and those who were with   Mt.27.54
Now a *c.* had a slave who was dear   Lk.7.2
a *c.* of . . . the Italian Cohort   Acts 10.1
to a *c.* of the Augustan Cohort   Acts 27.1
CEPHAS
(Peter), Jn.1.42; 1 Cor.1.12; 3.22; 9.5; 15.5;
Gal.2.9; *see* PETER
CHAFF
like *c.* that the storm carries   Job 21.18
are like *c.* which the wind drives   Ps.1.4
Let them be like *c.* before the wind   Ps.35.5
but the *c.* he will burn with   Lk.3.17
CHAIN
Can you bind the *c.* of the Pleiades   Job 38.31
I . . . put . . . a *c.* on your neck   Ezek.16.11
a *c.* of gold was put about his neck   Dan.5.29
bind him any more, even with a *c.*   Mk.5.3
as I am—except for these *c.*   Acts 26.29
for which I am an ambassador in *c.*   Eph.6.20
in eternal *c.* in the nether gloom   Jude 6
CHANCE (noun)
time and *c.* happen to them all   Ec.9.11
by *c.* a priest was going down   Lk.10.31
on the *c.* that somehow they could   Acts 27.12
for he found no *c.* to repent   Heb.12.17
CHANGE (verb)
not fear though the earth should *c.*   Ps.46.2

has sworn and will not *c.* his mind   Ps.110.4
Can the Ethiopian *c.* his skin or   Jer.13.23
For I the LORD do not *c.*; therefore   Mal.3.6
will *c.* the customs which Moses   Acts 6.14
but we shall all be *c.*   1 Cor.15.51
are being *c.* into his likeness   2 Cor.3.18
who will *c.* our lowly body to be   Phil.3.21
has sworn and will not *c.* his mind   Heb.7.21
CHARGE (noun)
Who gave him *c.* over the earth   Job 34.13
give his angels *c.* of you to guard   Ps.91.11
He will give his angels *c.* of you   Mt.4.6
See how many *c.* they bring against   Mk.15.4
this *c.* I have received from my   Jn.10.18
Having received this *c.*, he put   Acts 16.24
Who shall bring . . . *c.* against God's   Rom.8.33
I may make the gospel free of *c.*   1 Cor.9.18
This *c.* I commit to you, Timothy   1 Tim.1.18
the flock of God that is your *c.*   1 Pet.5.2
CHARGE (verb)
Job did not . . . *c.* God with wrong   Job 1.22
Like warriors they *c.*, like soldiers   Jl.2.7
he strictly *c.* them that no one   Mk.5.43
And he *c.* them to tell no one   Mk.7.36
We strictly *c.* you not to teach   Acts 5.28
I *c.* you in the name of Jesus   Acts 16.18
I *c.* you to keep the commandment   1 Tim.6.14
I *c.* you in the presence of God   2 Tim.4.1
May it not be *c.* against them   2 Tim.4.16
CHARIOT
made him to ride in his second *c.*   Gen.41.43
picked *c.* and all the other *c.*   Ex.14.7
Sisera called out all his *c.*   Jg.4.13
A *c.* could be imported from Egypt   1 Kg.10.29
he burns the *c.* with fire   Ps.46.9
who makest the clouds thy *c.*   Ps.104.3
to Philip, "Go . . . join this *c.*"   Acts 8.29
CHASTEN
I will *c.* him with the rod of men   2 Sam.7.14
nor *c.* me in thy wrath   Ps.38.1
When thou dost *c.* man with rebukes   Ps.39.11
Blessed is the man whom thou dost *c.*   Ps.94.12
we are *c.* so that we may not be   1 Cor.11.32
CHASTISE
My father *c.* you with whips, but   1 Kg.12.11
He who chastens . . . does he not *c.*?   Ps.94.10
I will *c.* them for their wicked   Hos.7.12
I will therefore *c.* him and release   Lk.23.16
c. every son whom he receives   Heb.12.6
CHEEK
in the night, tears on her *c.*   Lam.1.2
let him give his *c.* to the smiter   Lam.3.30
one strikes you on the right *c.*   Mt.5.39
CHEERFUL
A glad heart makes a *c.* countenance   Pr.15.13
A *c.* heart is a good medicine   Pr.17.22
for God loves a *c.* giver   2 Cor.9.7
Is any *c.*? Let him sing praise   Jas.5.13
CHERUBIM
east of the garden . . . he placed the *c.*   Gen.3.24
And you shall make two *c.* of gold   Ex.25.18
He sits enthroned upon the *c.*   Ps.99.1
who art enthroned above the *c.*   Is.37.16
above it were the *c.* of glory   Heb.9.5
CHIEF (adjective)
The *c.* butler and the *c.* baker   Gen.40.2

O Belteshazzar, *c.* of the magicians | Dan.4.9
assembling all the *c.* priests | Mt.2.4
the elders and *c.* priests | Mt.16.21
Iscariot, went to the *c.* priests | Mt.26.14
he was a *c.* tax collector, and rich | Lk.19.2
the *c.* captain Lysias came | Acts 24.7
when the *c.* Shepherd is manifested | 1 Pet.5.4

CHILD
Shall a *c.* be born to a man who is | Gen.17.17
And Elijah took the *c.* | 1 Kg.17.23
Then he went up and lay upon the *c.* | 2 Kg.4.34
Train up a *c.* in the way he should | Pr.22.6
not withhold discipline from a *c.* | Pr.23.13
a *c.* left to himself brings shame | Pr.29.15
For to us a *c.* is born, to us a son | Is.9.6
a little *c.* shall lead them | Is.11.6
When Israel was a *c.*, I loved him | Hos.11.1
search diligently for the *c.* | Mt.2.8
Whoever humbles himself like this *c.* | Mt.18.4
The *c.* is not dead but sleeping | Mk.5.39
And the *c.* grew and became strong | Lk.2.40
When I was a *c.*, I spoke like a *c.* | 1 Cor.13.11
Titus, my true *c.* in a common faith | Tit.1.4
appeal to you for my *c.*, Onesimus | Philem.10
who loves the parent loves the *c.* | 1 Jn.5.1

CHILDREN
in pain you shall bring forth *c.* | Gen.3.16
the iniquity of fathers upon *c.* | Num.14.18
Moses set before the *c.* of Israel | Dt.4.44
When your *c.* ask their fathers | Jos.4.21
Even young *c.* despise me | Job 19.18
forsaken or his *c.* begging bread | Ps.37.25
our fathers to teach to their *c.* | Ps.78.5
As a father pities his *c.*, so the | Ps.103.13
May you see your children's *c.* | Ps.128.6
Her *c.* rise up and call her blessed | Pr.31.28
stones to raise up *c.* to Abraham | Mt.3.9
how to give good gifts to your *c.* | Mt.7.11
and *c.* will rise against parents | Mt.10.21
Let the *c.* come to me, and do not | Mt.19.14
our spirit that we are *c.* of God | Rom.8.16
do not be *c.* in your thinking | 1 Cor.14.20
C., obey your parents in the Lord | Eph.6.1
obedient *c.*, do not be conformed | 1 Pet.1.14
Beloved, we are God's *c.* now | 1 Jn.3.2

CHOOSE
c. this day whom you will serve | Jos.24.15
C. a man for yourselves | 1 Sam.17.8
Let us *c.* what is right | Job 34.4
to refuse the evil and *c.* the good | Is.7.15
Is not this the fast that I *c.* | Is.58.6
to whom the Son *c.* to reveal him | Lk.10.22
Did I not *c.* you, the twelve, and | Jn.6.70
You did not *c.* me, but I chose you | Jn.15.16
c. men from among them and send | Acts 15.22

CHOSE
Lot *c.* for himself all the . . . valley | Gen.13.11
He *c.* David his servant, and took | Ps.78.70
but I *c.* you out of the world | Jn.15.19
they *c.* Stephen, a man full of | Acts 6.5
God *c.* what is weak in the world to | 1 Cor.1.27
he *c.* us in him before the foundation | Eph.1.4
God *c.* you from the beginning | 2 Th.2.13

CHOSEN
your God has *c.* you to be a people | Dt.7.6
that you have *c.* the LORD | Jos.24.22

where I have *c.* to put my name | 1 Kg.11.36
The LORD is my *c.* portion and my | Ps.16.5
A good name is to be *c.* rather than | Pr.22.1
Holy One of Israel, who has *c.* you | Is.49.7
For many are called, but few are *c.* | Mt.22.14
Mary has *c.* the good portion, which | Lk.10.42
is the Christ of God, his *C.* One | Lk.23.35
I know whom I have *c.* | Jn.13.18
for he is a *c.* instrument of mine | Acts 9.15
as God's *c.* ones, holy and beloved | Col.3.12
c. and destined by God the Father | 1 Pet.1.2
that living stone . . . . *c.* and precious | 1 Pet.2.4
But you are a *c.* race, a royal | 1 Pet.2.9
those . . . are called and *c.* and faithful | Rev.17.14

CHRIST
The book of the genealogy of Jesus *C.* | Mt.1.1
Jesus was born, who is called *C.* | Mt.1.16
You are the *C.*, the Son of the | Mt.16.16
What do you think of the *C.?* | Mt.22.42
Are you the *C.*, the Son of the | Mk.14.61
found the Messiah" (which means *C.*) | Jn.1.41
I believe that you are the *C.* | Jn.11.27
God has made him both Lord and *C.* | Acts 2.36
and preaching Jesus as the *C.* | Acts 5.42
at the right time *C.* died for the | Rom.5.6
separate us from the love of *C.?* | Rom.8.35
But put on the Lord Jesus *C.* | Rom.13.14
All the churches of *C.* greet you | Rom.16.16
to Cephas," or "I belong to *C.*" | 1 Cor.1.12
C. the power of God and the wisdom | 1 Cor.1.24
But we have the mind of *C.* | 1 Cor.2.16
For *C.*, our paschal lamb, has been | 1 Cor.5.7
followed them, and the Rock was *C.* | 1 Cor.10.4
Be imitators of me, as I am of *C.* | 1 Cor.11.1
God was in *C.* reconciling the world | 2 Cor.5.19
I have been crucified with *C.* | Gal.2.20
C. redeemed us from the curse of | Gal.3.13
the unsearchable riches of *C.* | Eph.3.8
to me to live is *C.*, and to die | Phil.1.21
but *C.* is all, and in all | Col.3.11
appearing of our Savior *C.* Jesus | 2 Tim.1.10
Jesus *C.* is the same yesterday and | Heb.13.8
For *C.* also died for sins once for | 1 Pet.3.18
our God and Savior Jesus *C.* | 2 Pet.1.1
Jesus *C.* the faithful witness | Rev.1.5

CHRISTIAN
were for the first time called *C.* | Acts 11.26
you think to make me a *C.* | Acts 26.28
yet if one suffers as a *C.* | 1 Pet.4.16

CHURCH
on this rock I will build my *c.* | Mt.16.18
listen to them, tell it to the *c.* | Mt.18.17
great fear came upon the whole *c.* | Acts 5.11
But Saul laid waste the *c.* | Acts 8.3
feed the *c.* of the Lord which he | Acts 20.28
teach them everywhere in every *c.* | 1 Cor.4.17
to excel in building up the *c.* | 1 Cor.14.12
head over all things for the *c.* | Eph.1.22
as Christ is the head of the *c.* | Eph.5.23
cherishes it, as Christ does the *c.* | Eph.5.29
He is the head of the body, the *c.* | Col.1.18
which is the *c.* of the living God | 1 Tim.3.15

CIRCUMCISE
C. therefore the foreskin of your | Dt.10.16
eighth day they came to *c.* the child | Lk.1.59
you *c.* a man upon the sabbath | Jn.7.22

said, "It is necessary to *c.* them — Acts 15.5
he took him and *c.* him because of — Acts 16.3
CIRCUMCISION
Moses gave you *c.* (not that it is — Jn.7.22
And he gave him the covenant of *c.* — Acts 7.8
nor is true *c.* something external — Rom.2.28
He received *c.* as a sign or seal of — Rom.4.11
For neither *c.* counts for anything — Gal.6.15
we are the true *c.*, who worship God — Phil.3.3
CITIZEN
the ears of all the *c.* of Shechem — Jg.9.2
to one of the *c.* of that country — Lk.15.15
in Cilicia, a *c.* of no mean city — Acts 21.39
For this man is a Roman *c.* — Acts 22.26
CITY
he built a *c.*, and called — Gen.4.17
Come, let us build ourselves a *c.* — Gen.11.4
Israel, "Go every man to his *c.*" — 1 Sam.8.22
A *c.* set on a hill cannot be hid — Mt.5.14
to teach and preach in their *c.* — Mt.11.1
to upbraid the *c.* where most of — Mt.11.20
he went on through *c.* and villages — Lk.8.1
when he . . . saw the *c.* he wept — Lk.19.41
So he came to a *c.* of Samaria — Jn.4.5
was crucified was near the *c.* — Jn.19.20
the people of the *c.* were divided — Acts 14.4
they are disturbing our *c.* — Acts 16.20
for he has prepared for them a *c.* — Heb.11.16
For here we have no lasting *c.* — Heb.13.14
and the name of the *c.* of my God — Rev.3.12
I saw the holy *c.*, new Jerusalem — Rev.21.2
CLAY
Remember . . . thou hast made me of *c.* — Job 10.9
the potter be regarded as the *c.* — Is.29.16
Does the *c.* say to him who fashions — Is.45.9
we are the *c.*, and thou art our potter — Is.64.8
Jesus made *c.* and anointed my eyes — Jn.9.11
Has the potter no right over the *c.* — Rom.9.21
CLEAN (adjective)
seven pairs of all *c.* animals — Gen.7.2
can he who is born of woman be *c.*? — Job 25.4
He who has *c.* hands and a pure — Ps.24.4
Purge me with hyssop, and I shall be *c.* — Ps.51.7
Create in me a *c.* heart, O God — Ps.51.10
I will sprinkle *c.* water upon you — Ezek.36.25
that the outside also may be *c.* — Mt.23.26
(Thus he declared all foods *c.*) — Mk.7.19
behold, everything is *c.* for you — Lk.11.41
Everything is indeed *c.*, but it is — Rom.14.20
CLEANSE
first *c.* the inside of the cup and — Mt.23.26
Then said Jesus, "Were not ten *c.*? — Lk.17.17
What God has *c.*, you must not call — Acts 10.15
C. out the old leaven that you may — 1 Cor.5.7
having *c.* her by the washing of — Eph.5.26
If the worshipers had once been *c.* — Heb.10.2
C. your hands, you sinners — Jas.4.8
will forgive our sins and *c.* us — 1 Jn.1.9
CLEAR (adjective)
This is a *c.* omen to them of their — Phil.1.28
of the faith with a *c.* conscience — 1 Tim.3.9
and keep your conscience *c.* — 1 Pet.3.16
city was pure gold, *c.* as glass — Rev.21.18
CLEAR (verb)
he will by no means *c.* the guilty — Num.14.18
God will *c.* away these nations — Dt.7.22

C. thou me from hidden faults — Ps.19.12
I will not *c.* the guilty — Jl.3.21
CLEAVE
a man leaves . . . and *c.* to his wife — Gen.2.24
but *c.* to the LORD your God — Jos.23.8
Because he *c.* to me in love, I will — Ps.91.14
I *c.* to thy testimonies, O LORD — Ps.119.31
Let my tongue *c.* to the roof of my — Ps.137.6
CLEFT
I will put you in a *c.* of the rock — Ex.33.22
He *c.* rocks in the wilderness — Ps.78.15
he *c.* the rock and the water gushed — Is.48.21
hide it there in a *c.* of the rock — Jer.13.4
CLING
My soul *c.* to thee — Ps.63.8
the whole house of Judah *c.* to me — Jer.13.11
the dust of your town that *c.* to — Lk.10.11
CLOAK
a shepherd cleans his *c.* of vermin — Jer.43.12
let him have your *c.* as well — Mt.5.40
And they clothed him in a purple *c.* — Mk.15.17
takes away your *c.* do not withhold — Lk.6.29
bring the *c.* that I left . . . at Troas — 2 Tim.4.13
CLOSE (adjective)
Afflicted and *c.* to death — Ps.88.15
a whisperer separates *c.* friends — Pr.16.28
lying thus, *c.* to the breast of — Jn.13.25
I find . . . evil lies *c.* at hand — Rom.7.21
CLOSE (verb)
one of his ribs and *c.* up its place — Gen.2.21
They *c.* their hearts to pity — Ps.17.10
the pit *c.* its mouth over me — Ps.69.15
Do not *c.* thine ear to my cry — Lam.3.56
he *c.* the book, and gave it back — Lk.4.20
their eyes they have *c.* — Acts 28.27
if any one . . . *c.* his heart against — 1 Jn.3.17
CLOTH
unshrunk *c.* on an old garment — Mt.9.16
left the linen *c.* and ran away — Mk.14.52
wrapped him in swaddling *c.* — Lk.2.7
his face wrapped with a *c.* — Jn.11.44
he saw the linen *c.* lying — Jn.20.6
CLOTHE
God is *c.* with terrible majesty — Job 37.22
meadows *c.* themselves with flocks — Ps.65.13
Thou art *c.* with honor and majesty — Ps.104.1
priests be *c.* with righteousness — Ps.132.9
I *c.* the heavens with blackness — Is.50.3
will he not much more *c.* you — Mt.6.30
I was naked and you *c.* me — Mt.25.36
Now John was *c.* with camel's hair — Mk.1.6
who was *c.* in purple and fine linen — Lk.16.19
until you are *c.* with power from on — Lk.24.49
but that we would be further *c.* — 2 Cor.5.4
C. yourselves, all of you, with — 1 Pet.5.5
buy from me . . . garments to *c.* you — Rev.3.18
CLOTHING
bread to eat and *c.* to wear — Gen.28.20
Your *c.* did not wear out upon you — Dt.8.4
And why are you anxious about *c.*? — Mt.6.28
in sheep's *c.* but inwardly . . . wolves — Mt.7.15
for my *c.* they cast lots — Jn.19.24
we have food and *c.* . . . be content — 1 Tim.6.8
a poor man in shabby *c.* also comes — Jas.2.2
CLOUD
I set my bow in the *c.* — Gen.9.13

in a pillar of *c.* to lead them	Ex.13.21		by the way of concession, not of *c.*	1 Cor.7.6
And Moses entered the *c.*	Ex.24.18		I have no *c.* of the Lord, but	1 Cor.7.25
a *c.* filled the house of the LORD	1 Kg.8.10		I say this not as a *c.*, but	2 Cor.8.8
As the *c.* fades and vanishes, so he	Job 7.9		**COMMAND** (verb)	
In the daytime he led them with a *c.*	Ps.78.14		You shall speak all that I *c.* you	Ex.7.2
C. and thick darkness are round	Ps.97.2		he has *c.* his covenant for ever	Ps.111.9
who makest the *c.* thy chariot	Ps.104.3		For he *c.* and they were created	Ps.148.5
thy faithfulness reaches to the *c.*	Ps.108.4		*c.* these stones to become loaves	Mt.4.3
over her assemblies a *c.* by day	Is.4.5		to observe all that I have *c.* you	Mt.28.20
Your love is like a morning *c.*	Hos.6.4		he *c.* the unclean spirits	Lk.4.36
a bright *c.* overshadowed them	Mt.17.5		he *c.* even wind and water	Lk.8.25
coming on the *c.* of heaven with	Mt.24.30		but I do as the Father has *c.* me	Jn.14.31
When you see a *c.* rising in the	Lk.12.54		my friends if you do what I *c.* you	Jn.15.14
Son of man coming in a *c.* with power	Lk.21.27		*C.* and teach these things	1 Tim.4.11
our fathers were all under the *c.*	1 Cor.10.1		**COMMANDMENT**	
by so great a *c.* of witnesses	Heb.12.1		those who love me and keep my *c.*	Ex.20.6
Behold, he is coming with the *c.*	Rev.1.7		words of the covenant, the ten *c.*	Ex.34.28
he who sat upon the *c.* swung his	Rev.14.16		you shall keep my *c.* and do them	Lev.22.31
COAL			the *c.* of the LORD is pure	Ps.19.8
he will rain *c.* of fire	Ps.11.6		Thy *c.* makes me wiser than my	Ps.119.98
Let burning *c.* fall upon them	Ps.140.10		My son, keep your father's *c.*	Pr.6.20
will heap *c.* of fire on his head	Pr.25.22		He who keeps the *c.* keeps his life	Pr.19.16
having in his hand a burning *c.*	Is.6.6		This is the great and first *c.*	Mt.22.38
will heap burning *c.* upon his head	Rom.12.20		they rested according to the *c.*	Lk.23.56
COAT			A new *c.* I give to you, that you	Jn.13.34
he was armed with a *c.* of mail	1 Sam.17.5		This is my *c.*, that you love one	Jn.15.12
would sue you and take your *c.*	Mt.5.40		he had given *c.* through the Holy	Acts 1.2
answered them, "He who has two *c.*	Lk.3.11		Beloved, I am writing you no new *c.*	1 Jn.2.7
do not withhold your *c.* as well	Lk.6.29		All who keep his *c.* abide in him	1 Jn.3.24
c. and garments which Dorcas made	Acts 9.39		And his *c.* are not burdensome	1 Jn.5.3
COIN			**COMMEND**	
Bring me a *c.*, and let me look at	Mk.12.15		A man is *c.* according to his good	Pr.12.8
what woman, having ten silver *c.*	Lk.15.8		And now I *c.* you to God	Acts 20.32
a poor widow put in two copper *c.*	Lk.21.2		Food will not *c.* us to God	1 Cor.8.8
poured out . . . *c.* of . . . money-changers	Jn.2.15		Are we beginning to *c.* ourselves	2 Cor.3.1
COLD			some of those who *c.* themselves	2 Cor.10.12
c. and heat, summer and winter, day	Gen.8.22		**COMMISSION** (verb)	
who can stand before his *c.*?	Ps.147.17		you shall *c.* him in their sight	Num.27.19
Like the *c.* of snow in the time of	Pr.25.13		the LORD *c.* Joshua the son of Nun	Dt.31.23
Like *c.* water to a thirsty soul	Pr.25.25		with you in Christ, and has *c.* us	2 Cor.1.21
gives . . . even a cup of *c.* water	Mt.10.42		*c.* by God, in the sight of God we	2 Cor.2.17
most men's love will grow *c.*	Mt.24.12		**COMMIT**	
a charcoal fire, because it was *c.*	Jn.18.18		You shall not *c.* adultery	Ex.20.14
Would that you were *c.* or hot	Rev.3.15		to God would I *c.* my cause	Job 5.8
COMFORT (noun)			Into thy hand I *c.* my spirit	Ps.31.5
This is my *c.* in my affliction	Ps.119.50		*C.* your way to the LORD; trust	Ps.37.5
walking . . . in the *c.* of the Holy	Acts 9.31		*C.* your work to the LORD, and your	Pr.16.3
it is for your *c.* and salvation	2 Cor.1.6		Why do you *c.* this great evil	Jer.44.7
the *c.* with which he was comforted	2 Cor.7.7		You shall not *c.* adultery	Mt.19.18
gave us eternal *c.* and good hope	2 Th.2.16		into thy hands I *c.* my spirit	Lk.23.46
COMFORT (verb)			This charge I *c.* to you, Timothy	1 Tim.1.18
My bed will *c.* me, my couch will ease	Job 7.13		you *c.* sin, and are convicted by	Jas.2.9
How then will you *c.* me with empty	Job 21.34		No one born of God *c.* sin	1 Jn.3.9
thy rod and thy staff, they *c.* me	Ps.23.4		**COMMON**	
LORD, hast helped me and *c.* me	Ps.86.17		between the holy and the *c.*	Ezek.42.20
be ready to *c.* me according to thy	Ps.119.76		had all things in *c.*	Acts 2.44
C., *c.* my people, says your God	Is.40.1		not call any man *c.* or unclean	Acts 10.28
For the LORD has *c.* his people	Is.49.13		of the Spirit for the *c.* good	1 Cor.12.7
For the LORD will *c.* Zion	Is.51.3		write to you of our *c.* salvation	Jude 3
As one whom his mother *c.*, so I will	Is.66.13		**COMPANION**	
the LORD will again *c.* Zion	Zech.1.17		his brother, and every man his *c.*	Ex.32.27
who mourn, for they shall be *c.*	Mt.5.4		my *c.*, my familiar friend	Ps.55.13
to *c.* those who are in any affliction	2 Cor.1.4		My *c.* stretched out his hand	Ps.55.20
COMMAND (noun)			I am a *c.* of all who fear thee	Ps.119.63
The Lord gives the *c.*; great is	Ps.68.11		who were Paul's *c.* in travel	Acts 19.29
stormy wind fulfilling his *c.*	Ps.148.8			

COMPANY

the *c.* of the godless is barren	Job 15.34
a *c.* of evildoers encircle me	Ps.22.16
a *c.* of destroying angels	Ps.78.49
in the *c.* of the upright	Ps.111.1
not sit in the *c.* of merrymakers	Jer.15.17
the daughter . . . danced before the *c.*	Mt.14.6
Now the *c.* of those who believed	Acts 4.32
so spoke that a great *c.* believed	Acts 14.1
have enjoyed your *c.* for a little	Rom.15.24
Bad *c.* ruins good morals	1 Cor.15.33

COMPARE

none can *c.* with thee	Ps.40.5
For who . . . can be *c.* to the LORD?	Ps.89.6
nothing you desire can *c.* with her	Pr.3.15
With what can we *c.* the kingdom of	Mk.4.30
are not worth *c.* with the glory	Rom.8.18
c. themselves with one another	2 Cor.10.12

COMPASSION

Has he in anger shut up his *c.*?	Ps.77.9
let thy *c.* come speedily to meet us	Ps.79.8
his *c.* is over all that he has made	Ps.145.9
with everlasting love I will have *c.*	Is.54.8
will not pity or spare or have *c.*	Jer.13.14
I led them with cords of *c.*	Hos.11.4
He will again have *c.* upon us	Mic.7.19
he had *c.* on them, and healed	Mt.14.14
I have *c.* on the crowd, because	Mk.8.2
I will have *c.* on whom I have *c.*	Rom.9.15
c., kindness, lowliness, meekness	Col.3.12

COMPEL

men are *c.* to grind at the mill	Lam.5.13
this man they *c.* to carry his cross	Mt.27.32
c. people to come in, that my	Lk.14.23
how can you *c.* the Gentiles to live	Gal.2.14

COMPLAINT

Today also my *c.* is bitter	Job 23.2
Hear my voice, O God, in my *c.*	Ps.64.1
I pour out my *c.* before him	Ps.142.2
have a *c.* against any one	Acts 19.38
if one has a *c.* against another	Col.3.13

COMPLETE (adjective)

that the man of God may be *c.*	2 Tim.3.17
that you may be perfect and *c.*	Jas.1.4
to face, so that our joy may be *c.*	2 Jn.12
their brethren should be *c.*	Rev.6.11

COMPLETE (verb)

C. your work, your daily task, as	Ex.5.13
c. my joy by being of the same mind	Phil.2.2
in my flesh I *c.* what is lacking	Col.1.24
faith was *c.* by works	Jas.2.22

CONCEAL

slay our brother and *c.* his blood?	Gen.37.26
he will *c.* me under the cover of	Ps.27.5
I have not *c.* thy steadfast love	Ps.40.10
A prudent man *c.* his knowledge	Pr.12.23
He who *c.* his transgressions will	Pr.28.13
it was *c.* from them	Lk.9.45

CONCEIT

any who are wise in their own *c.*	Job 37.24
Lest you be wise in your own *c.*	Rom.11.25
slander, gossip, *c.*, and disorder	2 Cor.12.20
Do nothing from selfishness or *c.*	Phil.2.3
puffed up with *c.*, and fall into	1 Tim.3.6
swollen with *c.*, lovers of pleasure	2 Tim.3.4

CONCEIVE

in sin did my mother *c.* me	Ps.51.5
young woman shall *c.* and bear a son	Is.7.14
a virgin shall *c.* and bear a son	Mt.1.23
nor the heart of man *c.*	1 Cor.2.9
desire when it has *c.*, gives birth to sin	Jas.1.15

CONDEMN

Will you *c.* him who is righteous	Job 34.17
c. the innocent to death	Ps.94.21
they will *c.* him to death	Mt.20.18
c. not, and you will not be *c.*	Lk.6.37
God sent the Son . . . not to *c.* the world	Jn.3.17
Neither do I *c.* you; go, and do not	Jn.8.11
who is to *c.*? Is it Christ	Rom.8.34
But he who has doubts is *c.*	Rom.14.23
lest you come together to be *c.*	1 Cor.11.34
whenever our hearts *c.* us	1 Jn.3.20

CONDUCT (noun)

wise *c.* is pleasure to a man of	Pr.10.23
but the *c.* of the pure is right	Pr.21.8
not a terror to good *c.*, but to bad	Rom.13.3
to give you in our *c.* an example	2 Th.3.9
be holy yourselves in all your *c.*	1 Pet.1.15
Maintain good *c.* among the	1 Pet.2.12

CONFESS

he shall *c.* the sin he has committed	Lev.5.5
I will *c.* my transgressions to the	Ps.32.5
I *c.* my iniquity, I am sorry for my	Ps.38.18
any one should *c.* him to be Christ	Jn.9.22
if you *c.* with your lips that Jesus	Rom.10.9
every tongue *c.* that Jesus Christ	Phil.2.11
c. your sins to one another	Jas.5.16
If we *c.* our sins, he is faithful	1 Jn.1.9
I will *c.* his name before my Father	Rev.3.5

CONFIDENCE

will have *c.*, because there is hope	Job 11.18
in the LORD than to put *c.* in man	Ps.118.8
I have *c.* in the Lord that you will	Gal.5.10
And we have *c.* in the Lord about	2 Th.3.4
Let us then with *c.* draw near to	Heb.4.16
Through him you have *c.* in God	1 Pet.1.21
we have *c.* before God	1 Jn.3.21
this is the *c.* which we have in him	1 Jn.5.14

CONFIDENT

though war arise . . . yet I will be *c.*	Ps.27.3
If any one is *c.* that he is Christ's	2 Cor.10.7
have been made *c.* in the Lord	Phil.1.14
C. of your obedience, I write	Philem.21

CONFIRM

will *c.* my covenant with you	Lev.26.9
c. for ever the word which thou	2 Sam.7.25
C. to thy servant thy promise	Ps.119.38
Then *c.* your vows and perform	Jer.44.25
in order to *c.* the promises given	Rom.15.8
the more zealous to *c.* your call	2 Pet.1.10

CONFORM

men who do not *c.* to thy law	Ps.119.85
predestined to be *c.* to the image	Rom.8.29
Do not be *c.* to this world but be	Rom.12.2
do not be *c.* to the passions of	1 Pet.1.14

CONFOUND

You would *c.* the plans of the poor	Ps.14.6
turned back and *c.* who devise evil	Ps.35.4
Then the moon will be *c.*	Is.24.23
All of them are put to shame and *c.*	Is.45.16

are ashamed and *c.* and cover their	Jer.14.3
c. the Jews who lived in Damascus	Acts 9.22

CONFUSION

will throw into *c.* all the people	Ex.23.27
the LORD . . . threw them into *c.*	1 Sam.7.10
hast put to *c.* those who hate us	Ps.44.7
to us *c.* of face, as at this day	Dan.9.7
the city was filled with the *c.*	Acts 19.29
is not a God of *c.* but of peace	1 Cor.14.33

CONFUTE

there was none that *c.* Job	Job 32.12
you shall *c.* every tongue that	Is.54.17
for he powerfully *c.* the Jews in	Acts 18.28
also to *c.* those who contradict	Tit.1.9

CONGREGATION

All the *c.* of the people of Israel	Ex.17.1
nor sinners in the *c.* of the righteous	Ps.1.5
in the great *c.* I will bless the	Ps.26.12
I will thank thee in the great *c.*	Ps.35.18
Bless God in the great *c.*	Ps.68.26
Sanctify the *c.*; assemble the elders	Jl.2.16
midst of the *c.* I will praise thee	Heb.2.12

CONQUER

who through faith *c.* kingdoms	Heb.11.33
he went out conquering and to *c.*	Rev.6.2
they have *c.* him by the blood	Rev.12.11
the Lamb will *c.* them	Rev.17.14
He who *c.* shall have this heritage	Rev.21.7

CONSCIENCE

to have a clear *c.* toward God	Acts 24.16
while their *c.* also bears witness	Rom.2.15
my *c.* bears me witness in the Holy	Rom.9.1
their *c.*, being weak, is defiled	1 Cor.8.7
every man's *c.* in the sight of God	2 Cor.4.2
a good *c.* and sincere faith	1 Tim.1.5
liars whose *c.* are seared	1 Tim.4.2
perfect the *c.* of the worshiper	Heb.9.9
purify your *c.* from dead works	Heb.9.14
keep your *c.* clear, so that	1 Pet.3.16

CONSECRATE

C. to me all the first-born	Ex.13.2
You shall be men *c.* to me	Ex.22.31
I will *c.* the tent of meeting and	Ex.29.44
C. yourselves therefore, and be holy	Lev.20.7
whom the Father *c.* and sent into	Jn.10.36
And for their sake I *c.* myself	Jn.17.19
husband is *c.* through his wife	1 Cor.7.14
then it is *c.* by the word of God	1 Tim.4.5

CONSIDER

C. too that this nation is thy	Ex.33.13
Have you *c.* my servant Job, that	Job 1.8
C. and answer me, O LORD my God	Ps.13.3
Blessed is he who *c.* the poor	Ps.41.1
c. well her ramparts, go through her	Ps.48.13
C. how I love thy precepts	Ps.119.159
C. the work of God; who can	Ec.7.13
C. the lilies of the field, how they	Mt.6.28
C. the ravens: they neither sow nor	Lk.12.24
For *c.* your call, brethren	1 Cor.1.26
c. Jesus, the apostle and high priest	Heb.3.1
He *c.* that God was able to raise	Heb.11.19
C. him who endured from sinners	Heb.12.3
c. the outcome of their life	Heb.13.7

CONSOLATION

Are the *c.* of God too small for you	Job 15.11
the cup of *c.* to drink for his	Jer.16.7

looking for the *c.* of Israel	Lk.2.25
for you have received your *c.*	Lk.6.24
for their upbuilding . . . and *c.*	1 Cor.14.3

CONSUME

lest I *c.* you in the way	Ex.33.3
thou dost *c.* like a moth what is	Ps.39.11
For we are *c.* by thy anger	Ps.90.7
My soul is *c.* with longing for thy	Ps.119.20
but the lips of a fool *c.* him	Ec.10.12
moth and rust *c.* and where thieves	Mt.6.19
Zeal for thy house will *c.* me	Jn.2.17
were *c.* with passion for one another	Rom.1.27
that you are not *c.* by one another	Gal.5.15
fire which will *c.* the adversaries	Heb.10.27
for our God is a *c.* fire	Heb.12.29
came down from heaven and *c.* them	Rev.20.9

CONTEMPT

He pours *c.* on princes, and looses	Job 12.21
we have had more than enough of *c.*	Ps.123.3
When wickedness comes, *c.* comes also	Pr.18.3
for the son treats the father with *c.*	Mic.7.6
treated him with *c.* and mocked him	Lk.23.11
own account and hold him up to *c.*	Heb.6.6

CONTEND

Who is there that will *c.* with me?	Job 13.19
Shall a faultfinder *c.* with the	Job 40.2
Do not *c.* with a man for no reason	Pr.3.30
I will *c.* with those who *c.* with you	Is.49.25
For I will not *c.* for ever	Is.57.16
For we are not *c.* against flesh and	Eph.6.12
appealing to you to *c.* for the faith	Jude 3

CONTENT

Be *c.* with your glory, and stay	2 Kg.14.10
Yet you were not *c.* to walk in	Ezek.16.47
and be *c.* with your wages	Lk.3.14
I am *c.* with weaknesses, insults	2 Cor.12.10
in whatever state I am, to be *c.*	Phil.4.11
be *c.* with what you have	Heb.13.5

CONTINUALLY

of his heart was only evil *c.*	Gen.6.5
as he came he cursed *c.*	2 Sam.16.5
who *c.* stand before you and hear	2 Chr.9.7
his praise shall *c.* be in my mouth	Ps.34.1
In God we have boasted *c.*	Ps.44.8
May prayer be made for him *c.*	Ps.72.15
Let them be before the LORD *c.*	Ps.109.15
I will keep thy law *c.*, for ever	Ps.119.44
And the LORD will guide you *c.*	Is.58.11
My soul *c.* thinks of it and is	Lam.3.20
justice, and wait *c.* for your God	Hos.12.6
and were *c.* in the temple blessing	Lk.24.53
Through him then let us *c.* offer up	Heb.13.15

CONTINUE

that it may *c.* for ever before	2 Sam.7.29
O *c.* thy steadfast love to those	Ps.36.10
his fame *c.* as long as the sun	Ps.72.17
but *c.* in the fear of the LORD all	Pr.23.17
all night he *c.* in prayer to God	Lk.6.12
If you *c.* in my word, you are truly	Jn.8.31
urged them to *c.* in the grace of	Acts 13.43
exhorting them to *c.* in the faith	Acts 14.22
Are we to *c.* in sin that grace may	Rom.6.1
provided that you *c.* in the faith	Col.1.23
C. steadfastly in prayer	Col.4.2
Let brotherly love *c.*	Heb.13.1

CONTRIBUTE
For they all *c.* out of their	Mk.12.44
he who *c.*, in liberality; he who	Rom.12.8
C. to the needs of the saints	Rom.12.13

CONTRIBUTION
bring the *c.* into the house of	2 Chr.31.10
make some *c.* for the poor among	Rom.15.26
concerning the *c.* for the saints	1 Cor.16.1
so that *c.* need not be made when	1 Cor.16.2
generosity of your *c.* for them	2 Cor.9.13

CONTRITE
a broken and *c.* heart, O God, thou	Ps.51.17
who is of a *c.* and humble spirit	Is.57.15
to revive the heart of the *c.*	Is.57.15
he that is humble and *c.* in spirit	Is.66.2

CONTROVERSY
LORD has a *c.* with the inhabitants	Hos.4.1
craving for *c.* and for disputes	1 Tim.6.4
to do with stupid, senseless *c.*	2 Tim.2.23
But avoid stupid *c.*, genealogies	Tit.3.9

CONVERT (noun)
Jews and devout *c.* to Judaism	Acts 13.43
Epaenetus . . . was the first *c.* in Asia	Rom.16.5
were the first *c.* in Achaia	1 Cor.16.15
He must not be a recent *c.*, or he	1 Tim.3.6

CONVINCE
he will *c.* the world of sin and of	Jn.16.8
trying to *c.* them about Jesus	Acts 28.23
fully *c.* that God was able to do	Rom.4.21
are *c.* that one has died for all	2 Cor.5.14
C. of this, I know that I shall	Phil.1.25
c., rebuke, and exhort	2 Tim.4.2

COPPER
c. is smelted from the ore	Job 28.2
nor silver, nor *c.* in your belts	Mt.10.9
came, and put in two *c.* coins	Mk.12.42
you have paid the very last *c.*	Lk.12.59

CORD
this scarlet *c.* in the window	Jos.2.18
Pleiades, or loose the *c.* of Orion?	Job 38.31
The *c.* of death encompassed me	Ps.18.4
he has cut the *c.* of the wicked	Ps.129.4
threefold *c.* is not quickly broken	Ec.4.12
before the silver *c.* is snapped	Ec.12.6
lengthen your *c.* and strengthen	Is.54.2
I led them with *c.* of compassion	Hos.11.4
making a whip of *c.*, he drove them	Jn.2.15

CORINTH
Acts 18.1; 1 Cor.1.2; 2 Cor.1.1; 2 Tim.4.20

CORNELIUS
devout centurion, Acts 10.1; his prayer answered, Acts 10.3–4; sends for Peter, Acts 10.17; is baptized, Acts 10.48

CORNER
has become the head of the *c.*	Mt.21.42
let down by four *c.* upon the earth	Acts 10.11
for this was not done in a *c.*	Acts 26.26
has become the head of the *c.*	1 Pet.2.7
at the four *c.* of the earth, holding	Rev.7.1

CORNERSTONE
a precious *c.*, of a sure foundation	Is.28.16
Out of them shall come the *c.*	Zech.10.4
Christ Jesus himself being the *c.*	Eph.2.20
a *c.* chosen and precious	1 Pet.2.6

CORRUPT
Now the earth was *c.* in God's sight	Gen.6.11
They are *c.*, they do abominable	Ps.14.1
The heart is . . . desperately *c.*	Jer.17.9
They have deeply *c.* themselves as	Hos.9.9
and is *c.* through deceitful lusts	Eph.4.22
men of *c.* mind and counterfeit	2 Tim.3.8
but to the *c.* and unbelieving	Tit.1.15

CORRUPTION
nor let thy Holy One see *c.*	Acts 2.27
the dead, no more to return to *c.*	Acts 13.34
he whom God raised up saw no *c.*	Acts 13.37
flesh will from the flesh reap *c.*	Gal.6.8
escape from the *c.* . . . . in the world	2 Pet.1.4
they themselves are slaves of *c.*	2 Pet.2.19

COSTLY
the ransom of his life is *c.*	Ps.49.8
with precious stones and *c.* gifts	Dan.11.38
jar of ointment . . . very *c.*	Mk.14.3
Mary took a pound of *c.* ointment	Jn.12.3
or gold or pearls or *c.* attire	1 Tim.2.9
of ivory, all articles of *c.* wood	Rev.18.12

COUNCIL
feared in the *c.* of the holy ones	Ps.89.7
brother shall be liable to the *c.*	Mt.5.22
for they will deliver you up to *c.*	Mk.13.9
He was a member of the *c.*	Lk.23.50
called together the *c.* and all	Acts 5.21
Pharisee in the *c.* named Gamaliel	Acts 5.34
when he had conferred with his *c.*	Acts 25.12

COUNSEL (noun)
forsaking the *c.* which the old men	1 Kg.12.13
Rehoboam took *c.* with the old men	2 Chr.10.6
took *c.* with the young men	2 Chr.10.8
he has *c.* and understanding	Job 12.13
The *c.* of the wicked is far from me	Job 21.16
walks not in the *c.* of the wicked	Ps.1.1
I bless the LORD who gives me *c.*	Ps.16.7
The *c.* of the LORD stands for ever	Ps.33.11
the *c.* of the wicked are treacherous	Pr.12.5
Give *c.*, grant justice; make your	Is.16.3
counselors of Pharaoh give stupid *c.*	Is.19.11
Has *c.* perished from the prudent?	Jer.49.7
the people took *c.* against Jesus	Mt.27.1
declaring . . . the whole *c.* of God	Acts 20.27
according to the *c.* of his will	Eph.1.11

COUNSELOR
an abundance of *c.* there is safety	Pr.11.14
name will be called "Wonderful *C.*	Is.9.6
among these there is no *c.*	Is.41.28
he will give you another *C.*	Jn.14.16
But the *C.*, the Holy Spirit, whom	Jn.14.26
when the *C.* comes, whom I shall	Jn.15.26
the *C.* will not come to you	Jn.16.7
the Lord, or who has been his *c.*?	Rom.11.34

COUNT
I can *c.* all my bones–they stare	Ps.22.17
If I would *c.* them, they are more	Ps.139.18
first sit down and *c.* the cost	Lk.14.28
that they were *c.* worthy to suffer	Acts 5.41
sin is not *c.* where there is no law	Rom.5.13
but in humility *c.* others better	Phil.2.3
did not *c.* equality with God a	Phil.2.6
Indeed I *c.* everything as loss	Phil.3.8
C. it all joy, my brethren, when you	Jas.1.2

COUNTENANCE
The LORD lift up his *c.* upon you	Num.6.26
his *c.* was like the *c.* of the angel	Jg.13.6

thy arm, and the light of thy *c.*	Ps.44.3	strangers to the *c.* of promise	Eph.2.12
secret sins in the light of thy *c.*	Ps.90.8	Jesus the surety of a better *c.*	Heb.7.22
A glad heart makes a cheerful *c.*	Pr.15.13	This is the *c.* that I will make	Heb.8.10
At that saying his *c.* fell	Mk.10.22	he is the mediator of a new *c.*	Heb.9.15
appearance of his *c.* was altered	Lk.9.29	Jesus, the mediator of a new *c.*	Heb.12.24

COUNTRY

so is good news from a far *c.*	Pr.25.25	by the blood of the eternal *c.*	Heb.13.20
to their own *c.* by another way	Mt.2.12	**COVER**	
who was coming in from the *c.*	Mk.15.21	O earth, *c.* not my blood	Job 16.18
and took his journey into a far *c.*	Lk.15.13	thou dost *c.* him with favor	Ps.5.12
prophet has no honor in his own *c.*	Jn.4.44	Blessed is he . . . whose sin is *c.*	Ps.32.1
as it is, they desire a better *c.*	Heb.11.16	who *c.* thyself with light as with	Ps.104.2

COURAGE

		If I say, "Let only darkness *c.* me	Ps.139.11
Be of good *c.*, and bring some of	Num.13.20	but love *c.* all offenses	Pr.10.12
Be strong and of good *c.*, do not	Dt.31.6	shall say to the mountains, *C.* us	Hos.10.8
Be . . . of good *c.*, be not frightened	Jos.1.9	some began . . . to *c.* his face	Mk.14.65
Be strong, and let your heart take *c.*	Ps.31.24	Nothing is *c.* up that will not be	Lk.12.2
says to his brother, "Take *c.!*"	Is.41.6	Blessed are those . . . whose sins are *c.*	Rom.4.7
Take *c.*, for as you have testified	Acts 23.11	a man ought not to *c.* his head	1 Cor.11.7
Paul thanked God and took *c.*	Acts 28.15	will *c.* a multitude of sins	Jas.5.20
So we are always of good *c.*	2 Cor.5.6	since love *c.* a multitude of sins	1 Pet.4.8
we had *c.* in our God to declare to	1 Th.2.2	**COVERING (noun)**	
nor lose *c.* when you are punished	Heb.12.5	before God . . . Abaddon has no *c.*	Job 26.6

COURAGEOUS

		He made darkness his *c.* around him	Ps.18.11
Only be strong and very *c.*	Jos.1.7	He spread a cloud for a *c.*	Ps.105.39
Be *c.* and be valiant	2 Sam.13.28	the *c.* too narrow to wrap	Is.28.20
His heart was *c.* in the ways of	2 Chr.17.6	every precious stone was your *c.*	Ezek.28.13
in your faith, be *c.*, be strong	1 Cor.16.13	her hair is given to her for a *c.*	1 Cor.11.15

COURSE

		COVET	
and like a strong man runs its *c.*	Ps.19.5	shall not *c.* your neighbor's wife	Ex.20.17
and the third day I finish my *c.*	Lk.13.32	you shall not *c.* the silver	Dt.7.25
as John was finishing his *c.*	Acts 13.25	They *c.* fields, and seize them	Mic.2.2
accomplish my *c.* and the ministry	Acts 20.24	I *c.* no one's silver or gold	Acts 20.33
following the *c.* of this world	Eph.2.2	not have known what it is to *c.*	Rom.7.7

COURT

		You shall not *c.*	Rom.13.9
yea, faints for the *c.* of the LORD	Ps.84.2	you *c.* and cannot obtain	Jas.4.2
For a day in thy *c.* is better than	Ps.84.10	**CRAFTSMAN**	
Enter . . . his *c.* with praise	Ps.100.4	a thing made by the hands of a *c.*	Dt.27.15
while you are going with him to *c.*	Mt.5.25	a skilful *c.* to set up an image	Is.40.20
he entered the *c.* of the high	Jn.18.15	no little business to the *c.*	Acts 19.24
a member of the *c.* of Herod	Acts 13.1	Demetrius and the *c.* with him	Acts 19.38
judged by you or by any human *c.*	1 Cor.4.3	a *c.* . . . shall be found . . . no more	Rev.18.22
is it not they who drag you into *c.?*	Jas.2.6	**CRAFTY**	

COVENANT

		Jonadab was a very *c.* man	2 Sam.13.3
I will establish my *c.* with you	Gen.6.18	He frustrates the devices of the *c.*	Job 5.12
a sign of the *c.* between me and	Gen.9.13	you choose the tongue of the *c.*	Job 15.5
establish my *c.* . . . an everlasting *c.*	Gen.17.19	They lay *c.* plans against thy people	Ps.83.3
God remembered his *c.* with Abraham	Ex.2.24	I was *c.*, you say, and got the	2 Cor.12.16
Then he took the book of the *c.*	Ex.24.7	**CREATE**	
the ark of the *c.* of the LORD went	Num.10.33	In the beginning God *c.* the heavens	Gen.1.1
the faithful God who keeps *c.*	Dt.7.9	So God *c.* man in his own image	Gen.1.27
Joshua made a *c.* with the people	Jos.24.25	*C.* in me a clean heart, O God	Ps.51.10
he read . . . the book of the *c.* which	2 Chr.34.30	the LORD will *c.* . . . a cloud by day	Is.4.5
I have made a *c.* with my eyes	Job 31.1	the Holy One of Israel has *c.* it	Is.41.20
Have regard for thy *c.*	Ps.74.20	whom I *c.* for my glory	Is.43.7
He is mindful of his *c.* for ever	Ps.105.8	For behold, I *c.* new heavens	Is.65.17
will make a new *c.* with the house	Jer.31.31	Has not one God *c.* us?	Mal.2.10
make with them an everlasting *c.*	Jer.32.40	of those who *c.* dissensions	Rom.16.17
an everlasting *c.* which will never	Jer.50.5	*c.* in Christ Jesus for good works	Eph.2.10
be an everlasting *c.* with them	Ezek.37.26	*c.* after the likeness of God	Eph.4.24
My *c.* with him was a *c.* of life	Mal.2.5	for in him all things were *c.*	Col.1.16
for this is my blood of the *c.*	Mt.26.28	For everything *c.* by God is good	1 Tim.4.4
sons . . . of the *c.* which God gave	Acts 3.25	world was *c.* by the word of God	Heb.11.3
This cup is the new *c.* in my blood	1 Cor.11.25	who *c.* heaven and what is in it	Rev.10.6
to be ministers of a new *c.*	2 Cor.3.6	**CREATION**	
allegory: these women are two *c.*	Gal.4.24	But from the beginning of *c.*	Mk.10.6
		Ever since the *c.* of the world	Rom.1.20

the *c.* waits with eager longing — Rom.8.19
the whole *c.* has been groaning — Rom.8.22
nor anything else in all *c.* — Rom.8.39
in Christ, he is a new *c.* — 2 Cor.5.17
nor uncircumcision, but a new *c.* — Gal.6.15
the first-born of all *c.* — Col.1.15
they were from the beginning of *c.* — 2 Pet.3.4

CREATOR
Remember also your *C.* in the days — Ec.12.1
the *C.* of the ends of the earth — Is.40.28
the *C.* of Israel, your King — Is.43.15
the creature rather than the *C.* — Rom.1.25
their souls to a faithful *C.* — 1 Pet.4.19

CREATURE
bring forth swarms of living *c.* — Gen.1.20
the man called every living *c.* — Gen.2.19
the life of every *c.* is its blood — Lev.17.14
there is not . . . a *c.* without fear — Job 41.33
the earth is full of thy *c.* — Ps.104.24
served the *c.* rather than the — Rom.1.25
preached to every *c.* under heaven — Col.1.23
And before him no *c.* is hidden — Heb.4.13
I heard every *c.* in heaven and — Rev.5.13

CRETE
under the lee of *C.* off Salmone — Acts 27.7
a harbor of *C.*, looking northeast — Acts 27.12
This is why I left you in *C.* — Tit.1.5

CRY (noun)
God does not hear an empty *c.* — Job 35.13
attend to my *c.*! Give ear — Ps.17.1
he inclined to me and heard my *c.* — Ps.40.1
may there be no *c.* of distress in — Ps.144.14
And Jesus uttered a loud *c.* — Mk.15.37
she exclaimed with a loud *c.* — Lk.1.42
from heaven with a *c.* of command — 1 Th.4.16
the *c.* of the harvesters have — Jas.5.4

CRY (verb)
to my God I *c.* for help — Ps.18.6
in his temple all *c.*, "Glory!" — Ps.29.9
This poor man *c.*, and the LORD — Ps.34.6
Out of the depths I *c.* to thee — Ps.130.1
Wisdom *c.* aloud in the street — Pr.1.20
A voice *c.*: "In the wilderness — Is.40.3
A voice says, "*C.*!" And I said — Is.40.6
He will not *c.* or lift up his voice — Is.42.2
prophets . . . who *c.* "Peace" — Mic.3.5
and beginning to sink he *c.* out — Mt.14.30
they *c.* out the more, "Lord, have — Mt.20.31
Jesus . . . with a loud voice — Mt.27.46
those who followed *c.* out, "Hosanna — Mk.11.9
they *c.* out again, "Crucify him — Mk.15.13
seizes him, and he suddenly *c.* out — Lk.9.39
who *c.* to him day and night? — Lk.18.7
the very stones would *c.* out — Lk.19.40
voice of one *c.* in the wilderness — Jn.1.23
When we *c.*, "Abba! Father!" — Rom.8.15

CROOKED
are a perverse and *c.* generation — Dt.32.5
with the *c.* thou dost show — Ps.18.26
Put away from you *c.* speech — Pr.4.24
A man of *c.* mind does not prosper — Pr.17.20
The way of the guilty is *c.* — Pr.21.8
What is *c.* cannot be made straight — Ec.1.15
and the *c.* shall be made straight — Lk.3.5
yourselves from this *c.* generation — Acts 2.40
the midst of a *c.* . . . generation — Phil.2.15

CROSS (noun)
not take his *c.* and follow me — Mt.10.38
let him come down now from the *c.* — Mt.27.42
and take up his *c.* and follow me — Mk.8.34
Simon of Cyrene . . . to carry his *c.* — Mk.15.21
and take up his *c.* daily — Lk.9.23
he went out, bearing his own *c.* — Jn.19.17
wrote a title and put it on the *c.* — Jn.19.19
lest the *c.* of Christ be emptied — 1 Cor.1.17
the word of the *c.* is folly to — 1 Cor.1.18
except in the *c.* of our Lord Jesus — Gal.6.14
to God in one body through the *c.* — Eph.2.16
unto death, even death on a *c.* — Phil.2.8
making peace by the blood of his *c.* — Col.1.20
was set before him endured the *c.* — Heb.12.2

CROWN (noun)
good wife is the *c.* of her husband — Pr.12.4
The *c.* of the wise is their wisdom — Pr.14.24
Grandchildren are the *c.* of the aged — Pr.17.6
does a *c.* endure to all generations? — Pr.27.24
LORD of hosts will be a *c.* of glory — Is.28.5
plaiting a *c.* of thorns they — Mt.27.29
wearing the *c.* of thorns — Jn.19.5
my joy and *c.*, stand firm thus — Phil.4.1
obtain the unfading *c.* of glory — 1 Pet.5.4
and I will give you the *c.* of life — Rev.2.10
cast their *c.* before the throne — Rev.4.10
on her head a *c.* of twelve stars — Rev.12.1
with a golden *c.* on his head — Rev.14.14

CRUCIFY
to be mocked and scourged and *c.* — Mt.20.19
all the more, "Let him be *c.*" — Mt.27.23
Then two robbers were *c.* with him — Mt.27.38
And they cried out again, "*C.* him." — Mk.15.13
they cried out, "*C.* him, *c.* him!" — Jn.19.6
away with him, *c.* him — Jn.19.15
this Jesus . . . you *c.* and killed — Acts 2.23
Jesus . . . whom you *c.* . . . . God raised — Acts 4.10
our old self was *c.* with him — Rom.6.6
but we preach Christ *c.* — 1 Cor.1.23
he was *c.* in weakness, but lives — 2 Cor.13.4
I have been *c.* with Christ — Gal.2.20
since they *c.* the Son of God — Heb.6.6

CRUEL
but a *c.* man hurts himself — Pr.11.17
Wrath is *c.*, anger is overwhelming — Pr.27.4
jealousy is *c.* as the grave — S.of S.8.6
daughter of my people has become *c.* — Lam.4.3

CUBIT
can add one *c.* to his span of life? — Mt.6.27

CUNNING
yea, their *c.* is in vain — Ps.119.118
we refuse to practice *c.* — 2 Cor.4.2
serpent deceived Eve by his *c.* — 2 Cor.11.3
by the *c.* of men, by their craftiness — Eph.4.14

CUP
is my chosen portion and my *c.* — Ps.16.5
my head with oil, my *c.* overflows — Ps.23.5
lift up the *c.* of salvation — Ps.116.13
have drunk . . . the *c.* of his wrath — Is.51.17
give him the *c.* of consolation — Jer.16.7
gives . . . even a *c.* of cold water — Mt.10.42
to drink the *c.* that I am to drink? — Mt.20.22
you cleanse the outside of the *c.* — Mt.23.25
And he took a *c.*, and when he had — Mt.26.27
possible, let this *c.* pass from me — Mt.26.39

The *c.* of blessing which we bless   1 Cor.10.16
This *c.* is the new covenant   1 Cor.11.25
eat this bread and drink the *c.*   1 Cor.11.26
unmixed into the *c.* of his anger   Rev.14.10

CURE
He would *c.* him of his leprosy   2 Kg.5.3
he is not able to *c.* you or heal   Hos.5.13
and the boy was *c.* instantly   Mt.17.18
gave them power . . . to *c.* diseases   Lk.9.1
Jews said to the man who was *c.*   Jn.5.10
had diseases also came and were *c.*   Acts 28.9

CURSE (noun)
you this day a blessing and a *c.*   Dt.11.26
God turned the *c.* into a blessing   Dt.23.5
with all the *c.* of the covenant   Dt.29.21
God turned the *c.* into a blessing   Neh.13.2
Therefore a *c.* devours the earth   Is.24.6
I will send the *c.* upon you   Mal.2.2
began to invoke a *c.* on himself   Mt.26.74
their mouth is full of *c.* and   Rom.3.14
who rely on works . . . are under a *c.*   Gal.3.10
redeemed us from the *c.* of the law   Gal.3.13

CURSE (verb)
c. is the ground because of you   Gen.3.17
I will never again *c.* the ground   Gen.8.21
You shall not *c.* the deaf or put   Lev.19.14
his wife said, ". . . *C.* God, and die."   Job 2.9
but inwardly they *c.*   Ps.62.4
Let them *c.*, but do thou bless   Ps.109.28
C. is the man who trusts in man   Jer.17.5
fig tree which you *c.* has withered   Mk.11.21
bless those who *c.* you   Lk.6.28
bless and do not *c.* them   Rom.12.14
of God ever says "Jesus be *c.*!"   1 Cor.12.3
and with it we *c.* men   Jas.3.9

CURTAIN
stretches out the heavens like a *c.*   Is.40.22
And the *c.* of the temple was torn   Mk.15.38
the inner shrine behind the *c.*   Heb.6.19

CUSTOM
Now this was the *c.* in former times   Ru.4.7
for the *c.* of the peoples are false   Jer.10.3
as his *c.* was, he taught them   Mk.10.1
as his *c.* was, on the sabbath day   Lk.4.16
a *c.* that I should release one man   Jn.18.39
as is the burial *c.* of the Jews   Jn.19.40

CUT
So Moses *c.* two tables of stone   Ex.34.4
For the wicked shall be *c.* off   Ps.37.9
May his posterity be *c.* off   Ps.109.13
does not bear good fruit is *c.* down   Mt.3.10
c. it off and throw it from you   Mt.18.8
the man whose ear Peter had *c.* off   Jn.18.26
At Cenchreae he *c.* his hair   Acts 18.18
otherwise you too will be *c.* off   Rom.11.22

CYMBAL
Asaph was to sound the *c.*   1 Chr.16.5
with *c.*, to praise the LORD   Ezra 3.10
praise him with loud clashing *c.*   Ps.150.5
I am a noisy gong or a clanging *c.*   1 Cor.13.1

CYPRUS
Is.23.1; Ezek.27.6; Acts 11.20; 15.39; 27.4

CYRENE
Mt.27.32; Acts 2.10; 11.20; 13.1

CYRUS
king of Persia, 2 Chr.36.22; prophecies con-

cerning, Is.44.28; 45.1; *see* Dan.6.28; 10.1;
his proclamation for rebuilding the temple,
2 Chr.36.22–23; Ezra 1

DAILY
Blessed be the Lord, who *d.* bears us   Ps.68.19
Yet they seek me *d.*, and delight   Is.58.2
Give us this day our *d.* bread   Mt.6.11
take up his cross *d.* and follow me   Lk.9.23
he was teaching *d.* in the temple   Lk.19.47
they increased in numbers *d.*   Acts 16.5
examining the scriptures *d.* to see   Acts 17.11
priests, to offer sacrifices *d.*   Heb.7.27

DAMASCUS
the capital of Syria; first mentioned, Gen.14.15;
subjugated by David, 2 Sam.8.6; 1 Chr.18.6;
Elisha's prophecy there, 2 Kg.8.7–13; taken by
Tiglath-pileser, king of Assyria, 2 Kg.16.9;
restored to Israel by Jeroboam, 2 Kg.14.28;
king Ahaz copies an altar there, 2 Kg.16.10;
Paul's journey to, Acts 9; 22.6; Paul restored to
sight, and baptized there, Acts 9.17,18;
prophecies concerning, Is.7.8; 8.4; 17.1;
Jer.49.23; Am.1.3

DAN
(1) son of Jacob, by Rachel's handmaid, Gen.
30.6; (2) tribe of, numbered, Num.1.39;
26.42–43; their inheritance, Jos.19.40; blessed
by Jacob, Gen.49.16; blessed by Moses,
Dt.33.22; win Laish, and call it Dan, Jg.18.29;
set up idolatry, Jg.18.30; 1 Kg.12.29

DANCE (verb)
David *d.* before the LORD with all   2 Sam.6.14
a time to mourn, and a time to *d.*   Ec.3.4
We piped to you, and you did not *d.*   Mt.11.17
Herodias' daughter came in and *d.*   Mk.6.22
to eat and drink and rose up to *d.*   1 Cor.10.7

DANIEL
(1) (Belteshazzar), with other captives, taken
from Jerusalem to Babylon, Dan.1.3–6; taught
the learning of the Chaldeans, Dan.1.4; will not
take the king's meat or drink, Dan.1.8; has
understanding in dreams, Dan.1.17; interprets
the royal dreams, Dan.2; 4, and handwriting
on wall, Dan.5.17; made chief president by
Darius, Dan.6.2; conspired against by the
princes, Dan.6.4; idolatrous decree against,
issued, Dan.6.9; cast into the lions' den, Dan.
6.16; preservation in, Dan.6.22; his visions,
Dan.7–8; his prayer, Dan.9.3; promise of return
from captivity, Dan.9.24; name mentioned,
Ezek.14.14,20; 28.3; (2) others, 1 Chr.3.1;
Ezra 8.2

DARE
nor . . . did any one *d.* to ask him any   Mt.22.46
For they no longer *d.* to ask him   Lk.20.40
none of the disciples *d.* ask him   Jn.21.12
for a good man one will *d.* even to die   Rom.5.7
does he *d.* go to law before the   1 Cor.6.1
I also *d.* to boast of that   2 Cor.11.21

DARIUS
Ezra 4.5; Neh.12.22; Dan.6.1; Hag.1.1; Zech.
1.1

DARK (noun)
They grope in the *d.* without light   Job 12.25

The murderer rises in the *d.*   Job 24.14
What I tell you in the *d.*, utter   Mt.10.27
DARK (adjective)
even the darkness is not *d.* to thee   Ps.139.12
I am very *d.*, but comely   S.of S.1.5
to the tomb . . . while it was still *d.*   Jn.20.1
as to a lamp shining in a *d.* place   2 Pet.1.19
DARKENED
Let their eyes be *d.*, so that   Ps.69.23
The sun and the moon are *d.*   Jl.2.10
after . . . those days the sun will be *d.* Mt.24.29
their senseless minds were *d.*   Rom.1.21
they are *d.* in their understanding   Eph.4.18
sun and . . . air were *d.* with the smoke Rev.9.2
DARKNESS
d. was upon the face of the deep   Gen.1.2
and the *d.* he called Night   Gen.1.5
land of Egypt, a *d.* to be felt   Ex.10.21
as the blind grope in *d.*   Dt.28.29
the wicked shall be cut off in *d.*   1 Sam.2.9
He made *d.* around him his canopy   2 Sam.22.12
and my God lightens my *d.*   2 Sam.22.29
I am hemmed in by *d.*, and thick *d.*   Job 23.17
when I waited for light, *d.* came   Job 30.26
the LORD my God lightens my *d.*   Ps.18.28
nor the pestilence that stalks in *d.*   Ps.91.6
Let only *d.* cover me, and the light   Ps.139.11
who walked in *d.* have seen a great   Is.9.2
I form light and create *d.*   Is.45.7
For behold, *d.* shall cover the earth   Is.60.2
who makes the morning *d.*   Am.4.13
and turns deep *d.* into the morning   Am.5.8
Is not the day of the LORD *d.*   Am.5.20
who sat in *d.* have seen a great   Mt.4.16
and cast him into the outer *d.*   Mt.22.13
there was *d.* over all the land   Mt.27.45
The light shines in the *d.*   Jn.1.5
men loved *d.* rather than light   Jn.3.19
believes in me may not remain in *d.*   Jn.12.46
cast off the works of *d.* and   Rom.13.12
what fellowship has light with *d.*?   2 Cor.6.14
we are not of the night or of *d.*   1 Th.5.5
out of *d.* into his marvelous light   1 Pet.2.9
in him is no *d.* at all   1 Jn.1.5
DAUGHTER
saw that the *d.* of men were fair   Gen.6.2
and said, "Tell me whose *d.* you are   Gen.24.23
Now the *d.* of Pharaoh came down to   Ex.2.5
When a man sells his *d.* as a slave   Ex.21.7
And she said to her, "Go, my *d.*"   Ru.2.2
Now Saul's *d.* Michal loved David   1 Sam.18.20
his sons and *d.* were eating   Job 1.13
Hear, O *d.*, consider, and incline   Ps.45.10
O *d.* of Babylon, you devastator   Ps.137.8
sons and your *d.* shall prophesy   Jl.2.28
saying, "My *d.* has just died   Mt.9.18
a *d.* against her mother, and a   Mt.10.35
the *d.* of Herodias danced before   Mt.14.6
Tell the *d.* of Zion, Behold, your   Mt.21.5
D., your faith has made you well   Mk.5.34
Fear not, *d.* of Zion   Jn.12.15
and you shall be my sons and *d.*   2 Cor.6.18
be called the son of Pharaoh's *d.*   Heb.11.24
DAVID
anointed king by Samuel, 1 Sam.16.8–13; plays
the harp before Saul, 1 Sam.16–23; his zeal and

faith, 1 Sam.17.26,34–36; kills Goliath, 1 Sam.
17.49; at first honored by Saul, 1 Sam.18.5;
Saul jealous of, tries to kill, 1 Sam.18.8–12;
afterwards persecuted by him, 1 Sam.19; 20;
loved by Jonathan, 1 Sam.18.1; 19.1; 20;
23.16; overcomes the Philistines, 1 Sam.18.27;
19.8; flees to Gath, and feigns madness, 1
Sam.21.10, 13; dwells in the cave of Adullam,
1 Sam.22; escapes Saul's pursuit, 1 Sam.23;
twice spares Saul's life, 1 Sam.24.4; 26.9–11;
dwells at Ziklag, 1 Sam.27; laments the death of
Saul and Jonathan, 2 Sam.1.17; becomes king of
Judah, 2 Sam.2.4; forms a league with Abner, 2
Sam.3.13; avenges the murder of Ish-bosheth,
2 Sam.4.9–12; becomes king of all Israel, 2
Sam.5.3; 1 Chr.11; his victories, 2 Sam.2;
5; 8; 10; 12.29; 21.15–22; 1 Chr.18–20; brings
the ark to Jerusalem, 2 Sam.6; 1 Chr.13; 15;
desires to build God a house, 2 Sam.7.2–3, and
is forbidden by Nathan, 1 Chr.17.4; God's
promises to him, 2 Sam.7.11; 1 Chr.17.10; his
prayer and thanksgiving, 2 Sam.7.18–29; 1
Chr.17.16–27; his kindness to Mephibosheth,
2 Sam.9; his sin involving Bathsheba and Uriah,
2 Sam.11; 12; repents at Nathan's parable of
the ewe lamb, 2 Sam.12; Ps.51; grieves over
Absalom's death, 2 Sam.18.33; 19.1; Sheba's
conspiracy against, 2 Sam.20; makes expiation
for the Gibeonites, 2 Sam.21; regulates the
service of the tabernacle, 1 Chr.23–26; exhorts
the congregation to fear God, 1 Chr.28; appoints Solomon his successor, 1 Kg.1; his
charge to Solomon, 1 Kg.2; 1 Chr.28.9; his last
words, 2 Sam.23; his death, 1 Kg.2; 1 Chr.
29.26–28
DAWN (verb)
and shadow of death light has *d.*   Mt.4.16
the day shall *d.* upon us from on   Lk.1.78
As day was about to *d.*, Paul urged   Acts 27.33
until the day *d.* and the morning   2 Pet.1.19
DAY
God called the light *D.*   Gen.1.5
the greater light to rule the *d.*   Gen.1.16
So God blessed the seventh *d.*   Gen.2.3
This *d.* shall be . . . a memorial *d.*   Ex.12.14
Remember the *d.* of old, consider the   Dt.32.7
This *d.* is a *d.* of good news   2 Kg.7.9
of his salvation from *d.* to *d.*   1 Chr.16.23
This *d.* is holy to the LORD your   Neh.8.9
and cursed the *d.* of his birth   Job 3.1
for our *d.* on earth are a shadow   Job 8.9
on his law he meditates *d.* and night   Ps.1.2
D. to *d.* pours forth speech   Ps.19.2
follow me all the *d.* of my life   Ps.23.6
tell . . . of thy praise all the *d.* long Ps.35.28
Thine is the *d.*, thine also the   Ps.74.16
In the *d.* of my trouble I seek the   Ps.77.2
For a *d.* in thy courts is better   Ps.84.10
tell of his salvation from *d.* to *d.*   Ps.96.2
As for man, his *d.* are like grass   Ps.103.15
This is the *d.* which the LORD has   Ps.118.24
The sun shall not smite you by *d.*   Ps.121.6
the night is bright as the *d.*   Ps.139.12
not know what a *d.* may bring forth   Pr.27.1
the *d.* of death, than the *d.* of birth   Ec.7.1
In the *d.* of prosperity be joyful   Ec.7.14

O *D.* Star, son of Dawn! How you Is.14.12
Cursed be the *d.* on which I was Jer.20.14
my covenant with *d.* and night and Jer.33.25
three times a *d.* and prayed and Dan.6.10
For the *d.* of the LORD is near Jl.1.15
Is not the *d.* of the LORD darkness Am.5.20
Give us this *d.* our daily bread Mt.6.11
own trouble be sufficient for the *d.* Mt.6.34
more tolerable on the *d.* of judgment Mt.10.15
and on the third *d.* be raised Mt.16.21
of that *d.* and hour no one knows Mt.24.36
since it was the *d.* of Preparation Mk.15.42
born this *d.* in the city of David Lk.2.11
When the *d.* of Pentecost had come Acts 2.1
sealed for the *d.* of redemption Eph.4.30
in the last *d.* . . . times of stress 2 Tim.3.1
laid up treasure for the last *d.* Jas.5.3
both now and to the *d.* of eternity 2 Pet.3.18
was in the Spirit on the Lord's *d.* Rev.1.10

DEACONS
Philippi, with the bishops and *d.* Phil.1.1
D. likewise must be serious, not 1 Tim.3.8
if . . . blameless let them serve as *d.* 1 Tim.3.10
those who serve well as *d.* gain 1 Tim.3.13

DEAD
not forsaken the living or the *d.* Ru.2.20
look upon a *d.* dog such as I? 2 Sam.9.8
out of mind like one who is *d.* Ps.31.12
the *d.* do not praise the LORD Ps.115.17
D. flies make the perfumer's ointment Ec.10.1
Thy *d.* shall live, their bodies Is.26.19
Weep not for him who is *d.* Jer.22.10
raise the *d.*, cleanse lepers, cast Mt.10.8
the Son of man is raised from the *d.* Mt.17.9
he is not God of the *d.*, but of Mt.22.32
And the *d.* man sat up, and began to Lk.7.15
Leave the *d.* to bury their own *d.* Lk.9.60
do you seek the living among the *d.?* Lk.24.5
raises the *d.* and gives them life Jn.5.21
whom God raised from the *d.* Acts 3.15
be judge of the living and the *d.* Acts 10.42
raised from the *d.* Jesus our Lord Rom.4.24
consider yourselves *d.* to sin Rom.6.11
your bodies are *d.* because of sin Rom.8.10
Christ . . . raised from the *d.* 1 Cor.15.20
baptized in behalf of the *d.* 1 Cor.15.29
the *d.* will be raised imperishable 1 Cor.15.52
And the *d.* in Christ will rise 1 Th.4.16
repentance from *d.* works and Heb.6.1
so faith apart from works is *d.* Jas.2.26
Blessed are the *d.* who die in the Rev.14.13

DEAF
be not *d.* to me, lest, if thou be Ps.28.1
the ears of the *d.* unstopped Is.35.5
lepers are cleansed and the *d.* hear Mt.11.5
You dumb and *d.* spirit, I command Mk.9.25

DEAL (verb)
May the LORD *d.* kindly with you Ru.1.8
He does not *d.* with us according Ps.103.10
D. bountifully with thy servant Ps.119.17
those who *d.* with the world as 1 Cor.7.31
He can *d.* gently with the ignorant Heb.5.2
not to *d.* with sin but to save Heb.9.28

DEATH
I do not know the day of my *d.* Gen.27.2
Let me die the *d.* of the righteous Num.23.10

if even *d.* parts me from you Ru.1.17
who long for *d.*, but it comes not Job 3.21
Abaddon and *D.* say, 'We have heard Job 28.22
Have the gates of *d.* been revealed Job 38.17
For in *d.* there is no remembrance Ps.6.5
lest I sleep the sleep of *d.* Ps.13.3
the valley of the shadow of *d.* Ps.23.4
D. shall be their shepherd Ps.49.14
What man can live and never see *d.?* Ps.89.48
hast delivered my soul from *d.* Ps.116.8
he has not given me over to *d.* Ps.118.18
but righteousness delivers from *d.* Pr.11.4
for love is strong as *d.* S.of S.8.6
We have made a covenant with *d.* Is.28.15
my soul is . . . sorrowful, even to *d.* Mt.26.38
darkness and in the shadow of *d.* Lk.1.79
but has passed from *d.* to life Jn.5.24
having loosed the pangs of *d.* Acts 2.24
Yet *d.* reigned from Adam to Moses Rom.5.14
The *d.* he died he died to sin, once Rom.6.10
For the wages of sin is *d.* Rom.6.23
deliver me from this body of *d.?* Rom.7.24
For I am sure that neither *d.* Rom.8.38
you proclaim the Lord's *d.* until 1 Cor.11.26
D. is swallowed up in victory 1 Cor.15.54
O *d.*, where is thy victory? 1 Cor.15.55
The sting of *d.* is sin 1 Cor.15.56
Now if the dispensation of *d.* 2 Cor.3.7
d. is at work in us, but life in 2 Cor.4.12
obedient unto *d.*, even *d.* on a cross Phil.2.8
becoming like him in his *d.* Phil.3.10
Put to *d.* therefore what is earthly Col.3.5
who abolished *d.* and brought life 2 Tim.1.10
we have passed out of *d.* into life 1 Jn.3.14
He who does not love remains in *d.* 1 Jn.3.14
Be faithful unto *d.*, and I will Rev.2.10
horse, and its rider's name was *D.* Rev.6.8
Over such the second *d.* has no Rev.20.6
Then *D.* and Hades were thrown into Rev.20.14

DEBORAH
Jg.4.4–10; 5.1

DEBT
and every one who was in *d.* 1 Sam.22.2
And forgive us our *d.* Mt.6.12
released him and forgave him the *d.* Mt.18.27
indeed they are in *d.* to them Rom.15.27

DECEIT
in whose spirit there is no *d.* Ps.32.2
D. is in the heart of those who Pr.12.20
Bread gained by *d.* is sweet to a Pr.20.17
there was no *d.* in his mouth Is.53.9
d., licentiousness, envy, slander Mk.7.22
makes a prey of you by . . . empty *d.* Col.2.8

DECEITFUL
from *d.* and unjust men deliver me Ps.43.1
Charm is *d.*, and beauty is vain Pr.31.30
The heart is *d.* above all things Jer.17.9
d. workmen, disguising themselves 2 Cor.11.13
by their craftiness in *d.* wiles Eph.4.14
by giving heed to *d.* spirits 1 Tim.4.1

DECEIVE
Why then have you *d.* me? Gen.29.25
Every one *d.* his neighbor, and no Jer.9.5
The pride of your heart has *d.* you Ob.3
they use their tongues to *d.* Rom.3.13
Let no one *d.* himself 1 Cor.3.18

serpent *d.* Eve by his cunning   2 Cor.11.3
Let no one *d.* you with empty words   Eph.5.6
we *d.* ourselves, and the truth is   1 Jn.1.8
DECLARE
to *d.* to you the word of the LORD   Dt.5.5
D. his glory among the nations   1 Chr.16.24
they had *d.* Job to be in the wrong   Job 32.3
The heavens *d.* his righteousness   Ps.50.6
D. his glory among the nations   Ps.96.3
I will *d.* thy greatness   Ps.145.6
let us *d.* in Zion the work of . . . God   Jer.51.10
(Thus he *d.* all foods clean.)   Mk.7.19
d. how much God has done for you   Lk.8.39
take what is mine and *d.* it to you   Jn.16.15
d. that God is really among you   1 Cor.14.25
that I may *d.* it boldly, as I ought   Eph.6.20
to *d.* the mystery of Christ   Col.4.3
D. these things; exhort and reprove   Tit.2.15
For if the message *d.* by angels was   Heb.2.2
that you may *d.* the wonderful deeds   1 Pet.2.9
DECREE (noun)
I will tell of the *d.* of the LORD   Ps.2.7
Thy *d.* are very sure   Ps.93.5
I have heard a *d.* of destruction   Is.28.22
So the *d.* went forth that the wise   Dan.2.13
In those days a *d.* went out from   Lk.2.1
they know God's *d.* that those   Rom.1.32
DEDICATE
the people of Israel *d.* to the LORD   Lev.22.3
When a man *d.* his house to be holy   Lev.27.14
these . . . King David *d.* to the LORD   2 Sam.8.11
I am about to . . . *d.* it to him for   2 Chr.2.4
DEDICATION
offerings for the *d.* of the altar   Num.7.10
celebrated the *d.* of this house   Ezra 6.16
the *d.* of the wall of Jerusalem   Neh.12.27
the feast of the *D.* at Jerusalem   Jn.10.22
DEED
O LORD . . . terrible in glorious *d.*   Ex.15.11
Tell among the peoples his *d.*   Ps.9.11
By dread *d.* thou dost answer us   Ps.65.5
I still proclaim thy wondrous *d.*   Ps.71.17
tell . . . the glorious *d.* of the LORD   Ps.78.4
Praise him for his mighty *d.*   Ps.150.2
what good *d.* must I do, to have   Mt.19.16
mighty in *d.* and word before God   Lk.24.19
because their *d.* were evil   Jn.3.19
I did one *d.,* and you all marvel   Jn.7.21
he was mighty in his words and *d.*   Acts 7.22
put to death the *d.* of the body   Rom.8.13
disobedient, unfit for any good *d.*   Tit.1.16
let us . . . love . . . in *d.* and in truth   1 Jn.3.18
Great and wonderful are thy *d.*   Rev.15.3
the fine linen is the righteous *d.*   Rev.19.8
DEEP (adjective)
God caused a *d.* sleep to fall upon   Gen.2.21
find out the *d.* things of God?   Job 11.7
O LORD! Thy thoughts are very *d.*   Ps.92.5
a man's mind is like *d.* water   Pr.20.5
who dwelt in a land of *d.* darkness   Is.9.2
to draw with, and the well is *d.*   Jn.4.11
for us with sighs too *d.* for words   Rom.8.26
some call the *d.* things of Satan   Rev.2.24
DEEP (noun)
darkness was upon the face of the *d.*   Gen.1.2
D. calls to *d.* at the thunder of   Ps.42.7

who says to the *d.,* "Be dry   Is.44.27
out into the *d.* and let down your   Lk.5.4
DEFEND
d. my cause against an ungodly   Ps.43.1
May he *d.* the cause of the poor of   Ps.72.4
d. the fatherless, plead for the widow   Is.1.17
he *d.* the oppressed man   Acts 7.24
DEFENSE
God has shown himself a sure *d.*   Ps.48.3
to make a *d.* to the people   Acts 19.33
as he thus made his *d.,* Festus   Acts 26.24
my *d.* to those who would examine   1 Cor.9.3
put here for the *d.* of the gospel   Phil.1.16
DEFILE
You shall not *d.* yourselves with   Lev.11.44
You shall not *d.* the land in which   Num.35.34
they have *d.* thy holy temple   Ps.79.1
For your hands are *d.* with blood   Is.59.3
They have *d.* my holy name by their   Ezek.43.8
These are what *d.* a man   Mt.15.20
his disciples ate with hands *d.*   Mk.7.2
and he has *d.* this holy place   Acts 21.28
their conscience, being weak, is *d.*   1 Cor.8.7
and by it the many become *d.*   Heb.12.15
have not *d.* themselves with women   Rev.14.4
DEITY
to think that the *D.* is like gold   Acts 17.29
namely, his eternal power and *d.*   Rom.1.20
whole fulness of *d.* dwells bodily   Col.2.9
DELAY (verb)
saw that Moses *d.* to come down   Ex.32.1
not *d.* to keep thy commandments   Ps.119.60
d. not, for thy own sake, O my God   Dan.9.19
My master is *d.* in coming   Lk.12.45
DELIGHT (noun)
that it was a *d.* to the eyes   Gen.3.6
his *d.* is in the law of the LORD   Ps.1.2
For thou hast no *d.* in sacrifice   Ps.51.16
LORD, but a just weight is his *d.*   Pr.11.1
his *d.* shall be in the fear of the   Is.11.3
then you shall take *d.* in the LORD   Is.58.14
take no *d.* in your solemn assemblies   Am.5.21
the *d.* in riches choke the word   Mt.13.22
DELIGHT (verb)
delivered me, because he *d.* in me   Ps.18.19
I *d.* to do thy will, O my God   Ps.40.8
my chosen, in whom my soul *d.*   Is.42.1
For I *d.* in the law of God   Rom.7.22
DELIVER
I have come down to *d.* them out of   Ex.3.8
I will *d.* you from their bondage   Ex.6.6
the LORD will *d.* you into my hand   1 Sam.17.46
Thou dost *d.* a humble people   2 Sam.22.28
D. my life from the wicked by thy   Ps.17.13
D. my soul from the sword   Ps.22.20
D. me from all my transgressions   Ps.39.8
Be pleased, O God, to *d.* me   Ps.70.1
d. you from the snare of the fowler   Ps.91.3
d. me from the hand of aliens   Ps.144.11
but righteousness *d.* from death   Pr.11.4
he . . . will defend and *d.* them   Is.19.20
saying, "The LORD will surely *d.* us   Is.36.15
who . . . will *d.* you out of my hands?   Dan.3.15
But *d.* us from evil   Mt.6.13
Brother will *d.* up brother to death   Mt.10.21
let God *d.* him now, if he desires   Mt.27.43

for they will *d.* you up to councils Mk.13.9
he who *d.* me to you has . . . greater sin Jn.19.11
this Jesus, *d.* up according to the Acts 2.23
the customs which Moses *d.* to us Acts 6.14
received the law as *d.* by angels Acts 7.53
will *d.* me from this body of death? Rom.7.24
if I *d.* my body to be burned 1 Cor.13.3
when he *d.* the kingdom to God 1 Cor.15.24
our hope that he will *d.* us again 2 Cor.1.10
Jesus who *d.* us from the wrath to 1 Th.1.10
whom I have *d.* to Satan that they 1 Tim.1.20
and *d.* all those who through fear Heb.2.15
was once for all *d.* to the saints Jude 3

DELIVERER
the LORD raised up a *d.* for the people Jg.3.9
The LORD . . . my fortress, and my *d.* 2 Sam.22.2
my *d.*, my God, my rock, in whom I Ps.18.2
Thou art my help and my *d.* Ps.40.17
The *D.* will come from Zion Rom.11.26

DELUSION
men of high estate are a *d.* Ps.62.9
Behold, they are all a *d.* Is.41.29
you have uttered *d.* and seen lies Ezek.13.8
God sends upon them a strong *d.* 2 Th.2.11

DEMON
sacrificed to *d.* which were no gods Dt.32.17
sacrificed their sons . . . to the *d.* Ps.106.37
He casts out *d.* by the prince of *d.* Mt.9.34
and they say, 'He has a *d.*' Mt.11.18
and the *d.* came out of him Mt.17.18
who had the spirit of an unclean *d.* Lk.4.33
The people answered, "You have a *d.* Jn.7.20
Jesus answered, "I have not a *d.* Jn.8.49
Can a *d.* open the eyes of the blind? Jn.10.21
they offer to *d.* and not to God 1 Cor.10.20
cup of the Lord and the cup of *d.* 1 Cor.10.21
giving heed to . . . doctrines of 1 Tim.4.1
Even the *d.* believe–and shudder Jas.2.19
has become a dwelling place of *d.* Rev.18.2

DEN
shall be cast into the *d.* of lions Dan.6.7
a young lion cry out from his *d.* Am.3.4
you have made it a *d.* of robbers Mk.11.17
in *d.* and caves of the earth Heb.11.38

DENY
I also will *d.* before my Father who Mt.10.33
let him *d.* himself and take up his Mt.16.24
crows, you will *d.* me three times Mt.26.34
Peter again *d.* it; and at once Jn.18.27
you *d.* the Holy and Righteous One Acts 3.14
if we *d.* him, he also will *d.* us 2 Tim.2.12
but they *d.* him by their deeds Tit.1.16
No one who *d.* the Son has the 1 Jn.2.23
and you did not *d.* my faith even Rev.2.13

DEPART
The scepter shall not *d.* from Judah Gen.49.10
They say to God, '*D.* from us Job 21.14
to *d.* from evil is understanding Job 28.28
D. from evil and do good Ps.34.14
D. from me, you evildoers Ps.119.115
when he is old he will not *d.* from Pr.22.6
shall not *d.* out of your mouth Is.59.21
d. from me, you evildoers Mt.7.23
D. from me, you cursed, into the Mt.25.41
D. from me, for I am a sinful man Lk.5.8
Gerasenes asked him to *d.* from them Lk.8.37

d. from me, all you workers of Lk.13.27
his hour . . . to *d.* out of this world Jn.13.1
them not to *d.* from Jerusalem Acts 1.4
My desire is to *d.* and be with Phil.1.23
some will *d.* from the faith 1 Tim.4.1
Let every one . . . *d.* from iniquity 2 Tim.2.19

DEPARTURE
in glory and spoke of his *d.* Lk.9.31
after my *d.* fierce wolves will Acts 20.29
the time of my *d.* has come 2 Tim.4.6
that after my *d.* you may be able 2 Pet.1.15

DEPEND
on these two commandments *d.* all Mt.22.40
That is why it *d.* on faith, in order Rom.4.16
So it *d.* not upon man's will or Rom.9.16
so far as it *d.* upon you, live Rom.12.18
righteousness . . . that *d.* on faith Phil.3.9

DEPTH
from the *d.* of the earth thou wilt Ps.71.20
In his hand are the *d.* of the earth Ps.95.4
Out of the *d.* I cry to thee, O LORD Ps.130.1
to Sheol, to the *d.* of the Pit Is.14.15
cast . . . sins into the *d.* of the sea Mic.7.19
since they had no *d.* of soil Mt.13.5
to be drowned in the *d.* of the sea Mt.18.6
nor height, nor *d.*, nor anything Rom.8.39
O the *d.* of the riches and wisdom Rom.11.33
everything, even the *d.* of God 1 Cor.2.10
and length and height and *d.* Eph.3.18

DESCEND
straight to the grave they *d.* Ps.49.14
with those who *d.* into the Pit Ezek.26.20
I saw the Spirit *d.* as a dove Jn.1.32
something *d.*, like a great sheet Acts 11.5
or "Who will *d.* into the abyss?" Rom.10.7
the Lord himself will *d.* from heaven 1 Th.4.16

DESCENDANT
To your *d.* I will give this land Gen.12.7
multiply your *d.* that they cannot Gen.16.10
no offspring or *d.* among his people Job 18.19
I will establish your *d.* for ever Ps.89.4
His *d.* will be mighty in the land Ps.112.2
I will pour my Spirit upon your *d.* Is.44.3
We are *d.* of Abraham, and have Jn.8.33
The promise to Abraham and his *d.* Rom.4.13
Are they *d.* of Abraham? So am I 2 Cor.11.22
And those *d.* of Levi who receive Heb.7.5

DESERT (noun)
often they . . . grieved him in the *d.* Ps.78.40
He turns rivers into a *d.*, springs Ps.107.33
the *d.* shall rejoice and blossom Is.35.1
make straight in the *d.* a highway Is.40.3
her *d.* like the garden of the LORD Is.51.3
enough in the *d.* to feed so great Mt.15.33
driven by the demon into the *d.* Lk.8.29
wandering over *d.* and mountains Heb.11.38

DESERTED
but a poor man is *d.* by his friend Pr.19.4
For Gaza shall be *d.*, and Ashkelon Zeph.2.4
are so quickly *d.* him who called Gal.1.6
Demas . . . has *d.* me and gone to 2 Tim.4.10
no one took my part; all *d.* me 2 Tim.4.16

DESERVE
for the laborer *d.* his food Mt.10.10
anything for which I *d.* to die Acts 25.11
those who do such things *d.* to die Rom.1.32

The laborer *d.* his wages   1 Tim.5.18
be *d.* by the man who has spurned   Heb.10.29
to each of you as your works *d.*   Rev.2.23

DESIGNATED
and *d.* Son of God in power according   Rom.1.4
being *d.* by God a high priest after   Heb.5.10
long ago were *d.* for this condemnation   Jude 4

DESIRE (noun)
your *d.* shall be for your husband   Gen.3.16
May he grant you your heart's *d.*   Ps.20.4
the *d.* of the wicked man comes to   Ps.112.10
He fulfils the *d.* of all who fear   Ps.145.19
a *d.* fulfilled is a tree of life   Pr.13.12
my heart's *d.* and prayer to God for   Rom.10.1
but having his *d.* under control   1 Cor.7.37
do not gratify the *d.* of the flesh   Gal.5.16
following the *d.* of body and mind   Eph.2.3
My *d.* is to depart and be with   Phil.1.23

DESIRE (verb)
More to be *d.* are they than gold   Ps.19.10
Sacrifice and offering thou dost not *d.*   Ps.40.6
upon earth that I *d.* besides thee   Ps.73.25
Do not *d.* her beauty in your heart   Pr.6.25
no beauty that we should *d.* him   Is.53.2
For I *d.* steadfast love and not   Hos.6.6
I *d.* mercy, and not sacrifice   Mt.9.13
and kings *d.* to see what you see   Lk.10.24
Father, I *d.* that they also, whom   Jn.17.24
earnestly *d.* the higher gifts   1 Cor.12.31
all who *d.* to live a godly life   2 Tim.3.12
they *d.* a better country , . . a heavenly   Heb.11.16

DESOLATE
he has made *d.* all my company   Job 16.7
He drew me up from the *d.* pit   Ps.40.2
God gives the *d.* a home to dwell in   Ps.68.6
the rights of all who are left *d.*   Pr.31.8
lay waste the earth and make it *d.*   Is.24.1
your land shall no more be termed *D.*   Is.62.4
streets of Jerusalem that are *d.*   Jer.33.10
your house is forsaken and *d.*   Mt.23.38
I will not leave you *d.*; I will come   Jn.14.18

DESOLATION
and your land shall be a *d.*   Lev.26.33
how he has wrought *d.* in the earth   Ps.46.8
It is a *d.*, without man or beast   Jer.32.43
I will bring *d.* upon the land   Ezek.30.12
know that its *d.* has come near   Lk.21.20

DESPAIR (noun)
my heart, so that I am in *d.*   Ps.69.20
the prince is wrapped in *d.*   Ezek.7.27
perplexed, but not driven to *d.*   2 Cor.4.8

DESPISE
Thus Esau *d.* his birthright   Gen.25.34
How long will this people *d.* me?   Num.14.11
Even young children *d.* me   Job 19.18
I *d.* myself, and repent in dust   Job 42.6
a broken . . . heart . . . thou wilt not *d.*   Ps.51.17
son, do not *d.* the LORD's discipline   Pr.3.11
not *d.* your mother when she is old   Pr.23.22
He was *d.* and rejected by men   Is.53.3
I hate, I *d.* your feasts, and I take   Am.5.21
See that you do not *d.* one of these   Mt.18.10
devoted to the one and *d.* the other   Lk.16.13
they were righteous and *d.* others   Lk.18.9
Or do you *d.* the church of God   1 Cor.11.22
do not *d.* prophesying   1 Th.5.20

Let no one *d.* your youth, but set   1 Tim.4.12
endured the cross, *d.* the shame   Heb.12.2

DESTINED
and he is *d.* for the sword   Job 15.22
He *d.* us in love to be his sons   Eph.1.5
have been *d.* and appointed to live   Eph.1.12
For God has not *d.* us for wrath   1 Th.5.9
chosen and *d.* by God the Father   1 Pet.1.2
He was *d.* before the foundation of   1 Pet.1.20

DESTROY
I will *d.* them with the earth   Gen.6.13
neither will I ever again *d.* every   Gen.8.21
wilt thou then *d.* the place   Gen.18.24
now thou dost turn about and *d.* me   Job 10.8
D. their plans, O Lord, confuse their   Ps.55.9
The wicked lie in wait to *d.* me   Ps.119.95
not hurt or *d.* in all my holy   Is.65.25
I will utterly *d.* them, and make   Jer.25.9
I will *d.* you, O Israel   Hos.13.9
I will seek to *d.* all the nations   Zech.12.9
to search for the child, to *d.* him   Mt.2.13
fear him who can *d.* both soul and   Mt.10.28
lawful . . . to save life or to *d.* it?   Lk.6.9
D. this temple, and in three days I   Jn.2.19
d. God's temple, God will *d.* him   1 Cor.3.17
and were *d.* by the Destroyer   1 Cor.10.10
The last enemy to be *d.* is death   1 Cor.15.26
struck down, but not *d.*   2 Cor.4.9
if the earthly tent we live in is *d.*   2 Cor.5.1
through death he might *d.* him who   Heb.2.14

DESTROYER
not allow the *d.* to enter your   Ex.12.23
be a refuge to them from the *d.*   Is.16.4
suddenly the *d.* will come upon us   Jer.6.26
for a *d.* has come upon her   Jer.51.56
and were destroyed by the *D.*   1 Cor.10.10
so that the *D.* of the first-born   Heb.11.28

DESTRUCTION
Let their own eyes see their *d.*   Job 21.20
nor the *d.* that wastes at noonday   Ps.91.6
they are doomed to *d.* for ever   Ps.92.7
and delivered them from *d.*   Ps.107.20
Pride goes before *d.*, and a haughty   Pr.16.18
Before *d.* a man's heart is haughty   Pr.18.12
held back my life from the pit of *d.*   Is.38.17
the gate is wide . . . that leads to *d.*   Mt.7.13
the vessels of wrath made for *d.*   Rom.9.22
to Satan for the *d.* of the flesh   1 Cor.5.5
then sudden *d.* will come upon them   1 Th.5.3
the punishment of eternal *d.* and   2 Th.1.9
that plunge men into ruin and *d.*   1 Tim.6.9
of judgment and *d.* of ungodly men   2 Pet.3.7
unstable twist to their own *d.*   2 Pet.3.16

DETERMINE
I have *d.* to make an end of all   Gen.6.13
that God has *d.* to destroy you   2 Chr.25.16
Since his days are *d.*   Job 14.5
Who *d.* its measurements–surely   Job 38.5
He *d.* the number of the stars   Ps.147.4
not heard that I *d.* it long ago?   Is.37.26
The LORD *d.* to lay in ruins the wall   Lam.2.8
for what is *d.* shall be done   Dan.11.36
Son of man goes as it has been *d.*   Lk.22.22
having *d.* allotted periods and   Acts 17.26

DEVICES
He frustrates the *d.* of the crafty   Job 5.12

men in whose hands are evil *d.*	Ps.26.10	Give me children, or I shall *d.*	Gen.30.1
but a man of evil *d.* he condemns	Pr.12.2	Let me *d.* the death of . . . righteous	Num.23.10
but they have sought out many *d.*	Ec.7.29	where you *d.* I will *d.*, and there	Ru.1.17
not good, following their own *d.*	Is.65.2	integrity? Curse God, and *d.*	Job 2.9

DEVIL

		and wisdom will *d.* with you	Job 12.2
the enemy who sowed them is the *d.*	Mt.13.39	If a man *d.*, shall he live again?	Job 14.14
prepared for the *d.* and his angels	Mt.25.41	you shall *d.* like men, and fall like	Ps.82.7
in the wilderness, tempted by the *d.*	Lk.4.2	they *d.* and return to their dust	Ps.104.29
the twelve, and one of you is a *d.?*	Jn.6.70	I shall not *d.*, but I shall live	Ps.118.17
give no opportunity to the *d.*	Eph.4.27	he who pursues evil will *d.*	Pr.11.19
stand against the wiles of the *d.*	Eph. 6.11	he who hates reproof will *d.*	Pr.15.10
reproach and the snare of the *d.*	1 Tim.3.7	a time to be born, and a time to *d.*	Ec.3.2
power of death, that is, the *d.*	Heb.2.14	eat and drink, for tomorrow we *d.*	Is.22.13
Resist the *d.* and he will flee from	Jas.4.7	If I must *d.* with you, I will not	Mk.14.31
the *d.* has sinned from the beginning	1 Jn.3.8	for they cannot *d.* any more	Lk.20.36
Michael, contending with the *d.*	Jude 9	a man may eat of it and not *d.*	Jn.6.50
who is called the *D.* and Satan	Rev.12.9	will seek me and *d.* in your sin	Jn.8.21

DEVISE

		though he *d.*, yet shall he live	Jn.11.25
to *d.* artistic designs, to work in	Ex.35.32	expedient . . . that one man should *d.*	Jn.11.50
Do they not err that *d.* evil?	Pr.14.22	Christ *d.* for the ungodly	Rom.5.6
for their minds *d.* violence	Pr.24.2	one will hardly *d.* for a righteous man	Rom.5.7
yet they *d.* evil against me	Hos.7.15	How can we who *d.* to sin still live	Rom.6.2
Woe to those who *d.* wickedness	Mic.2.1	For he who has *d.* is freed from sin	Rom.6.7
did not follow cleverly *d.* myths	2 Pet.1.16	you have *d.* to the law through	Rom.7.4

DEVOTE

		according to the flesh you will *d.*	Rom.8.13
will be *d.* to the one and despise	Lk.16.13	and if we *d.*, we *d.* to the Lord	Rom.14.8
they *d.* themselves to the . . . teaching	Acts 2.42	For as in Adam all *d.*, so also	1 Cor.15.22
But we will *d.* ourselves to prayer	Acts 6.4	eat and drink, for tomorrow we *d.*	1 Cor.15.32
that you may *d.* yourselves to	1 Cor.7.5	live is Christ, and to *d.* is gain	Phil.1.21
Practice these duties, *d.* yourself	1 Tim.4.15	it is appointed for men to *d.* once	Heb.9.27

DEVOTION

		d. to sin and live to righteousness	1 Pet.2.24
I remember the *d.* of your youth	Jer.2.2	For Christ also *d.* for sins once	1 Pet.3.18
your undivided *d.* to the Lord	1 Cor.7.35	I *d.*, and behold I am alive for	Rev.1.18
a sincere and pure *d.* to Christ	2 Cor.11.3	the dead who *d.* in the Lord	Rev.14.13
in promoting rigor of *d.*	Col.2.23	**DIFFERENT**	

DEVOUR

		servants he will call by a *d.* name	Is.65.15
LORD was like a *d.* fire on the top	Ex.24.17	For who sees anything *d.* in you?	1 Cor.4.7
For the LORD your God is a *d.* fire	Dt.4.24	if you receive a *d.* spirit from	2 Cor.11.4
and my sword shall *d.* flesh	Dt.32.42	so quickly . . . turning to a *d.* gospel	Gal.1.6
You love all words that *d.*	Ps.52.4	not to teach any *d.* doctrine	1 Tim.1.3
to *d.* the poor from off the earth	Pr.30.14	**DILIGENTLY**	
You *d.* men, and you bereave your	Ezek.36.13	Only take heed, and keep your soul *d.*	Dt.4.9
they fly like an eagle swift to *d.*	Hab.1.8	You shall *d.* keep the commandments	Dt.6.17
scribes . . . who *d.* widows' houses	Mk.12.40	those who seek me *d.* find me	Pr.8.17
But if you bite and *d.* one another	Gal.5.15	He who *d.* seeks good seeks favor	Pr.11.27
lion, seeking some one to *d.*	1 Pet.5.8	if you will *d.* obey the voice of	Zech.6.15

DEVOUT

		Go and search *d.* for the child	Mt.2.8
this man was righteous and *d.*	Lk.2.25	sweep the house and seek *d.* until	Lk.15.8
d. men from every nation under	Acts 2.5	**DINNER**	
D. men buried Stephen, and made	Acts 8.2	came to the *d.* that Esther had	Est.5.5
a *d.* man who feared God with all	Acts 10.2	Better is a *d.* of herbs where love	Pr.15.17
Jews and *d.* converts to Judaism	Acts 13.43	Behold, I have made ready my *d.*	Mt.22.4
many of the *d.* Greeks and not a	Acts 17.4	he did not first wash before *d.*	Lk.11.38
a *d.* man according to the law	Acts 22.12	When you give a *d.* or a banquet	Lk.14.12

DEW

		if one . . . invites you to *d.* and	1 Cor.10.27
God give you of the *d.* of heaven	Gen.27.28	**DIPPED**	
in the morning *d.* lay round about	Ex.16.13	and *d.* the robe in the blood	Gen.37.31
my speech distil as the *d.*	Dt.32.2	went down and *d.* himself seven	2 Kgs.5.14
if there is *d.* on the fleece alone	Jg.6.37	He who has *d.* his hand in the dish	Mt.26.23
like *d.* your youth will come to you	Ps.110.3	when he had *d.* the morsel, he gave	Jn.13.26
favor is like *d.* upon the grass	Pr.19.12	He is clad in a robe *d.* in blood	Rev.19.13
him be wet with the *d.* of heaven	Dan.4.15	**DIRECT** (verb)	
like the *d.* that goes early away	Hos.6.4	and *d.* your heart to the LORD	1 Sam.7.3

DIE

		d. their hearts toward thee	1 Chr.29.18
that you eat of it you shall *d.*	Gen.2.17	I *d.* my steps by all thy precepts	Ps.119.128
said to the woman, "You will not *d.*	Gen.3.4	but the LORD *d.* his steps	Pr.16.9

and *d.* your mind in the way	Pr.23.19
Who has *d.* the Spirit of the LORD	Is.40.13
our Lord Jesus, *d.* our way to you	1 Th.3.11
May the Lord *d.* your hearts to the	2 Th.3.5

DISAPPOINT

Behold, the hope of a man is *d.*	Job 41.9
in thee they trusted, and were not *d.*	Ps.22.5
and hope does not *d.* us	Rom.5.5

DISCERN

angel of God to *d.* good and evil	2 Sam.14.17
Cannot my taste *d.* calamity?	Job 6.30
But who can *d.* his errors?	Ps.19.12
thou *d.* my thoughts from afar	Ps.139.2
because they are spiritually *d.*	1 Cor.2.14
without *d.* the body eats and	1 Cor.11.29
d. the thoughts and intentions	Heb.4.12

DISCERNMENT

takes away the *d.* of the elders	Job 12.20
The wise of heart is . . . a man of *d.*	Pr.16.21
For this is a people without *d.*	Is.27.11
with knowledge and all *d.*	Phil.1.9

DISCIPLE

seal the teaching among my *d.*	Is.8.16
he called to him his twelve *d.*	Mt.10.1
A *d.* is not above his teacher, nor	Mt.10.24
all the *d.* forsook him and fled	Mt.26.56
and come after me, cannot be my *d.*	Lk.14.27
baptizing more *d.* than John	Jn.4.1
men will know that you are my *d.*	Jn.13.35
the *d.* whom he loved standing near	Jn.19.26
the number of the *d.* multiplied	Acts 6.7
Now there was a *d.* at Damascus	Acts 9.10
at Joppa a *d.* named Tabitha	Acts 9.36
A *d.* was there, named Timothy	Acts 16.1
Mnason of Cyprus, an early *d.*	Acts 21.16

DISCIPLINE (noun)

you hate *d.*, and you cast my words	Ps.50.17
despise not the LORD'S *d.* or be weary	Pr.3.11
He dies for lack of *d.*, and because	Pr.5.23
Whoever loves *d.* loves knowledge	Pr.12.1
Do not withhold *d.* from a child	Pr.23.13
Fathers . . . bring them up in the *d.*	Eph.6.4
do not regard lightly the *d.* of the	Heb.12.5
For the moment all *d.* seems painful	Heb.12.11

DISCIPLINE (verb)

his voice, that he might *d.* you	Dt.4.36
loves him is diligent to *d.* him	Pr.13.24
D. your son while there is hope	Pr.19.18
For the Lord *d.* him whom he loves	Heb.12.6

DISCRETION

may the LORD grant you *d.*	1 Chr.22.12
My son, keep sound wisdom and *d.*	Pr.3.21
I find knowledge and *d.*	Pr.8.12
is a beautiful woman without *d.*	Pr.11.22
but a man of *d.* is patient	Pr.14.17

DISEASE

skin of his body, it is a leprous *d.*	Lev.13.3
the priest shall examine the *d.*	Lev.13.50
By *d.* his skin is consumed	Job 18.13
who heals all your *d.*	Ps.103.3
but sent a wasting *d.* among them	Ps.106.15
healing every *d.* and every infirmity	Mt.4.23
in peace, and be healed of your *d.*	Mk.5.34
d. left them and the evil spirits	Acts 19.12
people on the island who had *d.*	Acts 28.9

DISGRACE

and thus put *d.* upon all Israel	1 Sam.11.2
All day long my *d.* is before me	Ps.44.15
for ever; let them perish in *d.*	Ps.83.17
When pride comes, then comes *d.*	Pr.11.2
Poverty and *d.* come to him who	Pr.13.18
because I bore the *d.* of my youth	Jer.31.19
So be ashamed . . . bear your *d.*	Ezek.16.52

DISGUISE (verb)

Saul *d.* himself and put on other	1 Sam.28.8
I will *d.* myself and go into	1 Kg.22.30
Satan *d.* himself as an angel	2 Cor.11.14
his servants also *d.* themselves	2 Cor.11.15

DISHONOR (noun)

May my accusers be clothed with *d.*	Ps.109.29
and with *d.* comes disgrace	Pr.18.3
worthy to suffer *d.* for the name	Acts 5.41
sown in *d.*, it is raised in glory	1 Cor.15.43
in honor and *d.*, in ill repute and	2 Cor.6.8

DISHONOR (verb)

I honor my Father, and you *d.* me	Jn.8.49
do you *d.* God by breaking the law?	Rom.2.23
with her head unveiled *d.* her head	1 Cor.11.5
But you have *d.* the poor man	Jas.2.6

DISMAY

be not frightened, neither be *d.*	Jos.1.9
thou didst hide thy face, I was *d.*	Ps.30.7
be put to shame and *d.* for ever	Ps.83.17
And your mighty men shall be *d.*	Ob.9

DISOBEDIENCE

For as by one man's *d.* many were	Rom.5.19
received mercy because of their *d.*	Rom.11.30
For God has consigned all men to *d.*	Rom.11.32
being ready to punish every *d.*	2 Cor.10.6
is now at work in the sons of *d.*	Eph.2.2
no one fall by the same sort of *d.*	Heb.4.11

DISOBEDIENT

not *d.* to the heavenly vision	Acts 26.19
inventors of evil, *d.* to parents	Rom.1.30
to a *d.* and contrary people	Rom.10.21
you were once *d.* to God but now	Rom.11.30
d. to their parents, ungrateful	2 Tim.3.2
d., unfit for any good deed	Tit.1.16
not perish with those who were *d.*	Heb.11.31

DISPUTE (noun)

both parties to the *d.* shall appear	Dt.19.17
If there is a *d.* between men	Dt.25.1
controversy and for *d.* about words	1 Tim.6.4
in all their *d.* an oath is final	Heb.6.16
It is beyond *d.* that the inferior	Heb.7.7

DISPUTE (verb)

is not able to *d.* with one stronger	Ec.6.10
The Jews then *d.* among themselves	Jn.6.52
some . . . arose and *d.* with Stephen	Acts 6.9
he . . . *d.* against the Hellenists	Acts 9.29
Michael . . . *d.* about the body of Moses	Jude 9

DISSENSION

had no small *d.* and debate with	Acts 15.2
a *d.* arose between the Pharisees	Acts 23.7
who create *d.* and difficulties	Rom.16.17
that there be no *d.* among you	1 Cor.1.10
selfishness, *d.*, party spirit	Gal.5.20
d., slander, base suspicions	1 Tim.6.4

DISTINCTION

the LORD makes a *d.* between the	Ex.11.7
have made no *d.* between the holy	Ezek.22.26

he made no *d.* between us and Acts 15.9
there is no *d.* . . . all have sinned Rom.3.22
no *d.* between Jew and Greek Rom.10.12
have you not made *d.* among yourselves Jas.2.4
DISTINGUISH
You are to *d.* between the holy and Lev.10.10
how to *d.* between the unclean and Ezek.44.23
the ability to *d.* between spirits 1 Cor.12.10
by practice to *d.* good from evil Heb.5.14
DISTRESS (noun)
In my *d.* I called upon the LORD 2 Sam.22.7
d. and anguish terrify him Job 15.24
In my *d.* I called upon the LORD Ps.18.6
In *d.* you called, and I delivered Ps.81.7
when *d.* and anguish come upon you Pr.1.27
O LORD, in *d.* they sought thee Is.26.16
great *d.* shall be upon the earth Lk.21.23
tribulation and *d.* for every human Rom.2.9
or *d.*, persecution, or famine Rom.8.35
in view of the impending *d.* it 1 Cor.7.26
in all our *d.* and affliction we 1 Th.3.7
DISTRIBUTE
d. the portions to their brethren 2 Chr.31.15
duty was to *d.* to their brethren Neh.13.13
sell all . . . and *d.* to the poor Lk.18.22
sold their . . . goods and *d.* them Acts 2.45
gifts . . . *d.* according to his own will Heb.2.4
DIVINATION
any one who practices *d.* Dt.18.10
rebellion is as the sin of *d.* 1 Sam.15.23
used *d.* and sorcery 2 Kg.17.17
worthless *d.*, and the deceit of Jer.14.14
and uttered a lying *d.* Ezek.13.7
slave girl who had a spirit of *d.* Acts 16.16
DIVIDE
D. the living child in two 1 Kg.3.25
they *d.* my garments among them Ps.22.18
Thou didst *d.* the sea by thy might Ps.74.13
as men rejoice when they *d.* the spoil Is.9.3
Therefore I will *d.* him a portion Is.53.12
PERES, your kingdom is *d.* and given Dan.5.28
Every kingdom *d.* against itself is Mt.12.25
they *d.* his garments among them by Mt.27.35
he *d.* the two fish among them Mk.6.41
bid my brother *d.* the inheritance Lk.12.13
Take . . . and *d.* it among yourselves Lk.22.17
they cast lots to *d.* his garments Lk.23.34
Is Christ *d.*? Was Paul crucified 1 Cor.1.13
DIVINE (adjective)
Your *d.* throne endures for ever and Ps.45.6
because in his *d.* forbearance he Rom.3.25
but have *d.* power to destroy 2 Cor.10.4
according to the *d.* office which Col.1.25
the *d.* training that is in faith 1 Tim.1.4
men of old received *d.* approval Heb.11.2
His *d.* power has granted to us 2 Pet.1.3
become partakers of the *d.* nature 2 Pet.1.4
DIVISION
Thus I will put a *d.* between my Ex.8.23
No, I tell you, but rather *d.* Lk.12.51
So there was a *d.* among the people Jn.7.43
There was again a *d.* among the Jews Jn.10.19
I hear that there are *d.* among you 1 Cor.11.18
Piercing to the *d.* of soul and Heb.4.12
DIVORCE (noun)
he writes her a bill of *d.* Dt.24.1

For I hate *d.*, says the LORD Mal.2.16
let him give her a certificate of *d.* Mt.5.31
why then . . . give a certificate of *d.* Mt.19.7
DIVORCE (verb)
marry a woman *d.* from her husband Lev.21.7
Joseph . . . resolved to *d.* her quietly Mt.1.19
marries a *d.* woman commits adultery Mt.5.32
Is it lawful to *d.* one's wife for Mt.19.3
Whoever *d.* his wife and marries Mk.10.11
Every one who *d.* his wife and Lk.16.18
husband should not *d.* his wife 1 Cor.7.11
DOCTRINE
My *d.* is pure, and I am clean in Job 11.4
opposition to the *d.* which you Rom.16.17
carried about with every wind of *d.* Eph.4.14
according to human precepts and *d.* Col.2.22
not to teach any different *d.* 1 Tim.1.3
teach what befits sound *d.* Tit.2.1
may adorn the *d.* of God our Savior Tit.2.10
leave the elementary *d.* of Christ Heb.6.1
does not abide in the *d.* of Christ 2 Jn.9
DOG
Am I a *d.*, that you come to me 1 Sam.17.43
who takes a passing *d.* by the ears Pr.26.17
a living *d.* is better than a dead lion Ec.9.4
Do not give *d.* what is holy Mt.7.6
even the *d.* under the table eat Mk.7.28
the *d.* came and licked his sores Lk.16.21
Look out for the *d.*, look out Phil.3.2
The *d.* turns back to his . . . vomit 2 Pet.2.22
DOMINION
let them have *d.* over the fish of Gen.1.26
D. and fear are with God Job 25.2
Thou hast given him *d.* over the Ps.8.6
For *d.* belongs to the LORD, and he Ps.22.28
his works, in all places of his *d.* Ps.103.22
and thy *d.* endures throughout all Ps.145.13
for his *d.* is an everlasting *d.* Dan.4.34
death no longer has *d.* over him Rom.6.9
For sin will have no *d.* over you Rom.6.14
and authority and power and *d.* Eph.1.21
delivered us from the *d.* of darkness Col.1.13
To him be honor and eternal *d.* 1 Tim.6.16
glory and *d.* for ever and ever 1 Pet.4.11
to him be the *d.* for ever and 1 Pet. 5.11
d., and authority, before all time Jude 25
be glory and *d.* for ever and ever Rev.1.6
DOOMED
preserve those *d.* to die Ps.79.11
they are *d.* to destruction for ever Ps.92.7
LORD our God has *d.* us to perish Jer.8.14
rulers . . . who are *d.* to pass away 1 Cor.2.6
thus he is *d.* to be killed Rev.11.5
DOOR
sin is couching at the *d.* Gen.4.7
keep watch over the *d.* of my lips Ps.141.3
As a *d.* turns on its hinges, so Pr.26.14
make . . . Valley of Achor a *d.* of hope Hos.2.15
shut the *d.* and pray to your Father Mt.6.6
great stone to the *d.* of the tomb Mt.27.60
Strive to enter by the narrow *d.* Lk.13.24
you will . . . knock at the *d.*, saying Lk.13.25
enters by the *d.* is the shepherd Jn.10.2
I am the *d.*; if any one enters Jn.10.9
The *d.* were shut, but Jesus came Jn.20.26
opened a *d.* of faith to the Gentiles Acts 14.27

for a wide *d*. for effective work 1 Cor.16.9
a *d*. was opened for me in the Lord 2 Cor.2.12
may open to us a *d*. for the word Col.4.3
I have set before you an open *d*. Rev.3.8
Behold, I stand at the *d*. and knock Rev.3.20
and lo, in heaven an open *d*. Rev.4.1
DORCAS
raised from death by Peter, Acts 9.36–41
DOUBT (verb)
of little faith, why did you *d*.? Mt.14.31
if you have faith and never *d*. Mt.21.21
they worshiped him; but some *d*. Mt.28.17
he who *d*. is like a wave of the sea Jas.1.6
And convince some, who *d*. Jude 22
DOVE
Then he sent forth a *d*. from him Gen.8.8
O that I had wings like a *d*. Ps.55.6
My *d*., my perfect one, is only S.of S.6.9
Spirit of God descending like a *d*. Mt.3.16
wise as serpents and innocent as *d*. Mt.10.16
DRAGON
the heads of the *d*. on the waters Ps.74.13
he will slay the *d*. . . . in the sea Is.27.1
the great *d*. that lies in the Ezek.29.3
like a lamb and it spoke like a *d*. Rev.13.11
seized the *d*., that ancient serpent Rev.20.2
DRAW
D. near to me . . . set me free Ps.69.18
the Holy One of Israel *d*. near Is.5.19
they delight to *d*. near to God Is.58.2
she does not *d*. near to her God Zeph.3.2
a woman of Samaria to *d*. water Jn.4.7
d. near to the throne of grace Heb.4.16
through which we *d*. near to God Heb.7.19
let us *d*. near with a true heart Heb.10.22
whoever would *d*. near to God must Heb.11.6
D. near to God and he will *d*. near Jas.4.8
DREAD (noun)
the *d*. of you . . . upon every beast Gen.9.2
the *d*. of the Lord fell upon 1 Sam.11.7
preserve my life from *d*. Ps.64.1
for *d*. of them had fallen upon it Ps.105.38
do not fear . . . nor be in *d*. Is.8.12
they shall turn in *d*. to the Lord Mic.7.17
DREAM (noun)
angel of God said to me in the *d*. Gen.31.11
Now Joseph had a *d*., and . . . he told it Gen.37.5
and Pharaoh told them his *d*. Gen.41.8
Lord appeared to Solomon in a *d*. 1 Kg.3.5
They are like a *d*. when one awakes Ps.73.20
I had a *d*., and my spirit is troubled Dan.2.3
This *d*. I, King Nebuchadnezzar, saw Dan.4.18
an angel . . . appeared to him in a *d*. Mt.1.20
appeared to Joseph in a *d*. and said Mt.2.13
and your old men shall dream *d*. Acts 2.17
DRINK (noun)
Wine is a mocker, strong *d*. a brawler Pr.20.1
or for rulers to desire strong *d*. Pr.31.4
that they may run after strong *d*. Is.5.11
valiant men in mixing strong *d*. Is.5.22
I was thirsty and you gave me *d*. Mt.25.35
Jesus said to her, "Give me a *d*." Jn.4.7
if he is thirsty, give him *d*. Rom.12.20
not to be slanderers or slaves to *d*. Tit.2.3
DRINK (verb)
D. no wine nor strong drink Lev.10.9

You shall *d*. from the brook 1 Kg.17.4
But David would not *d*. of it 1 Chr.11.18
wine to *d*. that made us reel Ps.60.3
they gave me vinegar to *d*. Ps.69.21
is thirsty, give him water to *d*. Pr.25.21
it is not for kings to *d*. wine Pr.31.4
Let us eat and *d*., for tomorrow we Is.22.13
vegetables to eat and water to *d*. Dan.1.12
be not anxious . . . what you shall *d*. Mt.6.25
able to *d*. the cup that I am to *d*.? Mt.20.22
D. of it, all of you Mt.26.27
on a reed and gave it to him to *d*. Mk.15.36
he who eats my flesh and *d*. my blood Jn.6.54
thirst, let him come to me and *d*. Jn.7.37
cannot *d*. the cup of the Lord 1 Cor.10.21
Do this, as often as you *d*. it 1 Cor.11.25
No longer *d*. only water, but use 1 Tim.5.23
shall *d*. the wine of God's wrath Rev.14.10
DRIVE
For the Lord has *d*. out before you Jos.23.9
Jehu . . . for he *d*. furiously 2 Kg.9.20
like chaff which the wind *d*. away Ps.1.4
thou didst *d*. out the nations Ps.80.8
D. out a scoffer, and strife will go Pr.22.10
and began to *d*. out those who sold Lk.19.45
D. out the wicked person from 1 Cor.5.13
DROSS
the wicked . . . thou dost count as *d*. Ps.119.119
Take away the *d*. from the silver Pr.25.4
Your silver has become *d*., your Is.1.22
Because you have all become *d*. Ezek.22.19
DRUNK
I have *d*. neither wine nor strong 1 Sam.1.15
Be *d*., but not with wine Is.29.9
these . . . are not *d*., as you suppose Acts 2.15
And do not get *d*. with wine Eph.5.18
d. with the blood of the saints Rev.17.6
nations have *d*. the wine of her Rev.18.3
DRUNKARD
he is a glutton and a *d*. Dt.21.20
Behold, a glutton and a *d*. Mt.11.19
not to associate with any . . . *d*. 1 Cor.5.11
nor *d*., nor revilers, nor robbers 1 Cor.6.10
no *d*., not violent but gentle 1 Tim.3.3
must not be . . . quick-tempered or a *d*. Tit.1.7
DRY
God called the *d*. land Earth Gen.1.10
the midst of the sea on *d*. ground Ex.14.22
the priests . . . stood on *d*. ground Jos.3.17
He turned the sea into *d*. land Ps.66.6
for his hands formed the *d*. land Ps.95.5
the Red Sea, and it became *d*. Ps.106.9
Nile will diminish and *d*. up Is.19.6
I will *d*. up her sea and make her Jer.51.36
in a *d*. and thirsty land Ezek.19.13
And I will *d*. up the Nile Ezek.30.12
O *d*. bones, hear the word of the Ezek.37.4
who made the sea and the *d*. land Jon.1.9
what will happen when it is *d*.? Lk.23.31
DULL
The *d*. man cannot know, the stupid Ps.92.6
his ear *d*., that it cannot hear Is.59.1
this people's heart has grown *d*. Mt.13.15
you have become *d*. of hearing Heb.5.11
DUMB
Let the lying lips be *d*. Ps.31.18

I was *d.* and silent, I held my peace Ps.39.2
the tongue of the *d.* sing for joy Is.35.6
that before its shearers is *d.* Is.53.7
a blind and *d.* demoniac was brought Mt.12.22
when they saw the *d.* speaking Mt.15.31
the deaf hear and the *d.* speak Mk.7.37
a lamb before its shearer is *d.* Acts 8.32
a *d.* ass spoke with human voice 2 Pet.2.16

DUST
formed man of *d.* from the ground Gen.2.7
you are *d.*, and to *d.* you . . . return Gen.3.19
Who can count the *d.* of Jacob Num.23.10
He raises up the poor from the *d.* 1 Sam.2.8
and wilt thou turn me to *d.* again? Job 10.9
I have become like *d.* and ashes Job 30.19
Will the *d.* praise thee? Will it Ps.30.9
Thou turnest man back to the *d.* Ps.90.3
My soul cleaves to the *d.* Ps.119.25
Shake yourself from the *d.*, arise Is.52.2
shake off the *d.* from your feet as Lk.9.5
from the earth, a man of *d.* 1 Cor.15.47

DUTY
rights and *d.* of the kingship 1 Sam.10.25
And they cast lots for their *d.* 1 Chr.25.8
for this is the whole *d.* of man Ec.12.13
we have only done what was our *d.* Lk.17.10
Practice these *d.*, devote yourself 1 Tim.4.15
Teach and urge these *d.* 1 Tim.6.2

DWELL
the father of those who *d.* in tents Gen.4.20
Who shall *d.* on thy holy hill? Ps.15.1
I shall *d.* in the house of the LORD Ps.23.6
the world and those who *d.* therein Ps.24.1
how good . . . when brothers *d.* in unity Ps.133.1
the wicked will not *d.* in the land Pr.10.30
The wolf shall *d.* with the lamb Is.11.6
justice will *d.* in the wilderness Is.32.16
I *d.* in the high and holy place Is.57.15
upon all who *d.* upon the face of Lk.21.35
the Most High does not *d.* in houses Acts 7.48
that nothing good *d.* within me Rom.7.18
if the Spirit of God really *d.* in you Rom.8.9
and that God's Spirit *d.* in you? 1 Cor.3.16
that Christ may *d.* in your hearts Eph.3.17
word of Christ *d.* in you richly Col.3.16
O heaven and you that *d.* therein Rev.12.12

DWELLING
Where is the way to the *d.* of light Job 38.19
let them bring me . . . to thy *d.* Ps.43.3
How lovely is thy *d.* place Ps.84.1
My *d.* place shall be with them Ezek.37.27
we . . . long to put on our heavenly *d.* 2 Cor.5.2
built into it for a *d.* place of God Eph.2.22

EAGER
I am *e.* to preach the gospel Rom.1.15
the creation waits with *e.* longing Rom.8.19
e. to maintain the unity of the Eph.4.3
it is my *e.* expectation and hope Phil.1.20
searched for me *e.* and found me 2 Tim.1.17
those who are *e.* waiting for him Heb.9.28
not for shameful gain but *e.* 1 Pet.5.2
being very *e.* to write to you Jude 3

EAGLE
I bore you on *e.* wings and brought Ex.19.4
like an *e.* swooping on the prey Job 9.26

your youth is renewed like the *e.* Ps.103.5
shall mount up with wings like *e.* Is.40.31
his horses are swifter than *e.* Jer.4.13
had the face of an *e.* at the back Ezek.1.10
A great *e.* with great wings Ezek.17.3
make yourselves as bald as the *e.* Mic.1.16
there the *e.* will be gathered Mt.24.28
living creature like a flying *e.* Rev.4.7
the two wings of the great *e.* Rev.12.14

EAR
Give *e.*, O heavens, and I will Dt.32.1
Incline thy *e.*, O LORD, and hear 2 Kg.19.16
let thy *e.* be attentive, and thy eyes Neh.1.6
by the hearing of the *e.* Job 42.5
O LORD, and give *e.* to my cry Ps.39.12
We have heard with our *e.* Ps.44.1
the deaf adder that stops its *e.* Ps.58.4
He who planted the *e.*, does he not Ps.94.9
making your *e.* attentive to wisdom Pr.2.2
The hearing *e.* and the seeing eye Pr.20.12
He who closes his *e.* to the cry Pr.21.13
nor the *e.* filled with hearing Ec.1.8
did not obey or incline their *e.* Jer.7.24
two legs, or a piece of an *e.* Am.3.12
He who has *e.* to hear, let him hear Mt.11.15
high priest, and cut off his *e.* Mt.26.51
What no eye has seen, nor *e.* heard 1 Cor.2.9
If thy whole body were an *e.* 1 Cor.12.17
his *e.* are open to their prayer 1 Pet.3.12
He who has an *e.*, let him hear Rev.2.7

EARTH
God created the heavens and the *e.* Gen.1.1
wickedness . . . was great in the *e.* Gen.6.5
the covenant between me and the *e.* Gen.9.13
the Judge of all the *e.* do right? Gen.18.25
I call heaven and *e.* to witness Dt.4.26
Then the *e.* reeled and rocked 2 Sam.22.8
From going to and fro on the *e.* Job 1.7
at last he will stand upon the *e.* Job 19.25
The kings of the *e.* set themselves Ps.2.2
The *e.* is the LORD's and the fulness Ps.24.1
Let all the *e.* fear the LORD Ps.33.8
not fear though the *e.* should change Ps.46.2
from the end of the *e.* I call to thee Ps.61.2
Thou visitest the *e.* and waterest it Ps.65.9
that thy way may be known upon *e.* Ps.67.2
In his hand are the depths of the *e.* Ps.95.4
for he comes to judge the *e.* Ps.98.9
the heavens are high above the *e.* Ps.103.11
dust returns to the *e.* as it was Ec.12.7
sits above the circle of the *e.* Is.40.22
who formed the *e.* and made it Is.45.18
the heavens are higher than the *e.* Is.55.9
I create new heavens and a new *e.* Is.65.17
for they shall inherit the *e.* Mt.5.5
I have come to bring peace on *e.* Mt.10.34
e. will pass away, but my words Mt.24.35
and on *e.* peace among men with whom Lk.2.14
I came to cast fire upon the *e.* Lk.12.49
wheat falls into the *e.* and dies Jn.12.24
my throne, and *e.* my footstool Acts 7.49
to live on all the face of the *e.* Acts 17.26
voice has gone out to all the *e.* Rom.10.18
strangers and exiles on the *e.* Heb.11.13
a new *e.* in which righteousness 2 Pet.3.13
I saw a new heaven and a new *e.* Rev.21.1

EARTHLY
If I have told you *e.* things	Jn.3.12
if the *e.* tent we live in is destroyed	2 Cor.5.1
with minds set on *e.* things	Phil.3.19
regulations for . . . an *e.* sanctuary	Heb.9.1
but is *e.*, unspiritual, devilish	Jas.3.15

EARTHQUAKE
but the LORD was not in the *e.*	1 Kg.19.11
famines and *e.* in various places	Mt.24.7
And behold, there was a great *e.*	Mt.28.2
suddenly there was a great *e.*	Acts 16.26

EASIER
For which is *e.*, to say, 'Your sins	Mt.9.5
it is *e.* for a camel to go through	Mt.19.24
But it is *e.* for heaven and earth	Lk.16.17

EAST
a garden in Eden, in the *e.*	Gen.2.8
in the land of Nod, *e.* of Eden	Gen.4.16
the LORD brought an *e.* wind upon	Ex.10.13
as far as the *e.* is from the west	Ps.103.12
house of the LORD, which faces *e.*	Ezek.11.1
God appointed a sultry *e.* wind	Jon.4.8
we have seen his star in the *E.*	Mt.2.2
And men will come from *e.* and west	Lk.13.29

EAT
You may freely *e.* of every tree	Gen.2.16
You shall not *e.* of any tree of	Gen.3.1
Let me *e.* some of that red pottage	Gen.25.30
Only you shall not *e.* the blood	Dt.12.16
These are the animals you may *e.*	Dt.14.4
And the dogs shall *e.* Jezebel	2 Kg.9.10
who *e.* up my people as they *e.* bread	Ps.14.4
you shall *e.* the good of the land	Is.1.19
The fathers have *e.* sour grapes	Jer.31.29
e. this scroll, and go, speak to	Ezek.3.1
be made to *e.* grass like an ox	Dan.4.25
do not be anxious . . . what you shall *e.*	Mt.6.25
your teacher *e.* with tax collectors	Mt.9.11
John came neither *e.* nor drinking	Mt.11.18
Take, *e.*; this is my body	Mt.26.26
Why do you *e.* and drink with tax	Lk.5.30
I have food to *e.* of which you do	Jn.4.32
He who *e.* my flesh and drinks my	Jn.6.56
Rise, Peter; kill and *e.*	Acts 10.13
and he was *e.* by worms and died	Acts 12.23
One believes he may *e.* anything	Rom.14.2
it is right not to *e.* meat or drink	Rom.14.21
I will never *e.* meat, lest I cause	1 Cor.8.13
whether you *e.* or drink, or	1 Cor.10.31
as often as you *e.* this bread	1 Cor.11.26
Let us *e.* and drink, for tomorrow	1 Cor.15.32
I will grant to *e.* of the tree of	Rev.2.7

EBED-MELECH
Ethiopian eunuch, intercedes with king Zedediah for Jeremiah, Jer.38.7–13; deliverance promised to, Jer.39.16–18

EDEN
(1) Garden of, Gen.2.8; Adam driven from, Gen.3.24; mentioned, Is.51.3; Ezek.28.13; 31.9; 36.35; Jl.2.3; (2) 2 Kg.19.12; (3) 2 Chr.29.12

EDIFY
please his neighbor . . . to *e.* him	Rom.15.2
who speaks in a tongue *e.* himself	1 Cor.14.4
but the other man is not *e.*	1 Cor.14.17
but only such as is good for *e.*	Eph.4.29

EGG
For she leaves her *e.* to the earth	Job 39.14
They hatch adders' *e.*, they weave	Is.59.5
if he asks for an *e.*, will give	Lk.11.12

EGYPT
Abram goes down into, Gen.12.10; Joseph sold into, Gen.37.36; his advancement, fall, imprisonment, and restoration there, Gen.39–41; Jacob's sons go to buy food in, Gen.42; Jacob and all his descendants go there, Gen.46.6; plagued on account of Israelites, Ex.7–11; children of Israel depart from, Ex.13.17; army of, pursue, and perish in the Red Sea, Ex.14; kings of, harass Judah, 1 Kg.14.25; 2 Kg.23.29; 2 Chr.12.2; 35.20; 36.3; Jer.37.5; the remnant of Judah go there, Jer.43.5–7; Jesus taken to, Mt.2.13

ELDER
the *e.* shall serve the younger	Gen.25.23
Moses called all the *e.* of Israel	Ex.12.21
and seventy of the *e.* of Israel	Ex.24.1
conferred with the *e.* of Israel	2 Sam.3.17
according to the tradition of the *e.*	Mk.7.5
rejected by the *e.* and chief priests	Lk.9.22
Now his *e.* son was in the field	Lk.15.25
called . . . the *e.* of the church	Acts 20.17
Let the *e.* who rule well be	1 Tim.5.17
call for the *e.* of the church	Jas.5.14
as a fellow *e.* and a witness of	1 Pet.5.1
The *e.* to the elect lady and her	2 Jn.1
The *e.* to the beloved Gaius	3 Jn.1

ELEAZAR
(1) son of Aaron, and chief priest, Ex.6.23; 28.1; Num.3.2,32; 4.16; 16.37; 20.26–28; 27.22; 31.13; 34.17; Jos.17.4; 24.33; (2) son of Abinadab, keeps the ark, 1 Sam.7.1; (3) one of David's captains, 2 Sam.23.9; 1 Chr.11.12

ELECT
for the sake of the *e.* those days	Mt.24.22
lead astray, if possible, the *e.*	Mk.13.22
And will not God vindicate his *e.*	Lk.18.7
bring any charge against God's *e.*?	Rom.8.33
of the *e.* angels I charge you	1 Tim.5.21
everything for the sake of the *e.*	2 Tim.2.10
The elder to the *e.* lady and her	2 Jn.1
The children of your *e.* sister greet	2 Jn.13

ELECTION
God's purpose of *e.* might continue	Rom.9.11
as regards *e.* they are beloved	Rom.11.28
to confirm your call and *e.*	2 Pet.1.10

ELI
high priest and judge, blesses Hannah, who bears Samuel, 1 Sam.1.17,20; Samuel brought to, 1 Sam.1.25; wickedness of his sons, 1 Sam. 2.22; rebuked by man of God, 1 Sam.2.27–36; his sons slain, 1 Sam.4.11; his death, 1 Sam.4.18

ELIHU
reproves Job's friends, Job 32, and Job's impatience, Job 33.8–11, and self-righteousness, Job 34.5; declares God's justice, Job 33.12; 34.10; 35.13, power, Job 33–37, and mercy, Job 33.23-28; 34.28

ELIJAH
the Tishbite, prophet, predicts great drought, 1 Kg.17.1; Lk.4.25; Jas.5.17; hides at the brook Cherith, and is fed by ravens, 1 Kg.17.5–6

(19.5); raises the widow's son, 1 Kg.17.21; his sacrifice at Carmel, 1 Kg.18.38; kills the prophets of Baal at the brook Kishon, 1 Kg. 18.40; flees from Jezebel into the wilderness of Beersheba, 1 Kg.19; anoints Elisha, 1 Kg.19.19; by God's command denounces Ahab in Naboth's vineyard, 1 Kg.21.17; his prediction fulfilled, 1 Kg.22.38; 2 Kg.9.36; 10.10; divides Jordan, 2 Kg.2.8; taken up by chariot of fire, 2 Kg.2.11; his mantle taken by Elisha, 2 Kg.2.13; appears at Christ's transfiguration, Mt.17.3; Mk.9.4; Lk.9.30; precursor of John the Baptist, Mal.4.5; Mt.11.14; 16.14; Lk.1.17; 9.8,19; Jn.1.21

ELIPHAZ
reproves Job, Job 4; 5; 15; 22; God's wrath against him, Job 42.7; he offers burnt offering, and Job prays for him, Job 42.8

ELISHA
succeeds Elijah, 1 Kg. 19.16; receives his mantle, and divides Jordan, 2 Kg.2.13–14; bears destroy the children who mock him, 2 Kg.2.24; his miracles: water, 2 Kg.3.16–20; oil, 4.4; Shunammite's son, 4.32; death in the pot, 4.40; feeds a hundred men with twenty loaves, 4.44; Naaman's leprosy, 5.1–14; iron floats, 6.5–7; Syrians struck blind, 6.18; prophesies abundance in Samaria when besieged, 2 Kg.7.1; sends to anoint Jehu, 2 Kg.9.1–3; his death, 2 Kg.13.20; miracle wrought by his bones, 2 Kg.13.21

ELOI
E., E., lama sabachthani?   Mk.15.34

ELOQUENT
Moses said . . . I am not e.   Ex.4.10
He was an e. man, well versed   Acts 18.24
to preach . . . not with e. wisdom   1 Cor.1.17

EMBRACE
Laban . . . e. him and kissed him   Gen.29.13
a time to e., and a time to refrain   Ec.3.5
ran and e. him and kissed him   Lk.15.20
all wept and e. Paul and kissed   Acts 20.37

EMPEROR
custody for the decision of the e.   Acts 25.21
he himself appealed to the e.   Acts 25.25
be subject . . . to the e. as supreme   1 Pet.2.13
Fear God. Honor the e.   1 Pet.2.17

EMPTY (adjective)
The pit was e., there was no water   Gen.37.24
And none shall appear before me e.   Ex.34.20
the LORD has brought me back e.   Ru.1.21
e. vessels and not too few   2 Kg.4.3
Job opens his mouth in e. talk   Job 35.16
it shall not return to me e.   Is.55.11
he has made me an e. vessel   Jer.51.34
in praying do not heap up e. phrases   Mt.6.7
when he comes he finds it e.   Mt.12.44
the rich he has sent e. away   Lk.1.53
Let no one deceive you with e. words   Eph.5.6
by philosophy and e. deceit   Col.2.8
e. talkers and deceivers   Tit.1.10

ENCAMP
Though a host e. against me   Ps.27.3
angel of the LORD e. around those   Ps.34.7
And I will e. against you   Is.29.3
E. . . . . about her; let no one escape   Jer.50.29

ENCOMPASS
The cords of death e. me   Ps.18.4
Many bulls e. me, strong bulls of   Ps.22.12
thou dost e. me with deliverance   Ps.32.7
The snares of death e. me   Ps.116.3

ENCOURAGE
the brethren e. him, and wrote to   Acts 18.27
Then they all were e. and ate   Acts 27.36
be mutually e. by each other's faith   Rom.1.12
that he may e. your hearts   Col.4.8
Therefore e. one another and build   1 Th.5.11
e. the fainthearted, help the weak   1 Th.5.14
e. one another, and all the more   Heb.10.25

ENCOURAGEMENT
When he . . . had given them much e.   Acts 20.2
by the e. of the scriptures we   Rom.15.4
the God of steadfastness and e.   Rom.15.5
upbuilding and e. and consolation   1 Cor.14.3
So if there is any e. in Christ   Phil.2.1
have strong e. to seize the hope   Heb.6.18

END (noun)
to make an e. of all flesh   Gen.6.13
what is my e., that I . . . be patient?   Job 6.11
LORD, let me know my e.   Ps.39.4
wars cease to the e. of the earth   Ps.46.9
from the e. of the earth I call   Ps.61.2
its e. is the way to death   Pr.16.25
Better is the e. of a thing than   Ec.7.8
Of making many books there is no e.   Ec.12.12
LORD of hosts, will make a full e.   Is.10.23
my indignation will come to an e.   Is.10.25
I will not make a full e. of you   Jer.5.18
great houses shall come to an e.   Am.3.15
I will make an e. of the pride   Zech.9.6
endures to the e. will be saved   Mt.10.22
but the e. is not yet   Mk.13.7
of his kingdom there will be no e.   Lk.1.33
came from the e. of the earth   Lk.11.31
For Christ is the e. of the law   Rom.10.4
their words to the e. of the world   Rom.10.18
Then comes the e., when he   1 Cor.15.24
beginning of days nor e. of life   Heb.7.3
The e. of all things is at hand   1 Pet.4.7
who keeps my works until the e.   Rev.2.26
I am . . . the beginning and the e.   Rev.21.6

ENDURANCE
By your e. you will gain your lives   Lk.21.19
knowing that suffering produces e.   Rom.5.3
e. produces character   Rom.5.4
through great e., in afflictions   2 Cor.6.4
for all e. and patience with joy   Col.1.11
For you have need of e.   Heb.10.36
the kingdom and the patient e.   Rev.1.9
your toil and your patient e.   Rev.2.2
a call for the e. of the saints   Rev.14.12

ENDURE
his prosperity will not e.   Job 20.21
May he live while the sun e.   Ps.72.5
his steadfast love e. for ever   Ps.100.5
They will perish, but thou dost e.   Ps.102.26
the glory of the LORD e. for ever   Ps.104.31
faithfulness of the LORD e. for ever   Ps.117.2
whatever God does e. for ever   Ec.3.14
Who can e. the heat of his anger?   Nah.1.6
who can e. the day of his coming   Mal.3.2
he has no root . . . but e. for a while   Mt.13.21

the food which *e.* to eternal life | Jn.6.27
hopes all things, *e.* all things | 1 Cor.13.7
Therefore I *e.* everything | 2 Tim.2.10
if we *e.*, we shall also reign | 2 Tim.2.12
at Lystra, what persecutions I *e.* | 2 Tim.3.11
he *e.* as seeing him who is invisible | Heb.11.27
e. the cross, despising the shame | Heb.12.2

ENEMY
I will be an *e.* to your *e.* | Ex.23.22
Saul was David's *e.* continually | 1 Sam.18.29
Have you found me, O my *e.?* | 1 Kg.21.20
And Esther said, "A foe and *e.* | Est.7.6
to still the *e.* and the avenger | Ps.8.2
He delivered me from my strong *e.* | Ps.18.17
God arise, let his *e.* be scattered | Ps.68.1
till I make your *e.* your footstool | Ps.110.1
Deliver me, O LORD, from my *e.* | Ps.143.9
If your *e.* is hungry, give him bread | Pr.25.21
Love your *e.* and pray for those who | Mt.5.44
till I put thy *e.* under thy feet | Mk.12.36
that we should be saved from our *e.* | Lk.1.71
while we were *e.* we were reconciled | Rom.5.10
if your *e.* is hungry, feed him | Rom.12.20
The last *e.* to be destroyed is | 1 Cor.15.26

ENJOY
shall rest, and *e.* its sabbaths | Lev.26.34
dwell in the land, and *e.* security | Ps.37.3
that a man should *e.* his work | Ec.3.22
God does not give . . . power to *e.* them | Ec.6.2
E. life with the wife whom you love | Ec.9.9
than to *e.* the . . . pleasures of sin | Heb.11.25

ENLIGHTEN
The true light that *e.* every man | Jn.1.9
a zeal for God, but it is not *e.* | Rom.10.2
having the eyes of your hearts *e.* | Eph.1.18
those who have once been *e.* | Heb.6.4
after you were *e.*, you endured | Heb.10.32

ENMITY
put *e.* between you and the woman | Gen.3.15
Because you cherished perpetual *e.* | Ezek.35.5
had been at *e.* with each other | Lk.23.12
e., strife, jealousy, anger | Gal.5.20
with the world is *e.* with God? | Jas.4.4

ENRAGED
he was angry and greatly *e.* | Neh.4.1
At this the king was *e.* | Est.1.12
the LORD is *e.* against all the nations | Is.34.2
the princes were *e.* at Jeremiah | Jer.37.15
were *e.* and wanted to kill them | Acts 5.33
were *e.*, and . . . ground their teeth | Acts 7.54
When they heard this they were *e.* | Acts 19.28

ENRICH
king will *e.* with great riches | 1 Sam.17.25
waterest it, thou greatly *e.* it | Ps.65.9
who trusts in the LORD will be *e.* | Pr.28.25
were *e.* in him with all speech | 1 Cor.1.5
You will be *e.* in every way | 2 Cor.9.11

ENROLLED
All . . . were *e.* by genealogies | 1 Chr.5.17
priests were *e.* with all their | 2 Chr.31.18
the people to be *e.* by genealogy | Neh.7.5
not be *e.* among the righteous | Ps.69.28
that all the world should be *e.* | Lk.2.1
to be *e.* with Mary, his betrothed | Lk.2.5
he was *e.* with the eleven | Acts 1.26

Let a widow be *e.* if she is not less | 1 Tim.5.9
first-born who are *e.* in heaven | Heb.12.23

ENSIGN
stand as an *e.* to the peoples | Is.11.10
will raise an *e.* for the nations | Is.11.12
lift up an *e.* over the peoples | Is.62.10
was your sail, serving as your *e.* | Ezek.27.7

ENSLAVE
so that no one should *e.* a Jew | Jer.34.9
the hand of those who *e.* them | Ezek.34.27
we might no longer be *e.* to sin | Rom.6.6
but I will not be *e.* by anything | 1 Cor.6.12
overcomes a man, to that he is *e.* | 2 Pet.2.19

ENSNARE
that he should not *e.* the people | Job 34.30
the cords of the wicked *e.* me | Ps.119.61
The iniquities of the wicked *e.* him | Pr.5.22
An evil man is *e.* by the transgression | Pr.12.13

ENTANGLE
the cords of Sheol *e.* me | 2 Sam.22.6
counsel how to *e.* him in his talk | Mt.22.15
No soldier . . . gets *e.* in civilian | 2 Tim.2.4
they are again *e.* in them | 2 Pet.2.20

ENTER
not allow the destroyer to *e.* your | Ex.12.23
No . . . Moabite shall *e.* the assembly | Dt.23.3
no one *e.* the house of the LORD | 2 Chr.23.6
E. his gates with thanksgiving | Ps.100.4
E. not into judgment with thy | Ps.143.2
Do not *e.* the path of the wicked | Pr.4.14
Do not *e.* the house of mourning | Jer.16.5
But the Spirit *e.* into me and set | Ezek.3.24
E. by the narrow gate; for the gate | Mt.7.13
and *e.* no town of the Samaritans | Mt.10.5
can one *e.* a strong man's house | Mt.12.29
If you would *e.* life, keep the | Mt.19.17
e. into the joy of your master | Mt.25.21
that you may not *e.* into temptation | Mt.26.41
how hard it is to *e.* the kingdom | Mk.10.24
like a child shall not *e.* it | Lk.18.17
a rich man to *e.* the kingdom of God | Lk.18.25
Then Satan *e.* into Judas | Lk.22.3
he cannot *e.* the kingdom of God | Jn.3.5
he who does not *e.* the sheepfold | Jn.10.1
They shall never *e.* my rest | Heb.3.11
But nothing unclean shall *e.* it | Rev.21.27

ENTHRONED
LORD who sits *e.* above the cherubim | 1 Chr.13.6
the LORD sits *e.* as king for ever | Ps.29.10
But thou, O LORD, art *e.* for ever | Ps.102.12

ENTICE
E. your husband to tell us what | Jg.14.15
my heart has been secretly *e.* | Job 31.27
if sinners *e.* you, do not consent | Pr.1.10
A man of violence *e.* his neighbor | Pr.16.29
is lured and *e.* by his own desire | Jas.1.14
They *e.* unsteady souls | 2 Pet.2.14
they *e.* with licentious passions | 2 Pet.2.18

ENTREAT
E. the LORD to take away the frogs | Ex.8.8
E. me not to leave you or to | Ru.1.16
E. now the favor of the LORD | 1 Kg.13.6
now *e.* the favor of God, that he | Mal.1.9
His father came out and *e.* him | Lk.15.28
I, Paul . . . *e.* you, by the meekness | 2 Cor.10.1
I *e.* Euodia and I *e.* Syntyche | Phil.4.2

ENTRUST

Moses . . . is *e*. with all my house	Num.12.7
who will *e*. to you the true riches?	Lk.16.11
Jews are *e*. with the oracles of God	Rom.3.2
I am *e*. with a commission	1 Cor.9.17
e. to us the message of	2 Cor.5.19
Peter had been *e*. with the gospel	Gal.2.7
and *e*. their souls to a faithful	1 Pet.4.19

ENVIOUS

be not *e*. of wrongdoers	Ps.37.1
For I was *e*. of the arrogant	Ps.73.3
Be not *e*. of evil men, nor desire to	Pr.24.1
and be not *e*. of the wicked	Pr.24.19

ENVY (noun)

the anger and *e*. which you showed	Ezek.35.11
out of *e*. that they had delivered	Mt.27.18
e., slander, pride, foolishness	Mk.7.22
Full of *e*., murder, strife, deceit	Rom.1.29
e., drunkenness, carousing	Gal.5.21
preach Christ from *e*. and rivalry	Phil.1.15
passing our days in malice and *e*.	Tit.3.3
insincerity and *e*. and all slander	1 Pet.2.1

EPHESUS

Acts 18.19; 19.35; 1 Cor.15.32; 1 Tim.1.3; Rev.2.1

EPHOD

they shall make the *e*. of gold	Ex.28.6
the skilfully woven band of the *e*.	Lev.8.7
Gideon made an *e*. of it	Jg.8.27
persons who wore the linen *e*.	1 Sam.22.18
David was girded with a linen *e*.	2 Sam.6.14
without *e*. or teraphim	Hos.3.4

EPHRAIM

younger son of Joseph, Gen.41.52; Jacob blesses Ephraim and Manasseh, Gen.48.14; his descendants numbered, Num.1.10,32; 2.18; 26.35; 1 Chr.7.20; their possessions, Jos.16.5; 17.17; Jg.1.29; quarrel with Gideon, Jg.8.1, and Jephthah, Jg.12; revolt from the house of David, 1 Kg.12.25; carried into captivity, 2 Kg.17.5–6; Ps.78.9,67; Jer.7.15

EQUAL

Gold and glass cannot *e*. it	Job 28.17
to whom will you . . . make me *e*.	Is.46.5
have made them *e*. to us who have	Mt.20.12
they are *e*. to angels and are sons	Lk.20.36
making himself *e*. with God	Jn.5.18
a faith of *e*. standing with ours	2 Pet.1.1
breadth and height are *e*.	Rev.21.16

EQUALITY

that there may be *e*.	2 Cor.8.14
did not count *e*. with God a thing	Phil.2.6

EQUIPMENT

all the *e*. for their service	Num.4.26
war and the *e*. of his chariots	1 Sam.8.12
for the *e*. of the saints, for the	Eph.4.12
with the *e*. of the gospel of peace	Eph.6.15

ERR

make me understand how I have *e*.	Job 6.24
They are a people who *e*. in heart	Ps.95.10
they *e*. in vision, they stumble in	Is.28.7
and fools shall not *e*. therein	Is.35.8

ERROR

my *e*. remains with myself	Job 19.4
sinned through *e*. or ignorance	Ezek.45.20
no *e*. or fault was found in him	Dan.6.4

the due penalty for their *e*.	Rom.1.27
and for the *e*. of the people	Heb.9.7
By this we know . . . the spirit of *e*.	1 Jn.4.6
abandon themselves . . . to Balaam's *e*.	Jude 11

ESAU

son of Isaac, Gen.25.25 (Mal.1.2; Rom.9.13); sells his birthright, Gen.25.29 (Heb.12.16); deprived of the blessing, Gen.27.38; his anger against Jacob, Gen.27.41, and reconciliation, Gen.33; his riches and descendants, Gen.36; 1 Chr.1.35

ESCAPE (verb)

I am shut in so that I cannot *e*.	Ps.88.8
Let them not *e*. from your sight	Pr.4.21
And we, how shall we *e*.?	Is.20.6
And those who *e*. the sword shall	Jer.44.28
Can a man *e*. who does such things	Ezek.17.15
E. to Zion, you who dwell with the	Zech.2.7
how are you to *e*. being sentenced	Mt.23.33
but he *e*. from their hands	Jn.10.39
were seeking to *e*. from the ship	Acts 27.30
you will *e*. the judgment of God?	Rom.2.3
how shall we *e*. if we neglect such	Heb.2.3
much less shall we *e*. if we reject	Heb.12.25

ESTABLISH

But I will *e*. my covenant with you	Gen.6.18
The LORD will *e*. you as a people	Dt.28.9
that the LORD may *e*. his word	1 Kg.2.4
I will *e*. his kingdom for ever	1 Chr.28.7
the Most High himself will *e*. her	Ps.87.5
and *e*. thou the work of our hands	Ps.90.17
The LORD has *e*. his throne in the	Ps.103.19
In righteousness you shall be *e*.	Is.54.14
I will *e*. with you an everlasting	Ezek.16.60
to *e*. you in your faith and	1 Th.3.2
comfort your hearts and *e*. them	2 Th.2.17
when I will *e*. a new covenant with	Heb.8.8
E. your hearts, for the coming of	Jas.5.8

ESTEEM

so that his name was highly *e*.	1 Sam.18.30
yet we *e*. him stricken, smitten by	Is.53.4
One man *e*. one day as better than	Rom.14.5
who are least *e*. by the church?	1 Cor.6.4

ESTHER

(Hadassah), Est.2.7; made queen in the place of Vashti, Est.2.17; pleads for her people, Est. 7.3–4; the feast of Purim and Mordecai's advancement, Est.9–10

ETERNAL

The *e*. God is your dwelling place	Dt.33.27
What . . . must I do, to have *e*. life?	Mt.19.16
will go away into *e*. punishment	Mt.25.46
but the righteous into *e*. life	Mt.25.46
believes in him may have *e*. life	Jn.3.15
of water welling up to *e*. life	Jn.4.14
the food which endures to *e*. life	Jn.6.27
You have the words of *e*. life	Jn.6.68
this is *e*. life, that they know thee	Jn.17.3
as many as were ordained to *e*.	Acts 13.48
gift of God is *e*. life in Christ	Rom.6.23
the things that are unseen are *e*.	2 Cor.4.18
gave us *e*. comfort and good hope	2 Th.2.16
who through the *e*. Spirit offered	Heb.9.14
by the blood of the *e*. covenant	Heb.13.20
This is the true God and *e*. life	1 Jn.5.20
angels . . . kept by him in *e*. chains	Jude 6

undergoing a punishment of *e.* fire Jude 7
with an *e.* gospel to proclaim Rev.14.6
ETERNITY
he has put *e.* into man's mind Ec.3.11
high and lofty One who inhabits *e.* Is.57.15
both now and to the day of *e.* 2 Pet.3.18
ETHIOPIA
Ps.87.4; Jer.46.9; Ezek.30.5; Zeph.3.10
EUNUCH
the seven *e.* who served King Est.1.10
the chief of the *e.* said to Daniel Dan.1.10
For there are *e.* who have been so Mt.19.12
a *e.,* a minister of Candace Acts 8.27
EUPHRATES
Gen.2.14; Dt.1.7; 2 Sam.10.16; Jer.13.4;
Rev.9.14
EVANGELIST
entered the house of Philip the *e.* Acts 21.8
some *e.,* some pastors and teachers Eph.4.11
do the work of an *e.* 2 Tim.4.5
EVE
created, Gen.1.27; 2.18–22; her fall and fate,
Gen.3; 2 Cor.11.3
EVERLASTING
remember the *e.* covenant between Gen.9.16
the name of the LORD, the *E.* God Gen.21.33
The enemy have vanished in *e.* ruins Ps.9.6
from *e.* to *e.* thou art God Ps.90.2
love of the LORD is from *e.* to *e.* Ps.103.17
Thy kingdom is an *e.* kingdom Ps.145.13
Mighty God, *E.* Father, Prince of Peace Is.9.6
The LORD is the *e.* God, the Creator Is.40.28
e. joy shall be upon their heads Is.51.11
but the LORD will be your *e.* light Is.60.19
I will make an *e.* covenant with them Is.61.8
I have loved you with an *e.* love Jer.31.3
His kingdom is an *e.* kingdom Dan.4.3
EVERMORE
shall be peace from the LORD for *e.* 1 Kg.2.33
in thy right hand are pleasures for *e.* Ps.16.11
from this time forth and for *e.* Ps.113.2
glory for *e.* through Jesus Christ Rom.16.27
I died, and behold I am alive for *e.* Rev.1.18
EVIDENCE
to death on the *e.* of witnesses Num.35.30
speaks the truth gives honest *e.* Pr.12.17
by the *e.* of two or three witnesses Mt.18.16
e. of the righteous judgment of God 2 Th.1.5
their rust will be *e.* against you Jas.5.3
EVIL
of the knowledge of good and *e.* Gen.2.9
his heart was only *e.* continually Gen.6.5
Why have you returned *e.* for good? Gen.44.4
And God sent an *e.* spirit between Jg.9.23
to avert the *e.* design of Haman Est.8.3
feared God, and turned away from *e.* Job 1.1
Depart from me, all you workers of *e.* Ps.6.8
Keep your tongue from *e.,* and your Ps.34.13
Depart from *e.,* and do good Ps.34.14
The LORD loves those who hate *e.* Ps.97.10
The LORD will keep you from all *e.* Ps.121.7
Do not plan *e.* against your neighbor Pr.3.29
to preserve you from the *e.* woman Pr.6.24
The fear of the LORD is hatred of *e.* Pr.8.13
Be not envious of *e.* men, nor desire Pr.24.1
ointment give off an *e.* odor Ec.10.1

There is an *e.* which I have seen Ec.10.5
I will punish the world for its *e.* Is.13.11
Their feet run to *e.* Is.59.7
This *e.* people, who refuse to hear Jer.13.10
No *e.* shall come upon you Jer.23.17
Hate *e.,* and love good Am.5.15
Do not resist one who is *e.* Mt.5.39
sun rise on the *e.* and on the good Mt.5.45
who are *e.,* know how to give good Mt.7.11
He who speaks *e.* of father or mother Mt.15.4
Lazarus in like manner *e.* things Lk.16.25
shouldst keep them from the *e.* one Jn.17.15
some were . . . speaking *e.* of the Way Acts 19.9
deliver us from the present *e.* age Gal.1.4
Let no *e.* talk come out of your Eph.4.29
liars, *e.* beasts, lazy gluttons Tit.1.12
Do not speak *e.* against one another Jas.4.11
you have overcome the *e.* one 1 Jn.2.14
he who does *e.* has not seen God 3 Jn.11
EVILDOER
Break thou the arm of the . . . *e.* Ps.10.15
The face of the LORD is against *e.* Ps.34.16
Fret not yourself because of *e.* Pr.24.19
If this man were not an *e.,* we Jn.18.30
Let the *e.* still do evil, and the Rev.22.11
EXALT
didst *e.* me above my adversaries 2 Sam.22.49
Be *e.,* O LORD, in thy strength Ps.21.13
let us *e.* his name together Ps.34.3
Prize her highly, and she will *e.* you Pr.4.8
Righteousness *e.* a nation, but sin Pr.14.34
Capernaum, will you be *e.* to heaven? Mt.11.23
every one who *e.* himself will be Lk.14.11
God *e.* him at his right hand Acts 5.31
Therefore God has highly *e.* him Phil.2.9
who opposes and *e.* himself against 2 Th.2.4
with unutterable and *e.* joy 1 Pet.1.8
EXAMINE
Let us test and *e.* our ways Lam.3.40
if we are being *e.* today concerning Acts 4.9
e. the scriptures daily to see if Acts 17.11
Let a man *e.* himself, and so eat 1 Cor.11.28
E. yourselves, to see whether you 2 Cor.13.5
EXAMPLE
For I have given you an *e.,* that you Jn.13.15
also follow the *e.* of the faith Rom.4.12
so live as you have an *e.* in us Phil.3.17
become an *e.* to all the believers 1 Th.1.7
in our conduct an *e.* to imitate 2 Th.3.9
an *e.* in speech and conduct 1 Tim.4.12
As an *e.* of suffering and patience Jas.5.10
suffered for you, leaving you an *e.* 1 Pet.2.21
EXCELLENT
because an *e.* spirit was in him Dan.6.3
for you, most *e.* Theophilus Lk.1.3
by your provision, most *e.* Felix Acts 24.2
I am not mad, most *e.* Festus Acts 26.25
and approve what is *e.* Rom.2.18
show you a still more *e.* way 1 Cor.12.31
so that you may approve what is *e.* Phil.1.10
EXCUSE (noun)
But they all alike began to make *e.* Lk.14.18
now they have no *e.* for their sin Jn.15.22
So they are without *e.* Rom.1.20
Therefore you have no *e.,* O man Rom.2.1

EXECUTE

to *e.* the LORD's vengeance	Num.31.3
He *e.* justice for the fatherless	Dt.10.18
will *e.* judgment among the nations	Ps.110.6
by fire will the LORD *e.* judgment	Is.66.16
E. justice in the morning, and	Jer.21.12
given him authority to *e.* judgment	Jn.5.27
to *e.* his wrath on the wrongdoer	Rom.13.4

EXERCISE

kings of the Gentiles *e.* lordship	Lk.22.25
if they cannot *e.* self-control	1 Cor.7.9
Every athlete *e.* self-control	1 Cor.9.25
it was allowed to *e.* authority	Rev.13.5

EXHORT

he *e.* them all to remain faithful	Acts 11.23
e. the brethren with many words	Acts 15.32
we beseech and *e.* you in the Lord	1 Th.4.1
we command and *e.* in the Lord	2 Th.3.12
e. and reprove with all authority	Tit.2.15
But *e.* one another every day	Heb.3.13
So I *e.* the elders among you	1 Pet.5.1

EXILE (noun)

He took into *e.* in Babylon those	2 Chr.36.20
of Israel who had returned from *e.*	Ezra 6.21
The survivors . . . who escaped *e.*	Neh.1.3
Prepare yourselves baggage for *e.*	Jer.46.19
Judah has gone into *e.* because of	Lam.1.3
they carried into *e.* a whole people	Am.1.6
take you into *e.* beyond Damascus	Am.5.27
half of the city shall go into *e.*	Zech.14.2
Moses . . . became an *e.* in the land	Acts 7.29
throughout the time of your *e.*	1 Pet.1.17

EXIST

there is one God . . . for whom we *e.*	1 Cor.8.6
must believe that he *e.*	Heb.11.6
jealousy and selfish ambition *e.*	Jas.3.16
by the word of God heavens *e.*	2 Pet.3.5
by thy will they *e.* and were created	Rev.4.11

EXPIATION

sprinkle the water of *e.* upon them	Num.8.7
no *e.* can be made for the land	Num.35.33
e. for the land of his people	Dt.32.43
how shall I make *e.,* that	2 Sam.21.3
put forward as an *e.* by his blood	Rom.3.25
make *e.* for the sins of the people	Heb.2.17
he is the *e.* for our sins	1 Jn.2.2
his Son to be the *e.* for our sins	1 Jn.4.10

EXPLAIN

Moses undertook to *e.* the law	Dt.1.5
e. riddles, and solve problems	Dan.5.12
E. to us the parable of the weeds	Mt.13.36
much to say which is hard to *e.*	Heb.5.11

EXTEND

has *e.* to us his steadfast love	Ezra 9.9
thy . . . love . . . *e.* to the heavens	Ps.36.5
the Lord will *e.* his hand yet a	Is.11.11
I will *e.* prosperity to her like a	Is.66.12
as grace *e.* to more and more	2 Cor.4.15

EXTOL

For this I will *e.* thee, O LORD	2 Sam.22.50
and *e.* thy righteousness	Ps.89.16
E. the LORD our God, and worship at	Ps.99.9
E. him, all peoples	Ps.117.1
I will *e.* thee, my God and King	Ps.145.1
e. and honor the King of heaven	Dan.4.37
the name of the Lord Jesus was *e.*	Acts 19.17

EXULT

let the field *e.*	1 Chr.16.32
I will be glad and *e.* in thee	Ps.9.2
let not my enemies *e.* over me	Ps.25.2
how long shall the wicked *e.?*	Ps.94.3
my soul shall *e.* in my God	Is.61.10
their hearts shall *e.* in the LORD	Zech.10.7
rejoice and *e.* and give him glory	Rev.19.7

EYE

Then the *e.* of both were opened	Gen.3.7
as a memorial between your *e.*	Ex.13.9
e. for *e.,* tooth for tooth	Ex.21.24
his *e.* was not dim, nor his natural	Dt.34.7
is under the *e.* of the LORD	Jg.18.6
But the *e.* of their God was upon	Ezra 5.5
my *e.* pours out tears to God	Job 16.20
I have made a covenant with my *e.*	Job 31.1
Keep me as the apple of the *e.*	Ps.17.8
LORD is pure, enlightening the *e.*	Ps.19.8
my *e.* grows dim through sorrow	Ps.88.9
who formed the *e.,* does he not see?	Ps.94.9
The *e.* of the LORD are in every	Pr.15.3
the *e.* is not satisfied with seeing	Ec.1.8
no *e.* has seen a God besides thee	Is.64.4
touches the apple of his *e.*	Zech.2.8
The *e.* is the lamp of the body	Mt.6.22
speck that is in your brother's *e.*	Mt.7.3
if your *e.* causes you to sin	Mt.18.9
go through the *e.* of a needle	Mt.19.24
What no *e.* has seen, nor ear heard	1 Cor.2.9
Because I am not an *e.*	1 Cor.12.16
in the twinkling of an *e.*	1 Cor.15.52
and every *e.* will see him	Rev.1.7

EYEWITNESS

were *e.* and ministers of the word	Lk.1.2
we were *e.* of his majesty	2 Pet.1.16

EZEKIEL

sent to the house of Israel, Ezek.2–3; 33.7; his visions of God's glory, Ezek.1; 8; 10; 11.22; of the resurrection of dry bones, Ezek.37; his vision of the measuring of the temple, Ezek.40–42; intercedes for Israel, Ezek.9.8; 11.13; his dumbness, Ezek.3.26; 24.27; 33.22; his parables, Ezek.15–17; 19; 23–24; exhorts Israel against idolatry, Ezek.14.1–11; 20.1–44; predicts Israel's and the nations' doom, Ezek.21; 25

EZRA

goes from Babylonia to Jerusalem, Ezra 7.1–6; 8.1; his commission from Artaxerxes to rebuild the temple, Ezra 7.11–26; fast ordered by, Ezra 8.21; reproves the people, Ezra 10.9–11; reads the book of the law, Neh.8; reforms corruptions, Ezra 10; Neh.13

FACE

moving over the *f.* of the waters	Gen.1.2
In the sweat of your *f.* you shall eat	Gen.3.19
Then Abram fell on his *f.*	Gen.17.3
For I have seen God *f.* to *f.*	Gen.32.30
Moses hid his *f.,* for he was afraid	Ex.3.6
you cannot see my *f.*	Ex.33.20
the skin of his *f.* shone because	Ex.34.29
put the veil upon his *f.* again	Ex.34.35
The LORD make his *f.* to shine upon	Num.6.25
Hezekiah turned his *f.* to the wall	2 Kg.20.2
not turn away the *f.* of thy anointed	2 Chr.6.42

I . . . blush to lift my *f.* to thee	Ezra 9.6	*f.* in his name, has made this man	Acts 3.16
he will curse thee to thy *f.*	Job 1.11	full of *f.* and of the Holy Spirit	Acts 6.5
Thou hast said, "Seek ye my *f.*"	Ps.27.8	full of the Holy Spirit and of *f.*	Acts 11.24
Make thy *f.* shine upon thy servant	Ps.119.135	for I have *f.* in God that it will	Acts 27.25
Hide not thy *f.* from me, lest I be	Ps.143.7	he justifies him who has *f.* in Jesus	Rom.3.26
A wicked man puts on a bold *f.*	Pr.21.29	those who share the *f.* of Abraham	Rom.4.16
As in water *f.* answers to *f.*	Pr.27.19	So *f.* comes from what is heard	Rom.10.17
by grinding the *f.* of the poor?	Is.3.15	As for the man who is weak in *f.*	Rom.14.1
wings: with two he covered his *f.*	Is.6.2	whatever . . . not . . . from *f.* is sin	Rom.14.23
I have set my *f.* like a flint	Is.50.7	*f.*, hope, love abide, these three	1 Cor.13.13
Then I turned my *f.* to the Lord God	Dan.9.3	Be watchful, stand firm in your *f.*	1 Cor.16.13
anoint your head and wash your *f.*	Mt.6.17	for we walk by *f.*, not by sight	2 Cor.5.7
always behold the *f.* of my Father	Mt.18.10	that we might be justified by *f.*	Gal.3.24
he fell on his *f.* and prayed	Mt.26.39	but *f.* working through love	Gal.5.6
they spat in his *f.*, and struck	Mt.26.67	one Lord, one *f.*, one baptism	Eph.4.5
his *f.* was like the *f.* of an angel	Acts 6.15	provided that you continue in the *f.*	Col.1.23
glory of God in the *f.* of Christ	2 Cor.4.6	supply what is lacking in your *f.*?	1 Th.3.10
I opposed him to his *f.*	Gal.2.11	Timothy, my true child in the *f.*	1 Tim.1.2
the *f.* of the Lord is against	1 Pet.3.12	have made shipwreck of their *f.*	1 Tim.1.19
his *f.* was like the sun shining	Rev.1.16	Fight the good fight of the *f.*	1 Tim.6.12
fell on their *f.* and worshiped God	Rev.11.16	I am reminded of your sincere *f.*	2 Tim.1.5
they shall see his *f.*	Rev.22.4	my righteous one shall live by *f.*	Heb.10.38

FADE

As the cloud *f.* and vanishes, so he	Job 7.9	Now *f.* is the assurance of things	Heb.11.1
For they will soon *f.* like the grass	Ps.37.2	without *f.* it is impossible to please	Heb.11.6
in the evening it *f.* and withers	Ps.90.6	By *f.* Abraham obeyed when he was	Heb.11.8
We all *f.* like a leaf, and our	Is.64.6	By *f.* Moses, when he was grown up	Heb.11.24
its brightness, *f.* as this was	2 Cor.3.7	that *f.* apart from works is barren?	Jas.2.20
see the end of the *f.* splendor	2 Cor.3.13	so *f.* apart from works is dead	Jas.2.26
the rich man *f.* away in the midst	Jas.1.11	the prayer of *f.* will save the sick	Jas.5.15

FAIL

I will not *f.* you or forsake you	Jos.1.5	your *f.* and hope are in God	1 Pet.1.21
shall never *f.* you a man before me	1 Kg.8.25	that overcomes the world, our *f.*	1 Jn.5.4
My flesh and my heart may *f.*	Ps.73.26	contend for the *f.* . . . once . . . delivered	Jude 3
that your faith may not *f.*	Lk.22.32	did not deny my *f.* even in the	Rev.2.13
unless . . . you *f.* to meet the test	2 Cor.13.5	the endurance and *f.* of the saints	Rev.13.10
that no one *f.* to obtain the grace	Heb.12.15	**FAITHFUL**	
I will never *f.* you nor forsake	Heb.13.5	the *f.* God who keeps covenant and	Dt.7.9
keeps the . . . law but *f.* in one point	Jas.2.10	the LORD preserves the *f.*, but	Ps.31.23

FAINT

I call to thee, when my heart is *f.*	Ps.61.2	The LORD is *f.* in all his words	Ps.145.13
f. for the courts of the LORD	Ps.84.2	A *f.* witness does not lie, but a	Pr.14.5
When my spirit is *f.*, thou knowest	Ps.142.3	*F.* are the wounds of a friend	Pr.27.6
If you *f.* in the day of adversity	Pr.24.10	Who then is the *f.* and wise servant	Mt.24.45
is sick, and the whole heart *f.*	Is.1.5	you have been *f.* over a little	Mt.25.23
He does not *f.* or grow weary	Is.40.28	all to remain *f.* to the Lord	Acts 11.23
Even youths shall *f.* and be weary	Is.40.30	God is *f.*, by whom you were called	1 Cor.1.9
head of Jonah so that he was *f.*	Jon.4.8	who are also *f.* in Christ Jesus	Eph.1.1
hungry, lest they *f.* on the way	Mt.15.32	But the Lord is *f.*	2 Th.3.3
f. with fear and with foreboding	Lk.21.26	he remains *f.* . . . he cannot deny	2 Tim.2.13

FAIR

saw that the daughters of men were *f.*	Gen.6.2	a merciful and *f.* high priest	Heb.2.17
Queen Vashti . . . was *f.* to behold	Est.1.11	but Christ was *f.* over God's house	Heb.3.6
no women so *f.* as Job's daughters	Job 42.15	entrust their souls to a *f.* Creator	1 Pet.4.19
f. as the moon, bright as the sun	S.of S.6.10	Be *f.* unto death, and I will give	Rev.2.10
you say, 'It will be *f.* weather	Mt.16.2	He . . . is called *F.* and True	Rev.19.11
treat your slaves justly and *f.*	Col.4.1	**FAITHFULNESS**	

FAITH

a breach of *f.* against the LORD	Lev.6.2	abounding in steadfast love and *f.*	Ex.34.6
by breaking *f.* with the LORD	Num.5.6	A God of *f.* and without iniquity	Dt.32.4
have *f.* in him that he will return	Job 39.12	thy *f.* to the clouds	Ps.36.5
because they had no *f.* in God	Ps.78.22	thy *f.* is firm as the heavens	Ps.89.2
clothe you, O men of little *f.*?	Mt.6.30	his *f.* is a shield and buckler	Ps.91.4
when Jesus saw their *f.* he said to	Mt.9.2	the *f.* of the LORD endures forever	Ps.117.2
if you have *f.* as a grain of mustard	Mt.17.20	faithlessness nullify the *f.* of God?	Rom.3.3
Go . . . your *f.* has made you well	Mk.10.52	patience, kindness, goodness, *f.*	Gal.5.22

FAITHLESS

who were *f.* to the LORD God	2 Chr.30.7
I look at the *f.* with disgust	Ps.119.158
Return, O *f.* children, says the LORD	Jer.3.14
Why then are we *f.* to one another	Mal.2.10

O *f.* and perverse generation, how   Mt.17.17
do not be *f.*, but believing   Jn.20.27
if we are *f.*, he remains faithful   2 Tim.2.13
as for the cowardly, the *f.*   Rev.21.8
FALL (verb)
The lines have *f.* for me in pleasant   Ps.16.6
though he *f.*, he shall not be cast   Ps.37.24
terrors of death have *f.* upon me   Ps.55.4
May all kings *f.* down before him   Ps.72.11
A thousand may *f.* at your side, ten   Ps.91.7
The LORD upholds all who are *f.*   Ps.145.14
Where . . . is no guidance, a people *f.*   Pr.11.14
He who digs a pit will *f.* into it   Pr.26.27
And the Assyrian shall *f.* by a sword   Is.31.8
and young men shall *f.* exhausted   Is.40.30
whoever does not *f.* down and worship   Dan.3.11
and to the hills, *F.* upon us   Hos.10.8
You will all *f.* away because of me   Mt.26.31
I saw Satan *f.* like lightning from   Lk.10.18
a grain of wheat *f.* into the earth   Jn.12.24
lest I cause my brother to *f.*   1 Cor.8.13
those who desire to be rich *f.*   1 Tim.6.9
if you do this you will never *f.*   2 Pet.1.10
is able to keep you from *f.*   Jude 24
F., *f.* is Babylon the great, she who   Rev.14.8
FALSE
You shall not bear *f.* witness   Ex.20.16
For he was *f.* to the LORD his God   2 Chr.26.16
Put *f.* ways far from me   Ps.119.29
therefore I hate every *f.* way   Ps.119.104
A *f.* balance is an abomination to   Pr.11.1
A *f.* witness will not go unpunished   Pr.19.5
Beware of *f.* prophets, who come to   Mt.7.15
F. Christs and *f.* prophets will arise   Mk.13.22
many bore *f.* witness against him   Mk.14.56
Jewish *f.* prophet, named Bar-Jesus   Acts 13.6
For such men are *f.* apostles   2 Cor.11.13
f. brethren secretly brought in   Gal.2.4
there will be *f.* teachers among you   2 Pet.2.1
the beast and the *f.* prophet were   Rev.20.10
FALSEHOOD
my lips will not speak *f.*   Job 27.4
I hate and abhor *f.*, but I love   Ps.119.163
A righteous man hates *f.*, but   Pr.13.5
Remove far from me *f.* and lying   Pr.30.8
They have spoken *f.* and divined a   Ezek.13.6
in him there is no *f.*   Jn.7.18
putting away *f.*, let every one speak   Eph.4.25
every one who loves and practices *f.*   Rev.22.15
FAME
the *f.* of David went out into   1 Chr.14.17
heard of the *f.* of Solomon she came   2 Chr.9.1
not heard my *f.* or seen my glory   Is.66.19
tetrarch heard about the *f.* of Jesus   Mt.14.1
And at once his *f.* spread everywhere   Mk.1.28
FAMILY
went forth by *f.* out of the ark   Gen.8.19
These are the *f.* of the sons of   Gen.10.32
O *f.* of the peoples, ascribe to the   Ps.96.7
the God of all the *f.* of Israel   Jer.31.1
known of all the *f.* of the earth   Am.3.2
all the *f.* of the earth be blessed   Acts 3.25
from whom every *f.* . . . is named   Eph.3.15
FAMINE
for the *f.* was severe in the land   Gen.12.10
besides the former *f.* that was in   Gen.26.1

seven years of *f.* began to come   Gen.41.54
three years of *f.* come to you   2 Sam.24.13
Now the *f.* was severe in Samaria   1 Kg.18.2
When he summoned a *f.* on the land   Ps.105.16
Sword and *f.* shall not come   Jer.14.15
against you my deadly arrows of *f.*   Ezek.5.16
not a *f.* of bread, nor a thirst for   Am.8.11
there will be *f.* and earthquakes   Mt.24.7
a great *f.* arose in that country   Lk.15.14
or *f.*, or nakedness, or peril, or   Rom.8.35
pestilence and mourning and *f.*   Rev.18.8
FAMOUS
name of Solomon more *f.* than yours   1 Kg.1.47
f. men, heads of their fathers'   1 Chr.5.24
slew *f.* kings, for his steadfast   Ps.136.18
How the *f.* city is forsaken   Jer.49.25
the brother who is *f.* among all   2 Cor.8.18
FAR
Thus *f.* shall you come, and no   Job 38.11
But thou, O LORD, be not *f.* off   Ps.22.19
Perverseness . . . shall be *f.* from me   Ps.101.4
who looks *f.* down upon the heavens   Ps.113.6
The LORD is *f.* from the wicked   Pr.15.29
Remove *f.* from me falsehood   Pr.30.8
for a comforter is *f.* from me   Lam.1.16
but their heart is *f.* from me   Mt.15.8
You are not *f.* from the kingdom of   Mk.12.34
took his journey into a *f.* country   Lk.15.13
saw Abraham *f.* off and Lazarus   Lk.16.23
he led them out as *f.* as Bethany   Lk.24.50
is able to do *f.* more abundantly   Eph.3.20
with Christ, for that is *f.* better   Phil.1.23
FARMER
he had *f.* and vinedressers in   2 Chr.26.10
the *f.* are ashamed, they cover their   Jer.14.4
shall call the *f.* to mourning   Am.5.16
hard-working *f.* who ought to have   2 Tim.2.6
Behold, the *f.* waits for the precious   Jas.5.7
FAST (verb)
Why have we *f.*, and thou seest it not?   Is.58.3
Though they *f.*, I will not hear   Jer.14.12
And when you *f.*, do not look dismal   Mt.6.16
but your disciples do not *f.*?   Mt.9.14
the disciples of the Pharisees *f.*   Mk.2.18
I *f.* twice a week, I give tithes of   Lk.18.12
FASTING
with *f.* and weeping and lamenting   Est.4.3
I afflicted myself with *f.*   Ps.35.13
F. like yours this day will not   Is.58.4
that their *f.* may be seen by men   *Mt.6.16
worshiping with *f.* and prayer   Lk.2.37
Then after *f.* and praying they laid   Acts 13.3
every church, with prayer and *f.*   Acts 14.23
FAT
seven cows sleek and *f.*   Gen.41.2
But Jeshurun waxed *f.*, and kicked   Dt.32.15
Now Eglon was a very *f.* man   Jg.3.17
ate, and were filled and became *f.*   Neh.9.25
Make the heart of this people *f.*   Is.6.10
they have grown *f.* and sleek   Jer.5.28
between the *f.* sheep and the lean   Ezek.34.20
my oxen and my *f.* calves are killed   Mt.22.4
FATE
are visited by the *f.* of all men   Num.16.29
This is the *f.* of those who have   Ps.49.13

since one *f*. comes to all, to the	Ec.9.2	**FAULT**	
grief at the *f*. of all the maidens	Lam.3.51	the people found *f*. with Moses	Ex.17.2
FATHER		I have found no *f*. in him	1 Sam.29.3
a man leaves his *f*. and his mother	Gen.2.24	for no *f*. of mine, they run and make	Ps.59.4
Honor your *f*. and your mother	Ex.20.12	go and tell him his *f*.	Mt.18.15
Whoever curses his *f*. or his mother	Ex.21.17	that no *f*. may be found with our	2 Cor.6.3
my son, know the God of your *f*.	1 Chr.28.9	he finds *f*. with them when he	Heb.8.8
I was a *f*. to the poor	Job 29.16	**FAVOR (noun)**	
F. of the fatherless and protector	Ps.68.5	Noah found *f*. in the eyes of the LORD	Gen.6.8
Thou art my *F*., my God	Ps.89.26	So Joseph found *f*. in his sight	Gen.39.4
As a *f*. pities his children, so the	Ps.103.13	Entreat now the *f*. of the LORD	1 Kg.13.6
A wise son makes a glad *f*.	Pr.15.20	Remember this also in my *f*.	Neh.13.22
A stupid son is a grief to a *f*.	Pr.17.21	Esther found *f*. in the eyes of all	Est.2.15
If one curses his *f*. or his mother	Pr.20.20	cover him with *f*. as with a shield	Ps.5.12
Everlasting *F*., Prince of Peace	Is.9.6	Let the *f*. of the Lord our God be	Ps.90.17
thou, O LORD, art our *F*.	Is.63.16	obtains *f*. from the LORD	Pr.8.35
Yet, O LORD, thou art our *F*.; we are	Is.64.8	A good man obtains *f*. from the LORD	Pr.12.2
The *f*. have eaten sour grapes	Jer.31.29	Good sense wins *f*., but the way	Pr.13.15
Have we not all one *f*.? Has not one	Mal.2.10	Many seek the *f*. of a generous man	Pr.19.6
glory to your *F*. who is in heaven	Mt.5.16	God gave Daniel *f*. and compassion	Dan.1.9
be sons of your *F*. who is in heaven	Mt.5.45	to entreat the *f*. of the LORD	Zech.7.2
Our *F*. who art in heaven, Hallowed	Mt.6.9	for you have found *f*. with God	Lk.1.30
your heavenly *F*. knows that you need	Mt.6.32	and the *f*. of God was upon him	Lk.2.40
I also will deny before my *F*.	Mt.10.33	and in *f*. with God and man	Lk.2.52
F., Lord of heaven and earth	Mt.11.25	praising God and having *f*. with all	Acts 2.47
no one knows the Son except the *F*.	Mt.11.27	**FEAR (noun)**	
Come, O blessed of my *F*., inherit	Mt.25.34	God of Abraham and the *F*. of Isaac	Gen.31.42
comes in the glory of his *F*.	Mk.8.38	Serve the LORD with *f*.	Ps.2.11
nor the Son, but only the *F*.	Mk.13.32	no *f*. of God before his eyes	Ps.36.1
your *f*. and I have been looking	Lk.2.48	The *f*. of the LORD is the beginning	Ps.111.10
merciful . . . as your *F*. is merciful	Lk.6.36	The *f*. of the LORD is the beginning	Pr.1.7
the heavenly *F*. give the Holy Spirit	Lk.11.13	The *f*. of the LORD is hatred of	Pr.8.13
F., give me the share of property	Lk.15.12	The *f*. of the LORD prolongs life	Pr.10.27
F., I have sinned against heaven	Lk.15.21	The *f*. of the LORD leads to life	Pr.19.23
F., if thou art willing, remove	Lk.22.42	Take heart, it is I; have no *f*.	Mk.6.50
And Jesus said, "*F*., forgive them	Lk.23.34	*F*. seized them all; and they glorified	Lk.7.16
F., into thy hands I commit my	Lk.23.46	through *f*. of death were subject	Heb.2.15
Son, who is in the bosom of the *F*.	Jn.1.18	but perfect love casts out *f*.	1 Jn.4.18
worship the *F*. in spirit and truth	Jn.4.23	**FEAR (verb)**	
My *F*. is working . . . and I am working	Jn.5.17	*F*. not, Abram, I am your shield	Gen.15.1
Our *f*. ate the manna in the wilderness	Jn.6.31	*F*. not, stand firm, and see the	Ex.14.13
All that the *F*. gives me will come	Jn.6.37	You shall not *f*. them; for it is the	Dt.3.22
knew me, you would know my *F*. also	Jn.8.19	You shall *f*. the LORD your God	Dt.10.20
as the *F*. knows me and I know the *F*.	Jn.10.15	You shall not *f*. other gods or bow	2 Kg.17.35
I and the *F*. are one	Jn.10.30	Does Job *f*. God for nought?	Job 1.9
He who has seen me has seen the *F*.	Jn.14.9	You who *f*. the LORD, praise him	Ps.22.23
I am in the *F*. and the *F*. in me	Jn.14.11	whom shall I *f*.? The LORD is	Ps.27.1
but I do as the *F*. has commanded me	Jn.14.31	Let all the earth *f*. the LORD	Ps.33.8
All that the *F*. has is mine	Jn.16.15	the LORD pities those who *f*. him	Ps.103.13
Holy *F*., keep them in thy name which	Jn.17.11	*F*. God, and keep his commandments	Ec.12.13
As the *F*. has sent me, even so I send	Jn.20.21	thou didst say, 'Do not *f*.!'	Lam.3.57
from God our *F*. and the Lord Jesus	Rom.1.7	*f*. not, peace be with you	Dan.10.19
When we cry, "Abba! *F*.!"	Rom.8.15	you shall *f*. evil no more	Zeph.3.15
Blessed be the God and *F*. of our	2 Cor.1.3	*F*. not, therefore; you are of more	Mt.10.31
a man shall leave his *f*. and mother	Eph.5.31	But I will warn you whom to *f*.	Lk.12.5
F., do not provoke your children	Col.3.21	*F*. not, little flock, for it is your	Lk.12.32
be subject to the *F*. of spirits	Heb.12.9	Men of Israel, and you that *f*. God	Acts 13.16
coming down from the *F*. of lights	Jas.1.17	*F*. God. Honor the emperor	1 Pet.2.17
we have an advocate with the *F*.	1 Jn.2.1	*F*. not, I am the first and the last	Rev.1.17
No one who denies . . . Son has the *F*.	1 Jn.2.23	**FEARFUL**	
sat down with my *F*. on his throne	Rev.3.21	Whoever is *f*. and trembling, let	Jg.7.3
FATHERLESS		for thou art *f*. and wonderful	Ps.139.14
justice for the *f*. and the widow	Dt.10.18	Say to those who are of a *f*. heart	Is.35.4
thou hast been the helper of the *f*.	Ps.10.14	he shall cause *f*. destruction	Dan.8.24
Father of the *f*. . . . protector of widows	Ps.68.5	a *f*. prospect of judgment	Heb.10.27
they judge not . . . cause of the *f*.	Jer.5.28		

It is a f. thing to fall into the | Heb.10.31
so f. was that plague | Rev.16.21

FEAST (noun)
So he made them a f., and they ate | Gen.26.30
for we must hold a f. to the LORD | Ex.10.9
You shall keep the f. of unleavened | Ex.23.15
You shall keep the f. of harvest | Ex.23.16
shall keep the f. of ingathering | Ex.23.16
You shall keep the f. of booths | Dt.16.13
f. of weeks, and at the f. of booths | Dt.16.16
the yearly f. of the LORD at Shiloh | Jg.21.19
Solomon held the f. for seven days | 2 Chr.7.8
among the Jews, a f. and a holiday | Est.8.17
your appointed f. my soul hates | Is.1.14
I hate, I despise your f. | Am.5.21
I will turn your f. into mourning | Am.8.10
gave a marriage f. for his son | Mt.22.2
before . . . the f. of Unleavened Bread | Mk.14.1
After this there was a f. of the Jews | Jn.5.1
It was the f. of the Dedication | Jn.10.22
These are blemishes on your love f. | Jude 12

FEEBLE
but the f. gird on strength | 1 Sam.2.4
What are these f. Jews doing? | Neh.4.2
you have made firm the f. knees | Job 4.4
hands, and make firm the f. knees | Is.35.3
will melt and all hands will be f. | Ezek.21.7

FEED
commanded . . . ravens to f. you there | 1 Kg.17.4
commanded a widow there to f. you | 1 Kg.17.9
I would f. you with the finest of | Ps.81.16
The lips of the righteous f. many | Pr.10.21
the mouths of fools f. on folly | Pr.15.14
The cow and the bear shall f. | Is.11.7
He will f. his flock like a shepherd | Is.40.11
Aliens shall stand and f. your flocks | Is.61.5
wolf and the lamb shall f. together | Is.65.25
I will f. them with wormwood | Jer.23.15
should not shepherds f. the sheep? | Ezek.34.2
yet your heavenly Father f. them | Mt.6.26
when did we see thee hungry and f. | Mt.25.37
Jesus said to him, "F. my sheep | Jn.21.17
to f. the church of the Lord | Acts 20.28
if your enemy is hungry, f. him | Rom.12.20

FEET
put off your shoes from your f. | Ex.3.5
the great toes of their right f. | Lev.8.24
Put off your shoes from your f. | Jos.5.15
a son who was crippled in his f. | 2 Sam.4.4
He made my f. like hinds' f. | 2 Sam.22.34
the f. and the palms of her hands | 2 Kg.9.35
Thou puttest my f. in the stocks | Job 13.27
thou hast put all things under his f. | Ps.8.6
they have pierced my hands and f. | Ps.22.16
He . . . set my f. upon a rock | Ps.40.2
my f. had almost stumbled, my steps | Ps.73.2
Thy word is a lamp to my f. | Ps.119.105
spreads a net for his f. | Pr.29.5
Their f. run to evil, and they make | Is.59.7
Son of man, stand upon your f. | Ezek.2.1
its f. partly of iron and partly of | Dan.2.33
shake off the dust from your f. | Mt.10.14
than with two f. to be thrown into | Mk.9.45
has anointed my f. with ointment | Lk.7.46
sat at the Lord's f. and listened | Lk.10.39
began to wash the disciples' f. | Jn.13.5

brought up . . . at the f. of Gamaliel | Acts 22.3
shod your f. with the equipment of | Eph.6.15
whose f. are like burnished bronze | Rev.2.18

FELIX
Acts 23.24; 24.2,25,27; 25.14

FELLOW
regard this ill-natured f., Nabal | 1 Sam.25.25
for I set every man against his f. | Zech.8.10
have had mercy on your f. servant | Mt.18.33
Away with such a f. from the earth | Acts 22.22
and f. heirs with Christ | Rom.8.17
my f. workers in Christ Jesus | Rom.16.3
Timothy, my f. worker, greets you | Rom.16.21
For we are f. workers for God | 1 Cor.3.9
you are f. citizens with the saints | Eph.2.19
among my f. workers for the kingdom | Col.4.11
that we may be f. workers in the truth | 3 Jn.8
I am a f. servant with you | Rev.22.9

FELLOWSHIP
within God's house we walked in f. | Ps.55.14
to the apostles' teaching and f. | Acts 2.42
were called into the f. of his Son | 1 Cor.1.9
and the f. of the Holy Spirit | 2 Cor.13.14
gave . . . the right hand of f. | Gal.2.9
our f. is with the Father and | 1 Jn.1.3

FEMALE
male and f., went into the ark | Gen.7.9
two hundred male and f. singers | Ezra 2.65
there is neither male nor f. | Gal.3.28

FESTIVAL
thanksgiving, a multitude keeping f. | Ps.42.4
do on the day of appointed f. | Hos.9.5
celebrate the f., not with the old | 1 Cor.5.8
with regard to a f. or a new moon | Col.2.16

FESTUS
Acts 24.27; 25.9,14; 26.24-25

FETTERS
Gaza, and bound him with bronze f. | Jg.16.21
of Zedekiah, and bound him in f. | 2 Kg.25.7
been bound with f. and chains | Mk.5.4
every one's f. were unfastened | Acts 16.26
Remember my f. | Col.4.18
I am suffering and wearing f. | 2 Tim.2.9

FEVER
The LORD will smite you . . . with f. | Dt.28.22
mother-in-law lying sick with a f. | Mt.8.14
at the seventh hour the f. left him | Jn.4.52
lay sick with f. and dysentery | Acts 28.8

FEW
from saving by many or by f. | 1 Sam.14.6
When they were f. in number | 1 Chr.16.19
I and a f. men with me | Neh.2.12
born of a woman is of f. days | Job 14.1
therefore let your words be f. | Ec.5.2
grinders cease because they are f. | Ec.12.3
life, and those who find it are f. | Mt.7.14
plentiful, but the laborers are f. | Mt.9.37
many are called, but f. are chosen | Mt.22.14
But I have a f. things against you | Rev.2.14
you have still a f. names in Sardis | Rev.3.4

FIELD
when no plant of the f. was yet in | Gen.2.5
when they were in the f., Cain rose | Gen.4.8
the f. of Ephron in Machpelah | Gen.23.17
Six years you shall sow your f. | Lev.25.3
gleaned in the f. after the reapers | Ru.2.3

Come, let us go out into the *f.* 1 Sam.20.11
oxen, and also the beasts of the *f.* Ps.8.7
let the *f.* exult, and everything in Ps.96.12
She considers a *f.* and buys it Pr.31.16
trees of the *f.* shall clap their hands Is.55.12
Zion shall be plowed as a *f.* Jer.26.18
And I bought the *f.* at Anathoth Jer.32.9
God so clothes the grass of the *f.* Mt.6.30
the parable of the weeds of the *f.* Mt.13.36
bought with them the potter's *f.* Mt.27.7
there were shepherds out in the *f.* Lk.2.8
Now his elder son was in the *f.* Lk.15.25
see how the *f.* are already white Jn.4.35
Akeldama, that is, *F.* of Blood Acts 1.19
you are God's *f.*, God's building 1 Cor.3.9

FIERCE
the *f.* anger of the LORD may turn Num.25.4
f. wrath of our God . . . be averted Ezra 10.14
the *f.* anger of the LORD has not Jer.4.8
He has cut down in *f.* anger all the Lam.2.3
repent and turn from his *f.* anger Jon.3.9
after my departure *f.* wolves will Acts 20.29

FIERY
Then the LORD sent *f.* serpents Num.21.6
be cast into a burning *f.* furnace Dan.3.6
surprised at the *f.* ordeal which 1 Pet.4.12

FIG
and they sewed *f.* leaves together Gen.3.7
And the trees said to the *f.* tree Jg.9.10
Let them take a cake of *f.* Is.38.21
every man . . . under his *f.* tree Mic.4.4
from thorns, or *f.* from thistles? Mt.7.16
And the *f.* tree withered at once Mt.21.19
From the *f.* tree learn its lesson Mk.13.28
I saw you under the *f.* tree Jn.1.50
Can a *f.* tree, my brethren, yield Jas.3.12

FIGHT
the LORD your God who *f.* for you Dt.3.22
I myself will *f.* against you Jer.21.5
this world, my servants would *f.* Jn.18.36
F. the good *f.* of the faith 1 Tim.6.12
I have fought the good *f.* 2 Tim.4.7
you covet . . . so you *f.* and wage war Jas.4.2
beast, and who can *f.* against it? Rev.13.4

FILL
multiply and *f.* the waters in the Gen.1.22
F. me with joy and gladness Ps.51.8
My mouth is *f.* with thy praise Ps.71.8
Open your mouth . . . I will *f.* it Ps.81.10
Let the sea roar, and all that *f.* it Ps.98.7
the hungry he *f.* with good things Ps.107.9
the wicked are *f.* with trouble Pr.12.21
he will *f.* Zion with justice Is.33.5
the glory of the LORD *f.* the temple Ezek.43.5
glorified God and were *f.* with awe Lk.5.26
were all *f.* with the Holy Spirit Acts 2.4
why has Satan *f.* your heart to lie Acts 5.3
the disciples were *f.* with joy Acts 13.52
May the God of hope *f.* you with all Rom.15.13
but be *f.* with the Spirit Eph.5.18
the temple was *f.* with smoke Rev.15.8

FIND
Can you *f.* out the deep things of God? Job 11.7
that I knew where I might *f.* him Job 23.3
The Almighty—we cannot *f.* him Job 37.23
under his wings you will *f.* refuge Ps.91.4

I *f.* my delight in thy commandments Ps.119.47
So you will *f.* favor and good Pr.3.4
those who seek me diligently *f.* me Pr.8.17
A good wife who can *f.*? She is far Pr.31.10
for you will *f.* it after many days Ec.11.1
the LORD, but they will not *f.* him Hos.5.6
seek, and you will *f.*; knock Mt.7.7
He who *f.* his life will lose it Mt.10.39
you will *f.* rest for your souls Mt.11.29
will *f.* a babe wrapped in swaddling Lk.2.12
on entering you will *f.* a colt tied Lk.19.30
I *f.* no crime in this man Lk.23.4
f. grace to help in time of need Heb.4.16

FINGER
to Pharaoh, "This is the *f.* of God." Ex.8.19
stone, written with the *f.* of God Ex.31.18
who had six *f.* on each hand 2 Sam.21.20
thy heavens, the work of thy *f.* Ps.8.3
the *f.* of a man's hand appeared Dan.5.5
But if it is by the *f.* of God that Lk.11.20
Put your *f.* here, and see my hands Jn.20.27

FINISH
Thus the heavens and the earth were *f.* Gen.2.1
when Moses had *f.* speaking with them Ex.34.33
When Moses had *f.* writing the words Dt.31.24
Solomon built the house, and *f.* it 1 Kg.6.14
So Hiram *f.* all the work that he 1 Kg.7.40
the wall was *f.* on the twenty-fifth Neh.6.15
When the Lord has *f.* all his work Is.10.12
And when Jesus *f.* these sayings Mt.7.28
Jesus . . . said, "It is *f.*" Jn.19.30
I have *f.* the race, I have kept the 2 Tim.4.7
And when they have *f.* their testimony Rev.11.7

FIRE
the LORD descended upon it in *f.* Ex.19.18
an offering by *f.* to the LORD Ex.29.18
burnt offering, an offering by *f.* Lev.1.13
F. shall be kept burning upon the Lev.6.13
f. came forth from before the LORD Lev.9.24
offered unholy *f.* before the LORD Num.3.4
the *f.* of the LORD burned among them Num.11.1
And *f.* came forth from the LORD Num.16.35
the LORD . . . is a devouring *f.* Dt.4.24
God who answers by *f.*, he is God 1 Kg.18.24
after the *f.* a still small voice 1 Kg.19.12
a chariot of *f.* and horses of *f.* 2 Kg.2.11
f. came down from heaven 2 Chr.7.1
The *f.* of God fell from heaven Job 1.16
As I mused, the *f.* burned Ps.39.3
he burns the chariots with *f.* Ps.46.9
Can a man carry *f.* in his bosom and Pr.6.27
will heap coals of *f.* on his head Pr.25.22
For behold, the LORD will come in *f.* Is.66.15
Is not my word like *f.*, says the Jer.23.29
and *f.* flashing forth continually Ezek.1.4
walking in the midst of the *f.* Dan.3.25
he will burn with unquenchable *f.* Mt.3.12
to be thrown into the eternal *f.* Mt.18.8
eternal *f.* prepared for the devil Mt.25.41
with the Holy Spirit and with *f.* Lk.3.16
I came to cast *f.* upon the earth Lk.12.49
Sinai, in a flame of *f.* in a bush Acts 7.30
for our God is a consuming *f.* Heb.12.29
And the tongue is a *f.* Jas.3.6
his eyes were like a flame of *f.* Rev.1.14
the lake of *f.* and brimstone Rev.20.10

FIRM

stand *f.*, and see the salvation of	Ex.14.13
you have made *f.* the feeble knees	Job 4.4
thy faithfulness is *f.* as the heavens	Ps.89.2
my covenant will stand *f.* for him	Ps.89.28
shall stand *f.* and take action	Dan.11.32
stand *f.* in your faith	1 Cor.16.13
But God's *f.* foundation stands	2 Tim.2.19
Resist him, *f.* in your faith	1 Pet.5.9

FIRMAMENT

Let there be a *f.* in the midst of	Gen.1.6
and the *f.* proclaims his handiwork	Ps.19.1
shine like the brightness of the *f.*	Dan.12.3

FIRST

Noah was the *f.* tiller of the soil	Gen.9.20
the *f.* fruits of your labor	Ex.23.16
two tables of stone like the *f.*	Dt.10.3
Your *f.* father sinned, and your	Is.43.27
I am the *f.* and I am the last	Is.44.6
But seek *f.* his kingdom and his	Mt.6.33
You hypocrite, *f.* take the log out	Mt.7.5
But many that are *f.* will be last	Mt.19.30
This is the great and *f.* commandment	Mt.22.38
on the *f.* day of Unleavened Bread	Mt.26.17
the dawn of the *f.* day of the week	Mt.28.1
He *f.* found his brother Simon	Jn.1.41
This, the *f.* of his signs, Jesus did	Jn.2.11
In the *f.* book, O Theophilus, I have	Acts 1.1
were . . . *f.* . . . called Christians	Acts 11.26
On the *f.* day of the week, when we	Acts 20.7
On the *f.* day of every week, each	1 Cor.16.2
we hold our *f.* confidence firm to	Heb.3.14
We love, because he *f.* loved us	1 Jn.4.19
I am the *f.* and the last	Rev.1.17
abandoned the love you had at *f.*	Rev.2.4
This is the *f.* resurrection	Rev.20.5
for the *f.* heaven and the *f.* earth	Rev.21.1

FIRST-BORN

Consecrate to me all the *f.*	Ex.13.2
He smote all the *f.* in Egypt	Ps.78.51
offer by fire all their *f.*	Ezek.20.26
Shall I give my *f.* for my transgression	Mic.6.7
she gave birth to her *f.* son	Lk.2.7
the *f.* of all creation	Col.1.15
assembly of the *f.* who are enrolled	Heb.12.23

FISH (noun)

dominion over the *f.* of the sea	Gen.1.26
and the *f.* of the sea, whatever	Ps.8.8
appointed a great *f.* to swallow up	Jon.1.17
he took the seven loaves and the *f.*	Mt.15.36
they enclosed a great shoal of *f.*	Lk.5.6
instead of a *f.* give him a serpent	Lk.11.11
has five barley loaves and two *f.*	Jn.6.9
hauled the net . . . full of large *f.*	Jn.21.11

FISHERS

Behold, I am sending for many *f.*	Jer.16.16
and I will make you *f.* of men	Mt.4.19
I will make you become *f.* of men	Mk.1.17

FIXED

means that the thing is *f.* by God	Gen.41.32
Thou hast *f.* all the bounds of the	Ps.74.17
thy word is . . . *f.* in the heavens	Ps.119.89
he *f.* their bounds which cannot be	Ps.148.6
a great chasm has been *f.*	Lk.16.26
seasons which the Father has *f.*	Acts 1.7
because he has *f.* a day on which	Acts 17.31

FLAME (noun)

a *f.* comes forth from his mouth	Job 41.21
makest . . . fire and *f.* thy ministers	Ps.104.4
and his Holy One a *f.*	Is.10.17
anger and a *f.* of devouring fire	Is.30.30
his throne was fiery *f.*	Dan.7.9
for I am in anguish in this *f.*	Lk.16.24
winds, and his servants *f.* of fire	Heb.1.7
his eyes were like a *f.* of fire	Rev.1.14

FLASH

His sneezings *f.* forth light	Job 41.18
F. forth the lightning and scatter	Ps.144.6
a light from heaven *f.* about him	Acts 9.3
From the throne issue *f.* of lightning	Rev.4.5
there were *f.* of lightning	Rev.16.18

FLATTER

they *f.* with their tongue	Ps.5.9
But they *f.* him with their mouths	Ps.78.36
and a *f.* mouth works ruin	Pr.26.28
by fair and *f.* words they deceive	Rom.16.18
f. people to gain advantage	Jude 16

FLEE

Should such a man as I *f.*?	Neh.6.11
F. like a bird to the mountains	Ps.11.1
whither . . . *f.* from thy presence?	Ps.139.7
The wicked *f.* when no one pursues	Pr.28.1
To whom will you *f.* for help	Is.10.3
sorrow and sighing shall *f.* away	Is.51.11
both man and beast shall *f.* away	Jer.50.3
But Jonah rose to *f.* to Tarshish	Jon.1.3
f. to Egypt, and remain there till	Mt.2.13
warned you to *f.* from the wrath to	Mt.3.7
persecute you in one town, *f.* to	Mt.10.23
in Judea *f.* to the mountains	Mk.13.14
He *f.* because he is a hireling	Jn.10.13
Resist the devil and he will *f.* from	Jas.4.7

FLEECE

the first of the *f.* of your sheep	Dt.18.4
if there is dew on the *f.* alone	Jg.6.37
it was dry on the *f.* only	Jg.6.40

FLESH

bone of my bones and *f.* of my *f.*	Gen.2.23
all *f.* died that moved upon the earth	Gen.7.21
the life of the *f.* is in the blood	Lev.17.11
My *f.* is clothed with worms and dirt	Job 7.5
then from my *f.* I shall see God	Job 19.26
my *f.* faints for thee, as in a dry	Ps.63.1
My *f.* and my heart may fail, but God	Ps.73.26
He remembered that they were but *f.*	Ps.78.39
he who gives food to all *f.*	Ps.136.25
All *f.* is grass, and all its beauty	Is.40.6
All *f.* shall see that I the LORD	Ezek.20.48
You eat *f.* with the blood	Ezek.33.25
f. and blood has not revealed this	Mt.16.17
spirit . . . is willing . . . *f.* is weak	Mk.14.38
the Word became *f.* and dwelt among	Jn.1.14
That which is born of the *f.* is *f.*	Jn.3.6
you eat the *f.* of the Son of man	Jn.6.53
pour out my Spirit upon all *f.*	Acts 2.17
To set the mind on the *f.* is death	Rom.8.6
we are debtors, not to the *f.*	Rom.8.12
f. and blood cannot inherit the	1 Cor.15.50
a thorn was given me in the *f.*	2 Cor.12.7
Now the works of the *f.* are plain	Gal.5.19
not contending against *f.* and blood	Eph.6.12
we . . . put no confidence in the *f.*	Phil.3.3

He was manifested in the *f.* 1 Tim.3.16
curtain, that is, through his *f.* Heb.10.20
since . . . Christ suffered in the *f.* 1 Pet.4.1

FLOCK
Jacob fed the rest of Laban's *f.* Gen.30.36
Then we . . . the *f.* of thy pasture Ps.79.13
will feed his *f.* like a shepherd Is.40.11
LORD's *f.* has been taken captive Jer.13.17
as a shepherd keeps his *f.* Jer.31.10
I will save my *f.*, they shall no Ezek.34.22
LORD took me from following the *f.* Am.7.15
Shepherd . . . the *f.* of thy inheritance Mic.7.14
LORD of hosts cares for his *f.* Zech.10.3
sheep of the *f.* will be scattered Mt.26.31
keeping watch over their *f.* Lk.2.8
Fear not, little *f.*, for it Lk.12.32
So there shall be one *f.* Jn.10.16
Take heed . . . to all the *f.* Acts 20.28
Tend the *f.* of God that is your 1 Pet.5.2
but being examples to the *f.* 1 Pet.5.3

FLOOD
I will bring a *f.* of waters upon Gen.6.17
abroad on the earth after the *f.* Gen.10.32
Terrors overtake him like a *f.* Job 27.20
The LORD sits enthroned over the *f.* Ps.29.10
Let the *f.* clap their hands Ps.98.8
and the *f.* was round about me Jon.2.3
the *f.* came, and the winds blew Mt.7.25
to sweep her away with the *f.* Rev.12.15

FLOURISH
In his days may righteousness *f.* Ps.72.7
in the morning it *f.* and is renewed Ps.90.6
The righteous *f.* like the palm tree Ps.92.12
he *f.* like a flower of the field Ps.103.15
the righteous will *f.* like a green Pr.11.28
the tent of the upright will *f.* Pr.14.11
they shall *f.* as a garden Hos.14.7
Grain shall make the young men *f.* Zech.9.17

FLOW
A river *f.* out of Eden to water Gen.2.10
a land which *f.* with milk and honey Num.14.8
caused waters to *f.* down like rivers Ps.78.16
for from it *f.* the springs of life Pr.4.23
all the nations shall *f.* to it Is.2.2
my eyes *f.* with tears Lam.1.16
and peoples shall *f.* to it Mic.4.1
waters shall *f.* out from Jerusalem Zech.14.8
out of his heart shall *f.* rivers of Jn.7.38

FLOWER
flourishes like a *f.* of the field Ps.103.15
beauty is like the *f.* of the field Is.40.6
The grass withers, the *f.* fades Is.40.8
its *f.* falls . . . its beauty perishes Jas.1.11
all its glory like the *f.* of grass 1 Pet.1.24

FLY
and let birds *f.* above the earth Gen.1.20
He will *f.* away like a dream Job 20.8
they are soon gone, and we *f.* away Ps.90.10
I answered, "I see a *f.* scroll Zech.5.2
living creature like a *f.* eagle Rev.4.7
saw another angel *f.* in midheaven Rev.14.6

FOAL
Binding his *f.* to the vine and his Gen.49.11
on a colt the *f.* of an ass Zech.9.9
and on a colt, the *f.* of an ass Mt.21.5

FOE
And Esther said, "A *f.* and enemy Est.7.6
O LORD, how many are my *f.* Ps.3.1
hast not let my *f.* rejoice over me Ps.30.1
Through thee we push down our *f.* Ps.44.5
But thou hast saved us from our *f.* Ps.44.7
a man's *f.* will be those of his Mt.10.36
fire pours . . . and consumes their *f.* Rev.11.5

FOLLOW
not learn to *f.* the abominable Dt.18.9
you will *f.* the LORD your God 1 Sam.12.14
and did not wholly *f.* the LORD 1 Kg.11.6
mercy shall *f.* me all the days Ps.23.6
the upright in heart will *f.* it Ps.94.15
who stubbornly *f.* their own heart Jer.13.10
F. me, and I will make you fishers Mt.4.19
I will *f.* you wherever you go Mt.8.19
his cross and *f.* me is not worthy Mt.10.38
and take up his cross and *f.* me Mt.16.24
Jesus . . . said to him, "*F.* me." Jn.1.43
the sheep *f.* him, for they know his Jn.10.4
If any one serves me, he must *f.* me Jn.12.26
but you shall *f.* afterward Jn.13.36
we did not *f.* cleverly devised 2 Pet.1.16
as indeed you do *f.* the truth 3 Jn.3
it is these who *f.* the Lamb Rev.14.4
labors, for their deeds *f.* them Rev.14.13

FOLLY
deal with you according to your *f.* Job 42.8
O God, thou knowest my *f.* Ps.69.5
but a fool flaunts his *f.* Pr.13.16
f. is the garland of fools Pr.14.24
F. is . . . in the heart of a child Pr.22.15
Answer not a fool according to his *f.* Pr.26.4
wisdom excels *f.* as light excels Ec.2.13
the cross is *f.* to those who 1 Cor.1.18
for they are *f.* to him 1 Cor.2.14

FOOD
have given every green plant for *f.* Gen.1.30
saw that the tree was good for *f.* Gen.3.6
prepare . . . savory *f.* for your father Gen.27.9
and we loathe this worthless *f.* Num.21.5
So none of the people tasted *f.* 1 Sam.14.24
he gives *f.* in abundance Job 36.31
My tears have been my *f.* day and Ps.42.3
he sent them *f.* in abundance Ps.78.25
give them their *f.* in due season Ps.104.27
He gives to the beasts their *f.* Ps.147.9
and provides *f.* for her household Pr.31.15
dust shall be the serpent's *f.* Is.65.25
the children beg for *f.*, but no one Lam.4.4
youths who ate the king's rich *f.* Dan.1.15
that there may be *f.* in my house Mal.3.10
his *f.* was locusts and wild honey Mt.3.4
Is not life more than *f.*, and Mt.6.25
for I was hungry and you gave me *f.* Mt.25.35
he who has *f.*, let him do likewise Lk.3.11
I have *f.* to eat of which you do Jn.4.32
not labor for the *f.* which perishes Jn.6.27
For my flesh is *f.* indeed Jn.6.55
they partook of *f.* with glad and Acts 2.46
the kingdom . . . does not mean *f.* Rom.14.17
Now concerning *f.* offered to idols 1 Cor.8.1
F. will not commend us to God 1 Cor.8.8
But solid *f.* is for the mature Heb.5.14

FOOL

The *f.* says in his heart, "There is	Ps.14.1
he who utters slander is a *f.*	Pr.10.18
The way of a *f.* is right in his own	Pr.12.15
A *f.* despises his father's instruction	Pr.15.5
Even a *f.* who keeps silent is	Pr.17.28
Answer not a *f.* according to his	Pr.26.4
the wise man dies just like the *f.*	Ec.2.16
and whoever says, 'You *f.!*'	Mt.5.22
But God said to him, '*F.!* This night	Lk.12.20
become a *f.* he may become	1 Cor.3.18
We are *f.* for Christ's sake	1 Cor.4.10
I have been a *f.!* You forced me	2 Cor.12.11

FOOLISH

A *f.* woman is noisy; she is wanton	Pr.9.13
a *f.* son is a sorrow to his mother	Pr.10.1
a *f.* man despises his mother	Pr.15.20
Woe to the *f.* prophets who follow	Ezek.13.3
Five of them were *f.*, and five were	Mt.25.2
O *f.* men, and slow of heart to	Lk.24.25
God made *f.* the wisdom of the	1 Cor.1.20
You *f.* man! What you sow	1 Cor.15.36
O *f.* Galatians! Who has bewitched	Gal.3.1

FOOT

dove found no place to set her *f.*	Gen.8.9
hand for hand, *f.* for *f.*	Ex.21.24
you strike your *f.* against a stone	Mt.4.6
except to be . . . trodden under *f.* by men	Mt.5.13
And if your *f.* causes you to sin	Mk.9.45
If the *f.* should say, "Because	1 Cor.12.15

FOOTSTOOL

worship at his *f.!* Holy is he	Ps.99.5
till I make your enemies your *f.*	Ps.110.1
says the LORD . . . the earth is my *f.*	Is.66.1
or by the earth, for it is his *f.*	Mt.5.35
Heaven is my throne . . . earth my *f.*	Acts 7.49

FORBEARANCE

In thy *f.* take me not away	Jer.15.15
his kindness and *f.* and patience	Rom.2.4
f., kindness . . . genuine love	2 Cor.6.6
Let all men know your *f.*	Phil.4.5
count the *f.* of our Lord	2 Pet.3.15

FORBID

rebuke him, saying, "God *f.*, Lord	Mt.16.22
Jesus said to him, "Do not *f.* him	Lk.9.50
Can any one *f.* water for baptizing	Acts 10.47
having been *f.* by the Holy Spirit	Acts 16.6
f. marriage and enjoin abstinence	1 Tim.4.3

FOREFATHER

remember the covenant with their *f.*	Lev.26.45
the iniquities of our *f.*	Ps.79.8
back to the iniquities of their *f.*	Jer.11.10
our *f.* according to the flesh?	Rom.4.1
children by one man, our *f.* Isaac	Rom.9.10
beloved for the sake of their *f.*	Rom.11.28

FOREHEAD

It shall be upon Aaron's *f.*	Ex.28.38
baldness on your *f.* for the dead	Dt.14.1
struck the Philistine on his *f.*	1 Sam.17.49
marked on the right hand or the *f.*	Rev.13.16
on her *f.* was written a name of	Rev.17.5

FOREIGN

all the *f.* gods that they had	Gen.35.4
forsake the LORD and serve *f.* gods	Jos.24.20
King Solomon loved many *f.* women	1 Kg.11.1
He took away the *f.* altars	2 Chr.14.3

by marrying *f.* women	Neh.13.27
sing the LORD's song in a *f.* land?	Ps.137.4
and served *f.* gods in your land	Jer.5.19
to be a preacher of *f.* divinities	Acts 17.18
as in a *f.* land, living in tents	Heb.11.9

FOREST

For every beast of the *f.* is mine	Ps.50.10
the beasts of the *f.* creep forth	Ps.104.20
O *f.*, and every tree in it	Is.44.23
Does a lion roar in the *f.*	Am.3.4
How great a *f.* is set ablaze by a	Jas.3.5

FORGET

Take heed lest you *f.* the LORD	Dt.8.11
to Sheol . . . the nations that *f.* God	Ps.9.17
and not *f.* the works of God	Ps.78.7
I will never *f.* thy precepts	Ps.119.93
If I *f.* you, O Jerusalem, let my	Ps.137.5
Can a woman *f.* her sucking child	Is.49.15
f. what lies behind and straining	Phil.3.13

FORGIVE

Now therefore, *f.* my sin, I pray	Ex.10.17
But thou art a God ready to *f.*	Neh.9.17
f. our sins, for thy name's sake	Ps.79.9
I will *f.* their iniquity, and I	Jer.31.34
O LORD, *f.*; O LORD, give heed	Dan.9.19
And *f.* us our debts, As we also have	Mt.6.12
against the Spirit will not be *f.*	Mt.12.31
if you do not *f.* your brother from	Mt.18.35
and if he repents, *f.* him	Lk.17.3
And Jesus said, "Father, *f.* them	Lk.23.34
has *f.* you, so you also must *f.*	Col.3.13
will *f.* our sins and cleanse us	1 Jn.1.9

FORGIVENESS

there is *f.* with thee, that thou	Ps.130.4
to . . . our God belong mercy and *f.*	Dan.9.9
repentance for the *f.* of sins	Lk.3.3
for the *f.* of your sins	Acts 2.38
we have . . . the *f.* of our trespasses	Eph.1.7
we have redemption, the *f.* of sins	Col.1.14

FORGOTTEN

For the needy shall not always be *f.*	Ps.9.18
yet I have not *f.* thy statutes	Ps.119.83
O Israel, you will not be *f.* by me	Is.44.21
But my people have *f.* me	Jer.18.15
you have *f.* me, says the Lord	Ezek.22.12
For Israel has *f.* his Maker	Hos.8.14
not one of them is *f.* before God	Lk.12.6

FORM (noun)

The earth was without *f.* and void	Gen.1.2
and his *f.* beyond that of the sons	Is.52.14
he had no *f.* or comeliness that we	Is.53.2
likeness as it were of a human *f.*	Ezek.1.26
descended upon him in bodily *f.*	Lk.3.22
the *f.* of this world is passing	1 Cor.7.31
who, though he was in the *f.* of God	Phil.2.6
abstain from every *f.* of evil	1 Th.5.22
holding the *f.* of religion but	2 Tim.3.5

FORM (verb)

then the LORD God *f.* man of dust	Gen.2.7
I too was *f.* from a piece of clay	Job 33.6
or ever thou hadst *f.* the earth and	Ps.90.2
For thou didst *f.* my inward parts	Ps.139.13
the thing *f.* say of him who *f.* it	Is.29.16
who *f.* you from the womb and will	Is.44.2
I *f.* light and create darkness	Is.45.7
Before I *f.* you in the womb I knew	Jer.1.5

travail until Christ be *f.* in you Gal.4.19
For Adam was *f.* first, then Eve 1 Tim.2.13

FORSAKE
he will not fail you or *f.* you Dt.31.6
I will not fail you or *f.* you Jos.1.5
If you *f.* the LORD and serve Jos.24.20
if you *f.* him, he will *f.* you 2 Chr.15.2
My God, my God, why hast thou *f.* me? Ps.22.1
f. me not, O God of my salvation Ps.27.9
If his children *f.* my law and do Ps.89.30
Do not *f.* the work of thy hands Ps.138.8
Do not *f.* her, and she will keep you Pr.4.6
who *f.* the LORD shall be consumed Is.1.28
your house is *f.* and desolate Mt.23.38
God, my God, why hast thou *f.* me? Mt.27.46
I will never fail you nor *f.* you Heb.13.5

FORSOOK
and they *f.* the LORD, the God of Jg.2.12
they *f.* all the commandments of 2 Kg.17.16
For a brief moment I *f.* you, but Is.54.7
all the disciples *f.* him and fled Mt.26.56

FORTRESS
The LORD is my rock, and my *f.* 2 Sam.22.2
Yea, thou art my rock and my *f.* Ps.31.3
thou . . . art my *f.*, the God who shows Ps.59.17
to the LORD, "My refuge and my *f.* Ps.91.2
All your *f.* are like fig trees with Nah.3.12

FORTY
The flood continued *f.* days upon Gen.7.17
At the end of *f.* days they returned Num.13.25
f. years, and you shall know my Num.14.34
F. stripes may be given him, but not Dt.25.3
So the land had rest *f.* years Jg.3.11
f. days and *f.* nights to Horeb 1 Kg.19.8
F. years didst thou sustain them in Neh.9.21
Yet *f.* days, and Nineveh shall be Jon.3.4
he fasted *f.* days and *f.* nights Mt.4.2
appearing to them during *f.* days Acts 1.3
There were more than *f.* who made Acts 23.13

FOUNDATION
to lay the *f.* of the house with 1 Kg.5.17
The *f.* was of costly stones, huge 1 Kg.7.10
if the *f.* are destroyed, what can Ps.11.3
thou didst lay the *f.* of the earth Ps.102.25
I am laying in Zion for a *f.* a stone Is.28.16
My hand laid the *f.* of the earth Is.48.13
the day that the *f.* of the LORD's Hag.2.18
hidden since the *f.* of the world Mt.13.35
a house on the ground without a *f.* Lk.6.49
lest I build on another man's *f.* Rom.15.20
For no other *f.* can any one lay 1 Cor.3.11
built upon the *f.* of the apostles Eph.2.20
But God's firm *f.* stands 2 Tim.2.19
before the *f.* of the world 1 Pet.1.20
from the *f.* of the world Rev.17.8
the wall of the city had twelve *f.* Rev.21.14

FOX
if a *f.* goes up on it he will break Neh.4.3
Catch us the *f.*, the little *f.* S.of S.2.15
F. have holes, and birds of the air Mt.8.20
said to them, "Go and tell that *f.* Lk.13.32

FRAGRANT
Aaron shall burn *f.* incense on it Ex.30.7
your robes are all *f.* with myrrh Ps.45.8
a *f.* offering and sacrifice to God Eph.5.2
a *f.* offering . . . pleasing to God Phil.4.18

FRANKINCENSE
pour oil upon it, and put *f.* on it Lev.2.1
the *f.*, the vessels, and the tithes Neh.13.5
They shall bring gold and *f.* Is.60.6
gifts, gold and *f.* and myrrh Mt.2.11
f., wine, oil, fine flour Rev.18.13

FREE
The man shall be *f.* from iniquity Num.5.31
the LORD answered me and set me *f.* Ps.118.5
The LORD sets the prisoners *f.* Ps.146.7
said to him, "Then the sons are *f.* Mt.17.26
and the truth will make you *f.* Jn.8.32
the *f.* gift is not like the trespass Rom.5.15
and, having been set *f.* from sin Rom.6.18
the *f.* gift of God is eternal life Rom.6.23
I want you to be *f.* from anxieties 1 Cor.7.32
I . . . make the gospel *f.* of charge 1 Cor.9.18
But the Jerusalem above is *f.* Gal.4.26
For freedom Christ has set us *f.* Gal.5.1
Live as *f.* men, yet without using 1 Pet.2.16
both *f.* and slave, both small and Rev.19.18

FREED
you are *f.* from your infirmity Lk.13.12
believes is *f.* from everything Acts 13.39
could not be *f.* by the law of Acts 13.39
For he who has died is *f.* from sin Rom.6.7
and has *f.* us from our sins by Rev.1.5

FREEDOM
But if you can gain your *f.* 1 Cor.7.21
where the Spirit . . . is, there is *f.* 2 Cor.3.17
For *f.* Christ has set us free Gal.5.1
For you were called to *f.*, brethren Gal.5.13
using your *f.* as a pretext for evil 1 Pet.2.16
They promise them *f.*, but they 2 Pet.2.19

FREELY
You may *f.* eat of every tree of Gen.2.16
You shall give to him *f.*, and your Dt.15.10
He has distributed *f.*, he has given Ps.112.9
I will love them *f.*, for my anger Hos.14.4
and began to talk *f.* about it Mk.1.45
and to him I speak *f.* Acts 26.26
grace which he *f.* bestowed on us Eph.1.6

FRESH
thou hast poured over me *f.* oil Ps.92.10
shall obtain *f.* joy in the LORD Is.29.19
waters of the sea may become *f.* Ezek.47.9
new wine is put into *f.* wineskins Mt.9.17
same opening *f.* water and brackish? Jas.3.11

FRIEND
as a man speaks to his *f.* Ex.33.11
Ammon had a *f.*, whose name was 2 Sam.13.3
Zabud was priest and king's *f.* 1 Kg.4.5
the descendants of Abraham thy *f.* 2 Chr.20.7
Job's three *f.* heard of all this Job 2.11
Even my bosom *f.* in whom I trusted Ps.41.9
my companion, my familiar *f.* Ps.55.13
A *f.* loves at all times, and a Pr.17.17
a *f.* who sticks closer than a brother Pr.18.24
a poor man is deserted by his *f.* Pr.19.4
Faithful are the wounds of a *f.* Pr.27.6
a *f.* of tax collectors and sinners Mt.11.19
F., lend me three loaves Lk.11.5
may say to you, '*F.*, go up higher' Lk.14.10
that I might make merry with my *f.* Lk.15.29
Our *f.* Lazarus has fallen asleep Jn.11.11
You are my *f.* if you do what I Jn.15.14

you are not Caesar's *f.*   Jn.19.12
Abraham . . . was called the *f.* of God   Jas.2.23
wishes to be a *f.* of the world   Jas.4.4

FRIGHTEN
be not *f.*, neither be dismayed   Jos.1.9
For they all wanted to *f.* us   Neh.6.9
Terrors *f.* him on every side   Job 18.11
I was *f.* and fell upon my face   Dan.8.17
and as they were *f.* and bowed their   Lk.24.5
But they were startled and *f.*   Lk.24.37
near to the boat. They were *f.*   Jn.6.19
and not *f.* in anything by your   Phil.1.28

FROST
destroyed . . . their sycamores with *f.*   Ps.78.47
snow and *f.*, stormy wind fulfilling   Ps.148.8
heat by day and the *f.* by night   Jer.36.30
there shall be neither cold nor *f.*   Zech.14.6

FRUIT
f. trees bearing *f.* in which is   Gen.1.11
may eat of the *f.* of the trees of   Gen.3.2
The land will yield its *f.*   Lev.25.19
will give back the *f.* of his toil   Job 20.18
that yields its *f.* in its season   Ps.1.3
They still bring forth *f.* in old age   Ps.92.14
the *f.* of the womb a reward   Ps.127.3
all hills, *f.* trees and all cedars   Ps.148.9
My *f.* is better than gold, even fine   Pr.8.19
The *f.* of the righteous is a tree   Pr.11.30
shall eat the *f.* of their deeds   Is.3.10
and yield your *f.* to my people   Ezek.36.8
will bear fresh *f.* every month   Ezek.47.12
And I said, "A basket of summer *f.*"   Am.8.2
Bear *f.* that befits repentance   Mt.3.8
A sound tree cannot bear evil *f.*   Mt.7.18
again of this *f.* of the vine until   Mt.26.29
and gathers *f.* for eternal life   Jn.4.36
but if it dies, it bears much *f.*   Jn.12.24
Every branch of mine that bears no *f.*   Jn.15.2
that we may bear *f.* for God   Rom.7.4
But the *f.* of the Spirit is love   Gal.5.22
bearing *f.* in every good work   Col.1.10
twelve kinds of *f.*, yielding its *f.*   Rev.22.2

FRUITFUL
Be *f.* and multiply and fill the   Gen.1.22
I will make you exceedingly *f.*   Gen.17.6
God has made me *f.* in the land   Gen.41.52
like a *f.* vine within your house   Ps.128.3
and they shall increase and be *f.*   Ezek.36.11
that means *f.* labor for me   Phil.1.22

FULFIL
I will *f.* the number of your days   Ex.23.26
spoken, and will he not *f.* it?   Num.23.19
May the LORD *f.* all your petitions   Ps.20.5
and I will *f.* to you my promise   Jer.29.10
Behold, I will *f.* my words against   Jer.39.16
for us to *f.* all righteousness   Mt.3.15
not to abolish them but to *f.* them   Mt.5.17
loves his neighbor has *f.* the law   Rom.13.8
and so *f.* the law of Christ   Gal.6.2
See that you *f.* the ministry which   Col.4.17
may *f.* every good resolve   2 Th.1.11
of an evangelist, *f.* your ministry   2 Tim.4.5
If you really *f.* the royal law   Jas.2.8
the scripture was *f.* which says   Jas.2.23
until the words of God shall be *f.*   Rev.17.17

FULL
f. of the blessing of the LORD   Dt.33.23
Joshua . . . was *f.* of the spirit of   Dt.34.9
For I am *f.* of words, the spirit   Job 32.18
voice of the LORD is *f.* of majesty   Ps.29.4
the river of God is *f.* of water   Ps.65.9
For my soul is *f.* of troubles   Ps.88.3
the earth is *f.* of thy creatures   Ps.104.24
lest I be *f.*, and deny thee   Pr.30.9
your hands are *f.* of blood   Is.1.15
the whole earth is *f.* of his glory   Is.6.3
earth shall be *f.* of the knowledge   Is.11.9
I will not make a *f.* end of you   Jer.5.18
city shall be *f.* of boys and girls   Zech.8.5
Bring the *f.* tithes into the storehouse   Mal.3.10
whole body will be *f.* of light   Mt.6.22
then the *f.* grain in the ear   Mk.4.28
And Jesus, *f.* of the Holy Spirit   Lk.4.1
Woe to you that are *f.* now   Lk.6.25
the Word . . . *f.* of grace and truth   Jn.1.14
and that your joy may be *f.*   Jn.15.11
And Stephen, *f.* of grace and power   Acts 6.8
She was *f.* of good works and acts   Acts 9.36
until the *f.* number of the Gentiles   Rom.11.25
realizing the *f.* assurance of hope   Heb.6.11
f. of mercy and good fruits   Jas.3.17
They have eyes *f.* of adultery   2 Pet.2.14
with golden bowls *f.* of incense   Rev.5.8
golden bowls *f.* of the wrath of God   Rev.15.7

FULNESS
best gifts of the earth and its *f.*   Dt.33.16
in thy presence there is *f.* of joy   Ps.16.11
is the LORD's and the *f.* thereof   Ps.24.1
And from his *f.* have we all received   Jn.1.16
in the *f.* of the blessing of Christ   Rom.15.29
a plan for the *f.* of time, to unite   Eph.1.10
the *f.* of him who fills all in all   Eph.1.23
the stature of the *f.* of Christ   Eph.4.13
For in him all the *f.* of God was   Col.1.19
in him the whole *f.* of deity dwells   Col.2.9

FURNACE
went up like the smoke of a *f.*   Gen.19.28
smoke, and my bones burn like a *f.*   Ps.102.3
us from the burning fiery *f.*   Dan.3.17
throw them into the *f.* of fire   Mt.13.42
smoke like the smoke of a great *f.*   Rev.9.2

FURY
I will walk contrary to you in *f.*   Lev.26.28
he will . . . terrify them in his *f.*   Ps.2.5
to render his anger in *f.*   Is.66.15
So will I satisfy my *f.* on you   Ezek.16.42
Thou didst bestride the earth in *f.*   Hab.3.12
But they were filled with *f.* and   Lk.6.11
there will be wrath and *f.*   Rom.2.8
a *f.* of fire which will consume   Heb.10.27
the cup of the *f.* of his wrath   Rev.16.19
the *f.* of the wrath of God   Rev.19.15

FUTILE
they became *f.* in their thinking   Rom.1.21
the thoughts of the wise are *f.*   1 Cor.3.20
your faith is *f.* and you are   1 Cor.15.17
for they are unprofitable and *f.*   Tit.3.9
from the *f.* ways inherited from   1 Pet.1.18

FUTURE
Surely there is a *f.*, and your hope   Pr.23.18
for the evil man has no *f.*   Pr.24.20

There is hope for your *f*.   Jer.31.17
present or the *f*., all are yours   1 Cor.3.22
a good foundation for the *f*.   1 Tim.6.19

GABRIEL
Dan.8.16; 9.21; Lk.1.19,26

GAIN (noun)
every one is greedy for unjust *g*.   Jer.6.13
the dishonest *g*. which you have   Ezek.22.13
to live is Christ, and to die is *g*.   Phil.1.21
But whatever *g*. I had, I counted as   Phil.3.7
There is great *g*. in godliness   1 Tim.6.6
by teaching for base *g*. what they   Tit.1.11
we will . . . trade and get *g*.   Jas.4.13

GAIN (verb)
to *g*. the whole world and forfeit   Mk.8.36
Whoever seeks to *g*. his life will   Lk.17.33
What do I *g*. if, humanly speaking   1 Cor.15.32
in order that I may *g*. Christ   Phil.3.8
merchants . . . who *g*. wealth from her   Rev.18.15

GALATIA
Acts 16.6; 1 Cor.16.1; 2 Tim.4.10; 1 Pet.1.1

GALILEE
Is.9.1; Mt.3.13; Mk.1.9; Lk.3.1; Jn.1.43; 21.2

GAMALIEL
(1) Num.1.10; 10.23; (2) Acts 5.34; 22.3

GARDEN
the LORD God planted a *g*. in Eden   Gen.2.8
Let my beloved come to his *g*.   S.of S.4.16
her desert like the *g*. of the LORD   Is.51.3
you shall be like a watered *g*.   Is.58.11
as a *g*. causes what is sown in it   Is.61.11
has become like the *g*. of Eden   Ezek.36.35
where he was crucified . . . was a *g*.   Jn.19.41
in the *g*. a new tomb where no one   Jn.19.41

GARMENT
the LORD God made . . . *g*. of skins   Gen.3.21
coverest . . . with light as with a *g*.   Ps.104.2
the earth will wear out like a *g*.   Is.51.6
clothed me with the *g*. of salvation   Is.61.10
rend your hearts and not your *g*.   Jl.2.13
Remove the filthy *g*. from him   Zech.3.4
Now John wore a *g*. of camel's hair   Mt.3.4
to herself, "If I only touch his *g*.   Mt.9.21
saw a man who had no wedding *g*.   Mt.22.11
of unshrunk cloth on an old *g*.   Mk.2.21
throwing their *g*. on the colt they   Lk.19.35
They parted my *g*. among them   Jn.19.24
they will all grow old like a *g*.   Heb.1.11
hating even the *g*. spotted by the   Jude 23

GATE
and this is the *g*. of heaven   Gen.28.17
Enter his *g*. with thanksgiving   Ps.100.4
This is the *g*. of the LORD   Ps.118.20
and turn aside the needy in the *g*.   Am.5.12
Enter by the narrow *g*.   Mt.7.13
at the Beautiful *G*. of the temple   Acts 3.10
Peter was standing at the *g*.   Acts 12.14
outside the *g*. in order to sanctify   Heb.13.12
and its *g*. shall never be shut   Rev.21.25

GATHER
I will *g*. you to your fathers   2 Kg.22.20
and *g*. us from among the nations   Ps.106.47
and a time to *g*. stones together   Ec.3.5
and *g*. his wheat into the granary   Mt.3.12
neither sow nor . . . *g*. into barns   Mt.6.26

G. the weeds first and bind them   Mt.13.30
two or three are *g*. in my name   Mt.18.20
often would I have *g*. your children   Mt.23.37
he who does not *g*. with me scatters   Lk.11.23
as a hen *g*. her brood under her   Lk.13.34
G. up the fragments left over, that   Jn.6.12

GENEALOGY
of Noah, according to their *g*.   Gen.10.32
not enrolled in the *g*. according to   1 Chr.5.1
So all Israel was enrolled by *g*.   1 Chr.9.1
this is the *g*. of those who went up   Ezra 8.1
the people to be enrolled by *g*.   Neh.7.5
The book of the *g*. of Jesus Christ   Mt.1.1

GENERATION
that you may tell the next *g*.   Ps.48.13
be recorded for a *g*. to come   Ps.102.18
One *g*. shall laud thy works to   Ps.145.4
A *g*. goes, and a *g*. comes, but the   Ec.1.4
to what shall I compare this *g*.?   Mt.11.16
adulterous *g*. seeks for a sign   Mt.16.4
this *g*. will not pass away till all   Mt.24.34
O faithless *g*., how long am I to   Mk.9.19
henceforth all *g*. will call me blessed   Lk.1.48
from early *g*. Moses has had in   Acts 15.21
glory . . . in Christ Jesus to all *g*.   Eph.3.21
the mystery hidden for ages and *g*.   Col.1.26

GENEROUS
the righteous is *g*. and gives   Ps.37.21
Many seek the favor of a *g*. man   Pr.19.6
partook of food with glad and *g*. hearts   Acts 2.46
in good deeds, liberal and *g*.   1 Tim.6.18

GENTILE
in his name will the *G*. hope   Mt.12.21
be . . . as a *G*. and a tax collector   Mt.18.17
a light for revelation to the *G*.   Lk.2.32
the times of the *G*. are fulfilled   Lk.21.24
Why did the *G*. rage, and the   Acts 4.25
set you to be a light for the *G*.   Acts 13.47
how God first visited the *G*.   Acts 15.14
From now on I will go to the *G*.   Acts 18.6
Is he not the God of *G*. also?   Rom.3.29
the full number of the *G*. come in   Rom.11.25
if the *G*. have come to share in   Rom.15.27
I might preach him among the *G*.   Gal.1.16
you compel the *G*. to live like Jews   Gal.2.14
how the *G*. are fellow heirs, members   Eph.3.6
preach to the *G*. the unsearchable   Eph.3.8

GENTLE
A *g*. tongue is a tree of life, but   Pr.15.4
I was like a *g*. lamb led to the   Jer.11.19
for I am *g*. and lowly in heart   Mt.11.29
be *g*., and . . . show perfect courtesy   Tit.3.2
g., open to reason, full of mercy   Jas.3.17

GENTLENESS
by the meekness and *g*. of Christ   2 Cor.10.1
g., self-control; against such   Gal.5.23
restore him in a spirit of *g*.   Gal.6.1
correcting his opponents with *g*.   2 Tim.2.25

GETHSEMANE
Mt.26.36; Mk.14.32

GIANTS
one of the descendants of the *g*.   2 Sam.21.16
were descended from the *g*. in Gath   1 Chr.20.8

GIBEAH
(1) a city of Judah, Jos.15.57; (2) a city of
Benjamin, Jg.19.14; sin of its inhabitants,

Jg.19.22; their punishment, Jg.20; the city of Saul, 1 Sam.10.26; 11.4; 14.2; 15.34; 2 Sam. 21.6

GIBEON situated about five miles north of Jerusalem Jos.9.3; its inhabitants deceive Joshua, Jos.9; delivered by him from the five kings, Jos.10; Saul persecutes them, 2 Sam.21.1; David makes atonement, 2 Sam.21.3–9; Solomon's dream at, 1 Kg.3.5; site of the tabernacle under David and Solomon, 1 Chr.16.39; 21.29; 2 Chr.1.3–6

GIDEON God appoints him to deliver Israel from the Midianites, Jg.6.11,14; destroys the altar and grove of Baal, Jg.6.25–27; called Jerubbaal, Jg.6.32; God gives him two signs, Jg.6.36–40; his army reduced, and selected by a test of water, Jg.7.2–7; his stratagem, Jg.7.16; subdues the Midianites, Jg.7.19–8.28; makes an ephod of the spoil, Jg.8.24–27; his death, Jg.8.32

GIFT
he shall offer his *g*. to the LORD	Num.6.14
A *g*. in secret averts anger	Pr.21.14
it is God's *g*. in man that every	Ec.3.13
to give good *g*. to your children	Lk.11.13
her, "If you knew the *g*. of God	Jn.4.10
receive the *g*. of the Holy Spirit	Acts 2.38
the free *g*. is not like the trespass	Rom.5.15
the free *g*. of God is eternal life	Rom.6.23
Having *g*. that differ according to	Rom.12.6
Now concerning spiritual *g*.	1 Cor.12.1
to God for his inexpressible *g*.	2 Cor.9.15
to the measure of Christ's *g*.	Eph.4.7
Do not neglect the *g*. you have	1 Tim.4.14
who have tasted the heavenly *g*.	Heb.6.4
every perfect *g*. is from above	Jas.1.17
As each has received a *g*.	1 Pet.4.10

GIRD
G. up your loins like a man	Job 40.7
the God who *g*. me with strength	Ps.18.32
the mountains, being *g*. with might	Ps.65.6
G. yourselves with sackcloth	Jer.49.3
Let your loins be *g*. and your	Lk.12.35
the towel with which he was *g*.	Jn.13.5
having *g*. your loins with truth	Eph.6.14
g. up your minds, be sober	1 Pet.1.13

GIRL
and have sold a *g*. for wine	Jl.3.3
boys and *g*. playing in its streets	Zech.8.5
her by the hand, and the *g*. arose	Mt.9.25
Little *g*., I say to you, arise	Mk.5.41
a slave *g*. . . . who had a spirit	Acts 16.16

GLAD
Let the heavens be *g*., and let	1 Chr.16.31
The righteous see it and are *g*.	Job 22.19
dost make him *g*. with the joy of	Ps.21.6
Be *g*. in the LORD, and rejoice	Ps.32.11
let the afflicted hear and be *g*.	Ps.34.2
streams make *g*. the city of God	Ps.46.4
Let the nations be *g*. and sing for	Ps.67.4
Make us *g*. as many days as thou	Ps.90.15
I was *g*. when they said to me, "Let	Ps.122.1
A wise son makes a *g*. father	Pr.10.1
by sadness . . . the heart is made *g*.	Ec.7.3
let us be *g*. and rejoice in his	Is.25.9

Rejoice and be *g*., O daughter of	Lam.4.21
Rejoice and be *g*., for your reward	Mt.5.12
see my day; he saw it and was *g*.	Jn.8.56
disciples were *g*. when they saw	Jn.20.20
I am *g*. and rejoice with you all	Phil.2.17

GLADNESS
anointed you with the oil of *g*.	Ps.45.7
Serve the LORD with *g*.! Come into	Ps.100.2
they shall obtain joy and *g*.	Is.51.11
And you will have joy and *g*.	Lk.1.14

GLEAN
you shall not *g*. it afterward	Dt.24.21
When she rose to *g*., Boaz instructed	Ru.2.15
as when one *g*. the ears of grain	Is.17.5
G. thoroughly as a vine	Jer.6.9
as when the vintage has been *g*.	Mic.7.1

GLOOM
Some sat in darkness and in *g*.	Ps.107.10
and your *g*. be as the noonday	Is.58.10
turns it into *g*. and makes it deep	Jer.13.16
a day of darkness and *g*.	Jl.2.2
darkness, and *g*., and a tempest	Heb.12.18
for them the nether *g*. of darkness	2 Pet.2.17

GLORIFY
I will *g*. thy name for ever	Ps.86.12
they *g*. God, who had given such	Mt.9.8
he taught . . . being *g*. by all	Lk.4.15
they *g*. God, saying, "A great	Lk.7.16
for the Son of man to be *g*.	Jn.12.23
the Father may be *g*. in the Son	Jn.14.13
I *g*. thee . . . having accomplished	Jn.17.4
thine are mine, and I am *g*. in them	Jn.17.10
they *g*. God, saying, "Then to	Acts 11.18
So *g*. God in your body	1 Cor.6.20
you will *g*. God by your obedience	2 Cor.9.13
Who shall not fear and *g*. thy name	Rev.15.4

GLORIOUS
terrible in *g*. deeds, doing wonders	Ex.15.11
Blessed be his *g*. name for ever	Ps.72.19
G. things are spoken of you, O city	Ps.87.3
the *g*. splendor of thy kingdom	Ps.145.12
the branch of the LORD shall be . . . *g*.	Is.4.2
to make for thyself a *g*. name	Is.63.14
A *g*. throne set on high	Jer.17.12
will . . . obtain the *g*. liberty of the	Rom.8.21
the riches of his *g*. inheritance	Eph.1.18
lowly body to be like his *g*. body	Phil.3.21
the *g*. gospel of the blessed God	1 Tim.1.11

GLORY (noun)
The *g*. of the LORD settled on Mount	Ex.24.16
I pray thee, show me thy *g*.	Ex.33.18
Then the *g*. of the LORD appeared	Num.14.10
The *g*. has departed from Israel	1 Sam.4.21
Declare his *g*. among the nations	1 Chr.16.24
Thou whose *g*. above the heavens is	Ps.8.1
Who is the King of *g*.? The LORD	Ps.24.8
Ascribe to the LORD the *g*. of his	Ps.29.2
May the *g*. of the LORD endure for	Ps.104.31
not to us, but to thy name give *g*.	Ps.115.1
A hoary head is a crown of *g*.	Pr.16.31
It is the *g*. of God to conceal	Pr.25.2
They shall see the *g*. of the LORD	Is.35.2
My *g*. I will not give to another	Is.48.11
lo, the *g*. of the LORD stood	Ezek.3.23
Ephraim's *g*. shall fly away like a	Hos.9.11
knowledge of the *g*. of the LORD	Hab.2.14

When the Son of man comes in his *g.* Mt.25.31
G. to God in the highest, and on Lk.2.14
Yet I do not seek my own *g.* Jn.8.50
you would see the *g.* of God Jn.11.40
The *g.* which thou hast given me Jn.17.22
and fall short of the *g.* of God Rom.3.23
not have crucified the Lord of *g.* 1 Cor.2.8
he is the image and *g.* of God 1 Cor.11.7
the Father of *g.*, may give you a Eph.1.17
To our God . . . be *g.* for ever Phil.4.20
Christ in you, the hope of *g.* Col.1.27
For you are our *g.* and joy 1 Th.2.20
the *g.* of our great God and Savior Tit.2.13
He reflects the *g.* of God and bears Heb.1.3
To him belong *g.* and dominion for 1 Pet.4.11
Blessing and *g.* and wisdom and Rev.7.12
Fear God and give him *g.* Rev.14.7
for the *g.* of God is its light Rev.21.23

GLUTTON
he is a *g.* and a drunkard Dt.21.20
the *g.* will come to poverty Pr.23.21
Behold, a *g.* and a drunkard Mt.11.19
always liars, evil beasts, lazy *g.* Tit.1.12

GOAT
but the *g.* on which the lot fell Lev.16.10
he who lets the *g.* go to Azazel Lev.16.26
separates the sheep from the *g.* Mt.25.32
the blood of *g.* and bulls and with Heb.9.13
went about in skins of . . . *g.* Heb.11.37

GOD
In the beginning *G.* created the Gen.1.1
So *G.* created man in his own image Gen.1.27
the LORD *G.* planted a garden in Gen.2.8
But *G.* remembered Noah and all the Gen.8.1
G. said to Moses, "I AM WHO I AM." Ex.3.14
a *G.* merciful and gracious, slow to Ex.34.6
I am the LORD your *G.*, who brought Lev.25.38
is a devouring fire, a jealous *G.* Dt.4.24
a people holy to the LORD your *G.* Dt.14.2
A *G.* of faithfulness and without Dt.32.4
O Lord *G.*, remember me, I pray thee Jg.16.28
the spirit of *G.* is in my nostrils Job 27.3
Behold, *G.* does all these things Job 33.29
By the breath of *G.* ice is given Job 37.10
Answer me . . . O *G.* of my right Ps.4.1
G. is a righteous judge, and a Ps.7.11
My *G.*, my *G.*, why hast thou forsaken Ps.22.1
G. is our refuge and strength Ps.46.1
Behold, *G.* is my helper; the Lord is Ps.54.4
Our *G.* is a *G.* of salvation Ps.68.20
but *G.* is the strength of my heart Ps.73.26
When *G.* heard, he was full of wrath Ps.78.59
For the LORD *G.* is a sun and shield Ps.84.11
It is the glory of *G.* to conceal Pr.25.2
G. will judge the righteous and the Ec.3.17
for the LORD *G.* is my strength Is.12.2
The Spirit of the Lord *G.* is upon me Is.61.1
I will be their *G.*, and they shall Jer.31.33
for I am *G.* and not man, the Holy Hos.11.9
thou art a gracious *G.* and merciful Jon.4.2
and to walk humbly with your *G.*? Mic.6.8
LORD is a jealous *G.* and avenging Nah.1.2
Emmanuel'' (which means, *G.* with us) Mt.1.23
You cannot serve *G.* and mammon Mt.6.24
No one is good but *G.* alone Lk.18.19
Word was with *G.*, and the Word was *G.* Jn.1.1

For *G.* so loved the world that he Jn.3.16
G. is spirit, and those who worship Jn.4.24
I proceeded and came forth from *G.* Jn.8.42
answered him, "My Lord and my *G.* Jn.20.28
For *G.* shows no partiality Rom.2.11
Is he not the *G.* of Gentiles also? Rom.3.29
But *G.* shows his love for us in Rom.5.8
the free gift of *G.* is eternal life Rom.6.23
in everything *G.* works for good Rom.8.28
G. is faithful, by whom you were 1 Cor.1.9
G. is faithful, and he will not 1 Cor.10.13
G. was in Christ reconciling 2 Cor.5.19
G. is not mocked, for whatever a man Gal.6.7
one *G.* and Father of us all, who is Eph.4.6
He is the image of the invisible *G.* Col.1.15
For there is one *G.*, and there 1 Tim.2.5
of our great *G.* and Savior Jesus Tit.2.13
for our *G.* is a consuming fire Heb.12.29
for *G.* cannot be tempted with evil Jas.1.13
G. opposes the proud, but gives Jas.4.6
G. is light and in him is no darkness 1 Jn.1.5
G. is love, and he who abides in 1 Jn.4.16
the Lord *G.* Almighty, who was and is Rev.4.8
and *G.* will wipe away every tear Rev.7.17

GODLINESS
great gain in *g.* with contentment 1 Tim.6.6
the truth which accords with *g.* Tit.1.1
and *g.* with brotherly affection 2 Pet.1.7

GODLY
has set apart the *g.* for himself Ps.4.3
Preserve my life, for I am *g.* Ps.86.2
g. grief produces a repentance 2 Cor.7.10
to live a *g.* life in Christ Jesus 2 Tim.3.12
how to rescue the *g.* from trial 2 Pet.2.9

GOG
1 Chr.5.4; Ezek.38.2; 39.1; Rev.20.8

GOLD
More to be desired are they than *g.* Ps.19.10
and its profit better than *g.* Pr.3.14
To get wisdom is better than *g.* Pr.16.16
like apples of *g.* in a setting of Pr.25.11
g. like the dirt of the streets Zech.9.3
think that the Deity is like *g.* Acts 17.29
builds on the foundation with *g.* 1 Cor.3.12
the street of the city was pure *g.* Rev.21.21

GOLGOTHA
Mt.27.33; Mk.15.22; Jn.19.17

GOLIATH
1 Sam.17.4; 21.9; 2 Sam.21.19; 1 Chr.20.5

GOOD (adjective)
And God saw that the light was *g.* Gen.1.4
It is not *g.* that the man should Gen.2.18
but God meant it for *g.* Gen.50.20
God is bringing you into a *g.* land Dt.8.7
Be strong and of *g.* courage Dt.31.23
the *g.* hand of my God was upon me Neh.2.8
G. and upright is the LORD Ps.25.8
who seek the LORD lack no *g.* thing Ps.34.10
Truly God is *g.* to the upright Ps.73.1
The LORD is *g.* to all, and his Ps.145.9
A cheerful heart is a *g.* medicine Pr.17.22
A *g.* name is to be chosen rather Pr.22.1
A *g.* wife who can find? She is Pr.31.10
He has showed you, O man, what is *g.* Mic.6.8
how to give *g.* gifts to your Mt.7.11
Why do you ask me about what is *g.*? Mt.19.17

No one is *g*. but God alone	Mk.10.18	May God be *g*. to us and bless us	Ps.67.1
Mary has chosen the *g*. portion	Lk.10.42	*G*. is the LORD, and righteous	Ps.116.5
I am the *g*. shepherd	Jn.10.11	A *g*. woman gets honor	Pr.11.16
She was full of *g*. works and acts	Acts 9.36	for he is *g*. and merciful, slow to	Jl.2.13
a *g*. man, full of the Holy Spirit	Acts 11.24	Father, for such was thy *g*. will	Mt.11.26
Bad company ruins *g*. morals	1 Cor.15.33	Let your speech always be *g*.	Col.4.6
everything created by God is *g*.	1 Tim.4.4	GRAIN	
Fight the *g*. fight of the faith	1 Tim.6.12	seven ears of *g*., plump and good	Gen.41.5
I have fought the *g*. fight, I have	2 Tim.4.7	a cereal offering of new *g*. to	Num.28.26
Every *g*. endowment . . . is from above	Jas.1.17	thou providest their *g*., for so thou	Ps.65.9
Maintain *g*. conduct among the	1 Pet.2.12	valleys deck themselves with *g*.	Ps.65.13
GOOD (noun)		and gave them the *g*. of heaven	Ps.78.24
we receive *g*. at the hand of God	Job 2.10	it was I who gave her the *g*.	Hos.2.8
I have no *g*. apart from thee	Ps.16.2	threshing floors shall be full of *g*.	Jl.2.24
one sinner destroys much *g*.	Ec.9.18	on good soil and brought forth *g*.	Mt.13.8
God works for *g*. with those who	Rom.8.28	is like a *g*. of mustard seed which	Mt.13.31
let us do *g*. to all men . . . especially	Gal.6.10	have faith as a *g*. of mustard seed	Mt.17.20
has the world's *g*. and sees his	1 Jn.3.17	unless a *g*. of wheat falls into the	Jn.12.24
He who does *g*. is of God	3 Jn.11	GRANT	
GOODNESS		may God Almighty *g*. you mercy	Gen.43.14
make all my *g*. pass before you	Ex.33.19	may the LORD *g*. you discretion	1 Chr.22.12
Surely *g*. and mercy shall follow me	Ps.23.6	O *g*. us help against the foe	Ps.60.11
O how abundant is thy *g*., which	Ps.31.19	*G*. us to sit, one at your right	Mk.10.37
thy *g*., O God, thou didst provide	Ps.68.10	May the Lord *g*. mercy to the	2 Tim.1.16
be radiant over the *g*. of the LORD	Jer.31.12	I will *g*. him to sit with me on my	Rev.3.21
but when the *g*. and loving kindness	Tit.3.4	GRAPE	
tasted the *g*. of the word of God	Heb.6.5	you may eat your fill of *g*.	Dt.23.24
GOSPEL		When I looked for it to yield *g*.	Is.5.4
preaching the *g*. of the kingdom	Mt.4.23	The fathers have eaten sour *g*.	Jer.31.29
beginning of the *g*. of Jesus Christ	Mk.1.1	you shall tread *g*., but not drink	Mic.6.15
they departed . . . preaching the *g*.	Lk.9.6	Are *g*. gathered from thorns, or figs	Mt.7.16
For I am not ashamed of the *g*.	Rom.1.16	GRASS	
my ambition to preach the *g*.	Rom.15.20	For they will soon fade like the *g*.	Ps.37.2
woe . . . if I do not preach the *g*.	1 Cor.9.16	like *g*. which is renewed in the	Ps.90.5
want to pervert the *g*. of Christ	Gal.1.7	As for man, his days are like *g*.	Ps.103.15
to proclaim the mystery of the *g*.	Eph.6.19	All flesh is *g*., and all its beauty	Is.40.6
by God to be entrusted with the *g*.	1 Th.2.4	Nebuchadnezzar . . . ate *g*. like an ox	Dan.4.33
during my imprisonment for the *g*.	Philem.13	like showers upon the *g*.	Mic.5.7
with an eternal *g*. to proclaim to	Rev.14.6	God so clothes the *g*. of the field	Mt.6.30
GOSSIP (noun)		Now there was much *g*. in the place	Jn.6.10
the talk and evil *g*. of the people	Ezek.36.3	the flower of *g*. The *g*. withers	1 Pet.1.24
deceit, malignity, they are *g*.	Rom.1.29	GRAVE (noun)	
g., conceit, and disorder	2 Cor.12.20	man was cast into the *g*. of Elisha	2 Kg.13.21
not only idlers but *g*.	1 Tim.5.13	come to your *g*. in ripe old age	Job 5.26
GRACE		straight to the *g*. they descend	Ps.49.14
g. is poured upon your lips	Ps.45.2	jealousy is cruel as the *g*.	S.of S.8.6
g. and truth came through Jesus	Jn.1.17	you are like *g*. which are not seen	Lk.11.44
When he came and saw the *g*. of God	Acts 11.23	Their throat is an open *g*.	Rom.3.13
to the gospel of the *g*. of God	Acts 20.24	GRAVEN	
g. abounded all the more	Rom.5.20	not make for yourself a *g*. image	Ex.20.4
there is a remnant, chosen by *g*.	Rom.11.5	set up Micah's *g*. image which he	Jg.18.31
G. to you and peace from God our	2 Cor.1.2	he makes it a *g*. image and falls	Is.44.15
For you know the *g*. of our Lord	2 Cor.8.9	GREECE	
My *g*. is sufficient for you	2 Cor.12.9	Dan.11.2; Zech.9.13; Acts 20.2	
you have fallen away from *g*.	Gal.5.4	GREED	
For by *g*. you have been saved	Eph.2.8	His *g*. is as wide as Sheol	Hab.2.5
G., mercy, and peace from God	1 Tim.1.2	he is guilty of immorality or *g*.	1 Cor.5.11
strong in the *g*. that is in Christ	2 Tim.2.1	as you know, or a cloak for *g*.	1 Th.2.5
draw near to the throne of *g*.	Heb.4.16	They have hearts trained in *g*.	2 Pet.2.14
be strengthened by *g*., not by foods	Heb.13.9	GREEK	
But grow in the *g*. and knowledge	2 Pet.3.18	Now the woman was a *G*.	Mk.7.26
who pervert the *g*. of our God into	Jude 4	in Hebrew, in Latin, and in *G*.	Jn.19.20
The *g*. of the Lord Jesus be with	Rev.22.21	Timothy . . . his father was a *G*.	Acts 16.1
GRACIOUS		of the devout *G*. and not a few of	Acts 17.4
g. and merciful, slow to anger and	Neh.9.17	to the Jew first and also to the *G*.	Rom.1.16
Be *g*. to me . . . for I am languishing	Ps.6.2	There is neither Jew nor *G*.	Gal.3.28

GREEN

have given every *g.* plant for food	Gen.1.30
he makes me lie down in *g.* pastures	Ps.23.2
I the LORD . . . dry up the *g.* tree	Ezek.17.24
they do this when the wood is *g.*	Lk.23.31

GRIEF

My eye has grown dim from *g.*	Job 17.7
A stupid son is a *g.* to a father	Pr.17.21
man of sorrows . . . acquainted with *g.*	Is.53.3
has borne our *g.* and carried our	Is.53.4
godly *g.* produces a repentance	2 Cor.7.10
but worldly *g.* produces death	2 Cor.7.10

GRIEVE

Was not my soul *g.* for the poor?	Job 30.25
rebelled and *g.* his holy Spirit	Is.63.10
not willingly . . . *g.* the sons of men	Lam.3.33
g. at their hardness of heart	Mk.3.5
Peter was *g.* because he said to	Jn.21.17
because you were *g.* into repenting	2 Cor.7.9
do not *g.* the Holy Spirit of God	Eph.4.30

GROAN

despoiled, because the needy *g.*	Ps.12.5
the wicked rule, the people *g.*	Pr.29.2
gates are desolate, her priests *g.*	Lam.1.4
has been *g.* in travail together	Rom.8.22
Here indeed we *g.*, and long to put	2 Cor.5.2

GROW

God made to *g.* every tree that is	Gen.2.9
he makes grass *g.* upon the hills	Ps.147.8
He does not faint or *g.* weary	Is.40.28
Consider the lilies, how they *g.*	Lk.12.27
let us not *g.* weary in well-doing	Gal.6.9
may not *g.* weary or fainthearted	Heb.12.3
But *g.* in the grace and knowledge	2 Pet.3.18

GUARD (verb)

to *g.* the way to the tree of life	Gen.3.24
will *g.* the feet of his faithful	1 Sam.2.9
G. them and keep them until you	Ezra 8.29
Oh *g.* my life, and deliver me	Ps.25.20
G. me, O LORD, from the hands of	Ps.140.4
understanding will *g.* you	Pr.2.11
G. your steps when you go to the	Ec.5.1
angels charge of you, to *g.* you	Lk.4.10
I have *g.* them, and none of them is	Jn.17.12
strengthen you and *g.* you from evil	2 Th.3.3
g. what has been entrusted	1 Tim.6.20
g. the truth . . . entrusted to you	2 Tim.1.14

GUARDIAN

the *g.* cherub drove you out	Ezek.28.16
the Holy Spirit has made you *g.*	Acts 20.28
but he is under *g.* and trustees	Gal.4.2
the Shepherd and *G.* of your souls	1 Pet.2.25

GUIDE (verb)

or can you *g.* the Bear with its	Job 38.32
thy name's sake lead me and *g.* me	Ps.31.3
thou dost . . . *g.* the nations upon earth	Ps.67.4
and *g.* them with skilful hand	Ps.78.72
the LORD will *g.* you continually	Is.58.11
to *g.* our feet into the way of peace	Lk.1.79
he will *g.* you into all the truth	Jn.16.13
he will *g.* them to springs of	Rev.7.17

GUILE

said, "Your brother came with *g.*	Gen.27.35
Israelite indeed, in whom is no *g.*	Jn.1.47
keep . . . his lips from speaking *g.*	1 Pet.3.10

GUILT

less than your *g.* deserves	Job 11.6
Make them bear their *g.*, O God	Ps.5.10
pardon my *g.*, for it is great	Ps.25.11
didst forgive the *g.* of my sin	Ps.32.5
your *g.* is taken away, and your sin	Is.6.7
inhabitants suffer for their *g.*	Is.24.6
Because your *g.* is great	Jer.30.15
is full of *g.* against the Holy One	Jer.51.5
were blind, you would have no *g.*	Jn.9.41

GUILTY

who will by no means clear the *g.*	Ex.34.7
although thou knowest that I am not *g.*	Job 10.7
of him who walks in his *g.* ways	Ps.68.21
The way of the *g.* is crooked	Pr.21.8
who will declare me *g.*? Behold, all	Is.50.9
LORD will by no means clear the *g.*	Nah.1.3
but is *g.* of an eternal sin	Mk.3.29
I did not find this man *g.* of any	Lk.23.14
commits sin is *g.* of lawlessness	1 Jn.3.4

HABITATION

Look down from thy holy *h.*	Dt.26.15
I love the *h.* of thy house, and the	Ps.26.8
made . . . the Most High your *h.*	Ps.91.9
O *h.* of righteousness, O holy hill	Jer.31.23
receive you into the eternal *h.*	Lk.16.9
Let his *h.* become desolate, and let	Acts 1.20
asked leave to find a *h.* for the	Acts 7.46

HAGAR

Gen.16.1; 21.9; 25.12; Gal.4.24

HAIL (noun)

I will cause very heavy *h.* to fall	Ex.9.18
He destroyed their vines with *h.*	Ps.78.47
like a storm of *h.*, a destroying	Is.28.2
with blight and mildew and *h.*	Hag.2.17
and there followed *h.* and fire	Rev.8.7
an earthquake, and heavy *h.*	Rev.11.19
cursed . . . for the plague of the *h.*	Rev.16.21

HAIR

Do not let the *h.* of your heads	Lev.10.6
the *h.* of his head began to grow	Jg.16.22
sling a stone at a *h.*, and not miss	Jg.20.16
the *h.* of my flesh stood up	Job 4.15
are more than the *h.* of my head	Ps.40.12
beauty of old men is their gray *h.*	Pr.20.29
Now John wore a garment of camel's *h.*	Mt.3.4
cannot make one *h.* white or black	Mt.5.36
the *h.* of your head are all numbered	Lk.12.7
not a *h.* of your head will perish	Lk.21.18
and wiped his feet with her *h.*	Jn.11.2
At Cenchreae he cut his *h.*	Acts 18.18
his head and his *h.* were white as	Rev.1.14

HALLOW

blessed the seventh day and *h.* it	Gen.2.3
And you shall *h.* the fiftieth year	Lev.25.10
which he had *h.* in Jerusalem	2 Chr.36.14
who art in heaven, *H.* be thy name	Mt.6.9

HAM

Gen.5.32; 14.5; Ps.78.51; 106.22

HAMAN

Est.3.1; 5.5; 6.11; 7.8,10; 9.14

HAND

Do not lay your *h.* on the lad or	Gen.22.12
h. for *h.*, foot for foot	Ex.21.24
he shall lay his *h.* upon the head	Lev.1.4

LORD has given Sisera into your *h*.	Jg.4.14
The *h*. of God was very heavy there	1 Sam.5.11
I have taken my life in my *h*.	1 Sam.28.21
His right *h*. and his holy arm have	Ps.98.1
I hold my life in my *h*.	Ps.119.109
LORD is your shade on your right *h*.	Ps.121.5
Whatever your *h*. finds to do, do it	Ec.9.10
for the kingdom of heaven is at *h*.	Mt.3.2
do not let your left *h*. know what	Mt.6.3
And if your *h*. or your foot causes	Mt.18.8
to my Lord, Sit at my right *h*.	Mt.22.44
The Teacher says, My time is at *h*.	Mt.26.18
has dipped his *h*. in the dish with	Mt.26.23
seated at the right *h*. of Power	Mt.26.64
standing at the right *h*. of God	Acts 7.55
And the *h*. of the Lord was with	Acts 11.21
gave . . . the right *h*. of fellowship	Gal.2.9
at his right *h*. in the heavenly	Eph.1.20
the coming of the Lord is at *h*.	Jas.5.8
under the mighty *h*. of God	1 Pet.5.6
But he laid his right *h*. upon me	Rev.1.17

HANG

Pharaoh will . . . *h*. you on a tree	Gen.40.19
for a *h*. man is accursed by God	Dt.21.23
So they *h*. Haman on the gallows	Est.7.10
and he went and *h*. himself	Mt.27.5
criminals who were *h*. railed at him	Lk.23.39
you killed by *h*. him on a tree	Acts 5.30

HANNAH

1 Sam.1.2,13; 2.1,21

HAPPY

Behold, *h*. is the man whom God	Job 5.17
H. the people whose God is the LORD	Ps.144.15
H. is the man who finds wisdom	Pr.3.13
h. are those who keep my ways	Pr.8.32
but *h*. is he who is kind to the poor	Pr.14.21
and *h*. is he who trusts in the LORD	Pr.16.20
h. is he who has no reason to judge	Rom.14.22
we call those *h*. who were steadfast	Jas.5.11

HARD

Is anything too *h*. for the LORD?	Gen.18.14
I weep for him whose day was *h*.?	Job 30.25
Disaster follows *h*. on disaster	Jer.4.20
Nothing is too *h*. for thee	Jer.32.17
gate is narrow and the way is *h*.	Mt.7.14
it will be *h*. for a rich man to	Mt.19.23
Master, I knew you to be a *h*. man	Mt.25.24
Many . . . said, "This is a *h*. saying	Jn.6.60
But by your *h*. and impenitent heart	Rom.2.5
I am *h*. pressed between the two	Phil.1.23
much to say which is *h*. to explain	Heb.5.11
things in them *h*. to understand	2 Pet.3.16

HARDEN

but I will *h*. his heart, so that he	Ex.4.21
you shall not *h*. your heart or shut	Dt.15.7
H. not your hearts, as at Meribah	Ps.95.8
err from thy ways and *h*. our heart	Is.63.17
he *h*. the heart of whomever he	Rom.9.18
But their minds were *h*.	2 Cor.3.14
do not *h*. your hearts as in the	Heb.3.8

HARDNESS

for your *h*. of heart Moses allowed	Mt.19.8
grieved at their *h*. of heart	Mk.3.5
due to their *h*. of heart	Eph.4.18

HARLOT

They shall not marry a *h*. or a woman	Lev.21.7

shall not bring the hire of a *h*.	Dt.23.18
only Rahab the *h*. and all who are	Jos.6.17
Israel . . . played the *h*. after the Baals	Jg.8.33
For a *h*. is a deep pit	Pr.23.27
How the faithful city has become a *h*.	Is.1.21
have left their God to play the *h*.	Hos.4.12
tax collectors and the *h*. go into the	Mt.21.31
has devoured your living with *h*.	Lk.15.30
was not . . . Rahab the *h*. justified by	Jas.2.25
the judgment of the great *h*. who	Rev.17.1

HARM (noun)

he feared that *h*. might befall him	Gen.42.4
If any *h*. follows, then you shall	Ex.21.23
for I will no more do you *h*.	1 Sam.26.21
will do us more *h*. than Absalom	2 Sam.20.6
on the sabbath to do good or to do *h*.	Mk.3.4
the demon . . . having done him no *h*.	Lk.4.35

HARMONY

Live in *h*. with one another	Rom.12.16
live in such *h*. with one another	Rom.15.5
everything together in perfect *h*.	Col.3.14

HARP

from the high place with *h*.	1 Sam.10.5
with the *h*. for thy faithfulness	Ps.71.22
a ten-stringed *h*. I will play to	Ps.144.9
praise him with lute and *h*.	Ps.150.3
h., bagpipe, and every kind of music	Dan.3.5
such as the flute or the *h*.	1 Cor.14.7
before the Lamb, each holding a *h*.	Rev.5.8

HARVEST (noun)

seedtime and *h*., cold and heat	Gen.8.22
You shall keep the feast of *h*.	Ex.23.16
fruits of your *h*. to the priest	Lev.23.10
gathers her sustenance in *h*.	Pr.6.8
son who sleeps in *h*. brings shame	Pr.10.5
Like . . . snow in the time of *h*. is	Pr.25.13
The *h*. is past, the summer is ended	Jer.8.20
Put in the sickle, for the *h*. is ripe	Jl.3.13
pray therefore the Lord of the *h*.	Mt.9.38
because the *h*. has come	Mk.4.29
The *h*. is plentiful, but the laborers	Lk.10.2
fields are already white for *h*.	Jn.4.35
the *h*. of your righteousness	2 Cor.9.10
the *h*. of righteousness is sown	Jas.3.18

HATE (verb)

You shall not *h*. your brother in	Lev.19.17
those who *h*. the righteous will	Ps.34.21
The LORD loves those who *h*. evil	Ps.97.10
therefore I *h*. every false way	Ps.119.104
Do I not *h*. them that *h*. thee	Ps.139.21
How long will . . . fools *h*. knowledge?	Pr.1.22
a time to love, and a time to *h*.	Ec.3.8
I *h*. robbery and wrong	Is.61.8
H. evil, and love good	Am.5.15
you who *h*. the good and love the	Mic.3.2
these things I *h*., says the LORD	Zech.8.17
For I *h*. divorce, says the LORD	Mal.2.16
love your neighbor and *h*. your enemy	Mt.5.43
either he will *h*. the one and love	Mt.6.24
Blessed are you when men *h*. you	Lk.6.22
do good to those who *h*. you	Lk.6.27
you will be *h*. by all for my name's	Lk.21.17
The world cannot *h*. you, but it	Jn.7.7
h. what is evil, hold fast to what	Rom.12.9

HAUGHTY

upon the *h*. to bring them down	2 Sam.22.28

HAZAEL

and a *h.* spirit before a fall	Pr.16.18
the eyes of the *h.* are humbled	Is.5.15
They were *h.*, and did abominable	Ezek.16.50
h., boastful, inventors of evil	Rom.1.30
do not be *h.*, but associate with	Rom.12.16
charge them not to be *h.*	1 Tim.6.17

HAZAEL

king of Syria, 1 Kg.19.15; Elisha's prediction, 2 Kg.8.7–10; slays Ben-hadad, 2 Kg.8.15; oppresses Israel, 2 Kg.9.14; 10.32; 12.17; 13.22

HEAD

he shall bruise your *h.*, and you	Gen.3.15
his blood shall be upon his *h.*	Jos.2.19
Sisera a blow, she crushed his *h.*	Jg.5.26
them over to me, I will be your *h.*	Jg.11.9
No razor shall come upon his *h.*	Jg.13.5
of oil and poured it on his *h.*	1 Sam.10.1
took the *h.* of the Philistine	1 Sam.17.54
to his father, "Oh, my *h.*, my *h.*!"	2 Kg.4.19
his axe *h.* fell into the water	2 Kg.6.5
Behold, God is with us at our *h.*	2 Chr.13.12
his foot to the crown of his *h.*	Job 2.7
thou anointest my *h.* with oil	Ps.23.5
A hoary *h.* is a crown of glory	Pr.16.31
will heap coals of fire on his *h.*	Pr.25.22
And do not swear by your *h.*	Mt.5.36
Son of man has nowhere to lay his *h.*	Mt.8.20
Give me the *h.* of John the Baptist	Mt.14.8
has become the *h.* of the corner	Mt.21.42
a crown of thorns . . . on his *h.*	Mt.27.29
not a hair of your *h.* will perish	Lk.21.18
he bowed his *h.* and gave up his	Jn.19.30
heap burning coals upon his *h.*	Rom.12.20
the *h.* of every man is Christ	1 Cor.11.3
and the *h.* of Christ is God	1 Cor.11.3
made him the *h.* over all things	Eph.1.22
husband is the *h.* of the wife as	Eph.5.23
He is the *h.* of the body, the church	Col.1.18
his *h.* and his hair were white as	Rev.1.14

HEAL

forgive their sin and *h.* their	2 Chr.7.14
h. me, for my bones are troubled	Ps.6.2
who *h.* all your diseases	Ps.103.3
He *h.* the brokenhearted, and binds	Ps.147.3
with his stripes we are *h.*	Is.53.5
H. me, O Lord, and I shall be *h.*	Jer.17.14
I will *h.* their faithlessness	Hos.14.4
H. the sick, raise the dead, cleanse	Mt.10.8
Is it lawful to *h.* on the sabbath?	Mt.12.10
proverb, 'Physician, *h.* yourself	Lk.4.23
thou stretchest out thy hand to *h.*	Acts 4.30
By his wounds you have been *h.*	1 Pet.2.24

HEALING (noun)

I will bring to it health and *h.*	Jer.33.6
cured those who had need of *h.*	Lk.9.11
this sign of *h.* was performed	Acts 4.22
gifts of *h.* by the one Spirit	1 Cor.12.9
Do all possess gifts of *h.*?	1 Cor.12.30
were for the *h.* of the nations	Rev.22.2

HEAP (verb)

will *h.* coals of fire on his head	Pr.25.22
do not *h.* up empty phrases	Mt.6.7
h. burning coals upon his head	Rom.12.20
for her sins are *h.* high as heaven	Rev.18.5

HEAR

God does not *h.* an empty cry	Job 35.13
But thou didst *h.* my supplications	Ps.31.22
H. my prayer, O Lord, and give ear	Ps.39.12
O thou who *h.* prayer! To thee shall	Ps.65.2
They have ears, but do not *h.*	Ps.115.6
h., that your soul may live	Is.55.3
tell John what you *h.* and see	Mt.11.
He who has ears to *h.*, let him *h.*	Mt.11.15
H., O Israel: The Lord our God	Mk.12.29
when you *h.* of wars and tumults	Lk.21.9
when the dead will *h.* the voice of	Jn.5.25
My sheep *h.* my voice, and I know	Jn.10.27
Let every man be quick to *h.*, slow	Jas.1.19
we know that he *h.* us in whatever	1 Jn.5.15

HEART

imagination . . . of his *h.* was only evil	Gen.6.5
Lord hardened the *h.* of Pharaoh	Ex.9.12
with all your *h.* and with all your	Dt.4.29
The fool says in his *h.*, ". . . no God."	Ps.14.1
meditation of my *h.* be acceptable	Ps.19.14
He who has clean hands and a pure *h.*	Ps.24.4
For he knows the secrets of the *h.*	Ps.44.21
Create in me a clean *h.*, O God	Ps.51.10
a broken and contrite *h.*, O God	Ps.51.17
Search me, O God, and know my *h.*	Ps.139.23
for wisdom will come into your *h.*	Pr.2.10
Trust in the Lord with all your *h.*	Pr.3.5
Anxiety in a man's *h.* weighs him	Pr.12.25
Hope deferred makes the *h.* sick	Pr.13.12
A glad *h.* makes a cheerful	Pr.15.13
A wise man's *h.* inclines him toward	Ec.10.2
Say to those who are of a fearful *h.*	Is.35.
when you seek me with all your *h.*	Jer.29.13
Let not your *h.* faint, and be not	Jer.51.46
How lovesick is your *h.*, says	Ezek.16.30
Blessed are the pure in *h.*	Mt.5.8
out of the *h.* come evil thoughts	Mt.15.19
love the Lord . . . with all your *h.*	Mt.22.37
kept all these things in her *h.*	Lk.2.51
ought always to pray and not lose *h.*	Lk.18.
Let not your *h.* be troubled	Jn.14.
in singleness of *h.*, as to Christ	Eph.6.
doing the will of God from the *h.*	Eph.6.
Refresh my *h.* in Christ	Philem.20
God is greater than our *h.*	1 Jn.3.20
I am he who searches mind and *h.*	Rev.2.23

HEAVEN

God created the *h.* and the earth	Gen.1.1
And God called the firmament *H.*	Gen.1.8
Most High, maker of *h.* and earth	Gen.14.19
Elijah up to *h.* by a whirlwind	2 Kg.2.
the Lord's throne is in *h.*	Ps.11.4
Let *h.* and earth praise him	Ps.69.34
the Lord, who made *h.* and earth	Ps.121.
If I ascend to *h.*, thou art there	Ps.139.8
Who has ascended to *h.* and come down?	Pr.30.
I create new *h.* and a new earth	Is.65.17
H. is my throne and the earth is	Is.66.
for the kingdom of *h.* is at hand	Mt.3.
a voice from *h.*, saying, "This is my	Mt.3.17
for the kingdom of *h.* is at hand	Mt.4.1
for your reward is great in *h.*	Mt.5.12
till *h.* and earth pass away, not an	Mt.5.18
Our Father who art in *h.*	Mt.6.9
before my Father who is in *h.*	Mt.10.33

I thank thee . . . Lord of *h.* and earth	Mt.11.25	And take the *h.* of salvation	Eph.6.17
H. and earth will pass away, but my	Mt.24.35	and for a *h.* the hope of salvation	1 Th.5.8
the Spirit descend as a dove from *h.*	Jn.1.32	**HELP** (noun)	
He gave them bread from *h.* to eat	Jn.6.31	The God of my father was my *h.*	Ex.18.4
H. is my throne, and earth my	Acts 7.49	In truth I have no *h.* in me	Job 6.13
Then I saw a new *h.* and a new earth	Rev.21.1	soul of the wounded cries for *h.*	Job 24.12

HEAVENLY

O *h.* beings, ascribe to the LORD	Ps.29.1	there is no *h.* for him in God	Ps.3.2
as your *h.* Father is perfect	Mt.5.48	the LORD; he is our *h.* and shield	Ps.33.20
multitude of the *h.* host praising	Lk.2.13	Thou art my *h.* and my deliverer	Ps.40.17
believe if I tell you *h.* things?	Jn.3.12	a very present *h.* in trouble	Ps.46.1
not disobedient to the *h.* vision	Acts 26.19	He is their *h.* and their shield	Ps.115.9
and save me for his *h.* kingdom	2 Tim.4.18	My *h.* comes from the LORD, who made	Ps.121.2
copies of the *h.* things . . . purified	Heb.9.23	Our *h.* is in the name of the LORD	Ps.124.8
h. Jerusalem, and to innumerable	Heb.12.22	the *h.* of the Spirit of Jesus	Phil.1.19

HEAVY

HELP (verb)

Your father made our yoke *h.*	1 Kg.12.4	God has power to *h.* or to cast	2 Chr.25.8
his hand is *h.* in spite of my	Job 23.2	Fear not, I will *h.* you	Is.41.13
Thy wrath lies *h.* upon me	Ps.88.7	before him, saying, "Lord, *h.* me."	Mt.15.25
all who labor and are *h.* laden	Mt.11.28	said, "I believe; *h.* my unbelief!"	Mk.9.24
They bind *h.* burdens, hard to bear	Mt.23.4	He has *h.* his servant Israel	Lk.1.54
sleeping, for their eyes were *h.*	Mt.26.43	toiling one must *h.* the weak	Acts 20.35
their ears are *h.* of hearing	Acts 28.27	Likewise the Spirit *h.* us in our	Rom.8.26

HEBRON

You also must *h.* us by prayer	2 Cor.1.11
h. the weak, be patient with them	1 Th.5.14
find grace to *h.* in time of need	Heb.4.16

a city about 19 miles southwest of Jerusalem; Abraham dwells there, Gen.13.18; 23.2; the spies come to, Num.13.22; captured, Jos.10.36–37; given to Caleb, Jos.14.13; 15.13; David reigns there, 2 Sam.2.1; 3.2; 5.1; 1 Chr.11; 12.38; 29.27

HELPER

		I will make him a *h.* fit for him	Gen.2.18
		hast been the *h.* of the fatherless	Ps.10.14
		Behold, God is my *h.*; the Lord is	Ps.54.4

HEED (noun)

Take *h.* lest you forget the LORD	Dt.8.11	he delivers . . . him who has no *h.*	Ps.72.12
thou hast taken *h.* of my adversities	Ps.31.7	healers, *h.*, administrators	1 Cor.12.28
Take *h.* what you hear	Mk.4.24	confidently say, "The Lord is my *h.*	Heb.13.6
he stands take *h.* lest he fall	1 Cor.10.12	**HERITAGE**	

HEED (verb)

wise of heart will *h.* commandments	Pr.10.8	For they are thy people and thy *h.*	Dt.9.29
he who *h.* reproof is honored	Pr.13.18	the *h.* decreed for him by God	Job 20.29
h. the word of the LORD	Jer.2.31	yea, I have goodly *h.*	Ps.16.6
they have not all *h.* the gospel	Rom.10.16	given me the *h.* of those who fear	Ps.61.5
h. my appeal, agree with one	2 Cor.13.11	he will not abandon his *h.*	Ps.94.14

HEIFER

bring you a red *h.* without defect	Num.19.2	and he abhorred his *h.*	Ps.106.40
If you had not plowed with my *h.*	Jg.14.18	Lo, sons are a *h.* from the LORD	Ps.127.3
A beautiful *h.* is Egypt	Jer.46.20	gave their land as a *h.*	Ps.135.12
Like a stubborn *h.*, Israel is	Hos.4.16	Blessed be . . . Israel my *h.*	Is.19.25
Ephraim was a trained *h.*	Hos.10.11	the *h.* of the servants of the LORD	Is.54.17
the ashes of a *h.* sanctifies for	Heb.9.13	and made my *h.* an abomination	Jer.2.7

HEIR

shall not be *h.* with my son Isaac	Gen.21.10	and make not thy *h.* a reproach	Jl.2.17
Has Israel no sons? Has he no *h.*?	Jer.49.1	left his *h.* to jackals of the desert	Mal.1.3
and if children, then *h.*, *h.* of God	Rom.8.17	He who conquers shall have this *h.*	Rev.21.7
offspring, *h.* according to promise	Gal.3.29	**HEROD**	
and if a son then an *h.*	Gal.4.7		

(1) (the Great) king of Judea, Mt.2.1; troubled at Jesus' birth, Mt.2.3; kills the male children in Bethlehem, Mt.2.16; (2) (Antipas) reproved by John the Baptist, imprisons him, Lk.3.19; beheads him, Mt.14; Mk.6.14–28; desires to see Jesus, Lk.9.9; scourges him, and is reconciled to Pilate, Lk.23.7–12; Acts 4.27; (3) (Agrippa I) persecutes the church, Acts 12.1; his pride and miserable death, Acts 12.23; (4) (Agrippa II) visit to Festus, Acts 25.13; Paul's defense before, Acts 26

he appointed the *h.* of all things	Heb.1.2
are joint *h.* of the grace of life	1 Pet.3.7

HELL

shall be liable to the *h.* of fire	Mt.5.22
destroy both soul and body in *h.*	Mt.10.28
twice as much a child of *h.* as	Mt.23.15
has power to cast into *h.*	Lk.12.5
The tongue is . . . set on fire by *h.*	Jas.3.6
God . . . cast them into *h.*	2 Pet.2.4

HEW

H. two tables of stone like the	Dt.10.1
you shall *h.* down the graven images	Dt.12.3
to the rock from which you were *h.*	Is.51.1

HELMET

Ephraim is my *h.*; Judah is my scepter	Ps.60.7
a *h.* of salvation upon his head	Is.59.17

h. out cisterns for themselves	Jer.2.13
which had been *h.* out of the rock	Mk.15.46

HEZEKIAH

king of Judah, 2 Kg.16.19–20 (2 Chr.28.27); abolishes idolatry, 2 Kg.18; attacked by the Assyrians, his prayer and deliverance, 2 Kg.19; his life lengthened, shadow of dial goes backward, displays his treasure, Isaiah's prediction, 2 Kg.20 (Is.38); his passover, 2 Chr.30.13; his piety and good reign, 2 Chr.29; his death, 2 Kg.20.20–21

HID

I was naked; and I h. myself	Gen.3.10
Moses h. his face, for he was afraid	Ex.3.6
You shall be h. from the scourge	Job 5.21
It is h. from the eyes of all	Job 28.21
let the net which they h. ensnare	Ps.35.8
My way is h. from the LORD, and my	Is.40.27
in the shadow of his hand he h. me	Is.49.2
for thou hast h. thy face from us	Is.64.7
Compassion is h. from my eyes	Hos.13.14
A city set on a hill cannot be h.	Mt.5.14
nothing h., except to come to light	Mk.4.22
now they are h. from your eyes	Lk.19.42
Jesus h. himself, and went out	Jn.8.59
in whom are h. all the treasures of	Col.2.3
your life is h. with Christ in God	Col.3.3

HIDE

And when she could h. him no longer	Ex.2.3
long wilt thou h. thy face from me?	Ps.13.1
h. me in the shadow of thy wings	Ps.17.8
For he will h. me in his shelter	Ps.27.5
H. not thy face from thy servant	Ps.69.17
the wicked rise, men h. themselves	Pr.28.12
thou art a God who h. thyself	Is.45.15
I will not h. my face any more	Ezek.39.29
Though they h. themselves . . . I will	Am.9.3
he will h. his face from them	Mic.3.4
Fall on us and h. us from the face	Rev.6.16

HIGH

Is not God h. in the heavens?	Job 22.12
He beholds everything that is h.	Job 41.34
the name of the LORD, the Most H.	Ps.7.17
men of h. estate are a delusion	Ps.62.9
the heavens are h. above the earth	Ps.103.11
The LORD is h. above all nations	Ps.113.4
For though the LORD is h.	Ps.138.6
it is h., I cannot attain it	Ps.139.6
is poured upon us from on h.	Is.32.15
Lift up your eyes on h. and see	Is.40.26
your nest as h. as the eagle's	Jer.49.16
and abase that which is h.	Ezek.21.26
led them up a h. mountain apart	Mt.17.1
day shall dawn upon us from on h.	Lk.1.78
mother-in-law . . . ill with a h. fever	Lk.4.38
are clothed with power from on h.	Lk.24.49
right hand of the Majesty on h.	Heb.1.3
have not a h. priest who is unable	Heb.4.15
exalt himself to be made a h. priest	Heb.5.5
her sins are heaped h. as heaven	Rev.18.5

HIGHWAY

we will go by the King's H.	Num.21.22
The h. of the upright turns aside	Pr.16.17
there will be a h. from Assyria	Is.11.16
a h. shall be there . . . the Holy Way	Is.35.8
in the desert a h. for our God	Is.40.3
Go out to the h. and hedges	Lk.14.23

HILKIAH

2 Kg.18.18; 2 Chr.34.9; Is.22.20

HILL

set my king on Zion, my holy h.	Ps.2.6
Who shall dwell on thy holy h.?	Ps.15.1
Who shall ascend the h. of the LORD?	Ps.24.3
the cattle on a thousand h.	Ps.50.10
I lift up my eyes to the h.	Ps.121.1
before the h., I was brought forth	Pr.8.25
every mountain and h. be made low	Is.40.4
weighed . . . the h. in a balance?	Is.40.12
their altars, upon every high h.	Ezek.6.13
thy city Jerusalem, thy holy h.	Dan.9.16
A city set on a h. cannot be hid	Mt.5.14
went with haste into the h. country	Lk.1.39
through all the h. country of Judea	Lk.1.65
mountain and h. shall be brought low	Lk.3.5
led him to the brow of the h.	Lk.4.29
and to the h., 'Cover us.'	Lk.23.30
Jesus went up into the h.	Jn.6.3
the seven heads are seven h.	Rev.17.9

HINDER

for nothing can h. the LORD from	1 Sam.14.6
who can h. him? Who will say	Job 9.12
I work and who can h. it?	Is.43.13
children come to me, do not h. them	Mk.10.14
who h. you from obeying the truth?	Gal.5.7
again and again–but Satan h. us	1 Th.2.18
that your prayers may not be h.	1 Pet.3.7

HIRAM

2 Sam.5.11; 1 Kg.5.1,8; 1 Chr.14.1

HIRE

wages of a h. servant shall not	Lev.19.13
You shall not oppress a h. servant	Dt.24.14
early in the morning to h. laborers	Mt.20.1
my father's h. servants have bread	Lk.15.17

HISS

will be astonished, and will h.	1 Kg.9.8
a thing to be h. at for ever	Jer.18.16
they h., they gnash their teeth	Lam.2.16
merchants . . . h. at you	Ezek.27.36
Every one who passes by her h.	Zeph.2.15

HITTITE

Gen.23.10; Ex.23.28; 2 Sam.11.6; 2 Chr.1.17

HOLD

Do you still h. fast your integrity?	Job 2.9
I h. fast my righteousness	Job 27.6
trembling took h. of them there	Ps.48.6
thou dost h. my right hand	Ps.73.23
do not h. thy peace . . . O God	Ps.83.1
I h. my life in my hand	Ps.119.109
H. me up, that I may be safe	Ps.119.117
and thy right hand shall h. me	Ps.139.10
Let your heart h. fast my words	Pr.4.4
h. fast to love and justice	Hos.12.6
shall take h. of the robe of a Jew	Zech.8.23
Do not h. me, for I have not yet	Jn.20.17
h. fast to what is good	Rom.12.9
let us h. true to what we have	Phil.3.16
in him all things h. together	Col.1.17
take h. of the eternal life	1 Tim.6.12
let us h. fast our confession	Heb.4.14
you h. fast my name	Rev.2.13
h. fast what you have, until I	Rev.2.25

HOLINESS

Who is like thee, majestic in h.   Ex.15.11

Once for all I have sworn by my *h*.	Ps.89.35	**HOME**	
h. befits thy house, O Lord	Ps.93.5	The Lord grant that you may find a *h*.	Ru.1.9
I will manifest my *h*. among you	Ezek.20.41	Even the sparrow finds a *h*.	Ps.84.3
vindicate my *h*. before their eyes	Ezek.38.16	because man goes to his eternal *h*.	Ec.12.5
in *h*. and righteousness before him	Lk.1.75	Go *h*. to your friends, and tell them	Mk.5.19
according to the Spirit of *h*.	Rom.1.4	Return to your *h*., and declare how	Lk.8.39
with *h*. and godly sincerity	2 Cor.1.12	have left our *h*. and followed you	Lk.18.28
unblamable in *h*. before our God	1 Th.3.13	to him and make our *h*. with him	Jn.14.23
and love and *h*., with modesty	1 Tim.2.15	rather be . . . at *h*. with the Lord	2 Cor.5.8
that we may share his *h*.	Heb.12.10	So whether we are at *h*. or away	2 Cor.5.9
h. without which no one will see	Heb.12.14	**HONEST**	
lives of *h*. and godliness	2 Pet.3.11	How forceful are *h*. words	Job 6.25
HOLLOW		hold it fast in an *h*. and good heart	Lk.8.15
he touched the *h*. of Jacob's thigh	Gen.32.32	doing *h*. work with his hands	Eph.4.28
he made it *h*., with boards	Ex.38.7	to be ready for any *h*. work	Tit.3.1
waters in the *h*. of his hand	Is.40.12	**HONEY**	
HOLY		a land flowing with milk and *h*.	Ex.3.8
you are standing is *h*. ground	Ex.3.5	What is sweeter than *h*.?	Jg.14.18
the sabbath day, to keep it *h*.	Ex.20.8	sweeter than *h*. to my mouth	Ps.119.103
He made the *h*. anointing oil also	Ex.37.29	the lips of a loose woman drip *h*.	Pr.5.3
whoever touches them shall become *h*.	Lev.6.18	it was in my mouth as sweet as *h*.	Ezek.3.3
between the *h*. and the common	Lev.10.10	his food was locusts and wild *h*.	Mt.3.4
be *h*., for I am *h*.	Lev.11.44	it was sweet as *h*. in my mouth	Rev.10.10
wearing the *h*. linen garments	Lev.16.32	**HONOR (noun)**	
Consecrate yourselves . . . and be *h*.	Lev.20.7	*H*. and majesty are before him	Ps.96.6
the seventh day is a *h*. convocation	Lev.23.8	Full of *h*. and majesty is his work	Ps.111.3
the place where you stand is *h*.	Jos.5.15	humility goes before *h*.	Pr.15.33
he is a *h*. God; he is a jealous	Jos.24.19	so *h*. is not fitting for a fool	Pr.26.1
the *h*. race has mixed itself with	Ezra 9.2	If . . . I am a father, where is my *h*.?	Mal.1.6
The Lord is in his *h*. temple	Ps.11.4	A prophet is not without *h*.	Mk.6.4
who shall stand in his *h*. place?	Ps.24.3	*h*. to whom *h*. is due	Rom.13.7
give thanks to his *h*. name	Ps.30.4	in *h*. and dishonor, in ill repute	2 Cor.6.8
take not thy *h*. Spirit from me	Ps.51.11	To him be *h*. and eternal dominion	1 Tim.6.16
Worship the Lord in *h*. array	Ps.96.9	Let marriage be held in *h*. among all	Heb.13.4
worship at his *h*. mountain	Ps.99.9	glory and *h*. at the revelation	1 Pet.1.7
he looked down from his *h*. height	Ps.102.19	to receive glory and *h*. and power	Rev.4.11
H. and terrible is his name	Ps.111.9	be blessing and *h*. and glory	Rev.5.13
H., *h*., *h*., is the Lord of hosts	Is.6.3	**HONOR (verb)**	
I dwell in the high and *h*. place	Is.57.15	*H*. your father and your mother	Ex.20.12
put in the midst . . . his *h*. Spirit	Is.63.11	*H*. your father and mother	Mt.19.19
you have drunk upon my *h*. mountain	Ob.16	This people *h*. me with their lips	Mk.7.6
But the Lord is in his *h*. temple	Hab.2.20	He who does not *h*. the Son does not	Jn.5.23
all the *h*. ones with him	Zech.14.5	if one member is *h*., all rejoice	1 Cor.12.26
conceived in her is of the *H*. Spirit	Mt.1.20	*H*. widows who are real widows	1 Tim.5.3
Do not give dogs what is *h*.	Mt.7.6	Fear God. *H*. the emperor	1 Pet.2.17
baptize you with the *H*. Spirit	Mk.1.8	**HONORABLE**	
The *H*. Spirit will come upon you	Lk.1.35	insolent . . . the base fellow to the *h*.	Is.3.5
the *H*. Spirit was upon him	Lk.2.25	call . . . the holy day of the Lord *h*.	Is.58.13
that you are the *H*. One of God	Jn.6.69	parts of the body . . . less *h*.	1 Cor.12.23
H. Father, keep them in thy name	Jn.17.11	we aim at what is *h*.	2 Cor.8.21
said to them, "Receive the *H*. Spirit	Jn.20.22	whatever is *h*., whatever is just	Phil.4.8
be baptized with the *H*. Spirit	Acts 1.5	they who blaspheme that *h*. name	Jas.2.7
the promise of the *H*. Spirit	Acts 2.33	**HOOF**	
you are standing is *h*. ground	Acts 7.33	not a *h*. shall be left behind	Ex.10.26
directed by a *h*. angel to send	Acts 10.22	that chew the cud or part the *h*.	Lev.11.4
H. Spirit fell on all who heard	Acts 10.44	parts the *h*. and has the *h*. cloven	Dt.14.6
his prophets in the *h*. scriptures	Rom.1.2	their horses' *h*. seem like flint	Is.5.28
Greet one another with a *h*. kiss	Rom.16.16	I will make . . . your *h*. bronze	Mic.4.13
For God's temple is *h*.	1 Cor.3.17	**HOOK**	
called us with a *h*. calling	2 Tim.1.9	I will put my *h*. in your nose	2 Kg.19.28
as he who called you is *h*., be *h*.	I Pet.1.15	beat . . . their spears into pruning *h*.	Is.2.4
You shall be *h*., for I am *h*.	1 Pet.1.16	I will put my *h*. in your nose	Is.37.29
the Lord came with his *h*. myriads	Jude 14	Beat . . . your pruning *h*. into spears	Jl.3.10
H., *h*., *h*., is the Lord God Almighty	Rev.4.8	go to the sea and cast a *h*.	Mt.17.27
For thou alone art *h*.	Rev.15.4	**HOPE (noun)**	
I saw the *h*. city, new Jerusalem	Rev.21.2	for what do I wait? My *h*. is in thee	Ps.39.7

H. deferred makes the heart sick — Pr.13.12
Discipline . . . son while there is *h.* — Pr.19.18
your *h.* will not be cut off — Pr.24.14
There is more *h.* for a fool than — Pr.26.12
are dried up, and our *h.* is lost — Ezek.37.11
the Valley of Achor a door of *h.* — Hos.2.15
for this *h.* I am accused by Jews — Acts 26.7
For in this *h.* we were saved — Rom.8.24
Now *h.* that is seen is not *h.* — Rom.8.24
that . . . we might have *h.* — Rom.15.4
May the God of *h.* fill you with — Rom.15.13
So faith, *h.*, love abide — 1 Cor.13.13
know what is the *h.* to which — Eph.1.18
having no *h.* and without God — Eph.2.12
Christ in you, the *h.* of glory — Col.1.27
what is our *h.* or joy or crown — 1 Th.2.19
grieve as others . . . who have no *h.* — 1 Th.4.13
for a helmet the *h.* of salvation — 1 Th.5.8
awaiting our blessed *h.* — Tit.2.13
born anew to a living *h.* — 1 Pet.1.3
account for the *h.* that is in you — 1 Pet.3.15

HOPE (verb)

be upon us, even as we *h.* in thee — Ps.33.22
But I will *h.* continually — Ps.71.14
O Israel, *h.* in the LORD — Ps.131.3
in his name will the Gentiles *h.* — Mt.12.21
those from whom you *h.* to receive — Lk.6.34
if we *h.* for what we do not see — Rom.8.25
in him shall the Gentiles *h.* — Rom.15.12
Love . . . *h.* all things, endures all — 1 Cor.13.7
is the assurance of things *h.* for — Heb.11.1
holy women who *h.* in God — 1 Pet.3.5
one who thus *h.* in him purifies — 1 Jn.3.3

HOREB

a mountain (Sinai), Ex.3.1; 17.6; 33.6; Dt.1.6;
laws given, Ex.19; 20; Dt.4–5; 18.16; 1 Kg.8.9;
Mal.4.4; Moses twice there for forty days,
Ex.24.18; 34.28; Dt.9.9; Elijah there, 1 Kg.19.8

HORN

Fill your *h.* with oil, and go — 1 Sam.16.1
and the *h.* of my salvation — Ps.18.2
hast exalted my *h.* like that of — Ps.92.10
his *h.* is exalted in honor — Ps.112.9
has raised up a *h.* for his people — Ps.148.14
a fourth beast . . . had ten *h.* — Dan.7.7
Blow the *h.* in Gibeah — Hos.5.8
has raised up a *h.* of salvation — Lk.1.69
with seven *h.* and with seven eyes — Rev.5.6

HORROR

shall be a *h.* to all the kingdoms — Dt.28.25
he has made them an object of *h.* — 2 Chr.29.8
and *h.* overwhelms me — Ps.55.5
My mind reels, *h.* has appalled me — Is.21.4
make them a *h.* to all the kingdoms — Jer.29.18
that Bozrah shall become a *h.* — Jer.49.13
and a taunt, a warning and a *h.* — Ezek.5.15
A cup of *h.* and desolation — Ezek.23.33

HORSE

the *h.* and his rider he has thrown — Ex.15.1
Some boast of chariots . . . some of *h.* — Ps.20.7
Be not like a *h.* or a mule — Ps.32.9
The war *h.* is a vain hope for victory — Ps.33.17
A whip for the *h.*, a bridle for the — Pr.26.3
like a *h.* plunging headlong — Jer.8.6
break in pieces the *h.* and . . . rider — Jer.51.21

behold, a man riding upon a red *h.* — Zech.1.8
I will strike every *h.* with panic — Zech.12.4
a white *h.*, and its rider had a bow — Rev.6.2
and behold, a white *h.* — Rev.19.11

HOSANNA

H. to the Son of David! Blessed be — Mt.21.9
H. in the highest — Mk.11.10
went out to meet him, crying, "*H.* — Jn.12.13

HOST

The LORD of *h.*, he is the King of — Ps.24.10
Though a *h.* encamp against me, my — Ps.27.3
LORD will punish the *h.* of heaven — Is.24.21
who brings out their *h.* by number — Is.40.26
the moon and all the *h.* of heaven — Jer.8.2
h. of heaven cannot be numbered — Jer.33.22
Bring up a *h.* against them — Ezek.23.46
the heavenly *h.* praising God — Lk.2.13
to worship the *h.* of heaven — Acts 7.42
Gaius, who is *h.* to me and to the — Rom.16.23
on high he led a *h.* of captives — Eph.4.8
the spiritual *h.* of wickedness — Eph.6.12

HOT

went out from Pharaoh in *h.* anger — Ex.11.8
dancing, Moses' anger burned *h.* — Ex.32.19
In *h.* anger he went back to his — Jg.14.19
when it is *h.*, they vanish — Job 6.17
my heart became *h.* within me — Ps.39.3
I speak in my *h.* jealousy against — Ezek.36.5
My anger is *h.* against the — Zech.10.3
you are neither cold nor *h.* — Rev.3.15

HOUR

will be given to you in that *h.* — Mt.10.19
of that day and *h.* no one knows — Mt.24.36
And about the ninth *h.* Jesus cried — Mt.27.46
Could you not watch one *h.*? — Mk.14.37
My *h.* has not yet come — Jn.2.4
But the *h.* is coming, and now is — Jn.4.23
Father, save me from this *h.* — Jn.12.27
you know what *h.* it is — Rom.13.11
Why am I in peril every *h.*? — 1 Cor.15.30
Children, it is the last *h.* — 1 Jn.2.18
the *h.* of his judgment has come — Rev.14.7

HOUSE

is none other than the *h.* of God — Gen.28.17
of Egypt, from the *h.* of bondage — Ex.13.14
and peace be to your *h.* — 1 Sam.25.6
I dwell in a *h.* of cedar — 2 Sam.7.2
saying, 'I will build you a *h.*' — 2 Sam.7.27
The *h.* which King Solomon built — 1 Kg.6.2
the glory of the LORD filled the *h.* — 1 Kg.8.11
the LORD, 'Set your *h.* in order — 2 Kg.20.1
the *h.* appointed for all living — Job 30.23
dwell in the *h.* of the LORD for ever — Ps.23.6
I love the habitation of thy *h.* — Ps.26.8
For zeal for thy *h.* has consumed me — Ps.69.9
doorkeeper in the *h.* of my God — Ps.84.10
holiness befits thy *h.* — Ps.93.5
Wealth and riches are in his *h.* — Ps.112.3
Let us go to the *h.* of the LORD — Ps.122.1
Unless the LORD builds the *h.* — Ps.127.1
Wisdom has built her *h.*, she has — Pr.9.1
the *h.* of the righteous will stand — Pr.12.7
better to go to the *h.* of mourning — Ec.7.2
brought me to the banqueting *h.* — S.ofS.2.4
Woe to those who join *h.* to *h.* — Is.5.8
my *h.* shall be called a *h.* of prayer — Is.56.7

Our holy and beautiful *h.*	Is.64.11
I will drive them out of my *h.*	Hos.9.15
while this *h.* lies in ruins?	Hag.1.4
man who built his *h.* upon the rock	Mt.7.24
As you enter the *h.*, salute it	Mt.10.12
and no city or *h.* divided against	Mt.12.25
My *h.* shall be called a *h.* of prayer	Mt.21.13
your *h.* is forsaken and desolate	Mt.23.38
who has left *h.* or brothers	Mk.10.29
that I must be in my Father's *h.*?	Lk.2.49
make my Father's *h.* a *h.* of trade	Jn.2.16
Zeal for thy *h.* will consume me	Jn.2.17
In my Father's *h.* are many rooms	Jn.14.2
a *h.* not made with hands, eternal	2 Cor.5.1
gadding about from *h.* to *h.*	1 Tim.5.13
For every *h.* is built by some one	Heb.3.4
faithful over God's *h.* as a son	Heb.3.6
yourselves built into a spiritual *h.*	1 Pet.2.5

HOUSEHOLD

into the ark, you and all your *h.*	Gen.7.1
foes will be those of his own *h.*	Mt.10.36
he himself believed, and all his *h.*	Jn.4.53
you will be saved, you and your *h.*	Acts 16.31
those who are of the *h.* of faith	Gal.6.10
He must manage his own *h.* well	1 Tim.3.4
an ark for the saving of his *h.*	Heb.11.7
to begin with the *h.* of God	1 Pet.4.17

HOUSEHOLDER

is like a *h.* who brings out of his	Mt.13.52
is like a *h.* who went out early	Mt.20.1
a *h.* who planted a vineyard	Mt.21.33
if the *h.* had known at what	Lk.12.39
tell the *h.*, 'The Teacher says	Lk.22.11

HOUSETOP

I am like a lonely bird on the *h.*	Ps.102.7
a corner of the *h.* than in a house	Pr.21.9
proclaim upon the *h.*	Mt.10.27
let him who is on the *h.* not go	Mk.13.15
Peter went up on the *h.* to pray	Acts 10.9

HUMAN

was so marred, beyond *h.* semblance	Is.52.14
a stone was cut out by no *h.* hand	Dan.2.34
no *h.* being would be saved; but	Mt.24.22
nor is he served by *h.* hands	Acts 17.25
For no *h.* being will be justified	Rom.3.20
not taught by *h.* wisdom but taught	1 Cor.2.13
but on tablets of *h.* hearts	2 Cor.3.3
Christ from a *h.* point of view	2 Cor.5.16
being found in *h.* form he humbled	Phil.2.8
no *h.* being can tame the tongue	Jas.3.8
a dumb ass spoke with *h.* voice	2 Pet.2.16
their faces were like *h.* faces	Rev.9.7

HUMBLE

He leads the *h.* in what is right	Ps.25.9
he adorns the *h.* with victory	Ps.149.4
but to the *h.* he shows favor	Pr.3.34
Better is a man of *h.* standing	Pr.12.9
who is of a contrite and *h.* spirit	Is.57.15
he that is *h.* and contrite in spirit	Is.66.2
proud, but gives grace to the *h.*	Jas.4.6

HUMBLE (verb)

that we might *h.* ourselves before	Ezra 8.21
Whoever *h.* himself like this child	Mt.18.4
one who exalts himself will be *h.*	Lk.14.11
he *h.* himself and became obedient	Phil.2.8
H. yourselves therefore under the	1 Pet.5.6

HUMILITY

and *h.* goes before honor	Pr.15.33
reward for *h.* . . . . is riches and . . . life	Pr.22.4
serving the Lord with all *h.*	Acts 20.19
in *h.* count others better than	Phil.2.3
with *h.* toward one another	1 Pet.5.5

HUNGER (verb)

Blessed are those who *h.* and thirst	Mt.5.6
he who comes to me shall not *h.*	Jn.6.35
To the present hour we *h.* and	1 Cor.4.11
They shall *h.* no more, neither	Rev.7.16

HUNGRY

If I were *h.*, I would not tell you	Ps.50.12
the *h.* he fills with good things	Ps.107.9
If your enemy is *h.*, give him bread	Pr.25.21
to share your bread with the *h.*	Is.58.7
his disciples were *h.*, and they	Mt.12.1
am unwilling to send them away *h.*	Mt.15.32
for I was *h.* and you gave me food	Mt.25.35
he has filled the *h.* with good things	Lk.1.53
read what David did when he was *h.*	Lk.6.3
if your enemy is *h.*, feed him	Rom.12.20
one is *h.* and another is drunk	1 Cor.11.21
if any one is *h.*, let him eat at	1 Cor.11.34

HUNT

to the field, and *h.* game for me	Gen.27.3
thou dost *h.* me like a lion	Job 10.16
let evil *h.* down the violent man	Ps.140.11
they shall *h.* them from every	Jer.16.16
I have been *h.* like a bird by	Lam.3.52
Will you *h.* down souls belonging	Ezek.13.18

HURT (noun)

who swears to his own *h.* and does	Ps.15.4
those who seek my *h.* speak of ruin	Ps.38.12
brought to dishonor who desire my *h.*	Ps.70.2
while man lords it over man to his *h.*	Ec.8.9
Lord binds up the *h.* of his people	Is.30.26
Your *h.* is incurable	Jer.30.12

HURT (verb)

but a cruel man *h.* himself	Pr.11.17
and nothing shall *h.* you	Lk.10.19
It *h.* . . . . to kick against the goads	Acts 26.14
shall not be *h.* by the second death	Rev.2.11

HUSBAND

bereft of her two sons and her *h.*	Ru.1.5
A good wife is the crown of her *h.*	Pr.12.4
The heart of her *h.* trusts in her	Pr.31.11
For your Maker is your *h.*	Is.54.5
her *h.* Joseph, being a just man	Mt.1.19
if she divorces her *h.* and marries	Mk.10.12
Go, call your *h.*, and come here	Jn.4.16
and each woman her own *h.*	1 Cor.7.2
is consecrated through her *h.*	1 Cor.7.14
is bound to her *h.* as long as he	1 Cor.7.39
as a pure bride to her one *h.*	2 Cor.11.2
For the *h.* is the head of the wife	Eph.5.23
H., love your wives, as Christ loved	Eph.5.25
Wives, be subject to your *h.*	Col.3.18
to love their *h.* and children	Tit.2.4
to be . . . submissive to their *h.*	Tit.2.5
wives, be submissive to your *h.*	1 Pet.3.1
as a bride adorned for her *h.*	Rev.21.2

HYMN

And when they had sung a *h.*	Mt.26.30
come together, each one has a *h.*	1 Cor.14.26

in psalms and *h*. and spiritual — Eph.5.19
psalms and *h*. and spiritual songs — Col.3.16
HYPOCRITE
as the *h*. do in the synagogues — Mt.6.2
Why put me to the test, you *h*.? — Mt.22.18
Woe to you, scribes and . . . *h*. — Mt.23.15
You *h*., first take the log out of — Lk.6.42
You *h*.! You know how to interpret — Lk.12.56
the Lord answered him, "You *h*. — Lk.13.15
HYSSOP
Take a bunch of *h*. and dip it in — Ex.12.22
then a clean person shall take *h*. — Num.19.18
Purge me with *h*., and I shall be — Ps.51.7
a sponge full of the vinegar on *h*. — Jn.19.29
with water and scarlet wool and *h*. — Heb.9.19

IDLE
he said, "You are *i*., you are *i*. — Ex.5.17
an *i*. person will suffer hunger — Pr.19.15
Why do you stand here *i*. all day? — Mt.20.6
these words seemed . . . an *i*. tale — Lk.24.11
admonish the *i*., encourage the — 1 Th.5.14
we were not *i*. when we were with you — 2 Th.3.7
their condemnation has not been *i*. — 2 Pet.2.3
IDOL
Do not turn to *i*. or . . . molten gods — Lev.19.4
all the gods of the peoples are *i*. — Ps.96.5
make their boast in worthless *i*. — Ps.97.7
The *i*. of the nations are silver — Ps.135.15
who carry about their wooden *i*. — Is.45.20
Their *i*. are like scarecrows in a — Jer.10.5
Ephraim is joined to *i*. — Hos.4.17
abstain from the pollutions of *i*. — Acts 15.20
saw that the city was full of *i*. — Acts 17.16
Now concerning food offered to *i*. — 1 Cor.8.1
to eat food offered to *i*. — 1 Cor.8.10
you were led astray to dumb *i*. — 1 Cor.12.2
how you turned to God from *i*. — 1 Th.1.9
children, keep yourselves from *i*. — 1 Jn.5.21
to eat food sacrificed to *i*. — Rev.2.20
IDOLATRY
the penalty for your sinful *i*. — Ezek.23.49
i., sorcery, enmity, strife — Gal.5.20
covetousness, which is *i*. — Col.3.5
revels, carousing, and lawless *i*. — 1 Pet.4.3
IGNORANCE
has sinned through error or *i*. — Ezek.45.20
I know that you acted in *i*. — Acts 3.17
The times of *i*. God overlooked — Acts 17.30
because of the *i*. that is in them — Eph.4.18
to the passions of your former *i*. — 1 Pet.1.14
IGNORANT
I was stupid and *i*. — Ps.73.22
being *i*. of the righteousness — Rom.10.3
we are not *i*. of his designs — 2 Cor.2.11
deal gently with the *i*. and wayward — Heb.5.2
which the *i*. and unstable twist — 2 Pet.3.16
ILL
No *i*. befalls the righteous — Pr.12.21
Lord, he whom you love is *i*. — Jn.11.3
in *i*. repute and good repute — 2 Cor.6.8
because you heard that he was *i*. — Phil.2.26
Indeed he was *i*., near to death — Phil.2.27
Trophimus I left *i*. at Miletus — 2 Tim.4.20
IMAGE
Let us make man in our *i*. — Gen.1.26

for God made man in his own *i*. — Gen.9.6
not make yourself a graven *i*. — Ex.20.4
in Horeb and worshiped a molten *i*. — Ps.106.19
to set up an *i*. that will not move — Is.40.20
be conformed to the *i*. of his Son — Rom.8.29
a man . . . is the *i*. and glory of God — 1 Cor.11.7
bear the *i*. of the man of heaven — 1 Cor.15.49
He is the *i*. of the invisible God — Col.1.15
after the *i*. of its creator — Col.3.10
not worship the *i*. of the beast — Rev.13.15
IMAGINATION
that every *i*. . . . was only evil — Gen.6.5
the *i*. of man's heart is evil — Gen.8.21
proud in the *i*. of their hearts — Lk.1.51
representation by the art and *i*. — Acts 17.29
IMITATE
join in *i*. me, and mark those who — Phil.3.17
know how you ought to *i*. us — 2 Th.3.7
to give you . . . an example to *i*. — 2 Th.3.9
your leaders . . . *i*. their faith — Heb.13.7
Beloved, do not *i*. evil but *i*. good — 3 Jn.11
IMITATORS
I urge you, then, be *i*. of me — 1 Cor.4.16
Be *i*. of me, as I am of Christ — 1 Cor.11.1
be *i*. of God, as beloved children — Eph.5.1
you became *i*. of us and of the Lord — 1 Th.1.6
became *i*. of the churches of God — 1 Th.2.14
i. of those who . . . inherit the promises — Heb.6.12
IMMORAL
not to associate with *i*. men — 1 Cor.5.9
the *i*. man sins against his own — 1 Cor.6.18
Be sure . . . that no *i*. or impure man — Eph.5.5
that no one be *i*. or irreligious — Heb.12.16
will judge the *i*. and adulterous — Heb.13.4
IMMORALITY
reported . . . there is *i*. among you — 1 Cor.5.1
The body is not meant for *i*. — 1 Cor.6.13
Shun *i*. Every other sin — 1 Cor.6.18
But *i*. . . . must not even be named — Eph.5.3
that you abstain from *i*. — 1 Th.4.3
she refuses to repent of her *i*. — Rev.2.21
nor did they repent of . . . their *i*. — Rev.9.21
IMMORTALITY
those who . . . seek for . . . honor and *i*. — Rom.2.7
mortal nature must put on *i*. — 1 Cor.15.53
when . . . the mortal puts on *i*. — 1 Cor.15.54
who alone has *i*. and dwells in — 1 Tim.6.16
brought life and *i*. to light — 2 Tim.1.10
IMPERISHABLE
a perishable wreath, but we an *i*. — 1 Cor.9.25
what is raised is *i*. — 1 Cor.15.42
the dead will be raised *i*. — 1 Cor.15.52
the perishable puts on the *i*. — 1 Cor.15.54
to an inheritance which is *i*. — 1 Pet.1.4
not of perishable seed but of *i*. — 1 Pet.1.23
the *i*. jewel of a gentle . . . spirit — 1 Pet.3.4
IMPOSSIBLE
nothing will be *i*. to you — Mt.17.20
said to them, "With men this is *i*. — Mt.19.26
For with God nothing will be *i*. — Lk.1.37
is *i*. to restore again to repentance — Heb.6.4
i. that God should prove false — Heb.6.18
it is *i*. that the blood of bulls — Heb.10.4
without faith it is *i*. to please him — Heb.11.6
IMPRISONMENT
confiscation of his goods or for *i*. — Ezra 7.26

i. and afflictions await me — Acts 20.23
nothing deserving death or *i.* — Acts 23.29
partakers with me . . . both in my *i.* and Phil.1.7
thinking to afflict me in my *i.* — Phil.1.17
during my *i.* for the gospel — Philem.13
even chains and *i.* — Heb.11.36

IMPURITY
as in the days of her *i.* — Lev.15.25
takes his brother's wife, it is *i.* — Lev.20.21
approach a woman in her time of *i.* — Ezek.18.6
in the lusts of their hearts to *i.* — Rom.1.24
you once yielded your members to *i.* — Rom.6.19
have not repented of the *i.* — 2 Cor.12.21
immorality, *i.*, licentiousness — Gal.5.19
immorality and all *i.* — Eph.5.3
i., passion, evil desire — Col.3.5

INCENSE
Aaron shall burn fragrant *i.* on it — Ex.30.7
laid *i.* on it, and offered unholy — Lev.10.1
i. is an abomination to me — Is.1.13
they burned *i.* upon the mountains — Is.65.7
they have burned *i.* to other gods — Jer.1.16
When we burned *i.* to the queen of — Jer.44.19
in every place *i.* is offered to my — Mal.1.11
praying outside at the hour of *i.* — Lk.1.10
having the golden altar of *i.* — Heb.9.4
with golden bowls full of *i.* — Rev.5.8
smoke of the *i.* rose with the prayers — Rev.8.4

INCLINE
I. thy ear, O LORD, and hear — 2 Kg.19.16
he *i.* to me and heard my cry — Ps.40.1
I will *i.* my ear to a proverb — Ps.49.4
I *i.* my heart to perform thy — Ps.119.112
I. thy ear, O LORD, and hear — Is.37.17
O my God, *i.* thy ear and hear — Dan.9.18

INCREASE
the land shall yield its *i.* — Lev.26.4
if riches *i.*, set not your heart on — Ps.62.10
The earth has yielded its *i.* — Ps.67.6
Thou wilt *i.* my honor, and comfort — Ps.71.21
May the LORD give you *i.* — Ps.115.14
he will *i.* in learning — Pr.9.9
when they perish, the righteous *i.* — Pr.28.28
For when dreams *i.*, empty words — Ec.5.7
Of the *i.* of his government and — Is.9.7
who has no might he *i.* strength — Is.40.29
Jesus *i.* in wisdom and in stature — Lk.2.52
said to the Lord, "*I.* our faith!" — Lk.17.5
He must *i.*, but I must decrease — Jn.3.30
but where sin *i.*, grace abounded — Rom.5.20
make you *i.* and abound in love — 1 Th.3.12

INDIGNANT
they were *i.* at the two brothers — Mt.20.24
were *i.*, saying, "Why this waste? — Mt.26.8
when Jesus saw it he was *i.* — Mk.10.14
i. because Jesus had healed on the — Lk.13.14
is made to fall, and I am not *i.*? — 2 Cor.11.29

INDIGNATION
Pour out thy *i.* upon them — Ps.69.24
put away thy *i.* toward us — Ps.85.4
Hot *i.* seizes me because of the — Ps.119.53
his *i.* is against his enemies — Is.66.14
the nations cannot endure his *i.* — Jer.10.10
Who can stand before his *i.*? — Nah.1.6
see . . . what *i.*, what alarm, what — 2 Cor.7.11

INFERIOR
I also know; I am not *i.* to you — Job 13.2
the greater honor to the *i.* part — 1 Cor.12.24
I am not at all *i.* to these — 2 Cor.12.11
the *i.* is blessed by the superior — Heb.7.7

INFIRMITY
thou healest all his *i.* — Ps.41.3
He took our *i.* and bore our — Mt.8.17
to hear and to be healed of their *i.* — Lk.5.15
had a spirit of *i.* for eighteen — Lk.13.11

INHABITANTS
let all the *i.* of the world stand — Ps.33.8
Give ear, all *i.* of the world — Ps.49.1
its *i.* are like grasshoppers — Is.40.22
known to all the *i.* of Jerusalem — Acts 1.19
its *i.* worship the first beast — Rev.13.12

INHERIT
they shall *i.* it for ever — Ex.32.13
The wise will *i.* honor, but fools — Pr.3.35
my chosen shall *i.* it — Is.65.9
for they shall *i.* the earth — Mt.5.5
a hundredfold, and *i.* eternal life — Mt.19.29
i. the kingdom prepared for you — Mt.25.34
what must I do to *i.* eternal life? — Mk.10.17
will not *i.* the kingdom of God? — 1 Cor.6.9
cannot *i.* the kingdom of God — 1 Cor.15.50
shall not *i.* the kingdom of God — Gal.5.21
faith and patience *i.* the promises — Heb.6.12
when he desired to *i.* the blessing — Heb.12.17
futile ways *i.* from your fathers — 1 Pet.1.18

INHERITANCE
LORD your God gives you for an *i.* — Dt.4.21
the heathen have come into thy *i.* — Ps.79.1
i. gotten hastily in the beginning — Pr.20.21
Wisdom is good with an *i.* — Ec.7.11
Our *i.* . . . . turned over to strangers — Lam.5.2
let us kill him and have his *i.* — Mt.21.38
my brother divide the *i.* with me — Lk.12.13
he gave them their land as an *i.* — Acts 13.19
For if the *i.* is by the law, it is — Gal.3.18
guarantee of our *i.* until we acquire — Eph.1.14
has any *i.* in the kingdom of Christ — Eph.5.5
to share in the *i.* of the saints — Col.1.12
will receive the *i.* as your reward — Col.3.24
receive the promised eternal *i.* — Heb.9.15
to an *i.* which is imperishable — 1 Pet.1.4

INIQUITY
visiting the *i.* of the fathers upon — Ex.20.5
for our *i.* have risen higher than — Ezra 9.6
my sins, and blot out all my *i.* — Ps.51.9
Thou hast set our *i.* before thee — Ps.90.8
who forgives all your *i.* — Ps.103.3
If thou . . . shouldst mark *i.*, Lord — Ps.130.3
The *i.* of the wicked ensnare him — Pr.5.22
you have wearied me with your *i.* — Is.43.24
he was bruised for our *i.* — Is.53.5
and he shall bear their *i.* — Is.53.11
but your *i.* have made a separation — Is.59.2
Your *i.* have turned these away — Jer.5.25
Though our *i.* testify against us — Jer.14.7
By the multitude of your *i.* — Ezek.28.18
I will punish you for all your *i.* — Am.3.2
Blessed . . . whose *i.* are forgiven — Rom.4.7
name of the Lord depart from *i.* — 2 Tim.2.19
to redeem us from all *i.* — Tit.2.14

I will be merciful toward their *i.* Heb.8.12
and God has remembered her *i.* Rev.18.5

INJUSTICE
You shall do no *i.* in judgment Lev.19.15
than great revenues with *i.* Pr.16.8
He who sows *i.* will reap calamity Pr.22.8
i. has blossomed, pride has budded Ezek.7.10
iniquity, you have reaped *i.* Hos.10.13
is there *i.* on God's part? Rom.9.14

INK
I wrote them with *i.* on the scroll Jer.36.18
not with *i.* but with the Spirit of 2 Cor.3.3
would rather not use paper and *i.* 2 Jn.12
rather not write with pen and *i.* 3 Jn.13

INNER
The *i.* sanctuary he prepared in 1 Kg.6.19
into the *i.* court of the house Ezek.8.16
down into the *i.* part of the ship Jon.1.5
he put them into the *i.* prison Acts 16.24
our *i.* nature is being renewed 2 Cor.4.16
through his Spirit in the *i.* man Eph.3.16
hope . . . enters into the *i.* shrine Heb.6.19

INNOCENT
Lord, wilt thou slay an *i.* people? Gen.20.4
takes a bribe to slay an *i.* person Dt.27.25
who that was *i.* ever perished? Job 4.7
Though I am *i.*, I cannot answer him Job 9.15
he mocks at the calamity of the *i.* Job 9.23
I am *i.*, and God has taken away my Job 34.5
not take a bribe against the *i.* Ps.15.5
and *i.* of great transgression Ps.19.13
they poured out *i.* blood Ps.106.38
deprive the *i.* of his right Is.5.23
nor shed *i.* blood in this place Jer.22.3
wise as serpents and *i.* as doves Mt.10.16
I am *i.* of this man's blood Mt.27.24
said, "Certainly this man was *i.*!" Lk.23.47
that you may be blameless and *i.* Phil.2.15

INQUIRE
I. of God, we pray thee, that we may Jg.18.5
I. first for the word of the LORD 1 Kg.22.5
i. of the LORD for me and for 2 Chr.34.21
and to *i.* in his temple Ps.27.4
My people *i.* of a thing of wood Hos.4.12
do not seek the LORD or *i.* of him Zeph.1.6
prophets . . . *i.* about this salvation 1 Pet.1.10

INSCRIBE
Oh that they were *i.* in a book Job 19.23
i. it in a book, that it may be Is.30.8
this is the writing that was *i.* Dan.5.25
i. on the bells of the horses Zech.14.20
has a name *i.* which no one knows Rev.19.12

INSCRIPTION
pure gold, and wrote upon it an *i.* Ex.39.30
the *i.* of the charge against him Mk.15.26
Whose likeness and *i.* has it? Lk.20.24
I found also an altar with this *i.* Acts 17.23

INSIGHT
his words are without *i.* Job 34.35
understand words of *i.* Pr.1.2
whatever you get, get *i.* Pr.4.7
knowledge of the Holy One is *i.* Pr.9.10
in all wisdom and *i.* the mystery of Eph.1.9
my *i.* into the mystery of Christ Eph.3.4

INSOLENT
For *i.* men have risen against me Ps.54.3

Thou dost rebuke the *i.* Ps.119.21
the youth will be *i.* to the elder Is.3.5
You will see no more the *i.* people Is.33.19
i., haughty, boastful, inventors of Rom.1.30

INSPIRE
And he has *i.* him to teach Ex.35.34
I. decisions are on the lips of a Pr.16.10
David, *i.* by the Spirit, calls him Mt.22.43
And *i.* by the Spirit he came into Lk.2.27
which he mightily *i.* within me Col.1.29
with joy *i.* by the Holy Spirit 1 Th.1.6
All scripture is *i.* by God 2 Tim.3.16

INSTRUCT
gavest thy good Spirit to *i.* them Neh.9.20
I will *i.* you and teach you the way Ps.32.8
or as his counselor has *i.* him? Is.40.13
able to *i.* one another Rom.15.14
mind of the Lord so as to *i.* him? 1 Cor.2.16
are able to *i.* you for salvation 2 Tim.3.15
he was *i.* by God, saying, "See that Heb.8.5

INSTRUCTION
Receive *i.* from his mouth Job 22.22
fools despise wisdom and *i.* Pr.1.7
Keep hold of *i.*, do not let go Pr.4.13
Listen to advice and accept *i.* Pr.19.20
whatever . . . was written for our *i.* Rom.15.4
were written down for our *i.* 1 Cor.10.11
the discipline and *i.* of the Lord Eph.6.4
be able to give *i.* in sound doctrine Tit.1.9

INSTRUMENT
the forger of all *i.* of bronze Gen.4.22
accompanied by the *i.* of David 2 Chr.29.27
stringed *i.* make you glad Ps.45.8
he is a chosen *i.* of mine to carry Acts 9.15
not yield . . . to sin as *i.* of wickedness Rom.6.13
to God as *i.* of righteousness Rom.6.13
If even lifeless *i.*, . . . do not give 1 Cor.14.7

INTEGRITY
He still holds fast his *i.* Job 2.3
let God know my *i.* Job 31.6
May *i.* and uprightness preserve me Ps.25.21
O LORD, for I have walked in my *i.* Ps.26.1
The *i.* of the upright guides them Pr.11.3
who walks in *i.* will be delivered Pr.28.18
in your teaching show *i.*, gravity Tit.2.7

INTERCEDE
who can *i.* for him? 1 Sam.2.25
let them *i.* with the LORD of hosts Jer.27.18
Spirit himself *i.* for us with sighs Rom.8.26
Christ Jesus . . . indeed *i.* for us? Rom.8.34

INTERCESSION
made *i.* for the transgressors Is.53.12
I urge that . . . *i.* . . . be made 1 Tim.2.1
always lives to make *i.* for them Heb.7.25

INTEREST
you shall not exact *i.* from him Ex.22.25
received what was my own with *i.* Mt.25.27
and his *i.* are divided 1 Cor.7.34
look not only to his own *i.* Phil.2.4

INTERPRET
and understanding to *i.* dreams Dan.5.12
how to *i.* the appearance of the sky Mt.16.3
he *i.* to them in all the scriptures Lk.24.27
speak with tongues? Do all *i.*? 1 Cor.12.30
should pray for the power to *i.* 1 Cor.14.13

INTERPRETATION

This is its *i*.: the three branches	Gen.40.12
This is its *i*.: the three baskets	Gen.40.18
show me the dream and its *i*.	Dan.2.6
This is the *i*. of the matter: MENE	Dan.5.26
to another the *i*. of tongues	1 Cor.12.10
a revelation, a tongue, or an *i*.	1 Cor.14.26
is a matter of one's own *i*.	2 Pet.1.20

INVISIBLE

his *i*. nature . . . has been . . . perceived	Rom.1.20
He is the image of the *i*. God	Col.1.15
To the King of ages, immortal, *i*.	1 Tim.1.17
he endured as seeing him who is *i*.	Heb.11.27

INVITE

one of you will *i*. his neighbor	Zech.3.10
i. to the marriage feast as many	Mt.22.9
when you are *i*. . . . sit in the lowest	Lk.14.10
i. the poor, the maimed, the lame	Lk.14.13
he *i*. Philip to come up and sit	Acts 8.31
the unbelievers *i*. you to dinner	1 Cor.10.27
those who are *i*. to the marriage	Rev.19.9

INVOKE

the king *i*. the LORD your God	2 Sam.14.11
he began to *i*. a curse on himself	Mt.26.74
By faith Isaac *i*. future blessings	Heb.11.20
you *i*. as Father him who judges	1 Pet.1.17

INWARD

desirest truth in the *i*. being	Ps.51.6
the *i*. mind and heart . . . are deep	Ps.64.6
For thou didst form my *i*. parts	Ps.139.13
shall be hunger in your *i*. parts	Mic.6.14
but *i*. are ravenous wolves	Mt.7.15
He is a Jew who is one *i*.	Rom.2.29
groan *i*. as we wait for adoption	Rom.8.23

IOTA

Not an *i*., not a dot, will pass from	Mt.5.18

IRON

I. is taken out of the earth	Job 28.2
You shall break them with a rod of *i*.	Ps.2.9
I. sharpens *i*.	Pr.27.17
image on its feet of *i*. and clay	Dan.2.34
came to the *i*. gate leading into	Acts 12.10
they had scales like *i*. breastplates	Rev.9.9
he will rule them with a rod of *i*.	Rev.19.15

ISAAC

his birth promised, Gen.17.16,19; 18.10; born, Gen.21.2; offered by Abraham, Gen.22.7–14; marries Rebekah, Gen.24.67; blesses his sons, Gen.27.28–40; dies, Gen.35.29

ISAIAH

prophet, Is.1.1; 2.1; sent to Ahaz, Is.7; sent to Hezekiah, 2 Kg.20.1–19; Is.37.6; 38.5; 39.3; prophesies concerning various nations, Is.7–8; 10; 13–23; 45–47; referred to in Mt.3.3; 4.14; 8.17; 12.17; 13.14; 15.7; Mk.1.2; Jn.1.23; Acts 8.28; Rom.9.27

ISCARIOT

Judas, Mt.10.4; Mk.3.19; his treachery, Mt.26.21–25; Mk.14.18–21; Lk.22.47–48; Jn. 18.3; death, Mt.27.5; Acts 1.18

ISHMAEL

(1) son of Abram, Gen.16.15; 17.20; 21.17; 25.17; his descendants, Gen.25.12; 1 Chr.1.29; (2) son of Nethaniah, kills Gedaliah, 2 Kg.25.25; Jer.40.14; 41; (3) others, 1 Chr.8.38; 2 Chr. 19.11; Ezra 10.22

ISRAEL

(1) Jacob so named after striving with God, Gen.32.28; 35.10; Hos.12.3; (2) the name of the ten tribes as distinguished from Judah, 2 Sam.2.9

ISSACHAR

(1) son of Jacob, Gen.30.18; 35.23; (2) tribe, Gen.46.13; Jg.5.15; 1 Chr.7.1; (3) territory, occupied by tribe, Jos.19.17; *see* Gen.49.14; Num.1.28; 26.23; Dt.33.18; Ezek.48.33; Rev.7.7

IVORY

king . . . made a great *i*. throne	1 Kg.10.18
silver, *i*., apes, and peacocks	1 Kg.10.22
From *i*. palaces stringed instruments	Ps.45.8
the houses of *i*. shall perish	Am.3.15
Woe to those who lie upon beds of *i*.	Am.6.4
scented wood, all articles of *i*.	Rev.18.12

JACOB

his birth, Gen.25.26; birthright, Gen.25.33; blessing, Gen.27.27; his vision of the ladder, and vow, Gen.28.10–22; marriages, Gen.29; sons, Gen.29.31–30.24; dealings with Laban, Gen.31; his vision of God's host, Gen.32.1; his prayer, Gen.32.9; wrestles with an angel, Gen.32.24; Hos.12.4; reconciled with Esau, Gen.33; builds an altar at Bethel, Gen.35.1; his grief for Joseph and Benjamin, Gen.37; 42.38; goes down to Egypt, Gen.46; brought before Pharaoh, Gen.47.7; blesses his sons, Gen.48–49; his death, and burial, Gen.49.33; 50; *see* Ps. 105.23; Mal.1.2; Rom.9.10-13; Heb.11.21

JAIRUS

Mk.5.22; Lk.8.41

JAMES

English form of Jacob in the New Testament; (1) (Apostle), son of Zebedee, called, Mt.4.21; Mk.1.19; Lk.5.10; appointed one of the twelve, Mt.10.2; Mk.3.14; Lk.6.13; witnesses Jesus' transfiguration, Mt.17.1–8; Mk.9.2–8; Lk.9.28–36; present at Gethsemane, Mt.26.36–37; Mk.14.32–33; killed by Herod, Acts 12.2; (2) (Apostle), son of Alphaeus, Mt.10.3; Mk.3.18; Lk.6.15; Acts 1.13; (3) (brother of Jesus), Mt.13.55; Mk.6.3; 1 Cor. 15.7; head of church at Jerusalem, Acts 12.17; 15.13; 21.18; Gal.1.19; 2.9; (4) (the father of the Apostle Judas), Lk.6.16; Acts 1.13

JAW

or pierce his *j*. with a hook?	Job 41.2
my tongue cleaves to my *j*.	Ps.22.15
to place on the *j*. of the peoples	Is.30.28
I will put hooks in your *j*.	Ezek.29.4
one who eases the yoke on their *j*.	Hos.11.4

JAWBONE

he found a fresh *j*. of an ass	Jg.15.15
with the *j*. of an ass have I slain	Jg.15.16

JEALOUS

I the LORD your God am a *j*. God	Ex.20.5
God is a devouring fire, a *j*. God	Dt.4.24
I have been very *j*. for the LORD	1 Kg.19.10
The LORD is a *j*. God and avenging	Nah.1.2
am *j*. for Zion with great jealousy	Zech.8.2
love is not *j*. or boastful	1 Cor.13.4

JEALOUSY

This is the law in cases of *j*.	Num.5.29

stirred me to *j*. with what is no god Dt.32.21
moved him to *j*. with their graven Ps.78.58
not in quarreling and *j*. Rom.13.13
there is *j*. and strife among you 1 Cor.3.3
I feel a divine *j*. for you 2 Cor.11.2
j., anger, selfishness, dissension Gal.5.20
where *j*. and selfish ambition exist Jas.3.16

JEHOAHAZ
(1) son of Jehu, king of Israel, 2 Kg.10.35;
13.4; (2) (Shallum), king of Judah, his evil
reign, 2 Kg.23.31–34; 2 Chr.36.1–3; Jer.22.11–12

JEHOIADA
2 Sam.8.18; high priest, deposes and slays
Athaliah, and restores Jehoash, 2 Kg.11; 2
Chr.23; repairs the temple, 2 Kg.12.7; 2
Chr.24.6–14; abolishes idolatry, 2 Chr.23.16–17

JEHORAM
(1) (son of Jehoshaphat), king of Judah, 1
Kg.22.50; 2 Kg.8.16; his cruelty and death,
2 Chr.21.4,18; (2) (Joram), king of Israel, son
of Ahab, 2 Kg.1.17; 3.1; his evil reign, 2
Kg.3.2; slain by Jehu, 2 Kg.9.24; (3) a priest,
2 Chr.17.8

JEHOSHAPHAT
(1) king of Judah; his good reign, 1 Kg.15.24;
2 Chr.17; his death, 1 Kg.22.50; 2 Chr.21.1;
(2) others, 2 Sam.8.16; 1 Kg.4.17; 2 Kg.9.2;
1 Chr.11.43; 15.24; (3) valley of, Jl.3.2

JEHU
(1) son of Hanani, prophesies against Baasha,
1 Kg.16.1; rebukes Jehoshaphat, 2 Chr.19.2;
20.34; (2) son of Nimshi, to be anointed king of
Israel, 1 Kg.19.16; 2 Kg.9.1–3; his reign, 2
Kg.9.4–10.36; (3) others, 1 Chr.2.38; 4.35;
12.3

JEPHTHAH
Jg.11.1,29; 12.7; 1 Sam.12.11; Heb.11.32

JEREMIAH
(1) prophet, his call and visions, Jer.1; his
mission, Jer.7; his complaint, Jer.20.14; his
message to Zedekiah, Jer.21.3; 34.2; arraigned,
condemned, but delivered, Jer.26; denounces
the false prophet Hananiah, Jer.28.5–17; his
promises of redemption to Israel, Jer.31; dic-
tates a scroll, Jer.36.4; Baruch reads it, Jer.36.8;
imprisoned by Zedekiah, Jer.37–38; released,
Jer.38.7–13; with all the remnant of Israel carried into Egypt, Jer.43.4–7; various predictions,
Jer.46–51; mentioned in Dan.9.2; Mt.2.17;
16.14; 27.9; (2) others, 2 Kg.23.31; 1 Chr.5.24;
12.4,10

JERICHO
15 miles northeast of Jerusalem, in the Jordan
valley, 5 miles from the river, Num.22.1; the
spies at, Jos.2.1; capture of, Jos.6.20 (Heb.
11.30); rebuilt by Hiel, 1 Kg.16.34; *see* Jos.6.26

JEROBOAM I
1 Kg.11.26; promoted by Solomon, 1 Kg.11.28;
Ahijah's prophecy to, 1 Kg.11.29–39; made
king, 1 Kg.12.20 (2 Chr.10); his idolatry,
withered hand, denunciation, 1 Kg.12; 13;
14; death, 1 Kg.14.20; evil example, 1 Kg.15.34

JEROBOAM II
2 Kg.13.13; 14.23–29

JERUSALEM
the religious capital of Palestine; Adoni-zedek,

king of, slain by Joshua, Jos.10; David reigns
there, 2 Sam.5.6–10; the ark brought there, 2
Sam.6; saved from the pestilence, 2 Sam.24.16–
25; temple built at, 1 Kg.5–8; 2 Chr.1–7; sufferings from war, 1 Kg.14.25; 2 Kg.14.14; 25;
2 Chr.12; 25.24; 36; capture and destruction by
Nebuchadrezzar, Jer.52.12–15; captives return,
and rebuilding of the temple begun by Cyrus,
Ezra 1–3; continued by Artaxerxes, Neh.2; wall
rebuilt and dedicated by Nehemiah, Neh.12.38;
abominations there, Ezek.16.2; presentation of
Christ at, Lk.2.22; Christ rides into, Mt.21.1–
11; Mk.11.7–11; Lk.19.28–38; Jn.12.12–15;
laments over it, Mt.23.37–39; Lk.13.34; 19.41;
foretells its destruction, Mt.24; Mk.13; Lk.13.34;
19.43; 21; disciples filled with the Holy Spirit
at, Acts 2.4; the new, Rev.21.2

JESSE
Ru.4.17; 1 Sam.16.10; Ps.72.20; Is.11.1;
Lk.3.32; Rom.15.12

JESUS
(1) his birth foretold, Lk.1.26–38; born,
Mt.1.18–25; Lk.2.1–7; is circumcised and presented in the temple, Lk.2.21–38; visited by
the wise men, Mt.2.1–12; taken to Egypt, Mt.
2.13–18; brought to Nazareth, Mt.2.19–23; Lk.
2.39; visits Jerusalem when twelve years of
age, Lk. 2.41–50; is baptized, Mt.3.13–17;
Mk.1.9–11; Lk.3.21–22; tempted by the devil,
Mt.4.1–11; Mk.1.12–13; Lk.4.1–13; calls his
disciples, Mt. 4.18–29; 9.9; Jn.1.35–51; delivers
the Sermon on the Mount, Mt.5–7; commis-
sions the twelve, Mt.10.1–4; Mk.3.13–19;
Lk.6.12–16; teaches in parables, Mt.13.1–52;
Mk.4.1–34; performs miracles, Mk.4.35–5.43;
Jn.2.1–11; foretells his death and resurrection,
Mt.16.21–26; Mk. 10.32–34; Lk.18.31–34;
is transfigured, Mt.17.1–8; Mk.9.2–8; Lk.
9.28–36; his triumphal entry into Jerusalem,
Mt.21.1–11; Mk.11.1–11; Lk.19.28–44; Jn.
12.12–19; institutes the Lord's supper, Mt.
26.26–29; Mk.14.22–25; Lk.22.15–20; 1 Cor.
11.23–25; farewell discourses to his disciples,
Jn.14–16; his high priestly prayer, Jn.17; is
betrayed, arrested, and forsaken, Mt.26.47–56;
Mk.14.43–50; Lk.22.47–53; Jn.18.2–14; crucified, Mt.27.33–56; Mk.15.22–41; Lk.23.33–49;
Jn.19.17–30; appears to his disciples after his
resurrection, Mt.28.9–20; Mk.16.9–18; Lk.
24.13–49; Jn.20.11–31; Acts 1.3–8; 1 Cor.
15.5–7; the great commission, Mt.28.18–20;
his ascension, Mk.16.19–20; Lk.24.50–53; Acts
1.9–11; *see* CHRIST; (2) Mt.27.16–17 note *k*;
(3) Justus, Col.4.11

JEWEL
for wisdom is better than *j*. Pr.8.11
She is far more precious than *j*. Pr.31.10
like . . . *j*. . . . they shall shine Zech.9.16
imperishable *j*. of a gentle . . . spirit 1 Pet.3.4
were adorned with every *j*. Rev.21.19

JEZEBEL
wife of Ahab, 1 Kg.16.31; kills the prophets, 1
Kg.18.4; 19.2; causes Naboth to be put to
death, 1 Kg.21; her violent death, 2 Kg.9.30–37

JEZREEL
Jos.17.16; 1 Sam.29.11; 2 Sam.4.4; 2 Kg.9.30

JOAB
(1) 2 Sam.2.13; nephew of David, and captain of the host, 2 Sam.8.16; kills Abner, 2 Sam. 3.27; intercedes for Absalom, 2 Sam.14; kills him in an oak, 2 Sam.18.14; reproves David's grief, 2 Sam.19.5–8; kills Amasa, 2 Sam.20.9–10; unwillingly numbers the people, 2 Sam.24.3–9 (1 Chr.21.3–6); joins Adonijah's usurpation, 1 Kg.1.7; killed by Solomon's command, 1 Kg.2.5-34; (2) Othniel's grandson, 1 Chr.4.14; (3) Ezra 2.6; 8.9; Neh.7.11

JOASH
(1) father of Gideon, Jg.6.11; (2) (Jehoash), king of Israel, 2 Kg.13.10; visits Elisha, 2 Kg.13.14; defeats the Syrians, 2 Kg.13.25; defeats Amaziah, 2 Kg.14.8–14; (3) king of Judah, 2 Chr.23.3; 24.1–14; repairs the temple, 2 Kg.12; 2 Chr.24; kills Zechariah, 2 Chr.24.22; killed by his servants, 2 Kg.12.19–21; 2 Chr.24.23–27; (4) others, 1 Kg.22.26; 1 Chr. 4.22; 12.3; 27.28

JOB
his character, Job 1.1,8; 2.3; Ezek.14.14,20; his afflictions and patience, Job 1.13–21; 2.7–10; Jas.5.11; complains of his life, Job 3; reproves his friends, Job 6–7; 9–10; 12–14; 16–17; 19; 21; 23–24; 26–30; solemnly protests his integrity, Job 31; humbles himself, Job 40.3–5; 42.1–6; God accepts and doubly blesses, Job 42.10

JOHN
English form of Johanan; (1) the Apostle, called, Mt.4.21; Mk.1.19; Lk.5.10; reproved, Mt.20. 20–23; Mk.10.35–40; Lk.9.49–50; sent to prepare the passover, Lk.22.8; his care for Mary the mother of Jesus, Jn.19.27; meets for prayer, Acts 1.13; accompanies Peter before the council, Acts 3–4; (2) (Mark) Acts 12.12, 25; see MARK; (3) the Baptist, his birth and circumcision, Lk.1.13–25,57–80; preaching and baptism of, Mt.3; Mk.1; Lk.3; Jn.1.6; 3.26; Acts 1.5; 13.24; imprisoned by Herod, Mt.4.12; Mk.1.14; Lk.3.20; beheaded, Mt.14; Mk.6.25; sends his disciples to Christ, Mt.11.2; Lk.7.19; Christ's testimony concerning, Mt.11.11; 17.12–13; Mk.9.11–13; Lk.7.27–28; his disciples receive the Holy Spirit, Acts 19.3–6; (4) Jewish dignitary, Acts 4.6; (5) the seer, Rev.1.4,9; 22.8

JOIN
I . . . j. words together against you   Job 16.4
Woe to those who j. house to house   Is.5.8
What therefore God has j. together   Mk.10.9
the whole structure is j. together   Eph.2.21
j. and knit together by every joint   Eph.4.16

JONAH
2 Kg.14.25;   Jon.1.1;   Mt.12.39–40;   16.4; Lk.11.32

JONATHAN
(1) son of Saul, defeats the Philistines, 1 Sam.13.2–3; 14.1–15; his love for David, 1 Sam.18.1; 19; 20; 23.16; killed by the Philistines, 1 Sam.31.2; David's lamentation for, 2 Sam. 1.17–27; (2) son of Abiathar, 2 Sam.15.27; 1 Kg.1.42; (3) one of David's nephews, 2

Sam.21.21; 1 Chr.20.7; (4) son of Gershom, Jg.18.30

JORDAN
river, waters of, divided for the Israelites, Jos.3; 4; Ps.114.3; by Elijah and Elisha, 2 Kg.2.8, 13–14; Naaman's leprosy cured at, 2 Kg.5.10–14; John baptizes there, Mt.3; Mk.1.5; Lk.3.3; see Job 40.23; Ps.42.6; Jer.12.5; 49.19; Zech.11.3

JOSEPH
(1) son of Jacob, Gen.30.24; see Ps.105.17; Acts 7.9; Heb.11.22; his dreams, and the jealousy of his brothers, Gen.37.5; sold to the Ishmaelites, Gen.37.28; slave to Potiphar, Gen.39; resists Potiphar's wife, Gen.39.7–13; interprets the dreams of Pharaoh's servants, Gen.40, and of Pharaoh, predicting famine, Gen.41.25; made ruler of Egypt, Gen.41.39–41; prepares for the famine, Gen.41.48–49; receives his brothers and father, Gen.42–46; gives direction concerning his bones, Gen.50.25; his death, Gen.50.26; (2) of Arimathea, Mt.27.57; Mk.15.42–43; Lk.23.50; Jn.19.38; (3) (Barsabbas), Justus, Acts 1.23; (4) others, Num.13.7; Ezra 10.42; Neh.12.14; Lk.3.24

JOSHUA
son of Nun, Num.14.6; 1 Chr.7.27; Heb.4.8; ministers to Moses, Ex.24.13; 32.17; 33.11; spies out Canaan, Num.13.16; appointed to succeed Moses, Num.27.18–23; 34.17; Dt.1.38; 3.28; 34.9; reassured by God, Jos.1; crosses river Jordan, Jos.3; erects memorial pillars, Jos.4; assaults and destroys Jericho, Jos.6; condemns Achan, Jos.7; subdues Ai, Jos.8; his victories, Jos.10–12; apportions the land, Jos. 14–21; his charge to the Reubenites, Jos.22; exhortation to the people, Jos.23; reminds them of God's mercies, Jos.24; renews the covenant, Jos.24.14–28; his death, Jos.24.29; Jg.2.8; his curse, Jos.6.26, fulfilled, 1 Kg.16.34; (2) others, 1 Sam.6.14; 2 Kg.23.8; Hag.1.1; Zech. 3.1–9

JOSIAH
(1) 2 Kg.21.24; prophecy concerning, 1 Kg.13.2; fulfilled, 2 Kg.23.15–18; reigns well, 2 Kg.22; repairs the temple, 2 Kg.22.3–7; hears the words of the book of the law, 2 Kg.22.8–13; Huldah's message from God to him, 2 Kg.22.14–20; reads the book of the covenant, 2 Kg.23; keeps the passover, 2 Chr.35; slain by Pharaoh Neco at Megiddo, 2 Kg.23.29; (2) son of Zephaniah, Zech.6.10

JOTHAM
(1) son of Jerubbaal (Gideon), Jg.9.5; (2) king of Judah, 2 Kg.15.32; 2 Chr.27

JOY
sing for j. before the LORD   1 Chr.16.33
there was great j. in Jerusalem   2 Chr.30.26
the j. of the LORD is your strength   Neh.8.10
the widow's heart to sing for j.   Job 29.13
all the sons of God shouted for j.?   Job 38.7
in thy presence there is fulness of j.   Ps.16.11
but j. comes with the morning   Ps.30.5
is the j. of all the earth   Ps.48.2
let thy saints shout for j.   Ps.132.9
they shall obtain j. and gladness   Is.35.10

I will turn their mourning into *j*. Jer.31.13
the *j*. of all the earth? Lam.2.15
rejoiced exceedingly with great *j*. Mt.2.10
more *j*. in heaven over one sinner Lk.15.7
but your sorrow will turn into *j*. Jn.16.20
my brethren . . . my *j*. and crown Phil.4.1
For you are our glory and *j*. 1 Th.2.20
Count it all *j*., my brethren, when Jas.1.2

JOYFUL
not distinguish . . . the *j*. shout from Ezra 3.13
for the LORD had made them *j*. Ezra 6.22
Make a *j*. noise to God, all the earth Ps.66.1
But let the righteous be *j*. Ps.68.3
Make a *j*. noise to the LORD, all Ps.100.1
city is forsaken, the *j*. city Jer.49.25

JUDAH
(1) son of Jacob, Gen.29.35; his descendants, Gen.38; 46.12; Num.1.26; 26.19; 1 Chr.4; pledges himself for Benjamin, Gen.43.9; his interview with Joseph, Gen.44.18–34; blessed by Jacob, Gen.49.8–12; (2) tribe of, their blessing by Moses, Dt.33.7; their inheritance, Jos.15; they make David king, 2 Sam.2.4; (3) others, Ezra 3.9; 10.23; Neh.11.9

JUDAS
Greek form of Judah, (1) Apostle, son of James, Lk.6.16; Jn.14.22; Acts 1.13; (2) the brother of Jesus, Mt.13.55; Mk.6.3; (3) of Galilee, Acts 5.37; (4) (Barsabbas), Acts 15.22

JUDAS ISCARIOT
Mt.10.4; Mk.3.19; Lk.6.16; Jn.6.70–71; betrays Jesus, Mt.26.14–16,47–56; Mk.14.10,43–50; Lk.22.3–6,47–53; Jn.13.26–30; 18.2–11; kills himself, Mt.27.5; Acts 1.18

JUDEA
Ezra 9.9; Mt.2.5; Mk.1.5; Jn.4.3; Acts 28.21; Gal.1.22

JUDGE (verb)
the LORD *j*. between me and you 1 Sam.24.12
for he comes to *j*. the earth 1 Chr.16.33
j. me . . . according to my righteousness Ps.7.8
j. the world with righteousness Ps.96.13
He shall *j*. between the nations Is.2.4
He shall not *j*. by what his eyes see Is.11.3
I will *j*. between sheep and Ezek.34.22
J. not, and you will not be *j*. Lk.6.37
The Father *j*. no one, but has given Jn.5.22
You *j*. according to the flesh, I *j*. Jn.8.15
the ruler of this world is *j*. Jn.16.11
then how could God *j*. the world? Rom.3.6
not know that we are to *j*. angels? 1 Cor.6.3
But when we are *j*. by the Lord 1 Cor.11.32
that you may not be *j*. Jas.5.9
dead were *j*. by what was written Rev.20.12

JUDGMENT
but I will bring *j*. on the nation Gen.15.14
You shall do no injustice in *j*. Lev.19.15
and enters into *j*. with you? Job 22.4
for any man to go before God in *j*. Job 34.23
the wicked will not stand in the *j*. Ps.1.5
but it is God who executes *j*. Ps.75.7
Teach me good *j*. and knowledge Ps.119.66
Enter not into *j*. with thy servant Ps.143.2
God will bring every deed into *j*. Ec.12.14
By oppression and *j*. he was taken Is.53.8

the court sat in *j*., and the books Dan.7.10
my *j*. goes forth as the light Hos.6.5
whoever kills shall be liable to *j*. Mt.5.21
arise at the *j*. with this generation Lk.11.32
but has given all *j*. to the Son Jn.5.22
my *j*. is true, for it is not I alone Jn.8.16
Now is the *j*. of this world Jn.12.31
God's righteous *j*. will be revealed Rom.2.5
all stand before the *j*. seat of God Rom.14.10
die once, and after that comes *j*. Heb.9.27
yet mercy triumphs over *j*. Jas.2.13
to be kept until the *j*. 2 Pet.2.4
pronounce a reviling *j*. upon him Jude 9
In one hour has thy *j*. come Rev.18.10
for his *j*. are true and just Rev.19.2

JUST
A full and *j*. weight you shall have Dt.25.15
Let me be weighed in a *j*. balance Job 31.6
For thou hast maintained my *j*. cause Ps.9.4
The LORD is *j*. in all his ways Ps.145.17
A *j*. balance and scales are the Pr.16.11
The way of the Lord is not *j*. Ezek.18.25
rain on the *j*. and on the unjust Mt.5.45
my judgment is *j*., because I seek Jn.5.30
Their condemnation is *j*. Rom.3.8
commandment is holy and *j*. and good Rom.7.12
God deems it *j*. to repay with 2 Th.1.6
received a *j*. retribution Heb.2.2
the spirits of *j*. men made perfect Heb.12.23
he is faithful and *j*. 1 Jn.1.9
for his judgments are true and *j*. Rev.19.2

JUSTICE
He executes *j*. for the fatherless Dt.10.18
You shall not pervert *j*. Dt.16.19
the Almighty will not pervert *j*. Job 34.12
to do *j*. to the fatherless Ps.10.18
For the LORD loves *j*. Ps.37.28
j. to the weak and the fatherless Ps.82.3
I will sing of loyalty and of *j*. Ps.101.1
A worthless witness mocks at *j*. Pr.19.28
but from the LORD a man gets *j*. Pr.29.26
seek *j*., correct oppression Is.1.17
For the LORD is a God of *j*. Is.30.18
For I the LORD love *j*. Is.61.8
Do *j*. and righteousness Jer.22.3
But let *j*. roll down like waters Am.5.24
LORD require of you but to do *j*. Mic.6.8
j. and mercy and faith Mt.23.23
serves to show the *j*. of God Rom.3.5

JUSTIFY
so that thou art *j*. in thy sentence Ps.51.4
Yet wisdom is *j*. by her deeds Mt.11.19
doers of the law who will be *j*. Rom.2.13
For if Abraham was *j*. by works Rom.4.2
since we are *j*. by faith, we have Rom.5.1
those whom he *j*. he also glorified Rom.8.30
man is not *j*. by works of the law Gal.2.16
God would *j*. the Gentiles by faith Gal.3.8
no man is *j*. before God by the law Gal.3.11
You see that a man is *j*. by works Jas.2.24

KEEP
you shall *k*. my covenant, you and Gen.17.9
would *k*. the passover to the LORD Ex.12.48
the sabbath day, to *k*. it holy Ex.20.8
So you shall *k*. my commandments Lev.22.31

The LORD bless you and *k*. you — Num.6.24
K. back thy servant also from — Ps.19.13
O God, do not *k*. silence — Ps.83.1
nor will he *k*. his anger for ever — Ps.103.9
to those who *k*. his covenant — Ps.103.18
I will *k*. thy law continually — Ps.119.44
The LORD will *k*. you from all evil — Ps.121.7
K. your heart with all vigilance — Pr.4.23
k. my teachings as the apple of — Pr.7.2
Fear God, and *k*. his commandments — Ec.12.13
Thou dost *k*. him in perfect peace — Is.26.3
If you *k*. my commandments — Jn.15.10
Holy Father, *k*. them in thy name — Jn.17.11
the women should *k*. silence — 1 Cor.14.34
will *k*. your hearts and your minds — Phil.4.7
let him *k*. his tongue from evil — 1 Pet.3.10
All who *k*. his commandments abide — 1 Jn.3.24
k. yourselves in the love of God — Jude 21

KIDRON
2 Sam.15.23; 2 Kg.23.6; Jer.31.40; Jn.18.1

KILL
his brother Abel, and *k*. him — Gen.4.8
heard of it, he sought to *k*. Moses — Ex.2.15
You shall not *k*. — Ex.20.13
Saul my father seeks to *k*. you — 1 Sam.19.2
the men of old, 'You shall not *k*. — Mt.5.21
for Herod wants to *k*. you — Lk.13.31
Do not *k*., Do not steal, Do not bear — Lk.18.20
Jews sought all the more to *k*. him — Jn.5.18
passed, the Jews plotted to *k*. him — Acts 9.23
Rise, Peter; *k*. and eat — Acts 10.13

KIN
any one near of *k*. to him — Lev.18.6
for you are next of *k*. — Ru.3.9
the king is near of *k*. to us — 2 Sam.19.42
in his own country . . . among his own *k*. — Mk.6.4

KIND
If you will be *k*. to his people — 2 Chr.10.7
A man who is *k*. benefits himself — Pr.11.17
He who is *k*. to the poor lends to — Pr.19.17
the Most High . . . is *k*. to the ungrateful — Lk.6.35
Love is patient and *k*. — 1 Cor.13.4
k. to one another, tenderhearted — Eph.4.32
it was *k*. of you to share my — Phil.4.14
k., and submissive to their husbands — Tit.2.5
be submissive . . . not only to the *k*. — 1 Pet.2.18

KINDLED
Jacob's anger was *k*. against Rachel — Gen.30.2
a fire is *k*. by my anger, and it — Dt.32.22
Eliab's anger was *k*. against David — 1 Sam.17.28
of the LORD was *k*. against Uzzah — 1 Chr.13.10
My wrath is *k*. against you — Job 42.7
a fire was *k*. against Jacob — Ps.78.21
and would that it were already *k*. — Lk.12.49
heavens will be *k*. and dissolved — 2 Pet.3.12

KINDLY
May the LORD deal *k*. with you — Ru.1.8
Julius treated Paul *k*. — Acts 27.3
remember us *k*. and long to see us — 1 Th.3.6
be . . . *k*. to every one — 2 Tim.2.24

KINDNESS
whose *k*. has not forsaken the living — Ru.2.20
I may show him *k*. for Jonathan's — 2 Sam.9.1
He who withholds *k*. from a friend — Job 6.14
For he did not remember to show *k*. — Ps.109.16
and to love *k*., and to walk humbly — Mic.6.8

God's *k*. is meant to lead you — Rom.2.4
Note then . . . God's *k*. to you — Rom.11.22
loving *k*. of God our Savior appeared — Tit.3.4
you have tasted the *k*. of the Lord — 1 Pet.2.3

KING
Now there arose a new *k*. over Egypt — Ex.1.8
there was no *k*. in Israel — Jg.18.1
but we will have a *k*. over us — 1 Sam.8.19
shouted, "Long live the *k*.!" — 1 Sam.10.24
that the *K*. of glory may come in — Ps.24.9
For God is the *K*. of all the earth — Ps.47.7
O LORD of hosts, my *k*. and my God — Ps.84.3
and a great *K*. above all gods — Ps.95.3
and faithfulness preserve the *k*. — Pr.20.28
In the year that *K*. Uzziah died — Is.6.1
for my eyes have seen the *K*. — Is.6.5
a *k*. will reign in righteousness — Is.32.1
the *K*. of Israel and his Redeemer — Is.44.6
for I am a great *K*., says the LORD — Mal.1.14
who has been born *k*. of the Jews? — Mt.2.2
your *k*. is coming to you, humble and — Mt.21.5
This is Jesus the *K*. of the Jews — Mt.27.37
salute him, "Hail, *K*. of the Jews!" — Mk.15.18
saying that he himself is Christ a *k*. — Lk.23.2
the Lord, even the *K*. of Israel — Jn.12.13
Pilate said . . . "So you are a *k*.?" — Jn.18.37
that there is another *k*., Jesus — Acts 17.7
Wherefore, O *K*. Agrippa, I was — Acts 26.19
K. of ages, immortal, invisible — 1 Tim.1.17
k. of Salem, that is, *k*. of peace — Heb.7.2
Just and true . . . O *K*. of the ages — Rev.15.3
K. of kings and Lord of lords — Rev.19.16

KINGDOM
The beginning of his *k*. was Babel — Gen.10.10
come to the *k*. for such a time as — Est.4.14
and his *k*. rules over all — Ps.103.19
the glorious splendor of thy *k*. — Ps.145.12
Thy *k*. is an everlasting *k*. — Ps.145.13
and the *k*. shall be the LORD's — Ob.21
for the *k*. of heaven is at hand — Mt.4.17
Thy *k*. come, Thy will be done — Mt.6.10
the *k*. of God has come upon you — Mt.12.28
the keys of the *k*. of heaven — Mt.16.19
Then the *k*. of heaven shall be — Mt.25.1
if a *k*. is divided against itself — Mk.3.24
The *k*. of God is as if a man should — Mk.4.26
You are not far from the *k*. of God — Mk.12.34
The *k*. of God has come near to you — Lk.10.9
k. of God is in the midst of you — Lk.17.21
as my Father appointed a *k*. for me — Lk.22.29
the *k*. of God does not mean food — Rom.14.17
the *k*. of God does not consist — 1 Cor.4.20
delivers the *k*. to God the Father — 1 Cor.15.24
who through faith conquered *k*. — Heb.11.33
receiving a *k*. that cannot be — Heb.12.28
made us a *k*., priests to his God — Rev.1.6
The *k*. of the world has become — Rev.11.15

KISS (noun)
profuse are the *k*. of an enemy — Pr.27.6
betray the Son of man with a *k*.? — Lk.22.48
Greet one another with a holy *k*. — Rom.16.16
Greet . . . with the *k*. of love — 1 Pet.5.14

KISS (verb)
k. his feet, lest he be angry — Ps.2.12
The one I shall *k*. is the man — Mt.26.48

she has not ceased to *k.* my feet	Lk.7.45	by *k.* the righteous are delivered	Pr.11.9
wept and embraced Paul and *k.* him	Acts 20.37	The tongue of the wise dispenses *k.*	Pr.15.2

KNEE

cried before him, "Bow the *k.!*"	Gen.41.43	God gives wisdom and *k.* and joy	Ec.2.26
and make firm the feeble *k.*	Is.35.3	give *k.* of salvation to his people	Lk.1.77
To me every *k.* shall bow	Is.45.23	through the law comes *k.* of sin	Rom.3.20
who have not bowed the *k.* to Baal	Rom.11.4	"*K.*" puffs up, but love builds up	1 Cor.8.1
every *k.* shall bow to me	Rom.14.11	understand all mysteries and all *k.*	1 Cor.13.2
name of Jesus every *k.* should bow	Phil.2.10	love of Christ which surpasses *k.*	Eph.3.19

KNEW

		of what is falsely called *k.*	1 Tim.6.20
and they *k.* that they were naked	Gen.3.7	the grace and *k.* of our Lord	2 Pet.3.18
that I *k.* where I might find him	Job 23.3		

LABAN

Before I formed you . . . I *k.* you	Jer.1.5	(1) hospitality of, Gen.24.29; gives Jacob his
I declare to them, 'I never *k.* you	Mt.7.23	two daughters, Gen.29; envies and oppresses
You *k.* that I reap where I have not	Mt.25.26	him, Gen.30.27; 31.1; his dream, Gen.31.24;
But he *k.* their thoughts, and he	Lk.6.8	his covenant with Jacob, Gen.31.43–50; (2) city,
yet the world *k.* him not	Jn.1.10	Dt.1.1
For Jesus *k.* from the first who	Jn.6.64	

LABOR (verb)

For he *k.* who was to betray him	Jn.13.11	Six days you shall *l.*, and do all	Ex.20.9
although they *k.* God they did not	Rom.1.21	those who build it *l.* in vain	Ps.127.1
made him to be sin who *k.* no sin	2 Cor.5.21	all who *l.* and are heavy-laden	Mt.11.28

KNOCK

k., and it will be opened to you	Mt.7.7	reap that for which you did not *l.*	Jn.4.38
Behold, I stand at the door and *k.*	Rev.3.20	Do not *l.* for the food which perishes	Jn.6.27

KNOW

		we *l.*, working with our own hands	1 Cor.4.12
that you may *k.* that I am the Lord	Ex.8.22	but rather let him *l.*	Eph.4.28
Moses did not *k.* that the skin of	Ex.34.29	did not run in vain or *l.* in vain	Phil.2.16
Now Samuel did not yet *k.* the Lord	1 Sam.3.7	those who *l.* in preaching	1 Tim.5.17

LABORER

Make me *k.* my transgression and my	Job 13.23	Sweet is the sleep of a *l.*	Ec.5.12
For I *k.* that my Redeemer lives	Job 19.25	is plentiful, but the *l.* are few	Mt.9.37
I *k.* that thou canst do all things	Job 42.2	The *l.* deserves his wages	1 Tim.5.18
Make me to *k.* thy ways, O Lord	Ps.25.4	wages of the *l.* who mowed your	Jas.5.4
Be still, and *k.* that I am God	Ps.46.10	

LAMB

K. that the Lord is God! It is he	Ps.100.3	Your *l.* shall be without blemish	Ex.12.5
For he *k.* our frame; he remembers	Ps.103.14	But if he cannot afford a *l.*	Lev.5.7
Search me, O God, and *k.* my heart	Ps.139.23	The wolf shall dwell with the *l.*	Is.11.6
Therefore my people shall *k.* my name	Is.52.6	like a *l.* . . . led to the slaughter	Is.53.7
'*K.* the Lord,' for they shall all	Jer.31.34	send you out as *l.* in the midst of	Lk.10.3
your left hand *k.* what your right	Mt.6.3	*L.* of God, who takes away the sin	Jn.1.29
no one *k.* the Son except the Father	Mt.11.27	or a *l.* before its shearer is dumb	Acts 8.32
I say to you, I do not *k.* you	Mt.25.12	paschal *l.*, has been sacrificed	1 Cor.5.7
k. how to give good gifts to your	Lk.11.13	like that of a *l.* without blemish	1 Pet.1.19
saying, "Woman, I do not *k.* him."	Lk.22.57	I saw a *L.* standing, as though it	Rev.5.6
Nathanael said . . . "How do you *k.* me?"	Jn.1.48	Worthy is the *L.* who was slain	Rev.5.12
you will *k.* the truth, and the truth	Jn.8.32	the throne of God and of the *L.*	Rev.22.1
We *k.* that God does not listen to	Jn.9.31	

LAME

I *k.* my own and my own *k.* me	Jn.10.14	he fell, and became *l.*	2 Sam.4.4
I *k.* that he will rise again	Jn.11.24	then shall the *l.* man leap like a	Is.35.6
they *k.* that everything that thou	Jn.17.7	to enter life *l.* than with two feet	Mk.9.45
We *k.* that in everything God works	Rom.8.28	the *l.* walk, lepers are cleansed	Lk.7.22
Now I *k.* in part; then I shall	1 Cor.13.12	And a man *l.* from birth was being	Acts 3.2
and to *k.* the love of Christ which	Eph.3.19	

LAMENT

that I may *k.* him and the power of	Phil.3.10	year by year to *l.* the daughter of	Jg.11.40
I *k.* how to be abased, and I *k.*	Phil.4.12	Gird on sackcloth and *l.*, O priests	Jl.1.13
for I *k.* whom I have believed	2 Tim.1.12	of women who bewailed and *l.* him	Lk.23.27
The Lord *k.* those who are his	2 Tim.2.19	I say to you, you will weep and *l.*	Jn.16.20
They profess to *k.* God, but	Tit.1.16	

LAMP

'*K.* the Lord,' for all shall *k.* me	Heb.8.11	thou art my *l.*, O Lord	2 Sam.22.29
you do not *k.* about tomorrow	Jas.4.14	Yea, thou dost light my *l.*	Ps.18.28
who says "I *k.* him" but disobeys	1 Jn.2.4	Thy word is a *l.* to my feet and a	Ps.119.105
who does not love does not *k.* God	1 Jn.4.8	spirit of man is the *l.* of the Lord	Pr.20.27

KNOWLEDGE

		l. of the wicked will be put out	Pr.24.20
the tree of the *k.* of good and evil	Gen.2.9	Nor do men light a *l.* and put it	Mt.5.15
for the Lord is a God of *k.*	1 Sam.2.3	For when the foolish took their *l.*	Mt.25.3
he multiplies words without *k.*	Job 35.16	Your eye is the *l.* of your body	Lk.11.34
Such *k.* is too wonderful for me	Ps.139.6	be girded and your *l.* burning	Lk.12.35

as to a *l.* shining in a dark	2 Pet.1.19	**LAZARUS**	
they need no light of *l.* or sun	Rev.22.5	(1) a poor man, Lk.16.20; (2) brother of	
LANGUAGE		Mary and Martha, raised from the dead,	
people, and they have all one *l.*	Gen.11.6	Jn.11; 12.1	
from a people of strange *l.*	Ps. 114.1	**LEAD**	
heard them speaking in his own *l.*	Acts 2.6	let them *l.* me, let them bring me to	Ps.43.3
not know the meaning of the *l.*	1 Cor.14.11	*L.* thou me to the rock that is higher	Ps.61.2
LAODICEA		*l.* me in the way everlasting	Ps.139.24
Col.2.1; 4.16; Rev.1.11; 3.14		a little child shall *l.* them	Is.11.6
LAST		gently *l.* those that are with young	Is.40.11
at *l.* he will stand upon the earth	Job 19.25	And *l.* us not into temptation	Mt.6.13
But many that are first will be *l.*	Mt.19.30	Can a blind man *l.* a blind man?	Lk.6.39
a loud cry, and breathed his *l.*	Mk.15.37	in Christ always *l.* us in triumph	2 Cor.2.14
I will raise him up at the *l.* day	Jn.6.40	repentance that *l.* to salvation	2 Cor.7.10
The *l.* enemy to be destroyed is	1 Cor.15.26	to *l.* a life worthy of God	1 Th.2.12
the *l.* Adam became a life-giving	1 Cor.15.45	that we may *l.* a quiet . . . life	1 Tim.2.2
at the *l.* trumpet	1 Cor.15.52	**LEADER**	
I am the first and the *l.*	Rev.1.17	the *l.* of the people of Judah being	Num.2.3
bowls full of the seven *l.* plagues	Rev.21.9	take one *l.* of every tribe	Num.34.18
LAUGH (verb)		to Jephthah, "Come and be our *l.*	Jg.11.6
Abraham fell on his face and *l.*	Gen.17.17	for he chose Judah as *l.*	1 Chr.28.4
He who sits in the heavens *l.*	Ps.2.4	a *l.* and commander for the peoples	Is.55.4
a time to weep, and a time to *l.*	Ec.3.4	the *l.* as one who serves	Lk.22.26
And they *l.* at him	Mt.9.24	at his right hand as *L.* and Savior	Acts 5.31
Woe to you that *l.* now	Lk.6.25	Remember your *l.*, those who spoke	Heb.13.7
LAUGHTER		Obey your *l.* and submit to them	Heb.13.17
Then our mouth was filled with *l.*	Ps.126.2	Greet all your *l.* and all the saints	Heb.13.24
Even in *l.* the heart is sad	Pr.14.13	**LEAF**	
Sorrow is better than *l.*	Ec.7.3	a freshly plucked olive *l.*	Gen.8.11
Let your *l.* be turned to mourning	Jas.4.9	its *l.* does not wither	Ps.1.3
LAW		be like an oak whose *l.* withers	Is.1.30
This is the *l.* which Moses set	Dt.4.44	We all fade like a *l.*	Is.64.6
This book of the *l.* shall not	Jos.1.8	in the distance a fig tree in *l.*	Mk.11.13
delight is in the *l.* of the LORD	Ps.1.2	**LEAH**	
The *l.* of the LORD is perfect	Ps.19.7	Gen.29.16,30; 30.19; 49.31; Ru.4.11	
refused to walk according to his *l.*	Ps.78.10	**LEAP**	
wondrous things out of thy *l.*	Ps.119.18	by my God I can *l.* over a wall	Ps.18.29
I will keep thy *l.* continually	Ps.119.44	then shall the lame man *l.* like a hart	Is.35.6
Oh, how I love thy *l.*! It is my	Ps.119.97	*l.* for joy, for behold, your reward	Lk.6.23
Great peace . . . who love thy *l.*	Ps.119.165	And *l.* up he stood and walked	Acts 3.8
He who keeps the *l.* is a wise son	Pr.28.7	**LEARN**	
out of Zion shall go forth the *l.*	Is.2.3	that you may *l.* to fear the LORD	Dt.14.23
I will put my *l.* within them	Jer.31.33	that I may *l.* thy commandments	Ps.119.73
out of Zion shall go forth the *l.*	Mic.4.2	O simple ones, *l.* prudence	Pr.8.5
For the *l.* was given through Moses	Jn.1.17	*l.* to do good; seek justice	Is.1.17
doers of the *l.* . . . will be justified	Rom.2.13	neither shall they *l.* war any more	Mic.4.3
For the *l.* brings wrath, but where	Rom.4.15	Take my yoke . . . and *l.* from me	Mt.11.29
L. came in, to increase the trespass	Rom.5.20	From the fig tree *l.* its lesson	Mk.13.28
That the *l.* is sin? By no means	Rom.7.7	I have *l.*, in whatever state I am	Phil.4.11
Apart from the *l.* sin lies dead	Rom.7.8	Let a woman *l.* in silence	1 Tim.2.11
For I delight in the *l.* of God	Rom.7.22	he *l.* obedience through what he	Heb.5.8
For Christ is the end of the *l.*	Rom.10.4	No one could *l.* that song except	Rev.14.3
does he dare go to *l.* before the	1 Cor.6.1	**LEAST**	
but the *l.* does not rest on faith	Gal.3.12	I am the *l.* in my family	Jg.6.15
So that the *l.* was our custodian	Gal.3.24	one of the *l.* of these commandments	Mt.5.19
and so fulfil the *l.* of Christ	Gal.6.2	yet he who is *l.* in the kingdom	Lk.7.28
Now we know that the *l.* is good	1 Tim.1.8	from the *l.* to the greatest	Acts 8.10
since the *l.* has but a shadow of	Heb.10.1	For I am the *l.* of the apostles	1 Cor.15.9
he who looks into the perfect *l.*	Jas.1.25	I am the very *l.* of all the saints	Eph.3.8
If you really fulfil the royal *l.*	Jas.2.8	**LEAVEN (noun)**	
keeps the whole *l.* but fails in one	Jas.2.10	put away *l.* out of your houses	Ex.12.15
LAWYER		is like *l.* which a woman took	Mt.13.33
a *l.*, asked him a question, to test	Mt.22.35	Beware of the *l.* of the Pharisees	Mt.16.11
behold a *l.* stood up to put him	Lk.10.25	Cleanse out the old *l.* that you	1 Cor.5.7
Woe to you *l.*! for you have taken	Lk.11.52	the *l.* of malice and evil	1 Cor.5.8
speed Zenas the *l.* and Apollos on	Tit.3.13	a little *l.* leavens the whole lump	Gal.5.9

LEBANON

Dt.1.7; 2 Chr.2.8; Ps.29.5; Is.35.2; Hos.14.6

LEND

You shall not *l.* him your money	Lev.25.37
I have *l.* him to the LORD	1 Sam.1.28
is kind to the poor *l.* to the LORD	Pr.19.17
and *l.*, expecting nothing in return	Lk.6.35

LENTILS

gave Esau bread and pottage of *l.*	Gen.25.34
parched grain, beans and *l.*	2 Sam.17.28
a plot of ground full of *l.*	2 Sam.23.11
beans and *l.*, millet and spelt	Ezek.4.9

LEPER

the law of the *l.* for . . . his cleansing	Lev.14.2
a . . . man of valor, but he was a *l.*	2 Kg.5.1
Uzziah was a *l.* to the day of	2 Chr.26.21
in the house of Simon the *l.*	Mt.26.6
And a *l.* came to him beseeching him	Mk.1.40
l. are cleansed, and the deaf hear	Lk.7.22
he was met by ten *l.*	Lk.17.12

LEPROSY

pronounce him unclean; it is *l.*	.Lev.13.8
that you may cure him of his *l.*	2 Kg.5.6
And immediately the *l.* left him	Lk.5.13

LETTER

Hezekiah received the *l.* from the	Is.37.14
I Tertius, the writer of this *l.*	Rom.16.22
l. of recommendation to you	2 Cor.3.1
His *l.* are weighty and strong	2 Cor.10.10
See with what large *l.* I am writing	Gal.6.11
speaking . . . as . . . in all his *l.*	2 Pet.3.16

LEVI

(1) son of Jacob, Gen.29.34; avenges Dinah, Gen.34.25; 49.5; (2) same as Matthew, Mk.2.14; (3) others, Lk.3.24,29

LEVITES

descendants of Levi, Ex.6.25; 32.26; their service, Ex.38.21; appointed over the tabernacle, Num.1.50; their divisions, Gershonites, Kohathites, Merarites, Num.3; duties of, Num.4; 8.23–26; 18; their consecration, Num.8.5; inheritance of, Num.35; Dt.18; Jos.21; not to be forsaken, Dt.12.19; 14.27; their genealogies, 1 Chr.6; 9; charged with the temple service, 1 Chr.23–27; organized into divisions by David, 1 Chr.23.6; redivided by Ezra, Ezra 6.18; their sin censured, Ezek.22.26; Mal.1.2

LIAR

a poor man is better than a *l.*	Pr.19.22
he is a *l.* and the father of lies	Jn.8.44
one . . . said, "Cretans are always *l.*	Tit.1.12
Who is the *l.* but he who denies	1 Jn.2.22
not believe God, has made him a *l.*	1 Jn.5.10
and all *l.*, their lot shall be in	Rev.21.8

LIBATION

you shall pour no *l.* thereon	Ex.30.9
there were the *l.* for the burnt	2 Chr.29.35
their *l.* of blood I will not pour	Ps.16.4
as a *l.* upon the sacrificial	Phil.2.17

LIBERTY

proclaim *l.* throughout the land	Lev.25.10
to proclaim *l.* to the captives	Is.61.1
to set at *l.* those who are oppressed	Lk.4.18
the glorious *l.* of the children of	Rom.8.21

why should my *l.* be determined	1 Cor.10.29
to be judged under the law of *l.*	Jas.2.12

LICENTIOUSNESS

not in debauchery and *l.*	Rom.13.13
immorality, impurity, *l.*	Gal.5.19
have given themselves up to *l.*	Eph.4.19
distressed by the *l.* of the wicked	2 Pet.2.7

LIFE

everything that has the breath of *l.*	Gen.1.30
the tree of *l.* also in the midst of	Gen.2.9
I have set before you *l.* and death	Dt.30.19
therefore choose *l.*; that you and	Dt.30.19
The LORD kills and brings to *l.*	1 Sam.2.6
Elisha had restored the dead to *l.*	2 Kg.8.5
Are not the days of my *l.* few?	Job 10.20
Deliver my *l.* from the wicked	Ps.17.13
follow me all the days of my *l.*	Ps.23.6
For my *l.* is spent with sorrow	Ps.31.10
The years of our *l.* are threescore	Ps.90.10
With long *l.* I will satisfy him	Ps.91.16
who redeems your *l.* from the Pit	Ps.103.4
give me *l.* according to thy promise	Ps.119.154
for from it flow the springs of *l.*	Pr.4.23
he who finds me finds *l.*	Pr.8.35
The fear of the LORD prolongs *l.*	Pr.10.27
A gentle tongue is a tree of *l.*	Pr.15.4
So I hated *l.*, because what is done	Ec.2.17
In my vain *l.* I have seen everything	Ec.7.15
awake, some to everlasting *l.*	Dan.12.2
didst bring up my *l.* from the Pit	Jon.2.6
Is not *l.* more than food	Mt.6.25
He who finds his *l.* will lose it	Mt.10.39
loses his *l.* for my sake will find	Mt.16.25
If you would enter *l.*, keep the	Mt.19.17
must I do to inherit eternal *l.*?	Mk.10.17
can add a cubit to his span of *l.*?	Lk.12.25
In him was *l.*, and the *l.* was the	Jn.1.4
believes in the Son has eternal *l.*	Jn.3.36
the Son gives *l.* to whom he will	Jn.5.21
said to them, "I am the bread of *l.*	Jn.6.35
I lay down my *l.* for the sheep	Jn.10.15
I am the resurrection and the *l.*	Jn.11.25
this is eternal *l.*, that they know	Jn.17.3
and killed the Author of *l.*	Acts 3.15
ordained to eternal *l.* believed	Acts 13.48
to eternal *l.* through Jesus Christ	Rom.5.21
who risked their necks for my *l.*	Rom.16.4
but the Spirit gives *l.*	2 Cor.3.6
whose names are in the book of *l.*	Phil.4.3
your *l.* is hid with Christ in God	Col.3.3
God who gives *l.* to all things	1 Tim.6.13
become heirs in hope of eternal *l.*	Tit.3.7
have passed out of death into *l.*	1 Jn.3.14
he who has not the Son . . . has not *l.*	1 Jn.5.12
grant to eat of the tree of *l.*	Rev.2.7
written in the Lamb's book of *l.*	Rev.21.27
take the water of *l.* without price	Rev.22.17

LIFETIME

Absalom in his *l.* had taken	2 Sam.18.18
and his favor is for a *l.*	Ps.30.5
my *l.* is as nothing in thy sight	Ps.39.5
you in your *l.* received your good	Lk.16.25

LIFT

The LORD *l.* up his countenance upon	Num.6.26
I cannot *l.* up my head, for I am	Job 10.15
L. up the light of thy countenance	Ps.4.6

L. up your heads, O gates! and be　　Ps.24.7
To thee, O LORD, I *l.* up my soul　　Ps.25.1
I *l.* up my eyes to the hills　　Ps.121.1
L. up your eyes on high and see　　Is.40.26
as Moses *l.* up the serpent in the　　Jn.3.14
when I am *l.* up from the earth　　Jn.12.32
he was *l.* up, and a cloud took him　　Acts 1.9
l. holy hands without anger or　　1 Tim.2.8

LIGHT
"Let there be *l.*"; and there was *l.*　　Gen.1.3
Israel had *l.* where they dwelt　　Ex.10.23
a pillar of fire to give them *l.*　　Ex.13.21
The Jews had *l.* and gladness　　Est.8.16
They grope in the dark without *l.*　　Job 12.25
and *l.* will shine on your ways　　Job 22.28
Lift up the *l.* of thy countenance　　Ps.4.6
The LORD is my *l.* and my salvation　　Ps.27.1
Oh send out thy *l.* and thy truth　　Ps.43.3
L. dawns for the righteous　　Ps.97.11
L. rises in the darkness for the　　Ps.112.4
to my feet and a *l.* to my path　　Ps.119.105
L. is sweet, and it is pleasant for　　Ec.11.7
I form *l.* and create darkness　　Is.45.7
And nations shall come to your *l.*　　Is.60.3
my judgment goes forth as the *l.*　　Hos.6.5
He will bring me forth to the *l.*　　Mic.7.9
You are the *l.* of the world　　Mt.5.14
Let your *l.* so shine before men　　Mt.5.16
a *l.* for revelation to the Gentiles　　Lk.2.32
lest the *l.* in you be darkness　　Lk.11.35
and the life was the *l.* of men　　Jn.1.4
I am the *l.* of the world　　Jn.8.12
Walk while you have the *l.*　　Jn.12.35
a *l.* to those who are in darkness　　Rom.2.19
Let *l.* shine out of darkness　　2 Cor.4.6
walk as children of *l.*　　Eph.5.8
walk in the *l.*, as he is in the *l.*　　1 Jn.1.7
By its *l.* shall the nations walk　　Rev.21.24
for the Lord God will be their *l.*　　Rev.22.5

LIGHTNING
he scatters his *l.* about him　　Job 36.30
his face like the appearance of *l.*　　Dan.10.6
His appearance was like *l.*　　Mt.28.3
I saw Satan fall like *l.* from heaven　　Lk.10.18
And there were flashes of *l.*　　Rev.16.18

LIKENESS
man in our image, after our *l.*　　Gen.1.26
or any *l.* of anything that is in　　Ex.20.4
own Son in the *l.* of sinful flesh　　Rom.8.3
of Christ, who is the *l.* of God　　2 Cor.4.4
being born in the *l.* of men　　Phil.2.7
who are made in the *l.* of God　　Jas.3.9

LILY
of Sharon, a *l.* of the valleys　　S.of S.2.1
as a *l.* among brambles, so is my　　S.of S.2.2
he shall blossom as the *l.*　　Hos.14.5
Consider the *l.* of the field　　Mt.6.28

LINE
Or who stretched the *l.* upon it?　　Job 38.5
His *l.* shall endure for ever　　Ps.89.36
l. upon *l.*, *l.* upon *l.*　　Is.28.10
eastward with a *l.* in his hand　　Ezek.47.3
with a plumb *l.* in his hand　　Am.7.7
with a measuring *l.* in his hand　　Zech.2.1

LINEN
David was girded with a *l.* ephod　　2 Sam.6.14

She makes *l.* garments and sells　　Pr.31.24
Go and buy a *l.* waistcloth, and put　　Jer.13.1
he said to the man clothed in *l.*　　Ezek.10.2
and behold, a man clothed in *l.*　　Dan.10.5
wrapped it in a clean *l.* shroud　　Mt.27.59
but he left the *l.* cloth and ran　　Mk.14.52
was clothed in purple and fine *l.*　　Lk.16.19
tomb; he saw the *l.* cloths lying　　Jn.20.6
for the fine *l.* is the righteous　　Rev.19.8

LION
honey from the carcass of the *l.*　　Jg.14.9
Save me from the mouth of the *l.*　　Ps.22.21
will tread on the *l.* and the adder　　Ps.91.13
the righteous are bold as a *l.*　　Pr.28.1
a living dog is better than a dead *l.*　　Ec.9.4
the *l.* shall eat straw like the ox　　Is.11.7
I was rescued from the *l.* mouth　　2 Tim.4.17
stopped the mouths of *l.*　　Heb.11.33
prowls around like a roaring *l.*　　1 Pet.5.8
lo, the *L.* of the tribe of Judah　　Rev.5.5

LIPS
Job did not sin with his *l.*　　Job 2.10
my *l.* will not speak falsehood　　Job 27.4
the LORD cut off all flattering *l.*　　Ps.12.3
Let the lying *l.* be dumb　　Ps.31.18
My *l.* will pour forth praise　　Ps.119.171
Truthful *l.* endure for ever　　Pr.12.19
Lying *l.* are an abomination to the　　Pr.12.22
The *l.* of the wise spread knowledge　　Pr.15.7
for I am a man of unclean *l.*　　Is.6.5
This people honors me with their *l.*　　Mt.15.8
he confesses with his *l.*　　Rom.10.10
no guile was found on his *l.*　　1 Pet.2.22

LISTEN
but they did not *l.* to Moses　　Ex.6.9; 16.20
Hear my cry, O God, *l.* to my prayer　　Ps.61.1
O that my people would *l.* to me　　Ps.81.13
L. to advice and accept instruction　　Pr.19.20
L. to me, my people, and give ear　　Is.51.4
melody of your harps I will not *l.*　　Am.5.23
This is my beloved Son; *l.* to him　　Mk.9.7
that God does not *l.* to sinners　　Jn.9.31
sent to the Gentiles; they will *l.*　　Acts 28.28
Whoever knows God *l.* to us　　1 Jn.4.6

LITTLE
hast made him *l.* less than God　　Ps.8.5
Better is a *l.* that the righteous　　Ps.37.16
Better is a *l.* with righteousness　　Pr.16.8
so a *l.* folly outweighs wisdom　　Ec.10.1
and a *l.* child shall lead them　　Is.11.6
here a *l.*, there a *l.*　　Is.28.13
You have sown much, and harvested *l.*　　Hag.1.6
more clothe you, O men of *l.* faith?　　Mt.6.30
but he who is forgiven *l.*, loves *l.*　　Lk.7.47
Fear not *l.* flock, for it is your　　Lk.12.32
L. children, yet a *l.* while I am　　Jn.13.33
A *l.* while, and you will not see me　　Jn.16.19
but use a *l.* wine for the sake of　　1 Tim.5.23
who for a *l.* while was made lower　　Heb.2.9
He had a *l.* scroll open in his hand　　Rev.10.2

LIVE
tree of life, and . . . *l.* for ever　　Gen.3.22
Long *l.* the king! Long *l.* the　　2 Sam.16.16
If a man die, shall he *l.* again?　　Job 14.14
For I know that my Redeemer *l.*　　Job 19.25
So I will bless thee as long as I *l.*　　Ps.63.4

What man can *l.* and never see death?	Ps.89.48	*L.*, Hebrews are coming out of	1 Sam.14.11
praise the LORD as long as I *l.*	Ps.146.2	But when I *l.* for good, evil came	Job 30.26
hear, that your soul may *l.*	Is.55.3	When I *l.* at thy heavens, the work of	Ps.8.3
by whose observance man shall *l.*	Ezek.20.13	*L.* to him, and be radiant	Ps.34.5
Son of man, can these bones *l.*?	Ezek.37.3	*L.* down from heaven, and see	Ps.80.14
Seek the LORD and *l.*, lest he break	Am.5.6	*l.* upon the face of thine anointed	Ps.84.9
Man shall not *l.* by bread alone	Mt.4.4	so our eyes *l.* to the LORD our God	Ps.123.2
who eats me will *l.* because of me	Jn.6.57	*l.* to the rock from which you were	Is.51.1
though he die, yet shall he *l.*	Jn.11.25	no . . . comeliness that we should *l.* at	Is.53.2
because I *l.*, you will *l.* also	Jn.14.19	*L.* down from heaven and see	Is.63.15
In him we *l.* and move and have	Acts 17.28	*L.* and see if there is any sorrow	Lam.1.12
L. in harmony with one another	Rom.12.16	I will *l.* to the LORD, I will wait	Mic.7.7
If we *l.*, we *l.* to the Lord	Rom.14.8	one who *l.* at a woman lustfully	Mt.5.28
no longer I who *l.*, but Christ	Gal.2.20	he *l.* around at them with anger	Mk.3.5
if we *l.* by the Spirit, let us also	Gal.5.25	Bring me a coin, and let me *l.* at it	Mk.12.15
For to me to *l.* is Christ, and to	Phil.1.21	*L.* at the fig tree, and all the	Lk.21.29
wake or sleep we might *l.* with him	1 Th.5.10	They shall *l.* on him whom they	Jn.19.37
L. as free men, yet without using	1 Pet.2.16	Let each of you *l.* not only to his	Phil.2.4
l. considerately with your wives	1 Pet.3.7	he *l.* forward to the city which	Heb.11.10
God who *l.* for ever and ever	Rev.15.7	**LOOSE**	

LIVING

Divide the *l.* child in two	1 Kg.3.25	or *l.* the cords of Orion?	Job 38.31
blotted out of the book of the *l.*	Ps.69.28	to *l.* the bonds of wickedness	Is.58.6
no man *l.* is righteous before thee	Ps.143.2	whatever you *l.* on earth shall be *l.*	Mt.16.19
a *l.* dog is better than a dead lion	Ec.9.4	having *l.* the pangs of death	Acts 2.24
For the *l.* know that they will die	Ec.9.5	Satan will be *l.* from his prison	Rev.20.7
see the LORD in the land of the *l.*	Is.38.11	**LORD**	
the Christ, the Son of the *l.* God	Mt.16.16	day that the *L.* God made the earth	Gen.2.4
not God of the dead, but of the *l.*	Mk.12.27	the *L.*, a God merciful and gracious	Ex.34.6
where do you get that *l.* water?	Jn.4.11	you might know that the *L.* is God	Dt.4.35
I am the *l.* bread which came down	Jn.6.51	The *L.* our God is one *L.*	Dt.6.4
he received *l.* oracles to give	Acts 7.38	the *L.* gave, and the *L.* has taken	Job 1.21
your bodies as a *l.* sacrifice	Rom.12.1	O *L.*, our *L.*, how majestic is thy name	Ps.8.1
we are the temple of the *l.* God	2 Cor.6.16	For who is God, but the *L.*?	Ps.18.31
born anew to a *l.* hope through the	1 Pet.1.3	Great is the *L.* and greatly to be	Ps.48.1
guide them to springs of *l.* water	Rev.7.17	For the *L.* God is a sun and shield	Ps.84.11
LOAVES		kneel before the *L.*, our Maker	Ps.95.6
these stones to become *l.* of bread	Mt.4.3	Know that the *L.* is God! It is he	Ps.100.3
taking the five *l.* and the two fish	Mt.14.19	on that day the *L.* will be one and	Zech.14.9
he took the seven *l.* and the fish	Mt.15.36	one after another, "Is it I, *L.*?"	Mt.26.22
to him, 'Friend, lend me three *l.*	Lk.11.5	Son of man is *l.* even of the sabbath	Mk.2.28
you ate your fill of the *l.*	Jn.6.26	said, "My soul magnifies the *L.*	Lk.1.46
LOCUST		You call me Teacher and *L.*	Jn.13.13
the *l.* came up over all the land	Ex.10.14	answered him, "My *L.* and my God!"	Jn.20.28
It will devour you like the *l.*	Nah.3.15	has made them both *L.* and Christ	Acts 2.36
his food was *l.* and wild honey	Mt.3.4	if you confess . . . that Jesus is *L.*	Rom.10.9
In appearance the *l.* were like horses	Rev.9.7	no one can say "Jesus is *L.*"	1 Cor.12.3
LOINS		be accursed. Our *L.*, come	1 Cor.16.22
Gird up your *l.* like a man	Job 40.7	the *L.* is the Spirit, and where	2 Cor.3.17
didst lay affliction on our *l.*	Ps.66.11	one *L.*, one faith, one baptism	Eph.4.5
faithfulness the girdle of his *l.*	Is.11.5	confess that Jesus Christ is *L.*	Phil.2.11
Let your *l.* be girded and your	Lk.12.35	For the *L.* himself will descend	1 Th.4.16
having girded your *l.* with truth	Eph.6.14	The *L.* be with your spirit	2 Tim.4.22
LONG (verb)		If the *L.* wills, we shall live and	Jas.4.15
who *l.* for death, but it comes not	Job 3.21	O Sovereign *L.*, holy and true	Rev.6.10
As a hart *l.* for . . . streams, so I	Ps.42.1	King of kings and *L.* of lords	Rev.19.16
My soul *l.*, yea, faints for the	Ps.84.2	Amen. Come, *L.* Jesus	Rev.22.20
righteous men *l.* to see what you	Mt.13.17	**LOSE**	
and *l.* to put on our heavenly	2 Cor.5.2	a time to seek, and a time to *l.*	Ec.3.6
brethren, whom I love and *l.* for	Phil.4.1	better that you *l.* one of your members	Mt.5.29
remember us kindly and *l.* to see us	1 Th.3.6	He who finds his life will *l.* it	Mt.10.39
l. for the pure spiritual milk	1 Pet.2.2	what woman . . . if she *l.* one coin	Lk.15.8
will *l.* to die, and death will fly	Rev.9.6	seeks to gain his life will *l.* it	Lk.17.33
LOOK		shall reap, if we do not *l.* heart	Gal.6.9
for he was afraid to *l.* at God	Ex.3.6	nor *l.* courage when . . . punished	Heb.12.5
L. down from thy holy habitation	Dt.26.15	**LOST**	
		asses that were *l.* three days ago	1 Sam.9.20

I have gone astray like a *l.* sheep	Ps.119.176	taught by God to *l.* one another	1 Th.4.9
but the memory of them is *l.*	Ec.9.5	Lord disciplines him whom he *l.*	Heb.12.6
but if salt has *l.* its taste	Mt.5.13	Without having seen him you *l.* him	1 Pet.1.8
only to the *l.* sheep of the house	Mt.15.24	*l.* one another earnestly from the	1 Pet.1.22
I have found my sheep which was *l.*	Lk.15.6	Do not *l.* the world or the things	1 Jn.2.15
came to seek and to save the *l.*	Lk.19.10	that we should *l.* one another	1 Jn.3.11
none of them is *l.* but the son of	Jn.17.12	We *l.,* because he first *l.* us	1 Jn.4.19

LOT

Abram's nephew, Gen.11.27; separates from Abram, Gen.13.10–12; captured by four kings, and rescued by Abram, Gen.14; entertains angel visitors, Gen.19.1–3; saved from Sodom, Gen. 19.16; 2 Pet.2.7; his wife turned into a pillar of salt, Gen.19.26; Lk.17.28,32

		To him who *l.* us and has freed us	Rev.1.5
		Those whom I *l.,* I reprove and	Rev.3.19

LOTS

they cast *l.* for their duties	1 Chr.25.8		
and for my raiment they cast *l.*	Ps.22.18		
let us cast *l.,* that we may know	Jon.1.7		
cast *l.* . . . to see whose it shall be	Jn.19.24		
And they cast *l.* for them	Acts 1.26		

LOW

when I was brought *l.,* he saved me	Ps.116.6		
who remembered us in our *l.* estate	Ps.136.23		
the sound of the grinding is *l.*	Ec.12.4		
every mountain and hill be made *l.*	Is.40.4		
regarded the *l.* estate of his	Lk.1.48		
and exalted those of *l.* degree	Lk.1.52		
God chose what is *l.* and despised	1 Cor.1.28		

LOVE (noun)

but *l.* covers all offenses	Pr.10.12		
his banner over me was *l.*	S. of S.2.4		
for *l.* is strong as death	S.of S.8.6		
loved you with an everlasting *l.*	Jer.31.3		
the abundance of his steadfast *l.*	Lam.3.32		
most men's *l.* will grow cold	Mt.24.12		
have not the *l.* of God within you	Jn.5.42		
Greater *l.* has no man than this	Jn.15.13		
L. does no wrong to a neighbor	Rom.13.10		
L. is patient and kind	1 Cor.13.4		
L. never ends; as for prophecies	1 Cor.13.8		
For the *l.* of Christ controls us	2 Cor.5.14		
But the fruit of the Spirit is *l.*	Gal.5.22		
and to know the *l.* of Christ which	Eph.3.19		
the *l.* of money is the root of	1 Tim.6.10		
Let brotherly *l.* continue	Heb.13.1		
Keep your life free from *l.* of money	Heb.13.5		
since *l.* covers a multitude of sins	1 Pet.4.8		
know God; for God is *l.*	1 Jn.4.8		
but perfect *l.* casts out fear	1 Jn.4.18		
abandoned the *l.* you had at first	Rev.2.4		

LOWLY

he sets on high those who are *l.*	Job 5.11		
the LORD is high, he regards the *l.*	Ps.138.6		
for I am gentle and *l.* in heart	Mt.11.29		
but associate with the *l.*	Rom.12.16		
will change our *l.* body to be like	Phil.3.21		

LOYALTY

I will sing of *l.* and of justice	Ps.101.1		
Let not *l.* and faithfulness forsake	Pr.3.3		
What is desired in a man is *l.*	Pr.19.22		
L. and faithfulness preserve the	Pr.20.28		
Those . . . forsake their true *l.*	Jon.2.8		

LUKE

Col.4.14; 2 Tim.4.11; Philem.24

LUST (noun)

are taken captive by their *l.*	Pr.11.6		
is corrupt through deceitful *l.*	Eph.4.22		
not in the passion of *l.* like	1 Th.4.5		
in the *l.* of defiling passion	2 Pet.2.10		
l. of the flesh and the *l.* of	1 Jn.2.16		
and indulged in unnatural *l.*	Jude 7		

LOVE (verb)

you shall *l.* your neighbor as yourself	Lev.19.18		
you shall *l.* the LORD your God	Dt.6.5		
I *l.* thee, O LORD, my strength	Ps.18.1		
I *l.* the habitation of thy house	Ps.26.8		
L. the LORD, all you his saints	Ps.31.23		
I *l.* the LORD, because he has heard	Ps.116.1		
Oh, how I *l.* thy law! It is my	Ps.119.97		
peace have those who *l.* thy law	Ps.119.165		
The LORD preserves all who *l.* him	Ps.145.20		
all who hate me *l.* death	Pr.8.36		
a time to *l.,* and a time to hate	Ec.3.8		
I the LORD *l.* justice, I hate robbery	Is.61.8		
to *l.* kindness, and to walk humbly	Mic.6.8		
L. your enemies and pray for those	Mt.5.44		
You shall *l.* the Lord your God	Mt.22.37		
You shall *l.* your neighbor as	Mk.12.31		
scribes . . . *l.* salutations in the market	Lk.20.46		
God so *l.* the world that he gave	Jn.3.16		
If you *l.* me, you will keep my	Jn.14.15		
As the Father has *l.* me, so have I *l.*	Jn.15.9		
I command you, to *l.* one another	Jn.15.17		
do you *l.* me more than these?	Jn.21.15		
Jacob I *l.,* but Esau I hated	Rom.9.13		

LYDIA

Acts 16.14,40

LYING

the LORD has put a *l.* spirit in	1 Kg.22.23		
Let the *l.* lips be dumb	Ps.31.18		
speaking against me with *l.* tongues	Ps.109.2		
haughty eyes, a *l.* tongue	Pr.6.17		
He who conceals hatred has *l.* lips	Pr.10.18		
L. lips are an abomination to the	Pr.12.22		
Remove far from me falsehood and *l.*	Pr.30.8		
there is swearing, *l.,* killing	Hos.4.2		

LYRE

all those who play the *l.* and pipe	Gen.4.21		
My *l.* is turned to mourning	Job 30.31		
Praise the LORD with the *l.*	Ps.33.2		
Awake, O harp and *l.*	Ps.57.8		
Sing praises to the LORD with the *l.*	Ps.98.5		
make melody to our God upon the *l.*	Ps.147.7		

MACEDONIA

Acts 16.9; Rom.15.26; 1 Cor.16.5; Phil.4.15; 1 Tim.1.3

MAD

He has a demon, and he is *m.*	Jn.10.20		
I am not *m.,* most excellent Festus	Acts 26.25		
will they not say that you are *m.*?	1 Cor.14.23		

MADE

God saw everything that he had *m.*	Gen.1.31		

God *m.* man in his own image   Gen.9.6
I have *m.* a covenant with my eyes   Job 31.1
The sea is his, for he *m.* it   Ps.95.5
This is the day . . . the LORD has *m.*   Ps.118.24
The LORD has *m.* everything for its   Pr.16.4
He has *m.* everything beautiful in   Ec.3.11
God *m.* man upright, but they   Ec.7.29
The sabbath was *m.* for man   Mk.2.27
God *m.* them male and female   Mk.10.6
all things were *m.* through him   Jn.1.3
For our sake he *m.* him to be sin   2 Cor.5.21
Christ Jesus has *m.* me his own   Phil.3.12
he had to be *m.* like his brethren   Heb.2.17

MAGICIAN
he . . . called for all the *m.* of Egypt   Gen.41.8
Then the king commanded that the *m.*   Dan.2.2
But Elymas the *m.* . . . . withstood them   Acts 13.8

MAGNIFY
O *m.* the LORD with me, and let us   Ps.34.3
And you *m.* yourselves against me   Ezek.35.13
And Mary said, "My soul *m.* the Lord   Lk.1.46
to the Gentiles, I *m.* my ministry   Rom.11.13

MAIDEN
The *m.* was very fair to look upon   Gen.24.16
Then Boaz said . . . "Whose *m.* is this?"   Ru.2.5
Young men and *m.* together, old men   Ps.148.12
and the way of a man with a *m.*   Pr.30.19
ten *m.* who took their lamps   Mt.25.1

MAINTAIN
m. the right of the afflicted   Ps.82.3
LORD *m.* the cause of the afflicted   Ps.140.12
eager to *m.* the unity of the Spirit   Eph.4.3
M. good conduct among the Gentiles   1 Pet.2.12

MAJESTIC
m. in holiness, terrible in glorious   Ex.15.11
how *m.* is thy name in all the earth   Ps.8.1
I will make you *m.* for ever   Is.60.15
was borne to him by the *M.* Glory   2 Pet.1.17

MAJESTY
Honor and *m.* are before him   1 Chr.16.27
God is clothed with terrible *m.*   Job 37.22
the voice of the LORD is full of *m.*   Ps.29.4
The LORD reigns; he is robed in *m.*   Ps.93.1
were astonished at the *m.* of God   Lk.9.43
the right hand of the *M.* on high   Heb.1.3
we were eyewitnesses of his *m.*   2 Pet.1.16
m., dominion, and authority   Jude 25

MAKER
Can a man be pure before his *M.*?   Job 4.17
let us kneel before the LORD, our *M.*   Ps.95.6
Let Israel be glad in his *M.*   Ps.149.2
He who mocks the poor insults his *M.*   Pr.17.5
the LORD is the *m.* of them all   Pr.22.2
Woe to him who strives with his *M.*   Is.45.9
For Israel has forgotten his *M.*   Hos.8.14
whose builder and *m.* is God   Heb.11.10

MALICE
They scoff and speak with *m.*   Ps.73.8
But Jesus, aware of their *m.*   Mt.22.18
the leaven of *m.* and evil   1 Cor.5.8
be put away from you, with all *m.*   Eph.4.31
m., slander, and foul talk   Col.3.8
passing our days in *m.* and envy   Tit.3.3
So put away all *m.* and all guile   1 Pet.2.1

MAN
So God created *m.* in his own image   Gen.1.27

God is not *m.*, that he should lie   Num.23.19
Can a *m.* be pure before his Maker?   Job 4.17
how can a *m.* be just before God?   Job 9.2
If a *m.* die, shall he live again?   Job 14.14
what is *m.* that thou art mindful of   Ps.8.4
The steps of a *m.* are from the LORD   Ps.37.23
for vain is the help of *m.*   Ps.60.11
for no *m.* living is righteous   Ps.143.2
A faithful *m.* will abound with   Pr.28.20
Turn away from *m.* in whose nostrils   Is.2.22
Who is the *m.* so wise that he can   Jer.9.12
Cursed is the *m.* who trusts in *m.*   Jer.17.5
I am God and not *m.*, the Holy One   Hos.11.9
M. shall not live by bread alone   Mt.4.4
No *m.* ever spoke like this *m.*   Jn.7.46
each *m.* take care how he builds   1 Cor.3.10
the head of every *m.* is Christ   1 Cor.11.3
For each *m.* will have to bear his   Gal.6.5
Blessed is the *m.* who endures trial   Jas.1.12
No *m.* has ever seen God   1 Jn.4.12

MANASSEH
(1) first-born son of Joseph, Gen.41.51; his blessing, Gen.48.20; his descendants numbered, Num.1.34; 26.29; Jos.22.1; 7.14; their inheritance, Num.32.33; 34.14; Jos.13.29; 17.1; desert to David's cause, 1 Chr. 12.19; 2 Chr.15.9; 30.11; (2) king of Judah, his reign, 2 Kg.21; 2 Chr.33; (3) others, Jg.18.30 note *z*; Ezra 10.30,33

MANIFEST
Let thy work be *m.* to thy servants   Ps.90.16
I will *m.* my glory in the midst   Ezek.28.22
will love him and *m.* myself to him   Jn.14.21
each man's work will become *m.*   1 Cor.3.13
that the life of Jesus may be *m.*   2 Cor.4.11
He was *m.* in the flesh, vindicated   1 Tim.3.16

MANNA
house of Israel called its name *m.*   Ex.16.31
Israel ate the *m.* forty years   Ex.16.35
Now the *m.* was like coriander seed   Num.11.7
he rained down upon them *m.* to eat   Ps.78.24
Your fathers ate the *m.* in the   Jn.6.49
a golden urn holding the *m.*   Heb.9.4
I will give some of the hidden *m.*   Rev.2.17

MARCH
the Egyptians were *m.* after them   Ex.14.10
You shall *m.* around the city   Jos.6.3
M. on, my soul, with might   Jg.5.21
the sound of *m.* in the tops of   1 Chr.14.15
thou didst *m.* through the wilderness   Ps.68.7
m. in the greatness of his strength   Is.63.1

MARK (John Mark)
(Evangelist), Acts 12.12; goes with Paul and Barnabas, Acts 12.25; 13.5; leaves them at Perga, Acts 13.13; contention about him, Acts 15.37; proves his usefulness, 2 Tim.4.11

MARK (noun)
And the LORD put a *m.* on Cain   Gen.4.15
It shall be as a *m.* on your hand   Ex.13.16
put a *m.* upon the foreheads of   Ezek.9.4
my finger in the *m.* of the nails   Jn.20.25
I bear on my body the *m.* of Jesus   Gal.6.17
buy or sell unless he has the *m.*   Rev.13.17
receives a *m.* on his forehead   Rev.14.9
who bore the *m.* of the beast   Rev.16.2
received its *m.* on their foreheads   Rev.20.4

MARKET
children sitting in the *m.* places	Mt.11.16
standing idle in the *m.* place	Mt.20.3
and salutations in the *m.* places	Mt.23.7
whatever is sold in the meat *m.*	1 Cor.10.25

MARRIAGE
a king who gave a *m.* feast for his	Mt.22.2
neither marry nor are given in *m.*	Mk.12.25
there was a *m.* at Cana in Galilee	Jn.2.1
free from a wife? Do not seek *m.*	1 Cor.7.27
who forbid *m.* and enjoin abstinence	1 Tim.4.3
Let *m.* be held in honor among all	Heb.13.4
for the *m.* of the Lamb has come	Rev.19.7

MARRY
They shall not *m.* a harlot or a	Lev.21.7
and *m.* another, commits adultery	Mt.19.9
they neither *m.*, nor are given in	Mk.12.25
I have *m.* a wife, and . . . cannot come	Lk.14.20
those whom *m.* will have worldly	1 Cor.7.28
So I would have younger widows *m.*	1 Tim.5.14

MARTHA
Lk.10.38; Jn.11.1,19,39; 12.2

MARVEL
When the disciples saw it they *m.*	Mt.21.20
And he *m.* because of their unbelief	Mk.6.6
Do not *m.* that I said to you	Jn.3.7
Do not *m.* at this; for the hour is	Jn.5.28

MARVELOUS
his *m.* works among all the peoples	1 Chr.16.24
and *m.* things without number	Job 9.10
for he has done *m.* things	Ps.98.1
and it is *m.* in our eyes	Mk.12.11
out of darkness into his *m.* light	1 Pet.2.9

MARY
Greek form of Miriam, (1) the Virgin, mother of Jesus, visited by the angel Gabriel, Lk.1.26–38; believes, and magnifies the Lord, Lk.1.38, 46; Jn.2.5; Jesus born of, Mt.1.18; Lk.2.5–7; witnesses the miracle at Cana, Jn.2.1–11; desires to speak with Jesus, Mt.12.46; Mk.3.31; Lk.8.19; commended to John by Jesus at his crucifixion, Jn.19.25–26; (2) Magdalene, Lk. 8.2; at the cross, Mt.27.56; Mk.15.40; Jn.19.25; Jesus appears first to, Jn.20.1–18; (3) sister of Lazarus, commended, Lk.10.42; Jesus' love for, Jn.11.5; anoints Jesus' feet, Jn.12.3; (4) mother of John Mark, Acts 12.12; (5) a Roman Christian, Rom.16.6

MASTER
no one can serve two *m.*; for either	Mt.6.24
for you have one *m.*, the Christ	Mt.23.10
M., you delivered to me five	Mt.25.20
betrayed him, said, "Is it I, *M.*?"	Mt.26.25
Jesus, *M.*, have mercy on us	Lk.17.13
a servant is not greater than his *m.*	Jn.13.16
the *M.* is able to make him stand	Rom.14.4
like a skilled *m.* builder I laid	1 Cor.3.10
M., treat your slaves justly	Col.4.1
you also have a *M.* in heaven	Col.4.1
denying the *M.* who bought them	2 Pet.2.1

MATTHEW
Mt.9.9; Mk.3.18; Lk.6.15; Acts 1.13

MATURE
among the *m.* we do impart wisdom	1 Cor.2.6
but in thinking be *m.*	1 Cor.14.20
let . . . us who are *m.* be thus minded	Phil.3.15

may present every man *m.* in Christ	Col.1.28
But solid food is for the *m.*	Heb.5.14

MEAL
The jar of *m.* shall not be spent	1 Kg.17.12
and hid in three measures of *m.*	Mt.13.33
one goes ahead with his own *m.*	1 Cor.11.21
sold his birthright for a single *m.*	Heb.12.16

MEASURE (noun)
Correct me, O Lord, but in just *m.*	Jer.10.24
I will chasten you in just *m.*	Jer.46.28
the scant *m.* that is accursed	Mic.6.10
m. you give will be the *m.* you get	Mt.7.2
good *m.*, pressed down, shaken	Lk.6.38
might become sinful beyond *m.*	Rom.7.13
according to the *m.* of faith which	Rom.12.3
according to the *m.* of Christ's gift	Eph.4.7

MEASURE (verb)
Who has *m.* the waters in the hollow	Is.40.12
If the heavens above can be *m.*	Jer.31.37
can be neither *m.* nor numbered	Hos.1.10
He stood and *m.* the earth	Hab.3.6
To *m.* Jerusalem, to see what is its	Zech.2.2
they *m.* themselves by one another	2 Cor.10.12
Rise and *m.* the temple of God	Rev.11.1
he *m.* the city with his rod	Rev.21.16

MEAT
and said, "O that we had *m.* to eat	Num.11.4
no *m.* or wine entered my mouth	Dan.10.3
not to eat *m.* or drink wine or do	Rom.14.21
I will never eat *m.*, lest I cause	1 Cor.8.13

MEDIATOR
a *m.*, one of the thousand	Job 33.23
there is one *m.* between God and	1 Tim.2.5
he is the *m.* of a new covenant	Heb.9.15
Jesus, the *m.* of a new covenant	Heb.12.24

MEDITATE
Isaac went out to *m.* in the field	Gen.24.63
you shall *m.* on it day and night	Jos.1.8
and on his law he *m.* day and night	Ps.1.2
I will *m.* on all thy work, and muse	Ps.77.12
I will *m.* on thy wondrous works	Ps.119.27
not to *m.* beforehand how to answer	Lk.21.14

MEDITATION
the *m.* of my heart be acceptable	Ps.19.14
m. of my heart . . . be understanding	Ps.49.3
May my *m.* be pleasing to him	Ps.104.34
thy law! It is my *m.* all the day	Ps.119.97
for thy testimonies are my *m.*	Ps.119.99

MEEK
Now the man Moses was very *m.*	Num.12.3
thou wilt hear the desire of the *m.*	Ps.10.17
But the *m.* shall possess the land	Ps.37.11
The *m.* shall obtain fresh joy	Is.29.19
Blessed are the *m.*, for they shall	Mt.5.5

MEEKNESS
the *m.* and gentleness of Christ	2 Cor.10.1
with all lowliness and *m.*	Eph.4.2
receive with *m.* the implanted word	Jas.1.21
show his works in the *m.* of wisdom	Jas.3.13

MEET
The rich and the poor *m.* together	Pr.22.2
went to *m.* the bridegroom	Mt.25.1
When you *m.* together, it is not	1 Cor.11.20
to *m.* the Lord in the air	1 Th.4.17
not neglecting to *m.* together	Heb.10.25
when you *m.* various trials	Jas.1.2

MELCHIZEDEK
Gen.14,18; Ps.110.4; Heb.5.6,10; 6.20; 7.1–17

MELODY
I will make *m.* to the Lord	Jg.5.3
I will sing and make *m.*	Ps.57.7
make *m.* to our God upon the lyre	Ps.147.7
to the *m.* of your harps I will not	Am.5.23
singing and making *m.* to the Lord	Eph.5.19

MELT
he utters his voice, the earth *m.*	Ps.46.6
The mountains *m.* like wax before	Ps.97.5
the elements will *m.* with fire	2 Pet.3.12

MEMBERS
Do not yield your *m.* to sin	Rom.6.13
now yield your *m.* to righteousness	Rom.6.19
For as in one body we have many *m.*	Rom.12.4
your bodies are *m.* of Christ?	1 Cor.6.15
If one *m.* suffers, all suffer	1 Cor.12.26
for we are *m.* one of another	Eph.4.25
the tongue is a little *m.* and boasts	Jas.3.5
passions that are at war in your *m.*?	Jas.4.1

MEMORIAL
This day shall be for you a *m.* day	Ex.12.14
Write this as a *m.* in a book	Ex.17.14
it shall be to the Lord for a *m.*	Is.55.13
have ascended as a *m.* before God	Acts 10.4

MEMORY
His *m.* perishes from the earth	Job 18.17
may his *m.* be cut off from the	Ps.109.15
The *m.* of the righteous is a blessing	Pr.10.7
will be told in *m.* of her	Mt.26.13

MEN
At that time *m.* began to call upon	Gen.4.26
So these three *m.* ceased to answer	Job 32.1
He recounts to *m.* his salvation	Job 33.26
nations know that they are but *m.*	Ps.9.20
You are the fairest of the sons of *m.*	Ps.45.2
nevertheless, you shall die like *m.*	Ps.82.7
M. are all a vain hope	Ps.116.11
Deliver me, O Lord, from evil *m.*	Ps.140.1
Young *m.* and maidens . . . old *m.*	Ps.148.12
the hearts of *m.* are full of evil	Ec.9.3
young *m.* shall fall exhausted	Is.40.30
He was despised and rejected by *m.*	Is.53.3
behold, wise *m.* from the East came to	Mt.2.1
God is stronger than *m.*	1 Cor.1.25
So let no one boast of *m.*	1 Cor.3.21
let us do good to all *m.*	Gal.6.10
Let all *m.* know your forbearance	Phil.4.5
who desires all *m.* to be saved	1 Tim.2.4
spirits of just *m.* made perfect	Heb.12.23
Honor all *m.* Love the brotherhood	1 Pet.2.17
the dwelling of God is with *m.*	Rev.21.3

MENTION
Among those who know me I *m.*	Ps.87.4
We must not *m.* the name of the Lord	Am.6.10
without ceasing I *m.* you always	Rom.1.9
made *m.* of the exodus of the	Heb.11.22

MEPHIBOSHETH
2 Sam.4.4; 9.11; 16.1; 19.30; 21.7

MERCHANDISE
perceives that her *m.* is profitable	Pr.31.18
Her *m.* . . . . will be dedicated	Is.23.18
vessels of bronze for your *m.*	Ezek.27.13
your *m.* and all your crew have	Ezek.27.34

MERCHANT
the fragrant powders of the *m.*?	S.of S.3.6
you were the *m.* of the nations	Is.23.3
set it in a city of *m.*	Ezek.17.4
you increased your *m.* more than	Nah.3.16
like a *m.* in search of fine pearls	Mt.13.45
And the *m.* of the earth weep and	Rev.18.11
thy *m.* were the great men of	Rev.18.23

MERCIFUL
a God *m.* and gracious, slow to anger	Ex.34.6
gracious and *m.*, slow to anger and	Neh.9.17
Be *m.* to me, O God, be *m.* to me	Ps.57.1
thou art a gracious God and *m.*	Jon.4.2
Blessed are the *m.*, for they	Mt.5.7
Be *m.*, even as your Father is *m.*	Lk.6.36
For I will be *m.* toward their	Heb.8.12
the Lord is compassionate and *m.*	Jas.5.11

MERCY
shall make a *m.* seat of pure gold	Ex.25.17
show *m.* on whom I will show *m.*	Ex.33.19
Lord, for his *m.* is very great	1 Chr.21.13
Surely goodness and *m.* shall follow	Ps.23.6
Be mindful of thy *m.*, O Lord	Ps.25.6
Have *m.* on me, O God, according to	Ps.51.1
Great is thy *m.*, O Lord	Ps.119.156
his *m.* never come to an end	Lam.3.22
in wrath remember *m.*	Hab.3.2
'I desire *m.*, and not sacrifice.'	Mt.9.13
Lord, have *m.* on my son, for he is	Mt.17.15
his *m.* is on those who fear him	Lk.1.50
the Lord had shown great *m.* to her	Lk.1.58
perform the *m.* promised to our	Lk.1.72
have *m.* upon me, and send Lazarus	Lk.16.24
Jesus, Master, have *m.* on us	Lk.17.13
I will have *m.* on whom I have *m.*	Rom.9.15
by the *m.* of God, to present your	Rom.12.1
the Father of *m.* and God of all	2 Cor.1.3
But God, who is rich in *m.*	Eph.2.4
I received *m.* because I had	1 Tim.1.13
By his great *m.* we have been born	1 Pet.1.3
Grace, *m.*, and peace will be with us	2 Jn.3

MERE
think that *m.* words are strategy	2 Kg.18.20
surely every man is a *m.* breath	Ps.39.11
but *m.* talk tends only to want	Pr.14.23
think that *m.* words are strategy	Is.36.5
They utter *m.* words; with empty	Hos.10.4
m. busybodies, not doing any work	2 Th.3.11

MERRY
King David dancing and making *m.*	1 Chr.15.29
heart of the king was *m.* with wine	Est.1.10
the voices of those who make *m.*	Jer.30.19
young men and the old shall be *m.*	Jer.31.13
take your ease, eat, drink, be *m.*	Lk.12.19
And they began to make *m.*	Lk.15.24
make *m.* and exchange presents	Rev.11.10

MESHACH
Dan.1.7; 2.49; 3.12,30

MESOPOTAMIA
Gen.24.10; 1 Chr.19.6; Acts 2.9; 7.2

MESSAGE
sends a *m.* by the hand of a fool	Pr.26.6
to the people with the Lord's *m.*	Hag.1.13
sent the *m.* of this salvation	Acts 13.26
to us the *m.* of reconciliation	2 Cor.5.19
for he strongly opposed our *m.*	2 Tim.4.15

For if the *m.* declared by angels	Heb.2.2
This is the *m.* we have heard from	1 Jn.1.5

MESSENGER

who makest the winds thy *m.*	Ps.104.4
Haggai, the *m.* of the Lord, spoke	Hag.1.13
I send my *m.* to prepare the way	Mal.3.1
the *m.* of the covenant in whom you	Mal.3.1
I send my *m.* before thy face	Mt.11.10
they are *m.* of the churches	2 Cor.8.23
a *m.* of Satan, to harass me	2 Cor.12.7

MESSIAH

We have found the *M.*	Jn.1.41
I know that *M.* is coming	Jn.4.25

METHUSELAH

Gen.5.21,27; 1 Chr.1.3; Lk.3.37

MICAIAH

1 Kg.22.8; 2 Chr.13.2; Jer.36.11

MICHAEL

Dan.10.13; 12.1; Jude 9; Rev.12.7

MIDNIGHT

About *m.* I will go forth in . . . Egypt	Ex.11.4
At *m.* the Lord smote all the	Ex.12.29
At *m.* I rise to praise thee	Ps.119.62
But at *m.* there was a cry, 'Behold	Mt.25.6
go to him at *m.* and say to him	Lk.11.5
But about *m.* Paul and Silas were	Acts 16.25
he prolonged his speech until *m.*	Acts 20.7

MIDST

the Lord in the *m.* of the earth	Ex.8.22
went into the *m.* of the sea on dry	Ex.14.22
art in the *m.* of this people	Num.14.14
God speaking out of the *m.* of fire	Dt.5.26
God walks in the *m.* of your camp	Dt.23.14
The sun stayed in the *m.* of heaven	Jos.10.13
God is in the *m.* of her, she shall	Ps.46.5
Though I walk in the *m.* of trouble	Ps.138.7
I dwell in the *m.* of a people of	Is.6.5
I will dwell in their *m.* for ever	Ezek.43.9
Is not the Lord in the *m.* of us?	Mic.3.11
and I will dwell in the *m.* of you	Zech.2.10
there am I in the *m.* of them	Mt.18.20
kingdom of God is in the *m.* of you	Lk.17.21
the Lamb in the *m.* of the throne	Rev.7.17

MIGHT (noun)

all your soul, and with all your *m.*	Dt.6.5
power and the *m.* of my hand have	Dt.8.17
In thy hand are power and *m.*	2 Chr.20.6
With God are wisdom and *m.*	Job 12.13
Do you give the horse his *m.?*	Job 39.19
But I will sing of thy *m.*	Ps.59.16
Thou didst divide the sea by thy *m.*	Ps.74.13
Stir up thy *m.*, and come to save us	Ps.80.2
proclaim the *m.* of thy terrible	Ps.145.6
I say that wisdom is better than *m.*	Ec.9.16
Behold, the Lord God comes with *m.*	Is.40.10
Not by *m.*, nor by power, but by my	Zech.4.6
the working of his great *m.*	Eph.1.19
strengthened with *m.* through his	Eph.3.16
according to his glorious *m.*	Col.1.11
and from the glory of his *m.*	2 Th.1.9
glory and *m.* for ever and ever	Rev.5.13
power and *m.* be to our God for	Rev.7.12

MIGHTY

These were the *m.* men that were of	Gen.6.4
Like Nimrod a *m.* hunter before the	Gen.10.9
has brought you out with a *m.* hand	Dt.7.8

The *M.* One, God, the Lord	Jos.22.22
How are the *m.* fallen	2 Sam.1.25
All the leaders and the *m.* men	1 Chr.29.24
a *m.* man of valor, with two	2 Chr.17.17
So Jotham became *m.*, because he	2 Chr.27.6
God is *m.*, and does not despise any	Job 36.5
strong and *m.*, the Lord, *m.* in battle	Ps.24.8
who is *m.* as thou art, O Lord	Ps.89.8
M. King, lover of justice, thou hast	Ps.99.4
Praise him for his *m.* deeds	Ps.150.2
M. God, Everlasting Father, Prince of	Is.9.6
The Lord goes forth like a *m.* man	Is.42.13
your Redeemer, the *M.* One of Jacob	Is.49.26
O great and *m.* God whose name is	Jer.32.18
and do many *m.* works in your name?	Mt.7.22
And he could do no *m.* work there	Mk.6.5
he was *m.* in his words and deeds	Acts 7.22
under the *m.* hand of God	1 Pet.5.6
Then a *m.* angel took up a stone	Rev.18.21

MILK

not boil a kid in its mother's *m.*	Ex.34.26
a land flowing with *m.* and honey	Lev.20.24
m. from the flock, with fat of lambs	Dt.32.14
He asked water and she gave him *m.*	Jg.5.25
buy wine and *m.* without money	Is.55.1
I fed you with *m.*, not solid food	1 Cor.3.2
You need *m.*, not solid food	Heb.5.12
long for the pure spiritual *m.*	1 Pet.2.2

MILLSTONE

cast an upper *m.* upon him from	2 Sam.11.21
to have a great *m.* fastened round	Mt.18.6
better for him if a *m.* were hung	Lk.17.2
like a great *m.* and threw it into	Rev.18.21
sound of the *m.* shall be heard in	Rev.18.22

MIND

man in whose *m.* the Lord had put	Ex.36.2
For the people had a *m.* to work	Neh.4.6
test my heart and my *m.*	Ps.26.2
the inward *m.* and heart of a man	Ps.64.6
Men of perverse *m.* . . . . an abomination	Pr.11.20
Apply your *m.* to instruction	Pr.23.12
who trusts in his own *m.* is a fool	Pr.28.26
the *m.* of a wise man will know	Ec.8.5
whose *m.* is stayed on thee	Is.26.3
I the Lord search the *m.* and try	Jer.17.10
let a beast's *m.* be given to him	Dan.4.16
Settle it therefore in your *m.*	Lk.21.14
he opened their *m.* to understand	Lk.24.45
serve the law of God with my *m.*	Rom.7.25
who has known the *m.* of the Lord	Rom.11.34
But we have the *m.* of Christ	1 Cor.2.16
blinded the *m.* of the unbelievers	2 Cor.4.4
Have this *m.* among yourselves	Phil.2.5
Set your *m.* on things that are above	Col.3.2
a tender heart and a humble *m.*	1 Pet.3.8
I am he who searches *m.* and heart	Rev.2.23

MINDFUL

m. of his covenant for ever	1 Chr.16.15
what is man that thou art *m.* of him	Ps.8.4
Be *m.* of thy mercy, O Lord, and of	Ps.25.6
He is *m.* of his covenant for ever	Ps.105.8
God will be *m.* of them and restore	Zeph.2.7

MINGLE

and *m.* tears with my drink	Ps.102.9
offered him wine *m.* with myrrh	Mk.15.23

whose blood Pilate had *m.* with their Lk.13.1
to be a sea of glass *m.* with fire Rev.15.2
MINISTER (noun)
Joshua . . . the *m.* of Moses, one of Num.11.28
for the authorities are *m.* of God Rom.13.6
to be *m.* of a new covenant 2 Cor.3.6
was made a *m.* according to the gift Eph.3.7
He is a faithful *m.* of Christ on our Col.1.7
of which I, Paul, became a *m.* Col.1.23
will be a good *m.* of Christ Jesus 1 Tim.4.6
a *m.* in the sanctuary and the true Heb.8.2
MINISTER (verb)
they come near the altar to *m.* Ex.30.20
that is blameless shall *m.* to me Ps.101.6
behold, angels came and *m.* to him Mt.4.11
in prison, and did not *m.* to thee? Mt.25.44
these hands *m.* to my necessities Acts 20.34
MINISTERING
Samuel was *m.* before the LORD 1 Sam.2.18
the Shunammite was *m.* to the king 1 Kg.1.15
many women there . . . *m.* to him Mt.27.55
Are they not all *m.* spirits sent Heb.1.14
MINISTRY
Jesus, when he began his *m.* Lk.3.23
to prayer and to the *m.* of the word Acts 6.4
I magnify my *m.* Rom.11.13
having this *m.* by the mercy of God 2 Cor.4.1
gave us the *m.* of reconciliation 2 Cor.5.18
no fault may be found with our *m.* 2 Cor.6.3
for the work of *m.*, for building up Eph.4.12
fulfil the *m.* which you have Col.4.17
an evangelist, fulfil your *m.* 2 Tim.4.5
Christ has obtained a *m.* which is as Heb.8.6
MIRACLE
Prove yourselves by working a *m.* Ex.7.9
seeing signs and great *m.* Acts 8.13
extraordinary *m.* by . . . Paul Acts 19.11
to another the working of *m.* 1 Cor.12.10
third teachers, then workers of *m.* 1 Cor.12.28
Do all work *m.*? 1 Cor.12.29
supplies the Spirit . . . and works *m.* Gal.3.5
bore witness by . . . various *m.* Heb.2.4
MIRE
God has cast me into the *m.* Job 30.19
I sink in deep *m.*, where there is Ps.69.2
rescue me from sinking in the *m.* Ps.69.14
and Jeremiah sank in the *m.* Jer.38.6
that your feet are sunk in the *m.* Jer.38.22
washed only to wallow in the *m.* 2 Pet.2.22
MIRIAM
Ex.15.20; Num.12.1,15; 20.1; Mic.6.4
MIRTH
sent you away with *m.* and songs Gen.31.27
heart of fools is in the house of *m.* Ec.7.4
The *m.* of the timbrels is stilled Is.24.8
I will put an end to all her *m.* Hos.2.11
MISCHIEF
They conceive *m.* and bring forth Job 15.35
His *m.* returns upon his own head Ps.7.16
He plots *m.* while on his bed Ps.36.4
let the *m.* of their lips overwhelm Ps.140.9
their lips talk of *m.* Pr.24.2
they conceive *m.* and bring forth Is.59.4
their minds shall be bent on *m.* Dan.11.27
MISERY
You will forget your *m.* Job 11.16

my strength fails because of my *m.* Ps.31.10
in their paths are ruin and *m.* Rom.3.16
howl for the *m.* that are coming Jas.5.1
MISSION
the LORD sent you on a *m.* 1 Sam.15.18
when they had fulfilled their *m.* Acts 12.25
in their boasted *m.* they work 2 Cor.11.12
Peter for the *m.* to the circumcised Gal.2.8
MIST
but a *m.* went up from the earth Gen.2.6
he distils his *m.* in rain Job 36.27
he makes the *m.* rise from the ends Jer.10.13
Immediately *m.* and darkness fell Acts 13.11
For you are a *m.* that appears for a Jas.4.14
MIXED
A *m.* multitude also went up with Ex.12.38
the holy race has *m.* itself with Ezra 9.2
and drink of the wine I have *m.* Pr.9.5
those who go to try *m.* wine Pr.23.30
you saw the iron *m.* with miry clay Dan.2.43
for her in the cup she *m.* Rev.18.6
MIZPAH
Gen.31.49; Jg.10.17; 1 Sam.7.5; 2 Chr.16.6;
Jer.40.10
MOAB
Gen.19.37; Dt.1.5; Ru.1.1; 2 Kg.3.4; Is.15.1;
Zeph.2.9
MOABITE
Dt.23.3; Jg.3.28; 2 Sam.8.2; 2 Kg.13.20
MOAN
noon I utter my complaint and *m.* Ps.55.17
I think of God, and I *m.* Ps.77.3
Therefore my soul *m.* like a lyre Is.16.11
we *m.* and *m.* like doves Is.59.11
MOANING
I am weary with my *m.*; every night Ps.6.6
there shall be *m.* and lamentation Is.29.2
all of them *m.*, every one over his Ezek.7.16
m. like doves, and beating their Nah.2.7
MOCK
has sent to *m.* the living God 2 Kg.19.4
All who see me *m.* at me Ps.22.7
He who *m.* the poor insults his Pr.17.5
he has sent to *m.* the living God Is.37.17
they will *m.* him, and spit upon Mk.10.34
all who see it begin to *m.* him Lk.14.29
The soldiers also *m.* him Lk.23.36
Now when they heard . . . some *m.* Acts 17.32
God is not *m.*, for whatever a man Gal.6.7
MOCKING
gloated over her, *m.* at her downfall Lam.1.7
others *m.* said, "They are filled Acts 2.13
Others suffered *m.* and scourging Heb.11.36
MOLECH
Lev.18.21; 1 Kg.11.7; 2 Kg.23.10; Jer.32.35
MOLTEN
have made for themselves a *m.* calf Ex.32.8
destroy all their *m.* images Num.33.52
m. images, provoking me to anger 1 Kg.14.9
their *m.* images are empty wind Is.41.29
who say to *m.* images, "You are our Is.42.17
MOMENT
that I may consume them in a *m.* Num.16.21
In a *m.* they die; at midnight Job 34.20
For his anger is but for a *m.* Ps.30.5
For a brief *m.* I forsook you, but Is.54.7

servant was healed at that very *m.* Mt.8.13
in a *m.*, in the twinkling of 1 Cor.15.52
For the *m.* all discipline seems Heb.12.11
MONEY
If you lend *m.* to any of my people Ex.22.25
does not put out his *m.* at interest Ps.15.5
will not be satisfied with *m.* Ec.5.10
and *m.* answers everything Ec.10.19
you shall be redeemed without *m.* Is.52.3
he who has no *m.*, come, buy and eat Is.55.1
Show me the *m.* for the tax Mt.22.19
gave a sum of *m.* to the soldiers Mt.28.12
Pharisees, who were lovers of *m.* Lk.16.14
because Judas had the *m.* box Jn.13.29
obtain the gift of God with *m.* Acts 8.20
the love of *m.* is the root of 1 Tim.6.10
lovers of *m.*, proud, arrogant 2 Tim.3.2
Keep your life free from love of *m.* Heb.13.5
MONEY-CHANGERS
tables of the *m.* and the seats of Mt.21.12
and the *m.* at their business Jn.2.14
MONUMENT
he set up a *m.* for himself 1 Sam.15.12
called Absalom's *m.* to this day 2 Sam.18.18
to set up his *m.* at the river 1 Chr.18.3
adorn the *m.* of the righteous Mt.23.29
MOON
the *m.* stayed, until the nation Jos.10.13
the *m.* and the stars which thou hast Ps.8.3
by day, nor the *m.* by night Ps.121.6
sun and *m.*, praise him, all you Ps.148.3
the *m.* shall not give its light Ezek.32.7
there will be signs in sun and *m.* Lk.21.25
and the *m.* into blood Acts 2.20
with the *m.* under her feet Rev.12.1
no need of sun or *m.* to shine Rev.21.23
MORDECAI
Ezra 2.2; Est.2.5; 3.2; 5.9; 9.4; 10.3
MORIAH
Gen.22.2; 2 Chr.3.1
MORNING
but joy comes with the *m.* Ps.30.5
Evening and *m.* and at noon I utter Ps.55.17
in the *m.* my prayer comes before Ps.88.13
If I take the wings of the *m.* Ps.139.9
early in the *m.* to hire laborers Mt.20.1
were at the tomb early in the *m.* Lk.24.22
the *m.* star rises in your hearts 2 Pet.1.19
I will give him the *m.* star Rev.2.28
MORSEL
or have eaten my *m.* alone Job 31.17
He casts forth his ice like *m.* Ps.147.17
Better is a dry *m.* with quiet than Pr.17.1
he to whom I shall give this *m.* Jn.13.26
Then after the *m.*, Satan entered Jn.13.27
MORTAL
Can *m.* man be righteous before God? Job 4.17
resembling *m.* man or birds or Rom.1.23
this *m.* nature must put on 1 Cor.15.53
may be manifested in our *m.* flesh 2 Cor.4.11
Here tithes are received by *m.* men Heb.7.8
committing what is not a *m.* sin 1 Jn.5.16
There is sin which is *m.* 1 Jn.5.16
but its *m.* wound was healed Rev.13.3
MOSES
born and hidden, Ex.2 (Acts 7.20; Heb.11.23);

escapes to Midian, Ex.2.25; revelation from
God, Ex.3; confirmed by signs, Ex.4; returns to
Egypt, Ex.4.20; intercedes with Pharaoh for
Israel, Ex.5–12; leads Israel forth, Ex.14;
meets God on Mount Sinai, Ex.19.3 (24.18);
brings the law to the people, Ex.19.25; 20–23;
35.1; Lev.1; Num.5–6; 15; 27–30; 36; Dt.12–
26; instructed to build the tabernacle, Ex.25–31;
35; 40; his grief at Israel's idolatry, Ex.32.10;
his intercession, Ex.32.11–14; again meets
God on the mount, Ex.34.2; skin of his face
shines, Ex.34.29 (2 Cor.3.7,13); sets apart
Aaron, Lev.8–9; numbers the people, Num.1;
26; sends out the spies to Canaan, Num.13;
intercedes for the murmuring people, Num.
14.13; Korah's sedition against, Num.16; for
his unbelief not allowed to enter Canaan,
Num.20.12; 27.12–14; Dt.1.37; 3.23–27; his
government of Israel in the wilderness, Num.
20–21; makes the bronze serpent, Num.21.9 (Jn.
3.14); his charge to Joshua, Dt.3.28; 31.7,23; his
death, Dt.34.5; his body, Jude 9; seen at Jesus'
transfiguration, Mt.17.3; Mk.9.4; Lk.9.30; his
meekness, Num.12.3; distinction, Dt.34.10;
faithfulness, Num.12.7; Heb.3.2
MOTH
the *m.* will eat them up Is.50.9
For the *m.* will eat them up like a Is.51.8
where *m.* and rust consume and where Mt.6.19
where . . . no *m.* destroys Lk.12.33
MOTHER
she was the *m.* of all living Gen.3.20
she shall be a *m.* of nations Gen.17.16
Honor your father and your *m.* Ex.20.12
father and my *m.* have forsaken me Ps.27.10
in sin did my *m.* conceive me Ps.51.5
a foolish son is a sorrow to his *m.* Pr.10.1
If one curses his father or his *m.* Pr.20.20
As one whom his *m.* comforts Is.66.13
took the child and his *m.* by night Mt.2.14
loves father or *m.* more than me is Mt.10.37
He who speaks evil of father or *m.* Mt.15.4
the *m.* of Jesus was there Jn.2.1
to the disciple, "Behold, your *m.*" Jn.19.27
the Jerusalem above . . . is our *m.* Gal.4.26
MOTHER-IN-LAW
and Orpah kissed her *m.* Ru.1.14
Then Naomi her *m.* said to her Ru.3.1
a daughter-in-law against her *m.* Mt.10.35
Simon's *m.* was ill with a high fever Lk.4.38
MOUNT OF OLIVES
Zech.14.4; Mt.21.1; Mk.11.1; Lk.19.37
MOUNTAIN
he was encamped at the *m.* of God Ex.18.5
Then Moses went up on the *m.* Ex.24.15
though the *m.* shake in the heart of Ps.46.2
Before the *m.* were brought forth Ps.90.2
and worship at his holy *m.* Ps.99.9
As the *m.* are round about Jerusalem Ps.125.2
Get you up to a high *m.*, O Zion Is.40.9
was cut from a *m.* by no human hand Dan.2.45
let us go up to the *m.* of the LORD Mic.4.2
devil took him to a very high *m.* Mt.4.8
who are in Judea flee to the *m.* Mt.24.16
every *m.* and hill shall be brought low Lk.3.5
Our fathers worshiped on this *m.* Jn.4.20

we were with him on the holy *m.*	2 Pet.1.18	a great *m.* from Galilee followed	Mk.3.7
every *m.* and island was removed	Rev.6.14	because all the *m.* was astonished	Mk.11.18
MOURN		In these lay a *m.* of invalids	Jn.5.3
those who *m.* are lifted to safety	Job 5.11	since love covers a *m.* of sins	1 Pet.4.8
a time to *m.*, and a time to dance	Ec.3.4	a great *m.* which no man could number	Rev.7.9
to comfort all who *m.*	Is.61.2	**MURDER**	
shall *m.* for him, as one *m.* for	Zech.12.10	fornication, theft, *m.*, adultery	Mk.7.21
Blessed are those who *m.*, for they	Mt.5.4	had committed *m.* in the insurrection	Mk.15.7
for you shall *m.* and weep	Lk.6.25	breathing threats and *m.* against	Acts 9.1
Ought you not rather to *m.*?	1 Cor.5.2	Full of envy, *m.*, strife, deceit	Rom.1.29
MOURNING (noun)		**MURDERER**	
My lyre is turned to *m.*	Job 30.31	the *m.* shall be put to death	Num.35.18
turned for me my *m.* into dancing	Ps.30.11	He was a *m.* from the beginning	Jn.8.44
your days of *m.* shall be ended	Is.60.20	and asked for a *m.* to be granted	Acts 3.14
the oil of gladness instead of *m.*	Is.61.3	let none of you suffer as a *m.*	1 Pet.4.15
I will turn their *m.* into joy	Jer.31.13	one who hates his brother is a *m.*	1 Jn.3.15
I will turn your feasts into *m.*	Am.8.10	know that no *m.* has eternal life	1 Jn.3.15
MOUTH		fornicators and *m.* and idolaters	Rev.22.15
He will yet fill your *m.* with laughter	Job 8.21	**MURMUR**	
by the *m.* of babes and infants, thou	Ps.8.2	And the people *m.* against Moses	Ex.15.24
Let the words of my *m.* and the	Ps.19.14	what are we, that you *m.* against us?	Ex.16.7
My *m.* shall speak wisdom	Ps.49.3	the Pharisees and the scribes *m.*	Lk.15.2
Open your *m.* wide, and I will fill	Ps.81.10	Do not *m.* among yourselves	Jn.6.43
tongue cleave to the roof of my *m.*	Ps.137.6	Hellenists *m.* against the Hebrews	Acts 6.1
My *m.* will speak the praise of	Ps.145.21	**MUSIC**	
He who guards his *m.* preserves his	Pr.13.3	leader of the *m.* of the singers	1 Chr.15.27
He who keeps his *m.* and his tongue	Pr.21.23	instruments for *m.* to the LORD	2 Chr.7.6
Be not rash with your *m.*	Ec.5.2	to the *m.* of the lute and the harp	Ps.92.3
And he touched my *m.*, and said	Is.6.7	I will stop the *m.* of your songs	Ezek.26.13
the *m.* of the LORD has commanded	Is.34.16	for themselves instruments of *m.*	Am.6.5
He made my *m.* like a sharp sword	Is.49.2	he heard *m.* and dancing	Lk.15.25
is dumb, so he opened not his *m.*	Is.53.7	**MUSTARD**	
And he opened his *m.* and taught	Mt.5.2	have faith as a grain of *m.* seed	Mt.17.20
I will open my *m.* in parables	Mt.13.35	It is like a grain of *m.* seed	Mk.4.31
abundance of the heart his *m.* speaks	Lk.6.45	**MYRRH**	
I will give you a *m.* and wisdom	Lk.21.15	fragrant with *m.* and aloes	Ps.45.8
no evil talk come out of your *m.*	Eph.4.29	perfumed with *m.* and frankincense	S.of S.3.6
I was rescued from the lion's *m.*	2 Tim.4.17	gold and frankincense and *m.*	Mt.2.11
I will spew you out of my *m.*	Rev.3.16	offered him wine mingled with *m.*	Mk.15.23
From his *m.* issues a sharp sword	Rev.19.15	bringing a mixture of *m.* and aloes	Jn.19.39
MOVE		*m.*, frankincense, wine, oil	Rev.18.13
does these things shall never be *m.*	Ps.15.5	**MYRTLE**	
I shall not be greatly *m.*	Ps.62.2	instead of . . . shall come up the *m.*	Is.55.13
For the righteous will never be *m.*	Ps.112.6	was standing among the *m.* trees	Zech.1.11
'*M.* hence to yonder place,' and it	Mt.17.20	**MYSTERY**	
M. with pity, he stretched out his	Mk.1.41	Then the *m.* was revealed to Daniel	Dan.2.19
he was deeply *m.* in spirit	Jn.11.33	I want you to understand this *m.*	Rom.11.25
in him we live and *m.* and have	Acts 17.28	if I . . . understand all *m.* and all	1 Cor.13.2
men *m.* by the Holy Spirit spoke	2 Pet.1.21	I tell you a *m.* We shall not all	1 Cor.15.51
MULE		my insight into the *m.* of Christ	Eph.3.4
Absalom was riding upon his *m.*	2 Sam.18.9	the plan of the *m.* hidden for ages	Eph.3.9
Solomon to ride on King David's *m.*	1 Kg.1.38	to declare the *m.* of Christ	Col.4.3
Be not like a horse or a *m.*	Ps.32.9	the *m.* of lawlessness is . . . at work	2 Th.2.7
MULTIPLY		As for the *m.* of the seven stars	Rev.1.20
Be fruitful and *m.* and fill the	Gen.1.22	**MYTHS**	
I will *m.* your descendants as the	Gen.26.4	with *m.* and endless genealogies	1 Tim.1.4
And when you have *m.* and increased	Jer.3.16	turn away . . . and wander into *m.*	2 Tim.4.4
disciples *m.* greatly in Jerusalem	Acts 6.7	giving heed to Jewish *m.*	Tit.1.14
But the word of God grew and *m.*	Acts 12.24	not follow cleverly devised *m.*	2 Pet.1.16
May grace and peace be *m.* to you	1 Pet.1.2		
MULTITUDE		**NAAMAN**	
be the father of a *m.* of nations	Gen.17.4	2 Kg.5.1,11,27; Lk.4.27	
A mixed *m.* also went up with them	Ex.12.38	**NABAL**	
Should a *m.* of words go unanswered	Job 11.2	1 Sam.25.3; 30.5; 2 Sam.2.2	
a *m.* keeping festival	Ps.42.4	**NAILS**	
M., *m.*, in the valley of decision	Jl.3.14	like *n.* firmly fixed are . . . sayings	Ec.12.11

his *n.* were like birds' claws	Dan.4.33	Jg.4.10; 5.18; 6.35; carried captive, 2 Kg.15.29;	
my finger in the mark of the *n.*	Jn.20.25	*see* Is.9.1; Mt.4.13-15	

NAKED

the man and his wife were both *n.*	Gen.2.25
N. I came from my mother's womb	Job 1.21
I was *n.* and you clothed me	Mt.25.36
left the linen cloth and ran away *n.*	Mk.14.52
we may not be found *n.*	2 Cor.5.3
they will make her desolate and *n.*	Rev.17.16

NAKEDNESS

covered the *n.* of their father	Gen.9.23
not uncover the *n.* of your father	Lev.18.7
so openly and flaunted her *n.*	Ezek.23.18
or *n.*, or peril, or sword?	Rom.8.35
shame of your *n.* from being seen	Rev.3.18

NAME (noun)

Abram called on the *n.* of the LORD	Gen.13.4
this is my *n.* for ever, and thus I	Ex.3.15
the LORD is his *n.*	Ex.15.3
blasphemed the *N.*, and cursed	Lev.24.11
what wilt thou do for thy great *n.*?	Jos.7.9
My *n.* shall be there	1 Kg.8.29
in thy *n.* we have come against	2 Chr.14.11
thou didst get thee a *n.*	Neh.9.10
blessed be the *n.* of the LORD	Job 1.21
how majestic is thy *n.* in all the earth	Ps.8.1
let us exalt his *n.* together	Ps.34.3
May his *n.* endure for ever	Ps.72.17
Ascribe . . . the glory due his *n.*	Ps.96.8
Give thanks to him, bless his *n.*	Ps.100.4
all . . . within me, bless his holy *n.*	Ps.103.1
Holy and terrible is his *n.*	Ps.111.9
Our help is in the *n.* of the LORD	Ps.124.8
Thy *n.*, O LORD, endures for ever	Ps.135.13
A good *n.* is to be chosen rather	Pr.22.1
A good *n.* is better than precious	Ec.7.1
and shall call his *n.* Immanuel	Is.7.14
I am the LORD, that is my *n.*	Is.42.8
the LORD of hosts is his *n.*	Is.48.2
whose *n.* is Holy: "I dwell in the	Is.57.15
our Redeemer from of old is thy *n.*	Is.63.16
no one that calls upon thy *n.*	Is.64.7
walk in the *n.* of the LORD our God	Mic.4.5
How have we despised thy *n.*?	Mal.1.6
you shall call his *n.* Jesus	Mt.1.21
who art in heaven, Hallowed be thy *n.*	Mt.6.9
in his *n.* will the Gentiles hope	Mt.12.21
two or three are gathered in my *n.*	Mt.18.20
because you bear the *n.* of Christ	Mk.9.41
that your *n.* are written in heaven	Lk.10.20
works that I do in my Father's *n.*	Jn.10.25
Whatever you ask in my *n.*, I will	Jn.14.13
I made known to them thy *n.*	Jn.17.26
is no other *n.* under heaven given	Acts 4.12
carry my *n.* before the Gentiles	Acts 9.15
the *n.* which is above every *n.*	Phil.2.9
whose *n.* are in the book of life	Phil.4.3
reproached for the *n.* of Christ	1 Pet.4.14
not blot his *n.* out of the book of	Rev.3.5

NAOMI

Ru.1.2,11,20; 4.5,17

NAPHTALI

(1) son of Jacob, Gen.30.8; 35.25; 46.24; 49.21; Dt.33.23; (2) tribe of, numbered, Num.1.42; 10.27; 13.14; 26.48; subdue the Canaanites,

NARD

my *n.* gave forth its fragrance	S.of S.1.12
alabaster jar of ointment of pure *n.*	Mk.14.3
Mary took . . . ointment of pure *n.*	Jn.12.3

NARROW

covering too *n.* to wrap oneself in	Is.28.20
The place is too *n.* for me	Is.49.20
the gate is *n.* and the way is hard	Mt.7.14
Strive to enter by the *n.* door	Lk.13.24

NATHAN

(1) the prophet, 2 Sam.7; 1 Chr.29.29; 2 Chr. 9.29; reproves David for his sin, 2 Sam.12.1-15; anoints Solomon king, 1 Kg.1.34; (2) son of David, 2 Sam.5.14; Zech.12.12; Lk.3.31; (3) others, 2 Sam.23.36; 1 Kg.4.5; Ezra 8.16; 10.39

NATHANAEL

Jn.1.45-49; 21.2

NATION

I will make of you a great *n.*	Gen.12.2
A *n.* which you have not known shall	Dt.28.33
Blessed is the *n.* whose God is the	Ps.33.12
Let the *n.* be glad and sing for joy	Ps.67.4
Declare his glory among the *n.*	Ps.96.3
The LORD is high above all *n.*	Ps.113.4
not dealt thus with any other *n.*	Ps.147.20
Righteousness exalts a *n.*	Pr.14.34
Against a godless *n.* I send him	Is.10.6
n. . . . not lift up sword against *n.*	Mic.4.3
robbing me; the whole *n.* of you	Mal.3.9
For *n.* will rise against *n.*	Mt.24.7
make disciples of all *n.*	Mt.28.19
a house of prayer for all the *n.*	Mk.11.17
that Jesus should die for the *n.*	Jn.11.51
men from every *n.* under heaven	Acts 2.5
he made from one every *n.* of men	Acts 17.26
In you shall all the *n.* be blessed	Gal.3.8
a holy *n.*, God's own people	1 Pet.2.9
from every . . . tongue and people and *n.*	Rev.5.9
over every . . . people and tongue and *n.*	Rev.13.7
All *n.* shall come and worship the	Rev.15.4
were for the healing of the *n.*	Rev.22.2

NATIVE

return no more to see his *n.* land	Jer.22.10
each of us in his own *n.* language	Acts 2.8
a *n.* of Pontus, lately come from	Acts 18.2
Apollos, a *n.* of Alexandria, came	Acts 18.24

NATURAL

not dim, nor his *n.* force abated	Dt.34.7
women exchanged *n.* relations for	Rom.1.26
because of your *n.* limitations	Rom.6.19
God did not spare the *n.* branches	Rom.11.21
observes his *n.* face in a mirror	Jas.1.23

NATURE

Does not *n.* itself teach you	1 Cor.11.14
this perishable *n.* must put on	1 Cor.15.53
our outer *n.* is wasting away	2 Cor.4.16
so we were by *n.* children of wrath	Eph.2.3
Put off your old *n.* which belongs	Eph.4.22
have put on the new *n.*	Col.3.10
become partakers of the divine *n.*	2 Pet.1.4
for God's *n.* abides in him	1 Jn.3.9

NAVE

in front of the *n.* of the house	1 Kg.6.3
The *n.* he lined with cypress	2 Chr.3.5

Then he brought me to the *n.*   Ezek.41.1
doorposts of the *n.* were squared   Ezek.41.21
NAZARENE
Mt.2.23; Mk.14.67; Acts 24.5
NAZARETH
Mt.2.23; 21.11; Lk.2.39; Jn.1.46; Acts 22.8
NAZIRITE
the vow of a *N.*, to separate   Num.6.2
I have been a *N.* to God from my Jg.16.17
But you made the *N.* drink wine Am.2.12
NEBUCHADNEZZAR
same as Nebuchadrezzar; King of Babylon, Jer.
21; 25; 27–28; 32; 34; Ezek.26.7; 29.19; cap-
tures Jerusalem, 2 Kg.24–25; 2 Chr.36; Jer.37–
39; 52; Dan.1.1; his dreams, Dan.2; 4; sets up
a golden image, Dan.3; his madness, Dan.4.33;
his restoration and confession, Dan.4.34
NECESSARY
For it is *n.* that temptations come Mt.18.7
Was it not *n.* that the Christ   Lk.24.26
hence it is *n.* for this priest also Heb.8.3
I found it *n.* to write appealing to Jude 3
NECK
stiffened his *n.* and hardened   2 Chr.36.13
stiffened their *n.* and would not Neh.9.29
bind them about your *n.*, write them Pr.3.3
stiffens his *n.* will suddenly be Pr.29.1
round his *n.* and to be drowned in Mt.18.6
yoke upon the *n.* of the disciples Acts 15.10
who risked their *n.* for my life Rom.16.4
NECROMANCER
a medium, or a wizard, or a *n.*   Dt.18.11
NEED (noun)
Those who are well have no *n.* of Mk.2.17
distributed them . . . as any had *n.* Acts 2.45
to the feet, "I have no *n.* of you 1 Cor.12.21
supply every *n.* of yours according Phil.4.19
find grace to help in time of *n.* Heb.4.16
For you have *n.* of endurance Heb.10.36
sees his brother in *n.*   1 Jn.3.17
the city has no *n.* of sun or moon Rev.21.23
NEED (verb)
knows what you *n.* before you ask him Mt.6.8
who has bathed does not *n.* to wash Jn.13.10
You *n.* milk, not solid food Heb.5.12
I have prospered, and I *n.* nothing Rev.3.17
NEEDLE
easier . . . through the eye of a *n.* than Mk.10.25
NEEDY
he lifts the *n.* from the ash heap 1 Sam.2.8
the *n.* shall not always be forgotten Ps.9.18
As for me, I am poor and *n.* Ps.40.17
For the LORD hears the *n.* Ps.69.33
He has pity on the weak and the *n.* Ps.72.13
to turn aside the *n.* from justice Is.10.2
they sell . . . the *n.* for a pair of shoes Am.2.6
you who trample upon the *n.* Am.8.4
was not a *n.* person among them Acts 4.34
NEGEB
Gen.12.9; Num.13.17; Jos.10.40; Jg.1.9; Ps.
126.4; Ezek.20.46
NEGLECT (verb)
will not *n.* the house of our God Neh.10.39
n. justice and the love of God Lk.11.42
their widows were *n.* in the daily Acts 6.1

Do not *n.* the gift you have 1 Tim.4.14
how shall we escape if we *n.* such Heb.2.3
NEHEMIAH
(1) Ezra 2.2; (2) Neh.3.16; (3) son of Hacali-
ah, his grief for Jerusalem, Neh.1.1–3; his
prayer for, Neh.1.5–11; his visit to, Neh.2.5,
11; his work at, Neh.4–6; 8–10; 13
NEIGHBOR
bear false witness against your *n.* Ex.20.16
not oppress your *n.* or rob him Lev.19.13
you shall love your *n.* as yourself Lev.19.18
takes up a reproach against his *n.* Ps.15.3
He who despises his *n.* is a sinner Pr.14.21
and every man against his *n.* Is.19.2
shall love your *n.* and hate your Mt.5.43
You shall love your *n.* as yourself Mt.22.39
said to Jesus, "And who is my *n.*?" Lk.10.29
Love does no wrong to a *n.* Rom.13.10
who are you that you judge your *n.*? Jas.4.12
NEIGHBORHOOD
women of the *n.* gave him a name Ru.4.17
beg Jesus to depart from their *n.* Mk.5.17
in the *n.* of that place were lands Acts 28.7
NEST
Like an eagle that stirs up its *n.* Dt.32.11
and the swallow a *n.* for herself Ps.84.3
Like a bird that strays from its *n.* Pr.27.8
birds of the air have *n.* Mt.8.20
NET
will pluck my feet out of the *n.* Ps.25.15
take me out of the *n.* which is Ps.31.4
They set a *n.* for my steps Ps.57.6
in vain is a *n.* spread in the sight Pr.1.17
he spread a *n.* for my feet Lam.1.13
they spread their *n.* over him Ezek.19.8
Immediately they left their *n.* and Mt.4.20
is like a *n.* which was thrown into Mt.13.47
Cast the *n.* on the right side of Jn.21.6
NETHER
heart . . . hard as the *n.* millstone Job 41.24
committed them to pits of *n.* gloom 2 Pet.2.4
the *n.* gloom of darkness 2 Pet.2.17
kept . . . in . . . chains in the *n.* gloom Jude 6
NEW
Now there arose a *n.* king over Egypt Ex.1.8
Sing to him a *n.* song Ps.33.3
Sing to the LORD a *n.* song Ps.149.1
there is nothing *n.* under the sun Ec.1.9
I create *n.* heavens and a *n.* earth Is.65.17
they are *n.* every morning Lam.3.23
A *n.* heart I will give you Ezek.36.26
Neither is *n.* wine put into old Mt.9.17
when I drink it *n.* with you in my Mt.26.29
A *n.* commandment I give to you Jn.13.34
in the garden a *n.* tomb where no Jn.19.41
They are filled with *n.* wine Acts 2.13
know what this *n.* teaching is Acts 17.19
This cup is the *n.* covenant in 1 Cor.11.25
in Christ, he is a *n.* creation 2 Cor.5.17
is the mediator of a *n.* covenant Heb.9.15
I am writing you a *n.* commandment 1 Jn.2.8
the *n.* Jerusalem which comes down Rev.3.12
I saw a *n.* heaven and a *n.* earth Rev.21.1
said,"Behold, I make all things *n.*" Rev.21.5
NEWS
This day is a day of good *n.* 2 Kg.7.9

told the glad *n.* of deliverance	Ps.40.9	I will make the sun go down at *n.*	Am.8.9
poor have good *n.* preached to them	Mt.11.5	about *n.* a great light from heaven	Acts 22.6
bring you good *n.* of a great joy	Lk.2.10	NOONDAY	
the good *n.* of the kingdom of God	Lk.8.1	you shall grope at *n.*	Dt.28.29
he told him the good *n.* of Jesus	Acts 8.35	your life . . . brighter than the *n.*	Job 11.17
feet of those who preach good *n.*	Rom.10.15	the destruction that wastes at *n.*	Ps.91.6
For good *n.* came to us just as to	Heb.4.2	your gloom be as the *n.*	Is.58.10

NICODEMUS
Jn.3.1,9; 7.50; 19.39

NICOLAITANS
Rev.2.6, 15

NIGHT

NOSE

		Can you put a rope in his *n.*	Job 41.2
on his law he meditates day and *n.*	Ps.1.2	pressing the *n.* produces blood	Pr.30.33
and *n.* to *n.* declares knowledge	Ps.19.2	Your *n.* is like a tower	S.of S.7.4
Weeping may tarry for the *n.*	Ps.30.5	my hook in your *n.* and my bit in	Is.37.29
I commune with my heart in the *n.*	Ps.77.6	NOSTRILS	
fire to give light by *n.*	Ps.105.39	breathed into his *n.* the breath of	Gen.2.7
nor the moon by *n.*	Ps.121.6	Smoke went up from his *n.*	2 Sam.22.9
Upon my bed by *n.* I sought him	S. of S.3.1	the spirit of God is in my *n.*	Job 27.3
Watchman, what of the *n.?*	Is.21.11	from man in whose *n.* is breath	Is.2.22
this very *n.*, before the cock crows	Mt.26.34	NOWHERE	
N. and day among the tombs	Mk.5.5	Go *n.* among the Gentiles, and enter	Mt.10.5
watch over their flock by *n.*	Lk.2.8	Son of man has *n.* to lay his head	Lk.9.58
we toiled all *n.* and took nothing	Lk.5.5	for I have *n.* to store my crops?	Lk.12.17
This *n.* your soul is required	Lk.12.20	NUMBER (verb)	
But if any one walks in the *n.*	Jn.11.10	Go, *n.* Israel and Judah	2 Sam.24.1
on the *n.* when he was betrayed	1 Cor.11.23	Who can *n.* the clouds by wisdom?	Job 38.37
will come like a thief in the *n.*	1 Th.5.2	go round about her, *n.* her towers	Ps.48.12
prayers *n.* and day	1 Tim.5.5	So teach us to *n.* our days that we	Ps.90.12
And *n.* shall be no more	Rev.22.5	God has *n.* the days of your kingdom	Dan.5.26

NILE
Gen.41.1; Ex.1.22; Is.18.2; Ezek.29.3; Zech. 10.11

NIMROD
Gen.10.8; 1 Chr.1.10; Mic.5.6

NINEVEH
Gen.10.11; 2 Kg.19.36; Jon.1.2; 4.11; Zeph. 2.13; Mt.12.41

NOAH
son of Lamech, Gen.5.29; finds favor with God, Gen.6.8; ordered to build the ark, Gen.6.14; with his family and animals enters into the ark, Gen.7; God blesses and makes a covenant with, Gen.9.8–17; is drunken, and mocked by Ham, Gen.9.22; his death, Gen.9.29

the hairs of your head are all *n.*	Mt.10.30
For he was *n.* among us	Acts 1.17
multitude which no man could *n.*	Rev.7.9

NURSE

Rebekah's *n.* died, and . . . was buried	Gen.35.8
a *n.* from the Hebrew women	Ex.2.7
as a *n.* carries the sucking child	Num.11.12

OATH

NOBLE

Hear, for I will speak *n.* things	Pr.8.6	Joshua laid an *o.* upon them	Jos.6.26
he who is *n.* things	Is.32.8	Saul laid an *o.* on the people	1 Sam.14.24
these Jews were more *n.* than	Acts 17.11	They took *o.* to the LORD with a	2 Chr.15.14
what is *n.* in the sight of all	Rom.12.17	have sworn an *o.* and confirmed	Ps.119.106
of bishop, he desires a *n.* task	1 Tim.3.1	may perform the *o.* which I swore	Jer.11.5
		promised with an *o.* to give her	Mt.14.7
		again he denied it with an *o.*	Mt.26.72

NOISE

There is a *n.* of war in the camp	Ex.32.17	the *o.* which he swore to our father	Lk.1.73
by the *n.* of the enemy	Ps.55.3	bound themselves by an *o.*	Acts 23.12
Make a joyful *n.* to God, all the	Ps.66.1	do not swear . . . with any other *o.*	Jas.5.12

The *n.* of battle is in the land | Jer.50.22 **OBADIAH**
Take away . . . the *n.* of your songs | Am.5.23 (1) prophet, his prediction, Ob.1–21; (2)
was like the *n.* of many chariots | Rev.9.9 Levite, gatekeeper in the temple, Neh.12.25; (3)
sent by Ahab to find water, 1 Kg.18.3; meets

NOISY
Elijah, 1 Kg.18.7; hid a hundred prophets, 1 Kg.

A foolish woman is *n.*; she is wanton	Pr.9.13
N. one who lets the hour go by	Jer.46.17
a *n.* multitude of men	Mic.2.12
am a *n.* gong or a clanging cymbal	1 Cor.13.1

18.4,13; (4) others, 1 Chr.7.3; 8.38; 9.16; 12.9; 27.19; 2 Chr.17.7; 34.12; Ezra 8.9

OBEDIENCE

by one man's *o.* many will be made	Rom.5.19
while your *o.* is known to all	Rom.16.19
Confident of your *o.*, I write to	Philem.21
learned *o.* through what he suffered	Heb.5.8

OBEDIENT

If you are willing and *o.*	Is.1.19
to Nazareth, and was *o.* to them	Lk.2.51
many . . . priests were *o.* to the faith	Acts 6.7
Slaves, be *o.* to those who are your	Eph.6.5
o. children, do not be conformed	1 Pet.1.14

NOON
called . . . Baal from morning until *n.* | 1 Kg.18.26

OBEISANCE
they bowed their heads and made *o.* | Gen.43.28

he fell to the ground and did *o*.   2 Sam.1.2
Bathsheba bowed and did *o*. to   1 Kg.1.16
Mordecai did not bow down or do *o*.   Est.3.2

OBEY
o. the commandments of the LORD   Dt.11.27
serve, and his voice we will *o*.   Jos.24.24
to *o*. is better than sacrifice   1 Sam.15.22
did not *o*. the voice of the LORD   Ps.106.25
O. now the voice of the LORD in   Jer.38.20
that even winds and sea *o*. him?   Mt.8.27
unclean spirits, and they *o*. him   Mk.1.27
he who does not *o*. the Son shall   Jn.3.36
We must *o*. God rather than men   Acts 5.29
are slaves of the one whom you *o*.   Rom.6.16
o. your parents in everything   Col.3.20
By faith Abraham *o*. when he was   Heb.11.8
O. your leaders and submit to them   Heb.13.17
formerly did not *o*., when God's   1 Pet.3.20
love God and *o*. his commandments   1 Jn.5.2

OBSERVE
O. what I command you this day   Ex.34.11
O. the sabbath day, to keep it   Dt.5.12
good care to *o*. the commandment   Jos.22.5
o. and seek . . . the commandments   1 Chr.28.8
Blessed are they who *o*. justice   Ps.106.3
that I may *o*. thy testimonies   Ps.119.146
o. carefully what is before you   Pr.23.1
He who *o*. the wind will not sow   Ec.11.4
so practice and *o*. whatever they   Mt.23.3
teaching them to *o*. all that I have   Mt.28.20
All these I have *o*. from my youth   Lk.18.21
You *o*. days, and months, and   Gal.4.10
like a man who *o*. his natural face   Jas.1.23

OBSTACLE
an *o*. in the way of the gospel   1 Cor.9.12
We put no *o*. in any one's way   2 Cor.6.3
We destroy . . . every proud *o*.   2 Cor.10.5

OBTAIN
lowly in spirit will *o*. honor   Pr.29.23
they shall *o*. joy and gladness   Is.35.10
merciful, for they shall *o*. mercy   Mt.5.7
Through him we have *o*. access to   Rom.5.2
So run that you may *o*. it   1 Cor.9.24
to *o*. salvation through our Lord   1 Th.5.9
you will *o*. the unfading crown of   1 Pet.5.4

OCCASION
seeking an *o*. against the Philistines   Jg.14.4
as fits the *o*., that it may impart   Eph.4.29
give the enemy no *o*. to revile   1 Tim.5.14
would have been no *o*. for a second   Heb.8.7

OCCUPATION
Pharaoh . . . says, 'What is your *o*.?'   Gen.46.33
What is your *o*.? And whence do   Jon.1.8
with the workmen of like *o*.   Acts 19.25

OCCUPY
Let us go up at once, and *o*. it   Num.13.30
they also *o*. the land which the   Dt.3.20
I do not *o*. myself with things too   Ps.131.1
nor to *o*. themselves with myths   1 Tim.1.4

ODOR
the LORD smelled the pleasing *o*.   Gen.8.21
by fire, a pleasing *o*. to the LORD   Lev.1.9
a burnt offering of pleasing *o*.   Num.28.13
pleasing *o*. to all their idols   Ezek.6.13
by this time there will be an *o*.   Jn.11.39

OFFENSE
but love covers all *o*.   Pr.10.12
it is his glory to overlook an *o*.   Pr.19.11
And they took *o*. at him. But Jesus   Mt.13.57
And they took *o*. at him   Mk.6.3
blessed is he who takes no *o*. at me   Lk.7.23
Give no *o*. to Jews or to Greeks   1 Cor.10.32

OFFER
when they *o*. unholy fire   Num.3.4
that the people *o*. themselves   Jg.5.2
I will *o*. in his tent sacrifices   Ps.27.6
O. . . . a sacrifice of thanksgiving   Ps.50.14
When you *o*. your gifts   Ezek.20.31
Even though you *o*. me your burnt   Am.5.22
And when you *o*. those that are lame   Mal.1.8
o. the gift that Moses commanded   Mt.8.4
to *o*. a sacrifice according to   Lk.2.24
Now concerning food *o*. to idols   1 Cor.8.1
to *o*. gifts and sacrifices for sins   Heb.5.1
Jesus . . . up prayers and supplications Heb.5.7
By faith Abel *o*. to God a more   Heb.11.4
By faith Abraham . . . *o*. up Isaac   Heb.11.17
to *o*. spiritual sacrifices   1 Pet.2.5

OFFERING (noun)
had regard for Abel and his *o*.   Gen.4.4
continual burnt *o*. throughout your   Ex.29.42
Sacrifice and *o*. thou dost not   Ps.40.6
With a freewill *o*. I will sacrifice   Ps.54.6
I will render thank *o*. to thee   Ps.56.12
come into thy house with burnt *o*.   Ps.66.13
bring an *o*., and come into his   Ps.96.8
he makes himself an *o*. for sin   Is.53.10
offer burnt *o*. and cereal *o*.   Jer.14.12
not accept an *o*. from your hand   Mal.1.10
make an *o*. for your cleansing   Lk.5.14
that the *o*. of the Gentiles may   Rom.15.16
write . . . about the *o*. for the saints 2 Cor.9.1
the sacrificial *o*. of your faith   Phil.2.17
the gifts you sent, a fragrant *o*.   Phil.4.18
by a single *o*. he has perfected   Heb.10.14

OFFICE
Matthew sitting at the tax *o*.   Mt.9.9
His *o*. let another take   Acts 1.20
the divine *o*. which was given to me   Col.1.25
one aspires to the *o*. of bishop   1 Tim.3.1
took their *o*. without an oath   Heb.7.21

OFFSPRING
Behold, thou hast given me no *o*.   Gen.15.3
All the *o*. of Jacob were seventy   Ex.1.5
Should women eat their *o*.   Lam.2.20
Being then God's *o*., we ought not   Acts 17.29
then you are Abraham's *o*.   Gal.3.29
I am the root and the *o*. of David   Rev.22.16

OFTEN
How *o*. they rebelled against him   Ps.78.40
He who is *o*. reproved, yet stiffens   Pr.29.1
for *o*. he falls into the fire   Mt.17.15
how *o*. shall my brother sin against   Mt.18.21
How *o*. would I have gathered your   Lk.13.34
For as *o*. as you eat this bread   1 Cor.11.26
o. without food, in cold and   2 Cor.11.27

OG
        Num.21.33; Dt.1.4; Jos.2.10; 1 Kg.4.19; Ps
        135.11

OIL
the cruse of *o*. shall not fail   1 Kg.17.14

thou anointest my head with *o.* Ps.23.5
anointed you with the *o.* of gladness Ps.45.7
o. to make his face shine Ps.104.15
like the precious *o.* upon the head Ps.133.2
and her speech is smoother than *o.* Pr.5.3
O. and perfume make the heart glad Pr.27.9
lamps, they took no *o.* with them Mt.25.3
Give us some of your *o.* Mt.25.8
You did not anoint my head with *o.* Lk.7.46
his wounds, pouring on *o.* and wine Lk.10.34

OINTMENT
good name is better than precious *o.* Ec.7.1
Why was the *o.* thus wasted? Mk.14.4
and anointed them with the *o.* Lk.7.38
pound of costly *o.* of pure nard Jn.12.3
Why was this *o.* not sold for three Jn.12.5

OLD
Now Abraham and Sarah were *o.* Gen.18.11
I have been young and now am *o.* Ps.37.25
I will remember thy wonders of *o.* Ps.77.11
thy throne is established from of *o.* Ps.93.2
child shall die a hundred years *o.* Is.65.20
your *o.* men shall dream dreams Jl.2.28
new wine put into *o.* wineskins Mt.9.17
Elizabeth in her *o.* age has also Lk.1.36
can a man be born when he is *o.?* Jn.3.4
Cleanse out the *o.* leaven 1 Cor.5.7
the *o.* has passed away, behold 2 Cor.5.17
Put off your *o.* nature Eph.4.22
God spoke of *o.* to our fathers Heb.1.1
will all grow *o.* like a garment Heb.1.11
an *o.* commandment which you had 1 Jn.2.7

OLIVE
there are two *o.* trees by it Zech.4.3
you, a wild *o.* shoot . . . grafted in Rom.11.17
Can a fig tree . . . yield *o.* Jas.3.12
These are the two *o.* trees Rev.11.4

OLIVET
Lk.19.29; 21.37; Acts 1.12

OMEGA
I am the Alpha and the *O.* Rev.1.8
is done! I am the Alpha and the *O.* Rev.21.6
the Alpha and the *O.*, the first Rev.22.13

OMEN
the men were watching for an *o.* 1 Kg.20.33
for they are men of good *o.* Zech.3.8
This is a clear *o.* to them of Phil.1.28

ONESIMUS
Col.4.9; Philem.10

ONIONS
the leeks, the *o.*, and the garlic Num.11.5

ONYX
bdellium and *o.* stone are there Gen.2.12
And you shall take two *o.* stones Ex.28.9
valued . . . in precious *o.* or sapphire Job 28.16
o., sapphire, carbuncle Ezek.28.13
the fifth *o.*, the sixth carnelian Rev.21.20

OPEN (verb)
Then the eyes of both were *o.* Gen.3.7
if he shuts a man in, none can *o.* Job 12.14
o. thou my lips, and my mouth Ps.51.15
O. your mouth wide, and I will fill it Ps.81.10
O. my eyes, that I may behold Ps.119.18
Thou *o.* thy hand, thou satisfiest Ps.145.16
O. your mouth, judge righteously Pr.31.9
to *o.* the eyes that are blind Is.42.7

if I will not *o.* the windows of Mal.3.10
saying, 'Lord, lord, *o.* to us Mt.25.11
And their eyes were *o.* and they Lk.24.31
hears my voice and *o.* the door Rev.3.20
Then God's temple in heaven was *o.* Rev.11.19

OPENING (noun)
with a woven binding around the *o.* Ex.28.32
Its *o.* was within a crown which 1 Kg.7.31
from the same *o.* fresh water and Jas.3.11

OPHIR
Gen.10.29; 1 Kg.9.28; Ps.45.9; Is.13.12

OPINION
go limping with two different *o.* 1 Kg.18.21
afraid to declare my *o.* to you Job 32.6
but not for disputes over *o.* Rom.14.1
but I give my *o.* as one who by 1 Cor.7.25

OPPORTUNITY
he sought an *o.* to betray him Mt.26.16
freedom, avail yourself of the *o.* 1 Cor.7.21
as we have *o.*, let us do good to all Gal.6.10
give no *o.* to the devil Eph.4.27

OPPOSE
when Cephas came . . . I *o.* him Gal.2.11
so these men also *o.* the truth 2 Tim.3.8
God *o.* the proud, but gives grace Jas.4.6
God *o.* the proud, but gives 1 Pet.5.5

OPPRESS
You shall not *o.* a stranger Ex.23.9
You shall not *o.* a hired servant Dt.24.14
The LORD is a stronghold for the *o.* Ps.9.9
Let the *o.* see it and be glad Ps.69.32
let not the godless *o.* me Ps.119.122
I will punish all who *o.* them Jer.30.20
who *o.* the poor, who crush the needy Am.4.1
not *o.* the widow, the fatherless Zech.7.10
who *o.* the hireling in his wages Mal.3.5
to set at liberty those who are *o.* Lk.4.18
Is it not the rich who *o.* you Jas.2.6

OPPRESSION
I have seen the *o.* with which the Ex.3.9
for he saw the *o.* of Israel 2 Kg.13.4
o. and fraud do not depart from its Ps.55.11
Redeem me from man's *o.* Ps.119.134
who despises the gain of *o.* Is.33.15

OPPRESSOR
Ransom me from the hand of *o.* Job 6.23
give deliverance . . . and crush the *o.* Ps.72.4
The poor man and the *o.* meet Pr.29.13
the rod of his *o.*, thou hast broken Is.9.4
And where is the fury of the *o.?* Is.51.13

ORACLE
The *o.* of Balaam the son of Beor Num.24.3
The *o.* concerning Babylon which Is.13.1
This *o.* concerns the prince in Ezek.12.10
An *o.* concerning Nineveh Nah.1.1
The *o.* of God which Habakkuk Hab.1.1
The *o.* of the word of the LORD to Mal.1.1
he received living *o.* to give to us Acts 7.38
are entrusted with the *o.* of God Rom.3.2
as one who utters *o.* of God 1 Pet.4.11

ORDAIN
Thus you shall *o.* Aaron and his sons Ex.29.9
thou wilt *o.* peace for us Is.26.12
the one *o.* by God to be judge Acts 10.42
as many as were *o.* to eternal life Acts 13.48
it was *o.* by angels through an Gal.3.19

ORDER

the LORD, 'Set your house in *o.*	2 Kg.20.1
for ever after the *o.* of Melchizedek	Ps.110.4
be done decently and in *o.*	1 Cor.14.40
But each in his own *o.*	1 Cor.15.23
priest after the *o.* of Melchizedek	Heb.5.10

ORDINANCE

This is the *o.* of the passover	Ex.12.43
the *o.* of the LORD are true	Ps.19.9
O LORD, and teach me thy *o.*	Ps.119.108
commandments and *o.* of the Lord	Lk.1.6
the law of commandments and *o.*	Eph.2.15

ORIGIN

city whose *o.* is from days of old	Is.23.7
in the land of your *o.*	Ezek.21.30
whose *o.* is from of old	Mic.5.2
who are sanctified have all one *o.*	Heb.2.11

ORPAH
Ru.1.4,14

ORPHAN

shall not afflict any widow or *o.*	Ex.22.22
In thee the *o.* finds mercy	Hos.14.3
who oppress . . . the widow and the *o.*	Mal.3.5
to visit *o.* and widows in their	Jas.1.27

OSTRICH

The wings of the *o.* wave proudly	Job 39.13
haunt of jackals, an abode for *o.*	Is.34.13
and *o.* shall dwell in her	Jer.50.39
jackals, and mourning like the *o.*	Mic.1.8

OUGHT

these you *o.* to have done	Lk.11.42
you also *o.* to wash one another's	Jn.13.14
we *o.* not to think that the Deity	Acts 17.29
more highly than he *o.* to think	Rom.12.3
We who are strong *o.* to bear with	Rom.15.1
declare it boldly, as I *o.* to speak	Eph.6.20
My brethren, this *o.* not to be so	Jas.3.10
Instead you *o.* to say, "If the Lord	Jas.4.15
we also *o.* to love one another	1 Jn.4.11

OUTER

cast him into the *o.* darkness	Mt.22.13
Though our *o.* nature is wasting	2 Cor.4.16
go continually into the *o.* tent	Heb.9.6

OUTSIDE

mother and his brothers stood *o.*	Mt.12.46
you cleanse the *o.* of the cup	Mt.23.25
into a man from *o.* cannot defile	Mk.7.18
But Mary stood weeping *o.* the tomb	Jn.20.11
that I might win those *o.* the law	1 Cor.9.21
let us go forth to him *o.* the camp	Heb.13.13
O. are the dogs and sorcerers	Rev.22.15

OUTSIDER

An *o.* shall not eat of a holy thing	Lev.22.10
how can . . . an *o.* say the "Amen"	1 Cor.14.16
and an unbeliever or *o.* enters	1 Cor.14.24
Conduct yourselves wisely towards *o.*	Col.4.5
you may command the respect of *o.*	1 Th.4.12
he must be well thought of by *o.*	1 Tim.3.7

OUTWARDLY

tombs, which *o.* appear beautiful	Mt.23.27
So you also *o.* appear righteous	Mt.23.28
he is not a real Jew who is one *o.*	Rom.2.28

OVEN

as a blazing *o.* when you appear	Ps.21.9
For like an *o.* their hearts burn	Hos.7.6

the day comes, burning like an *o.*	Mal.4.1
and tomorrow is thrown into the *o.*	Lk.12.28

OVERCOME

and the darkness has not *o.* it	Jn.1.5
of good cheer, I have *o.* the world	Jn.16.33
Do not be *o.* by evil, but *o.* evil	Rom.12.21
Who is it that *o.* the world but he	1 Jn.5.5

OVERFLOW

the Red Sea *o.* them as they	Dt.11.4
my head with oil, my cup *o.*	Ps.23.5
My heart *o.* with a goodly theme	Ps.45.1
shall again *o.* with prosperity	Zech.1.17
pour down for you an *o.* blessing	Mal.3.10

OVERPOWER

by what means we may *o.* him	Jg.16.5
the lions *o.* them and broke all	Dan.6.24
o. them, so that they fled out	Acts 19.16
are . . . entangled in them and *o.*	2 Pet.2.20

OVERSHADOW

o. the mercy seat with their wings	Ex.25.20
a cloud *o.* them, and a voice came out	Mk.9.7
power of the Most High will *o.* you	Lk.1.35
cherubim of glory *o.* the mercy seat	Heb.9.5

OVERTAKE

Terrors *o.* him like a flood	Job 27.20
let thy burning anger *o.* them	Ps.69.24
say, 'Evil shall not *o.* or meet us.'	Am.9.10
the plowman shall *o.* the reaper	Am.9.13
lest the darkness *o.* you	Jn.12.35
No temptation has *o.* you that	1 Cor.10.13
if a man is *o.* in any trespass, you	Gal.6.1

OVERTHROW

confront them, *o.* them! Deliver my	Ps.17.13
I will *o.* the wicked; I will cut off	Zeph.1.3
you will not be able to *o.* them	Acts 5.39
Do we . . . *o.* the law by this faith?	Rom.3.31

OVERWHELM

thou dost *o.* me with all thy waves	Ps.88.7
by thy wrath we are *o.*	Ps.90.7
the mischief of their lips *o.* them	Ps.140.9
Wrath is cruel, anger is *o.*; but	Pr.27.4
he may be *o.* by excessive sorrow	2 Cor.2.7

OWE

he said, 'Pay what you *o.*'	Mt.18.28
'And how much do you *o.*?'	Lk.16.7
O. no one anything, except to love	Rom.13.8

OWL

the *o.*, the cormorant, the ibis	Lev.11.17
like an *o.* of the waste places	Ps.102.6
the *o.* and the raven shall dwell in	Is.34.11
the *o.* shall hoot in the window	Zeph.2.14

OWNER

the *o.* of the ox shall be clear	Ex.21.28
the *o.* of the vineyard said to his	Mt.20.8
What will the *o.* of the vineyard do?	Mk.12.9
paid . . . attention . . . to the *o.* of	Acts 27.11
he is the *o.* of all the estate	Gal.4.1

OX

all sheep and *o.*, and also the beasts	Ps.8.7
an ass or an *o.* that has fallen	Lk.14.5
Is it for *o.* that God is concerned?	1 Cor.9.9
not muzzle an *o.* when . . . treading	1 Tim.5.18

PAGANS

that is not found even among *p.*	1 Cor.5.1
imply that what *p.* sacrifice	1 Cor.10.20

PAIN

in *p*. you shall bring forth children   Gen.3.16
chastened with *p*. upon his bed   Job 33.19
How long must I bear *p*. in my soul   Ps.13.2
But I am afflicted and in *p*.   Ps.69.29
For all his days are full of *p*.   Ec.2.23
Why is my *p*. unceasing   Jer.15.18
if I cause you *p*., who is there   2 Cor.2.2
nor crying nor *p*. any more   Rev.21.4

PAINFUL

not to make you another *p*. visit   2 Cor.2.1
discipline seems *p*. rather than   Heb.12.11

PAIR

Take with you seven *p*. of all clean   Gen.7.2
sell . . . the needy for a *p*. of shoes   Am.2.6
buy . . . the needy for a *p*. of sandals   Am.8.6
a *p*. of turtledoves, or two young   Lk.2.24

PALACE

burned all its *p*. with fire   2 Chr.36.19
as they enter the *p*. of the king   Ps.45.15
roof of the royal *p*. of Babylon   Dan.4.29
led him away inside the *p*.   Mk.15.16

PALE

no more shall his face grow *p*.   Is.29.22
Why has every face turned *p*.?   Jer.30.6
Hearts faint . . . all faces grow *p*.   Nah.2.10
I saw . . . a *p*. horse, and its rider's   Rev.6.8

PALLET

Rise, take up your *p*. and walk   Mk.2.9
to bring sick people on their *p*.   Mk.6.55
laid them on beds and *p*.   Acts 5.15

PALM

there were . . . seventy *p*. trees   Ex.15.27
righteous flourish like the *p*. tree   Ps.92.12
graven you on the *p*. of my hands   Is.49.16
a *p*. tree between cherub and   Ezek.41.18
they took branches of *p*. trees and   Jn.12.13
with *p*. branches in their hands   Rev.7.9

PAMPHYLIA

Acts 2.10; 14.24; 15.38; 27.5

PANGS

Many are the *p*. of the wicked   Ps.32.10
the *p*. of Sheol laid hold on me   Ps.116.3
having loosed the *p*. of death   Acts 2.24
pierced their hearts with many *p*.   1 Tim.6.10

PANIC

threw them into a *p*. before Israel   Jos.10.10
there was a *p*. in the camp   1 Sam.14.15
I will mock when *p*. strikes you   Pr.1.26
Do not be afraid of sudden *p*.   Pr.3.25
a great *p*. from the Lᴏʀᴅ shall   Zech.14.13

PARABLE

I will open my mouth in a *p*.   Ps.78.2
Hear then the *p*. of the sower   Mt.13.18
said nothing to them without a *p*.   Mt.13.34
With many such *p*. he spoke the word   Mk.4.33
but for others they are in *p*.   Lk.8.10

PARADISE

today you will be with me in *P*.   Lk.23.43
this man was caught up into *P*.   2 Cor.12.3
tree of life . . . in the *p*. of God   Rev.2.7

PARALYZED

my servant is lying *p*. at home   Mt.8.6
bringing on a bed a man who was *p*.   Lk.5.18
of invalids, blind, lame, *p*.   Jn.5.3

many who were *p*. or lame were healed   Acts 8.7
bedridden for . . . years and was *p*.   Acts 9.33

PARCHED

my throat is *p*. My eyes grow dim   Ps.69.3
thirsts for thee like a *p*. land   Ps.143.6
the river will be *p*. and dry   Is.19.5
their tongue is *p*. with thirst   Is.41.17

PARDON

p. our iniquity and our sin   Ex.34.9
P. the iniquity of this people   Num.14.19
dost thou not *p*. my transgression   Job 7.21
Lᴏʀᴅ, *p*. my guilt, for it is great   Ps.25.11
is ended, that her iniquity is *p*.   Is.40.2
our God, for he will abundantly *p*.   Is.55.7
I will *p*. those whom I leave   Jer.50.20

PARENT

his *p*. went to Jerusalem every year   Lk.2.41
wife or brothers or *p*. or children   Lk.18.29
who sinned, this man or his *p*.   Jn.9.2
Children, obey your *p*. in the Lord   Eph.6.1
abusive, disobedient to their *p*.   2 Tim.3.2
who loves the *p*. loves the child   1 Jn.5.1

PART

dwell in the uttermost *p*. of the sea   Ps.139.9
brought only a *p*. and laid it at   Acts 5.2
You have neither *p*. nor lot in   Acts 8.21
hardening has come upon *p*. of   Rom.11.25
there are many *p*., yet one body   1 Cor.12.20
Now I know in *p*.; then I shall   1 Cor.13.12
when each *p*. is working properly   Eph.4.16

PARTAKERS

p. of the promise in Christ   Eph.3.6
for you are all *p*. with me of grace   Phil.1.7
have become *p*. of the Holy Spirit   Heb.6.4
become *p*. of the divine nature   2 Pet.1.4

PARTIALITY

I will not show *p*. to any person   Job 32.21
P. in judging is not good   Pr.24.23
show no *p*., but truly teach the   Lk.20.21
I perceive that God shows no *p*.   Acts 10.34
For God shows no *p*.   Rom.2.11
there is no *p*. with him   Eph.6.9
But if you show *p*., you commit sin   Jas.2.9

PARTNER

to their *p*. in the other boat   Lk.5.7
not want you to be *p*. with demons   1 Cor.10.20
he is my *p*. and fellow worker   2 Cor.8.23
So if you consider me your *p*.   Philem.17

PARTY

the circumcision *p*. criticized him   Acts 11.2
belonged to the *p*. of the Pharisees   Acts 15.5
fearing the circumcision *p*.   Gal.2.12
selfishness, dissension, *p*. spirit   Gal.5.20

PASS

I will *p*. over you, and no plague   Ex.12.13
all our days *p*. away under thy wrath   Ps.90.9
When you *p*. through the waters   Is.43.2
till heaven and earth *p*. away   Mt.5.18
but my words will not *p*. away   Mt.24.35
the hour might *p*. from him   Mk.14.35
those who would *p*. from here to you   Lk.16.26
but has *p*. from death to life   Jn.5.24
all *p*. through the sea   1 Cor.10.1
as for prophecies, they will *p*. away   1 Cor.13.8
let no one *p*. judgment on you   Col.2.16
like . . . the grass he will *p*. away   Jas.1.10

heavens will *p*. away with a loud 2 Pet.3.10
we have *p*. out of death into life 1 Jn.3.14
for the former things have *p*. away Rev.21.4
PASSION
but *p*. makes the bones rot Pr.14.30
alive after his *p*. by many proofs Acts 1.3
consumed with *p*. for one another Rom.1.27
our sinful *p*., aroused by the law Rom.7.5
the flesh with its *p*. and desires Gal.5.24
once lived in the *p*. of our flesh Eph.2.3
So shun youthful *p*. and aim at 2 Tim.2.22
wrongly, to spend it on your *p*. Jas.4.3
p., drunkenness, revels, carousing 1 Pet.4.3
malcontents, following their own *p*. Jude 16
PASSOVER
This is the ordinance of the *p*. Ex.12.43
they kept the *p*. in the first month Num.9.5
keep the *p*. to the LORD your God Dt.16.1
Keep the *p*. to the LORD your God 2 Kg.23.21
Josiah kept a *p*. to the LORD 2 Chr.35.1
No *p*. like it had been kept in 2 Chr.35.18
I will keep the *p*. at your house Mt.26.18
Go and prepare the *p*. for us Lk.22.8
The *P*. of the Jews was at hand Jn.2.13
Now the *P*., the feast of the Jews Jn.6.4
Six days before the *P*., Jesus came Jn.12.1
intending after the *P*. to bring Acts 12.4
he kept the *P*. and sprinkled the Heb.11.28
PASTORS
evangelists, some *p*. and teachers Eph.4.11
PASTURE
he makes me lie down in green *p*. Ps.23.2
we thy people, the flock of thy *p*. Ps.79.13
the sheep of his *p*. Ps.100.3
and scatter the sheep of my *p*. Jer.23.1
I will restore Israel to his *p*. Jer.50.19
he . . . will go in and out and find *p*. Jn.10.9
PATH
Thou dost show me the *p*. of life Ps.16.11
He leads me in *p*. of righteousness Ps.23.3
lead me on a level *p*. because of my Ps.27.11
Thy word is . . . a light to my *p*. Ps.119.105
Thou searchest out my *p*. and my Ps.139.3
he will make straight your *p*. Pr.3.6
the *p*. of the upright is a level Pr.15.19
as he sowed, some fell along the *p*. Lk.8.5
make straight *p*. for your feet Heb.12.13
PATIENCE
and bring forth fruit with *p*. Lk.8.15
do not see, we wait for it with *p*. Rom.8.25
p., kindness, goodness Gal.5.22
with *p*., forbearing one another Eph.4.2
for all endurance and *p*. with joy Col.1.11
his perfect *p*. for an example 1 Tim.1.16
be unfailing in *p*. and in teaching 2 Tim.4.2
faith and *p*. inherit the promises Heb.6.12
As an example of suffering and *p*. Jas.5.10
God's *p*. waited in the days of 1 Pet.3.20
PATIENT
the *p*. in spirit is better than Ec.7.8
be *p*. in tribulation, be constant Rom.12.12
Love is *p*. and kind; love is not 1 Cor.13.4
help the weak, be *p*. with them all 1 Th.5.14
Be *p*., therefore, brethren, until Jas.5.7
I know . . . your *p*. endurance Rev.2.2
have kept my word of *p*. endurance Rev.3.10

PATIENTLY
before the LORD and wait *p*. for him Ps.37.7
I waited *p*. for the LORD Ps.40.1
I beg you to listen to me *p*. Acts 26.3
you *p*. endure the same sufferings 2 Cor.1.6
I know you are enduring *p*. Rev.2.3
PATMOS
Rev.1.9
PATTERN
concerning the *p*. of the tabernacle Ex.25.9
Follow the *p*. of the sound words 2 Tim.1.13
according to the *p*. which was shown Heb.8.5
PAUL
as a persecutor, Acts 7.58; 8.1; 9.1; 22.4; 26.9;
1 Cor.15.9; Gal.1.13; Phil.3.6; 1 Tim.1.13; as a
convert to the gospel, Acts 9.3–19; 22.6–16;
26.12–18; as a preacher, Acts 9.19–29; 13.1–15;
17.18; stoned at Lystra, Acts 14.8,19; is persecuted at Philippi, Acts 16; restores Eutychus,
Acts 20.10; his charge to the elders of Ephesus,
at Miletus, Acts 20.17; his return to Jerusalem,
and persecution there, Acts 21; his defense
before the people and the council, Acts 22–23;
before Felix, Acts 24; Festus, Acts 25; Agrippa,
Acts 26; appeals to Caesar at Rome, Acts
25.11; his voyage and shipwreck, Acts 27; at
Rome, reasons with the Jews, Acts 28.17–20; his
sufferings, 1 Cor.4.9; 2 Cor.11.23–28; 12.7;
Phil.1.12; 2 Tim.3.11; defends his apostleship,
1 Cor.9; 2 Cor.11–12; 2 Tim.3.10; rebukes
Peter, Gal.2.14; his letters mentioned in 2
Pet.3.15-16
PAVEMENT
as it were a *p*. of sapphire stone Ex.24.10
silver on a mosaic *p*. of porphyry Est.1.6
thirty chambers fronted on the *p*. Ezek.40.17
at a place called The *P*. Jn.19.13
PAY (verb)
thief is found, he shall *p*. double Ex.22.7
Go, sell the oil and *p*. your debts 2 Kg.4.7
my vows I will *p*. before those who Ps.22.24
I will *p*. my vows to the LORD in Ps.116.15
PAYMENT
whether in *p*. of a vow or as a Lev.22.18
all that he had, and *p*. to be made Mt.18.25
I have received full *p*., and more Phil.4.18
PEACE
The LORD . . . give you *p*. Num.6.26
I give to him my covenant of *p*. Num.25.12
P. be to you, and *p*. be to 1 Sam.25.6
In *p*. I will both lie down and Ps.4.8
do good; seek *p*., and pursue it Ps.34.14
Great *p*. have those who love thy Ps.119.165
Pray for the *p*. of Jerusalem Ps.122.6
his enemies to be at *p*. with him Pr.16.7
Everlasting Father, Prince of *P*. Is.9.6
Thou dost keep him in perfect *p*. Is.26.3
"There is no *p*.," says the LORD Is.48.22
who publishes *p*., who brings good Is.52.7
'*P*., *p*.,' when there is no *p*. Jer.6.14
I have not come to bring *p*., but a Mt.10.34
said to the sea, "*P*.! Be still!" Mk.4.39
be at *p*. with one another Mk.9.50
guide our feet into the way of *p*. Lk.1.79
on earth *p*. among men with whom Lk.2.14
lettest thou thy servant depart in *p*. Lk.2.29

P. in heaven and glory in the Lk.19.38
P. I leave with you; my p. I give Jn.14.27
we have p. with God through our Rom.5.1
The God of p. be with you all Rom.15.33
For he is our p., who has made us Eph.2.14
the p. of God, which passes all Phil.4.7
let the p. of Christ rule in your Col.3.15
Be at p. among yourselves 1 Th.5.13
Strive for p. with all men Heb.12.14
Now may the God of p. who brought Heb.13.20

PEACEABLE
those who are p. and faithful 2 Sam.20.19
we may lead a quiet and p. life 1 Tim.2.2
then p., gentle, open to reason Jas.3.17

PEACEFUL
will abide in a p. habitation Is.32.18
p. understanding shall be between Zech.6.13
the p. fruit of righteousness Heb.12.11

PEACEMAKERS
Blessed are the p. Mt.5.9

PEARL
the price of wisdom is above p. Job 28.18
do not throw your p. before swine Mt.7.6
finding one p. of great value Mt.13.46
or gold or p. or costly attire 1 Tim.2.9
the twelve gates were twelve p. Rev.21.21

PENALTY
man of great wrath will pay the p. Pr.19.19
You bear the p. of your lewdness Ezek.16.58
no reason for the death p. Acts 28.18
receiving . . . due p. for their error Rom.1.27

PENTECOST
When the day of P. had come Acts 2.1
if possible, on the day of P. Acts 20.16
I will stay in Ephesus until P. 1 Cor.16.8

PERCEIVE
see and see, but do not p. Is.6.9
they may indeed see but not p. Mk.4.12
lest they . . . p. with their heart Jn.12.40
Truly I p. that God shows no Acts 10.34
they should p. with their eyes Acts 28.27
been clearly p. in the things that Rom.1.20
they p. the grace that was given Gal.2.9

PERDITION
the torrents of p. assailed me Ps.18.4
none . . . is lost but the son of p. Jn.17.12
is revealed, the son of p. 2 Th.2.3
The beast . . . is to . . . go to p. Rev.17.8

PERFECT
This God—his way is p. 2 Sam.22.31
of him who is p. in knowledge Job 37.16
The law of the LORD is p., reviving Ps.19.7
Thou dost keep him in p. peace Is.26.3
be p., as your heavenly Father is p. Mt.5.48
what is good and acceptable and p. Rom.12.2
when the p. comes, the imperfect 1 Cor.13.10
my power is made p. in weakness 2 Cor.12.9
make . . . p. through suffering Heb.2.10
the spirits of just men made p. Heb.12.23
every p. gift is from above Jas.1.17
But he who looks into the p. law Jas.1.25
but p. love casts out fear 1 Jn.4.18
I have not found your works p. Rev.3.2

PERFECTION
the p. of beauty, God shines forth Ps.50.2
I have seen a limit to all p. Ps.119.96

which was called the p. of beauty Lam.2.15
Now if p. had been attainable Heb.7.11

PERFORM
to p. the words of the covenant 2 Chr.34.31
My vows to thee I must p., O God Ps.56.12
make vows to the LORD and p. them Is.19.21
am watching over my word to p. it Jer.1.12
that I may p. the oath which I Jer.11.5
turn to God and p. deeds worthy Acts 26.20

PERIL
our bread at the p. of our lives Lam.5.9
or nakedness, or p., or sword? Rom.8.35
Why am I in p. every hour? 1 Cor.15.30
delivered us from so deadly a p. 2 Cor.1.10

PERISH
Let the day p. wherein I was born Job 3.3
all flesh would p. together Job 34.15
but the way of the wicked will p. Ps.1.6
he is like the beasts that p. Ps.49.12
who are far from thee shall p. Ps.73.27
They will p., but thou dost endure Ps.102.26
A false witness will p. Pr.21.28
LORD our God has doomed us to p. Jer.8.14
all who take the sword will p. Mt.26.52
Teacher, do you not care if we p.? Mk.4.38
But not a hair of your head will p. Lk.21.18
should not p. but have eternal life Jn.3.16
Do not labor for the food which p. Jn.6.27
will also p. without the law Rom.2.12
is folly to those who are p. 1 Cor.1.18
not wishing that any should p. 2 Pet.3.9

PERISHABLE
They do it to receive a p. wreath 1 Cor.9.25
nor does the p. inherit the 1 Cor.15.50
not of p. seed but of imperishable 1 Pet.1.23

PERMIT
he will never p. the righteous to Ps.55.22
he would not p. the demons to speak Mk.1.34
time with you, if the Lord p. 1 Cor.16.7
I p. no woman to teach or to have 1 Tim.2.12
And this we will do if God p. Heb.6.3
its rider was p. to take peace from Rev.6.4

PERPETUAL
keep the sabbath . . . as a p. covenant Ex.31.16
shall be to you for a p. statute Num.10.8
the covenant of a p. priesthood Num.25.13
a p. barrier which it cannot pass Jer.5.22
everlasting reproach and p. shame Jer.23.40
shall sleep a p. sleep and not wake Jer.51.57
I will make you a p. desolation Ezek.35.9

PERPLEXED
When he heard him, he was much p. Mk.6.20
While they were p. about this Lk.24.4
all were amazed and p. Acts 2.12
for I am p. about you Gal.4.20

PERSECUTE
Princes p. me without cause Ps.119.161
Let those be put to shame who p. Jer.17.18
pray for those who p. you Mt.5.44
When they p. you in one town, flee Mt.10.23
If they p. me, they will p. you Jn.15.20
Saul, Saul, why do you p. me? Acts 9.4
Bless those who p. you; bless and Rom.12.14
when p., we endure 1 Cor.4.12
I p. the church of God violently Gal.1.13
live a godly life . . . will be p. 2 Tim.3.12

PERSECUTION
tribulation or *p.* arises on account	Mt.13.21
great *p.* arose against the church	Acts 8.1
or *p.*, or famine, or nakedness	Rom.8.35
in all your *p.* and in the afflictions	2 Th.1.4
my *p.*, my sufferings	2 Tim.3.11

PERSECUTOR
from the hand of my enemies and *p.*	Ps.31.15
Many are my *p.* and my adversaries	Ps.119.157
Deliver me from my *p.*	Ps.142.6
take vengeance for me on my *p.*	Jer.15.15
as to zeal a *p.* of the church	Phil.3.6

PERSIA
2 Chr.36.20; Ezra 1.1; Est.1.3; Ezek.27.10; Dan.8.20

PERSUADE
the elders *p.* the people to ask for	Mt.27.20
This man is *p.* men to worship God	Acts 18.13
for I am *p.* that none of these	Acts 26.26
I know and am *p.* in the Lord Jesus	Rom.14.14
the fear of the Lord, we *p.* men	2 Cor.5.11

PERVERSE
the *p.* tongue will be cut off	Pr.10.31
Men of *p.* mind are an abomination	Pr.11.20
A *p.* man spreads strife	Pr.16.28
and your mind utter *p.* things	Pr.23.33
O faithless and *p.* generation	Lk.9.41
will arise men speaking *p.* things	Acts 20.30
a crooked and *p.* generation	Phil.2.15

PERVERSENESS
P. of heart shall be far from me	Ps.101.4
delight in the *p.* of evil	Pr.2.14
and trust in oppression and *p.*	Is.30.12

PERVERT
You shall not *p.* the justice due	Ex.23.6
the Almighty will not *p.* justice	Job 34.12
We found this man *p.* our nation	Lk.23.2
and want to *p.* the gospel of Christ	Gal.1.7
such a person is *p.* and sinful	Tit.3.11
persons who *p.* the grace of our God	Jude 4

PESTILENCE
lest he fall upon us with *p.*	Ex.5.3
the Lord sent a *p.* upon Israel	1 Chr.21.14
he will deliver . . . from the deadly *p.*	Ps.91.3
nor the *p.* that stalks in darkness	Ps.91.6
by the sword, by famine, and by *p.*	Jer.14.12
I sent among you a *p.* after the	Am.4.10
in various places famines and *p.*	Lk.21.11
p. and mourning and famine	Rev.18.8

PETER
Apostle, called, Mt.4.18; Mk.1.16; Lk.5.1–11; Jn.1.35; sent forth, Mt.10.2–5; Mk.3.16; Lk. 6.14; tries to walk to Jesus on the sea, Mt.14.29; confesses Jesus to be the Christ, Mt.16.16; Mk.8.29; Lk.9.20; witnesses the transfiguration, Mt.17; Mk.9; Lk.9.28–36 (2 Pet.1.16–17); his self-confidence reproved, Lk.22.31; Jn.13.36; thrice denies Jesus, Mt.26.69–74; Mk.14.66–71; Lk.22.57–61; Jn.18.17; his repentance, Mt. 26.75; Mk.14.72; Lk.22.62; sermon at Pentecost, Acts 2.14–36; brought before the council, Acts 4; condemns Ananias and Sapphira, Acts 5; denounces Simon the magician, Acts 8.20–23; sent for by Cornelius, Acts 10; instructed in a vision not to despise the Gentiles, Acts 10.9–16; imprisoned, and liberated by an angel, Acts 12; his

decision about circumcision, Acts 15.7–11; rebuked by Paul, Gal.2.14

PHARAOH
when the princes of *P.* saw her	Gen.12.15
P. was angry with his two officers	Gen.40.2
P. dreamed that he was standing by	Gen.41.1
Then *P.* said to Joseph, "Behold	Gen.41.17
they built for *P.* store-cities	Ex.1.11
Then *P.* called Moses and Aaron	Ex.8.25
But *P.* hardened his heart this time	Ex.8.32
the Lord hardened the heart of *P.*	Ex.9.12
Then *P.* called Moses, and said, "Go	Ex.10.24
your God did to *P.* and to all Egypt	Dt.7.18
Joseph's family became known to *P.*	Acts 7.13
For the scripture says to *P.*	Rom.9.17

PHARISEES
notable Pharisees: Nicodemus, Jn.3.1; Simon, Lk.7.36–47; Gamaliel, Acts 5.34; Saul of Tarsus, Acts 23.6; 26.5; Phil.3.5; Jesus entertained by, Lk.7.36; 11.37; 14.1; Jesus utters woes against, Mt.23.13; Lk.11.42; Jesus questioned by, about: divorce, Mt.19.3; eating, Mt.9.11; 15.1; Mk.2.16; Lk.5.30; forgiveness of sin, Lk.5.21; sabbath, Mt.12.2,10; fasting, Mk.2.18; taxes, Mt.22.17; murmur against Jesus, Mt.9.34; Lk.15.2; denounced by Jesus, Mt.5.20; 16.6; 21.43; 23; Lk.11.39; people cautioned against, Mk.8.15; Lk.12.1; seek a sign from Jesus, Mt.12.38; 16.1; take counsel against Jesus, Mt.12.14; Mk.3.6; Nicodemus remonstrates with, Jn.7.51; cast out the man cured of blindness, Jn.9.34; dissensions among, Jn.9.16; send officers to arrest Jesus, Jn.7.32; contend about circumcision, Acts 15.5; their belief in the resurrection, Acts 23.8; and tax collector, Lk.18.10–14

PHILIP
(1) Apostle, called, Jn.1.43; sent forth, Mt.10.3; Mk.3.18; Lk.6.14; Jn.12.22; Acts 1.13; remonstrated with by Jesus, Jn.14.8; (2) the evangelist, Acts 6.5; preaches in Samaria, Acts 8.5; baptizes the Ethiopian, Acts 8.38; his four daughters prophesy, Acts 21.8–9; (3) Herod Philip, half-brother of Herod Antipas, and tetrarch of Trachonitis, Lk.3.1; (4) half-brother of (3) and of Herod Antipas, first husband of Herodias, and father of Salome, Mt.14.3; Mk.6.17; Lk.3.19

PHILIPPI
Mt.16.13; Acts 16.12; Phil.1.1; 1 Th.2.2

PHILISTIA
Ex.15.14; Ps.83.7, 108.9; Zech.9.6

PHILISTINES
Gen.10.14; Ex.13.17; Jos.13.2; 1 Sam.4.2; 18.27; 1 Chr.1.12; Zeph.2.5

PHILOSOPHERS
Epicurean and Stoic *p.* met him	Acts 17.18

PHILOSOPHY
makes a prey of you by *p.* and	Col.2.8

PHOENICIA
Ob.20; Acts 11.19; 15.3; 21.2

PHYSICIAN
who are well have no need of a *p.*	Mt.9.12
had suffered much under many *p.*	Mk.5.26
this proverb, '*P.*, heal yourself	Lk.4.23

who are well have no need of a *p*.	Lk.5.31
Luke the beloved *p*. and Demas greet	Col.4.14

PIECES

dash them in *p*. like a potter's vessel	Ps.2.9
thou that didst cut Rahab in *p*.	Is.51.9
little ones shall be dashed in *p*.	Hos.13.16
they paid him thirty *p*. of silver	Mt.26.15
twelve baskets of broken *p*.	Lk.9.17
on planks or on *p*. of the ship	Acts 27.44

PIERCE

they have *p*. my hands and feet	Ps.22.16
look on him whom they have *p*.	Zech.12.10
a sword will *p*. through your own soul	Lk.2.35
soldiers *p*. his side with a spear	Jn.19.34
will see him, every one who *p*. him	Rev.1.7

PIGEON

a turtledove, and a young *p*.	Gen.15.9
or young *p*. such as he can afford	Lev.14.30
and the seats of those who sold *p*.	Mt.21.12
he told those who sold the *p*.	Jn.2.16

PILATE

Pontius, governor of Judea during Jesus' ministry, sufferings, and death, Lk.3.1; admonished by his wife, examines Jesus, washes his hands, but delivers him to be crucified, Mt.27; Mk.15; Lk.23; Jn.18–19; grants request of Joseph of Arimathea, Mt.27.57–60; Mk.15.42–46; Lk. 23.50–53; Jn.19.38; *see* Acts 3.13; 4.27; 13.28; 1 Tim.6.13

PILLAR

Lot's wife . . . became a *p*. of salt	Gen.19.26
p. of cloud by day . . . *p*. of fire	Ex.13.22
erect no graven image or *p*.	Lev.26.1
And you shall not set up a *p*.	Dt.16.22
He spoke to them in the *p*. of cloud	Ps.99.7
who were reputed to be *p*.	Gal.2.9
the *p*. and bulwark of the truth	1 Tim.3.15
I will make him a *p*. in the temple	Rev.3.12

PISGAH

Num.21.20; Dt.3.17; Jos.12.3; 13.20

PIT

The *p*. was empty, there was no	Gen.37.24
His soul draws near the *P*.	Job 33.22
like those who go down to the *P*.	Ps.28.1
He drew me up from the desolate *p*.	Ps.40.2
who redeems your life from the *P*.	Ps.103.4
He who digs a *p*. will fall into it	Pr.26.27
falls into a *p*. on the sabbath	Mt.12.11
Will they not both fall into a *p*.?	Lk.6.39
the shaft of the bottomless *p*.	Rev.9.1

PITY (noun)

I looked for *p*., but there was none	Ps.69.20
He has *p*. on the weak and the needy	Ps.72.13
wilt arise and have *p*. on Zion	Ps.102.13
in his *p*. he redeemed them	Is.63.9
And Jesus in *p*. touched their eyes	Mt.20.34
Moved with *p*., he stretched out his	Mk.1.41

PITY (verb)

so the LORD *p*. those who fear him	Ps.103.13
said to him, "Call her name Not *p*.	Hos.1.6
And should not I *p*. Nineveh	Jon.4.11
we are of all men most to be *p*.	1 Cor.15.19

PLACE (noun)

for the *p*. on which you are standing	Ex.3.5
And who shall stand in his holy *p*.?	Ps.24.3
the *p*. where thy glory dwells	Ps.26.8

How lovely is thy dwelling *p*.	Ps.84.1
our dwelling *p*. in all generations	Ps.90.1
The eyes of the LORD are in every *p*.	Pr.15.3
I dwell in the high and holy *p*.	Is.57.15
and said, "This is a lonely *p*.	Mt.14.15
(which means the *p*. of a skull)	Mt.27.33
Come, see the *p*. where he lay	Mt.28.6
Jerusalem is the *p*. where men ought	Jn.4.20
that I go to prepare a *p*. for you?	Jn.14.2
they were all together in one *p*.	Acts 2.1
who in every *p*. call on the name	1 Cor.1.2
his right hand in the heavenly *p*.	Eph.1.20
a dwelling *p*. of God in the Spirit	Eph.2.22
enters the Holy *P*. yearly with	Heb.9.25

PLAGUE (noun)

the LORD sent a *p*. upon the people	Ex.32.35
companions stand aloof from my *p*.	Ps.38.11
diseases and *p*. and evil spirits	Lk.7.21
the seven angels with the seven *p*.	Rev.15.6
add to him the *p*. described in	Rev.22.18

PLAIN (adjective)

make it *p*. upon tablets, so he may	Hab.2.2
what can be known about God is *p*.	Rom.1.19
we have made this *p*. to you	2 Cor.11.6
Now the works of the flesh are *p*.	Gal.5.19
for their folly will be *p*. to all	2 Tim.3.9
that it might be *p*. that they all	1 Jn.2.19

PLAN (noun)

understands every *p*. and thought	1 Chr.28.9
that God had frustrated their *p*.	Neh.4.15
the definite *p*. and foreknowledge	Acts 2.23
whatever . . . thy *p*. had predestined	Acts 4.28
as a *p*. for the fulness of time	Eph.1.10
see what is the *p*. of the mystery	Eph.3.9

PLANT (noun)

have given every green *p*. for food	Gen.1.30
p. for man to cultivate, that he	Ps.104.14
grew up before him like a young *p*.	Is.53.2
Every *p*. which my heavenly Father	Mt.15.13

PLANT (verb)

the LORD God *p*. a garden in Eden	Gen.2.8
He is like a tree *p*. by streams of	Ps.1.3
but them thou didst *p*.	Ps.44.2
a time to *p*., and a time to pluck	Ec.3.2
I will *p*. you, and not pluck you up	Jer.42.10
I will *p*. them upon their land	Am.9.15
Father has not *p*. will be rooted up	Mt.15.13
A man *p*. a vineyard, and set a hedge	Mk.12.1
I *p*., Apollos watered, but God gave	1 Cor.3.6

PLATTER

the head of John . . . here on a *p*.	Mt.14.8

PLAYING

while David was *p*. the lyre	1 Sam.18.10
will make you stop *p*. the harlot	Ezek.16.41
boys and girls *p*. in its streets	Zech.8.5
sound of harpers *p*. on their harps	Rev.14.2

PLEAD

Arise, O God, *p*. thy cause	Ps.74.22
P. my cause and redeem me	Ps.119.154
for the LORD will *p*. their cause	Pr.22.23
p. for the widow	Is.1.17
how he *p*. with God against Israel?	Rom.11.2

PLEASANT

every tree that is *p*. to the sight	Gen.2.9
have fallen for me in *p*. places	Ps.16.6
how good and *p*. it is when brothers	Ps.133.1

bread eaten in secret is *p.*	Pr.9.17
P. words are like a honeycomb	Pr.16.24
you have planted *p.* vineyards	Am.5.11
the *p.* land was made desolate	Zech.7.14
seems painful rather than *p.*	Heb.12.11

PLEASE

Be *p.*, O God, to deliver me	Ps.70.1
When a man's ways *p.* the LORD	Pr.16.7
my . . . Son, with whom I am well *p.*	Mt.3.17
For Christ did not *p.* himself	Rom.15.3
I try to *p.* all men in everything	1 Cor.10.33
the fulness of God was *p.* to dwell	Col.1.19
without faith . . . impossible to *p.* him	Heb.11.6
such sacrifices are *p.* to God	Heb.13.16

PLEASURE

thy right hand are *p.* for evermore	Ps.16.11
Do good to Zion in thy good *p.*	Ps.51.18
I kept my heart from no *p.*	Ec.2.10
you will say, "I have no *p.* in them"	Ec.12.1
from doing your *p.* on my holy day	Is.58.13
For I have no *p.* in the death of	Ezek.18.32
Father's good *p.* to give you the	Lk.12.32
lovers of *p.* rather than lovers of	2 Tim.3.4
than to enjoy the fleeting *p.* of sin	Heb.11.25

PLEDGE (noun)

take your neighbor's garment in *p.*	Ex.22.26
an oath to bind himself by a *p.*	Num.30.2
they take the widow's ox for a *p.*	Job 24.3
A man without sense gives a *p.*	Pr.17.18
exacts no *p.*, commits no robbery	Ezek.18.16
having violated their first *p.*	1 Tim.5.12

PLEIADES

the *P.* and the chambers of the south	Job 9.9
Can you bind the chains of the *P.*	Job 38.31
He who made the *P.* and Orion	Am.5.8

PLENTEOUS

during the seven *p.* years	Gen.41.34
with him is *p.* redemption	Ps.130.7
the ground . . . will be rich and *p.*	Is.30.23

PLENTY

seven years of *p.* that prevailed	Gen.41.53
your barns will be filled with *p.*	Pr.3.10
You shall eat in *p.* and be satisfied	Jl.2.26
the secret of facing *p.* and hunger	Phil.4.12

PLOT (verb)

why do . . . the peoples *p.* in vain?	Ps.2.1
The wicked *p.* against the righteous	Ps.37.12
What do you *p.* against the LORD?	Nah.1.9
the Jews *p.* to kill him	Acts 9.23

PLOW

shall not *p.* with an ox and an ass	Dt.22.10
If you had not *p.* with my heifer	Jg.14.18
sluggard does not *p.* in the autumn	Pr.20.4
Does one *p.* the sea with oxen?	Am.6.12
his hand to the *p.* and looks back	Lk.9.62

PLOWMAN

the *p.* shall overtake the reaper	Am.9.13
the *p.* should plow in hope	1 Cor.9.10

PLOWSHARES

shall beat their swords into *p.*	Is.2.4
Beat your *p.* into swords, and your	Jl.3.10
shall beat their swords into *p.*	Mic.4.3

PLUCK

he will *p.* my feet out of the net	Ps.25.15
and a time to *p.* up what is planted	Ec.3.2
I will *p.* up the house of Judah	Jer.12.14

I will plant you, and not *p.* you up	Jer.42.10
a brand *p.* from the fire?	Zech.3.2
p. it out and throw it away	Mt.5.29
disciples began to *p.* ears of grain	Mk.2.23
eye causes you to sin, *p.* it out	Mk.9.47

PLUNDER (verb)

may strangers *p.* the fruits of his	Ps.109.11
shall *p.* the people of the east	Is.11.14
all who *p.* her shall be sated	Jer.50.10
your strongholds shall be *p.*	Am.3.11
Because you have *p.* many nations	Hab.2.8
Then indeed he may *p.* his house	Mt.12.29

POINT (noun)

Hezekiah . . . was at the *p.* of death	Is.38.1
my . . . daughter is at the *p.* of death	Mk.5.23
son, for he was at the *p.* of death	Jn.4.47
Christ from a human *p.* of view	2 Cor.5.16
The *p.* is this: he who sows	2 Cor.9.6
Now the *p.* in what we are saying is	Heb.8.1
to the *p.* of shedding your blood	Heb.12.4
fails in one *p.* has become guilty	Jas.2.10
remains and is on the *p.* of death	Rev.3.2

POISON (noun)

They gave me *p.* for food	Ps.69.21
under their lips is the *p.* of vipers	Ps.140.3
you have turned justice into *p.*	Am.6.12
a restless evil, full of deadly *p.*	Jas.3.8

POLLUTE

You shall not thus *p.* the land	Num.35.33
the land was *p.* with blood	Ps.106.38
You have *p.* the land with your vile	Jer.3.2
and *p.* yourself with their idols	Ezek.23.30
And you say, 'How have we *p.* it?'	Mal.1.7

POMP

splendor and *p.* of his majesty	Est.1.4
Man cannot abide in his *p.*	Ps.49.12
Your *p.* is brought down to Sheol	Is.14.11
Bernice came with great *p.*	Acts 25.23

POOR

be partial to a *p.* man in his suit	Ex.23.3
But if he is *p.* and cannot afford	Lev.14.21
For the *p.* will never cease out of	Dt.15.11
The LORD makes *p.* and makes rich	1 Sam.2.7
but he took the *p.* man's lamb	2 Sam.12.4
Was not my soul grieved for the *p.*	Job 30.25
This *p.* man cried, and the LORD heard	Ps.34.6
As for me, I am *p.* and needy	Ps.40.17
Blessed is he who considers the *p.*	Ps.41.1
He raises the *p.* from the dust	Ps.113.7
He who mocks the *p.* insults his	Pr.17.5
The rich and the *p.* meet together	Pr.22.2
Better is a *p.* man who walks in his	Pr.28.6
He who gives to the *p.* will not	Pr.28.27
or lest I be *p.*, and steal, and	Pr.30.9
Yet no one remembered that *p.* man	Ec.9.15
by grinding the face of the *p.*?	Is.3.15
hast been a stronghold to the *p.*	Is.25.4
Blessed are the *p.* in spirit	Mt.5.3
and the *p.* have good news preached	Mt.11.5
you always have the *p.* with you	Mt.26.11
a *p.* widow came, and put in two	Mk.12.42
at his gate lay a *p.* man . . . Lazarus	Lk.16.20
as *p.*, yet making many rich	2 Cor.6.10
yet for your sake he became *p.*	2 Cor.8.9
and a *p.* man in shabby clothing	Jas.2.2
pitiable, *p.*, blind, and naked	Rev.3.17

PORTION

I am your *p*. and your inheritance	Num.18.20
For the LORD'S *p*. is his people	Dt.32.9
This is the *p*. of a wicked man	Job 27.13
The LORD is my chosen *p*. and my cup	Ps.16.5
my *p*. in the land of the living	Ps.142.5
divide him a *p*. with the great	Is.53.12
Mary has chosen the good *p*.	Lk.10.42

POSITION

you do not regard the *p*. of men	Mt.22.16
one in the *p*. of an outsider	1 Cor.14.16
pride themselves on a man's *p*.	2 Cor.5.12
kings and all who are in high *p*.	1 Tim.2.2

POSSESS

to give you this land to *p*.	Gen.15.7
God has given you this land to *p*.	Dt.3.18
and his children shall *p*. the land	Ps.25.13
The righteous shall *p*. the land	Ps.37.29
your descendants will *p*. the nations	Is.54.3
many who were *p*. with demons	Mt.8.16
sell what you *p*. and give to the	Mt.19.21
any of the things which he *p*. was	Acts 4.32
truths to those who *p*. the Spirit	1 Cor.2.13
However, not all *p*. this knowledge	1 Cor.8.7
having nothing, and yet *p*.	2 Cor.6.10

POSSESSION

of Canaan, for an everlasting *p*.	Gen.17.8
the ends of the earth your *p*.	Ps.2.8
for himself, Israel as his own *p*.	Ps.135.4
no *p*. in Israel; I am their *p*.	Ezek.44.28
my special *p*. on the day when I act	Mal.3.17
sorrowful; for he had great *p*.	Mt.19.22
they sold their *p*. and goods	Acts 2.45
inheritance until we acquire *p*. of	Eph.1.14
had a better *p*. and an abiding one	Heb.10.34

POSSIBLE

but with God all things are *p*.	Mt.19.26
if it be *p*., let this cup pass from me	Mt.26.39
it was not *p*. for him to be held	Acts 2.24
If *p*., so far as it depends upon	Rom.12.18
if *p*., you would have plucked out	Gal.4.15
that if *p*. I may attain the	Phil.3.11

POSTERITY

the *p*. of the wicked shall be cut off	Ps.37.38
May his *p*. be cut off	Ps.109.13
to Abraham and to his *p*. for ever	Lk.1.55
in your *p*. shall all . . . be blessed	Acts 3.25
Of this man's *p*. God has brought	Acts 13.23

POTIPHAR

Gen.37.36; 39.1

POTTER

we are the clay, and thou art our *p*.	Is.64.8
as it seemed good to the *p*. to do	Jer.18.4
bought with them the *p*. field	Mt.27.7
Has the *p*. no right over the clay	Rom.9.21

POUND

your *p*. has made ten *p*. more	Lk.19.16
here is your *p*., which I kept	Lk.19.20
Mary took a *p*. of costly ointment	Jn.12.3
aloes, about a hundred *p*. weight	Jn.19.39

POUR

I am *p*. out like water, and all my	Ps.22.14
as I *p*. out my soul	Ps.42.4
P. out thy indignation upon them	Ps.69.24
My lips will *p*. forth praise	Ps.119.171
The mouths of fools *p*. out folly	Pr.15.2

because he *p*. out his soul to death	Is.53.12
P. out your heart like water before	Lam.2.19
I *p*. out my Spirit upon . . . Israel	Ezek.39.29
p. down for you an overflowing	Mal.3.10
I will *p*. out my Spirit upon all	Acts 2.17
love has been *p*. into our hearts	Rom.5.5
if I am to be *p*. as a libation	Phil.2.17
which he *p*. out upon us richly	Tit.3.6
Does a spring *p*. forth from the	Jas.3.11
p. out on the earth the seven bowls	Rev.16.1

POVERTY

A slack hand causes *p*.	Pr.10.4
Love not sleep, lest you come to *p*.	Pr.20.13
give me neither *p*. nor riches	Pr.30.8
she out of her *p*. put in all . . . she had	Lk.21.4
so that by his *p*. you might become	2 Cor.8.9
I know . . . your *p*. (but you are rich)	Rev.2.9

POWER

Thy right hand . . . glorious in *p*.	Ex.15.6
let the *p*. of the LORD be great as	Num.14.17
he who gives you *p*. to get wealth	Dt.8.18
save us from the *p*. of our enemies	1 Sam.4.3
God has *p*. to help or to cast down	2 Chr.25.8
you have helped him who has no *p*.	Job 26.2
Behold, God is exalted in his *p*.	Job 36.22
ransom my soul from the *p*. of Sheol	Ps.49.15
thy saving *p*. among all nations	Ps.67.2
he might make known his mighty *p*.	Ps.106.8
Great is our LORD . . . abundant in *p*.	Ps.147.5
No man has *p*. to retain the spirit	Ec.8.8
He gives *p*. to the faint	Is.40.29
he who made the earth by his *p*.	Jer.51.15
Daniel from the *p*. of the lions	Dan.6.27
nor by *p*., but by my Spirit	Zech.4.6
seated at the right hand of *P*.	Mt.26.64
p. of the Most High will overshadow	Lk.1.35
the *p*. of the Lord was with him	Lk.5.17
in a cloud with *p*. and great glory	Lk.21.27
he gave *p*. to become children of God	Jn.1.12
hast given him *p*. over all flesh	Jn.17.2
By what *p*. or by what name did you	Acts 4.7
And Stephen, full of grace and *p*.	Acts 6.8
p. of signs and wonders, by the *p*.	Rom.15.19
will also raise us up by his *p*.	1 Cor.6.14
my *p*. is made perfect in weakness	2 Cor.12.9
May you be strengthened with all *p*.	Col.1.11
upholding the universe by his . . . *p*.	Heb.1.3
with angels . . . and *p*. subject to him	1 Pet.3.22
honor and *p*. and might be to	Rev.7.12
glory and *p*. belong to our God	Rev.19.1

POWERFUL

The voice of the LORD is *p*.	Ps.29.4
like a *p*. army drawn up for battle	Jl.2.5
not many were *p*., not many were	1 Cor.1.26
He is not weak . . . but is *p*. in you	2 Cor.13.3

PRACTICE (verb)

You shall not *p*. augury or	Lev.19.26
I am the LORD who *p*. steadfast love	Jer.9.24
those who *p*. magic arts brought	Acts 19.19
refuse to *p*. cunning or to tamper	2 Cor.4.2
to *p*. every kind of uncleanness	Eph.4.19
P. these duties, devote yourself	1 Tim.4.15
P. hospitality ungrudgingly	1 Pet.4.9

PRACTICES (noun)

people still followed corrupt *p*.	2 Chr.27.2
Esther fixed these *p*. of Purim	Est.9.32

confessing and divulging their *p.*	Acts 19.18	**PRAYING**	
put off the old nature with its *p.*	Col.3.9	she continued *p.* before the LORD	1 Sam.1.12
PRAETORIUM		And whenever you stand *p.*, forgive	Mk.11.25
inside the palace (that is, the *p.*)	Mk.15.16	as he was *p.*, the appearance of	Lk.9.29
Pilate entered the *p.* again	Jn.18.33	where many . . . were *p.*	Acts 12.12
to be guarded in Herod's *p.*	Acts 23.35	*p.* earnestly night and day	1 Th.3.10
PRAISE (noun)		**PREACH**	
He is your *p.*; he is your God	Dt.10.21	From that time Jesus began to *p.*	Mt.4.17
in Sheol who can give thee *p.?*	Ps.6.5	the poor have good news *p.* to them	Mt.11.5
his *p.* shall continually be in my	Ps.34.1	they *p.*, but do not practice	Mt.23.3
P. is due to thee, O God, in Zion	Ps.65.1	anointed me to *p.* good news	Lk.4.18
My mouth is filled with thy *p.*	Ps.71.8	so I am eager to *p.* the gospel to	Rom.1.15
you shall call . . . your gates *P.*	Is.60.18	how can men *p.* unless they are	Rom.10.15
the mantle of *p.* instead of a faint	Is.61.3	but we *p.* Christ crucified	1 Cor.1.23
and the earth was full of his *p.*	Hab.3.3	what we *p.* is not ourselves, but	2 Cor.4.5
His *p.* is not from men but from God	Rom.2.29	*p.* to the Gentiles the unsearchable	Eph.3.8
to live for the *p.* of his glory	Eph.1.12	Some indeed *p.* Christ from envy	Phil.1.15
PRAISE (verb)		*p.* the word, be urgent in season	2 Tim.4.2
P. his people, O you nations	Dt.32.43	he . . . *p.* to the spirits in prison	1 Pet.3.19
You who fear the LORD, *p.* him	Ps.22.23	**PREACHER**	
for I shall again *p.* him, my help	Ps.42.5	The words of the *P.*, the son of David	Ec.1.1
Let the peoples *p.* thee, O God	Ps.67.3	he would be the *p.* for this people	Mic.2.11
the wrath of men shall *p.* thee	Ps.76.10	how are they to hear without a *p.?*	Rom.10.14
Seven times a day I *p.* thee	Ps.119.164	I was appointed a *p.* and apostle	1 Tim.2.7
the LORD, and greatly to be *p.*	Ps.145.3	I was appointed a *p.* and apostle	2 Tim.1.11
P. our God, all you his servants	Rev.19.5	**PREACHING** (noun)	
PRAY		they repented at the *p.* of Jonah	Mt.12.41
will *p.* for you, and you shall live	Gen.20.7	Paul was occupied with *p.*	Acts 18.5
So Moses *p.* for the people	Num.21.7	then our *p.* is in vain and your	1 Cor.15.14
I will *p.* to the LORD for you	1 Sam.7.5	famous . . . for his *p.* of the gospel	2 Cor.8.18
by ceasing to *p.* for you	1 Sam.12.23	who labor in *p.* and teaching	1 Tim.5.17
p. and seek my face, and turn	2 Chr.7.14	through the *p.* with which I have	Tit.1.3
what profit do we get if we *p.*	Job 21.15	**PRECEPT**	
P. for the peace of Jerusalem	Ps.122.6	the *p.* of the LORD are right	Ps.19.8
Then Jonah *p.* to the LORD his God	Jon.2.1	Make me understand . . . thy *p.*	Ps.119.27
And when you *p.*, you must not be like	Mt.6.5	Through . . . *p.* I get understanding	Ps.119.104
P. then like this: Our Father who art	Mt.6.9	For it is *p.* upon *p.*, *p.* upon *p.*	Is.28.10
Watch and *p.* that you may not enter	Mt.26.41	Not all men can receive this *p.*	Mt.19.11
teach us to *p.*, as John taught his	Lk.11.1	teaching as doctrines the *p.* of men	Mk.7.7
Two men went up into the temple to *p.*	Lk.18.10	uncircumcised keeps . . . *p.* of the law	Rom.2.26
I will *p.* with the mind also	1 Cor.14.15	according to human *p.* and doctrines	Col.2.22
P. at all times in the Spirit	Eph.6.18	**PRECIOUS**	
p. constantly	1 Th.5.17	How *p.* is thy steadfast love, O God	Ps.36.7
P. for us, for we are sure that	Heb.13.18	*P.* in the sight of the LORD is the	Ps.116.15
p. for one another, that you may	Jas.5.16	How *p.* to me are thy thoughts	Ps.139.17
PRAYER		She is more *p.* than jewels	Pr.3.15
my ears attentive to the *p.*	2 Chr.7.15	She is far more *p.* than jewels	Pr.31.10
and the LORD accepted Job's *p.*	Job 42.9	good name is better than *p.* ointment	Ec.7.1
Hear my *p.*, O LORD, and give ear to	Ps.39.12	*p.* cornerstone, of a sure foundation	Is.28.16
O thou who hearest *p.*! To thee shall	Ps.65.2	Because you are *p.* in my eyes	Is.43.4
May *p.* be made for him continually	Ps.72.15	*p.* stones, wood, hay, stubble	1 Cor.3.12
Let my *p.* come before thee	Ps.88.2	but with the *p.* blood of Christ	1 Pet.1.19
Let my *p.* be counted as incense	Ps.141.2	To you . . . who believe, he is *p.*	1 Pet.2.7
he hears the *p.* of the righteous	Pr.15.29	his *p.* and very great promises	2 Pet.1.4
whatever you ask in *p.*, you will	Mt.21.22	**PREDESTINED**	
with fasting and *p.* night and day	Lk.2.37	thy plan had *p.* to take place	Acts 4.28
My house shall be a house of *p.*	Lk.19.46	those whom he foreknew he also *p.*	Rom.8.29
devoted themselves to *p.*	Acts 1.14	And those whom he *p.* he also called	Rom.8.30
every church, with *p.* and fasting	Acts 14.23	**PREPARE**	
in tribulation, be constant in *p.*	Rom.12.12	Thou *p.* a table before me in the	Ps.23.5
You also must help us by *p.*	2 Cor.1.11	he *p.* rain for the earth	Ps.147.8
everything by *p.* and supplication	Phil.4.6	*p.* to meet your God, O Israel	Am.4.12
Continue steadfastly in *p.*	Col.4.2	*P.* the way of the Lord, make his	Mt.3.3
The *p.* of a righteous man has great	Jas.5.16	eternal fire *p.* for the devil and	Mt.25.41
his ears are open to their *p.*	1 Pet.3.12	has done it to *p.* me for burial	Mt.26.12
which are the *p.* of the saints	Rev.5.8	go before the Lord to *p.* his ways	Lk.1.76

Go and *p*. the passover for us	Lk.22.8	PREY (noun)	
when I go and *p*. a place for you	Jn.14.3	Who provides for the raven its *p*.	Job 38.41
affliction is *p*. for us an eternal	2 Cor.4.17	The young lions roar for their *p*.	Ps.104.21
Always be *p*. to make a defense to	1 Pet.3.15	not given us as *p*. to their teeth	Ps.124.6
p. as a bride adorned for her	Rev.21.2	slothful man will not catch his *p*.	Pr.12.27
PRESENCE		makes a *p*. of you by philosophy	Col.2.8
went away from the *p*. of the LORD	Gen.4.16	PRICE	
My *p*. will go with you, and I will	Ex.33.14	the *p*. of wisdom is above pearls	Job 28.18
went forth from the *p*. of the LORD	Job 1.12	give to God the *p*. of his life	Ps.49.7
in thy *p*. there is fulness of joy	Ps.16.11	milk without money and without *p*.	Is.55.1
Cast me not away from thy *p*.	Ps.51.11	*p*. of him on whom a *p*. had been set	Mt.27.9
Come into his *p*. with singing	Ps.100.2	You were bought with a *p*.	1 Cor.7.23
whither shall I flee from thy *p*.?	Ps.139.7	take the water of life without *p*.	Rev.22.17
mountains might quake at thy *p*.	Is.64.1	PRIDE	
Gabriel, who stand in the *p*. of God	Lk.1.19	let them be trapped in their *p*.	Ps.59.12
say, 'We ate and drank in your *p*.	Lk.13.26	*P*. goes before destruction	Pr.16.18
bring us with you into his *p*.	2 Cor.4.14	A man's *p*. will bring him low	Pr.29.23
In the *p*. of God and of Christ	1 Tim.5.21	the *p*. of men shall be humbled	Is.2.11
the table and the bread of the *P*.	Heb.9.2	We have heard of the *p*. of Moab	Is.16.6
will shelter them with his *p*.	Rev.7.15	I spoil the *p*. of Judah	Jer.13.9
from his *p*. earth and sky fled	Rev.20.11	bring to nought the *p*. of Egypt	Ezek.32.12
PRESENT (adjective)		I abhor the *p*. of Jacob, and hate	Am.6.8
God is . . . a very *p*. help in trouble	Ps.46.1	The *p*. of your heart has deceived	Ob.3
nor things *p*., nor things to come	Rom.8.38	*p*. of Assyria shall be laid low	Zech.10.11
absent in body I am *p*. in spirit	1 Cor.5.3	who *p*. themselves on a man's	2 Cor.5.12
to deliver us from the *p*. evil age	Gal.1.4	I have great *p*. in you	2 Cor.7.4
corresponds to the *p*. Jerusalem	Gal.4.25	our confidence and *p*. in our hope	Heb.3.6
world rulers of this *p*. darkness	Eph.6.12	lust of the eyes and the *p*. of life	I Jn.2.16
PRESENT (verb)		PRIEST	
Seven days you shall *p*. offerings	Lev.23.36	he was *p*. of God Most High	Gen.14.18
they *p*. themselves before God	Jos.24.1	You are a *p*. ever after the order	Ps.110.4
To them he *p*. himself alive after	Acts 1.3	as with the people, so with the *p*.	Is.24.2
to *p*. your bodies as a living	Rom.12.1	Both prophet and *p*. are ungodly	Jer.23.11
to *p*. you as a pure bride	2 Cor.11.2	No *p*. shall drink wine	Ezek.44.21
he might *p*. the church to himself	Eph.5.27	struck the slave of the high *p*.	Mt.26.51
to *p*. you holy and blameless	Col.1.22	but go, show yourself to the *p*.	Mk.1.44
Do your best to *p*. yourself to God	2 Tim.2.15	there was a *p*. named Zechariah	Lk.1.5
PRESERVE		Now by chance a *p*. was going down	Lk.10.31
God sent me before you to *p*. life	Gen.45.5	Would you revile God's high *p*.?	Acts 23.4
that he might *p*. us alive	Dt.6.24	high *p*. of our confession	Heb.3.1
P. me, O God, for in thee I take	Ps.16.1	have not a high *p*. who is unable	Heb.4.15
p. my life from dread of the enemy	Ps.64.1	that we should have such a high *p*.	Heb.7.26
P. my life according to thy	Ps.119.159	we have a great *p*. over the house	Heb.10.21
he who guards his way *p*. his life	Pr.16.17	a kingdom and *p*. to our God	Rev.5.10
whoever loses his life will *p*. it	Lk.17.33	PRIESTHOOD	
he . . . *p*. Noah, a herald of	2 Pet.2.5	I give your *p*. as a gift	Num.18.7
PRESS (verb)		but he holds his *p*. permanently	Heb.7.24
let us *p*. on to know the LORD	Hos.6.3	be a holy *p*., to offer spiritual	1 Pet.2.5
I will *p*. you down in your place	Am.2.13	a royal *p*., a holy nation	1 Pet.2.9
good measure, *p*. down	Lk.6.38	PRINCE	
the Pharisees began to *p*. him hard	Lk.11.53	Who made you a *p*. and a judge over	Ex.2.14
but I *p*. on to make it my own	Phil.3.12	a *p*. and a great man has fallen	2 Sam.3.38
I *p*. on toward the goal for the	Phil.3.14	die like men, and fall like any *p*.	Ps.82.7
PRETEND		*P*. persecute me without cause	Ps.119.161
why do you *p*. to be another?	1 Kg.14.6	Put not your trust in *p*.	Ps.146.3
There are friends who *p*. to be	Pr.18.24	*p*. and all rulers of the earth	Ps.148.11
sent spies, who *p*. to be sincere	Lk.20.20	by me *p*. rule, and nobles govern	Pr.8.16
with *p*. signs and wonders	2 Th.2.9	Everlasting Father, *P*. of Peace	Is.9.6
PREVAIL		shall even rise up against the *P*. of	Dan.8.25
When our transgressions *p*. over us	Ps.65.3	The *p*. of the kingdom of Persia	Dan.10.13
they shall not *p*. against you	Jer.1.19	the *p*. of Greece will come	Dan.10.20
He strove with the angel and *p*.	Hos.12.4	Your *p*. are like grasshoppers	Nah.3.17
death shall not *p*. against it	Mt.16.18	by the *p*. of demons he casts out	Mk.3.22
the word of the Lord grew and *p*.	Acts 19.20	the *p*. of the power of the air	Eph.2.2
and *p*. when thou art judged	Rom.3.4	PRINCIPALITIES	
		nor *p*., nor things present, nor	Rom.8.38

the *p*. and powers in the heavenly	Eph.3.10	*p*. to you the eternal life	1 Jn.1.2
we are . . . contending . . . against the *p*.	Eph.6.12	to *p*. to those who dwell on earth	Rev.14.6
dominions or *p*. or authorities	Col.1.16	PRODUCE (verb)	
He disarmed the *p*. and powers	Col.2.15	pressing anger *p*. strife	Pr.30.33
PRISCA (PRISCILLA)		The earth *p*. of itself, first the	Mk.4.28
Acts 18.2; Rom.16.3; 1 Cor.16.19; 2 Tim.4.19		suffering *p*. endurance	Rom.5.3
PRISON		godly grief *p*. a repentance	2 Cor.7.10
the *p*. where Joseph was confined	Gen.40.3	*p*. envy, dissension, slander	1 Tim.6.4
he ground at the mill in the *p*.	Jg.16.21	your faith *p*. steadfastness	Jas.1.3
Bring me out of *p*., that I may	Ps.142.7	PROFANE (verb)	
from the *p*. those . . . in darkness	Is.42.7	you shall not *p*. my holy name	Lev.22.32
opening of the *p*. to those . . . bound	Is.61.1	steal, and *p*. the name of my God	Pr.30.9
for he had not yet been put in *p*.	Jer.37.4	shall no more *p*. with your gifts	Ezek.20.39
John heard in *p*. about the deeds	Mt.11.2	Forces . . . appear and *p*. the temple	Dan.11.31
I was in *p*. and you came to me	Mt.25.36	you *p*. it when you say that the	Mal.1.12
went and beheaded him in the *p*.	Mk.6.27	how . . . the priests . . . *p*. the sabbath	Mt.12.5
delivering you up to the . . . *p*.	Lk.21.12	He even tried to *p*. the temple	Acts 24.6
to go with you to *p*. and to death	Lk.22.33	guilty of *p*. the body and blood	1 Cor.11.27
an angel . . . opened the *p*. doors	Acts 5.19	*p*. the blood of the covenant by	Heb.10.29
So Peter was kept in *p*.	Acts 12.5	PROFIT (verb)	
foundations of the *p*. were shaken	Acts 16.26	things which cannot *p*. or save	1 Sam.12.21
a favor, Felix left Paul in *p*.	Acts 24.27	Riches do not *p*. in the day of wrath	Pr.11.4
on account of which I am in *p*.	Col.4.3	that which does not *p*.	Jer.2.11
Remember those who are in *p*.	Heb.13.3	what does it *p*. a man if he gains	Lk.9.25
preached to the spirits in *p*.	1 Pet.3.19	What does it *p*., my brethren, if a	Jas.2.14
Satan will be loosed from his *p*.	Rev.20.7	PROFITABLE	
PRISONER		Can a man be *p*. to God?	Job 22.2
groans of the *p*. come before thee	Ps.79.11	an image, that is *p*. for nothing	Is.44.10
p. in affliction and in irons	Ps.107.10	All scripture is . . . *p*. for teaching	2 Tim.3.16
The LORD sets the *p*. free	Ps.146.7	these are excellent and *p*. to men	Tit.3.8
they had then a notorious *p*.	Mt.27.16	PROLONG	
a *p*. for Christ Jesus on behalf of	Eph.3.1	that you may *p*. your days in the land	Dt.4.40
Aristarchus my fellow *p*. greets you	Col.4.10	*P*. the life of the king	Ps.61.6
Paul, a *p*. for Christ Jesus	Philem.1	The fear of the LORD *p*. life	Pr.10.27
you had compassion on the *p*.	Heb.10.34	neither will he *p*. his days like a	Ec.8.13
PRIZE		he shall *p*. his days	Is.53.10
shall have his life as a *p*. of war	Jer.21.9	their lives were *p*. for a season	Dan.7.12
but only one receives the *p*.?	1 Cor.9.24	he *p*. his speech until midnight	Acts 20.7
for the *p*. of the upward call	Phil.3.14	PROMISE (noun)	
PROCEED		the *p*. of the LORD proves true	2 Sam.22.31
for they *p*. from evil to evil	Jer.9.3	Confirm to thy servant thy *p*.	Ps.119.38
every word that *p*. from the mouth	Mt.4.4	Uphold me according to thy *p*.	Ps.119.116
what comes out of the mouth *p*.	Mt.15.18	that I may meditate upon thy *p*.	Ps.119.148
I *p*. and came forth from God	Jn.8.42	I send the *p*. of my Father upon you	Lk.24.49
Spirit of truth . . . *p*. from the	Jn.15.26	to wait for the *p*. of the Father	Acts 1.4
does not *p*. from faith is sin	Rom.14.23	For the *p*. is to you and to your	Acts 2.39
PROCLAIM		*p*. to Abraham and his descendants	Rom.4.13
will *p*. before you my name	Ex.33.19	all the *p*. of God find their Yes	2 Cor.1.20
p. liberty throughout the land	Lev.25.10	receive the *p*. of the Spirit	Gal.3.14
the firmament *p*. his handiwork	Ps.19.1	heirs according to *p*.	Gal.3.29
I will *p*. thy name, for it is good	Ps.52.9	strangers to the covenants of *p*.	Eph.2.12
The heavens *p*. his righteousness	Ps.97.6	the first commandment with a *p*.	Eph.6.2
shall *p*. the praise of the LORD	Is.60.6	not slow about his *p*. as some count	2 Pet.3.9
to *p*. liberty to the captives	Is.61.1	PROMISE (verb)	
P. this among the nations: Prepare	Jl.3.9	and I *p*. that I will bring you up	Ex.3.17
p. to it the message that I tell you	Jon.3.2	I *p*. to keep thy words	Ps.119.57
p. upon the housetops	Mt.10.27	so that he *p*. with an oath to give	Mt.14.7
he shall *p*. justice to the Gentiles	Mt.12.18	perform the mercy *p*. to our fathers	Lk.1.72
go and *p*. the kingdom of God	Lk.9.60	which he *p*. beforehand through his	Rom.1.2
forgiveness of sins is *p*. to you	Acts 13.38	sealed with the *p*. Holy Spirit	Eph.1.13
p. to you the way of salvation	Acts 16.17	God, who never lies, *p*. ages ago	Tit.1.2
those who *p*. the gospel	1 Cor.9.14	receive the *p*. eternal inheritance	Heb.9.15
you *p*. the Lord's death until he	1 Cor.11.26	considered him faithful who had *p*.	Heb.11.11
to *p*. the mystery of the gospel	Eph.6.19	which God has *p*. to those who love	Jas.1.12
Him we *p*., warning every man	Col.1.28	They *p*. them freedom, but they	2 Pet.2.19
I will *p*. thy name to my brethren	Heb.2.12		

PROMOTE
King Ahasuerus *p.* Haman the Agagite Est.3.1
Then the king *p.* Shadrach, Meshach Dan.3.30
to *p.* good order and to secure 1 Cor.7.35
genealogies which *p.* speculations 1 Tim.1.4
your faith may *p.* the knowledge of Philem.6
PRONOUNCE
By you Israel will *p.* blessing Gen.48.20
for he could not *p.* it right Jg.12.6
judgment you *p.* you will be judged Mt.7.2
Is this blessing *p.* only upon the Rom.4.9
do not *p.* judgment before the time 1 Cor.4.5
do not *p.* a reviling judgment 2 Pet.2.11
PROOF
Why do you put the LORD to the *p.*? Ex.17.2
put me to the *p.* these ten times Num.14.22
tested me, and put me to the *p.* Ps.95.9
for a *p.* to the people Mk.1.44
alive after his passion by many *p.* Acts 1.3
give *p.*, before the churches, of 2 Cor.8.24
since you desire *p.* that Christ 2 Cor.13.3
PROPER
their food at the *p.* time Mt.24.45
is it *p.* for a woman to pray 1 Cor.11.13
be made manifest at the *p.* time 1 Tim.6.15
but left their *p.* dwelling Jude 6
PROPERTY
met him at the *p.* of Naboth 2 Kg.9.21
and entrusted to them his *p.* Mt.25.14
squandered his *p.* in loose living Lk.15.13
wife Sapphira sold a piece of *p.* Acts 5.1
accepted the plundering of your *p.* Heb.10.34
PROPHECY
Where there is no *p.* the people Pr.29.18
fulfilled the *p.* of Isaiah which Mt.13.14
if *p.*, in proportion to our faith Rom.12.6
as for *p.*, they will pass away 1 Cor.13.8
no *p.* of scripture is a matter 2 Pet.1.20
reads aloud the words of the *p.* Rev.1.3
the testimony . . . is the spirit of *p.* Rev.19.10
the words of the book of this *p.* Rev.22.19
PROPHESY
spirit rested upon them, they *p.* Num.11.25
other messengers . . . also *p.* 1 Sam.19.21
And all the prophets *p.* so 2 Chr.18.11
they *p.* by Baal and led my people Jer.23.13
as I *p.*, there was a noise Ezek.37.7
sons and your daughters shall *p.* Jl.2.28
did we not *p.* in your name, and cast Mt.7.22
prophets and the law *p.* until John Mt.11.13
his father Zechariah . . . *p.* Lk.1.67
that year he *p.* that Jesus should Jn.11.51
they spoke with tongues and *p.* Acts 19.6
four unmarried daughters, who *p.* Acts 21.9
but he who *p.* edifies the church 1 Cor.14.4
The prophets who *p.* of the grace 1 Pet.1.10
PROPHET
Aaron your brother shall be your *p.* Ex.7.1
that all the LORD's people were *p.* Num.11.29
If a *p.* arises among you, or a Dt.13.1
the LORD sent a *p.* to the people Jg.6.8
established as a *p.* of the LORD 1 Sam.3.20
sent a message by Nathan the *p.* 2 Sam.12.25
I only, am left a *p.* of the LORD 1 Kg.18.22
Is there no *p.* of the LORD here 2 Kg.3.11
there is no longer any *p.* Ps.74.9

my anointed ones, do my *p.* no harm Ps.105.15
I am no *p.*, nor a *p.'s* son Am.7.14
I am no *p.*, I am a tiller of the Zech.13.5
Elijah the *p.* before the great Mal.4.5
come to abolish the law and the *p.* Mt.5.17
Beware of false *p.*, who come to you Mt.7.15
receives a *p.* because he is a *p.* Mt.10.41
A *p.* is not without honor except Mt.13.57
This is the *p.* Jesus from Nazareth Mt.21.11
mouth of his holy *p.* from of old Lk.1.70
be called the *p.* of the Most High Lk.1.76
A great *p.* has arisen among us Lk.7.16
"Are you the *p.*?" And he answered Jn.1.21
Sir, I perceive that you are a *p.* Jn.4.19
God will raise up for you a *p.* Acts 7.37
a *p.* named Agabus came down from Acts 21.10
If any one thinks that he is a *p.* 1 Cor.14.37
foundation of the apostles and *p.* Eph.2.20
the beast and the false *p.* were Rev.20.10
PROPHETESS
Miriam, the *p.*, the sister of Aaron Ex.15.20
Now Deborah, a *p.*, the wife of Jg.4.4
Asaiah went to Huldah the *p.* 2 Kg.22.14
also the *p.* Noadiah and the rest of Neh.6.14
I went to the *p.*, and she conceived Is.8.3
And there was a *p.*, Anna Lk.2.36
calls herself a *p.* and is teaching Rev.2.20
PROPHETIC
through the *p.* writings is made Rom.16.26
if I have *p.* powers, and 1 Cor.13.2
p. utterances which pointed to 1 Tim.1.18
given you by *p.* utterance when 1 Tim.4.14
we have the *p.* word made more 2 Pet.1.19
PROSPER
all that he did to *p.* in his hands Gen.39.3
I know that the LORD will *p.* me Jg.17.13
you will *p.* if you are careful 1 Chr.22.13
The God of heaven will make us *p.* Neh.2.20
In all that he does, he *p.* Ps.1.3
May they *p.* who love you Ps.122.6
he who keeps understanding will *p.* Pr.19.8
p. in the thing for which I sent it Is.55.11
her enemies *p.*, because the LORD Lam.1.5
I have *p.*, and I need nothing Rev.3.17
PROSPERITY
the LORD will make you abound in *p.* Dt.28.11
in *p.* the destroyer will come upon Job 15.21
my *p.* has passed away like a cloud Job 30.15
I said in my *p.*, "I shall never be Ps.30.6
when I saw the *p.* of the wicked Ps.73.3
May you see the *p.* of Jerusalem Ps.128.5
In the day of *p.* be joyful Ec.7.14
abundance of *p.* and security Jer.33.6
shall again overflow with *p.* Zech.1.17
PROSTITUTE
be no cult *p.* of the daughters of Dt.23.17
also male cult *p.* in the land 1 Kg.14.24
harlots, and sacrifice with cult *p.* Hos.4.14
make them members of a *p.*? 1 Cor.6.15
PROSTRATE
Then I lay *p.* before the LORD Dt.9.18
There the evildoers lie *p.* Ps.36.12
I am utterly bowed down and *p.* Ps.38.6
princes . . . shall *p.* themselves Is.49.7
PROTECT
For my sake *p.* the young man 2 Sam.18.12

The name of the God of Jacob *p.* you   Ps.20.1
the LORD *p.* him and keeps him alive   Ps.41.2
I will *p.* him, because he knows my   Ps.91.14
he will *p.* and deliver it   Is.31.5
The LORD of hosts will *p.* them   Zech.9.15

PROUD
when he was strong he grew *p.*   2 Chr.26.16
God abases the *p.*, but he saves   Job 22.29
Look on every one that is *p.*   Job 40.12
to divide the spoil with the *p.*   Pr.16.19
against all that is *p.* and lofty   Is.2.12
be not *p.*, for the LORD has spoken   Jer.13.15
The *p.* one shall stumble and fall   Jer.50.32
scattered the *p.* in the imagination   Lk.1.51
So do not become *p.*, but stand in   Rom.11.20
p., arrogant, abusive, disobedient   2 Tim.3.2
it says, "God opposes the *p.*   Jas.4.6

PROVE
for God has come to *p.* you   Ex.20.20
P. me, O LORD, and try me   Ps.26.2
Which . . . *p.* neighbor to the man who   Lk.10.36
and so *p.* to be my disciples   Jn.15.8
that you may *p.* what is the will of   Rom.12.2
impossible that God should *p.* false   Heb.6.18
which comes upon you to *p.* you   1 Pet.4.12

PROVERB
a *p.*, and a byword among all the   Dt.28.37
He also uttered three thousand *p.*   1 Kg.4.32
Your maxims are *p.* of ashes   Job 13.12
I will incline my ear to a *p.*   Ps.49.4
The *p.* of Solomon, son of David   Pr.1.1
this *p.* shall no more be used by   Ezek.18.3
you will quote to me this *p.*   Lk.4.23
to them according to the true *p.*   2 Pet.2.22

PROVIDE
God will *p.* himself the lamb for a   Gen.22.8
thou *p.* their grain, for so thou   Ps.65.9
O God, thou didst *p.* for the needy   Ps.68.10
will also *p.* the way of escape   1 Cor.10.13
God is able to *p.* you with every   2 Cor.9.8
one does not *p.* for his relatives   1 Tim.5.8

PROVOCATION
because of the *p.* of his sons   Dt.32.19
all the *p.* with which Manasseh   2 Kg.23.26
my eye dwells on their *p.*   Job 17.2
a fool's *p.* is heavier than both   Pr.27.3
Ephraim has given bitter *p.*   Hos.12.14

PROVOKE
so as to *p.* him to anger   Dt.4.25
Ahab did more to *p.* the LORD   1 Kg.16.33
a people who *p.* me to my face   Is.65.3
when your fathers *p.* me to wrath   Zech.8.14
his spirit was *p.* within him as   Acts 17.16
Shall we *p.* the Lord to jealousy?   1 Cor.10.22
do not *p.* your children to anger   Eph.6.4
with whom was he *p.* forty years?   Heb.3.17

PRUDENCE
O simple ones, learn *p.*; O foolish   Pr.8.5
I, wisdom, dwell in *p.*   Pr.8.12
replied with *p.* and discretion to   Dan.2.14
the dishonest steward for his *p.*   Lk.16.8

PRUDENT
p. in speech, and a man of good   1 Sam.16.18
A son who gathers in summer is *p.*   Pr.10.5
he who restrains his lips is *p.*   Pr.10.19
but the *p.* man ignores an insult   Pr.12.16

but a *p.* wife is from the LORD   Pr.19.14
A *p.* man sees danger and hides   Pr.22.3

PRUNING
beat . . . their spears into *p.* hooks   Is.2.4
cut off the shoots with *p.* hooks   Is.18.5
Beat . . . your *p.* hooks into spears   Jl.3.10
beat . . . their spears into *p.* hooks   Mic.4.3

PSALM
sing praises with a *p.*   Ps.47.7
prophets and the *p.* must be fulfilled   Lk.24.44
addressing one another in *p.* and   Eph.5.19
as you sing *p.* and hymns and   Col.3.16

PUBLIC
from the *p.* square of Beth-shan   2 Sam.21.12
truth has fallen in the *p.* squares   Is.59.14
powerfully confuted the Jews in *p.*   Acts 18.28
teaching you in *p.* and from house to   Acts 20.20
and made a *p.* example of them   Col.2.15
the *p.* reading of scripture   1 Tim.4.13

PUBLISH
p. it not in . . . Ashkelon   2 Sam.1.20
they should *p.* and proclaim in all   Neh.8.15
who *p.* peace, who brings good tidings   Is.52.7
who *p.* salvation, who says to Zion   Is.52.7

PUFFED
that none of you may be *p.* up   1 Cor.4.6
p. up without reason by his sensuous   Col.2.18
he may be *p.* up with conceit   1 Tim.3.6
he is *p.* up with conceit   1 Tim.6.4

PUNISH
then I will *p.* their transgression   Ps.89.32
I will *p.* the world for its evil   Is.13.11
Behold, I will *p.* them   Jer.11.22
I will *p.* you for all your iniquities   Am.3.2
will *p.* him, and put him with the   Mt.24.51
ready to *p.* every disobedience   2 Cor.10.6
governors . . . to *p.* those who   1 Pet.2.14

PUNISHMENT
My *p.* is greater than I can bear   Gen.4.13
Add to them *p.* upon *p.*   Ps.69.27
The days of *p.* have come, the days   Hos.9.7
they will go away into eternal *p.*   Mt.25.46
what longing, what zeal, what *p.*   2 Cor.7.11
How much worse *p.* do you think   Heb.10.29
unrighteous under *p.* until the day   2 Pet.2.9
For fear has to do with *p.*   1 Jn.4.18

PURE
with the *p.* . . . . show thyself *p.*   2 Sam.22.27
Can a man be *p.* before his Maker?   Job 4.17
the commandment of the LORD is *p.*   Ps.19.8
who has clean hands and a *p.* heart   Ps.24.4
How can a young man keep his way *p.*?   Ps.119.9
ways of a man are *p.* in his own eyes   Pr.16.2
those who are *p.* in their own eyes   Pr.30.12
Thou who art of *p.* eyes than to   Hab.1.13
of the peoples to a *p.* speech   Zeph.3.9
Blessed are the *p.* in heart   Mt.5.8
ointment of *p.* nard and anointed   Jn.12.3
may be *p.* and blameless for the   Phil.1.10
whatever is *p.*, whatever is lovely   Phil.4.8
keep yourself *p.*   1 Tim.5.22
call upon the Lord from a *p.* heart   2 Tim.2.22
To the *p.* all things are *p.*, but   Tit.1.15
Religion that is *p.* and undefiled   Jas.1.27
the street of the city was *p.* gold   Rev.21.21

PURIFY

they should *p*. themselves and come	Neh.13.22
Many shall *p*. themselves, and make	Dan.12.10
not eat unless they *p*. themselves	Mk.7.4
take these men and *p*. yourself	Acts 21.24
p. your conscience from dead works	Heb.9.14
almost everything is *p*. with blood	Heb.9.22
p. your hearts, you men of double	Jas.4.8
p. himself as he is pure	1 Jn.3.3

PURITY

He who loves *p*. of heart, and whose	Pr.22.11
by *p*., knowledge, forbearance	2 Cor.6.6
in love, in faith, in *p*.	1 Tim.4.12
women like sisters, in all *p*.	1 Tim.5.2

PURPLE

Daniel was clothed with *p*.	Dan.5.29
they clothed him in a *p*. cloak	Mk.15.17
was clothed in *p*. and fine linen	Lk.16.19
crown of thorns and the *p*. robe	Jn.19.5
a seller of *p*. goods, who was a	Acts 16.14
was arrayed in *p*. and scarlet	Rev.17.4

PURPOSE (noun)

no *p*. of thine can be thwarted	Job 42.2
to God who fulfils his *p*. for me	Ps.57.2
The LORD will fulfil his *p*. for me	Ps.138.8
has made everything for its *p*.	Pr.16.4
p. of the LORD will be established	Pr.19.21
for I was sent for this *p*.	Lk.4.43
No, for this *p*. I have come to this	Jn.12.27
who are called according to his *p*.	Rom.8.28
that God's *p*. of election might	Rom.9.11
will disclose the *p*. of the heart	1 Cor.4.5
according to the *p*. of his will	Eph.1.5
the eternal *p*. which he has realized	Eph.3.11
unchangeable character of his *p*.	Heb.6.17
you have seen the *p*. of the Lord	Jas.5.11

PURSE

we will all have one *p*.	Pr.1.14
Those who lavish gold from the *p*.	Is.46.6
Carry no *p*., no bag, no sandals	Lk.10.4
let him who has a *p*. take it	Lk.22.36

PURSUE

in hot anger *p*. the manslayer	Dt.19.6
Why do you, like God, *p*. me?	Job 19.22
do good; seek peace, and *p*. it	Ps.34.14
The wicked flee when no one *p*.	Pr.28.1
Thou wilt *p*. them in anger	Lam.3.66
Let us . . . *p*. what makes for peace	Rom.14.19
let him seek peace and *p*. it	1 Pet.3.11

QUAILS

In the evening *q*. came up and	Ex.16.13
it brought *q*. from the sea	Num.11.31
the next day, and gathered the *q*.	Num.11.32
They asked, and he brought *q*.	Ps.105.40

QUAKE

the whole mountain *q*. greatly	Ex.19.18
The mountains *q*. before the LORD	Jg.5.5
Thou hast made the land to *q*.	Ps.60.2
mountains might *q*. at thy presence	Is.64.1
all . . . shall *q*. at my presence	Ezek.38.20

QUALIFIED

able men *q*. for the service	1 Chr.26.8
who has *q*. us to be ministers of	2 Cor.3.6
q. us to share in the inheritance	Col.1.12

QUARREL (verb)

said to them, "Do not *q*. on the way."	Gen.45.24
When men *q*. and one strikes the	Ex.21.18
they *q*. with one another in the	2 Sam.14.6
you fast only to *q*. and to fight	Is.58.4

QUARRELING (noun)

a wife's *q*. is a continual . . . rain	Pr.19.13
where . . . is no whisperer, *q*. ceases	Pr.26.20
not in *q*. and jealousy	Rom.13.13
that there is *q*. among you	1 Cor.1.11
holy hands without anger or *q*.	1 Tim.2.8
to avoid *q*., to be gentle, and to	Tit.3.2

QUARRELSOME

so is a *q*. man for kindling strife	Pr.26.21
not *q*., and no lover of money	1 Tim.3.3
must not be *q*. but kindly to	2 Tim.2.24

QUEEN

when the *q*. of Sheba had seen	1 Kg.10.4
But *Q*. Vashti refused to come at	Est.1.12
What is your petition, *Q*. Esther?	Est.7.2
stands the *q*. in gold of Ophir	Ps.45.9
and their *q*. your nursing mothers	Is.49.23
The *q*. of the South will arise at	Mt.12.42
Candace the *q*. of the Ethiopians	Acts 8.27
A *q*. I sit, I am no widow, mourning	Rev.18.7

QUENCH

lest you *q*. the lamp of Israel	2 Sam.21.17
Many waters cannot *q*. love	S.of S.8.7
dimly burning wick he will not *q*.	Is.42.3
or *q*. a smoldering wick	Mt.12.20
not die, and the fire is not *q*.	Mk.9.48
you can *q*. all the flaming darts	Eph.6.16
Do not *q*. the Spirit	1 Th.5.19
q. raging fire, escaped the edge	Heb.11.34

QUESTION (noun)

And Solomon answered all her *q*.	2 Chr.9.2
I also will ask you a *q*.	Mt.21.24
asked him a *q*., to test him	Mt.22.35
no one dared to ask him any *q*.	Mk.12.34
listening to them and asking them *q*.	Lk.2.46
in *q*. of food and drink or	Col.2.16

QUESTION (verb)

Why do you *q*. thus in your hearts?	Mk.2.8
and all men *q*. in their hearts	Lk.3.15
you . . . need none to *q*. you	Jn.16.30
And the high priest *q*. them	Acts 5.27

QUICK

A man of *q*. temper acts foolishly	Pr.14.17
Be not *q*. to anger, for anger lodges	Ec.7.9
Make friends *q*. with your accuser	Mt.5.25
not to be *q*. shaken in mind or	2 Th.2.2
Let every man be *q*. to hear	Jas.1.19

QUIET

Be *q*., for this day is holy	Neh.8.11
Better is a dry morsel with *q*. than	Pr.17.1
shall return and have *q*. and ease	Jer.30.10
like the sea which cannot be *q*.	Jer.49.23
should wait *q*. for the salvation	Lam.3.26
aspire to live *q*., to mind your	1 Th.4.11
may lead a *q*. and peaceable life	1 Tim.2.2
jewel of a gentle and *q*. spirit	1 Pet.3.4

QUIVER

Upon him rattle the *q*., the	Job 39.23
the man who has his *q*. full of them	Ps.127.5
in his *q*. he hid me away	Is.49.2

Their *q.* is like an open tomb   Jer.5.16
into my heart the arrows of his *q.*   Lam.3.13

RABBI
you are not to be called *r.*   Mt.23.8
"*R.*" (which means Teacher), "where   Jn.1.38
R., we know that you are a teacher   Jn.3.2
R., who sinned, this man or his   Jn.9.2

RACE
the holy *r.* has mixed itself   Ezra 9.2
the *r.* is not to the swift   Ec.9.11
my brethren, my kinsmen by *r.*   Rom.9.3
in a *r.* all the runners compete   1 Cor.9.24
I have finished the *r.*   2 Tim.4.7
run with perseverance the *r.*   Heb.12.1
But you are a chosen *r.*, a royal   1 Pet.2.9

RACHEL
Gen.29.6; 30.1; 35.19; Jer.31.15; Mt.2.18

RADIANT
Look to him, and be *r.*   Ps.34.5
My beloved is all *r.* and ruddy   S.of S.5.10
Then you shall see and be *r.*   Is.60.5
they shall be *r.* over the goodness   Jer.31.12

RAGE
The nations *r.*, the kingdoms totter   Ps.46.6
his heart *r.* against the LORD   Pr.19.3
The sword shall *r.* against their   Hos.11.6
The chariots *r.* in the streets   Nah.2.4
Why did the Gentiles *r.*   Acts 4.25
quenched *r.* fire, escaped the edge   Heb.11.34
The nations *r.*, but thy wrath came   Rev.11.18

RAHAB
Jos.2.1; 6.17; Mt.1.5; Heb.11.31; Jas.2.25

RAIMENT
and for my *r.* they cast lots   Ps.22.18
Thou changest them like *r.*   Ps.102.26
his *r.* was white as snow   Dan.7.9
To see a man clothed in soft *r.?*   Mt.11.8
and his *r.* white as snow   Mt.28.3
his *r.* became dazzling white   Lk.9.29

RAIN (noun)
I will send *r.* upon the earth   Gen.7.4
he made a decree for the *r.*   Job 28.26
Has the *r.* a father, or who has   Job 38.28
the early *r.* also covers it with   Ps.84.6
he prepares *r.* for the earth   Ps.147.8
If the clouds are full of *r.*   Ec.11.3
For as the *r.* and the snow come   Is.55.10
withheld the *r.* from you when   Am.4.7
Ask *r.* from the LORD in the season   Zech.10.1
sends *r.* on the just and on the   Mt.5.45
the *r.* fell, and the floods came   Mt.7.25

RAIN (verb)
not caused it to *r.* upon the earth   Gen.2.5
Then the LORD *r.* on Sodom and   Gen.19.24
On the wicked he will *r.* coals of   Ps.11.6
he *r.* down upon them manna to   Ps.78.24
let the skies *r.* down righteousness   Is.45.8
fire and brimstone *r.* from heaven   Lk.17.29
he prayed . . . that it might not *r.*   Jas.5.17

RAISE
I will *r.* up for them a prophet   Dt.18.18
He has *r.* up a horn for his people   Ps.148.14
Heal the sick, *r.* the dead, cleanse   Mt.10.8
and *r.* up children for his brother   Mk.12.19
has *r.* up a horn of salvation   Lk.1.69

able . . . to *r.* up children to Abraham   Lk.3.8
will you *r.* it up in three days?   Jn.2.20
I will *r.* him up at the last day   Jn.6.44
This Jesus God *r.* up, and of that   Acts 2.32
God will *r.* up for you a prophet   Acts 7.37
whom he did not *r.* if it is true   1 Cor.15.15
will *r.* us also with Jesus   2 Cor.4.14
who for their sake died and was *r.*   2 Cor.5.15
Father, who *r.* him from the dead   Gal.1.1
r. us up with him, and made us   Eph.2.6
you were also *r.* with him through   Col.2.12
If then you have been *r.* with Christ   Col.3.1
the Lord will *r.* him up   Jas.5.15
who *r.* him from the dead and gave   1 Pet.1.21

RAISINS
a hundred clusters of *r.*   1 Sam.25.18
portion of meat, and a cake of *r.*   2 Sam.6.19
clusters of *r.*, and wine and oil   1 Chr.12.40
Sustain me with *r.*, refresh me   S.of S.2.5
to other gods and love cakes of *r.*   Hos.3.1

RAMPART
it stood against the *r.*   2 Sam.20.15
consider well her *r.*, go through   Ps.48.13
her *r.* a sea, and water her wall?   Nah.3.8
Tyre has built herself a *r.*   Zech.9.3

RANSOM
R. me from the hand of oppressors   Job 6.23
God will *r.* my soul from . . . Sheol   Ps.49.15
the *r.* of the LORD shall return   Is.35.10
Shall I *r.* them from the power of   Hos.13.14
to give his life as a *r.* for many   Mt.20.28
who gave himself as a *r.* for all   1 Tim.2.6
that you were *r.* from the futile   1 Pet.1.18
by thy blood didst *r.* men for God   Rev.5.9

RASH
therefore my words have been *r.*   Job 6.3
he spoke words that were *r.*   Ps.106.33
There is one whose *r.* words are   Pr.12.18
Be not *r.* with your mouth, nor let   Ec.5.2
to be quiet and do nothing *r.*   Acts 19.36

RAVEN
sent forth a *r.* . . . . it went to and fro   Gen.8.7
commanded the *r.* to feed you there   1 Kg.17.4
Who provides for the *r.* its prey   Job 38.41
food . . . to the young *r.* which cry   Ps.147.9
the owl and the *r.* shall dwell in   Is.34.11
Consider the *r.*: they neither sow   Lk.12.24

RAZOR
No *r.* shall come upon his head   Jg.13.5
A *r.* has never come upon my head   Jg.16.17
Your tongue is like a sharp *r.*   Ps.52.2
shave with a *r.* which is hired   Is.7.20
as a barber's *r.* and pass it over   Ezek.5.1

REACH
his head *r.* to the clouds   Job 20.6
waters, they shall not *r.* him   Ps.32.6
thy praise *r.* to the ends of the   Ps.48.10
thy faithfulness *r.* to the clouds   Ps.108.4
r. out her hands to the needy   Pr.31.20
salvation may *r.* to the end of the   Is.49.6
that all should *r.* repentance   2 Pet.3.9

READ
afterward he *r.* all the words   Jos.8.34
he *r.* from the book of the law of   Neh.8.18
So Baruch *r.* it to them   Jer.36.15
so he may run who *r.* it   Hab.2.2

sabbath day. And he stood up to r.	Lk.4.16	harden your hearts as in the r.	Heb.3.8
prophets . . . are r. every sabbath	Acts 13.27	and perish in Korah's r.	Jude 11
to be known and r. by all men	2 Cor.3.2	REBELLIOUS	
when they r. the old covenant	2 Cor.3.14	You have been r. against the LORD	Dt.9.24
this letter has been r. among you	Col.4.16	This our son is stubborn and r.	Dt.21.20
this letter be r. to all the brethren	1 Th.5.27	let not the r. exalt themselves	Ps.66.7
READING		a stubborn and r. generation	Ps.78.8
that the people understood the r.	Neh.8.8	"Woe to the r. children," says the	Is.30.1
When you finish r. this book	Jer.51.63	has a stubborn and r. heart	Jer.5.23
Do you understand what you are r.?	Acts 8.30	be not r. like that r. house	Ezek.2.8
After the r. of the law and the	Acts 13.15	for they are a r. house. Therefore	Ezek.12.3
to the public r. of scripture	1 Tim.4.13	Woe to her that is r. and defiled	Zeph.3.1
READY		they that heard and yet were r.?	Heb.3.16
the grave is r. for me	Job 17.1	REBUILD	
is like the pen of a r. scribe	Ps.45.1	r. the walls of Jerusalem	Ps.51.18
blown the trumpet and made all r.	Ezek.7.14	r. them as they were at first	Jer.33.7
Therefore you also must be r.	Mt.24.44	and they shall r. the ruined cities	Am.9.14
Come; for all is now r.	Lk.14.17	I will r. the dwelling of David	Acts 15.16
r. for any good work	2 Tim.2.21	REBUKE (verb)	
a salvation r. to be revealed	1 Pet.1.5	He will surely r. you if in secret	Job 13.10
his Bride has made herself r.	Rev.19.7	O LORD, r. me not in thy anger	Ps.6.1
REAP		R. the beasts that dwell among the	Ps.68.30
sow in tears r. with shouts of joy	Ps.126.5	He r. the Red Sea, and it became dry	Ps.106.9
who sows injustice will r. calamity	Pr.22.8	Thou dost r. the insolent	Ps.119.21
who regards the clouds will not r.	Ec.11.4	lest he r. you, and you be found a	Pr.30.6
they shall r. the whirlwind	Hos.8.7	The LORD r. you, O Satan	Zech.3.2
neither sow nor r. nor gather into	Mt.6.26	Behold, I will r. your offspring	Mal.2.3
and r. what you did not sow	Lk.19.21	I will r. the devourer for you so	Mal.3.11
I sent you to r. that for which you	Jn.4.38	Peter took him and began to r. him	Mt.16.22
sparingly will also r. sparingly	2 Cor.9.6	he r. Peter, and said, "Get behind	Mk.8.33
a man sows, that he will also r.	Gal.6.7	But Jesus r. the unclean spirit	Lk.9.42
REAPER		to him, "Teacher, r. your disciples."	Lk.19.39
gleaned in the field after the r.	Ru.2.3	Do not r. an older man but exhort	1 Tim.5.1
the plowman shall overtake the r.	Am.9.13	Therefore r. them sharply	Tit.1.13
of the age, and the r. are angels	Mt.13.39	but said, "The Lord r. you."	Jude 9
that sower and r. may rejoice	Jn.4.36	RECEIVE	
REASON (noun)		He will r. blessing from the LORD	Ps.24.5
or even by r. of strength fourscore	Ps.90.10	afterward thou wilt r. me to glory	Ps.73.24
Do not contend with a man for no r.	Pr.3.30	let your ear r. the word of his	Jer.9.20
my r. returned to me, and I blessed	Dan.4.34	the Most High shall r. the kingdom	Dan.7.18
For this r. a man shall leave his	Mk.10.7	a prophet shall r. a prophet's	Mt.10.41
For this r. the Father loves me	Jn.10.17	Not all men can r. this precept	Mt.19.11
there was no r. for the death	Acts 28.18	will r. the greater condemnation	Mk.12.40
The r. the Son of God appeared was	1 Jn.3.8	the blind r. their sight, the lame	Lk.7.22
REASON (verb)		Whoever r. this child in my name r.	Lk.9.48
you shall r. with your neighbor	Lev.19.17	For every one who asks r.	Lk.11.10
an upright man could r. with him	Job 23.7	and his own people r. him not	Jn.1.11
let us r. together, says the LORD	Is.1.18	from his fulness have we all r.	Jn.1.16
like a child, I r. like a child	1 Cor.13.11	I do not r. glory from men	Jn.5.41
REBEKAH		said to them, "R. the Holy Spirit	Jn.20.22
Gen.24.15; 25.28; 26.35; 27.5; 49.31		you shall r. power when the Holy	Acts 1.8
REBEL (verb)		more blessed to give than to r.	Acts 20.35
Only, do not r. against the LORD	Num.14.9	Brother Saul, r. your sight	Acts 22.13
that we should r. against the LORD	Jos.22.29	What have you that you did not r.?	1 Cor.4.7
The king of Moab has r. against me	2 Kg.3.7	I r. from the Lord what I also	1 Cor.11.23
Zedekiah r. against the king of	2 Kg.24.20	that each one may r. good or evil	2 Cor.5.10
How often they r. against him in	Ps.78.40	that we may r. mercy and find grace	Heb.4.16
for they had r. against the words	Ps.107.11	You ask and do not r., because you	Jas.4.3
But they r. and grieved his holy	Is.63.10	If we r. the testimony of men, the	1 Jn.5.9
You have all r. against me, says	Jer.2.29	to r. power and wealth and wisdom	Rev.5.12
We have transgressed and r.	Lam.3.42	RECHABITES	
wickedly r. against my ordinances	Ezek.5.6	Jer.35.2, 18	
they r. against me	Hos.7.14	RECKON	
REBELLION		he r. it to him as righteousness	Gen.15.6
An evil man seeks only r.	Pr.17.11	He shall r. with him who bought	Lev.25.50
unless the r. comes first	2 Th.2.3	And he was r. with transgressors	Lk.22.37

it was *r.* to him as righteousness	Rom.4.3	O Lord, my rock and my *r.*	Ps.19.1
whom the Lord will not *r.* his sin	Rom.4.8	the Most High God their *r.*	Ps.78.35
RECOGNIZE		their *R.* is strong; he will plead	Pr.23.11
immediately the people *r.* him	Mk.6.54	your *R.* is the Holy One of Israel	Is.41.14
eyes were opened and they *r.* him	Lk.24.31	Their *R.* is strong; the Lord of	Jer.50.34
did not *r.* him nor understand	Acts 13.27	**REDEMPTION**	
we *r.* no other practice, nor do	1 Cor.11.16	shall give for the *r.* of his life	Ex.21.30
If any one does not *r.* this, he	1 Cor.14.38	you shall grant a *r.* of the land	Lev.25.24
RECOMPENSE (noun)		Moses gave the *r.* money to Aaron	Num.3.51
and see the *r.* of the wicked	Ps.91.8	He sent *r.* to his people	Ps.111.9
is with him, and his *r.* before him	Is.62.11	and with him is plenteous *r.*	Ps.130.7
for the Lord is a God of *r.*	Jer.51.56	and my year of *r.* has come	Is.63.
bringing my *r.*, to repay every one	Rev.22.12	through the *r.* which is in Christ	Rom.3.24
RECONCILE		the *r.* of our bodies	Rom.8.23
if while ... enemies we were *r.* to God	Rom.5.10	and sanctification and *r.*	1 Cor.1.30
God was in Christ *r.* the world to	2 Cor.5.19	In him we have *r.* through his blood	Eph.1.7
on behalf of Christ, be *r.* to God	2 Cor.5.20	you were sealed for the day of *r.*	Eph.4.30
and might *r.* us both to God in one	Eph.2.16	in whom we have *r.*, the forgiveness	Col.1.14
and through him to *r.* to himself	Col.1.20	blood, thus securing an eternal *r.*	Heb.9.12
RECONCILIATION		**REED**	
through whom we ... received our *r.*	Rom.5.11	seven cows ... fed in the *r.* grass	Gen.41.2
means the *r.* of the world	Rom.11.15	among the *r.* at the river's brink	Ex.2.3
and gave us the ministry of *r.*	2 Cor.5.18	a bruised *r.* he will not break	Is.42.3
entrusting to us the message of *r.*	2 Cor.5.19	A *r.* shaken by the wind?	Mt.11.7
RECORDER		took the *r.* and struck him on	Mt.27.30
the son of Ahilud was *r.*	2 Sam.8.16	put it on a *r.* and gave it to him	Mk.15.30
Joah the son of Asaph, the *r.*	Is.36.3	**REFINE**	
RECOUNT		I will *r.* them and test them	Jer.9.7
that I may *r.* all thy praises	Ps.9.14	*r.* them as one *r.* silver	Zech.13.9
we will *r.* thy praise	Ps.79.13	*r.* them like gold and silver	Mal.3.3
r. the deeds of the Lord	Ps.118.17	bronze, *r.* as in a furnace	Rev.1.15
I will *r.* the steadfast love of the	Is.63.7	to buy from me gold *r.* by fire	Rev.3.18
RECOVER		**REFRAIN**	
Shall I *r.* from this sickness?	2 Kg.8.8	*R.* from anger, and forsake wrath	Ps.37.8
lay it on the boil, that he may *r.*	2 Kg.20.7	he who *r.* from marriage will do	1 Cor.7.38
you shall die, you shall not *r.*	Is.38.1	will *r.* from burdening you in	2 Cor.11.9
if he has fallen asleep, he will *r.*	Jn.11.12	**REFRESH**	
RED		that you may *r.* yourselves	Gen.18.5
and drove them into the *R.* Sea	Ex.10.19	and good news *r.* the bones	Pr.15.30
to bring you a *r.* heifer without	Num.19.2	with joy and be *r.* in your company	Rom.15.32
He rebuked the *R.* Sea, and it became	Ps.106.9	they *r.* my spirit as well as yours	1 Cor.16.18
Do not look at wine when it is *r.*	Pr.23.31	Onesiphorus, for he often *r.* me	2 Tim.1.16
though they are *r.* like crimson	Is.1.18	*R.* my heart in Christ	Philem.20
Why is thy apparel *r.*, and thy	Is.63.2	**REFUGE**	
a man riding upon a *r.* horse	Zech.1.8	shall be the six cities of *r.*	Num.35.6
for the sky is *r.* and threatening	Mt.16.3	This God is my strong *r.*	2 Sam.22.33
out came another horse, bright *r.*	Rev.6.4	O Lord my God, in thee do I take *r.*	Ps.7.1
behold, a great *r.* dragon	Rev.12.3	Preserve me ... for in thee I take *r.*	Ps.16.1
REDEEM		In thee, O Lord, do I seek *r.*	Ps.31.1
I will *r.* you with an outstretched	Ex.6.6	God is our *r.* and strength, a very	Ps.46.1
all the first-born of my sons I *r.*	Ex.13.15	shadow of thy wings I will take *r.*	Ps.57.1
I cannot *r.* it for myself, lest I	Ru.4.6	under his wings you will find *r.*	Ps.91.4
In famine he will *r.* you from death	Job 5.20	But the Lord is a *r.* to his people	Jl.3.16
R. Israel, O God, out of all his	Ps.25.22	he knows those who take *r.* in him	Nah.1.7
who *r.* your life from the Pit	Ps.103.4	we who have fled for *r.* might	Heb.6.18
Let the *r.* of the Lord say so	Ps.107.2	**REFUSE**	
And he will *r.* Israel from all his	Ps.130.8	Pharaoh stubbornly *r.* to let us go	Ex.13.15
hand shortened, that it cannot *r.*?	Is.50.2	but *r.* to walk according to his law	Ps.78.10
you shall be *r.* without money	Is.52.3	I have called and you *r.* to listen	Pr.1.24
the Lord will *r.* you from the hand	Mic.4.10	But if you *r.* and rebel, you shall	Is.1.20
he was the one to *r.* Israel	Lk.24.21	do not *r.* him who would borrow	Mt.5.42
Christ *r.* us from the curse of the	Gal.3.13	Our fathers *r.* to obey him	Acts 7.39
to *r.* those who were under the law	Gal.4.5	If any one *r.* to obey what we say	2 Th.3.14
to *r.* us from all iniquity	Tit.2.14	See that you do not *r.* him who is	Heb.12.25
REDEEMER		**REGARD** (verb)	
For I know that my *R.* lives	Job 19.25	I *r.* not myself; I loathe my life	Job 9.21

nor *r*. the rich more than the poor   Job 34.19
will *r*. the prayer of the destitute   Ps.102.17
what is man that thou dost *r*. him   Ps.144.3
In that day men will *r*. their Maker   Is.17.7
for he has *r*. the low estate of his   Lk.1.48
I neither fear God nor *r*. man   Lk.18.4
we *r*. no one from a human point   2 Cor.5.16
do not *r*. lightly the discipline of   Heb.12.5

REHOBOAM
1 Kg.11.43; 14.21; 2 Chr.9.31; 11.5; 12.16

REIGN (verb)
The LORD will *r*. for ever and ever   Ex.15.18
No, but a king shall *r*. over us   1 Sam.12.12
Solomon your son shall *r*. after me   1 Kg.1.13
Say among the nations, "The LORD *r*.   Ps.96.10
The LORD *r*.; let the peoples tremble   Ps.99.1
The LORD will *r*. for ever, thy God   Ps.146.10
But thou, O LORD, dost *r*. for ever   Lam.5.19
he will *r*. over the house of Jacob   Lk.1.33
death *r*. through that one man   Rom.5.17
Let not sin . . . *r*. in your . . . bodies   Rom.6.12
he must *r*. until he has put all   1 Cor.15.25
if we endure, we shall also *r*.   2 Tim.2.12
and he shall *r*. for ever and ever   Rev.11.15
r. with Christ a thousand years   Rev.20.4

REJECT
God will not *r*. a blameless man   Job 8.20
and *r*. not your mother's teaching   Pr.1.8
He was despised and *r*. by men   Is.53.3
You have *r*. me, says the LORD   Jer.15.6
I *r*. you from being a priest to me   Hos.4.6
and be *r*. by the elders and chief   Lk.9.22
stone which was *r*. by you builders   Acts 4.11
commands of men who *r*. the truth   Tit.1.14
shall we escape if we *r*. him who   Heb.12.25
The . . . stone which the builders *r*.   1 Pet.2.7

REJOICE
And you shall *r*. before the LORD   Dt.12.12
r., O righteous, and shout for joy   Ps.32.11
Then my soul shall *r*. in the LORD   Ps.35.9
Only let them not *r*. over me   Ps.38.16
The righteous will *r*. when he sees   Ps.58.10
But the king shall *r*. in God   Ps.63.11
that we may *r*. and be glad all our   Ps.90.14
R. in the LORD, O you righteous   Ps.97.12
r. at thy word like one who finds   Ps.119.162
and *r*. in the wife of your youth   Pr.5.18
Do not *r*. when your enemy falls   Pr.24.17
the desert shall *r*. and blossom   Is.35.1
R. and exult with all your heart   Zeph.3.14
Sing and *r*., O daughter of Zion   Zech.2.10
R. greatly, O daughter of Zion   Zech.9.9
R. and be glad, for your reward is   Mt.5.12
and my spirit *r*. in God my Savior   Lk.1.47
R. in that day, and leap for joy   Lk.6.23
but *r*. that your names are written   Lk.10.20
Your father Abraham *r*. that he was   Jn.8.56
you . . . lament, but the world will *r*.   Jn.16.20
we *r*. in our sufferings, knowing   Rom.5.3
R. in your hope, be patient in   Rom.12.12
R. with those who *r*., weep with   Rom.12.15
it does not *r*. at wrong, but   1 Cor.13.6
R. in the Lord always; again . . . *R*.   Phil.4.4
Now I *r*. in my sufferings for your   Col.1.24
But *r*. in so far as you share   1 Pet.4.13
R. . . . O heaven and you that dwell   Rev.12.12

RELEASE (verb)
accustomed to *r*. for the crowd any   Mt.27.15
therefore chastise him and *r*. him   Lk.23.16
once more, desiring to *r*. Jesus   Lk.23.20
Upon this Pilate sought to *r*. him   Jn.19.12
When they were *r*. they went to   Acts 4.23
our brother Timothy has been *r*.   Heb.13.23
R. the four angels who are bound   Rev.9.14

RELIEF
the Jews got *r*. from their enemies   Est.9.22
to send *r*. to the brethren who   Acts 11.29
taking part in the *r*. of the saints   2 Cor.8.4

RELIGION
as befits women who profess *r*.   1 Tim.2.10
Great . . . is the mystery of our *r*.   1 Tim.3.16
holding the form of *r*. but denying   2 Tim.3.5
R. that is pure and undefiled   Jas.1.27

RELIGIOUS
in every way you are very *r*.   Acts 17.22
learn their *r*. duty to their own   1 Tim.5.4
If any one thinks he is *r*.   Jas.1.26

RELY
we *r*. on thee, and in thy name   2 Chr.14.11
and do not *r*. on your own insight   Pr.3.5
We *r*. on the LORD our God   Is.36.7
when you *r*. on Egypt for chariots   Is.36.9
if you . . . *r*. upon the law and boast   Rom.2.17
to make us *r*. not on ourselves   2 Cor.1.9
For all who *r*. on works of the law   Gal.3.10

REMAIN
While the earth *r*., seedtime and   Gen.8.22
r. every man of you in his place   Ex.16.29
his body shall not *r*. all night   Dt.21.23
even to death; *r*. here, and watch   Mk.14.34
you see the Spirit descend and *r*.   Jn.1.33
Every one should *r*. in the state   1 Cor.7.20
But to *r*. in the flesh is more   Phil.1.24
that what cannot be shaken may *r*.   Heb.12.27
strengthen what *r*. and is on the   Rev.3.2

REMEMBER
I will *r*. my covenant which is   Gen.9.15
the chief butler did not *r*. Joseph   Gen.40.23
R. the sabbath day, to keep it holy   Ex.20.8
R. what the LORD your God did to   Dt.24.9
R. now, O LORD, I beseech thee   2 Kg.20.3
R. that thou hast made me of clay   Job 10.9
R. not the sins of my youth, or my   Ps.25.7
Do not *r*. against us the iniquities   Ps.79.8
he *r*. that we are dust   Ps.103.14
sat down and wept, when we *r*. Zion   Ps.137.1
Yet no one *r*. that poor man   Ec.9.15
R. also your Creator in the days of   Ec.12.1
R. my affliction and my bitterness   Lam.3.19
And Peter *r*. the saying of Jesus   Mt.26.75
and to *r*. his holy covenant   Lk.1.72
R. Lot's wife   Lk.17.32
R. the word that I said to you   Jn.15.20
only they would have us *r*. the poor   Gal.2.10
and I will *r*. their sins no more   Heb.8.12
R. those who are in prison   Heb.13.3
R. your leaders, those who spoke   Heb.13.7

REMEMBRANCE
For in death there is no *r*. of thee   Ps.6.5
a book of *r*. was written before him   Mal.3.16
in *r*. of his mercy   Lk.1.54

Do this in *r*. of me 1 Cor.11.24
I thank my God in all my *r*. of you Phil.1.3
REMIND
to *r*. you of my ways in Christ 1 Cor.4.17
I *r*. you to rekindle the gift 2 Tim.1.6
R. them to be submissive to rulers Tit.3.1
Now I desire to *r*. you, though you Jude 5
REMINDER
have written to you . . . by way of *r*. Rom.15.15
there is a *r*. of sin year after Heb.10.3
to arouse you by way of *r*. 2 Pet.1.13
aroused your . . . mind by way of *r*. 2 Pet.3.1
REMNANT
to preserve for you a *r*. on earth Gen.45.7
one of the *r*. of the Rephaim Jos.12.4
but of the *r*. of the Amorites 2 Sam.21.2
prayer for the *r*. that is left 2 Kg.19.4
A *r*. will return, the *r*. of Jacob Is.10.21
out of Jerusalem shall go forth a *r*. Is.37.32
I will take the *r*. of Judah who Jer.44.12
I will cut off . . . the *r*. of Baal Zeph.1.4
only a *r*. of them will be saved Rom.9.27
at the present time there is a *r*. Rom.11.5
REMOVE
R. thy stroke from me; I am spent Ps.39.10
so far does he *r*. our transgressions Ps.103.12
The righteous will never be *r*. Pr.10.30
Do not *r*. an ancient landmark or Pr.23.10
R. far from me falsehood and lying Pr.30.8
r. this cup from me; nevertheless Lk.22.42
I will . . . *r*. your lampstand Rev.2.5
REND
lest like a lion they *r*. me Ps.7.2
a time to *r*., and a time to sew Ec.3.7
O that thou wouldst *r*. the heavens Is.64.1
r. your hearts and not your garments Jl.2.13
RENDER
I will *r*. thank offerings to thee Ps.56.12
What shall I *r*. to the LORD for Ps.116.12
R. true judgments, show kindness Zech.7.9
Then *r*. to Caesar the things that Lk.20.25
he will *r*. to every man according Rom.2.6
RENEW
go to Gilgal and . . . *r*. the kingdom 1 Sam.11.14
like grass which is *r*. in the morning Ps.90.5
your youth is *r*. like the eagle's Ps.103.5
the LORD shall *r*. their strength Is.40.31
be restored! *R*. our days as of old Lam.5.21
In the midst of the years *r*. it Hab.3.2
inner nature is being *r*. every day 2 Cor.4.16
be *r*. in the spirit of your minds Eph.4.23
which is being *r*. in knowledge Col.3.10
RENOUNCE
Why does the wicked *r*. God, and say Ps.10.13
Thou hast *r*. the covenant with thy Ps.89.39
have *r*. disgraceful, underhanded 2 Cor.4.2
training us to *r*. irreligion and Tit.2.12
REPAIR
And he *r*. the altar of the LORD 1 Kg.18.30
let them *r*. the house wherever 2 Kg.12.5
quarried stone to *r*. the house 2 Kg.22.6
r. the house of the LORD his God 2 Chr.34.8
they shall *r*. the ruined cities Is.61.4
REPAY
given to me, that I should *r*. him? Job 41.11
Do not say, "I will *r*. evil" Pr.20.22

I will *r*., yea, I will *r*. into their Is.65.6
then he will *r*. every man for what Mt.16.27
blessed, because they cannot *r*. you Lk.14.14
R. no one evil for evil, but take Rom.12.17
See that none of you *r*. evil for evil 1 Th.5.15
Vengeance is mine, I will *r*. Heb.10.30
and *r*. her double for her deeds Rev.18.6
REPENT
I *r*. that I have made Saul king 1 Sam.15.11
is not a man, that he should *r*. 1 Sam.15.29
I . . . *r*. in dust and ashes Job 42.6
God *r*. of the evil which he had Jon.3.10
R., for the kingdom of heaven is Mt.3.2
and preached that men should *r*. Mk.6.12
if he . . . says, 'I *r*.,' you must forgive Lk.17.4
R., and be baptized every one of Acts 2.38
commands all men everywhere to *r*. Acts 17.30
R. then. If not, I will come Rev.2.16
so be zealous and *r*. Rev.3.19
they did not *r*. and give him glory Rev.16.9
REPENTANCE
Bear fruit that befits *r*. Mt.3.8
a baptism of *r*. for the forgiveness Mk.1.4
not . . . the righteous, but sinners to *r*. Lk.5.32
that *r*. and forgiveness of sins Lk.24.47
give *r*. to Israel and forgiveness Acts 5.31
perform deeds worthy of their *r*. Acts 26.20
kindness is meant to lead you to *r*. Rom.2.4
grief produces a *r*. that leads to 2 Cor.7.10
impossible to restore again to *r*. Heb.6.4
but that all should reach *r*. 2 Pet.3.9
REPORT (noun)
You shall not utter a false *r*. Ex.23.1
brought up an evil *r*. of the land Num.14.37
in anguish over the *r*. about Tyre Is.23.5
She had heard the *r*. about Jesus Mk.5.27
a *r*. concerning him went out Lk.4.14
Lord, who has believed our *r*. Jn.12.38
REPROACH (noun)
takes away the *r*. from Israel? 1 Sam.17.26
nor takes up a *r*. against his Ps.15.3
for thy sake . . . I have borne *r*. Ps.69.7
but sin is a *r*. to any people Pr.14.34
fear not the *r*. of men, and be not Is.51.7
everlasting *r*. and perpetual shame Jer.23.40
You shall be a *r*. and a taunt Ezek.5.15
to take away my *r*. among men Lk.1.25
Now a bishop must be above *r*. 1 Tim.3.2
so that they may be without *r*. 1 Tim.5.7
REPROOF
Give heed to my *r*.; behold, I will Pr.1.23
he who rejects *r*. goes astray Pr.10.17
he who hates *r*. will die Pr.15.10
scripture is . . . profitable . . . for *r*. 2 Tim.3.16
REPROVE
Behold, happy is the man whom God *r*. Job 5.17
r. a wise man, and he will love you Pr.9.8
He who is often *r*., yet stiffens his Pr.29.1
exhort and *r*. with all authority Tit.2.15
Those whom I love, I *r*. and chasten Rev.3.19
REPUTE
LORD gave Solomon great *r*. 1 Chr.29.25
pick out . . . seven men of good *r*. Acts 6.3
in ill *r*. and good *r*. 2 Cor.6.8
who were of *r*. added nothing to me Gal.2.6

REQUEST
O that I might have my r. | Job 6.8
not withheld the r. of his lips | Ps.21.2
let your r. be made known to God | Phil.4.6
have obtained the r. made of him | 1 Jn.5.15
REQUIRE
I will surely r. a reckoning | Gen.9.5
sin offering thou hast not r. | Ps.40.6
there our captors r. of us songs | Ps.137.3
what does the Lord r. of you but to | Mic.6.8
This night thy soul is r. of you | Lk.12.20
is given, of him will much be r. | Lk.12.48
do by nature what the law r. | Rom.2.14
REQUITE
Lord r. the evildoer according | 2 Sam.3.39
They r. me evil for good; my soul | Ps.35.12
thou dost r. a man according to | Ps.62.12
nor r. us according to our iniquities | Ps.103.10
R. her according to her deeds | Jer.50.29
Thou wilt r. them, O Lord | Lam.3.64
will r. your deeds upon your head | Ezek.16.43
I will r. your deed upon your own | Jl.3.4
the Lord will r. him for his deeds | 2 Tim.4.14
RESCUE
Incline thy ear to me, r. me speedily | Ps.31.2
R. the weak and the needy | Ps.82.4
I will r. my sheep from their | Ezek.34.10
r. him out of all his afflictions | Acts 7.10
So I was r. from the lion's mouth | 2 Tim.4.17
Lord will r. me from every evil | 2 Tim.4.18
knows how to r. the godly from | 2 Pet.2.9
RESIST
Do not r. one who is evil. But if | Mt.5.39
you always r. the Holy Spirit | Acts 7.51
who r. the authorities r. what God | Rom.13.2
R. the devil and he will flee from | Jas.4.7
R. him, firm in your faith | 1 Pet.5.9
RESPECT (verb)
Do not r. their offering | Num.16.15
saying, 'They will r. my son.' | Mk.12.6
wife see that she r. her husband | Eph.5.33
to r. those who labor among you | 1 Th.5.12
to discipline us and we r. them | Heb.12.9
REST (noun)
until the Lord gives r. to your | Jos.1.15
Lord gave them r. on every side | Jos.21.44
I have no r.; but trouble comes | Job 3.26
I would fly away and be at r. | Ps.55.6
Return, O my soul, to your r. | Ps.116.7
the Spirit of the Lord gave them r. | Is.63.14
heavy laden, and I will give you r. | Mt.11.28
our bodies had no r. but we were | 2 Cor.7.5
They shall never enter my r. | Heb.3.11
a sabbath r. for the people of God | Heb.4.9
therefore strive to enter that r. | Heb.4.11
and they have no r., day or night | Rev.14.11
REST (verb)
on the seventh day you shall r. | Ex.34.21
in the night his mind does not r. | Ec.2.23
to a lonely place, and r. a while | Mk.6.31
power of Christ may r. upon me | 2 Cor.12.9
that they may r. from their labor | Rev.14.13
RESTORE
the Lord r. the fortunes of Job | Job 42.10
he r. my soul. He leads me in paths | Ps.23.3
R. to me the joy of thy salvation | Ps.51.12

thou didst r. the fortunes of Jacob | Ps.85.1
I will r. your judges as at the first | Is.1.26
R. us to thyself, O Lord, that we | Lam.5.21
I will r. the fortunes of Jacob | Ezek.39.25
Elijah . . . is to r. all things | Mt.17.11
if I . . . defrauded . . . I r. it fourfold | Lk.19.8
Lord, will you . . . r. the kingdom | Acts 1.6
impossible to r. again to repentance | Heb.6.4
RESTRAIN
Therefore I will not r. my mouth | Job 7.11
he does not r. the lightnings | Job 37.4
he r. his anger often, and did not | Ps.78.38
he who r. his lips is prudent | Pr.10.19
He who r. his words has knowledge | Pr.17.27
Who can r. her lust? None who | Jer.2.24
only he who now r. it will do so | 2 Th.2.7
RESURRECTION
in the r. they neither marry nor | Mt.22.30
In the r. whose wife will she be? | Mk.12.23
done evil, to the r. of judgment | Jn.5.29
to her, "I am the r. and the life | Jn.11.25
proclaiming . . . the r. from the dead | Acts 4.2
he preached Jesus and the r. | Acts 17.18
Sadducees say that there is no r. | Acts 23.8
united with him in a r. like his | Rom.6.5
So is it with the r. of the dead | 1 Cor.15.42
know him and the power of his r. | Phil.3.10
that the r. is past already | 2 Tim.2.18
Women received their dead by r. | Heb.11.35
through the r. of Jesus Christ | 1 Pet.3.21
were ended. This is the first r. | Rev.20.5
RETURN (verb)
we will r. with you to your people | Ru.1.10
and man would r. to dust | Job 34.15
Like a dog that r. to his vomit is | Pr.26.11
the spirit r. to God who gave it | Ec.12.7
A remnant will r., the remnant of | Is.10.21
the ransomed of the Lord shall r. | Is.51.11
let him r. to the Lord, that he may | Is.55.7
my word . . . shall not r. to me empty | Is.55.11
they have refused to r. to me | Hos.11.5
R., O Israel, to the Lord your God | Hos.14.1
R. to me, and I will r. to you | Mal.3.7
not worthy, let your peace r. to you | Mt.10.13
r. to the Shepherd and Guardian | 1 Pet.2.25
Do not r. evil for evil or | 1 Pet.3.9
REUBEN
Gen.29.32; 37.21; Dt.33.6; Jg.5.15; Rev.7.5
REVEAL
there God had r. himself to him | Gen.35.7
have been able to r. this mystery | Dan.2.47
to whom the Son chooses to r. him | Mt.11.27
Nothing . . . that will not be r. | Lk.12.2
After this Jesus r. himself again | Jn.21.1
wrath of God is r. from heaven | Rom.1.18
God has r. to us through the Spirit | 1 Cor.2.10
because it will be r. with fire | 1 Cor.3.13
was pleased to r. his Son to me | Gal.1.16
God will r. that also to you | Phil.3.15
then the lawless one will be r. | 2 Th.2.8
ready to be r. in the last time | 1 Pet.1.5
REVELATION
a light for r. to the Gentiles | Lk.2.32
according to the r. of the mystery | Rom.16.25
a r. . . . or an interpretation | 1 Cor.14.26
too elated by the abundance of r. | 2 Cor.12.7

came through a r. of Jesus Christ	Gal.1.12	Christ . . . though he was r., yet for	2 Cor.8.9
honor at the r. of Jesus Christ	1 Pet.1.7	God, who is r. in mercy, out of the	Eph.2.4
The r. of Jesus Christ, which God	Rev.1.1	who desire to be r. fall into	1 Tim.6.9
REVENUE		So will the r. man fade away in the	Jas.1.11
the royal r. will be impaired	Ezra 4.13	both r. and poor, both free and	Rev.13.16
than great r. with injustice	Pr.16.8	**RICHES**	
your r. was the grain of Shihor	Is.23.3	Both r. and honor come from thee	1 Chr.29.12
r. to whom r. is due	Rom.13.7	if r. increase, set not your heart	Ps.62.10
REVERENCE (noun)		Wealth and r. are in his house	Ps.112.3
shall not pay r. to the gods of the	Jg.6.10	in her left hand are r. and honor	Pr.3.16
Be subject . . . out of r. for Christ	Eph.5.21	R. do not profit in the day of wrath	Pr.11.4
acceptable worship, with r. and awe	Heb.12.28	He who trusts in his r. will wither	Pr.11.28
yet do it with gentleness and r.	1 Pet.3.15	good name . . . rather than great r.	Pr.22.1
REVILE		for r. do not last for ever	Pr.27.24
You shall not r. God, nor curse a	Ex.22.28	give me neither poverty nor r.	Pr.30.8
when men r. you and persecute you	Mt.5.11	the delight in r. choke the word	Mt.13.22
when they exclude you and r. you	Lk.6.22	to make known the r. of his glory	Rom.9.23
When r., we bless; when persecuted	1 Cor.4.12	O the depth of the r. and wisdom	Rom.11.33
give the enemy no occasion to r. us	1 Tim.5.14	immeasurable r. of his grace in	Eph.2.7
those who r. your good behavior	1 Pet.3.16	the unsearchable r. of Christ	Eph.3.8
not afraid to r. the glorious ones	2 Pet.2.10	Your r. have rotted and your	Jas.5.2
REVILING (noun)		**RIDDLE**	
and be not dismayed at their r.	Is.51.7	Let me now put a r. to you	Jg.14.12
heard all the r. which you uttered	Ezek.35.12	she told the r. to her countrymen	Jg.14.17
of Moab and the r. of the Ammonites	Zeph.2.8	I will solve my r. to the music of	Ps.49.4
not return evil for evil or r. for r.	1 Pet.3.9	propound a r. . . . speak an allegory	Ezek.17.2
REVIVE		to . . . explain r., and solve problems	Dan.5.12
Wilt thou not r. us again, that thy	Ps.85.6	**RIDE**	
r. me according to thy word	Ps.119.25	Solomon to r. on King David's mule	1 Kg.1.38
to r. the heart of the contrite	Is.57.15	So he had him r. in his chariot	2 Kg.10.16
After two days he will r. us	Hos.6.2	In your majesty r. forth victoriously	Ps.45.4
commandment came, sin r. and I died	Rom.7.9	didst let men r. over our heads	Ps.66.12
you have r. your concern for me	Phil.4.10	to him who r. in the heavens	Ps.68.33
REWARD (noun)		I will make you r. upon the heights	Is.58.14
in keeping them there is great r.	Ps.19.11	**RIDER**	
The r. for humility and fear of the	Pr.22.4	horse and his r. he has thrown into	Ex.15.1
behold, his r. is with him, and his	Is.40.10	both r. and horse lay stunned	Ps.76.6
who love you, what r. have you?	Mt.5.46	overthrow the chariots and their r.	Hag.2.22
he shall not lose his r.	Mt.10.42	white horse, and its r. had a bow	Rev.6.2
your r. is great in heaven	Lk.6.23	**RIGHT (adjective)**	
survives, he will receive a r.	1 Cor.3.14	Thy r. hand, O LORD, glorious in	Ex.15.6
REWARD (verb)		Let us choose what is r.; let us	Job 34.4
may the LORD r. you with good	1 Sam.24.19	in thy r. hand are pleasures for	Ps.16.11
The LORD r. me according to my	Ps.18.20	the precepts of the LORD are r.	Ps.19.8
So they r. me evil for good	Ps.109.5	He leads the humble in what is r.	Ps.25.9
and the LORD will r. you	Pr.25.22	put a new and r. spirit within me	Ps.51.10
who sees in secret will r. you	Mt.6.4	His r. hand and his holy arm have	Ps.98.1
God . . . r. those who seek him	Heb.11.6	Sit at my r. hand, till I make your	Ps.110.1
RICH		a way which seems r. to a man	Pr.16.25
The LORD makes poor and makes r.	1 Sam.2.7	if any one strikes you on the r. cheek	Mt.5.39
The r. man had very many flocks	2 Sam.12.2	seated at the r. hand of Power	Mt.26.64
nor regards the r. more than the	Job 34.19	and cut off his r. ear	Lk.22.50
low and high, r. and poor together	Ps.49.2	your heart is not r. before God	Acts 8.21
The blessing of the LORD makes r.	Pr.10.22	at the r. time Christ died for the	Rom.5.6
the r. has many friends	Pr.14.20	I can will what is r., but I cannot	Rom.7.18
The r. and the poor meet together	Pr.22.2	gave . . . the r. hand of fellowship	Gal.2.9
A r. man is wise in his own eyes	Pr.28.11	he sat down at the r. hand of God	Heb.10.12
and with a r. man in his death	Is.53.9	in his r. hand he held seven stars	Rev.1.16
hard for a r. man to enter the	Mt.19.23	**RIGHT (noun)**	
came a r. man from Arimathea	Mt.27.57	does the Almighty pervert the r.?	Job 8.3
Many r. people put in large sums	Mk.12.41	God has taken away my r.	Job 34.5
the r. he has sent empty away	Lk.1.53	and your r. as the noonday	Ps.37.6
But woe to you that are r.	Lk.6.24	yet surely my r. is with the LORD	Is.49.4
The land of a r. man brought forth	Lk.12.16	Do we not have the r. to be	1 Cor.9.5
and is not r. toward God	Lk.12.21	we have not made use of this r.	1 Cor.9.12
The r. man also died and was buried	Lk.16.22		

but rejoices in the r. — 1 Cor.13.6
have the r. to the tree of life — Rev.22.14

RIGHTEOUS
find at Sodom fifty r. in the city — Gen.18.26
to David, "You are more r. than — 1 Sam.24.17
The r. see it and are glad — Job 22.19
How then can man be r. before God? — Job 25.4
the LORD knows the way of the r. — Ps.1.6
are destroyed, what can the r. do"? — Ps.11.3
eyes of the LORD are toward the r. — Ps.34.15
The r. shall see, and fear — Ps.52.6
Light dawns for the r., and joy — Ps.97.11
For the r. will never be moved — Ps.112.6
no man living is r. before thee — Ps.143.2
LORD does not let the r. go hungry — Pr.10.3
but the r. is established for ever — Pr.10.25
The r. is delivered from trouble — Pr.11.8
The thoughts of the r. are just — Pr.12.5
he hears the prayer of the r. — Pr.15.29
Be not r. overmuch, and do not make — Ec.7.16
by his knowledge shall the r. one — Is.53.11
I will cause a r. Branch to spring — Jer.33.15
But when a r. man turns away from — Ezek.18.24
Then the r. will shine like the sun — Mt.13.43
I have not come to call the r. — Lk.5.32
O r. Father, the world has not known — Jn.17.25
But you denied the Holy and R. One — Acts 3.14
The prayer of a r. man has great — Jas.5.16
eyes of the Lord are upon the r. — 1 Pet.3.12

RIGHTEOUSNESS
he reckoned it to him as r. — Gen.15.6
Not because of your r. or the — Dt.9.5
recompensed . . . according to my r. — 2 Sam.22.25
ascribe r. to my Maker — Job 36.3
He loves r. and justice — Ps.33.5
May he judge thy people with r. — Ps.72.2
r. and peace will kiss each other — Ps.85.10
his r. to children's children — Ps.103.17
Let thy priests be clothed with r. — Ps.132.9
The r. of the upright delivers them — Pr.11.6
R. exalts a nation, but sin is a — Pr.14.34
To do r. and justice is more — Pr.21.3
R. shall be the girdle of his waist — Is.11.5
Behold, a king will reign in r. — Is.32.1
the effect of r. will be peace — Is.32.17
He put on r. as a breastplate — Is.59.17
be called: 'The LORD is our r.' — Jer.23.6
to bring in everlasting r. — Dan.9.24
those who hunger and thirst for r. — Mt.5.6
unless your r. exceeds that of the — Mt.5.20
seek first his kingdom and his r. — Mt.6.33
of sin and of r. and of judgment — Jn.16.8
the r. of God has been manifested — Rom.3.21
God reckons r. apart from works — Rom.4.6
we might become the r. of God — 2 Cor.5.21
partnership have r. and iniquity? — 2 Cor.6.14
put on the breastplate of r. — Eph.6.14
loved r. and hated lawlessness — Heb.1.9
yields the peaceful fruit of r. to — Heb.12.11
the harvest of r. is sown in peace — Jas.3.18
might die to sin and live to r. — 1 Pet.2.24
a new earth in which r. dwells — 2 Pet.3.13
in r. he judges and makes war — Rev.19.11

RING
seal it with the king's r. — Est.8.8
Like a gold r. in a swine's snout — Pr.11.22

put a r. on his hand, and shoes — Lk.15.22
a man with gold r. and in fine — Jas.2.2

RISE
a scepter shall r. out of Israel — Num.24.17
from those who r. up against me — Ps.59.1
R. up, O judge of the earth — Ps.94.2
At midnight I r. to praise thee — Ps.119.62
Her children r. up and call her — Pr.31.28
your light r. in the darkness — Is.58.10
the sun of righteousness shall r. — Mal.4.2
For nation will r. against nation — Mt.24.7
after three days he will r. — Mk.10.34
r., take up your bed and go home — Lk.5.24
Nation will r. against nation — Lk.21.10
no prophet is to r. from Galilee — Jn.7.52
I know that he will r. again in the — Jn.11.24
the dead in Christ will r. first — 1 Th.4.16
morning star r. in your hearts — 2 Pet.1.19

RIVER
A r. flowed out of Eden to water — Gen.2.10
r. of Damascus, better than all — 2 Kg.5.12
There is a r. whose streams make — Ps.46.4
baptized by him in the r. Jordan — Mk.1.5
shall flow r. of living water — Jn.7.38
the r. of the water of life — Rev.22.1

ROAR
though its waters r. and foam — Ps.46.3
Let the sea r., and all that fills — Ps.98.7
The LORD will r. from on high — Jer.25.30
The LORD r. from Zion, and utters — Am.1.2
devil prowls around like a r. lion — 1 Pet.5.8

ROB
Do not r. the poor, because he is — Pr.22.22
Will man r. God? Yet you are — Mal.3.8
R. no one by violence or by false — Lk.3.14
who abhor idols, do you r. temples? — Rom.2.22

ROBBER
But you have made it a den of r. — Mk.11.17
Have you come out as against a r. — Mk.14.48
to Jericho, and he fell among r. — Lk.10.30
Now Barabbas was a r. — Jn.18.40
nor r. will inherit the kingdom — 1 Cor.6.10

ROBBERY
shall restore what he took by r. — Lev.6.4
set no vain hopes on r. — Ps.62.10
I the LORD love justice, I hate r. — Is.61.8
commits no r., but gives his — Ezek.18.16
gives back what he had taken by r. — Ezek.33.15

ROBE
he made him a long r. with sleeves — Gen.37.3
he has covered me with the r. of — Is.61.10
put a scarlet r. upon him — Mt.27.28
Bring quickly the best r. — Lk.15.22
crown of thorns and the purple r. — Jn.19.5
Who are these, clothed in white r. — Rev.7.13
He is clad in a r. dipped in blood — Rev.19.13

ROCK
struck the r. with his rod — Num.20.11
scoffed at the R. of his salvation — Dt.32.15
The LORD is my r., and my fortress — Ps.18.2
Be thou a r. of refuge for me — Ps.31.2
He only is my r. and my salvation — Ps.62.2
look to the r. from which you were — Is.51.1
hide it there in a cleft of the r. — Jer.13.4
who built his house upon the r. — Mt.7.24

some fell on the *r.*	Lk.8.6	If you really fulfil the *r.* law	Jas.2.8
the *R.* was Christ	1 Cor.10.4	a *r.* priesthood, a holy nation	1 Pet.2.9

ROD

who have not yet received *r.* power — Rev.17.12

But Aaron's *r.* swallowed up their	Ex.7.12	**RUIN** (noun)	
shall break them with a *r.* of iron	Ps.2.9	Let *r.* come upon them unawares	Ps.35.8
thy *r.* and thy staff, they comfort	Ps.23.4	they have laid Jerusalem in *r.*	Ps.79.1
He who spares the *r.* hates his son	Pr.13.24	way of the wicked he brings to *r.*	Ps.146.9
if you beat him with a *r.*, he will	Pr.23.13	but a prating fool will come to *r.*	Pr.10.8
I said, "I see a *r.* of almond."	Jer.1.11	A foolish son is *r.* to his father	Pr.19.13
Aaron's *r.* that budded, and the	Heb.9.4	For vast as the sea is your *r.*	Lam.2.13
he measured the city with his *r.*	Rev.21.16	A *r.*, *r.*, *r.* I will make it	Ezek.21.27

ROLL (verb)

Jerusalem shall become a heap of *r.* — Mic.3.12

the skies *r.* up like a scroll	Is.34.4	a day of *r.* and devastation	Zeph.1.15
But let justice *r.* down like waters	Am.5.24	in their paths are *r.* and misery	Rom.3.16
Who will *r.* away the stone for us	Mk.16.3	plunge men into *r.* and destruction	1 Tim.6.9
like a mantle thou wilt *r.* them up	Heb.1.12	**RULE** (noun)	
like a scroll that is *r.* up	Rev.6.14	we might share the *r.* with you	1 Cor.4.8

ROMAN

This is my *r.* in all the churches — 1 Cor.7.17

the *R.* will come and destroy both	Jn.11.48	be upon all who walk by this *r.*	Gal.6.16
of Macedonia, and a *R.* colony	Acts 16.12	the head of all *r.* and authority	Col.2.10
men who are *R.* citizens, and have	Acts 16.37	to keep these *r.* without favor	1 Tim.5.21
scourge a man who is a *R.* citizen	Acts 22.25	**RULE** (verb)	
learned that he was a *R.* citizen	Acts 23.27	the greater light to *r.* the day	Gen.1.16

ROME

Acts 2.10; 28.16; Rom.1.7; 2 Tim.1.17

		husband, and he shall *r.* over you	Gen.3.16
ROOM		his kingdom *r.* over all	Ps.103.19
go into your *r.* and shut the door	Mt.6.6	stars to *r.* over the night	Ps.136.9
Teacher says, Where is my guest *r.*	Mk.14.14	The hand of the diligent will *r.*	Pr.12.24
In my Father's house are many *r.*	Jn.14.2	he who rises to *r.* the Gentiles	Rom.15.12
they went up to the upper *r.*	Acts 1.13	peace of Christ *r.* in your hearts	Col.3.15
prepare a guest *r.* for me	Philem.22	Let the elders who *r.* well be	1 Tim.5.17

ROOT (noun)

he will *r.* them with a rod of iron — Rev.19.15

the *r.* of the righteous stands firm	Pr.12.12	**RULER**	
Judah shall again take *r.* downward	Is.37.31	I will make him *r.* all the days	1 Kg.11.34
like a *r.* out of dry ground	Is.53.2	A *r.* who lacks understanding is a	Pr.28.16
axe is laid to the *r.* of the trees	Mt.3.10	Many seek the favor of a *r.*	Pr.29.26
they have no *r.* in themselves	Mk.4.17	is our judge, the LORD is our *r.*	Is.33.22
if the *r.* is holy, so are the	Rom.11.16	a *r.* who will govern my people Israel	Mt.2.6
of money is the *r.* of all evils	1 Tim.6.10	said to the *r.* of the synagogue	Mk.5.36
the *R.* of David, has conquered	Rev.5.5	Nicodemus, a *r.* of the Jews	Jn.3.1

ROPE

the *r.* of this world is coming — Jn.14.30

Can you put a *r.* in his nose	Job 41.2	in ignorance, as did also your *r.*	Acts 3.17
instead of a girdle, a *r.*	Is.3.24	For *r.* are not a terror to good	Rom.13.3
who draw sin as with cart *r.*	Is.5.18	None of the *r.* of this age	1 Cor.2.8
to Jeremiah in the cistern by *r.*	Jer.38.11	world *r.* of this present darkness	Eph.6.12

ROT

submissive to *r.* and authorities — Tit.3.1

but the name of the wicked will *r.*	Pr.10.7	Jesus Christ . . . the *r.* of kings on earth	Rev.1.5
passion makes the bones *r.*	Pr.14.30	**RUMOR**	
All the host of heaven shall *r.* away	Is.34.4	he shall hear a *r.* and return to	2 Kg.19.7
tongues shall *r.* in their mouths	Zech.14.12	We have heard a *r.* of it with our	Job 28.22
Your riches have *r.* and your	Jas.5.2	Hark, a *r.*! Behold, it comes	Jer.10.22

ROUGH

you will hear of wars and *r.* of wars — Mt.24.6

level, and the *r.* places a plain	Is.40.4	**RUN**	
the *r.* places into level ground	Is.42.16	*r.* in the way of thy commandments	Ps.119.32
the *r.* ways shall be made smooth	Lk.3.5	their feet *r.* to evil, and they make	Pr.1.16

ROUTED

All streams *r.* to the sea, but the — Ec.1.7

the LORD *r.* the Egyptians in the	Ex.14.27	that they may *r.* after strong drink	Is.5.11
And the LORD *r.* Sisera and all his	Jg.4.15	Many shall *r.* to and fro	Dan.12.4
they were *r.* before Israel	1 Sam.7.10	prize? So *r.* that you may obtain	1 Cor.9.24
flashed . . . lightnings, and *r.* them	Ps.18.14	lest somehow I . . . had *r.* in vain	Gal.2.2

ROYAL

let us *r.* with perseverance the — Heb.12.1

Your *r.* scepter is a scepter of	Ps.45.6	**RUSH** (verb)	
thy righteousness to the *r.* son	Ps.72.1	an evil spirit . . . *r.* upon Saul	1 Sam.18.10
a *r.* diadem in the hand of your God	Is.62.3	*r.* to and fro through the squares	Nah.2.4
spread his *r.* canopy over them	Jer.43.10	the whole herd *r.* down the steep	Mt.8.32
the LORD, and shall bear *r.* honor	Zech.6.13	he called for lights and *r.* in	Acts 16.29

RUST (noun)

Its *r*. is your filthy lewdness	Ezek.24.13
earth, where moth and *r*. consume	Mt.6.19
their *r*. will be evidence against	Jas.5.3

RUTHLESS

r. men seek my life; they do not	Ps.54.3
a band of *r*. men seek my life	Ps.86.14
redeem you from the grasp of the *r*.	Jer.15.21
foolish, faithless, heartless, *r*.	Rom.1.31

SABBATH

The LORD has given you the *s*.	Ex.16.29
Remember the *s*. day, to keep it holy	Ex.20.8
The *s*. of the land shall provide	Lev.25.6
On the *s*. day two male lambs	Num.28.9
It is neither new moon nor *s*.	2 Kg.4.23
do not bear a burden on the *s*. day	Jer.17.21
to keep the *s*. day holy, and not	Jer.17.27
on the *s*. day it shall be opened	Ezek.46.1
And the *s*., that we may offer wheat	Am.8.5
through the grainfields on the *s*.	Mt.12.1
the Son of man is lord of the *s*.	Mt.12.8
it is lawful to do good on the *s*.	Mt.12.12
The *s*. was made for man, not man for	Mk.2.27
And when the *s*. was past, Mary	Mk.16.1
what is not lawful to do on the *s*.?	Lk.6.2
because Jesus had healed on the *s*.	Lk.13.14
On the *s*. they rested according to	Lk.23.56
you circumcise a man upon the *s*.	Jn.7.22
Now it was a *s*. day when Jesus made	Jn.9.14
(for that *s*. was a high day)	Jn.19.31
a *s*. day's journey away	Acts 1.12
prophets which are read every *s*.	Acts 13.27
is read every *s*. in the synagogues	Acts 15.21
argued in the synagogue every *s*.	Acts 18.4
a festival or a new moon or a *s*.	Col.2.16
there remains a *s*. rest for the	Heb.4.9

SACKCLOTH

put *s*. upon his loins, and mourned	Gen.37.34
assembled with fasting and in *s*.	Neh.9.1
Mordecai . . . put on *s*. and ashes	Est.4.1
I have sewed *s*. upon my skin	Job 16.15
thou hast loosed my *s*. and girded me	Ps.30.11
I wore *s*., I afflicted myself with	Ps.35.13
in the streets they gird on *s*.	Is.15.3
to spread *s*. and ashes under him	Is.58.5
Gird yourselves with *s*., lament	Jer.49.3
with fasting and *s*. and ashes	Dan.9.3
put on *s*., from the greatest of	Jon.3.5
repented long ago in *s*. and ashes	Mt.11.21
the sun became black as *s*.	Rev.6.12

SACRED

make of these a *s*. anointing oil	Ex.30.25
fields . . . shall be *s*. to the LORD	Jer.31.40
her priests profane what is *s*.	Zeph.3.4
or the altar that makes the gift *s*.?	Mt.23.19
acquainted with the *s*. writings	2 Tim.3.15

SACRIFICE (noun)

Jacob offered a *s*. on the mountain	Gen.31.54
It is the *s*. of the LORD's passover	Ex.12.27
you offer a *s*. of peace offerings	Lev.19.5
offer to the LORD the yearly *s*.	1 Sam.1.21
to obey is better than *s*.	1 Sam.15.22
The *s*. acceptable to God is a broken	Ps.51.17
s. of the wicked is an abomination	Pr.21.27
They love *s*. . . . but the LORD	Hos.8.13

'I desire mercy, and not *s*.'	Mt. 9.13
wanted to offer *s*. with the people	Acts 14.13
present your bodies as a living *s*.	Rom.12.1
This has been offered in *s*.	1 Cor.10.28
a fragrant offering and *s*. to God	Eph.5.2
put away sin by the *s*. of himself	Heb.9.26
a more acceptable *s*. than Cain	Heb.11.4
offer up a *s*. of praise to God	Heb.13.15
such *s*. are pleasing to God	Heb.13.16
offer spiritual *s*. acceptable to	1 Pet.2.5

SACRIFICE (verb)

for we shall *s*. to the LORD our God	Ex.8.26
freewill offering I will *s*. to thee	Ps.54.6
Therefore he *s*. to his net and	Hab.1.16
already on the point of being *s*.	2 Tim.4.6

SACRIFICIAL

let their *s*. feasts be a trap	Ps.69.22
Can vows and *s*. flesh avert your	Jer.11.15
share in the *s*. offerings?	1 Cor.9.13
the *s*. offering of your faith	Phil.2.17

SAD

her countenance was no longer *s*.	1 Sam.1.18
Why should not my face be *s*.	Neh.2.3
I will put off my *s*. countenance	Job 9.27
Even in laughter the heart is *s*.	Pr.14.13
when he heard this he became *s*.	Lk.18.23
they stood still, looking *s*.	Lk.24.17

SADDUCEES

their controversies with Jesus, Mt.16.1; 22.23; Mk.12.18; Lk.20.27; with the apostles, Acts 4.1; with Paul, Acts 23.6; their beliefs, Mt.22.23; Mk.12.18; Acts 23.8

SADNESS

nothing else but *s*. of the heart	Neh.2.2
by *s*. of countenance the heart is	Ec.7.3

SAFE

I shall be *s*., though I walk in	Dt.29.19
God . . . has made my way *s*.	2 Sam.22.33
Their houses are *s*. from fear	Job 21.9
Oh to be *s*. under the shelter of	Ps.61.4
that I may be *s*. and have regard	Ps.119.117
righteous man runs into it and is *s*.	Pr.18.10
he who trusts in the LORD is *s*.	Pr.29.25
not irksome to me, and is *s*. for you	Phil.3.1

SAFELY

And Jacob came *s*. to the city of	Gen.33.18
He pursues them and passes on *s*.	Is.41.3
seize him and lead him away *s*.	Mk.14.44
charging the jailer to keep them *s*.	Acts 16.23
bring him *s*. to Felix the governor	Acts 23.24

SAFETY

The beloved . . . dwells in *s*. by him	Dt.33.12
those who mourn are lifted to *s*.	Job 5.11
thou . . . O LORD, makest me dwell in *s*.	Ps.4.8
He led them in *s*., so that they	Ps.78.53
Flee for *s*., O people of Benjamin	Jer.6.1
I will make them dwell in *s*.	Jer.32.37
I will make you lie down in *s*.	Hos.2.18

SAINT

As for the *s*. in the land, they are	Ps.16.3
O you his *s*., and give thanks to	Ps.30.4
he preserves the lives of his *s*.	Ps.97.10
Precious . . . is the death of his *s*.	Ps.116.15
the *s*. of the Most High shall	Dan.7.18
much evil he has done to thy *s*.	Acts 9.13

also to the *s.* that lived at Lydda — Acts 9.32
in Rome, who are called to be *s.* — Rom.1.7
Contribute to the needs of the *s.* — Rom.12.13
the *s.* will judge the world — 1 Cor.6.2
to the service of the *s.* — 1 Cor.16.15
glorious inheritance in the *s.* — Eph.1.18
the *s.* and members of the household — Eph.2.19
among you, as is fitting among *s.* — Eph.5.3
Greet every *s.* in Christ Jesus — Phil.4.21
the inheritance of the *s.* in light — Col.1.12
our Lord Jesus with all his *s.* — 1 Th.3.13
that day to be glorified in his *s.* — 2 Th.1.10
washed the feet of the *s.* — 1 Tim.5.10
hearts of the *s.* have been refreshed — Philem.7
faith . . . once for all delivered to the *s.* — Jude 3
which are the prayers of the *s.* — Rev.5.8
thy servants, the prophets and *s.* — Rev.11.18
make war on the *s.* and to conquer — Rev.13.7
is the righteous deeds of the *s.* — Rev.19.8
the Lord Jesus be with all the *s.* — Rev.22.21

SAKE
Are you jealous for my *s.?* — Num.11.29
show . . . kindness for Jonathan's *s.?* — 2 Sam.9.1
for David's *s.* the LORD . . . gave — 1 Kg.15.4
of righteousness for his name's *s.* — Ps.23.3
for the *s.* of thy steadfast love — Ps.115.1
persecuted for righteousness' *s.* — Mt.5.10
loses his life for my *s.* will find — Mt.10.39
for the *s.* of your tradition? — Mt.15.3
for the *s.* of the elect, whom he — Mk.13.20
for your *s.* I am glad that I was — Jn.11.15
for their *s.* I consecrate myself — Jn.17.19
accursed . . . for the *s.* of my brethren — Rom.9.3
but also for the *s.* of conscience — Rom.13.5
We are fools for Christ's *s.* — 1 Cor.4.10
do it all for the *s.* of the gospel — 1 Cor.9.23
For our *s.* he made him to be sin — 2 Cor.5.21
For the *s.* of Christ, then, I am — 2 Cor.12.10
afflictions for the *s.* of his body — Col.1.24
for love's *s.* I prefer to appeal — Philem.9
suffer for righteousness' *s.* — 1 Pet.3.14
your sins are forgiven for his *s.* — 1 Jn.2.12
bearing up for my name's *s.* — Rev.2.3

SALE
within a whole year after its *s.* — Lev.25.29
from the *s.* of his patrimony — Dt.18.8
yourselves for *s.* to your enemies — Dt.28.68
that we may offer wheat for *s.* — Am.8.5

SALEM
Gen.14.18; Ps.76.2; Heb.7.1

SALT
and she became a pillar of *s.* — Gen.19.26
the whole land brimstone and *s.* — Dt.29.23
his sons by a covenant of *s.* — 2 Chr.13.5
is tasteless be eaten without *s.* — Job 6.6
shall sprinkle *s.* upon them — Ezek.43.24
Have *s.* in yourselves, and be at — Mk.9.50
S. is good; but if *s.* has lost — Lk.14.34
your speech . . . seasoned with *s.* — Col.4.6
No more can *s.* water yield fresh — Jas.3.12

SALUTE
And thus you shall *s.* him — 1 Sam.25.6
If you meet any one, do not *s.* him — 2 Kg.4.29
And if you *s.* only your brethren — Mt.5.47
As you enter the house, *s.* it — Mt.10.12

they began to *s.* him, "Hail, King — Mk.15.18
and *s.* no one on the road — Lk.10.4

SALVATION
I wait for thy *s.,* O LORD — Gen.49.18
see the *s.* of the LORD, which he — Ex.14.13
my song, and he has become my *s.* — Ex.15.2
scoffed at the Rock of his *s.* — Dt.32.15
be my God, the rock of my *s.* — 2 Sam.22.47
Tell of his *s.* from day to day — 1 Chr.16.23
my heart shall rejoice in thy *s.* — Ps.13.5
for thou art the God of my *s.* — Ps.25.5
The LORD is my light and my *s.* — Ps.27.1
The *s.* of the righteous is from the — Ps.37.39
Restore to me the joy of thy *s.* — Ps.51.12
O God of our *s.,* who art the hope — Ps.65.5
Our God is a God of *s.;* and to God — Ps.68.20
tell . . . of thy deeds of *s.* all the — Ps.71.15
working *s.* in the midst of the earth — Ps.74.12
Surely his *s.* is at hand for those — Ps.85.9
joyful noise to the rock of our *s.* — Ps.95.1
tell of his *s.* from day to day — Ps.96.2
I will lift up the cup of *s.* and — Ps.116.13
he has become my *s.* — Ps.118.14
My soul languishes for thy *s.* — Ps.119.81
S. is far from the wicked, for — Ps.119.155
Behold, God is my *s.;* I will trust — Is.12.2
draw water from the wells of *s.* — Is.12.3
our *s.* in the time of trouble — Is.33.2
by the LORD with everlasting *s.* — Is.45.17
in a day of *s.* I have helped you — Is.49.8
LORD our God is the *s.* of Israel — Jer.3.23
wait quietly for the *s.* of the LORD — Lam.3.26
I will joy in the God of my *s.* — Hab.3.18
has raised up a horn of *s.* for us — Lk.1.69
for mine eyes have seen thy *s.* — Lk.2.30
Today *s.* has come to this house — Lk.19.9
for *s.* is from the Jews — Jn.4.22
And there is *s.* in no one else — Acts 4.12
power of God for *s.* to every one — Rom.1.16
s. is nearer to us now than when — Rom.13.11
behold, now is the day of *s.* — 2 Cor.6.2
heard . . . the gospel of your *s.* — Eph.1.13
And take the helmet of *s.* — Eph.6.17
work out your own *s.* with fear and — Phil.2.12
destined us . . . to obtain *s.* through — 1 Th.5.9
may obtain the *s.* which in Christ — 2 Tim.2.10
for the sake of those who . . . obtain *s.?* — Heb.1.14
if we neglect such a great *s.?* — Heb.2.3
eternal *s.* to all who obey him — Heb.5.9
better things that belong to *s.* — Heb.6.9
you obtain the *s.* of your souls — 1 Pet.1.9
that by it you may grow up to *s.* — 1 Pet.2.2
to write to you of our common *s.* — Jude 3
S. belongs to our God who sits — Rev.7.10

SAMARIA
(1) the district between Judea and Galilee,
Lk.17.11; Jn.4; (2) the city built by Omri,
king of Israel, 1 Kg.16.24; 20.1; 2 Kg.6.24;
destroyed by the Assyrians, 722–721 B.C., and
rebuilt by Herod

SAMARITAN
high places which the *S.* had made — 2 Kg.17.29
But a *S.,* as he journeyed, came to — Lk.10.33
Now he was a *S.* — Lk.17.16
For Jews have no dealings with *S.* — Jn.4.9
gospel to many villages of the *S.* — Acts 8.25

SAMSON
Jg.13–16; delivered up to Philistines, Jg.16.21;
his death, Jg.16.30
SAMUEL
born, and presented to the Lord, 1 Sam.1.19–20,
26–28; the Lord speaks to, 1 Sam.3.11; judges
Israel, 1 Sam.7; 8.1; Acts 13.20; anoints Saul
king, 1 Sam.10.1; rebukes Saul for sin, 1
Sam.13.13; 15.16; anoints David, 1 Sam.16;
his death, 1 Sam.25.1; 28.3; his spirit consulted
by Saul, 1 Sam.28.12; as a prophet, Acts 3.24
SANCTIFICATION
members to righteousness for s.   Rom.6.19
He is . . . righteousness and s.   1 Cor.1.30
your s.: that you abstain from   1 Th.4.3
through s. by the Spirit   2 Th.2.13
SANCTIFY
it shall be s. by my glory   Ex.29.43
I the LORD, who s. you, am holy   Lev.21.8
said to the people, "S. yourselves   Jos.3.5
the Levites s. themselves to   1 Chr.15.14
And the priests s. themselves in   2 Chr.30.24
they will s. the Holy One of Jacob   Is.29.23
Those who s. and purify themselves   Is.66.17
S. them in the truth; thy word is   Jn.17.17
those who are s. by faith in me   Acts 26.18
acceptable, s. by the Holy Spirit   Rom.15.16
to those s. in Christ Jesus   1 Cor.1.2
you were s., you were justified   1 Cor.6.11
he might s. her, having cleansed   Eph.5.26
God of peace himself s. you wholly   1 Th.5.23
those who are s. have all one origin   Heb.2.11
s. by the Spirit for obedience   1 Pet.1.2
SANCTUARY
the s., O LORD, which thy hands have   Ex.15.17
And let them make me a s.   Ex.25.8
reverence my s.: I am the LORD   Lev.19.30
May he send you help from the s.   Ps.20.2
I have looked upon thee in the s.   Ps.63.2
of my God, my King, into the s.   Ps.68.24
Terrible is God in his s.   Ps.68.35
until I went into the s. of God   Ps.73.17
built his s. like the high heavens   Ps.78.69
strength and beauty are in his s.   Ps.96.6
Praise God in his s.; praise him in   Ps.150.1
he will become a s., and a stone   Is.8.14
to beautify the place of my s.   Is.60.13
beginning is the place of our s.   Jer.17.12
scorned his altar, disowned his s.   Lam.2.7
I have been a s. to them   Ezek.11.16
the place of his s. was overthrown   Dan.8.11
at Bethel, for it is the king's s.   Am.7.13
between the s. and the altar   Mt.23.35
copy and shadow of the heavenly s.   Heb.8.5
to enter the s. by the blood of   Heb.10.19
SAND
as the s. which is on the seashore   Gen.22.17
descendants as the s. of the sea   Gen.32.12
be heavier than the s. of the sea   Job 6.3
s. is weighty, but a fool's   Pr.27.3
shall be like the s. of the sea   Hos.1.10
who built his house upon the s.   Mt.7.26
sons of Israel be as the s. of the sea Rom.9.27
grains of s. by the seashore   Heb.11.12
SANDAL
pull his s. off his foot   Dt.25.9

drew off his s. and gave it to the   Ru.4.7
two tunics, nor s., nor a staff   Mt.10.10
to wear s. and not put on two tunics   Mk.6.9
with no purse or bag or s.   Lk.22.35
thong of whose s. I am not worthy   Jn.1.27
SANG
the people of Israel s. this song to   Ex.15.1
And Miriam s. to them: "Sing to the   Ex.15.21
they s. responsively, praising   Ezra 3.11
the singers s. with Jezrahiah   Neh.12.42
when the morning stars s. together   Job 38.7
they s. a new song, saying, "Worthy   Rev.5.9
SAPPHIRE
as it were a pavement of s. stone   Ex.24.10
Its stones are the place of s.   Job 28.6
the beauty of their form was like s.   Lam.4.7
above them something like a s.   Ezek.10.1
the color of fire and of s.   Rev.9.17
the second s., the third agate   Rev.21.19
SARAH
Gen.17.15; 18.10; 20.2; 21.1–6; 23.1; Heb.11.11
SATAN
S. stood up against Israel   1 Chr.21.1
LORD said to S., "Whence have you   Job 1.7
if S. casts out S., he is divided   Mt.12.26
rebuked Peter . . . "Get behind me, S. Mk.8.33
I saw S. fall like lightning from   Lk.10.18
Then S. entered into Judas   Lk.22.3
why has S. filled your heart to lie   Acts 5.3
from the power of S. to God   Acts 26.18
will soon crush S. under your feet   Rom.16.20
you are to deliver this man to S.   1 Cor.5.5
keep S. from gaining the advantage   2 Cor.2.11
a messenger of S., to harass me   2 Cor.12.7
the activity of S. . . . with all power 2 Th.2.9
whom I have delivered to S.   1 Tim.1.20
some call the deep things of S.   Rev.2.24
S. will be loosed from his prison   Rev.20.7
SATISFY
you shall eat, and not be s.   Lev.26.26
I shall be s. with beholding thy   Ps.17.15
The afflicted shall eat and be s.   Ps.22.26
with honey . . . I would s. you   Ps.81.16
S. us in the morning with thy   Ps.90.14
With long life I will s. him   Ps.91.16
Sheol and Abaddon are never s.   Pr.27.20
see . . . travail of his soul and be s. Is.53.11
labor for that which does not s.?   Is.55.2
shall be s. with my goodness   Jer.31.14
They shall eat, but not be s.   Hos.4.10
righteousness, for they shall be s.   Mt.5.6
And they all ate and were s.   Mt.15.37
show us the Father . . . we shall be s. Jn.14.8
SATYR
no more slay their sacrifices for s.   Lev.17.7
appointed . . . priests . . . for the s. 2 Chr.11.15
the s. shall cry to his fellow   Is.34.14
SAUL
(1) king of Israel, his parentage, anointing by
Samuel, prophesying, and acknowledgment
as king, 1 Sam.9–10; his disobedience, and
rejection by God, 1 Sam.14.31–15.35; possessed
by an evil spirit, quieted by David, 1 Sam.16.14,
15,23; favors David, 1 Sam.18.5; seeks to kill
him, 1 Sam.18.10–11; pursues him, 1 Sam.20;
23–24; 26; inquires of the witch of Endor, 1

Sam.28.7; his ruin and suicide, 1 Sam.28.15; 31; 1 Chr.10; his posterity, 1 Chr.8.33; (2) of Tarsus, *see* PAUL

SAVE

s. us, and help us; for all the	Jos.10.6
said, "How can this man s. us?"	1 Sam.10.27
S. me, O God, by thy name	Ps.54.1
call upon God; and the LORD will s.	Ps.55.16
S. us, we beseech thee, O LORD	Ps.118.25
I am thine, s. me; for I have	Ps.119.94
I will s. the lame and gather	Zeph.3.19
to sink he cried out, "Lord, s. me."	Mt.14.30
For whoever would s. his life will	Mt.16.25
it in three days, s. yourself	Mt.27.40
to s. life or to kill?" But they were	Mk.3.4
He s. others; he cannot s. himself	Mk.15.31
to s. life or to destroy it?	Lk.6.9
s. me from this hour'? No, for this	Jn.12.27
day by day those who were being s.	Acts 2.47
among men by which we must be s.	Acts 4.12
Men, what must I do to be s.?	Acts 16.30
shall we be s. by his life	Rom.5.10
For in this hope we were s.	Rom.8.24
only a remnant of them will be s.	Rom.9.27
confesses with his lips . . . so is s.	Rom.10.10
and so all Israel will be s.	Rom.11.26
that his spirit may be s. in	1 Cor.5.5
(by grace you have been s.)	Eph.2.5
came into the world to s. sinners	1 Tim.1.15
The Lord will . . . s. me for his	2 Tim.4.18
the . . . word . . . is able to s. your souls	Jas.1.21
Can his faith s. him?	Jas.2.14

SAVIOR

the LORD gave Israel a s.	2 Kg.13.5
They forgot God, their S., who	Ps.106.21
the Holy One of Israel, your S.	Is.43.3
know that I am the LORD your S.	Is.49.26
my spirit rejoices in God my S.	Lk.1.47
to you is born this day . . . a S.	Lk.2.11
at his right hand as Leader and S.	Acts 5.31
God has brought to Israel a S.	Acts 13.23
as Christ . . . is himself its S.	Eph.5.23
is the S. of all men, especially	1 Tim.4.10
appearing of our S. Christ Jesus	2 Tim.1.10
adorn the doctrine of God our S.	Tit.2.10
our great God and S. Jesus Christ	Tit.2.13
through Jesus Christ our S.	Tit.3.6
our God and S. Jesus Christ	2 Pet.1.1
the commandment of the Lord and S.	2 Pet.3.2
our Lord and S. Jesus Christ	2 Pet.3.18
his Son as the S. of the world	1 Jn.4.14
our S. through Jesus Christ our	Jude 25

SAYINGS

I will utter dark s. from of old	Ps.78.2
These also are s. of the wise	Pr.24.23
The s. of the wise are like goads	Ec.12.11
when Jesus finished these s.	Mt.7.28
If any one hears my s. and does	Jn.12.47

SCALES

in the waters that has fins and s.	Lev.11.9
just balance and s. are the LORD's	Pr.16.11
weighed the mountains in s.	Is.40.12
something like s. fell from his eyes	Acts 9.18
They had s. like iron breastplates	Rev.9.9

SCARLET

bound on his hand a s. thread	Gen.38.28

blue and purple and s. stuff	Ex.25.4
bind this s. cord in the window	Jos.2.18
though your sins are like s.	Is.1.18
and put a s. robe upon him	Mt.27.28
with water and s. wool and hyssop	Heb.9.19
a woman sitting on a s. beast	Rev.17.3

SCATTER

the LORD s. them abroad from there	Gen.11.8
So the people were s. abroad	Ex.5.12
I will s. you among the nations	Lev.26.33
God will s. the bones of the ungodly	Ps.53.5
Let God arise, let his enemies be s.	Ps.68.1
all evildoers shall be s.	Ps.92.9
and all their flock is s.	Jer.10.21
I will s. you like chaff driven by	Jer.13.24
that the sheep may be s.	Zech.13.7
the sheep of the flock will be s.	Mt.26.31
has s. the proud in the imagination	Lk.1.51
children of God who are s. abroad	Jn.11.52
all who followed him were s.	Acts 5.37

SCEPTER

The s. shall not depart from Judah	Gen.49.10
a s. shall rise out of Israel	Num.24.17
held out the golden s. to Esther	Est.8.4
Your royal s. is a s. of equity	Ps.45.6
How the mighty s. is broken	Jer.48.17
righteous s. is the s. of thy kingdom	Heb.1.8

SCOFF

s. at the Rock of his salvation	Dt.32.15
They s. and speak with malice	Ps.73.8
remember how the impious s. at thee	Ps.74.22
Now therefore do not s., lest your	Is.28.22
heard all this, and they s. at him	Lk.16.14
but the rulers s. at him	Lk.23.35

SCOFFER

nor sits in the seat of s.	Ps.1.1
How long will s. delight in their	Pr.1.22
"S." is the name of the proud	Pr.21.24
Drive out a s., and strife will go	Pr.22.10
hear . . . you s., who rule this people	Is.28.14
Behold, you s., and wonder	Acts 13.41
s. will come in the last days	2 Pet.3.3
In the last time there will be s.	Jude 18

SCORN (noun)

I am the s. of all my adversaries	Ps.31.11
derision and s. of those about us	Ps.44.13
the LORD is to them an object of s.	Jer.6.10
shall bear the s. of the peoples	Mic.6.16

SCORPION

serpents and s. and thirsty ground	Dt.8.15
to tread upon serpents and s.	Lk.10.19
asks for an egg, will give him a s.?	Lk.11.12
was like the torture of a s.	Rev.9.5

SCOURGE (verb)

some you will s. in your synagogues	Mt.23.34
having s. Jesus, he delivered him	Mk.15.15
they will s. him and kill him	Lk.18.33
Is it lawful . . . to s. a . . . Roman	Acts 22.25

SCRIBE

a man of understanding and a s.	1 Chr.27.32
Shimshai the s. wrote a letter	Ezra 4.8
Ezra the s. stood on a wooden pulpit	Neh.8.4
and gave it to Baruch the s.	Jer.36.32
a s. came up and said to him	Mt.8.19
Therefore every s. who has been	Mt.13.52
teaching he said, "Beware of the s.	Mk.12.38

SCRIPTURE (continued)

Beware of the *s.*, who like to go	Lk.20.46
elders and *s.* were gathered	Acts 4.5
Where is the *s.*?	1 Cor.1.20

SCRIPTURE

Today this *s.* has been fulfilled	Lk.4.21
this *s.* must be fulfilled	Lk.22.37
Has not the *s.* said that the Christ	Jn.7.42
it is that the *s.* may be fulfilled	Jn.13.18
This was to fulfil the *s.*	Jn.19.24
for as yet they did not know the *s.*	Jn.20.9
the *s.* had to be fulfilled	Acts 1.16
the *s.* which he was reading was	Acts 8.32
examining the *s.* daily to see if	Acts 17.11
showing by the *s.* that the Christ	Acts 18.28
For what does the *s.* say?	Rom.4.3
may learn . . . to live according to *s.*	1 Cor.4.6
And the *s.*, foreseeing that God	Gal.3.8
attend to the public reading of *s.*	1 Tim.4.13
All *s.* is inspired by God	2 Tim.3.16
no prophecy of *s.* is a matter of	2 Pet.1.20

SCROLL

a *s.* was found on which this was	Ezra 6.2
the skies roll up like a *s.*	Is.34.4
Take a *s.* and write on it all the	Jer.36.2
I wrote them with ink on the *s.*	Jer.36.18
and saw, and behold, a flying *s.*	Zech.5.1
on the throne a *s.* written within	Rev.5.1
sky vanished like a *s.* that is rolled	Rev.6.14
He had a little *s.* open in his hand	Rev.10.2

SEA

dominion over the fish of the *s.*	Gen.1.26
LORD drove the *s.* back by a strong	Ex.14.21
didst divide the *s.* before them	Neh.9.11
By his power he stilled the *s.*	Job 26.12
Or who shut in the *s.* with doors	Job 38.8
He turned the *s.* into dry land	Ps.66.6
May he have dominion from *s.* to *s.*	Ps.72.8
Thou dost rule the raging of the *s.*	Ps.89.9
mightier than the waves of the *s.*	Ps.93.4
The *s.* is his, for he made it	Ps.95.5
Israel be as the sand of the *s.*	Is.10.22
by my rebuke I dry up the *s.*	Is.50.2
who brought up out of the *s.* the	Is.63.11
Your branches passed over the *s.*	Jer.48.32
our sins into the depths of the *s.*	Mic.7.19
He rebukes the *s.* and makes it dry	Nah.1.4
he . . . dwelt in Capernaum by the *s.*	Mt.4.13
As he walked by the *S.* of Galilee	Mt.4.18
he . . . rebuked the winds and the *s.*	Mt.8.26
of the house and sat beside the *s.*	Mt.13.1
he came to them, walking on the *s.*	Mt.14.25
Be taken up and cast into the *s.*	Mt.21.21
Moses in the cloud and in the *s.*	1 Cor.10.2
there is as it were a *s.* of glass	Rev.4.6
I saw a beast rising out of the *s.*	Rev.13.1
And the *s.* gave up the dead in it	Rev.20.13
passed away, and the *s.* was no more	Rev.21.1

SEAL (noun)

on him has God the Father set his *s.*	Jn.6.27
a sign or *s.* of the righteousness	Rom.4.11
he has put his *s.* upon us	2 Cor.1.22
bearing this *s.*: "The Lord knows	2 Tim.2.19
Lamb opened one of the seven *s.*	Rev.6.1

SEAL (verb)

s. the teaching among my disciples	Is.8.16
s. up the vision, for it pertains	Dan.8.26

were *s.* with the promised Holy Spirit	Eph.1.13
in whom you were *s.* for the day of	Eph.4.30
And I heard the number of the *s.*	Rev.7.4

SEARCH (verb)

thou dost . . . *s.* for my sin	Job 10.6
Who can *s.* out our crimes?	Ps.64.6
I meditate and *s.* my spirit	Ps.77.6
S. me, O God, and know my heart	Ps.139.23
glory of kings is to *s.* things out	Pr.25.2
to seek and to *s.* out by wisdom	Ec.1.13
I the LORD *s.* the mind and try the	Jer.17.10
I myself will *s.* for my sheep	Ezek.34.11
there I will *s.* out and take them	Am.9.3
I will *s.* Jerusalem with lamps	Zeph.1.12
Go and *s.* diligently for the child	Mt.2.8
You *s.* the scriptures, because you	Jn.5.39
he who *s.* the hearts of men	Rom.8.27
For the Spirit *s.* everything	1 Cor.2.10
I am he who *s.* mind and heart	Rev.2.23

SEASHORE

as the sand which is on the *s.*	Gen.22.17
saw the Egyptians dead upon the *s.*	Ex.14.30
as the sand which is upon the *s.*	Jg.7.12
against the *s.* he has appointed it	Jer.47.7
grains of sand by the *s.*	Heb.11.12

SEASON

let them be for signs and for *s.*	Gen.1.14
that yields its fruit in its *s.*	Ps.1.3
For everything there is a *s.*	Ec.3.1
God, who gives the rain in its *s.*	Jer.5.24
its saltness, how will you *s.* it?	Mk.9.50
for in due *s.* we shall reap, if we	Gal.6.9
be urgent in *s.* and out of *s.*	2 Tim.4.2

SEAT

shall make a mercy *s.* of pure gold	Ex.25.17
set the mercy *s.* above on the ark	Ex.40.20
that I might come even to his *s.*	Job 23.3
I prepared my *s.* in the square	Job 29.7
nor sits in the *s.* of scoffers	Ps.1.1
bring near the *s.* of violence?	Am.6.3
the Pharisees sit on Moses' *s.*	Mt.23.2
love the best *s.* in the synagogues	Lk.11.43
sat down on the judgment *s.* at	Jn.19.13
Herod . . . took his *s.* upon the throne	Acts 12.21
before the judgment *s.* of God	Rom.14.10
before the judgment *s.* of Christ	2 Cor.5.10
glory overshadowing the mercy *s.*	Heb.9.5

SECRET (noun)

So the *s.* of his strength was not	Jg.16.9
For he knows the *s.* of the heart	Ps.44.21
when I was being made in *s.*	Ps.139.15
bread eaten in *s.* is pleasant	Pr.9.17
A gift in *s.* averts anger	Pr.21.14
do not disclose another's *s.*	Pr.25.9
I did not speak in *s.*	Is.45.19
I have not spoken in *s.*	Is.48.16
revealing his *s.* to his servants	Am.3.7
who sees in *s.* will reward you	Mt.6.4
pray to your Father who is in *s.*	Mt.6.6
been given the *s.* of the kingdom	Mk.4.11
For no man works in *s.* if he seeks	Jn.7.4
the things that they do in *s.*	Eph.5.12
I have learned the *s.* of facing	Phil.4.12

SECRETARY

the king's *s.* and the high priest	2 Kg.12.10
Shaphan the *s.* came to the king	2 Kg.22.9

Hilkiah said to Shaphan the *s*.	2 Chr.34.15	demand signs and Greeks *s*. wisdom	1 Cor.1.22
Then the king's *s*. were summoned	Est.3.12	Let no one *s*. his own good	1 Cor.10.24
Baruch the *s*. and Jeremiah	Jer.36.26	*s*. the things that are above, where	Col.3.1
SECRETLY		nor did we *s*. glory from men	1 Th.2.6
For you did it *s*.; but I will	2 Sam.12.12	that he rewards those who *s*. him	Heb.11.6
Herod summoned the wise men *s*.	Mt.2.7	let him *s*. peace and pursue it	1 Pet.3.11
but *s*., for fear of the Jews	Jn.19.38	**SEER**	
Then they *s*. instigated men, who	Acts 6.11	a prophet was formerly called a *s*.	1 Sam.9.9
false brethren *s*. brought in	Gal.2.4	Samuel answered . . . "I am the *s*.	1 Sam.9.19
false teachers . . . will *s*. bring in	2 Pet.2.1	spoke to Gad, David's *s*., saying	1 Chr.21.9
admission has been *s*. gained by some	Jude 4	the visions of Iddo the *s*.	2 Chr.9.29
SECURE (adjective)		Hanani the *s*. went out to meet	2 Chr.19.2
you will be *s*., and will not fear	Job 11.15	words . . . of Asaph the *s*.	2 Chr.29.30
thy servants shall dwell *s*.	Ps.102.28	**SEIZE**	
You felt *s*. in your wickedness	Is.47.10	*S*. the prophets of Baal; let not	1 Kg.18.40
And they shall dwell *s*.	Mic.5.4	he lurks that he may *s*. the poor	Ps.10.9
go, make it as *s*. as you can	Mt.27.65	May the creditor *s*. all that he has	Ps.109.11
SECURITY		Pangs and agony will *s*. them	Is.13.8
He gives them *s*., and they are	Job 24.23	Have you come to *s*. spoil?	Ezek.38.13
dwell in the land, and enjoy *s*.	Ps.37.3	They covet fields, and *s*. them	Mic.2.2
I am oppressed; be thou my *s*.	Is.38.14	The one I . . . kiss is the man; *s*. him	Mt.26.48
abundance of prosperity and *s*.	Jer.33.6	For Herod had sent and *s*. John	Mk.6.17
people say, "There is peace and *s*."	1 Th.5.3	And amazement *s*. them all, and they	Lk.5.26
SEED		they *s*. one Simon of Cyrene	Lk.23.26
and between your *s*. and her *s*.	Gen.3.15	they *s*. Paul and dragged him out	Acts 21.30
tithe all the yield of your *s*.	Dt.14.22	that no one may *s*. your crown	Rev.3.11
shall carry much *s*. into the field	Dt.28.38	**SELF**	
bearing the *s*. for sowing,	Ps.126.6	thou didst swear by thine own *s*.	Ex.32.13
In the morning sow your *s*.	Ec.11.6	our old *s*. was crucified with him	Rom.6.6
rain for the *s*. with which you sow	Is.30.23	For men will be lovers of *s*.	2 Tim.3.2
giving *s*. to the sower and bread to	Is.55.10	your owing me even your own *s*.	Philem.19
a choice vine, wholly of pure *s*.	Jer.2.21	**SELF-CONTROL**	
He who sows the good *s*. is the Son	Mt.13.37	A man without *s*. is like a city	Pr.25.28
faith as a grain of mustard *s*.	Mt.17.20	Satan tempt you through lack of *s*.	1 Cor.7.5
A sower went out to sow his *s*.	Lk.8.5	athlete exercises *s*. in all things	1 Cor.9.25
to each kind of *s*. its own body	1 Cor.15.38	*s*.; against such there is no law	Gal.5.23
He who supplies *s*. to the sower	2 Cor.9.10	a spirit of power and love and *s*.	2 Tim.1.7
born anew, not of perishable *s*.	1 Pet.1.23	*s*. with steadfastness	2 Pet.1.6
SEEK		**SELFISHNESS**	
from there you will *s*. the LORD your	Dt.4.29	*s*., slander, gossip, conceit	2 Cor.12.20
have set your heart to *s*. God	2 Chr.19.3	anger, *s*., dissension, party spirit	Gal.5.20
never *s*. their peace or prosperity	Ezra 9.12	Do nothing from *s*. or conceit	Phil.2.3
I would *s*. God, and to God would I	Job 5.8	**SELL**	
the generation of those who *s*. him	Ps.24.6	"First *s*. me your birthright."	Gen.25.31
Thou hast said, "*S*. ye my face."	Ps.27.8	Buy truth, and do not *s*. it	Pr.23.23
In thee, O LORD, do I *s*. refuge	Ps.31.1	they *s*. the righteous for silver	Am.2.6
do good; *s*. peace, and pursue it	Ps.34.14	*s*. what you possess and give to the	Mt.19.21
S. the LORD and his strength	Ps.105.4	has no sword *s*. his mantle and buy	Lk.22.36
I applied my mind to *s*. and to	Ec.1.13	**SELLER**	
a time to *s*., and a time to lose	Ec.3.6	as with the buyer, so with the *s*.	Is.24.2
s. justice, correct oppression	Is.1.17	Lydia . . . a *s*. of purple goods	Acts 16.14
S. the LORD while he may be found	Is.55.6	**SEND**	
when you *s*. me with all your heart	Jer.29.13	he will *s*. his angel before you	Gen.24.7
do you *s*. great things for yourself?	Jer.45.5	May he *s*. you help from the sanctuary	Ps.20.2
they will *s*. peace, but there shall	Ezek.7.25	Oh *s*. out thy light and thy truth	Ps.43.3
I will *s*. the lost, and I will	Ezek.34.16	I said, "Here am I! *S*. me."	Is.6.8
return and *s*. the LORD their God	Hos.3.5	he will *s*. them a savior	Is.19.20
S. the LORD and live, lest he break	Am.5.6	to *s*. out laborers into his harvest	Mt.9.38
S. good, and not evil, that you may	Am.5.14	Behold, I *s*. you out as sheep in	Mt.10.16
S. the LORD, all you humble of the	Zeph.2.3	The Son of man will *s*. his angels	Mt.13.41
But *s*. first his kingdom and his	Mt.6.33	Therefore I *s*. you prophets and	Mt.23.34
s., and you will find; knock, and	Mt.7.7	behold, I *s*. you out as lambs in	Lk.10.3
Why do you *s*. the living among the	Lk.24.5	I *s*. the promise of my Father	Lk.24.49
I *s*. not my own will but	Jn.5.30	whom the Father will *s*. in my name	Jn.14.26
You will *s*. me and you will not find	Jn.7.36	but if I go, I will *s*. him to you	Jn.16.7
they should *s*. God, in the hope	Acts 17.27	believed that thou didst *s*. me	Jn.17.8

Christ did not s. me to baptize | 1 Cor.1.17
God s. upon them a strong delusion | 2 Th.2.11
SENNACHERIB
2 Kg.18.13; 2 Chr.32.1; Is.36.1; 37.37
SENSE
they gave the s., so that the people | Neh.8.8
He who commits adultery has no s. | Pr.6.32
but fools die for lack of s. | Pr.10.21
Good s. makes a man slow to anger | Pr.19.11
like a dove, silly and without s. | Hos.7.11
where would be the s. of smell? | 1 Cor.12.17
SENSELESS
O foolish and s. people, who have | Jer.5.21
their s. minds were darkened | Rom.1.21
into many s. and hurtful desires | 1 Tim.6.9
with stupid, s. controversies | 2 Tim.2.23
SENTENCE
This man deserves the s. of death | Jer.26.11
So Pilate gave s. that their demand | Lk.23.24
asking for s. against him | Acts 25.15
are summed up in this s. | Rom.13.9
we had received the s. of death | 2 Cor.1.9
SEPARATE
S. yourself from me. If you take | Gen.13.9
s. yourselves from the peoples of | Ezra 10.11
he will s. them one from another | Mt.25.32
shall s. us from the love of Christ? | Rom.8.35
be s. from them, says the Lord | 2 Cor.6.17
s. from sinners, exalted above the | Heb.7.26
SEPULCHRE
will withhold from you his s. | Gen.23.6
their throat is an open s. | Ps.5.9
there, sitting opposite the s. | Mt.27.61
made the s. secure by sealing | Mt.27.66
the other Mary went to see the s. | Mt.28.1
SERIOUS
or has any s. blemish whatever | Dt.15.21
Deacons likewise must be s. | 1 Tim.3.8
The women likewise must be s. | 1 Tim.3.11
s., sensible, sound in faith | Tit.2.2
SERPENT
Now the s. was more subtle than any | Gen.3.1
The Lord God said to the s. | Gen.3.14
Moses made a bronze s., and set it | Num.21.9
They have venom like . . . a s. | Ps.58.4
At the last it bites like a s. | Pr.23.32
If the s. bites before it is charmed | Ec.10.11
punish Leviathan the fleeing s. | Is.27.1
there I will command the s. | Am.9.3
be wise as s. and innocent as doves | Mt.10.16
You s., you brood of vipers, how | Mt.23.33
instead of a fish give him a s. | Lk.11.11
lifted up the s. in the wilderness | Jn.3.14
the s. deceived Eve by his cunning | 2 Cor.11.3
fly from the s. into the wilderness | Rev.12.14
that ancient s., who is the Devil | Rev.20.2
SERVANT
Moreover by them is thy s. warned | Ps.19.11
O Lord, I am thy s.; I am thy s. | Ps.116.16
the s. like his master. If they | Mt.10.25
Well done, good and faithful s. | Mt.25.21
great among you must be your s. | Mk.10.43
lettest thou thy s. depart in peace | Lk.2.29
that s. who knew his master's will | Lk.12.47
No s. can serve two masters | Lk.16.13
the s. does not know what his master | Jn.15.15

I should not be a s. of Christ | Gal.1.10
taking the form of a s. | Phil.2.7
makes . . . his s. flames of fire | Heb.1.7
S., be submissive to your masters | 1 Pet.2.18
have sealed the s. of our God | Rev.7.3
all you his s., you who fear him | Rev.19.5
to show his s. what must soon take | Rev.22.6
SERVE
the elder shall s. the younger | Gen.25.23
I will s. you seven years for your | Gen.29.18
that they may s. the Lord their God | Ex.10.7
not bow down to them or s. them | Dt.5.9
Because you did not s. the Lord | Dt.28.47
choose this day whom you will s. | Jos.24.15
The Lord our God we will s. | Jos.24.24
s. him faithfully with all your | 1 Sam.12.24
and also s. their graven images | 2 Kg.17.41
s. him with a whole heart and | 1 Chr.28.9
Almighty, that we should s. him? | Job 21.15
S. the Lord with fear, with trembling | Ps.2.11
S. the Lord with gladness | Ps.100.2
not go after other gods to s. them | Jer.35.15
Go s. every one of you his idols | Ezek.20.39
God, whom you s. . . . deliver you | Dan.6.16
No one can s. two masters | Mt.6.24
Lo, these many years I have s. you | Lk.15.29
You cannot s. God and mammon | Lk.16.13
Martha s., and Lazarus was one of | Jn.12.2
nor is he s. by human hands, as | Acts 17.25
God . . . whom I s. with my spirit in | Rom.1.9
with my flesh I s. the law of sin | Rom.7.25
to s. a living and true God | 1 Th.1.9
whom I s. with a clear conscience | 2 Tim.1.3
dead works to s. the living God | Heb.9.14
s. him day and night within his | Rev.7.15
SERVICE
What do you mean by this s.? | Ex.12.26
all the s. of the house of God | 1 Chr.28.21
think he is offering s. to God | Jn.16.2
there are varieties of s. | 1 Cor.12.5
and fellow worker in your s. | 2 Cor.8.23
rendering s. with a good will | Eph.6.7
high priest in the s. of God | Heb.2.17
whoever renders s., as one who | 1 Pet.4.11
SEVENTY
offspring of Jacob were s. persons | Ex.1.5
Gather for me s. men of the elders | Num.11.16
serve the king of Babylon s. years | Jer.25.11
seven times, but s. times seven | Mt.18.22
the Lord appointed s. others | Lk.10.1
SEVERE
Now the famine was s. in the land | Gen.43.1
a very s. plague upon your cattle | Ex.9.3
Why is the decree of the king so s.? | Dan.2.15
because you are a s. man | Lk.19.21
for in a s. test of affliction | 2 Cor.8.2
SHADE (noun)
Do the s. rise up to praise thee? | Ps.88.10
Lord is your s. on your right hand | Ps.121.5
It will be for a s. by day | Is.4.6
s. of a great rock in a weary land | Is.32.2
He sat under it in the s. | Jon.4.5
SHADOW
for our days on earth are a s. | Job 8.9
all my members are like a s. | Job 17.7
hide me in the s. of thy wings | Ps.17.8

the valley of the *s.* of death	Ps.23.4
take refuge in the *s.* of thy wings	Ps.36.7
abides in the *s.* of the Almighty	Ps.91.1
in the *s.* of his hand he hid me	Is.49.2
the region and *s.* of death	Mt.4.16
in darkness and in the *s.* of death	Lk.1.79
a copy and *s.* of the heavenly	Heb.8.5
no variation or *s.* due to change	Jas.1.17

SHADRACH

	Dan.1.7; 2.49; 3.12,30

SHAKE

trembling . . . made all my bones *s.*	Job 4.14
my foes rejoice because I am *s.*	Ps.13.4
foundations of the earth are *s.*	Ps.82.5
earth will be *s.* out of its place	Is.13.13
your walls will *s.* at the noise	Ezek.26.10
I am about to *s.* the heavens and	Hag.2.21
s off the dust from your feet as	Mt.10.14
I will *s.* not only the earth but	Heb.12.26

SHAME (noun)

let me not be put to *s.*	Ps.25.2
let the wicked be put to *s.*	Ps.31.17
s. has covered my face	Ps.44.15
Let not the downtrodden be put to *s.*	Ps.74.21
His enemies I will clothe with *s.*	Ps.132.18
she who brings *s.* is like rottenness	Pr.12.4
You have devised *s.* to your house	Hab.2.10
all his adversaries were put to *s.*	Lk.13.17
I say this to your *s.*	1 Cor.6.5
I shall not be put to *s.*	2 Cor.10.8
they glory in their *s.*	Phil.3.19

SHAMEFUL

it is a *s.* thing, and they shall	Lev.20.17
he has done a *s.* thing in Israel	Jos.7.15
s. for a woman to speak in church	1 Cor.14.35
not for *s.* gain but eagerly	1 Pet.5.2

SHAMEFULLY

wicked man acts *s.* and disgracefully	Pr.13.5
will rule over a son who acts *s.*	Pr.17.2
treated them *s.*, and killed them	Mt.22.6
mocked and *s.* treated and spit upon	Lk.18.32
we had . . . been *s.* treated at Philippi	1 Th.2.2

SHARE (verb)

will *s.* the inheritance as one	Pr.17.2
Is it not to *s.* your bread with the	Is.58.7
let him *s.* with him who has none	Lk.3.11
those who *s.* the faith of Abraham	Rom.4.16
to *s.* the richness of the olive	Rom.11.17
that I may *s.* in its blessings	1 Cor.9.23
s. abundantly in Christ's sufferings	2 Cor.1.5
may *s.* his sufferings, becoming	Phil.3.10
we *s.* in Christ, if only we hold	Heb.3.14
choosing rather to *s.* ill-treatment	Heb.11.25
as you *s.* Christ's sufferings	1 Pet.4.13
he who *s.* in the first resurrection	Rev.20.6

SHARP

Your tongue is like a *s.* razor	Ps.52.2
their tongue *s.* as a serpent's	Ps.140.3
their arrows are *s.*, all their bows	Is.5.28
And there arose a *s.* contention	Acts 15.39
s. than any two-edged sword	Heb.4.12
from his mouth issues a *s.* sword	Rev.19.15

SHAVE

then he shall *s.* his head	Num.6.9
Nazirite shall *s.* his consecrated	Num.6.18
had him *s.* off the seven locks	Jg.16.19

their beards *s.* and their clothes	Jer.41.5
so that they may *s.* their heads	Acts 21.24
the same as if her head were *s.*	1 Cor.11.5

SHEBA

(1) men, Gen.25.3; 2 Sam.20.1; (2) places, Job 6.19; Ps.72.10; Jer.6.20; Ezek.27.22; 38.13;	
queen of, visits Solomon, 1 Kg.10; 2 Chr.9;	Mt.12.42

SHED

by man shall his blood be *s.*	Gen.9.6
lest innocent blood be *s.*	Dt.19.10
having *s.* blood without cause	1 Sam.25.31
You have *s.* much blood and have	1 Chr.22.8
My eyes *s.* streams of tears	Ps.119.136
they make haste to *s.* blood	Pr.1.16
all the righteous blood *s.* on earth	Mt.23.35
Their feet are swift to *s.* blood	Rom.3.15
For men have *s.* the blood of saints	Rev.16.6

SHEEP

Now Abel was a keeper of *s.*	Gen.4.2
He was shearing his *s.* in Carmel	1 Sam.25.2
He had seven thousand *s.*	Job 1.3
all *s.* and oxen, and also the beasts	Ps.8.7
accounted as *s.* for the slaughter	Ps.44.22
we are . . . the *s.* of his pasture	Ps.100.3
All we like *s.* have gone astray	Is.53.6
My people have been lost *s.*	Jer.50.6
go . . . to the lost *s.* of the house of	Mt.10.6
If a man has a hundred *s.*, and one	Mt.18.12
and the *s.* will be scattered	Mk.14.27
selling oxen and *s.* and pigeons	Jn.2.14
calls his own *s.* by name and leads	Jn.10.3
I lay down my life for the *s.*	Jn.10.15
I have other *s.*, that are not	Jn.10.16
Jesus said to him, "Feed my *s.*"	Jn.21.17
went about in skins of *s.* and goats	Heb.11.37
Jesus, the great shepherd of the *s.*	Heb.13.20

SHEEPFOLD

We will build *s.* here for our	Num.32.16
Why did you tarry among the *s.*	Jg.5.16
though they stay among the *s.*	Ps.68.13
took him from the *s.*	Ps.78.70
not enter the *s.* by the door but	Jn.10.1

SHEKEL

twenty gerahs shall make a *s.*	Lev.27.25
a measure of fine meal for a *s.*	2 Kg.7.18
the ephah small and the *s.* great	Am.8.5
open its mouth you will find a *s.*	Mt.17.27

SHELTER (noun)

cling to the rock for want of *s.*	Job 24.8
will hide me in his *s.* in the day of	Ps.27.5
be safe under the *s.* of thy wings	Ps.61.4
dwells in the *s.* of the Most High	Ps.91.1
a refuge and a *s.* from the storm	Is.4.6
a *s.* from the storm and a shade	Is.25.4

SHEM

	Gen.5.32; 10.1; 1 Chr.1.4; Lk.3.36

SHEOL

I shall go down to *S.* to my son	Gen.37.35
it burns to the depths of *S.*	Dt.32.22
Deeper than *S.*—what can you know?	Job 11.8
Will it go down to the bars of *S.*?	Job 17.16
S. is naked before God	Job 26.6
The wicked shall depart to *S.*	Ps.9.17
the cords of *S.* entangled me	Ps.18.5
let them go down to *S.* alive	Ps.55.15

my life draws near to S.	Ps.88.3
If I make my bed in S., thou art	Ps.139.8
Her house is the way to S.	Pr.7.27
S. and Abaddon are never satisfied	Pr.27.20
Your pomp is brought down to S.	Is.14.11
For S. cannot thank thee	Is.38.18
ransom them from the power of S.?	Hos.13.14
out of the belly of S. I cried	Jon.2.2
His greed is as wide as S.	Hab.2.5

SHEPHERD (noun)

The LORD is my s., I shall not want	Ps.23.1
Give ear, O S. of Israel, thou who	Ps.80.1
He will feed his flock like a s.	Is.40.11
I myself will be the s. of my sheep	Ezek.34.15
are afflicted for want of a s.	Zech.10.2
Woe to my worthless s.	Zech.11.17
they were like sheep without a s.	Mk.6.34
there were s. out in the field	Lk.2.8
the s. said to one another, "Let us	Lk.2.15
I am the good s. The good s. lays	Jn.10.11
Jesus, the great s. of the sheep	Heb.13.20
returned to the S. and Guardian	1 Pet.2.25
when the chief S. is manifested	1 Pet.5.4
the Lamb . . . will be their s.	Rev.7.17

SHIBBOLETH

"Then say S." . . . he said, "Sibboleth"	Jg.12.6

SHIELD

Fear not, Abram, I am your s.	Gen.15.1
he is a s. for all those who	2 Sam.22.31
thou . . . art a s. about me, my glory	Ps.3.3
he is a s. for all those who take	Ps.18.30
The LORD is my strength and my s.	Ps.28.7
For the LORD God is a sun and s.	Ps.84.11
he is a s. to those who take refuge	Pr.30.5
above all taking the s. of faith	Eph.6.16

SHILOH

Jos.18.1; Jg.18.31; 1 Sam.1.3; Ps.78.60; Jer.26.6	

SHINE

LORD make his face to s. upon you	Num.6.25
light will s. on your ways	Job 22.28
Let thy face s. on thy servant	Ps.31.16
make his face to s. upon us	Ps.67.1
Make thy face s. upon thy servant	Ps.119.135
A man's wisdom makes his face s.	Ec.8.1
Arise, s.; for your light has come	Is.60.1
wise shall s. like the brightness	Dan.12.3
Let your light so s. before men	Mt.5.16
the righteous will s. like the sun	Mt.13.43
The light s. in the darkness	Jn.1.5
Let light s. out of darkness	2 Cor.4.6
among whom you s. as lights in the	Phil.2.15
no need of sun or moon to s. upon	Rev.21.23

SHIP

There go the s., and Leviathan	Ps.104.26
Some went down to the sea in s.	Ps.107.23
the way of a s. on the high seas	Pr.30.19
and found a s. going to Tarshish	Jon.1.3
centurion found a s. of Alexandria	Acts 27.6
on planks or on pieces of the s.	Acts 27.44
Look at the s. also; though they	Jas.3.4

SHOES

put off your s. from your feet	Ex.3.5
Put off your s. from your feet	Jos.5.15
sell . . . the needy for a pair of s.	Am.2.6

ring on his hand, and s. on his feet	Lk.15.22
Take off the s. from your feet	Acts 7.33

SHOOT (noun)

come forth a s. from the stump of	Is.11.1
the s. of my planting, the work of	Is.60.21
as the earth brings forth its s.	Is.61.11
you, a wild olive s., were grafted in	Rom.11.17

SHORT

Thou hast cut s. the days of his	Ps.89.45
For the bed is too s. to stretch	Is.28.20
In a s. time you think to make me	Acts 26.28
devil . . . knows that his time is s.	Rev.12.12

SHOUT (verb)

all the sons of God s. for joy?	Job 38.7
s. for joy, all you upright in heart	Ps.32.11
My lips will s. for joy, when I	Ps.71.23
S. aloud, O daughter of Jerusalem	Zech.9.9
they s. out, "Crucify, crucify him!"	Lk.23.21
Rejoice . . . break forth and s.	Gal.4.27

SHOWER

to the s. and the rain	Job 37.6
its ridges, softening it with s.	Ps.65.10
like s. that water the earth	Ps.72.6
Therefore the s. have been withheld	Jer.3.3
send down the s. in their season	Ezek.34.26
like s. upon the grass	Mic.5.7
you say at once, 'A s. is coming'	Lk.12.54

SHRINK

for I did not s. from declaring	Acts 20.27
if he s. back, my soul has no	Heb.10.38
those who s. back and are destroyed	Heb.10.39
not s. from him in shame	1 Jn.2.28

SHUT

I am s. in so that I cannot escape	Ps.88.8
his angel and s. the lions' mouths	Dan.6.22
your room and s. the door and pray	Mt.6.6
The doors were s., but Jesus came	Jn.20.26
who opens and no one shall s.	Rev.3.7

SICK

Hope deferred makes the heart s.	Pr.13.12
The whole head is s., and the	Is.1.5
Heal the s., raise the dead, cleanse	Mt.10.8
I was s. and you visited me	Mt.25.36
prayer of faith will save the s.	Jas.5.15

SICKNESS

I will take s. away from . . . you	Ex.23.25
Shall I recover from this s.?	2 Kg.8.8
A man's spirit will endure s.	Pr.18.14
Hezekiah . . . had recovered from his s.	Is.38.9
s. and wounds are ever before me	Jer.6.7

SIDON

Gen.10.15; Is.23.2; Jer.25.22; Mt.11.21; Acts 12.20	

SIGHT

the earth was corrupt in God's s.	Gen.6.11
turn aside and see this great s.	Ex.3.3
the stars are not clean in his s.	Job 25.5
precious is their blood in his s.	Ps.72.14
Precious in the s. of the LORD is	Ps.116.15
And I will cast you out of my s.	Jer.7.15
Jesus said to him, "Receive your s.	Lk.18.42
Brother Saul, receive your s.	Acts 22.13
walk by faith, not by s.	2 Cor.5.7
is acceptable in the s. of God	1 Tim.5.4
in God's s. chosen and precious	1 Pet.2.4

SIGN (noun)

it shall be a *s.* of the covenant	Gen.9.13
The blood shall be a *s.* for you	Ex.12.13
It is a *s.* for ever between me and	Ex.31.17
This is the *s.* that the LORD has	1 Kg.13.3
those who dwell . . . are afraid at thy *s.*	Ps.65.8
when he wrought his *s.* in Egypt	Ps.78.43
Show me a *s.* of thy favor	Ps.86.17
the Lord himself will give you a *s.*	Is.7.14
Thus shall Ezekiel be to you a *s.*	Ezek.24.24
no *s.* . . . . except the *s.* of Jonah	Mt.16.4
then will appear the *s.* of the Son	Mt.24.30
the betrayer had given them a *s.*	Mk.14.44
hoping to see some *s.* done by him	Lk.23.8
was now the second *s.* that Jesus did	Jn.4.54
they saw the *s.* which he did on	Jn.6.2
For this man performs many *s.*	Jn.11.47
did many other *s.* in the presence	Jn.20.30
circumcision as a *s.* or seal of	Rom.4.11
with *s.* and wonders and mighty	2 Cor.12.12
bore witness by *s.* and wonders	Heb.2.4
It works great *s.*, even making fire	Rev.13.13

SILAS

Acts 15.22; 16.19; 18.5

SILENCE

For God alone my soul waits in *s.*	Ps.62.5
O God, do not keep *s.*; do not hold	Ps.83.1
a time to keep *s.*, and a time	Ec.3.7
all the earth keep *s.* before him	Hab.2.20
should keep *s.* in the churches	1 Cor.14.34
Let a woman learn in *s.* with all	1 Tim.2.11
there was *s.* in heaven for about	Rev.8.1

SILENT

if thou be *s.* to me, I become like	Ps.28.1
be not *s.*! O Lord, be not far	Ps.35.22
I was dumb and *s.*, I held my peace	Ps.39.2
For Zion's sake I will not keep *s.*	Is.62.1
Be *s.*, all flesh, before the LORD	Zech.2.13
Jesus was *s.* And the high priest	Mt.26.63
if these were *s.*, the very stones	Lk.19.40
speak and do not be *s.*	Acts 18.9

SILLY

s. and without sense, calling to	Hos.7.11
nor *s.* talk, nor levity, which are	Eph.5.4
to do with godless and *s.* myths	1 Tim.4.7

SILVANUS

2 Cor.1.19; 1 Th.1.1; 2 Th.1.1; 1 Pet.5.12

SILVER

the *s.* cup, in the mouth of the sack	Gen.44.2
Though he heap up *s.* like dust	Job 27.16
thou hast tried us as *s.* is tried	Ps.66.10
Take my instruction instead of *s.*	Pr.8.10
apples of gold in a setting of *s.*	Pr.25.11
before the *s.* cord is snapped	Ec.12.6
they sell the righteous for *s.*	Am.2.6
they paid him thirty pieces of *s.*	Mt.26.15
I have no *s.* and gold, but I give	Acts 3.6
who made *s.* shrines of Artemis	Acts 19.24
perishable things such as *s.* or gold	1 Pet.1.18

SIMEON

(1) son of Jacob, Gen.29.33; 34.25; 42.24; his descendants, Gen.46.10; Ex.6.15; Num.1.22; 26.12; 1 Chr.4.24; 12.25; prophecy concerning, Gen.49.5; (2) blesses Christ, Lk.2.25–32; (3) (Niger), Acts 13.1

SIMON

(1) brother of Jesus, Mt.13.55; Mk.6.3; (2) Apostle, Mt.10.4; Mk.3.18; Lk.6.15; (3) (Pharisee), reproved, Lk.7.36–47; (4) (leper), Mt.26.6; Mk.14.3; (5) (of Cyrene), bears the cross of Jesus, Mt.27.32; Mk.15.21; Lk.23.26; (6) (a tanner), Peter's vision in his house, Acts 9.43; 10.6; (7) (a sorcerer), baptized, Acts 8.9–13; rebuked by Peter, Acts 8.18; (8) Peter, *see* PETER

SIN (noun)

s. is couching a he door	Gen.4.7
forgive my *s.*, I ray you	Ex.10.17
make atonement for him for his *s.*	Lev.4.26
I acknowledged my *s.* to thee	Ps.32.5
cleanse me from my *s.*	Ps.51.2
in *s.* did my mother conceive me	Ps.51.5
s. is a reproach) any people	Pr.14.34
that they may a d *s.* to *s.*	Is.30.1
of my body for ae *s.* of my soul?	Mic.6.7
but is guilty of an eternal *s.*	Mk.3.29
who takes away the *s.* of the world	Jn.1.29
who commits *s.* is a slave to *s.*	Jn.8.34
do not hold this *s.* against them	Acts 7.60
to continue in *s.* that grace may	Rom.6.1
Let not *s.* therefore reign in your	Rom.6.12
For the wages of *s.* is death	Rom.6.23
but *s.* which dwells within me	Rom.7.20
does not proceed from faith is *s.*	Rom.14.23
The sting of death is *s.*	1 Cor.15.56
gave himself for our *s.* to deliver	Gal.1.4
redemption, the forgiveness of *s.*	Col.1.14
s. of some men are conspicuous	1 Tim.5.24
he had made purification for *s.*	Heb.1.3
confess your *s.* to one another	Jas.5.16
bore our *s.* in his body on the tree	1 Pet.2.24
If we confess our *s.*, he is faithful	1 Jn.1.9
freed us from our *s.* by his blood	Rev.1.5

SIN (verb)

there is no man who does not *s.*	1 Kg.8.46
foreign women made even him to *s.*	Neh.13.26
Job did not *s.* or charge God with	Job 1.22
that I may not *s.* with my tongue	Ps.39.1
that I might not *s.* against thee	Ps.119.11
And if your eye causes you to *s.*	Mt.18.9
S. no more, that nothing worse	Jn.5.14
who *s.*, this man or his parents	Jn.9.2
all who have *s.* under the law will	Rom.2.12
all have *s.* and fall short of the	Rom.3.23
Be angry but do not *s.*	Eph.4.26
For if we *s.* deliberately after	Heb.10.26
he cannot *s.* because he is born of	1 Jn.3.9

SINAI

Ex.16.1; 19.20; Lev.7.38; Num.1.1; Ps.68.8; Gal.4.24

SINCERE

sent spies, who pretended to be *s.*	Lk.20.20
a good conscience and *s.* faith	1 Tim.1.5
I am reminded of your *s.* faith	2 Tim.1.5
for a *s.* love of the brethren	1 Pet.1.22
I have aroused your *s.* mind	2 Pet.3.1

SINCERITY

serve him in *s.* and in faithfulness	Jos.24.14
unleavened bread of *s.* and truth	1 Cor.5.8
with holiness and godly *s.*	2 Cor.1.12
men of *s.*, as commissioned by God	2 Cor.2.17

SINFUL
were sick through their *s.* ways Ps.107.17
Ah, *s.* nation, a people laden with Is.1.4
this adulterous and *s.* generation Mk.8.38
from me, for I am a *s.* man, O Lord Lk.5.8
delivered into the hands of *s.* men Lk.24.7
our *s.* passions, aroused by the law Rom.7.5
SING
S. to the LORD, for he has triumphed Ex.15.21
and *s.* praises to thy name 2 Sam.22.50
rejoice, let them ever *s.* for joy Ps.5.11
S. to him a new song, play skilfully Ps.33.3
How shall we *s.* the LORD's song in Ps.137.4
S. for joy, O heavens, and exult Is.49.13
I will *s.* with the mind also 1 Cor.14.15
day and night they never cease to *s.* Rev.4.8
they *s.* a new song before the throne Rev.14.3
SINGERS
Therefore the ballad *s.* say Num.21.27
these are the *s.*, the heads of 1 Chr.9.33
the *s.* sang, and the trumpeters 2 Chr.29.28
The *s.*: the sons of Asaph, a hundred Neh.7.44
portions for the *s.* and the Neh.12.47
the *s.* in front, the minstrels last Ps.68.25
S. and dancers alike say, "All my Ps.87.7
SINK
make my assailants *s.* under me Ps.18.39
I *s.* in deep mire, where there is no Ps.69.2
Thus shall Babylon *s.* Jer.51.64
beginning to *s.* he cried out Mt.14.30
Let these words *s.* into your ears Lk.9.44
SINNER
nor stands in the way of *s.* Ps.1.1
Let *s.* be consumed from the earth Ps.104.35
My son, if *s.* entice you, do not Pr.1.10
Let not your heart envy *s.* Pr.23.17
a friend of tax collectors and *s.* Mt.11.19
Even *s.* lend to *s.*, to receive Lk.6.34
God, be merciful to me a *s.* Lk.18.13
know that God does not listen to *s.* Jn.9.31
while we were yet *s.* Christ died for us Rom.5.8
came into the world to save *s.* 1 Tim.1.15
Cleanse your hands, you *s.* Jas.4.8
which ungodly *s.* have spoken Jude 15
SISERA
Jg.4.2; 5.20; 1 Sam.12.9; Ps.83.9
SISTER
Say you are my *s.*, that it may go Gen.12.13
And his *s.* stood at a distance Ex.2.4
the worm, 'My mother,' or 'My *s.*' Job 17.14
We have a little *s.*, and she has S.of S.8.8
and are not his *s.* here with us? Mk.6.3
village of Mary and her *s.* Martha Jn.11.1
I commend to you our *s.* Phoebe Rom.16.1
Apphia our *s.* and Archippus our Philem.2
If a brother or *s.* is ill-clad and Jas.2.15
SKILFUL
Esau was a *s.* hunter Gen.25.27
s. in playing, a man of valor 1 Sam.16.18
Do you see a man *s.* in his work? Pr.22.29
he seeks out a *s.* craftsman to set Is.40.20
send for the *s.* women to come Jer.9.17
handsome and *s.* in all wisdom Dan.1.4
SKILL
every willing man who has *s.* 1 Chr.28.21
showed good *s.* in the service 2 Chr.30.22

toiled with . . . knowledge and *s.* Ec.2.21
learning and *s.* in all letters Dan.1.17
SKIN
Satan answered . . . "*S.* for *s.*! All that Job 2.4
have escaped by the *s.* of my teeth Job 19.20
Can the Ethiopian change his *s.* Jer.13.23
the new wine will burst the *s.* Lk.5.37
SKULL
Abimelech's head, and crushed his *s.* Jg.9.53
found no more of her than the *s.* 2 Kg.9.35
the place which is called The *S.* Lk.23.33
SKY
righteousness . . . down from the *s.* Ps.85.11
be fair weather; for the *s.* is red Mt.16.2
lights up the *s.* from one side to Lk.17.24
sacred stone that fell from the *s.* Acts 19.35
the *s.* vanished like a scroll that Rev.6.14
SLACK
he will not be *s.* with him who Dt.7.10
care not to be *s.* in this matter Ezra 4.22
A *s.* hand causes poverty Pr.10.4
He who is *s.* in his work is a Pr.18.9
SLAIN
I have *s.* a man for wounding me Gen.4.23
for thy sake we are *s.* all the day Ps.44.22
breathe upon these *s.* Ezek.37.9
Worthy is the Lamb who was *s.* Rev.5.12
SLANDER (noun)
uttering *s.* against me Ps.27.2
he who utters *s.* is a fool Pr.10.18
envy, *s.*, pride, foolishness Mk.7.22
s., gossip, conceit 2 Cor.12.20
insincerity and envy and all *s.* 1 Pet.2.1
SLANDERERS
s., haters of God, insolent Rom.1.30
no *s.*, but temperate, faithful in all 1 Tim.3.11
s., profligates, fierce, haters of good 2 Tim.3.3
not to be *s.* or slaves to drink Tit.2.3
SLAUGHTER (noun)
Thou hast made us like sheep for *s.* Ps.44.11
as an ox goes to the *s.* Pr.7.22
like a lamb that is led to the *s.* Is.53.7
As a sheep led to the *s.* or Acts 8.32
fattened your hearts in a day of *s.* Jas.5.5
SLAVE
Cast out this *s.* woman with her Gen.21.10
became a *s.* at forced labor Gen.49.15
When a man strikes the eye of his *s.* Ex.21.26
borrower is the *s.* of the lender Pr.22.7
would be first . . . must be your *s.* Mt.20.27
one who commits sin is a *s.* to sin Jn.8.34
I have made myself a *s.* to all 1 Cor.9.19
there is neither *s.* nor free Gal.3.28
S., obey in everything those who Col.3.22
not to be slanderers or *s.* to drink Tit.2.3
no longer as a *s.* but more than a *s.* Philem.16
SLAVERY
did not receive the spirit of *s.* Rom.8.15
for she is in *s.* with her children Gal.4.25
not submit again to a yoke of *s.* Gal.5.1
all . . . under the yoke of *s.* regard 1 Tim.6.1
SLAY
whoever finds me will *s.* me Gen.4.14
took the knife to *s.* his son Gen.22.10
Behold, he will *s.* me; I have no Job 13.15
O that thou wouldst *s.* the wicked Ps.139.19

SLEEP (noun)
God caused a deep s. to fall upon the	Gen.2.21
he gives to his beloved s.	Ps.127.2
A little s., a little slumber	Pr.6.10
Love not s., lest you come to	Pr.20.13
Sweet is the s. of a laborer	Ec.5.12

SLEEP (verb)
Rouse thyself! Why s. thou, O Lord?	Ps.44.23
a son who s. in harvest brings shame	Pr.10.5
he said to them, "Why do you s.?	Lk.22.46
We shall not all s., but we shall	1 Cor.15.51

SLING (noun)
his s. was in his hand	1 Sam.17.40
David prevailed . . . with a s.	1 Sam.17.50
as from the hollow of a s.	1 Sam.25.29
one who binds the stone in the s.	Pr.26.8

SLIP
ready for those whose feet s.	Job 12.5
and my feet did not s.	Ps.18.36
his steps do not s.	Ps.37.31
has not let our feet s.	Ps.66.9
who s. in to spy out our freedom	Gal.2.4

SLOTHFUL
the s. will be put to forced labor	Pr.12.24
A s. man will not catch his prey	Pr.12.27
You wicked and s. servant	Mt.25.26

SLOW
I am s. of speech and of tongue	Ex.4.10
The LORD is s. to anger, and	Num.14.18
Good sense makes a man s. to anger	Pr.19.11
The LORD is s. to anger and of	Nah.1.3
s. of heart to believe all that	Lk.24.25
quick to hear, s. to speak, s. to	Jas.1.19
Lord is not s. about his promise	2 Pet.3.9

SLUGGARD
Go to the ant, O s.; consider her	Pr.6.6
The s. buries his hand in the dish	Pr.19.24
The s. does not plow in the autumn	Pr.20.4
The s. is wiser in his own eyes	Pr.26.16

SLUMBER (verb)
he who keeps you will not s.	Ps.121.3
will neither s. nor sleep	Ps.121.4
dreaming, lying down, loving to s.	Is.56.10
O king of Assyria; your nobles s.	Nah.3.18
was delayed, they all s. and slept	Mt.25.5

SMALL
after the fire a still s. voice	1 Kg.19.12
fear the LORD, both s. and great	Ps.115.13
I am s. and despised, yet I	Ps.119.141
because he was s. of stature	Lk.19.3

SMELL (noun)
s. of my son is as the s. of a field	Gen.27.27
no s. of fire had come upon them	Dan.3.27
where would be the sense of s.?	1 Cor.12.17

SMITE
I will s. all the first-born in	Ex.12.12
The sun shall not s. you by day	Ps.121.6
lest I come and s. the land with a	Mal.4.6
to s. the earth with every plague	Rev.11.6

SMITH
Now there was no s. to be found	1 Sam.13.19
all the craftsmen and the s.	2 Kg.24.14
the s. who blows the fire	Is.54.16
Then the LORD showed me four s.	Zech.1.20

SMOKE (noun)
| Mount Sinai was wrapped in s. | Ex.19.18 |

Out of his nostrils comes forth s.	Job 41.20
For my days pass away like s.	Ps.102.3
the house was filled with s.	Is.6.4
the s. of their torment goes up	Rev.14.11

SMOOTH
is a hairy man, and I am a s. man	Gen.27.11
the s. tongue of the adventuress	Pr.6.24
thou dost make s. the path of the	Is.26.7
speak to us s. things, prophesy	Is.30.10
the rough ways shall be made s.	Lk.3.5

SNARE (noun)
their gods shall be a s. to you	Jg.2.3
from the s. of the fowler	Ps.91.3
The s. of death encompassed me	Ps.116.3
fall into . . . the s. of the devil	1 Tim.3.7
escape from the s. of the devil	2 Tim.2.26

SNATCH
were s. away before their time	Job 22.16
who seek to s. away my life	Ps.40.14
one comes and s. away what is sown	Mt.13.19
no one shall s. them out of my hand	Jn.10.28

SNOW
If I wash myself with s.	Job 9.30
entered the storehouses of the s.	Job 38.22
wash me . . . I shall be whiter than s.	Ps.51.7
they shall be as white as s.	Is.1.18

SOBER
but let us keep awake and be s.	1 Th.5.6
to live s., upright, and godly lives	Tit.2.12
be s., set your hope fully upon	1 Pet.1.13
Be s., be watchful. Your adversary	1 Pet.5.8

SODOM
Gen.10.19; its iniquity and destruction, Gen. 13.13; 18.20; 19.4–24; Lot's deliverance from, 13.19; Lam.4.6; Mt.10.15; Lk.17.29; Jude 7; Rev.11.8

SOFT
Will he speak to you s. words?	Job 41.3
A s. answer turns away wrath, but a	Pr.15.1
a s. tongue will break a bone	Pr.25.15
A man clothed in s. raiment?	Lk.7.25

SOIL
Noah was the first tiller of the s.	Gen.9.20
wash away the s. of the earth	Job 14.19
Be confounded, O tillers of the s.	Jl.1.11
I am a tiller of the s.	Zech.13.5
fell on good s. and brought forth	Mt.13.8

SOJOURN (verb)
Abram went down to Egypt to s. there	Gen.12.10
We have come to s. in the land	Gen.47.4
evil may not s. with thee	Ps.5.4
O LORD, who shall s. in thy tent?	Ps.15.1
the outcasts of Moab s. among you	Is.16.4
the strangers that s. in Israel	Ezek.14.7
By faith he s. in the land of promise	Heb.11.9

SOJOURNER
I am a stranger and a s. among you	Gen.23.4
I have been a s. in a foreign land	Ex.2.22
the s. who is within your gates	Ex.20.10
Love the s. therefore; for you were	Dt.10.19
perverts the justice due to the s.	Dt.27.19
They slay the widow and the s.	Ps.94.6
I am a s. on earth; hide not thy	Ps.119.19
those who thrust aside the s.	Mal.3.5
you are no longer strangers and s.	Eph.2.19

SOLD

s. his birthright to Jacob	Gen.25.33
And the LORD s. them into the hand	Jg.4.2
for your iniquities you were s.	Is.50.1
Are not two sparrows s. for a penny?	Mt.10.29
they s., they planted, they built	Lk.17.28
he told those who s. the pigeons	Jn.2.16
they s. their possessions	Acts 2.45
Sapphira s. a piece of property	Acts 5.1
but I am carnal, s. under sin	Rom.7.14
s. his birthright for a single meal	Heb.12.16

SOLDIER

to them, "You have a guard of s.	Mt.27.65
his s. treated him with contempt	Lk.23.11
When the s. had crucified Jesus	Jn.19.23
Peter was sleeping between two s.	Acts 12.6
fellow worker and fellow s.	Phil.2.25
as a good s. of Christ Jesus	2 Tim.2.3
No s. on service gets entangled in	2 Tim.2.4

SOLEMN

the first day shall be a s. rest	Lev.23.39
Sanctify a s. assembly for Baal	2 Kg.10.20
Thy s. processions are seen, O God	Ps.68.24
Sanctify a fast, call a s. assembly	Jl.1.14
take no delight in your s. assemblies	Am.5.21

SOLOMON

2 Sam.5.14; king of Israel, 2 Sam.12.24; 1 Kg.1; 2.24; 1 Chr.28.9; 29; asks of God wisdom, 1 Kg.3.9 (4.29); 2 Chr.1.10; the wise judgment of, 1 Kg.3.16–28; his league with Hiram for building the temple, 1 Kg.5; 2 Chr.2; builds the temple, (2 Sam.7.13; 1 Chr.17.12); 1 Kg.6–7; 2 Chr. 3–5; the dedication, 1 Kg.8; 2 Chr.6; God's covenant with, 1 Kg.9; 2 Chr.7.12; the queen of Sheba visits, 1 Kg.10; 2 Chr.9; Mt. 6.29; 12.42; his idolatry, rebuke, and death, 1 Kg.11; 2 Chr.9.29; Neh.13.26

SON

my s., today I have begotten you	Ps.2.7
and the s. of man that thou dost	Ps.8.4
My s., if sinners entice you, do not	Pr.1.10
My s., do not forget my teaching	Pr.3.1
My s., be attentive to my words	Pr.4.20
He who spares the rod hates his s.	Pr.13.24
Discipline your s. while there is	Pr.19.18
Discipline your s., and he will	Pr.29.17
woman shall conceive and bear a s.	Is.7.14
a child is born, to us a s. is given	Is.9.6
out of Egypt I called my s.	Hos.11.1
saying, "This is my beloved S.	Mt.3.17
one knows the S. except the Father	Mt.11.27
The S. of man will send his angels	Mt.13.41
My s., your sins are forgiven	Mk.2.5
Boanerges, that is, s. of thunder	Mk.3.17
her first-born s. and wrapped him	Lk.2.7
as of the only S. from the Father	Jn.1.14
so loved . . . that he gave his only S.	Jn.3.16
his mother, "Woman, behold your s.!"	Jn.19.26
conformed to the image of his S.	Rom.8.29
I live by faith in the S. of God	Gal.2.20
to wait for his S. from heaven	1 Th.1.10
For you are all s. of light	1 Th.5.5
God is treating you as s.	Heb.12.7
He who has the S. has life	1 Jn.5.12
one like a s. of man	Rev.1.13

SONG

The LORD is my strength and my s.	Ex.15.2
So Moses wrote this s. the same day	Dt.31.22
at night his s. is with me	Ps.42.8
O sing to the LORD a new s.	Ps.96.1
psalms and hymns and spiritual s.	Eph.5.19
they sing a new s. before the	Rev.14.3
and the s. of the Lamb, saying	Rev.15.3

SORCERER

summoned the wise men and the s.	Ex.7.11
soothsayer, or an augur, or a s.	Dt.18.10
will consult the idols and the s.	Is.19.3
enchanters, the s., and the Chaldeans	Dan.2.2
be a swift witness against the s.	Mal.3.5
s., idolaters and all liars	Rev.21.8
the dogs and s. and fornicators	Rev.22.15

SORCERY

used divination and s.	2 Kg.17.17
soothsaying and augury and s.	2 Chr.33.6
I will cut off s. from your hand	Mic.5.12
idolatry, s., enmity, strife	Gal.5.20
nations were deceived by thy s.	Rev.18.23

SORROW

my eye grows dim through s.	Ps.88.9
a foolish son is a s. to his mother	Pr.10.1
Who has s.? Who has strife?	Pr.23.29
S. is better than laughter, for by	Ec.7.3
s. and sighing shall flee away	Is.35.10
a man of s., and acquainted with	Is.53.3
borne our griefs and carried our s.	Is.53.4
found them sleeping for s.	Lk.22.45
s. has filled your hearts	Jn.16.6
have great s. and unceasing anguish	Rom.9.2
lest I should have s. upon s.	Phil.2.27

SORROWFUL

a very great and s. lamentation	Gen.50.10
they were very s., and began	Mt.26.22
countenance fell . . . he went away s.	Mk.10.22
They began to be s., and to say to	Mk.14.19
My soul is very s., even to death	Mk.14.34
as s., yet always rejoicing	2 Cor.6.10

SORRY

the LORD was s. that he had made man	Gen.6.6
I am s. for my sin	Ps.38.18
the king was exceedingly s.	Mk.6.26
if I made you s. with my letter	2 Cor.7.8

SOUL

March on, my s., with might	Jg.5.21
now my s. is poured out within	Job 30.16
LORD is perfect, reviving the s.	Ps.19.7
he restores my s. He leads me	Ps.23.3
My s. thirsts for God	Ps.42.2
O my s. . . . why are you disquieted	Ps.43.5
Awake, my s.! Awake, O harp and	Ps.57.8
My s. longs, yea, faints for the	Ps.84.2
Bless the LORD, O my s.	Ps.103.1
The s. of the wicked desires evil	Pr.21.10
My s. yearns for thee in the night	Is.26.9
he poured out his s. to death	Is.53.12
destroy both s. and body in hell	Mt.10.28
My s. is very sorrowful, even to	Mk.14.34
said, "My s. magnifies the Lord	Lk.1.46
I will say to my s., S., you have	Lk.12.19
Now is my s. troubled. And what	Jn.12.27
spirit and s. and body be kept	1 Th.5.23
which is able to save your s.	Jas.1.21

Shepherd and Guardian of your *s.* 1 Pet.2.25
I know that it is well with your *s.* 3 Jn.2
I saw the *s.* of those who had Rev.20.4

SOUND (noun)
they heard the *s.* of the LORD Gen.3.8
Hearken to the *s.* of my cry, my King Ps.5.2
when the *s.* of the grinding is low Ec.12.4
suddenly a *s.* came from heaven Acts 2.2
the *s.* of a trumpet, and a voice Heb.12.19
was like the *s.* of harpers playing Rev.14.2

SOUND (adjective)
My son, keep *s.* wisdom and discretion Pr.3.21
if your eye is *s.,* your whole body Mt.6.22
A *s.* tree cannot bear evil fruit Mt.7.18
body be kept *s.* and blameless at 1 Th.5.23
is contrary to *s.* doctrine 1 Tim.1.10
the pattern of the *s.* words which 2 Tim.1.13
s. in faith, in love, and in Tit.2.2

SOVEREIGN
S. Lord, who didst make the heaven Acts 4.24
by the blessed and only *S.* 1 Tim.6.15
O *S.* Lord, holy and true, how long Rev.6.10

SOW (verb)
you shall *s.* your seed in vain Lev.26.16
May those who *s.* in tears reap with Ps.126.5
He who observes the wind will not *s.* Ec.11.4
S. for yourselves righteousness Hos.10.12
Listen! A sower went out to *s.* Mk.4.3
One *s.* and another reaps Jn.4.37
he who *s.* sparingly will also reap 2 Cor.9.6
whatever a man *s.* . . . will also reap Gal.6.7

SPAIN
Rom.15.24,28

SPARE
In thy steadfast love *s.* my life Ps.119.88
He who *s.* the rod hates his son Pr.13.24
I will *s.* them as a man *s.* his son Mal.3.17
He who did not *s.* his own Son but Rom.8.32
For if God did not *s.* the angels 2 Pet.2.4

SPARROW
Even the *s.* finds a home Ps.84.3
Like a *s.* in its flitting, like a swallow Pr.26.2
Are not two *s.* sold for a penny? Mt.10.29
you are of more value than many *s.* Lk.12.7

SPEAK
LORD used to *s.* to Moses face to Ex.33.11
S., LORD, for thy servant hears 1 Sam.3.9
My mouth will *s.* the praise of Ps.145.21
to keep silence, and a time to *s.* Ec.3.7
s. to us smooth things, prophesy Is.30.10
S. tenderly to Jerusalem, and cry to Is.40.2
S. the truth to one another Zech.8.16
Woe . . . when all men *s.* well of you Lk.6.26
abundance of the heart his mouth *s.* Lk.6.45
began to *s.* in other tongues Acts 2.4
If I *s.* in the tongues of men and 1 Cor.13.1
Rather, *s.* the truth in love Eph.4.15
slow to *s.,* slow to anger Jas.1.19

SPEAR
LORD saves not with sword and *s.* 1 Sam.17.47
pin David to the wall with the *s.* 1 Sam.19.10
whose *s.* weighed three hundred 2 Sam.21.16
beat . . . their *s.* into pruning hooks Is.2.4
Beat . . . your pruning hooks into *s.* Jl.3.10
soldiers pierced his side with a *s.* Jn.19.34

SPEECH
may not understand one another's *s.* Gen.11.7
but I am slow of *s.* and of tongue Ex.4.10
Day to day pours forth *s.* Ps.19.2
Put away from you crooked *s.* Pr.4.24
to a pure *s.,* that all . . . may call Zeph.3.9
Let your *s.* always be gracious Col.4.6
sound *s.* that cannot be censured Tit.2.8

SPEED (verb)
let him *s.* his work that we may see Is.5.19
that you may *s.* me on my journey 1 Cor.16.6
S. him on his way in peace 1 Cor.16.11
the word of the Lord may *s.* on 2 Th.3.1
Do your best to *s.* Zenas the lawyer Tit.3.13

SPEND
Why do you *s.* your money for that Is.55.2
and whatever more you *s.* Lk.10.35
I will most gladly *s.* and be *s.* 2 Cor.12.15

SPEW
I will *s.* you out of my mouth Rev.3.16

SPICES
s. for the anointing oil and for Ex.25.6
a very great quantity of *s.* 1 Kg.10.10
His cheeks are like beds of *s.* S.of S.5.13
prepared *s.* and ointments Lk.23.56
in linen cloths with the *s.* Jn.19.40

SPIES
We are honest men, we are not *s.* Gen.42.31
men secretly from Shittim as *s.* Jos.2.1
David sent out *s.,* and learned of 1 Sam.26.4
s., who pretended to be sincere Lk.20.20
given friendly welcome to the *s.* Heb.11.31

SPIRIT
the *S.* of God was moving over Gen.1.2
My *s.* shall not abide in man for Gen.6.3
Then the *S.* of the LORD came upon Jg.11.29
evil *s.* from God was upon Saul 1 Sam.16.23
inherit a double share of your *s.* 2 Kg.2.9
The *s.* of Elijah rests on Elisha 2 Kg.2.15
A *s.* glided past my face; the hair Job 4.15
Into thy hand I commit my *s.* Ps.31.5
take not thy holy *S.* from me Ps.51.11
Whither shall I go from thy *S.*? Ps.139.2
but the LORD weighs the *s.* Pr.16.7
The *s.* of man is the lamp of the Pr.20.27
No man has power to retain the *s.* Ec.8.8
the *s.* returns to God who gave it Ec.12.7
Who has directed the *S.* of the LORD Is.40.13
the *S.* entered into me and set me Ezek.2.2
I will pour out my *s.* on all flesh Jl.2.28
Blessed are the poor in *s.* Mt.5.3
will baptize you with the Holy *S.* Mk.1.8
my *s.* rejoices in God my Savior Lk.1.47
The *S.* of the Lord is upon me Lk.4.18
the Holy *S.* will teach you in Lk.12.12
into thy hands I commit my *s.* Lk.23.46
God is *s.,* and those who worship him Jn.4.24
When the *S.* of truth comes, he will Jn.16.13
said to them, "Receive the Holy *S.* Jn.20.22
will pour out my *S.* upon all flesh Acts 2.17
prayed, "Lord Jesus, receive my *s.*" Acts 7.59
shall be baptized with the Holy *S.* Acts 11.16
Now the Lord is the *S.* 2 Cor.3.17
walk by the *S.,* and do not gratify Gal.5.16
But the fruit of the *S.* is love Gal.5.22
do not grieve the Holy *S.* of God Eph.4.30

Do not quench the *S*.   1 Th.5.19
Christ . . . through the eternal *S*.   Heb.9.14
because the *S*. is the truth   1 Jn.5.7
I was in the *S*. on the Lord's day   Rev.1.10
The *S*. and the Bride say, "Come."   Rev.22.17
SPIRITS
and he cast out the *s*. with a word   Mt.8.16
seven other *s*. more evil than   Mt.12.45
authority over the unclean *s*.   Mk.6.7
diseases and plagues and evil *s*.   Lk.7.21
unclean *s*. came out of many who   Acts 8.7
ability to distinguish between *s*.   1 Cor.12.10
the weak and beggarly elemental *s*.   Gal.4.9
giving heed to deceitful *s*.   1 Tim.4.1
the *s*. of just men made perfect   Heb.12.23
preached to the *s*. in prison   1 Pet.3.19
test the *s*. to see whether they   1 Jn.4.1
three foul *s*. like frogs   Rev.16.13
they are demonic *s*., performing   Rev.16.14
SPIRITUAL
to God, which is your *s*. worship   Rom.12.1
interpreting *s*. truths to those   1 Cor.2.13
Now concerning *s*. gifts, brethren   1 Cor.12.1
there is also a *s*. body   1 Cor.15.44
you who are *s*. should restore him   Gal.6.1
against the *s*. hosts of wickedness   Eph.6.12
yourselves built into a *s*. house   1 Pet.2.5
SPIT
I am one before whom men *s*.   Job 17.6
when he had *s*. on his eyes   Mk.8.23
s. upon him, and scourge him   Mk.10.34
And some began to *s*. on him   Mk.14.65
shamefully treated and *s*. upon   Lk.18.32
SPLENDOR
clothe yourself with glory and *s*.   Job 40.10
the glorious *s*. of thy kingdom   Ps.145.12
The latter *s*. of this house shall   Hag.2.9
earth was made bright with his *s*.   Rev.18.1
SPOIL (noun)
shall enjoy the *s*. of your enemies   Dt.20.14
But the people took of the *s*.   1 Sam.15.21
to divide the *s*. with the proud   Pr.16.19
divide the *s*. with the strong   Is.53.12
will make a *s*. of your riches   Ezek.26.12
and divides his *s*.   Lk.11.22
SPOT
his skin or the leopard his *s*.?   Jer.13.23
without *s*. or wrinkle or any such   Eph.5.27
a lamb without blemish or *s*.   1 Pet.1.19
found by him without *s*. or blemish   2 Pet.3.14
SPREAD
O LORD; I *s*. out my hands to thee   Ps.88.9
The lips of the wise *s*. knowledge   Pr.15.7
So his fame *s*. throughout all Syria   Mt.4.24
many *s*. their garments on the road   Mk.11.8
so death *s*. to all men because   Rom.5.12
SPRING (noun)
of Baca they make it a place of *s*.   Ps.84.6
from it flow the *s*. of life   Pr.4.23
become in him a *s*. of water   Jn.4.14
Does a *s*. pour forth from the same   Jas.3.11
These are waterless *s*. and mists   2 Pet.2.17
guide them to *s*. of living water   Rev.7.17
SPRING (verb)
sang this song: "*S*. up, O well   Num.21.17
Faithfulness will *s*. up from the   Ps.85.11

before they *s*. forth I tell you of   Is.42.9
a . . . Branch to *s*. forth for David   Jer.33.15
SPURN
if you *s*. my statutes, and if your   Lev.26.15
s. the counsel of the Most High   Ps.107.11
Do not *s*. us, for thy name's sake   Jer.14.21
the man who has *s*. the Son of God   Heb.10.29
SPY (verb)
Send men to *s*. out the land   Num.13.2
whom Joshua sent to *s*. out Jericho   Jos.6.25
overthrow and to *s*. out the land?   1 Chr.19.3
slipped in to *s*. out our freedom   Gal.2.4
STAFF
lay my *s*. upon the . . . child   2 Kg.4.29
thy rod and thy *s*., they comfort me   Ps.23.4
has broken the *s*. of the wicked   Is.14.5
I took my *s*. Grace, and I broke it   Zech.11.10
no *s*., nor bag, nor bread, nor money   Lk.9.3
STAND (verb)
to *s*. before the LORD to minister   Dt.10.8
you cannot *s*. before your enemies   Jos.7.13
Who is able to *s*. before the LORD   1 Sam.6.20
at last he will *s*. upon the earth   Job 19.25
Why dost thou *s*. afar off, O LORD?   Ps.10.1
And who shall *s*. in his holy place?   Ps.24.3
he will *s*. before kings   Pr.22.29
but who can *s*. before jealousy?   Pr.27.4
word of our God will *s*. for ever   Is.40.8
And he shall *s*. and feed his flock   Mic.5.4
Who can *s*. before his indignation?   Nah.1.6
they love to *s*. and pray in the   Mt.6.5
why do you *s*. looking into heaven?   Acts 1.11
shall all *s*. before the judgment   Rom.14.10
s. firm thus in the Lord   Phil.4.1
Behold, I *s*. at the door and knock   Rev.3.20
STANDARD
shall encamp each by his own *s*.   Num.2.2
Raise a *s*. toward Zion, flee for   Jer.4.6
Set up a *s*. against the walls of   Jer.51.12
obedient . . . to the *s*. of teaching   Rom.6.17
were wise according to worldly *s*.   1 Cor.1.26
STAR
he made the *s*. also   Gen.1.16
descendants as the *s*. of heaven   Ex.32.13
a *s*. shall come forth out of Jacob   Num.24.17
when the morning *s*. sang together   Job 38.7
the *s*. which thou hast established   Ps.8.3
He determines the number of the *s*.   Ps.147.4
we have seen his *s*. in the East   Mt.2.2
the seven *s*. are the angels of the   Rev.1.20
STATURE
we saw in it . . . men of great *s*.   Num.13.32
an Egyptian, a man of great *s*.   1 Chr.11.23
increased in wisdom and in *s*.   Lk.2.52
because he was small of *s*.   Lk.19.3
measure of the *s*. of the fulness   Eph.4.13
STATUTE
And it shall be a *s*. to you for   Lev.16.29
for a perpetual *s*. throughout your   Num.10.8
shall keep his *s*. and commandments   Dt.4.40
I will observe thy *s*.; O forsake   Ps.119.8
I will meditate on thy *s*.   Ps.119.48
you have turned aside from my *s*.   Mal.3.7
STEADFAST
Thou hast led in thy *s*. love the   Ex.15.13
Remember thy *s*. love for David   2 Chr.6.42

hast granted me life and s. love	Job 10.12	you saw that a s. was cut from a	Dan.2.45
But I have trusted in thy s. love	Ps.13.5	asks . . . for bread, will give him a s.?	Mt.7.9
Thy s. love, O LORD, extends to the	Ps.36.5	they found the s. rolled away	Lk.24.2
Their heart was not s. toward him	Ps.78.37	sacred s. that fell from the sky	Acts 19.35
his s. love endures for ever	Ps.100.5	Come to him, to that living s.	1 Pet.2.4
thank the LORD for his s. love	Ps.107.8	I will give him a white s.	Rev.2.17
He who is s. in righteousness will	Pr.11.19	STONE (verb)	
be s., immovable, always	1 Cor.15.58	you shall s. that man or woman	Dt.17.5
as a sure and s. anchor of the soul	Heb.6.19	We s. you for no good work but for	Jn.10.33
STEADFASTNESS		they s. Paul and dragged him out	Acts 14.19
the God of s. and encouragement	Rom.15.5	They were s. . . . were sawn in two	Heb.11.37
my patience, my love, my s.	2 Tim.3.10	STOREHOUSE	
testing of your faith produces s.	Jas.1.3	Have you entered the s. of the snow	Job 38.22
You have heard of the s. of Job	Jas.5.11	brings forth the wind from his s.	Ps.135.7
STEAL		Bring the full tithes into the s.	Mal.3.10
You shall not s.	Ex.20.15	they have neither s. nor barn	Lk.12.24
where thieves break in and s.	Mt.6.19	STORM	
Do not s., Do not bear false	Mk.10.19	he made the s. be still	Ps.107.29
preach against stealing, do you s.?	Rom.2.21	when panic strikes you like a s.	Pr.1.27
Let the thief no longer s.	Eph.4.28	a shelter from the s. and rain	Is.4.6
STEPHEN		Behold, the s. of the LORD! Wrath	Jer.23.19
Acts 6.5; 7.2; 8.2; 11.19; 22.20		And a great s. of wind arose	Mk.4.37
STEPS		STRAIGHT	
The s. of a man are from the LORD	Ps.37.23	make thy way s. before me	Ps.5.8
they lurk, they watch my s.	Ps.56.6	he will make s. your paths	Pr.3.6
Keep steady my s. according to	Ps.119.133	What is crooked cannot be made s.	Ec.1.15
A man's s. are ordered by the LORD	Pr.20.24	make s. in the desert a highway for	Is.40.3
the dial of Ahaz turn back ten s.	Is.38.8	immediately she was made s.	Lk.13.13
that you should follow in his s.	1 Pet.2.21	go to the street called S.	Acts 9.11
STEWARD		STRANGE	
owner of the vineyard said to his s.	Mt.20.8	There shall be no s. god among you	Ps.81.9
There was a rich man who had a s.	Lk.16.1	Your eyes will see s. things	Pr.23.33
When the s. of the feast tasted the	Jn.2.9	We have seen s. things today	Lk.5.26
is required of s. that they be	1 Cor.4.2	led . . . by diverse and s. teachings	Heb.13.9
as good s. of God's varied grace	1 Pet.4.10	STRANGER	
STIFF-NECKED		You shall not oppress a s.	Ex.23.9
and behold, it is a s. people	Ex.32.9	if a s. sojourns among you	Num.9.14
Israel, 'You are a s. people	Ex.33.5	I have become a s. to my brethren	Ps.69.8
Do not now be s. as your fathers	2 Chr.30.8	A s. they will not follow, but they	Jn.10.5
You s. people, uncircumcised in	Acts 7.51	s. to the covenants of promise	Eph.2.12
STILL		show hospitality to s.	Heb.13.2
after the fire a s. small voice	1 Kg.19.12	STRAW	
He leads me beside s. waters	Ps.23.2	no longer give . . . s. to make bricks	Ex.5.7
Be s., and know that I am God	Ps.46.10	No s. is given to your servants	Ex.5.16
"Peace! Be s.!" And the wind	Mk.4.39	they are like s. before the wind	Job 21.18
My Father is working s.	Jn.5.17	the lion shall eat s. like the ox	Is.65.25
STIR (verb)		STREAM (noun)	
S. up thy might, and come to save us	Ps.80.2	like a tree planted by s. of water	Ps.1.3
s. up the spirit of a destroyer	Jer.51.1	As a hart longs for flowing s.	Ps.42.1
He s. up the people, teaching	Lk.23.5	a river whose s. make glad the city	Ps.46.4
s. up persecution against Paul	Acts 13.50	fountain of wisdom is a gushing s.	Pr.18.4
your zeal has s. up most of them	2 Cor.9.2	All s. run to the sea, but the sea	Ec.1.7
consider how to s. up one another	Heb.10.24	STREET	
STOCKS		Wisdom cries aloud in the s.	Pr.1.20
Thou puttest my feet in s.	Job 13.27	boys and girls playing in its s.	Zech.8.5
he puts my feet in the s.	Job 33.11	in the synagogues and at the s. corners	Mt.6.5
released Jeremiah from the s.	Jer.20.3	go to the s. called Straight	Acts 9.11
fastened their feet in the s.	Acts 16.24	the s. of the city was pure gold	Rev.21.21
STONE (noun)		STRENGTH	
And they had brick for s.	Gen.11.3	the God who girded me with s.	Ps.18.32
So Jacob took a s., and set it up	Gen.31.45	May the LORD give s. to his people	Ps.29.11
LORD gave me the two tables of s.	Dt.9.11	God is our refuge and s.	Ps.46.1
His heart is hard as a s.	Job 41.24	gives power and s. to his people	Ps.68.35
lest you dash your foot against a s.	Ps.91.12	They go from s. to s.	Ps.84.7
The s. which the builders rejected	Ps.118.22	s. and beauty are in his sanctuary	Ps.96.6
a tested s., a precious cornerstone	Is.28.16	the LORD GOD is my s. and my song	Is.12.2

for the LORD shall renew their s.	Is.40.31		**STUBBLE**	
O LORD, my s. and my stronghold	Jer.16.19		to gather s. for straw	Ex.5.12
He has shown s. with his arm	Lk.1.51		Clubs are counted as s.; he laughs	Job 41.29
not . . . be tempted beyond your s.	1 Cor.10.13		tempest carries them off like s.	Is.40.24
STRENGTHEN			they are consumed, like dry s.	Nah.1.10
but now, O God, s. thou my hands	Neh.6.9		all evildoers will be s.	Mal.4.1
s. me according to thy word	Ps.119.28		precious stones, wood, hay, s.	1 Cor.3.12
lengthen . . . cords and s. . . . stakes	Is.54.2		**STUBBORN**	
s. your brethren	Lk.22.32		for you are a s. people	Dt.9.6
the churches were s. in the faith	Acts 16.5		This our son is s. and rebellious	Dt.21.20
is able to s. you according to	Rom.16.25		I gave them over to their s. hearts	Ps.81.12
can do all things in him who s. me	Phil.4.13		Like a s. heifer, Israel is s.	Hos.4.16
May you be s. with all power	Col.1.11		when some were s. and disbelieved	Acts 19.9
he will s. you and guard you from	2 Th.3.3		**STUMBLE**	
STRIFE			they shall s. and fall	Ps.27.2
Let there be no s. between you and	Gen.13.8		as for me, my feet had almost s.	Ps.73.2
deliver me from s. with the peoples	Ps.18.43		and if you run, you will not s.	Pr.4.12
Hatred stirs up s., but love covers	Pr.10.12		a stone that will make men s.	Rom.9.33
A perverse man spreads s.	Pr.16.28		anything that makes your brother s.	Rom.14.21
Who has s.? Who has complaining?	Pr.23.29		for they s. because they disobey	1 Pet.2.8
there is jealousy and s. among you	1 Cor.3.3		**STUPID**	
s., jealousy, anger, selfishness	Gal.5.20		I was s. and ignorant, I was like a	Ps.73.22
STRIKE			A s. son is a grief to a father	Pr.17.21
you shall s. the rock, and water	Ex.17.6		man is s. and without knowledge	Jer.10.14
Let a good man s. or rebuke me in	Ps.141.5		nothing to do with s., senseless	2 Tim.2.23
But if any one s. you on the right	Mt.5.39		avoid s. controversies, genealogies	Tit.3.9
lest you s. your foot against a stone	Lk.4.11		**SUBDUE**	
God shall s. you, you whitewashed	Acts 23.3		fill the earth and s. it	Gen.1.28
the sun shall not s. them, nor any	Rev.7.16		I would soon s. their enemies	Ps.81.14
STRIPE			no one had the strength to s. him	Mk.5.4
wound for wound, s. for s.	Ex.21.25		I pommel my body and s. it	1 Cor.9.27
Forty s. may be given him, but not	Dt.25.3		**SUBJECT**	
and with his s. we are healed	Is.53.5		the demons are s. to us	Lk.10.17
STRIPPED			the creation was s. to futility	Rom.8.20
Hezekiah s. the gold from the	2 Kg.18.16		Let every person be s. to the	Rom.13.1
stouthearted were s. of their spoil	Ps.76.5		As the church is s. to Christ	Eph.5.24
I will go s. and naked; I will make	Mic.1.8		Wives, be s. to your husbands	Col.3.18
they s. him of the purple cloak	Mk.15.20		younger be s. to the elders	1 Pet.5.5
s. him and beat him, and departed	Lk.10.30		**SUBJECTION**	
STRIVE			brought into s. under their power	Ps.106.42
Woe to him who s. with his Maker	Is.45.9		brought them into s. as slaves	Jer.34.11
S. to enter by the narrow door	Lk.13.24		all things in s. under his feet	1 Cor.15.27
For to this end we toil and s.	1 Tim.4.10		everything in s. under his feet	Heb.2.8
Let us therefore s. to enter that	Heb.4.11		**SUBMISSIVE**	
S. for peace with all men	Heb.12.14		his children s. and respectful in	1 Tim.3.4
STRONG			Bid slaves to be s. to their masters	Tit.2.9
Drink no wine nor s. drink	Lev.10.9		Remind them to be s. to rulers	Tit.3.1
Be s. and of good courage	Dt.31.7		be s. to your husbands, so that	1 Pet.3.1
Out of the s. came something sweet	Jg.14.14		**SUBMIT**	
He delivered me from my s. enemy	Ps.18.17		did not s. to God's righteousness	Rom.10.3
be s., and let your heart take	Ps.27.14		do not s. again to a yoke of slavery	Gal.5.1
Wine is a mocker; s. drink a brawler	Pr.20.1		Obey your leaders and s. to them	Heb.13.17
for love is s. as death	S.of S.8.6		S. yourselves therefore to God	Jas.4.7
shall divide the spoil with the s.	Is.53.12		**SUCCEED**	
And he shall make a s. covenant	Dan.9.27		devise mischief, they will not s.	Ps.21.11
can one enter a s. man's house	Mt.12.29		with many advisers they s.	Pr.15.22
shall drink no wine nor s. drink	Lk.1.15		a man who shall not s. in his days	Jer.22.30
We who are s. ought to bear with	Rom.15.1		says the LORD . . . you shall not s.	Jer.32.5
when I am weak, then I am s.	2 Cor.12.10		Will he s.? Can a man escape	Ezek.17.15
STRONGHOLD			**SUCCESS**	
The LORD is a s. for the oppressed	Ps.9.9		the LORD your God granted me s.	Gen.27.20
my s. The LORD is a s., my deliverer, my shield	Ps.144.2		may have good s. wherever you go	Jos.1.7
The LORD is a s. to him whose way	Pr.10.29		had s. in all his undertakings	1 Sam.18.14
O LORD, my strength and my s.	Jer.16.19		so that their hands achieve no s.	Job 5.12
have divine power to destroy s.	2 Cor.10.4		LORD, we beseech thee, give us s.	Ps.118.25

SUCCOTH
Gen.33.17; Num.33.5; Jg.8.5; Ps.60.6

SUFFER
The young lions *s.* want and hunger	Ps.34.10
the simple go on, and *s.* for it	Pr.22.3
the Son of man must *s.* many things	Mk.8.31
that the Christ must *s.*	Acts 26.23
if one member *s.*, all *s.* together	1 Cor.12.26
So Jesus also *s.* outside the gate	Heb.13.12
is better to *s.* for doing right	1 Pet.3.17
Do not fear what you are . . . to *s.*	Rev.2.10

SUFFERING (noun)
saw that his *s.* was very great	Job 2.13
knowing that *s.* produces endurance	Rom.5.3
your share of *s.* for the gospel	2 Tim.1.8
As an example of *s.* and patience	Jas.5.10
so far as you share Christ's *s.*	1 Pet.4.13

SUFFICIENT
and lend him *s.* for his need	Dt.15.8
own trouble be *s.* for the day	Mt.6.34
Who is *s.* for these things?	2 Cor.2.16
My grace is *s.* for you, for my	2 Cor.12.9

SUMMER
s. and winter, day and night	Gen.8.22
thou hast made *s.* and winter	Ps.74.17
A son who gathers in *s.* is prudent	Pr.10.5
behold, a basket of *s.* fruit	Am.8.1
know that the *s.* is already near	Lk.21.30

SUN
S., stand thou still at Gibeon	Jos.10.12
In them he has set a tent for the *s.*	Ps.19.4
the LORD God is a *s.* and shield	Ps.84.11
The *s.* shall not smite you by day	Ps.121.6
Praise him, *s.* and moon, praise him	Ps.148.3
there is nothing new under the *s.*	Ec.1.9
So the *s.* turned back on the dial	Is.38.8
the *s.* beat upon the head of Jonah	Jon.4.8
he makes his *s.* rise on the evil	Mt.5.45
when the *s.* rose it was scorched	Mk.4.6
signs in *s.* and moon and stars	Lk.21.25
a woman clothed with the *s.*	Rev.12.1

SUPPER
There they made him a *s.*; Martha	Jn.12.2
rose from *s.*, laid aside his garments	Jn.13.4
after *s.*, saying, "This cup is	1 Cor.11.25
to the marriage *s.* of the Lamb	Rev.19.9

SUPPLICATION
The LORD has heard my *s.*	Ps.6.9
and hide not thy self from my *s.*	Ps.55.1
Let my *s.* come before thee	Ps.119.170
making *s.* for all the saints	Eph.6.18
by prayer and *s.* with thanksgiving	Phil.4.6
continues in *s.* and prayers night	1 Tim.5.5
Jesus offered up prayers and *s.*	Heb.5.7

SUPPLY
their abundance may *s.* your want	2 Cor.8.14
by every joint with which it is *s.*	Eph.4.16
my God will *s.* every need of yours	Phil.4.19
s. what is lacking in your faith?	1 Th.3.10
by the strength which God *s.*	1 Pet.4.11

SUPPORT
the land could not *s.* both of them	Gen.13.6
Those who *s.* Egypt shall fall	Ezek.30.6
it is not you that *s.* the root	Rom.11.18
So we ought to *s.* such men	3 Jn.8

SURE
the testimony of the LORD is *s.*	Ps.19.7
All thy commandments are *s.*	Ps.119.86
then all your ways will be *s.*	Pr.4.26
like a peg in a *s.* place	Is.22.23
plans formed of old, faithful and *s.*	Is.25.1
Temptations to sin are *s.* to come	Lk.17.1
I am *s.* that neither death, nor	Rom.8.38
The saying is *s.* and worthy of	1 Tim.1.15
The saying is *s.* I desire you to	Tit.3.8
the prophetic word made more *s.*	2 Pet.1.19

SURETY
I will be *s.* for him; of my hand	Gen.43.9
Be *s.* for thy servant for good	Ps.119.122
He who gives *s.* for a stranger will	Pr.11.15
This makes Jesus the *s.* of a better	Heb.7.22

SURROUND
steadfast love *s.* him who trusts	Ps.32.10
They *s.* me, *s.* me on every side	Ps.118.11
you see Jerusalem *s.* by armies	Lk.21.20
we are *s.* by so great a cloud of	Heb.12.1

SURVIVE
those who *s.* will be very few	Is.16.14
in this city who *s.* the pestilence	Jer.21.7
anger of the LORD none escaped or *s.*	Lam.2.22
Then every one that *s.* of all the	Zech.14.16
work . . . built on the foundation *s.*	1 Cor.3.14

SUSTAIN
thou *s.* them in the wilderness	Neh.9.21
The LORD *s.* him on his sickbed	Ps.41.3
on the LORD, and he will *s.* you	Ps.55.22
may know how to *s.* with a word him	Is.50.4
who will *s.* you to the end	1 Cor.1.8

SWALLOW (verb)
But Aaron's rod *s.* up their rods	Ex.7.12
opened its mouth and *s.* them up	Num.16.32
LORD will *s.* them up in his wrath	Ps.21.9
a great fish to *s.* up Jonah	Jon.1.17
Death is *s.* up in victory	1 Cor.15.54
what is mortal may be *s.* up by life	2 Cor.5.4

SWEAR
you shall not *s.* by my name	Lev.19.12
who *s.* to his own hurt and does not	Ps.15.4
Do not *s.* at all, either by heaven	Mt.5.34
a curse on himself and to *s.*	Mt.26.74
had no one greater by whom to *s.*	Heb.6.13
do not *s.*, either by heaven or by	Jas.5.12

SWEAT
In the *s.* of your face you shall	Gen.3.19
with anything that causes *s.*	Ezek.44.18
his *s.* became like great drops	Lk.22.44

SWEEP
S. me not away with sinners	Ps.26.9
Thou dost *s.* men away	Ps.90.5
Then they *s.* by like the wind	Hab.1.11
light a lamp and *s.* the house	Lk.15.8
to *s.* her away with the flood	Rev.12.15

SWEET
and the water became *s.*	Ex.15.25
the *s.* psalmist of Israel	2 Sam.23.1
wickedness is *s.* in his mouth	Job 20.12
How *s.* are thy words to my taste	Ps.119.103
Stolen water is *s.*, and bread	Pr.9.17
S. is the sleep of a laborer	Ec.5.12

SWIFT
My days are *s.* than a weaver's	Job 7.6

the race is not to the *s.*   Ec.9.11
Flight shall perish from the *s.*   Am.2.14
Their feet are *s.* to shed blood   Rom.3.15
upon themselves *s.* destruction   2 Pet.2.1

SWINE
Like a gold ring in a *s.* snout is a   Pr.11.22
do not throw your pearls before *s.*   Mt.7.6
Now a great herd of *s.* was feeding   Mk.5.11
sent him into his fields to feed *s.*   Lk.15.15

SWORD
a flaming *s.* which turned every   Gen.3.24
Put every man his *s.* on his side   Ex. 32.27
not draw *s.* out of his belly   Jg.3.22
LORD saves not with *s.* and spear   1 Sam.17.47
The *s.* of Goliath the Philistine   1 Sam.21.9
Deliver my soul from the *s.*   Ps.22.20
Rescue me from the cruel *s.*   Ps.144.11
rash words are like *s.* thrusts   Pr.12.18
beat their *s.* into plowshares   Is.2.4
not lift up *s.* against nation   Is.2.4
Ah, *s.* of the LORD! How long till   Jer.47.6
Beat your plowshares into *s.*   Jl.3.10
not come to bring peace, but a *s.*   Mt.10.34
a *s.* will pierce through your own soul Lk.2.35
Put your *s.* into its sheath   Jn.18.11
the *s.* of the Spirit, which is   Eph.6.17
the *s.* that issues from his mouth   Rev.19.21

SYCAMORE
as the *s.* of the Shephelah   1 Kg.10.27
and a dresser of *s.* trees   Am.7.14
climbed up into a *s.* tree to see him   Lk.19.4

SYNAGOGUE
he entered the *s.* and taught   Mk.1.21
Then came one of the rulers of the *s.*   Mk.5.22
he went to the *s.*, as his custom   Lk.4.16
he was to be put out of the *s.*   Jn.9.22
belonged to the *s.* of the Freedmen   Acts 6.9
letters to the *s.* at Damascus   Acts 9.2
he argued in the *s.* every sabbath   Acts 18.4
Sosthenes, the ruler of the *s.*   Acts 18.17
in every *s.* I imprisoned   Acts 22.19
and are not, but are a *s.* of Satan   Rev.2.9

SYRIA
Jg.10.6; 1 Kg.10.29; 1 Chr.18.6; Mt.4.24; Gal.
1.21

SYROPHOENICIAN
the woman was a Greek, a *S.* by birth Mk.7.26

TABERNACLE
concerning the pattern of the *t.*   Ex.25.9
anoint the *t.* and all that is in it   Ex.40.9
Moses erected the *t.*; he laid its   Ex.40.18
the glory of the LORD filled the *t.*   Ex.40.35
anointed the *t.* and all that was in   Lev.8.10
and the feast of *t.*   2 Chr.8.13
the Jews' feast of *T.* was at hand   Jn.7.2

TABLE
So Moses cut two *t.* of stone like   Ex.34.4
he wrote them upon two *t.* of stone   Dt.5.22
Thou preparest a *t.* before me in   Ps.23.5
and sit at *t.* with Abraham   Mt.8.11
dogs under the *t.* eat the children's   Mk.7.28
the *t.* of the moneychangers   Mk.11.15
was sitting at *t.* in the Pharisee's   Lk.7.37
Now no one at the *t.* knew why he   Jn.13.28

at *t.* in an idol's temple   1 Cor.8.10
t. of the Lord and the *t.* of demons   1 Cor.10.21

TABLET
write them on the *t.* of your heart   Pr.7.3
make it plain upon *t.*, so he may run   Hab.2.2
And he asked for a writing *t.*   Lk.1.63
not on *t.* of stone but on *t.* of   2 Cor.3.3

TABOR
Jos.19.22; Jg.4.6; 1 Chr.6.77; Ps.89.12; Hos.5.1

TALENT
Of a *t.* of pure gold shall it be   Ex.25.39
weight of it was a *t.* of gold   2 Sam.12.30
else you shall pay a *t.* of silver   1 Kg.20.39
who owed him ten thousand *t.*   Mt.18.24
But he who had received the one *t.*   Mt.25.18
take the *t.* from him, and give it   Mt.25.28

TALK (noun)
Job opens his mouth in empty *t.*   Job 35.16
I am the *t.* of those who sit in the   Ps.69.12
put devious *t.* far from you   Pr.4.24
how to entangle him in his *t.*   Mt.22.15
not consist in *t.* but in power   1 Cor.4.20
Let no evil *t.* come out of your   Eph.4.29
nor silly *t.*, nor levity   Eph.5.4
foul *t.* from your mouth   Col.3.8

TALK (verb)
because he had been *t.* with God   Ex.34.29
T. no more so very proudly   1 Sam.2.3
my tongue will *t.* of thy . . . help   Ps.71.24
their lips *t.* of mischief   Pr.24.2
while he *t.* to us on the road   Lk.24.32
I will no longer *t.* much with you   Jn.14.30
to see you and *t.* with you face to   2 Jn.12

TARRY
Weeping may *t.* for the night   Ps.30.5
my deliverer; O LORD, do not *t.*   Ps.70.5
Those who *t.* long over wine   Pr.23.30
my salvation will not *t.*   Is.46.13
one shall come and shall not *t.*   Heb.10.37

TARSHISH
Gen.10.4; Ps.48.7; Is.2.16; Jer.10.9; Jon.1.3

TARSUS
Acts 9.11; 11.25; 21.39; 22.3

TASK
all your *t.* of making bricks   Ex.5.14
each to his *t.* and to his burden   Num.4.19
Arise, for it is your *t.*   Ezra 10.4
it seemed to me a wearisome *t.*   Ps.73.16
Whatever your *t.*, work heartily   Col.3.23
he desires a noble *t.*   1 Tim.3.1

TASTE (verb)
O *t.* and see that the LORD is good   Ps.34.8
How sweet are thy words to my *t.*   Ps.119.103
who will not *t.* death before   Lk.9.27
he will never *t.* death   Jn.8.52
Do not *t.*, Do not touch   Col.2.21
he might *t.* death for every one   Heb.2.9
have *t.* the kindness of the Lord   1 Pet.2.3

TAUGHT
from my youth thou hast *t.* me   Ps.71.17
I have *t.* you the way of wisdom   Pr.4.11
your sons shall be *t.* by the LORD   Is.54.13
he entered the synagogue and *t.*   Lk.6.6
And they shall all be *t.* by God   Jn.6.45
speak thus as the Father *t.* me   Jn.8.28
in words not *t.* by human wisdom   1 Cor.2.13

Let him who is *t.* the word share Gal.6.6
have been *t.* by God to love one 1 Th.4.9

TAX
Do not even the *t.* collectors do Mt.5.46
Matthew sitting at the *t.* office Mt.9.9
the *t.* collectors and the harlots Mt.21.31
Is it lawful to pay *t.* to Caesar Mk.12.14
But the *t.* collector, standing far Lk.18.13
t. to whom *t.* are due, revenue to Rom.13.7

TEACH
will *t.* you what you shall do Ex.4.15
you shall *t.* them diligently to Dt.6.7
Will any *t.* God knowledge Job 21.22
T. me thy way, O LORD; and lead me Ps.27.11
I will *t.* you the fear of the LORD Ps.34.11
I will *t.* transgressors thy ways Ps.51.13
t. the way of God truthfully Mt.22.16
Spirit will *t.* you in that very hour Lk.12.12
he will *t.* you all things Jn.14.26
charged you not to *t.* in this name Acts 5.28
Command and *t.* these things 1 Tim.4.11
will be able to *t.* others also 2 Tim.2.2
no need that any one should *t.* you 1 Jn.2.27

TEACHER
more understanding than all my *t.* Ps.119.99
A disciple is not above his *t.* Mt.10.24
fully taught will be like his *t.* Lk.6.40
said to him, "Rabbi" (which means *T.*) Jn.1.38
You call me T. and Lord Jn.13.13
dignified, hospitable, an apt *t.* 1 Tim.3.2
by this time you ought to be *t.* Heb.5.12
Let not many of you become *t.* Jas.3.1
there will be false *t.* among you 2 Pet.2.1

TEACHING (noun)
Give ear, O my people, to my *t.* Ps.78.1
My son, do not forget my *t.* Pr.3.1
The *t.* of the wise is a fountain of Pr.13.14
they were astonished at his *t.* Mt.22.33
A new *t.*! With authority Mk.1.27
Mary . . . listened to his *t.* Lk.10.39
My *t.* is not mine, but his who sent Jn.7.16
Take heed to yourself and to your *t.* 1 Tim.4.16
All scripture . . . profitable for *t.* 2 Tim.3.16
people will not endure sound *t.* 2 Tim.4.3
who hold the *t.* of Balaam Rev.2.14

TEAR (noun)
My *t.* have been my food day and Ps.42.3
put thou my *t.* in thy bottle Ps.56.8
who sow in *t.* reap with shouts of Ps.126.5
my eyes a fountain of *t.* Jer.9.1
my eyes flow with rivers of *t.* Lam.3.48
began to wet his feet with her *t.* Lk.7.38
to admonish every one with *t.* Acts 20.31
anguish of heart and with many *t.* 2 Cor.2.4
with loud cries and *t.* Heb.5.7
though he sought it with *t.* Heb.12.17
wipe away every *t.* from their eyes Rev.21.4

TEETH
have escaped by the skin of my *t.* Job 19.20
dost break the *t.* of the wicked Ps.3.7
gnashing at me with their *t.* Ps.35.16
his *t.* shall be set on edge Jer.31.30
the children's *t.* are set on edge Ezek.18.2
men will weep and gnash their *t.* Mt.13.50
they ground their *t.* against him Acts 7.54
and their *t.* like lions' *t.* Rev.9.8

TEKOA
2 Sam.14.2; 2 Chr.11.6; Jer.6.1; Am.1.1

TEMPERATE
t., sensible, dignified 1 Tim.3.2
t., faithful in all things 1 Tim.3.11
Bid the older men be *t.*, serious Tit.2.2

TEMPEST
t. carries them off like stubble Is.40.24
a *t.* in the day of the whirlwind Am.1.14
there was a mighty *t.* on the sea Jon.1.4
and no small *t.* lay on us Acts 27.20
darkness and gloom, and a *t.* Heb.12.18

TEMPLE
were building a *t.* to the LORD Ezra 4.1
The LORD is in his holy *t.* Ps.11.4
the LORD, and to inquire in his *t.* Ps.27.4
they have defiled thy holy *t.* Ps.79.1
and his train filled the *t.* Is.6.1
their backs to the *t.* of the LORD Ezek.8.16
The songs of the *t.* shall become Am.8.3
I again look upon thy holy *t.?* Jon.2.4
will suddenly come to his *t.* Mal.3.1
set him on the pinnacle of the *t.* Mt.4.5
greater than the *t.* is here Mt.12.6
curtain of the *t.* was torn in two Mk.15.38
She did not depart from the *t.* Lk.2.37
Two men went up into the *t.* to pray Lk.18.10
But he spoke of the *t.* of his body Jn.2.21
at the Beautiful Gate of the *t.* Acts 3.10
You who abhor idols, do you rob *t.?* Rom.2.22
God's *t.* is holy, and that *t.* you 1 Cor.3.17
we are the *t.* of the living God 2 Cor.6.16
him a pillar in the *t.* of my God Rev.3.12
Then God's *t.* in heaven was opened Rev.11.19
for its *t.* is the Lord God Rev.21.22

TEMPT
You shall not *t.* the Lord your God Lk.4.12
to *t.* the Spirit of the Lord? Acts 5.9
lest Satan *t.* you through lack of 1 Cor.7.5
not . . . be *t.* beyond your strength 1 Cor.10.13
is able to help those who are *t.* Heb.2.18
in every respect . . . *t.* as we are Heb.4.15
God cannot be *t.* with evil Jas.1.13

TEMPTATION
And lead us not into *t.*, But deliver Mt.6.13
woe to the man by whom the *t.* comes Mt.18.7
pray that you may not enter into *t.* Mk.14.38
when the devil had ended every *t.* Lk.4.13
T. to sin are sure to come; but woe Lk.17.1
No *t.* has overtaken you that is 1 Cor.10.13
who desire to be rich fall into *t.* 1 Tim.6.9

TEMPTER
And the *t.* came and said to him, "If Mt.4.3
for fear that somehow the *t.* had 1 Th.3.5

TEND
his sons shall *t.* it from evening Ex.27.21
And I *t.* the sheep Zech.11.7
He said to him, "*T.* my sheep." Jn.21.16
Who *t.* a flock without getting some 1 Cor.9.7
T. the flock of God that is your 1 Pet.5.2

TENDER
no more be called *t.* and delicate Is.47.1
amid the *t.* grass of the field Dan.4.15
branch becomes *t.* and puts forth Mt.24.32
through the *t.* mercy of our God Lk.1.78
a *t.* heart and a humble mind 1 Pet.3.8

TENDERLY

he loved the maiden and spoke *t*.	Gen.34.3
Speak *t*. to Jerusalem, and cry to	Is.40.2
and speak *t*. to her	Hos.2.14

TENT

every man to his *t*., O Israel	2 Sam.20.1
In them he has set a *t*. for the sun	Ps.19.4
Let me dwell in thy *t*. for ever	Ps.61.4
than dwell in the *t*. of wickedness	Ps.84.10
stretched out the heavens like a *t*.	Ps.104.2
if the earthly *t*. we live in is	2 Cor.5.1
the true *t*. which is set up	Heb.8.2
go continually into the outer *t*.	Heb.9.6

TERRIBLE

t. in glorious deeds, doing wonders?	Ex.15.11
the *t*. God, who is not partial	Dt.10.17
the angel of God, very *t*.	Jg.13.6
the Lord, who is great and *t*.	Neh.4.14
God is clothed with *t*. majesty	Job 37.22
Say to God, "How *t*. are thy deeds	Ps.66.3
T. is God in his sanctuary	Ps.68.35
Holy and *t*. is his name	Ps.111.9
the day of the LORD is . . . very *t*.	Jl.2.11
the great and *t*. day of the LORD	Mal.4.5

TERRIFY

when he rises to *t*. the earth	Is.2.19
they were *t*., saying, "It is a ghost!"	Mt.14.26
of wars and tumults, do not be *t*.	Lk.21.9
do right and let nothing *t*. you	1 Pet.3.6
the rest were *t*. and gave glory to	Rev.11.13

TERROR

a *t*. from God fell upon the cities	Gen.35.5
I will send my *t*. before you	Ex.23.27
I will appoint over you sudden *t*.	Lev.26.16
For I was in *t*. of calamity from	Job 31.23
There they shall be in great *t*.	Ps.14.5
You will not fear the *t*. of the night	Ps.91.5
T., and the pit, and the snare	Is.24.17
T., pit, and snare are before you	Jer.48.43
there will be *t*. and great signs	Lk.21.11
are not a *t*. to good conduct	Rom.13.3

TEST (noun)

said to them, "Why put me to the *t*.?	Mk.12.15
We must not put the Lord to the *t*.	1 Cor.10.9
for in a severe *t*. of affliction	2 Cor.8.2
has stood the *t*. he will receive	Jas.1.12

TEST (verb)

After these things God *t*. Abraham	Gen.22.1
he might humble you and *t*. you	Dt.8.16
The LORD *t*. the righteous and the	Ps.11.5
T. your servants for ten days	Dan.1.12
This he said to *t*. him, for he . . . knew	Jn.6.6
T. yourselves. Do you not realize	2 Cor.13.5
But let each one *t*. his own work	Gal.6.4
t. everything; hold fast what is good	1 Th.5.21
though perishable is *t*. by fire	1 Pet.1.7
t. the spirits to see whether	1 Jn.4.1

TESTIFY

and our sins *t*. against us	Is.59.12
Though our iniquities *t*. against us	Jer.14.7
many things they *t*. against you?	Mt.27.13
I *t*. of it that its works are evil	Jn.7.7
t. to the gospel of the grace of God	Acts 20.24
we *t*. of God that he raised Christ	1 Cor.15.15
I *t*. again to every man who receives	Gal.5.3

have seen and *t*. that the Father	1 Jn.4.14
He who *t*. to these things says	Rev.22.20

TESTIMONY

placed it before the *t*., to be kept	Ex.16.34
these are the *t*., the statutes	Dt.4.45
the *t*. of the LORD is sure, making	Ps.19.7
Thy *t*. are wonderful; therefore	Ps.119.129
Bind up the *t*., seal the teaching	Is.8.16
To the teaching and to the *t*.	Is.8.20
sought false *t*. against Jesus	Mt.26.59
for a *t*. against them	Mk.6.11
to bear *t*. before them	Mk.13.9
a time for you to bear *t*.	Lk.21.13
And this is the *t*. of John	Jn.1.19
But the *t*. which I have is greater	Jn.5.36
the *t*. of two men is true	Jn.8.17
gave their *t*. to the resurrection	Acts 4.33
in his *t*. before Pontius Pilate	1 Tim.6.13
the *t*. of God is greater	1 Jn.5.9
And this is the *t*., that God gave	1 Jn.5.11
For the *t*. of Jesus is the spirit	Rev.19.10

TESTING (noun)

They were for the *t*. of Israel	Jg.3.4
For it will not be a *t*.	Ezek.21.13
on the day of *t*. in the wilderness	Heb.3.8
know that the *t*. of your faith	Jas.1.3

TETRARCH

Herod the *t*. heard about the fame of	Mt.14.1
Philip *t*. of the region of Ituraea	Lk.3.1
Now Herod the *t*. heard of all that	Lk.9.7
court of Herod the *t*., and Saul	Acts 13.1

THADDAEUS

James the son of Alphaeus, and *T*.	Mt.10.3
and *T*., and Simon the Cananaean	Mk.3.18

THANK

I will *t*. thee for ever, because	Ps.52.9
I *t*. thee, Father, Lord of heaven	Mt.11.25
I *t*. thee that I am not like other	Lk.18.11
I *t*. thee that thou hast heard me	Jn.11.41
I *t*. my God in all my remembrance	Phil.1.3
I *t*. him who has given me strength	1 Tim.1.12

THANKFUL

I am *t*. that I baptized none of	1 Cor.1.14
t. for . . . partnership in the gospel	Phil.1.5
And be *t*.	Col.3.15

THANKFULNESS

If I partake with *t*., why am I	1 Cor.10.30
with *t*. in your hearts to God	Col.3.16

THANKS

O give *t*. to the LORD, for he	1 Chr.16.34
We give *t*. to thee, O God; we give *t*.	Ps.75.1
we may give *t*. to thy holy name	Ps.106.47
All thy works shall give *t*. to thee	Ps.145.10
I give *t*. and praise, for thou hast	Dan.2.23
having given *t*. he broke them	Mk.8.6
that very hour she gave *t*. to God	Lk.2.38
and when he had given *t*.	Jn.6.11
T. be to God through Jesus Christ	Rom.7.25
But *t*. be to God, who gives us	1 Cor.15.57
T. be to God for his inexpressible	2 Cor.9.15
We give *t*. to God always for you	1 Th.1.2
bound to give *t*. to God always for	2 Th.2.13
honor and *t*. to him who is seated	Rev.4.9

THANKSGIVING

the leader to begin the *t*. in prayer	Neh.11.17
Offer to God a sacrifice of *t*.	Ps.50.14

come into his presence with *t.*	Ps.95.2
Enter his gates with *t.*, and his	Ps.100.4
Sing to the LORD with *t.*	Ps.147.7
say the "Amen" to your *t.*	1 Cor.14.16
by . . . supplication with *t.* let your	Phil.4.6
I urge that . . . *t.* be made for all	1 Tim.2.1
wisdom and *t.* and honor and	Rev.7.12

THEOPHILUS

account for you, most excellent *T.*	Lk.1.3
O *T.*, I have dealt with all that	Acts 1.1

THESSALONICA

Acts 17.1; 27.2; Phil.4.16; 2 Tim.4.10

THIEF

If a *t.* is found breaking in, and is	Ex.22.2
where *t.* break in and steal	Mt.6.19
part of the night the *t.* was coming	Mt.24.43
where no *t.* approaches and no moth	Lk.12.33
that man is a *t.* and a robber	Jn.10.1
but because he was a *t.*	Jn.12.6
Let the *t.* no longer steal, but	Eph.4.28
that day to surprise you like a *t.*	1 Th.5.4
a *t.*, or a wrongdoer, or a	1 Pet.4.15
Lo, I am coming like a *t.*	Rev.16.15

THIGH

Put your hand under my *t.*	Gen.24.2
Jacob's *t.* was put out of joint	Gen.32.25
the *t.* of the priests' portion	Ex.29.27
Gird your sword upon your *t.*	Ps.45.3
Smite therefore upon your *t.*	Ezek.21.12
on his *t.* he has a name inscribed	Rev.19.16

THING

You shall not eat any abominable *t.*	Dt.14.3
I know that thou canst do all *t.*	Job 42.2
hast put all *t.* under his feet	Ps.8.6
One *t.* have I asked of the LORD	Ps.27.4
No good *t.* does the LORD withhold	Ps.84.11
Behold, I am doing a new *t.*	Is.43.19
she has done a beautiful *t.* to me	Mt.26.10
and said to him, "You lack one *t.*	Mk.10.21
for all *t.* are possible with God	Mk.10.27
to Caesar the *t.* that are Caesar's	Mk.12.17
she has done a beautiful *t.* to me	Mk.14.6
one *t.* is needful. Mary has chosen	Lk.10.42
one *t.* I know, that though I was	Jn.9.25
but I do the very *t.* I hate	Rom.7.15
one *t.* I do, forgetting what	Phil.3.13
It is a fearful *t.* to fall into	Heb.10.31
with perishable *t.* such as silver	1 Pet.1.18
The end of all *t.* is at hand	1 Pet.4.7
said, "Behold, I make all *t.* new."	Rev.21.5

THINK

man that thou dost *t.* of him?	Ps.144.3
T. not that I have come to abolish	Mt.5.17
Why do you *t.* evil in your hearts?	Mt.9.4
What do you *t.* of the Christ?	Mt.22.42
Do not *t.* that I shall accuse you	Jn.5.45
short time you *t.* to make me a	Acts 26.28
more highly than he ought to *t.*	Rom.12.3
For if any one *t.* he is something	Gal.6.3
more . . . than all that we ask or *t.*	Eph.3.20

THIRD

he will be raised on the *t.* day	Mt.17.23
he . . . prayed for the *t.* time	Mt.26.44
the *t.* hour, when they crucified	Mk.15.25
crucified, and on the *t.* day rise	Lk.24.7

it is only the *t.* hour of the day	Acts 2.15
was caught up to the *t.* heaven	2 Cor.12.2

THIRST (verb)

My soul *t.* for God, for the living	Ps.42.2
who hunger and *t.* for righteousness	Mt.5.6
whoever drinks . . . will never *t.*	Jn.4.14
If any one *t.*, let him come to me	Jn.7.37
(to fulfil the scripture), "I *t.*"	Jn.19.28
hunger no more, neither *t.* any more	Rev.7.16

THISTLE

thorns and *t.* it shall bring forth	Gen.3.18
A *t.* on Lebanon sent to a cedar	2 Kg.14.9
Thorn and *t.* shall grow up on their	Hos.10.8
gathered from thorns, or figs from *t.*?	Mt.7.16
But if it bears thorns and *t.*	Heb.6.8

THOMAS

Mt.10.3; Jn.11.16; 14.5; 20.24; 21.2; Acts 1.13

THORN

as the crackling of *t.* under a pot	Ec.7.6
Instead of the *t.* shall come up the	Is.55.13
Are grapes gathered from *t.*	Mt.7.16
Other seeds fell upon *t.*	Mt.13.7
the soldiers plaited a crown of *t.*	Jn.19.2
a *t.* was given me in the flesh	2 Cor.12.7

THOUGHT (noun)

but the Lord takes *t.* for me	Ps.40.17
there is no work or *t.* . . . . in Sheol	Ec.9.10
For my *t.* are not your *t.*, neither	Is.55.8
For out of the heart come evil *t.*	Mt.15.19
But he knew their *t.*, and he said	Lk.6.8
but take *t.* for what is noble in	Rom.12.17
take every *t.* captive to obey	2 Cor.10.5
discerning the *t.* and intentions	Heb.4.12
arm yourselves with the same *t.*	1 Pet.4.1

THOUGHT (verb)

We have *t.* on thy steadfast love	Ps.48.9
feared the LORD and *t.* on his name	Mal.3.16
on the sea they *t.* it was a ghost	Mk.6.49
Why is it *t.* incredible by any of	Acts 26.8
I *t.* like a child, I reasoned	1 Cor.13.11

THREAD

I would not take a *t.* or a sandal	Gen.14.23
he snapped the ropes . . . like a *t.*	Jg.16.12
Your lips are like a scarlet *t.*	S.of S.4.3
the *t.* of your life is cut	Jer.51.13

THREEFOLD

A *t.* cord is not quickly broken	Ec.4.12

THRESHING

a fleece of wool on the *t.* floor	Jg.6.37
To buy the *t.* floor of you	2 Sam.24.21
is not threshed with a *t.* sledge	Is.28.27
The *t.* floors shall be full of	Jl.2.24
will clear his *t.* floor and gather	Mt.3.12

THREW

the blood and *t.* it upon the people	Ex.24.8
Moses *t.* the blood upon the altar	Lev.8.24
took up Jonah and *t.* him into the	Jon.1.15
into vessels but *t.* away the bad	Mt.13.48
millstone and *t.* it into the sea	Rev.18.21
t. him into the pit, and shut it	Rev.20.3

THROAT

their *t.* is an open sepulchre	Ps.5.9
my *t.* is parched. My eyes grow dim	Ps.69.3
and seizing him by the *t.* he said	Mt.18.28
Their *t.* is an open grave	Rom.3.13

THRONE

set up the *t.* of David over	2 Sam.3.10
the LORD's *t.* is in heaven	Ps.11.4
God sits on his holy *t.*	Ps.47.8
thy *t.* is established from of old	Ps.93.2
established his *t.* in the heavens	Ps.103.19
I saw the Lord sitting upon a *t.*	Is.6.1
Heaven is my *t.* and the earth is	Is.66.1
A glorious *t.* set on high	Jer.17.12
he will sit on his glorious *t.*	Mt.25.31
give to him the *t.* of his father	Lk.1.32
put down the mighty from their *t.*	Lk.1.52
Thy *t.*, O God, is for ever and ever	Heb.1.8
at the right hand of the *t.* of God	Heb.12.2
sat down with my Father on his *t.*	Rev.3.21
Round the *t.* were twenty-four *t.*	Rev.4.4
Therefore are they before the *t.*	Rev.7.15
a great white *t.* and him who sat	Rev.20.11
from the *t.* of God and of the Lamb	Rev.22.1

THRONG (noun)

in the mighty *t.* I will praise thee	Ps.35.18
praise him in the midst of the *t.*	Ps.109.30
As he went ashore he saw a great *t.*	Mt.14.14
And the great *t.* heard him gladly	Mk.12.37

THRUST

your God has *t.* them out before you	Dt.9.4
They only plan to *t.* him down from	Ps.62.4
they will be *t.* into thick darkness	Is.8.22
and you yourselves *t.* out	Lk.13.28
which God *t.* out before our fathers	Acts 7.45

THUNDER (noun)

the LORD sent *t.* and hail	Ex.9.23
But the *t.* of his power who can	Job 26.14
Hearken to the *t.* of his voice	Job 37.2
The crash of thy *t.* was in the	Ps.77.18
Mightier than the *t.* of many waters	Ps.93.4
at the sound of thy *t.* they	Ps.104.7
Boanerges, that is, sons of *t.*	Mk.3.17
say, as with a voice of *t.*, "Come!"	Rev.6.1
and like the sound of loud *t.*	Rev.14.2

THYATIRA

Acts 16.14; Rev.1.11; 2.18,24

TIBERIAS

Jn.6.1,23; 21.1

TIGRIS (Hiddekel)

Gen.2.14; Dan.10.4

TIMBRELS

after her with *t.* and dancing	Ex.15.20
meet him with *t.* and with dances	Jg.11.34
between them maidens playing *t.*	Ps.68.25
The mirth of the *t.* is stilled	Is.24.8
you shall adorn yourself with *t.*	Jer.31.4

TIME

the kingdom for such a *t.* as this?	Est.4.14
reserved for the *t.* of trouble	Job 38.23
My *t.* are in thy hand; deliver me	Ps.31.15
their refuge in the *t.* of trouble	Ps.37.39
has appointed a *t.* for every matter	Ec.3.17
For man does not know his *t.*	Ec.9.12
the *t.* of singing has come	S.of S.2.12
it is the *t.* to seek the LORD	Hos.10.12
interpret the signs of the *t.*	Mt.16.3
not . . . seven *t.*, but seventy *t.* seven	Mt.18.22
The Teacher says, My *t.* is at hand	Mt.26.18
The *t.* is fulfilled, and the kingdom	Mk.1.15
you will deny me three *t.*	Mk.14.72

how to interpret the present *t.*?	Lk.12.56
saying . . . 'The *t.* is at hand!'	Lk.21.8
until the *t.* of the Gentiles are	Lk.21.24
for my *t.* has not yet fully come	Jn.7.8
will you at this *t.* restore the	Acts 1.6
In a short *t.* you think to make me	Acts 26.28
Behold, now is the acceptable *t.*	2 Cor.6.2
when the *t.* had fully come, God	Gal.4.4
as a plan for the fulness of *t.*	Eph.1.10
the *t.* is coming when people	2 Tim.4.3
t. would fail me to tell of Gideon	Heb.11.32
the *t.* has come for judgment to	1 Pet.4.17
In the last *t.* there will be scoffers	Jude 18
written therein; for the *t.* is near	Rev.1.3

TIMOTHY

Paul's fellow worker, Acts 16.3; 17.14–15; Rom. 16.21; 2 Cor.1.1,19; commended, 1 Cor.16.10; Phil.2.19

TITHE (noun)

all the *t.* of herds and flocks	Lev.27.32
to the LORD, a *t.* of the *t.*	Num.18.26
paying all the *t.* of your produce	Dt.26.12
when the Levites receive the *t.*	Neh.10.38
Bring the full *t.* into the storehouse	Mal.3.10
I give *t.* of all that I get	Lk.18.12
Levi . . . who receives *t.*, paid *t.*	Heb.7.9

TITUS

Gal.2.3; Paul's love for, 2 Cor.2.13; 7.6,13

TODAY

my son, *t.* I have begotten you	Ps.2.7
O that *t.* you would hearken to his	Ps.95.7
which *t.* is alive and tomorrow is	Mt.6.30
t. you will be with me in Paradise	Lk.23.43
T., when you hear his voice	Heb.3.7
same yesterday and *t.* and for ever	Heb.13.8
T. or tomorrow we will go into	Jas.4.13

TOIL (noun)

in *t.* you shall eat of it all the days	Gen.3.17
their span is but *t.* and trouble	Ps.90.10
In all *t.* there is profit	Pr.14.23
yet there is no end to all his *t.*	Ec.4.8
remember our labor and *t.*, brethren	1 Th.2.9
your *t.* and your patient endurance	Rev.2.2

TOIL (verb)

make them *t.* at the brickkilns	2 Sam.12.31
Do not *t.* to acquire wealth	Pr.23.4
by a man who did not *t.* for it	Ec.2.21
they neither *t.* nor spin	Mt.6.28
we *t.* all night and took nothing	Lk.5.5
to this end we *t.* and strive	1 Tim.4.10

TOMB

it is the pillar of Rachel's *t.*	Gen.35.20
It is the *t.* of the man of God	2 Kg.23.17
Their quiver is like an open *t.*	Jer.5.16
for you are like whitewashed *t.*	Mt.23.27
you build the *t.* of the prophets	Mt.23.29
the *t.* also were opened, and many	Mt.27.52
who lived among the *t.*; and no one	Mk.5.3
a stone against the door of the *t.*	Mk.15.46
already been in the *t.* four days	Jn.11.17
Magdalene came to the *t.* early	Jn.20.1
outran Peter and reached the *t.* first	Jn.20.4

TOMORROW

Do not boast about *t.*, for you do not	Pr.27.1
Therefore do not be anxious about *t.*	Mt.6.34
field today and *t.* is thrown into	Lk.12.28

eat and drink, for *t*. we die	1 Cor.15.32	*t*. the young women to love	Tit.2.4
whereas you do not know about *t*.	Jas.4.14	those who have been *t*. by it	Heb.12.11

TONGUE

Keep your *t*. from evil	Ps.34.13
my *t*. is like the pen of a ready	Ps.45.1
Your *t*. is like a sharp razor	Ps.52.2
Let my *t*. cleave to the roof of my	Ps.137.6
Even before a word is on my *t*.	Ps.139.4
a lying *t*. is but for a moment	Pr.12.19
answer of the *t*. is from the LORD	Pr.16.1
and the *t*. of the dumb sing for joy	Is.35.6
have taught their *t*. to speak lies	Jer.9.5
his *t*. was released, and he spoke	Mk.7.35
and began to speak in other *t*.	Acts 2.4
If I speak in the *t*. of men	1 Cor.13.1
He who speaks in a *t*. edifies	1 Cor.14.4
and every *t*. confess that Jesus	Phil.2.11
not bridle his *t*. but deceives his	Jas.1.26
And the *t*. is a fire	Jas.3.6

TOOTH

t. for *t*., hand for hand	Ex.21.24; Dt.19.21
If he knocks out the *t*. of his slave	Ex.21.27
An eye for an eye and a *t*. for a *t*.	Mt.5.38

TORMENT

come here to *t*. us before the time?	Mt.8.29
being in *t*., he lifted up his eyes	Lk.16.23
smoke of their *t*. goes up for ever	Rev.14.11
they will be *t*. day and night for	Rev.20.10

TOTTER

The nations rage, the kingdoms *t*.	Ps.46.6
make them *t*. by thy power	Ps.59.11
When the earth *t*., and all its	Ps.75.3
my steps *t*. beneath me	Hab.3.16

TOUCH

neither shall you *t*. it	Gen.3.3
T. not my anointed ones	1 Chr.16.22
there shall no evil *t*. you	Job 5.19
t. no unclean thing; go out from	Is.52.11
If I only *t*. his garment, I shall	Mt.9.21
Do not taste, Do not *t*.	Col.2.21
looked upon and *t*. with our hands	1 Jn.1.1
the evil one does not *t*. him	1 Jn.5.18

TOWER

a *t*. with its top in the heavens	Gen.11.4
go round about her, number her *t*.	Ps.48.12
a strong *t*. against the enemy	Ps.61.3
The name of the LORD is a strong *t*.	Pr.18.10
Your neck is like an ivory *t*.	S.of S.7.4
built a *t*., and let it out to tenants	Mk.12.1
upon whom the *t*. in Siloam fell	Lk.13.4
desiring to build a *t*.	Lk.14.28

TRADE

by your great wisdom in *t*. you	Ezek.28.5
my Father's house a house of *t*.	Jn.2.16
for by *t*. they were tentmakers	Acts 18.3
all whose *t*. is on the sea	Rev.18.17

TRADITION

transgress the *t*. of the elders	Mt.15.2
observing the *t*. of the elders	Mk.7.3
and hold fast the *t*. of men	Mk.7.8
deceit, according to human *t*.	Col.2.8
hold to the *t*. which you were	2 Th.2.15

TRAIN (verb)

who were *t*. in singing to the LORD	1 Chr.25.7
T. up a child in the way he should	Pr.22.6
T. yourself in godliness	1 Tim.4.7

TRAMPLE

my enemies *t*. upon me all day long	Ps.56.2
T. under foot those who lust after	Ps.68.30
the serpent you will *t*. under foot	Ps.91.13
they that *t*. the head of the poor	Am.2.7
lest they *t*. them under foot	Mt.7.6
they will *t*. over the holy city	Rev.11.2

TRANSGRESS

if you *t*. the covenant of the LORD	Jos.23.16
my mouth does not *t*.	Ps.17.3
We have *t*. and rebelled, and thou	Lam.3.42
All Israel has *t*. thy law	Dan.9.11
Come to Bethel, and *t*.; to Gilgal	Am.4.4
why do you *t*. the commandment	Mt.15.3

TRANSGRESSION

forgiving iniquity and *t*. and sin	Ex.34.7
Make me know my *t*. and my sin	Job 13.23
blameless, and innocent of great *t*.	Ps.19.13
Blessed is he whose *t*. is forgiven	Ps.32.1
I know my *t*., and my sin is ever	Ps.51.3
so far does he remove our *t*. from	Ps.103.12
But he was wounded for our *t*.	Is.53.5
What is the *t*. of Jacob? Is it not	Mic.1.5
Shall I give my first-born for my *t*.	Mic.6.7
sins were not like the *t*. of Adam	Rom.5.14
was rebuked for his own *t*.	2 Pet.2.16

TRANSGRESSOR

t. shall be altogether destroyed	Ps.37.38
Then I will teach *t*. thy ways	Ps.51.13
but *t*. stumble in them	Hos.14.9
the woman . . . became a *t*.	1 Tim.2.14
you have become a *t*. of the law	Jas.2.11

TRAP

Arrogant men have hidden a *t*.	Ps.140.5
Keep me from the *t*. which they have	Ps.141.9
a *t*. and a snare to the inhabitants	Is.8.14
They set a *t*.; they catch men	Jer.5.26
Let their feast become . . . a *t*.	Rom.11.9

TRAVAIL

anguish as of a woman in *t*.	Ps.48.6
groaning in *t*. together until now	Rom.8.22
I am again in *t*. until Christ be	Gal.4.19
upon them as *t*. comes upon a woman	1 Th.5.3

TREACHEROUS

be ashamed who are wantonly *t*.	Ps.25.3
crookedness of the *t*. destroys them	Pr.11.3
the *t*. are taken captive by their lust	Pr.11.6
For the *t*. deal treacherously	Is.24.16
Why do all who are *t*. thrive?	Jer.12.1
t., reckless, swollen with conceit	2 Tim.3.4

TREACHERY

What is this *t*. which you have	Jos.22.16
and meditate *t*. all the day long	Ps.38.12
their houses are full of *t*.	Jer.5.27
all the *t*. they have practiced	Ezek.39.26

TREAD

t. down the wicked where they	Job 40.12
it is he who will *t*. down our foes	Ps.60.12
will *t*. on the lion and the adder	Ps.91.13
you shall *t*. down the wicked	Mal.4.3
authority to *t*. upon serpents	Lk.10.19
an ox when it is *t*. out the grain	1 Cor.9.9
he will *t*. the wine press	Rev.19.15

TREASURE (noun)

T. gained by wickedness do not	Pr.10.2
the t. of all nations shall come in	Hag.2.7
For where your t. is, there will	Mt.6.21
is like t. hidden in a field	Mt.13.44
you will have t. in heaven	Mk.10.21
out of the good t. of his heart	Lk.6.45
we have this t. in earthen vessels	2 Cor.4.7
in whom are hid all the t. of wisdom	Col.2.3
greater wealth than the t. of Egypt	Heb.11.26
have laid up t. for the last days	Jas.5.3

TREE

every t. with seed in its fruit	Gen.1.29
the t. of the knowledge of good	Gen.2.17
to guard the way to the t. of life	Gen.3.24
And the t. said to the fig t.	Jg.9.10
He is like a t. planted by streams	Ps.1.3
She is a t. of life to those who	Pr.3.18
a desire fulfilled is a t. of life	Pr.13.12
in the place where the t. falls	Ec.11.3
who say to a t., 'You are my father'	Jer.2.27
A sound t. cannot bear evil fruit	Mt.7.18
the fig t. withered at once	Mt.21.19
From the fig t. learn its lesson	Mk.13.28
axe is laid to the root of the t.	Lk.3.9
you could say to this sycamine t.	Lk.17.6
they took him down from the t.	Acts 13.29
bore our sins in his body on the t.	1 Pet.2.24
grant to eat of the t. of life	Rev.2.7
leaves of the t. were for the healing	Rev.22.2

TREMBLE

The pillars of heaven t.	Job 26.11
the mountains t. with its tumult	Ps.46.3
t. before him, all the earth	Ps.96.9
let the peoples t.	Ps.99.1
Do you not t. before me?	Jer.5.22
The inhabitants of Samaria t. for	Hos.10.5
the guards t. and became like dead	Mt.28.4
Moses t. and did not dare to look	Acts 7.32
Moses said, "I t. with fear."	Heb.12.21

TREMBLING (noun)

Serve the LORD with fear, with t.	Ps.2.11
t. took hold of them there, anguish	Ps.48.6
came in fear and t. and fell down	Mk.5.33
I was . . . in much fear and t.	1 Cor.2.3
with fear and t., in singleness of	Eph.6.5
your own salvation with fear and t.	Phil.2.12

TRESPASS (noun)

if you do not forgive men their t.	Mt.6.15
Father . . . may forgive you your t.	Mk.11.25
many died through one man's t.	Rom.5.15
Law came in, to increase the t.	Rom.5.20
Now if their t. means riches for	Rom.11.12
if a man is overtaken in any t.	Gal.6.1
when we were dead through our t.	Eph.2.5
having forgiven us all our t.	Col.2.13

TRIAL

have continued with me in my t.	Lk.22.28
I stand here on t. for hope in the	Acts 26.6
Blessed is the man who endures t.	Jas.1.12
you may have to suffer various t.	1 Pet.1.6
how to rescue the godly from t.	2 Pet.2.9
the hour of t. which is coming on	Rev.3.10

TRIBES

these are the twelve t. of Israel	Gen.49.28
according to the twelve t. of Israel	Ex.24.4

the t. of the LORD, as was decreed	Ps.122.4
judging the twelve t. of Israel	Lk.22.30
To the twelve t. in the Dispersion	Jas.1.1
from all t. and peoples and tongues	Rev.7.9

TRIBULATION

may he deliver me out of all t.	1 Sam.26.24
For then there will be great t.	Mt.24.21
when t. or persecution arises	Mk.4.17
In the world you have t.; but be	Jn.16.33
through many t. we must enter the	Acts 14.22
Shall t., or distress, or persecution	Rom.8.35
be patient in t., be constant in	Rom.12.12
who have come out of the great t.	Rev.7.14

TRIBUTE

May the kings . . . render him t.	Ps.72.10
where is he who weighed the t.?	Is.33.18
do kings of the earth take toll or t.?	Mt.17.25
lawful for us to give t. to Caesar	Lk.20.22

TRIUMPH (verb)

the LORD, for he has t. gloriously	Ex.15.1
thou wilt not let them t.	Job 17.4
my enemy has not t. over me	Ps.41.11
When the righteous t., there is	Pr.28.12
Israel shall t. and glory	Is.45.25
a public example of them, t. over	Col.2.15
yet mercy t. over judgment	Jas.2.13

TROAS

Acts 16.8; 20.5; 2 Cor.2.12; 2 Tim.4.13

TROUBLE (noun)

The LORD brings t. on you today	Jos.7.25
those who . . . sow t. reap the same	Job 4.8
man is born to t. as the sparks fly	Job 5.7
Man . . . is of few days, and full of t.	Job 14.1
The LORD answer you in the day of t.	Ps.20.1
their refuge in the time of t.	Ps.37.39
call upon me in the day of t.	Ps.50.15
They are not in t. as other men are	Ps.73.5
I will be with him in t.	Ps.91.15
T. and anguish have come upon me	Ps.119.143
his tongue keeps himself out of t.	Pr.21.23
the day's own t. be sufficient for	Mt.6.34
who marry will have worldly t.	1 Cor.7.28

TROUBLE (verb)

my spirit is t. to know the dream	Dan.2.3
he was t., and all Jerusalem with him	Mt.2.3
he began to be sorrowful and t.	Mt.26.37
Why t. the Teacher any further?	Mk.5.35
anxious and t. about many things	Lk.10.41
Now is my soul t. And what shall I	Jn.12.27
Let not your hearts be t.	Jn.14.1
some who t. you and want to pervert	Gal.1.7

TRUE

thou art God, and thy words are t.	2 Sam.7.28
Israel was without the t. God	2 Chr.15.3
right ordinances and t. laws	Neh.9.13
the ordinances of the LORD are t.	Ps.19.9
that the word of the LORD is t.	Ps.141.6
But the LORD is the t. God	Jer.10.10
Teacher, we know that you are t.	Mt.22.16
The t. light that enlightens every	Jn.1.9
when the t. worshipers will worship	Jn.4.23
gives you the t. bread from heaven	Jn.6.32
the testimony of two men is t.	Jn.8.17
I am the t. vine, and my Father is	Jn.15.1
they know thee the only t. God	Jn.17.3
whatever is t., whatever is	Phil.4.8

to serve a living and *t*. God | 1 Th.1.9
draw near with a *t*. heart | Heb.10.22
This is the *t*. God and eternal life | 1 Jn.5.20
Just and *t*. are thy ways, O King of | Rev.15.3
He . . . is called Faithful and *T*. | Rev.19.11
These words are trustworthy and *t*. | Rev.22.6

TRUMPET

lift up your voice like a *t*. | Is.58.1
Give heed to the sound of the *t*. | Jer.6.17
Blow the *t*. in Zion; sanctify a fast | Jl.2.15
sound no *t*. before you | Mt.6.2
in a moment . . . at the last *t*. | 1 Cor.15.52
the sound of a *t*., and a voice | Heb.12.19
I heard . . . a loud voice like a *t*. | Rev.1.10
seven *t*. were given to them | Rev.8.2
Then the seventh angel blew his *t*. | Rev.11.15

TRUST (verb)

T. in the LORD, and do good | Ps.37.3
I *t*. in the steadfast love of God | Ps.52.8
blessed is the man who *t*. in thee | Ps.84.12
He who *t*. in his own mind is a fool | Pr.28.26
T. in the LORD for ever | Is.26.4
to some who *t*. in themselves that | Lk.18.9
Jesus did not *t*. himself to them | Jn.2.24
t. him who justifies the ungodly | Rom.4.5

TRUTH

Oh send out thy light and thy *t*. | Ps.43.3
thou desirest *t*. in the inward being | Ps.51.6
to all who call upon him in *t*. | Ps.145.18
Buy *t*., and do not sell it | Pr.23.23
and no one speaks the *t*. | Jer.9.5
therefore love *t*. and peace | Zech.8.19
grace and *t*. came through Jesus | Jn.1.17
must worship in spirit and *t*. | Jn.4.24
and the *t*. will make you free | Jn.8.32
the Spirit of *t*., whom the world | Jn.14.17
Pilate said to him, "What is *t*.?" | Jn.18.38
speaking the *t*. in love | Eph.4.15
the pillar and bulwark of the *t*. | 1 Tim.3.15
the *t*. that has been entrusted | 2 Tim.1.14
rightly handling the word of *t*. | 2 Tim.2.15
the way of *t*. will be reviled | 2 Pet.2.2
because the Spirit is the *t*. | 1 Jn.5.7
we may be fellow workers in the *t*. | 3 Jn.8

TUMULT

the *t*. in the camp . . . increased | 1 Sam.14.19
the mountains tremble with its *t*. | Ps.46.3
a day of *t*. and trampling | Is.22.5
my soul is in *t*. | Lam.2.11
lest there be a *t*. among the people | Mt.26.5
Why do you make a *t*. and weep? | Mk.5.39
when you hear of wars and *t*. | Lk.21.9

TURN

he is unchangeable . . . who can *t*. him? | Job 23.13
T. not thy servant away in anger | Ps.27.9
Let them be *t*. back and confounded | Ps.35.4
T. back, O children of men | Ps.90.3
I do not *t*. aside from thy | Ps.119.102
T. to me and be gracious to me | Ps.119.132
to *t*. aside the needy from justice | Is.10.2
T. to me and be saved, all the ends | Is.45.22
we have *t*. every one to his own way | Is.53.6
I will *t*. their mourning into joy | Jer.31.13
I will *t*. to you, and you shall | Ezek.36.9
The sun shall be *t*. to darkness | Jl.2.31
But you have *t*. justice into poison | Am.6.12

they shall *t*. in dread to the LORD | Mic.7.17
he will *t*. the hearts of children | Mal.4.6
unless you *t*. and become like | Mt.18.3
to *t*. the hearts of the fathers to | Lk.1.17
men who have *t*. the world upside | Acts 17.6
that they may *t*. from darkness to | Acts 26.18
let him *t*. away from evil | 1 Pet.3.11

TURTLEDOVE

if he cannot afford two *t*. | Lev.5.11
pigeon or a *t*. for a sin offering | Lev.12.6
the voice of the *t*. is heard | S.of S.2.12
a pair of *t*., or two young pigeons | Lk.2.24

TWELVE

these are the *t*. tribes of Israel | Gen.49.28
The names of the *t*. apostles are | Mt.10.2
more than *t*. legions of angels? | Mt.26.53
And they took up *t*. baskets full | Mk.6.43
appeared to Cephas, then to the *t*. | 1 Cor.15.5
the *t*. gates were *t*. pearls | Rev.21.21

TYCHICUS

Acts 20.4; Eph.6.21; Col.4.7; 2 Tim.4.12; Tit.
3.12

TYRE

Jos.19.29; 1 Kg.5.1; Ps.45.12; Jer.25.22; Mt.
11.21; Acts 12.20

UNBELIEF

he marveled because of their *u*. | Mk.6.6
I believe; help my *u*. | Mk.9.24
broken off because of their *u*. | Rom.11.20
I had acted ignorantly in *u*. | 1 Tim.1.13
were unable to enter because of *u*. | Heb.3.19

UNBELIEVER

has a wife who is an *u*. | 1 Cor.7.12
If one of the *u*. invites you to | 1 Cor.10.27
if . . . an *u*. or outsider enters | 1 Cor.14.24
a believer in common with an *u*.? | 2 Cor.6.15
is worse than an *u*. | 1 Tim.5.8

UNCHASTITY

except on the ground of *u*. | Mt.5.32
except for *u*., and marries another | Mt.19.9
abstain . . . from *u*. and from | Acts 15.20
from what is strangled and from *u*. | Acts 21.25

UNCIRCUMCISED

Any *u*. male who is not circumcised | Gen.17.14
the house of Israel is *u*. in heart | Jer.9.26
if a man who is *u*. keeps the . . . law | Rom.2.26
entrusted with the gospel to the *u*. | Gal.2.7

UNCIRCUMCISION

your circumcision becomes *u*. | Rom.2.25
neither circumcision . . . nor *u*. | 1 Cor.7.19
nor *u*., but a new creation | Gal.6.15
dead in . . . the *u*. of your flesh | Col.2.13

UNCLEAN

if any one touches an *u*. thing | Lev.5.2
Thus they became *u*. by their acts | Ps.106.39
I am a man of *u*. lips, and I dwell | Is.6.5
go out thence, touch no *u*. thing | Is.52.11
gave them authority over *u*. spirits | Mt.10.1
he commands even the *u*. spirits | Mk.1.27
not call any man common or *u*. | Acts 10.28
it is *u*. for . . . one who thinks it *u*. | Rom.14.14
be separate . . . and touch nothing *u*. | 2 Cor.6.17
nothing *u*. shall enter it | Rev.21.27

UNDERSTAND

thunder of his power who can *u*.? | Job 26.14

I have uttered what I did not *u.*   Job 42.3
Make me *u.* the way of thy precepts   Ps.119.27
I *u.* more than the aged, for I   Ps.119.100
Evil men do not *u.* justice   Pr.28.5
those who are wise shall *u.*   Dan.12.10
You shall indeed hear but never *u.*   Mt.13.14
they did not *u.* the saying   Mk.9.32
opened . . . minds to *u.* the scriptures   Lk.24.45
Why do you not *u.* what I say?   Jn.8.43
Do you *u.* what you are reading?   Acts 8.30
I do not *u.* my own actions   Rom.7.15
and *u.* all mysteries and all   1 Cor.13.2
By faith we *u.* that the world was   Heb.11.3
some things in them hard to *u.*   2 Pet.3.16

UNDERSTANDING (noun)
But I have *u.* as well as you   Job 12.3
Through thy precepts I get *u.*   Ps.119.104
his *u.* is beyond measure   Ps.147.5
from his mouth come knowledge and *u.*   Pr.2.6
He who is slow to anger has great *u.*   Pr.14.29
A ruler who lacks *u.* is a cruel   Pr.28.16
The shepherds also have no *u.*   Is.56.11
hidden . . . from the wise and *u.*   Lk.10.21
they are darkened in their *u.*   Eph.4.18
peace of God, which passes all *u.*   Phil.4.7
all the riches of assured *u.*   Col.2.2
will grant you *u.* in everything   2 Tim.2.7
the Son of God . . . has given us *u.*   1 Jn.5.20

UNFAITHFUL
he was *u.* to the LORD in that he   1 Chr.10.13
If you are *u.,* I will scatter you   Neh.1.8
the master . . . put him with the *u.*   Lk.12.46
What if some were *u.?*   Rom.3.3
U. creatures! Do you not know that   Jas.4.4

UNFRUITFUL
choke the word, and it proves *u.*   Mk.4.19
my spirit prays but my mind is *u.*   1 Cor.14.14
Take no part in the *u.* works of   Eph.5.11
ineffective or *u.* in the knowledge   2 Pet.1.8

UNGODLINESS
to practice *u.,* to utter error   Is.32.6
against all *u.* and wickedness   Rom.1.18
lead people into more and more *u.*   2 Tim.2.16
deeds of *u.* which they have done   Jude 15

UNGODLY
God gives me up to the *u.*   Job 16.11
will scatter the bones of the *u.*   Ps.53.5
Both prophet and priest are *u.*   Jer.23.11
right time Christ died for the *u.*   Rom.5.6
the law is . . . for the *u.* and sinners   1 Tim.1.9
u. persons who pervert the grace of   Jude 4
things which *u.* sinners have spoken   Jude 15

UNHOLY
shall offer no *u.* incense thereon   Ex.30.9
offered *u.* fire before the LORD   Lev.10.1
they offered *u.* fire before the LORD   Num.3.4
law is . . . for the *u.* and profane   1 Tim.1.9
disobedient . . . ungrateful, *u.*   2 Tim.3.2

UNITE
u. my heart to fear thy name   Ps.86.11
if we have been *u.* with him in   Rom.6.5
But he who is *u.* to the Lord   1 Cor.6.17
to *u.* all things in him, things in   Eph.1.10

UNITY
good . . . when brothers dwell in *u.*   Ps.133.1

eager to maintain the *u.* of the   Eph.4.3
have *u.* of spirit, sympathy, love   1 Pet.3.8

UNJUST
from deceitful and *u.* men deliver me   Ps.43.1
he who hates *u.* gain will prolong   Pr.28.16
every one is greedy for *u.* gain   Jer.6.13
sends rain on the just and on the *u.*   Mt.5.45
For God is not so *u.* as to overlook   Heb.6.10

UNLEAVENED
Seven days you shall eat *u.* bread   Ex.13.6
shall keep the feast of *u.* bread   Ex.23.15
on the first day of *U.* Bread   Mk.14.12
after the days of *U.* Bread   Acts 20.6
with the *u.* bread of sincerity   1 Cor.5.8

UNPUNISHED
an evil man will not go *u.*   Pr.11.21
A false witness will not go *u.*   Pr.19.9
hastens to be rich will not go *u.*   Pr.28.20
You shall not go *u.,* for I am   Jer.25.29
I will by no means leave you *u.*   Jer.46.28

UNRIGHTEOUS
and the *u.* man his thoughts   Is.55.7
by means of *u.* mammon   Lk.16.9
Hear what the *u.* judge says   Lk.18.6
The tongue is an *u.* world among   Jas.3.6
the righteous for the *u.*   1 Pet.3.18

UNRIGHTEOUSNESS
there is no *u.* in him   Ps.92.15
Woe . . . who builds his house by *u.*   Jer.22.13
but had pleasure in *u.*   2 Th.2.12
cleanse us from all *u.*   1 Jn.1.9

UNSEARCHABLE
the number of his years is *u.*   Job 36.26
his greatness is *u.*   Ps.145.3
his understanding is *u.*   Is.40.28
How *u.* are his judgments and how   Rom.11.33
to preach . . . the *u.* riches of Christ   Eph.3.8

UNSEEN
yet thy footprints were *u.*   Ps.77.19
the things that are *u.* are eternal   2 Cor.4.18
warned . . . concerning events as yet *u.*   Heb.11.7

UPHOLD
and *u.* me with a willing spirit   Ps.51.12
The LORD *u.* all who are falling   Ps.145.14
he *u.* the widow and the fatherless   Ps.146.9
Behold my servant, whom I *u.*   Is.42.1
On the contrary, we *u.* the law   Rom.3.31
u. the universe by his word of power   Heb.1.3

UPRIGHT
may the LORD be with the *u.*   2 Chr.19.11
Or where were the *u.* cut off?   Job 4.7
God, who saves the *u.* in heart   Ps.7.10
Good and *u.* is the LORD   Ps.25.8
For the word of the LORD is *u.*   Ps.33.4
joy for the *u.* in heart   Ps.97.11
Light . . . in the darkness for the *u.*   Ps.112.4
but the *u.* enjoy his favor   Pr.14.9
the prayer of the *u.* is his delight   Pr.15.8
I found, that God made man *u.*   Ec.7.29
an *u.* and God-fearing man   Acts 10.22
u., holy, and self-controlled   Tit.1.8

UR
    Gen.11.28; 15.7; 1 Chr.11.35; Neh.9.7

URIAH
    2 Sam.11.3,17; 12.10; 1 Kg.15.5; Mt.1.6

URIM

shall put the *U.* and the Thummim Ex.28.30
he put the *U.* and the Thummim Lev.8.8
judgment of the *U.* before the LORD Num.27.21
O LORD, God of Israel, give *U.* 1 Sam.14.41
a priest to consult *U.* and Thummim Ezra 2.63
a priest with *U.* and Thummim Neh.7.65

UTTERANCE

speak . . . as the Spirit gave them *u.* Acts 2.4
to another the *u.* of knowledge 1 Cor.12.8
that *u.* may be given me in opening Eph.6.19

UZ

(1) Gen.10.23; (2) Gen.36.28; (3) Job 1.1;
Jer.25.20; Lam.4.21

UZZIAH

2 Kg.15.13; 2 Chr.26.1; Is.1.1; 6.1; Am.1.1

VAIN

guiltless who takes his name in *v.* Ex.20.7
How long will you love *v.* words Ps.4.2
for *v.* is the help of man Ps.108.12
Men are all a *v.* hope Ps.116.11
It is in *v.* that you rise up early Ps.127.2
beauty is *v.*, but a woman who Pr.31.30
But I said, "I have labored in *v.* Is.49.4
the peoples imagine *v.* things Acts 4.25
turn from these *v.* things to Acts 14.15
in the Lord your labor is not in *v.* 1 Cor.15.58
did not run in *v.* or labor in *v.* Phil.2.16
this man's religion is *v.* Jas.1.26

VALIANT

only be *v.* for me and fight the 1 Sam.18.17
Be courageous and be *v.* 2 Sam.13.28
having an army of *v.* men of war 2 Chr.13.3
v. men in mixing strong drink Is.5.22

VALLEY

the *v.* of the shadow of death Ps.23.4
the *v.* deck themselves with grain Ps.65.13
As they go through the *v.* of Baca Ps.84.6
Every *v.* shall be lifted up Is.40.4
the *v.* shall perish, and the plain Jer.48.8
in the midst of the *v.* . . . of bones Ezek.37.1
multitudes, in the *v.* of decision Jl.3.14
Every *v.* shall be filled Lk.3.5

VALUE

on finding one pearl of great *v.* Mt.13.46
you are of more *v.* than many sparrows Lk.12.7
Of how much more *v.* are you than Lk.12.24
Or what is the *v.* of circumcision? Rom.3.1
godliness is of *v.* in every way 1 Tim.4.8

VANISH

for the heavens will *v.* like smoke Is.51.6
and he *v.* out of their sight Lk.24.31
growing old is ready to *v.* away Heb.8.13
the sky *v.* like a scroll that is Rev.6.14

VANITY

Turn my eyes from looking at *v.* Ps.119.37
v. of *v.*! All is *v.* Ec.1.2; 12.8
Everything before them is *v.* Ec.9.1
All that comes is *v.* Ec.11.8

VASHTI

Est.1.9; 2.1,17

VEGETATION

Let the earth put forth *v.* Gen.1.11
devoured all the *v.* in their land Ps.105.35
brings forth *v.* useful to those Heb.6.7

VEIL

shall make a *v.* of blue and purple Ex.26.31
Your *v.* also I will tear off Ezek.13.21
ought to have a *v.* on her head 1 Cor.11.10
a *v.* lies over their minds 2 Cor.3.15

VENGEANCE

v. shall be taken on him sevenfold Gen.4.15
V. is mine, and recompense Dt.32.35
thou God of *v.*, shine forth Ps.94.1
Behold, your God will come with *v.* Is.35.4
the day of *v.* of our God Is.61.2
this is the time of the LORD's *v.* Jer.51.6
for these are days of *v.* Lk.21.22
V. is mine, I will repay, says the Rom.12.19

VESSEL

them in pieces like a potter's *v.* Ps.2.9
I have become like a broken *v.* Ps.31.12
the *v.* he was making of clay Jer.18.4
like a *v.* for which no one cares Jer.48.38
lighting a lamp covers it with a *v.* Lk.8.16
to make . . . one *v.* for beauty and Rom.9.21
have this treasure in earthen *v.* 2 Cor.4.7
he will be a *v.* for noble use 2 Tim.2.21

VEXATION

Surely *v.* kills the fool Job 5.2
O that my *v.* were weighed Job 6.2
The *v.* of a fool is known at once Pr.12.16
For in much wisdom is much *v.* Ec.1.18
Remove *v.* from your mind Ec.11.10

VICTORY

Thy right hand is filled with *v.* Ps.48.10
and his holy arm have gotten him *v.* Ps.98.1
All . . . have seen the *v.* of our God Ps.98.3
but the *v.* belongs to the LORD Pr.21.31
then his own arm brought him *v.* Is.59.16
till he brings justice to *v.* Mt.12.20
Death is swallowed up in *v.* 1 Cor.15.54
O death, where is thy *v.*? 1 Cor.15.55
this is the *v.* that overcomes 1 Jn.5.4

VILE

do not do this *v.* thing Jg.19.23
make them like *v.* figs which are Jer.29.17
see the *v.* abominations that Ezek.8.9
disorder and every *v.* practice Jas.3.16

VINDICATE

V. me, O God, and defend my cause Ps.43.1
For the LORD will *v.* his people Ps.135.14
he who *v.* me is near Is.50.8
And will not God *v.* his elect Lk.18.7
v. in the Spirit, seen by angels 1 Tim.3.16

VINDICATION

Turn now, my *v.* is at stake Job 6.29
v. from the God of his salvation Ps.24.5
bring forth your *v.* as the light Ps.37.6
The LORD works *v.* and justice for Ps.103.6
her *v.* goes forth as brightness Is.62.1
The nations shall see your *v.* Is.62.2
The LORD has brought forth our *v.* Jer.51.10

VINE

a fruitful *v.* within your house Ps.128.3
every one . . . will eat of his own *v.* Is.36.16
Yet I planted you a choice *v.* Jer.2.21
it became a *v.*, and brought forth Ezek.17.6
every man under his *v.* and under Mic.4.4
not drink again of the fruit of the *v.* Mk.14.25
I am the *v.*, you are the branches Jn.15.5

VINEGAR

they gave me *v.* to drink	Ps.69.21
Like *v.* to the teeth, and smoke to	Pr.10.26
filling a sponge full of *v.*	Mk.15.36
a sponge full of the *v.* on hyssop	Jn.19.29

VINEYARD

possession of the *v.* of Naboth	1 Kg.21.15
shall plant *v.* and eat their fruit	Is.65.21
though they plant *v.*, they shall not	Zeph.1.13
to hire laborers for his *v.*	Mt.20.1
A man planted a *v.*, and set a hedge	Mk.12.1
Who plants a *v.* without eating any	1 Cor.9.7

VIOLENCE

my savior; thou savest me from *v.*	2 Sam.22.3
there is no *v.* in my hands	Job 16.17
didst deliver me from men of *v.*	Ps.18.48
From oppression and *v.* he redeems	Ps.72.14
A man of *v.* entices his neighbor	Pr.16.29
V. shall no more be heard in your	Is.60.18
do no wrong or *v.* to the alien	Jer.22.3
Put away *v.* and oppression	Ezek.45.9
For the *v.* done to your brother	Ob.10
Your rich men are full of *v.*	Mic.6.12
kingdom of heaven has suffered *v.*	Mt.11.12
great city be thrown down with *v.*	Rev.18.21

VIOLENT

I have avoided the ways of the *v.*	Ps.17.4
preserve me from *v.* men	Ps.140.1
the king laid *v.* hands upon some	Acts 12.1
not *v.* but gentle, not quarrelsome	1 Tim.3.3
a drunkard or *v.* or greedy for gain	Tit.1.7

VIPER

under their lips is the poison of *v.*	Ps.140.3
You brood of *v.*! how can you speak	Mt.12.34
you brood of *v.*, how are you to	Mt.23.33
a *v.* came out because of the heat	Acts 28.3

VIRGIN

If a man seduces a *v.* who is not	Ex.22.16
beautiful young *v.* to the harem	Est.2.3
how then could I look upon a *v.*?	Job 31.1
the *v.* daughter of my people is	Jer.14.17
Fallen, no more to rise, is the *v.*	Am.5.2
Behold, a *v.* shall conceive and	Mt.1.23
a *v.* betrothed to a man whose name	Lk.1.27

VISION

the LORD came to Abram in a *v.*	Gen.15.1
there was no frequent *v.*	1 Sam.3.1
thou dost . . . terrify me with *v.*	Job 7.14
chased away like a *v.* of the night	Job 20.8
speak in a *v.* to thy faithful one	Ps.89.19
The *v.* of Isaiah the son of Amoz	Is.1.1
prophets obtain no *v.* from the LORD	Lam.2.9
I saw in my *v.* by night, and behold	Dan.7.2
had understanding of the *v.*	Dan.10.1
The *v.* of Obadiah. Thus says the	Ob.1
The book of the *v.* of Nahum	Nah.1.1
commanded them, "Tell no one the *v.*	Mt.17.9
he had seen a *v.* in the temple	Lk.1.22
they had even seen a *v.* of angels	Lk.24.23
Lord said to him in a *v.*, "Ananias."	Acts 9.10
And a *v.* appeared to Paul	Acts 16.9
not disobedient to the heavenly *v.*	Acts 26.19
I will go on to *v.* and revelations	2 Cor.12.1
taking his stand on *v.*	Col.2.18

VISIT (verb)

I will *v.* their sin upon them	Ex.32.34

v. the iniquity of the fathers upon	Dt.5.9
Thou *v.* the earth and waterest it	Ps.65.9
the LORD will *v.* Tyre, and she will	Is.23.17
sick or in prison and *v.* thee?	Mt.25.39
he has *v.* and redeemed his people	Lk.1.68
return and *v.* the brethren in	Acts 15.36
I will *v.* you after passing through	1 Cor.16.5
I wanted to *v.* you on my way to	2 Cor.1.16
to *v.* orphans and widows in their	Jas.1.27

VOICE

The *v.* is Jacob's *v.*, but the	Gen.27.22
saw no form; there was only a *v.*	Dt.4.12
if you obey the *v.* of the LORD	Dt.15.5
after the fire a still small *v.*	1 Kg.19.12
there was silence, then . . . a *v.*	Job 4.16
God thunders wondrously with his *v.*	Job 37.5
their *v.* is not heard	Ps.19.3
Hear the *v.* of my supplication	Ps.28.2
The *v.* of the LORD flashes forth	Ps.29.7
he utters his *v.*, the earth melts	Ps.46.6
hearkening to the *v.* of his word	Ps.103.20
Give ear to my *v.*, when I call	Ps.141.1
one rises up at the *v.* of a bird	Ec.12.4
the *v.* of the turtledove is heard	S. of S.2.12
And I heard the *v.* of the Lord	Is.6.8
A *v.* cries: "In the wilderness	Is.40.3
He will not cry or lift up his *v.*	Is.42.2
lift up your *v.* like a trumpet	Is.58.1
A *v.* is heard in Ramah, lamentation	Jer.31.15
I heard the *v.* of one speaking	Ezek.1.28
lo, a *v.* from heaven, saying	Mt.3.17
Jesus cried with a loud *v.*	Mt.27.46
a *v.* came out of the cloud	Lk.9.35
will hear the *v.* of the Son of God	Jn.5.25
My sheep hear my *v.*	Jn.10.27
Then a *v.* came from heaven	Jn.12.28
hearing the *v.* but seeing no one	Acts 9.7
His *v.* then shook the earth	Heb.12.26
one hears my *v.* and opens the door	Rev.3.20
I heard a great *v.* from the throne	Rev.21.3

VOID

The earth was without form and *v.*	Gen.1.2
stretches out the north over the *v.*	Job 26.7
you have made *v.* the word of God	Mt.15.6
one dot of the law to become *v.*	Lk.16.17
faith is null and the promise is *v.*	Rom.4.14
so as to make the promise *v.*	Gal.3.17

VOMIT (noun)

a drunken man staggers in his *v.*	Is.19.14
For all tables are full of *v.*	Is.28.8
Moab shall wallow in his *v.*	Jer.48.26
The dog turns back to his own *v.*	2 Pet.2.22

VOMIT (verb)

the land *v.* out its inhabitants	Lev.18.25
be drunk and *v.*, fall and rise no	Jer.25.27
it *v.* out Jonah upon the dry land	Jon.2.10

VOW (noun)

the *v.* of a Nazirite, to separate	Num.6.2
Jephthah made a *v.* to the LORD	Jg.11.30
pay your *v.* to the Most High	Ps.50.14
to thee shall *v.* be performed	Ps.65.1
he cut his hair, for he had a *v.*	Acts 18.18

WAGE (noun)

w. of the righteous leads to life	Pr.10.16
the laborers and pay them their *w.*	Mt.20.8

and be content with your *w.* Lk.3.14
his *w.* are not reckoned as a gift Rom.4.4
For the *w.* of sin is death Rom.6.23
The laborer deserves his *w.* 1 Tim.5.18
Behold, the *w.* of the laborers who Jas.5.4

WAGE (verb)
that *w.* war against Jerusalem Zech.14.12
you may *w.* the good warfare 1 Tim.1.18
so you fight and *w.* war Jas.4.2
that *w.* war against your soul 1 Pet.2.11

WAIL
W., for the day of the LORD is near Is.13.6
W., you shepherds, and cry Jer.25.34
Cry and *w.*, son of man, for it is Ezek.21.12
and *w.*, all you drinkers of wine Jl.1.5
we *w.*, and you did not mourn Mt.11.17
the earth will *w.* on account of him Rev.1.7
kings . . . will weep and *w.* over her Rev.18.9

WAILING (noun)
the *w.* reaches to Beer-elim Is.15.8
For a sound of *w.* is heard Jer.9.19
in all vineyards there shall be *w.* Am.5.17
w. and loud lamentation, Rachel Mt.2.18

WAIT
I *w.* for thy salvation, O LORD Gen.49.18
W. for the LORD; be strong Ps.27.14
w. patiently for him; fret not Ps.37.7
The wicked lie in *w.* to destroy me Ps.119.95
I *w.* for the LORD, my soul *w.* Ps.130.5
w. for the LORD, and he will help Pr.20.22
but they who *w.* for the LORD shall Is.40.31
For the coastlands shall *w.* for me Is.60.9
LORD is good to those who *w.* for him Lam.3.25
will *w.* for the God of my salvation Mic.7.7
the creation *w.* with eager longing Rom.8.19
we *w.* for the hope of righteousness Gal.5.5
to *w.* for his Son from heaven 1 Th.1.10
God's patience *w.* in the days of 1 Pet.3.20
w. for the mercy of our Lord Jesus Jude 21

WALK
Enoch *w.* with God; and he was not Gen.5.24
w. before me, and be blameless Gen.17.1
keep my statutes and *w.* in them Lev.18.4
I will *w.* among you, and will be Lev.26.12
And if you will *w.* in my ways 1 Kg.3.14
Blessed is the man who *w.* not in Ps.1.1
though I *w.* through the valley of Ps.23.4
W. about Zion, go round about her Ps.48.12
from those who *w.* uprightly Ps.84.11
Though I *w.* in the midst of trouble Ps.138.7
do not *w.* in the way of evil men Pr.4.14
let us *w.* in the light of the LORD Is.2.5
The people who *w.* in darkness have Is.9.2
they shall *w.* and not faint Is.40.31
Do two *w.* together, unless they Am.3.3
and to *w.* humbly with your God? Mic.6.8
So Peter . . . *w.* on the water Mt.14.29
or to say, 'Rise and *w.*'? Lk.5.23
follows me will not *w.* in darkness Jn.8.12
W. while you have the light, lest Jn.12.35
for we *w.* by faith, not by sight 2 Cor.5.7
w. by the Spirit, and do not gratify Gal.5.16
w. in love, as Christ loved us Eph.5.2
if we *w.* in the light, as he is 1 Jn.1.7
By its light shall the nations *w.* Rev.21.24

WALL
waters being a *w.* to them on their Ex.14.22
the *w.* of the city will fall Jos.6.5
let us build the *w.* of Jerusalem Neh.2.17
Now when the *w.* had been built Neh.7.1
by my God I can leap over a *w.* Ps.18.29
Peace be within your *w.* Ps.122.7
Hezekiah turned his face to the *w.* Is.38.2
the dividing *w.* of hostility Eph.2.14
By faith the *w.* of Jericho fell Heb.11.30
the *w.* of the city had twelve Rev.21.14

WANDER
let me not *w.* from thy commandments Ps.119.10
Therefore the people *w.* like sheep Zech.10.2
Certain persons . . . have *w.* away 1 Tim.1.6
turn away . . . and *w.* into myths 2 Tim.4.4
if any one . . . *w.* from the truth Jas.5.19

WANTON
do not do this *w.* folly 2 Sam.13.12
But they had a *w.* craving Ps.106.14
she is *w.* and knows no shame Pr.9.13
Her prophets are *w.*, faithless men Zeph.3.4
when they grow *w.* against Christ 1 Tim.5.11
glorified herself and played the *w.* Rev.18.7

WAR (noun)
The LORD is a man of *w.* Ex.15.3
in the Book of the *W.* of the LORD Num.21.14
He trains my hands for *w.* Ps.18.34
though *w.* arise against me, yet I Ps.27.3
yet *w.* was in your heart Ps.55.21
but when I speak, they are for *w.* Ps.120.7
a time for *w.*, and a time for peace Ec.3.8
Wisdom is better than weapons of *w.* Ec.9.18
neither shall they learn *w.* any more Is.2.4
Prepare the nations for *w.* against Jer.51.28
to Sheol with their weapons of *w.* Ezek.32.27
neither shall they learn *w.* any more Mic.4.3
when you hear of *w.* and rumors of *w.* Mk.13.7
another law at *w.* with the law of Rom.7.23
your passions that are at *w.* Jas.4.1
that wage *w.* against your soul 1 Pet.2.11
Now *w.* arose in heaven, Michael and Rev.12.7
allowed to make *w.* on the saints Rev.13.7

WARFARE
cry to her that her *w.* is ended Is.40.2
weapons of our *w.* are not worldly 2 Cor.10.4
by them you may wage the good *w.* 1 Tim.1.18

WARN
I solemnly *w.* you this day that you Dt.8.19
didst *w.* them by thy Spirit Neh.9.30
But if you *w.* the wicked, and he Ezek.3.19
being *w.* in a dream not to return Mt.2.12
Who *w.* you to flee from the wrath Lk.3.7
But I will *w.* you whom to fear Lk.12.5
I *w.* you, as I *w.* you before Gal.5.21
I *w.* every one who hears the words Rev.22.18

WASH
let them *w.* their garments Ex.19.10
They shall *w.* their hands and their Ex.30.21
W. me thoroughly from my iniquity Ps.51.2
w. me, and I shall be whiter than Ps.51.7
W. yourselves; make yourselves clean Is.1.16
anoint your head and *w.* your face Mt.6.17
not eat unless they *w.* their hands Mk.7.3
began to *w.* the disciples' feet Jn.13.5
w. away your sins, calling on Acts 22.16

you were *w.*, you were sanctified 1 Cor.6.11
w. the feet of the saints 1 Tim.5.10
our bodies *w.* with pure water Heb.10.22
Blessed are those who *w.* their robes Rev.22.14

WASTE
the destruction that *w.* at noonday Ps.91.6
the LORD will lay *w.* the earth Is.24.1
earth and lo, it was *w.* and void Jer.4.23
made my flesh and my skin *w.* away Lam.3.4
indignant, saying, "Why this *w.?* Mt.26.8
But Saul laid *w.* the church Acts 8.3
In one hour she has been laid *w.* Rev.18.19

WATCH (noun)
whose eyes keep *w.* on the nations Ps.66.7
or as a *w.* in the night Ps.90.4
keep *w.* over the door of my lips Ps.141.3
keeping *w.* on the evil and the good Pr.15.3
keeping *w.* over their flock by night Lk.2.8

WATCH (verb)
The LORD *w.* between you and me Gen.31.49
love and faithfulness *w.* over him Ps.61.7
those who *w.* for my life consult Ps.71.10
Unless the LORD *w.* over the city Ps.127.1
so I will *w.* over them to build Jer.31.28
I will take my stand to *w.* Hab.2.1
W. therefore, for you know neither Mt.25.13
Could you not *w.* one hour? Mk.14.37
the scribes and the Pharisees *w.* him Lk.6.7

WATCHFUL
Be *w.*, stand firm in your faith 1 Cor.16.13
being *w.* in it with thanksgiving Col.4.2
Be sober, be *w.* 1 Pet.5.8

WATCHMAN
the *w.* stays awake in vain Ps.127.1
more than *w.* for the morning Ps.130.6
W., what of the night? *W.*, what of Is.21.11
His *w.* are blind, they are all Is.56.10
if the *w.* sees the sword coming Ezek.33.6

WATER (noun)
Unstable as *w.*, you shall not have Gen.49.4
how he made the *w.* of the Red Sea Dt.11.4
a tree planted by streams of *w.* Ps.1.3
I am poured out like *w.*, and all my Ps.22.14
He leads me beside still *w.* Ps.23.2
He opened the rock, and *w.* gushed Ps.105.41
Stolen *w.* is sweet, and bread eaten Pr.9.17
As in *w.* face answers to face, so Pr.27.19
Cast your bread upon the *w.* Ec.11.1
you will draw *w.* from the wells of Is.12.3
broken cisterns, that can hold no *w.* Jer.2.13
LORD, the fountain of living *w.* Jer.17.13
But let justice roll down like *w.* Am.5.24
gives . . . even a cup of cold *w.* Mt.10.42
he took *w.* and washed his hands Mt.27.24
he commands even wind and *w.* Lk.8.25
his finger in *w.* and cool my tongue Lk.16.24
tasted the *w.* now become wine Jn.2.9
unless one is born of *w.* and the Jn.3.5
Then he poured *w.* into a basin Jn.13.5
there came out blood and *w.* Jn.19.34
the washing of *w.* with the word Eph.5.26
No longer drink only *w.* 1 Tim.5.23
guide them to springs of living *w.* Rev.7.17
the river of the *w.* of life Rev.22.1

WAVE (noun)
shall your proud *w.* be stayed'? Job 38.11

all thy *w.* and thy billows have Ps.42.7
boat was being swamped by the *w.* Mt.8.24
rebuked the wind and the raging *w.* Lk.8.24
he who doubts is like a *w.* of the sea Jas.1.6

WAY
corrupted their *w.* upon the earth Gen.6.12
wilt prosper the *w.* which I go Gen.24.42
This God-his *w.* is perfect 2 Sam.22.31
I shall go the *w.* whence I shall not Job 16.22
But he knows the *w.* that I take Job 23.10
LORD knows the *w.* of the righteous Ps.1.6
Teach me thy *w.*, O LORD Ps.27.11
Commit your *w.* to the LORD Ps.37.5
that thy *w.* may be known upon earth Ps.67.2
Teach me thy *w.*, O LORD Ps.86.11
He made known his *w.* to Moses Ps.103.7
How can a . . . man keep his *w.* pure? Ps.119.9
lead me in the *w.* everlasting Ps.139.24
I walk in the *w.* of righteousness Pr.8.20
The *w.* of a fool is right in his Pr.12.15
Train up a child in the *w.* he should Pr.22.6
This is the *w.*, walk in it Is.30.21
let the wicked forsake his *w.* Is.55.7
Prepare the *w.* of the LORD, make his Mt.3.3
gate is wide and the *w.* is easy Mt.7.13
guide our feet into the *w.* of peace Lk.1.79
Make straight the *w.* of the Lord Jn.1.23
I am the *w.*, and the truth, and the Jn.14.6
the *w.* of God more accurately Acts 18.26
no little stir concerning the *W.* Acts 19.23
I persecuted this *W.* to the death Acts 22.4
the *w.* of peace they do not know Rom.3.17
and how inscrutable his *w.* Rom.11.33
will also provide the *w.* of escape 1 Cor.10.13
show you a . . . more excellent *w.* 1 Cor.12.31
Love does not insist on its own *w.* 1 Cor.13.5
new and living *w.* which he opened Heb.10.20
unstable in all his *w.* Jas.1.7
were ransomed from the futile *w.* 1 Pet.1.18
Just and true are thy *w.*, O King of Rev.15.3

WEAK
Leah's eyes were *w.*, but Rachel was Gen.29.17
you have strengthened the *w.* hands Job 4.3
He has pity on the *w.* and the needy Ps.72.13
all knees will be *w.* as water Ezek.21.7
spirit . . . is willing . . . flesh is *w.* Mk.14.38
toiling one must help the *w.* Acts 20.35
As for the man who is *w.* in faith Rom.14.1
God chose what is *w.* in the world 1 Cor.1.27
To the *w.* I became *w.*, that 1 Cor.9.22
when I am *w.*, then I am strong 2 Cor.12.10
help the *w.*, be patient with them 1 Th.5.14
and strengthen your *w.* knees Heb.12.12

WEAKNESS
the Spirit helps us in our *w.* Rom.8.26
the *w.* of God is stronger than men 1 Cor.1.25
It is sown in *w.*, it is raised 1 Cor.15.43
my power is made perfect in *w.* 2 Cor.12.9
unable to sympathize with our *w.* Heb.4.15

WEALTH
his *w.* will not endure Job 15.29
leave their *w.* to others Ps.49.10
W. and riches are in his house Ps.112.3
A rich man's *w.* is his strong city Pr.10.15
W. hastily gotten will dwindle Pr.13.11
W. brings many new friends Pr.19.4

God has given *w.* and possessions   Ec.5.19
the *w.* of the nations shall come to   Is.60.5
you have gotten *w.* for yourself   Ezek.28.4
put an end to the *w.* of Egypt   Ezek.30.10
and hurl her *w.* into the sea   Zech.9.4
power and *w.* and wisdom and might   Rev.5.12
ships at sea grew rich by her *w.*   Rev.18.19

WEAPON
every man with his *w.* in his hand   2 Kg.11.11
he goes out to meet the *w.*   Job 39.21
he has prepared his deadly *w.*   Ps.7.13
Wisdom is better than *w.* of war   Ec.9.18
You are my hammer and *w.* of war   Jer.51.20
with the *w.* of righteousness   2 Cor.6.7
the *w.* of our warfare are not   2 Cor.10.4

WEAR
Your clothing did not *w.* out upon you   Dt.8.4
will all *w.* out like a garment   Ps.102.26
the earth will *w.* out like a garment   Is.51.6
or 'What shall we *w.?*'   Mt.6.31
Jesus . . . *w.* the crown of thorns   Jn.19.5
I am suffering and *w.* fetters   2 Tim.2.9
to the one who *w.* the fine clothing   Jas.2.3

WEARY
I am *w.* with my moaning   Ps.6.6
as in a dry and *w.* land where no   Ps.63.1
lest he become *w.* of you and hate   Pr.25.17
that you *w.* my God also?   Is.7.13
shade of a great rock in a *w.* land   Is.32.2
Even youths shall faint and be *w.*   Is.40.30
let us not grow *w.* in well-doing   Gal.6.9
you may not grow *w.* or fainthearted   Heb.12.3

WEDDING
crowned him on the day of his *w.*   S.of S.3.11
The *w.* is ready, but those invited   Mt.22.8
a man who had no *w.* garment   Mt.22.11
Can the *w.* guests fast while the   Mk.2.19

WEEK
you shall observe the feast of *w.*   Ex.34.22
dawn of the first day of the *w.*   Mt.28.1
I fast twice a *w.,* I give tithes of all   Lk.18.12
But on the first day of the *w.*   Lk.24.1
that day, the first day of the *w.*   Jn.20.19
On the first day of the *w.*   Acts 20.7
On the first day of every *w.*   1 Cor.16.2

WEEP
a time to *w.,* and a time to laugh   Ec.3.4
For these things I *w.*   Lam.1.16
there men will *w.* and gnash their   Mt.8.12
Why do you make a tumult and *w.?*   Mk.5.39
do not *w.* for me, but *w.* for   Lk.23.28
w. with those who *w.*   Rom.12.15
you rich, *w.* and howl for the miseries   Jas.5.1
one of the elders said to me, "*W.* not   Rev.5.5

WEEPING (noun)
My face is red with *w.*   Job 16.16
the LORD has heard the sound of my *w.*   Ps.6.8
W. may tarry for the night, but joy   Ps.30.5
sound of *w.* and the cry of distress   Is.65.19
Take up *w.* and wailing for the   Jer.9.10

WEIGH
Let me be *w.* in a just balance   Job 31.6
w. like a burden too heavy for me   Ps.38.4
Anxiety in a man's heart *w.* him down   Pr.12.25
but the LORD *w.* the spirit   Pr.16.2
let the others *w.* what is said   1 Cor.14.29

WEIGHT
A full and just *w.* you shall have   Dt.25.15
but a just *w.* is his delight   Pr.11.1
food which you eat shall be by *w.*   Ezek.4.10
aloes, about a hundred pounds' *w.*   Jn.19.39
an eternal *w.* of glory   2 Cor.4.17
let us also lay aside every *w.*   Heb.12.1

WELCOME (verb)
Hezekiah *w.* them, and he showed   2 Kg.20.13
a stranger and you did not *w.* me   Mt.25.43
the Galileans *w.* him, having seen   Jn.4.45
they were *w.* by the church   Acts 15.4
W. one another, therefore, as Christ   Rom.15.7
he refuses . . . to *w.* the brethren   3 Jn.10

WELFARE
they asked each other of their *w.*   Ex.18.7
he sought the *w.* of his people   Est.10.3
delights in the *w.* of his servant   Ps.35.27
not pray for the *w.* of this people   Jer.14.11
seek the *w.* of the city where   Jer.29.7
be genuinely anxious for your *w.*   Phil.2.20

WELL (noun)
sang this song: "Spring up, O *w.*   Num.21.17
a *w.* of living water   S.of S.4.15
water from the *w.* of salvation   Is.12.3
or an ox that has fallen into a *w.*   Lk.14.5
Jacob's *w.* was there, and so Jesus   Jn.4.6

WEPT
Joseph *w.* when they spoke to him   Gen.50.17
You fasted and *w.* for the child   2 Sam.12.21
I sat down and *w.*   Neh.1.4
Babylon, there we sat down and *w.*   Ps.137.1
Peter . . . went out and *w.* bitterly   Mt.26.75
when he . . . saw the city he *w.* over it   Lk.19.41
Jesus *w.*   Jn.11.35
I *w.* much that no one was found   Rev.5.4

WHEAT
let thorns grow instead of *w.*   Job 31.40
feed you with the finest of the *w.*   Ps.81.16
gather his *w.* into the granary   Mt.3.12
enemy . . . sowed weeds among the *w.*   Mt.13.25
that he might sift you like *w.*   Lk.22.31
a grain of *w.* falls into the earth   Jn.12.24

WHEEL
or the *w.* broken at the cistern   Ec.12.6
as it were a *w.* within a *w.*   Ezek.1.16
the *w.* were full of eyes round   Ezek.10.12
rumble of *w.,* galloping horse   Nah.3.2

WHIRLWIND
Elijah went up by a *w.* into heaven   2 Kg.2.11
the LORD answered Job out of the *w.*   Job 40.6
your calamity comes like a *w.*   Pr.1.27
they shall reap the *w.*   Hos.8.7

WHITE
I shall be *w.* than snow   Ps.51.7
they shall be as *w.* as snow   Is.1.18
cannot make one hair *w.* or black   Mt.5.36
a young man . . . dressed in a *w.* robe   Mk.16.5
his raiment became dazzling *w.*   Lk.9.29
she saw two angels in *w.*   Jn.20.12
two men stood by them in *w.* robes   Acts 1.10
hair . . . *w.* as *w.* wool, *w.* as snow   Rev.1.14
a great multitude . . . clothed in *w.* robes   Rev.7.9
Then I saw a great *w.* throne   Rev.20.11

WHOLE
may his glory fill the *w.* earth   Ps.72.19

thanks to the LORD with my *w*. heart	Ps.111.1	If a *w*. has children or	1 Tim.5.4
for this is the *w*. duty of man	Ec.12.13	She who is a real *w*., and is left	1 Tim.5.5
The *w*. head is sick, and the *w*. heart	Is.1.5	orphans and *w*. in their affliction	Jas.1.27

WICKED / **WIFE** — continued below.

thanks to the LORD with my *w*. heart — Ps.111.1
for this is the *w*. duty of man — Ec.12.13
The *w*. head is sick, and the *w*. heart — Is.1.5
the *w*. earth is full of his glory — Is.6.3
your *w*. body will be full of light — Mt.6.22
it was restored, *w*. like the other — Mt.12.13
to gain the *w*. world and forfeit — Mk.8.36
gospel is preached in the *w*. world — Mk.14.9
the *w*. creation has been groaning — Rom.8.22
he is bound to keep the *w*. law — Gal.5.3
Put on the *w*. armor of God — Eph.6.11
the Head, from whom the *w*. body — Col.2.19
also for the sins of the *w*. world — 1 Jn.2.2

WICKED
Yea, the light of the *w*. is put out — Job 18.5
walks not in the counsel of the *w*. — Ps.1.1
On the *w*. he will rain coals of fire — Ps.11.6
Many are the pangs of the *w*. — Ps.32.10
how long shall the *w*. exult? — Ps.94.3
The *w*. have laid a snare for me — Ps.119.110
see if there be any *w*. way in me — Ps.139.24
but the name of the *w*. will rot — Pr.10.7
house of the *w*. will be destroyed — Pr.14.11
The soul of the *w*. desires evil — Pr.21.10
be not envious of the *w*. — Pr.24.19
The *w*. flee when no one pursues — Pr.28.1
they made his grave with the *w*. — Is.53.9
let the *w*. forsake his way, and the — Is.55.7
no peace, says my God, for the *w*. — Is.57.21
Why does the way of the *w*. prosper? — Jer.12.1
no pleasure in the death of the *w*. — Ezek.33.11
the *w*. turns from his wickedness — Ezek.33.19
You *w*. and slothful servant — Mt.25.26
Drive out the *w*. person from — 1 Cor.5.13

WICKEDLY
I have sinned, and I have done *w*. — 2 Sam.24.17
we . . . have acted perversely and *w*. — 1 Kg.8.47
Of a truth, God will not do *w*. — Job 34.12
committed iniquity, we have done *w*. — Ps.106.6
we have sinned, we have done *w*. — Dan.9.15

WICKEDNESS
LORD saw that the *w*. of man was great — Gen.6.5
Out of the wicked comes forth *w*. — 1 Sam.24.13
let not *w*. dwell in your tents — Job 11.14
thou art not a God who delights in *w*. — Ps.5.4
you love righteousness and hate *w*. — Ps.45.7
w. is an abomination to my lips — Pr.8.7
A man is not established by *w*. — Pr.12.3
Jerusalem, wash your heart from *w*. — Jer.4.14
when the wicked turns from his *w*. — Ezek.33.19
who devise *w*. and work evil upon — Mic.2.1
because *w*. is multiplied, most men's — Mt.24.12
coveting, *w*., deceit, licentiousness — Mk.7.22
you are full of extortion and *w*. — Lk.11.39
were filled with all manner of *w*. — Rom.1.29
hosts of *w*. in the heavenly places — Eph.6.12
put away all . . . rank growth of *w*. — Jas.1.21

WIDOW
I caused the *w*. heart to sing for — Job 29.13
he upholds the *w*. and the fatherless — Ps.146.9
How like a *w*. has she become — Lam.1.1
devour *w*. houses and for a pretense — Mk.12.40
a poor *w*. came, and put in two — Mk.12.42
as a *w*. till she was eighty-four — Lk.2.37
there was a *w*. in that city who — Lk.18.3
because their *w*. were neglected in — Acts 6.1

WIFE
a man leaves . . . and cleaves to his *w*. — Gen.2.24
And Abram took Sarai his *w*. — Gen.12.5
shall not covet your neighbor's *w*. — Ex.20.17
When the *w*. of Uriah heard that — 2 Sam.11.26
Then his *w*. said to him, "Do you — Job 2.9
rejoice in the *w*. of your youth — Pr.5.18
good *w*. is the crown of her husband — Pr.12.4
He who finds a *w*. finds a good — Pr.18.22
a prudent *w*. is from the LORD — Pr.19.14
A good *w*. who can find? — Pr.31.10
does not defile his neighbor's *w*. — Ezek.18.15
Go, take to yourself a *w*. of harlotry — Hos.1.2
do not fear to take Mary your *w*. — Mt.1.20
Whoever divorces his *w*., let him give — Mt.5.31
to which of the seven will she be *w*.? — Mt.22.28
Whoever divorces his *w*. and marries — Mk.10.11
your *w*. Elizabeth will bear you — Lk.1.13
Remember Lot's *w*. — Lk.17.32
a man is living with his father's *w*. — 1 Cor.5.1
husband should not divorce his *w*. — 1 Cor.7.11
is consecrated through his *w*. — 1 Cor.7.14
the husband is the head of the *w*. — Eph.5.23
W., be subject to your husbands, as — Col.3.18
take a *w*. for himself in holiness — 1 Th.4.4
live considerately with your *w*. — 1 Pet.3.7
the Bride, the *w*. of the Lamb — Rev.21.9

WILD
say that a *w*. beast has devoured — Gen.37.20
but it yielded *w*. grapes — Is.5.2
Go, assemble all the *w*. beasts — Jer.12.9
Even the *w*. beasts cry to thee — Jl.1.20
Now John . . . ate locusts and *w*. honey — Mk.1.6
you, a *w*. olive . . . were grafted in — Rom.11.17
w. waves of the sea, casting up — Jude 13

WILDERNESS
may hold a feast to me in the *w*. — Ex.5.1
they came into the *w*. of Sinai — Ex.19.1
shall let the goat go in the *w*. — Lev.16.22
have led you forty years in the *w*. — Dt.29.5
The voice of the LORD shakes the *w*. — Ps.29.8
Can God spread a table in the *w*.? — Ps.78.19
guided them in the *w*. like a flock — Ps.78.52
who led his people through the *w*. — Ps.136.16
In the *w*. prepare the way of the — Is.40.3
I will cast you forth into the *w*. — Ezek.29.5
It was I who knew you in the *w*. — Hos.13.5
did you go out into the *w*. to behold? — Mt.11.7
John the baptizer appeared in the *w*. — Mk.1.4
The voice of one crying in the *w*. — Lk.3.4
for forty days in the *w*., tempted by — Lk.4.2
leave the ninety-nine in the *w*. — Lk.15.4
lifted up the serpent in the *w*. — Jn.3.14
Our fathers ate the manna in the *w*. — Jn.6.31
they were overthrown in the *w*. — 1 Cor.10.5
on the day of testing in the *w*. — Heb.3.8

WILES
have harassed you with their *w*. — Num.25.18
their craftiness in deceitful *w*. — Eph.4.14
stand against the *w*. of the devil — Eph.6.11

WILL (noun)
I delight to do thy *w*., O my God — Ps.40.8

Teach me to do thy *w*., for thou	Ps.143.10	These also reel with *w*. and stagger	Is.28.7
Thy *w*. be done, On earth as it is in	Mt.6.10	Come, buy *w*. and milk without money	Is.55.1
but he who does the *w*. of my Father	Mt.7.21	I have trodden the *w*. press alone	Is.63.3
it is not the *w*. of my Father who	Mt.18.14	they answered, "We will drink no *w*.	Jer.35.6
Whoever does the *w*. of God is my	Mk.3.35	No priest shall drink *w*.	Ezek.44.21
Jesus he delivered up to their *w*.	Lk.23.25	They drank *w*., and praised the gods	Dan.5.4
nor of the *w*. of the flesh nor	Jn.1.13	wail, all you drinkers of *w*.	Jl.1.5
not my own *w*. but the *w*. of him who	Jn.5.30	Moreover, *w*. is treacherous	Hab.2.5
if any man's *w*. is to do his *w*., he	Jn.7.17	Neither is new *w*. put into old	Mt.9.17
The *w*. of the Lord be done	Acts 21.14	offered him *w*. mingled with myrrh	Mk.15.23
For who can resist his *w*.?	Rom.9.19	his wounds, pouring on oil and *w*.	Lk.10.34
according to the *w*. of our God	Gal.1.4	tasted the water now become *w*.	Jn.2.9
according to the counsel of his *w*.	Eph.1.11	They are filled with new *w*.	Acts 2.13
filled with the knowledge of his *w*.	Col.1.9	And do not get drunk with *w*.	Eph.5.18
Lo, I have come to do thy *w*.	Heb.10.7	not addicted to much *w*.	1 Tim.3.8
Of his own *w*. he brought us forth	Jas.1.18	use a little *w*. for the sake of	1 Tim.5.23
he who does the *w*. of God abides	1 Jn.2.17	shall drink the *w*. of God's wrath	Rev.14.10

WILLING

uphold me with a *w*. spirit	Ps.51.12		

WINGS

If you are *w*. and obedient, you	Is.1.19	under whose *w*. you have come to	Ru.2.12
spirit indeed is *w*., but the flesh	Mt.26.41	hide me in the shadow of thy *w*.	Ps.17.8
if thou art *w*., remove this cup	Lk.22.42	I say, "O that I had *w*. like a dove	Ps.55.6
not as an exaction but as a *w*. gift	2 Cor.9.5	safe under the shelter of thy *w*.	Ps.61.4

WILLOWS

the *w*. of the brook surround him	Job 40.22	under his *w*. you will find refuge	Ps.91.4
On the *w*. there we hung up our lyres	Ps.137.2	If I take the *w*. of the morning	Ps.139.9

WIND

		each had six *w*.: with two he covered	Is.6.2
God made a *w*. blow over the earth	Gen.8.1	each creature had two *w*.	Ezek.1.11
back by a strong east *w*. all night	Ex.14.21	shall rise, with healing in its *w*.	Mal.4.2
went forth a *w*. from the LORD	Num.11.31	hen gathers her brood under her *w*.	Lk.13.34
like chaff which the *w*. drives away	Ps.1.4	the noise of their *w*. was like the	Rev.9.9

WINNOW

w. passes over it, and it is gone	Ps.103.16	You shall *w*. them and the wind	Is.41.16
who ridest on the wings of the *w*.	Ps.104.3	I have *w*. them with a . . . fork	Jer.15.7
stormy *w*. fulfilling his command	Ps.148.8	gathering where you did not *w*.	Mt.25.24
has gathered the *w*. in his fists?	Pr.30.4	His *w*. fork is in his hand, to clear	Lk.3.17
was vanity and a striving after *w*.	Ec.2.11		

WINTER

He who observes the *w*. will not sow	Ec.11.4	thou hast made summer and *w*.	Ps.74.17
God appointed a sultry east *w*.	Jon.4.8	the *w*. is past, the rain is over	S.of S.2.11
the *w*. blew and beat upon that house	Mt.7.25	Pray that it may not happen in *w*.	Mk.13.18
A reed shaken by the *w*.?	Mt.11.7	it was *w*., and Jesus was walking in	Jn.10.23
And he awoke and rebuked the *w*.	Mk.4.39	harbor was not suitable to *w*. in	Acts 27.12
he commands even *w*. and water	Lk.8.25	Do your best to come before *w*.	2 Tim.4.21
The *w*. blows where it wills, and you	Jn.3.8		

WIPE

like the rush of a mighty *w*.	Acts 2.2	*w*. Jerusalem as one *w*. a dish	2 Kg.21.13
carried . . . with every *w*. of doctrine	Eph.4.14	the LORD our God will *w*. them out	Ps.94.23
he says, "Who makes his angels *w*.	Heb.1.7	Lord GOD will *w*. away tears from	Is.25.8
is driven and tossed by the *w*.	Jas.1.6	Mary . . . *w*. his feet with her hair	Jn.11.2

WINDOW

		to *w*. them with the towel	Jn.13.5
Noah opened the *w*. of the ark	Gen.8.6	God will *w*. away every tear	Rev.7.17
let David down through the *w*.	1 Sam.19.12		

WISDOM

that look through the *w*. are dimmed	Ec.12.3	so that Solomon's *w*. surpassed	1 Kg.4.30
I will . . . open the *w*. of heaven	Mal.3.10	And the LORD gave Solomon *w*.	1 Kg.5.12
Eutychus was sitting in the *w*.	Acts 20.9	W. is with the aged	Job 12.12
basket through a *w*. in the wall	2 Cor.11.33	With God are *w*. and might	Job 12.13

WINE

		But where shall *w*. be found?	Job 28.12
he drank of the *w*., and became	Gen.9.21	the price of *w*. is above pearls	Job 28.18
let us make our father drink *w*.	Gen.19.32	teach me *w*. in my secret heart	Ps.51.6
Drink no *w*. nor strong drink	Lev.10.9	In *w*. hast thou made them all	Ps.104.24
beware, and drink no *w*. or	Jg.13.4	For the LORD gives *w*.	Pr.2.6
hast given us *w*. to drink that	Ps.60.3	The beginning of *w*. is this: Get *w*.	Pr.4.7
w. to gladden the heart of man	Ps.104.15	for *w*. is better than jewels	Pr.8.11
W. is a mocker, strong drink a	Pr.20.1	of the LORD is the beginning of *w*.	Pr.9.10
Those who tarry long over *w*.	Pr.23.30	W. is . . . life to him who has it	Pr.16.22
Do not look at *w*. when it is red	Pr.23.31	For in much *w*. is much vexation	Ec.1.18
who are heroes at drinking *w*.	Is.5.22	W. is better than weapons of war	Ec.9.18
		the spirit of *w*. and understanding	Is.11.2

established the world by his *w.*   Jer.51.15
full of *w.* and perfect in beauty   Ezek.28.12
he gives *w.* to the wise   Dan.2.21
Yet *w.* is justified by her deeds   Mt.11.19
What is the *w.* given to him?   Mk.6.2
Jesus increased in *w.* and in stature   Lk.2.52
Therefore also the *W.* of God said   Lk.11.49
for I will give you a mouth and *w.*   Lk.21.15
I will destroy the *w.* of the wise   1 Cor.1.19
demand signs and Greeks seek *w.*   1 Cor.1.22
For the *w.* of this world is folly   1 Cor.3.19
teaching every man in all *w.*   Col.1.28
If any of you lacks *w.*, let him ask   Jas.1.5
But the *w.* from above is first pure   Jas.3.17
glory and *w.* and thanksgiving   Rev.7.12

WISE
was to be desired to make one *w.*   Gen.3.6
It is not the old that are *w.*   Job 32.9
is sure, making *w.* the simple   Ps.19.7
Whoever is *w.*, let him give heed   Ps.107.43
Be not *w.* in your own eyes   Pr.3.7
reprove a *w.* man, and he will love   Pr.9.8
A *w.* son makes a glad father   Pr.10.1
the fool will be servant to the *w.*   Pr.11.29
The *w.* man's path leads upward to   Pr.15.24
who keeps silent is considered *w.*   Pr.17.28
A *w.* man is mightier than a strong   Pr.24.5
lest he be *w.* in his own eyes   Pr.26.5
I said, "I will be *w.*"   Ec.7.23
The sayings of the *w.* are like goads   Ec.12.11
wisdom of their *w.* men shall perish   Is.29.14
Then all the king's *w.* men came in   Dan.5.8
w. men from the East came to Jerusalem Mt.2.1
so be *w.* as serpents and innocent   Mt.10.16
hast hidden these things from the *w.*   Mt.11.25
five were foolish, and five were *w.*   Mt.25.2
both to the *w.* and to the foolish   Rom.1.14
Lest you be *w.* in your own conceits   Rom.11.25
foolishness of God is *w.* than men   1 Cor.1.25
the thoughts of the *w.* are futile   1 Cor.3.20
Who is *w.* and understanding among   Jas.3.13

WISH (verb)
So whatever you *w.* that men would   Mt.7.12
Sir, we *w.* to see Jesus   Jn.12.21
could *w.* that I myself were accursed   Rom.9.3
I *w.* those who unsettle you would   Gal.5.12
Therefore whoever *w.* to be a friend   Jas.4.4
not *w.* that any should perish   2 Pet.3.9

WITHER
its leaf does not *w.*   Ps.1.3
O Jerusalem, let my right hand *w.*   Ps.137.5
The grass *w.*, the flower fades   Is.40.7
since they had no root they *w.* away   Mt.13.6
a man was there who had a *w.* hand   Mk.3.1
the fig tree *w.* away to its roots   Mk.11.20
grass *w.*, and the flower falls   1 Pet.1.24

WITHHOLD
you may not *w.* your help   Dt.22.3
Do not . . . *w.* thy mercy from me   Ps.40.11
Do not *w.* good from those to whom   Pr.3.27
Do not *w.* discipline from a child   Pr.23.13
do not *w.* your coat as well   Lk.6.29

WITHSTAND
could no longer *w.* their enemies   Jg.2.14
so that none is able to *w.* thee   2 Chr.20.6

But they could not *w.* the wisdom   Acts 6.10
who was I that I could *w.* God?   Acts 11.17
may be able to *w.* in the evil day   Eph.6.13

WITNESS (noun)
This heap is a *w.* between you and   Gen.31.48
not bear false *w.* against your   Ex.20.16
only on the evidence of two *w.*   Dt.19.15
A truthful *w.* saves lives   Pr.14.25
A false *w.* will not go unpunished   Pr.19.9
who bears false *w.* against his   Pr.25.18
I made him a *w.* to the peoples   Is.55.4
You shall not bear false *w.*   Mt.19.18
For many bore false *w.* against him   Mk.14.56
to bear *w.* to the light   Jn.1.7
Father who sent me bears *w.* to me   Jn.8.18
you shall be my *w.* in Jerusalem   Acts 1.8
from the dead. To this we are *w.*   Acts 3.15
the *w.* laid down their garments   Acts 7.58
did not leave himself without *w.*   Acts 14.17
blood of Stephen thy *w.* was shed   Acts 22.20
For God is my *w.*, whom I serve with   Rom.1.9
my conscience bears me *w.*   Rom.9.1
For God is my *w.*, how I yearn for   Phil.1.8
Holy Spirit also bears *w.* to us   Heb.10.15
surrounded by so great a cloud of *w.*   Heb.12.1
There are three *w.*, the Spirit   1 Jn.5.8

WOE
If I am wicked, *w.* to me   Job 10.15
Who has *w.*? Who has sorrow?   Pr.23.29
W. to those who rise early in the   Is.5.11
And I said: "*W.* is me! For I am lost   Is.6.5
W. to the shepherds who destroy   Jer.23.1
W. to the foolish prophets who   Ezek.13.3
W. to you, Chorazin! *W.* to you   Mt.11.21
W. to the world for temptations   Mt.18.7
W. to you, scribes and Pharisees   Mt.23.15
w. to that man by whom the Son of   Mk.14.21
w. to you that are rich   Lk.6.24
W. to you, when all men speak well   Lk.6.26
W. to me if I do not preach the   1 Cor.9.16
W., *w.*, *w.* to those who dwell on   Rev.8.13

WOLF
The *w.* shall dwell with the lamb   Is.11.6
but inwardly are ravenous *w.*   Mt.7.15
out as lambs the *w.* in the midst of *w.* Lk.10.3
sees the *w.* coming and leaves the   Jn.10.12
fierce *w.* will come in among you   Acts 20.29

WOMAN
the rib . . . he made into a *w.*   Gen.2.22
The *w.* said, "The serpent beguiled   Gen.3.13
men say of me, 'A *w.* killed him.'   Jg.9.54
Man . . . born of a *w.* is of few days   Job 14.1
the lips of a loose *w.* drip honey   Pr.5.3
A foolish *w.* is noisy; she is wanton   Pr.9.13
a house shared with a contentious *w.*   Pr.21.9
a *w.* who fears the LORD is . . . praised Pr.31.30
a young *w.* shall conceive and bear   Is.7.14
one who looks at a *w.* lustfully has   Mt.5.28
instantly the *w.* was made well   Mt.9.22
O *w.*, great is your faith   Mt.15.28
Two *w.* will be grinding at the mill   Mt.24.41
a *w.* came with an alabaster jar of   Mk.14.3
a *w.* named Martha received him   Lk.10.38
leaven which a *w.* took and hid in   Lk.13.21
whose wife will the *w.* be?   Lk.20.33

There came a *w*. of Samaria to draw   Jn.4.7
he said ..."*W*., behold, your son!"   Jn.19.26
the devout *w*. of high standing   Acts 13.50
the head of a *w*. is her husband   1 Cor.11.3
but *w*. is the glory of man   1 Cor.11.7
these *w*. are two covenants   Gal.4.24
Let a *w*. learn in silence   1 Tim.2.11
a *w*. clothed with the sun   Rev.12.1
and I saw a *w*. sitting on a scarlet   Rev.17.3

WOMB
to her, "Two nations are in your *w*.   Gen.25.23
Naked I came from my mother's *w*.   Job 1.21
From whose *w*. did the ice come   Job 38.29
he who took me from my mother's *w*.   Ps.71.6
From the *w*. of the morning like dew   Ps.110.3
The LORD called me from the *w*.   Is.49.1
Before I formed you in the *w*. I knew   Jer.1.5
blessed is the fruit of your *w*.   Lk.1.42
Blessed is the *w*. that bore you   Lk.11.27
into his mother's *w*. and be born?   Jn.3.4

WONDER (verb)
w. and be astounded. For I am doing   Hab.1.5
Pilate *w*. if he were already dead   Mk.15.44
they *w*. at his delay in the temple   Lk.1.21
w. at the gracious words which   Lk.4.22
why do you *w*. at this, or why do   Acts 3.12
Do not *w*. . . . that the world hates   1 Jn.3.13

WONDERFUL
Why . . . ask my name, seeing it is *w*.?   Jg.13.18
I have uttered things too *w*. for me   Job 42.3
Remember the *w*. works that he has   Ps.105.5
his *w*. works to the sons of men   Ps.107.15
Such knowledge is too *w*. for me   Ps.139.6
for thou art fearful and *w*.   Ps.139.14
Three things are too *w*. for me   Pr.30.18
his name will be called "*W*. Counselor   Is.9.6
what *w*. stones and what *w*. buildings   Mk.13.1
Great and *w*. are thy deeds, O Lord   Rev.15.3

WONDERS
did all these *w*. before Pharaoh   Ex.11.10
the LORD showed signs and *w*.   Dt.6.22
mindful of the *w*. which thou didst   Neh.9.17
Thou art the God who workest *w*.   Ps.77.14
Let the heavens praise thy *w*.   Ps.89.5
to him who alone does great *w*.   Ps.136.4
he works signs and *w*. in heaven   Dan.6.27
will arise and show signs and *w*.   Mk.13.22
Unless you see signs and *w*. you will   Jn.4.48
many *w*. and signs were done   Acts 2.43
signs and *w*. and mighty works   2 Cor.12.12
by signs and *w*. and various miracles   Heb.2.4

WONDROUS
consider the *w*. works of God   Job 37.14
telling all thy *w*. deeds   Ps.26.7
thou art great and doest *w*. things   Ps.86.10
I may behold *w*. things out of thy   Ps.119.18
I will meditate on thy *w*. works   Ps.119.27

WOOL
a fleece of *w*. on the threshing floor   Jg.6.37
He gives snow like *w*.   Ps.147.16
the hair of his head like pure *w*.   Dan.7.9
white as white *w*., white as snow   Rev.1.14

WORD
the *w*. of the LORD came to him   Gen.15.4
the LORD put a *w*. in Balaam's   Num.23.5

Let the *w*. of my mouth and the   Ps.19.14
By the *w*. of the LORD the heavens   Ps.33.6
he sent forth his *w*., and healed   Ps.107.20
I have laid up thy *w*. in my heart   Ps.119.11
Thy *w*. is a lamp to my feet   Ps.119.105
Even before a *w*. is on my tongue   Ps.139.4
but a harsh *w*. stirs up anger   Pr.15.1
a *w*. in season, how good it is   Pr.15.23
A *w*. fitly spoken is like apples of   Pr.25.11
Every *w*. of God proves true   Pr.30.5
The *w*. which Isaiah the son of Amoz   Is.2.1
but the *w*. of our God will stand   Is.40.8
so shall my *w*. be that goes forth   Is.55.11
Now the *w*. of the LORD came to me   Jer.1.4
but by every *w*. that proceeds from   Mt.4.4
for every careless *w*. they utter   Mt.12.36
the delight in riches choke the *w*.   Mt.13.22
thus making void the *w*. of God   Mk.7.13
The seed is the *w*. of God   Lk.8.11
is ashamed of me and of my *w*.   Lk.9.26
all the people hung upon his *w*.   Lk.19.48
but my *w*. will not pass away   Lk.21.33
In the beginning was the *W*.   Jn.1.1
And the *W*. became flesh and dwelt   Jn.1.14
You have the *w*. of eternal life   Jn.6.68
If you continue in my *w*.   Jn.8.31
a man loves me, he will keep my *w*.   Jn.14.23
thy *w*. is truth   Jn.17.17
And the *w*. of God increased   Acts 6.7
the *w*. of God grew and multiplied   Acts 12.24
received the *w*. with all eagerness   Acts 17.11
the *w*. of the cross is folly to   1 Cor.1.18
Let the *w*. of Christ dwell in you   Col.3.16
in every good work and *w*.   2 Th.2.17
But the *w*. of God is not fettered   2 Tim.2.9
the *w*. of God is living and active   Heb.4.12
world was created by the *w*. of God   Heb.11.3
be doers of the *w*., and not hearers   Jas.1.22
the *w*. of the Lord abides for ever   1 Pet.1.25
the prophetic *w*. made more sure   2 Pet.1.19
let us not love in *w*. or speech but   1 Jn.3.18
he is called . . . The *W*. of God   Rev.19.13

WORK (noun)
God finished his *w*. which he had   Gen.2.2
Let heavier *w*. be laid upon the men   Ex.5.9
shall labor, and do all your *w*.   Ex.20.9
Thus all the *w*. that Solomon did   2 Chr.5.1
this *w*. goes on diligently   Ezra 5.8
the *w*. of thy fingers, the moon and   Ps.8.3
establish thou the *w*. of our hands   Ps.90.17
the heavens are the *w*. of thy hands   Ps.102.25
Commit your *w*. to the LORD, and your   Pr.16.3
that a man should enjoy his *w*.   Ec.3.22
then I saw all the *w*. of God   Ec.8.17
bow down to the *w*. of their hands   Is.2.8
he could do no mighty *w*. there   Mk.6.5
does a mighty *w*. in my name will   Mk.9.39
This is the *w*. of God, that you   Jn.6.29
We must work the *w*. of him who sent   Jn.9.4
The *w*. that I do in my Father's name   Jn.10.25
greater *w*. than these will he do   Jn.14.12
by faith apart from *w*. of law   Rom.3.28
cast off the *w*. of darkness   Rom.13.12
If any man's *w*. is burned up   1 Cor.3.15
But let each one test his own *w*.   Gal.6.4

for the *w.* of ministry	Eph. 4.12	**WORLDLY**	
he who began a good *w.* in you will	Phil.1.6	wise according to *w.* standards	1 Cor.1.26
do the *w.* of an evangelist	2 Tim.4.5	but *w.* grief produces death	2 Cor.7.10
faith apart from *w.* is barren?	Jas.2.20	we are not carrying on a *w.* war	2 Cor.10.3
so faith apart from *w.* is dead	Jas.2.26	renounce irreligion and *w.* passions	Tit.2.12
was to destroy the *w.* of the devil	1 Jn.3.8	*w.* people, devoid of the Spirit	Jude 19
do the *w.* you did at first	Rev.2.5	**WORM**	
WORK (verb)		it bred *w.* and became foul	Ex.16.20
deliver me from those who *w.* evil	Ps.59.2	if I say . . . to the *w.*, 'My mother	Job 17.14
I *w.* and who can hinder it?	Is.43.13	But I am a *w.*, and no man	Ps.22.6
night comes, when no one can *w.*	Jn.9.4	God appointed a *w.* which attacked	Jon.4.7
to one who does not *w.* but trusts	Rom.4.5	where their *w.* does not die	Mk.9.48
in everything God *w.* for good	Rom.8.28	he was eaten by *w.* and died	Acts 12.23
Do all *w.* miracles?	1 Cor.12.29	**WORMWOOD**	
w. out your own salvation	Phil.2.12	but in the end she is bitter as *w.*	Pr.5.4
w. heartily, as serving the Lord	Col.3.23	I will feed this people with *w.*	Jer.9.15
command: If any one will not *w.*	2 Th.3.10	O you who turn justice to *w.*	Am.5.7
WORKER		The name of the star is *W.*	Rev.8.11
Depart from me, all you *w.* of evil	Ps.6.8	A third of the waters became *w.*	Rev.8.11
those who are *w.* of evil	Ps.28.3	**WORSHIP** (verb)	
What gain has the *w.* from his toil?	Ec.3.9	you shall *w.* no other god	Ex.34.14
Timothy, my fellow *w.*, greets you	Rom.16.21	that I may *w.* the LORD your God	1 Sam.15.30
fellow *w.* in your service	2 Cor.8.23	I will *w.* toward thy holy temple	Ps.5.7
fellow *w.* and fellow soldier	Phil.2.25	O come, let us *w.* and bow down	Ps.95.6
Demas, and Luke, my fellow *w.*	Philem.24	let us *w.* at his footstool	Ps.132.7
that we may be fellow *w.* in the truth	3 Jn.8	Egyptians will *w.* with the Assyrians	Is.19.23
WORKMAN		enter these gates to *w.* the LORD	Jer.7.2
I was beside him, like a master *w.*	Pr.8.30	fall down and *w.* the golden image	Dan.3.10
with the *w.* of like occupation	Acts 19.25	we . . . have come to *w.* him	Mt.2.2
For we are fellow *w.* for God	1 Cor.3.9	if you will fall down and *w.* me	Mt.4.9
such men are . . . deceitful *w.*	2 Cor.11.13	in vain do they *w.* me, teaching as	Mk.7.7
w. who has no need to be ashamed	2 Tim.2.15	You shall *w.* the Lord your God	Lk.4.8
WORLD		will *w.* the Father in spirit	Jn.4.23
he judges the *w.* with righteousness	Ps.9.8	fell down at his feet and *w.* him	Acts 10.25
the *w.* and those who dwell therein	Ps.24.1	what therefore you *w.* as unknown	Acts 17.23
hadst formed the earth and the *w.*	Ps.90.2	*w.* him who made heaven and earth	Rev.14.7
judge the *w.* with righteousness	Ps.96.13	*W.* God. For the testimony of	Rev.19.10
established the *w.* by his wisdom	Jer.10.12	**WORTHLESS**	
You are the light of the *w.*	Mt.5.14	Now the sons of Eli were *w.* men	1 Sam.2.12
the field is the *w.*, and the good	Mt.13.38	A *w.* man plots evil, and his speech	Pr.16.27
gain the whole *w.* and forfeit his	Mk.8.36	A *w.* witness mocks at justice	Pr.19.28
the *w.* was made through him	Jn.1.10	They are *w.*, a work of delusion	Jer.51.18
God so loved the *w.* that he gave his	Jn.3.16	Woe to my *w.* shepherd, who deserts	Zech.11.17
is indeed the Savior of the *w.*	Jn.4.42	cast the *w.* servant into the outer	Mt.25.30
saying, "I am the light of the *w.*	Jn.8.12	it is *w.* and near to being cursed	Heb.6.8
Now is the judgment of this *w.*	Jn.12.31	**WORTHY**	
not as the *w.* gives do I give to	Jn.14.27	I am not *w.* of the least of all	Gen.32.10
In the *w.* you have tribulation	Jn.16.33	the LORD, who is *w.* to be praised	Ps.18.3
My kingship is not of this *w.*	Jn.18.36	whose sandals I am not *w.* to carry	Mt.3.11
have turned the *w.* upside down	Acts 17.6	if the house is *w.*, let your peace	Mt.10.13
sin came into the *w.* through one	Rom.5.12	for I am not *w.* to have you come	Lk.7.6
made foolish the wisdom of the *w.*?	1 Cor.1.20	whose sandal I am not *w.* to untie	Jn.1.27
wisdom of this *w.* is folly with God	1 Cor.3.19	deeds *w.* of their repentance	Acts 26.20
the saints will judge the *w.*?	1 Cor.6.2	lead a life *w.* of the calling	Eph.4.1
the god of this *w.* has blinded	2 Cor.4.4	let your . . . life be *w.* of the gospel	Phil.1.27
no hope and without God in the *w.*	Eph.2.12	if there is anything *w.* of praise	Phil.4.8
you shine as lights in the *w.*	Phil.2.15	lead a life *w.* of God, who calls you	1 Th.2.12
came into the *w.* to save sinners	1 Tim.1.15	God may make you *w.* of his call	2 Th.1.11
we brought nothing into the *w.*	1 Tim.6.7	of whom the world was not *w.*	Heb.11.38
of whom the *w.* was not worthy	Heb.11.38	*W.* art thou, our Lord and God, to	Rev.4.11
keep oneself unstained from the *w.*	Jas.1.27	*W.* is the Lamb who was slain, to	Rev.5.12
Do not love the *w.* or the things	1 Jn.2.15	**WOUND** (noun)	
the *w.* passes away, and the lust	1 Jn.2.17	Who has *w.* without cause?	Pr.23.29
God sent his only Son into the *w.*	1 Jn.4.9	like vinegar on a *w.*	Pr.25.20
kingdom of the *w.* has become the	Rev.11.15	Faithful are the *w.* of a friend	Pr.27.6

healed the *w*. of my people lightly Jer.8.11
Why is . . . my *w*. incurable, refusing Jer.15.18
her *w*. is incurable; and it has Mic.1.9
By his *w*. you have been healed 1 Pet.2.24
WOUND (verb)
I *w*. and I heal; and there is none Dt.32.39
But he was *w*. for our transgressions Is.53.5
they *w*. him in the head Mk.12.4
by means of them they *w*. Rev.9.19
WRAP
Mount Sinai was *w*. in smoke Ex.19.18
too narrow to *w*. oneself in it Is.28.20
Thou hast *w*. thyself with anger Lam.3.43
w. him in the linen shroud Mk.15.46
find a babe *w*. in swaddling cloths Lk.2.12
WRATH
my *w*. will burn, and I will kill you Ex.22.24
why does thy *w*. burn hot against Ex.32.11
w. has gone forth from the LORD Num.16.46
you provoked the LORD to *w*. Dt.9.22
w. fell upon all the congregation Jos.22.20
great is the *w*. of the LORD 2 Kg.22.13
my *w*. will be poured out 2 Chr.34.25
He has kindled his *w*. against me Job 19.11
My *w*. is kindled against you Job 42.7
Then he will speak to them in his *w*. Ps.2.5
nor chasten me in thy *w*. Ps.38.1
the *w*. of men shall praise thee Ps.76.10
all our days pass away under thy *w*. Ps.90.9
A soft answer turns away *w*. Pr.15.1
A man of *w*. stirs up strife Pr.29.22
the bowl of my *w*. you shall drink Is.51.22
for in my *w*. I smote you Is.60.10
Pour out thy *w*. upon the nations Jer.10.25
will soon pour out my *w*. upon you Ezek.7.8
I will pour out my *w*. like water Hos.5.10
His *w*. is poured out like fire Nah.1.6
in *w*. remember mercy Hab.3.2
to flee from the *w*. to come? Mt.3.7
the *w*. of God rests upon him Jn.3.36
For the *w*. of God is revealed from Rom.1.18
For the law brings *w*. Rom.4.15
if God, desiring to show his *w*. Rom.9.22
we were by nature children of *w*. Eph.2.3
delivers us from the *w*. to come 1 Th.1.10
For God has not destined us for *w*. 1 Th.5.9
hide us . . . from the *w*. of the Lamb Rev.6.16
the seven bowls of the *w*. of God Rev.16.1
WRATHFUL
nor go with a *w*. man Pr.22.24
upon them with *w*. chastisements Ezek.25.17
the LORD is avenging and *w*. Nah.1.2
WRETCHED
W. man that I am! Who will deliver Rom.7.24
Be *w*. and mourn and weep Jas.4.9
not knowing that you are *w*. Rev.3.17
WRITE
W. this as a memorial in a book Ex.17.14
LORD said to Moses, "*W*. these words Ex.34.27
W. each man's name upon his rod Num.17.2
I will *w*. on the tables the words Dt.10.2
Now therefore *w*. this song Dt.31.19
we make a firm covenant and *w*. it Neh.9.38
w. them on the tablet of your heart Pr.7.3
W. in a book all the words that I Jer.30.2

I will *w*. it upon their hearts Jer.31.33
take a stick and *w*. on it Ezek.37.16
the LORD answered me: "*W*. the vision Hab.2.2
Do not *w*., 'The King of the Jews' Jn.19.21
I, Paul, *w*. this greeting with my Col.4.18
it is the way I *w*. 2 Th.3.17
I had much to *w*. to you, but I would 3 Jn.13
saying, "*W*. what you see in a book Rev.1.11
W. this: Blessed are those who are Rev.19.9
WRITINGS
But if you do not believe his *w*. Jn.5.47
through the prophetic *w*. is made Rom.16.26
with the sacred *w*. which are able 2 Tim.3.15
WRONG (noun)
Is there any *w*. on my tongue? Job 6.30
had declared Job to be in the *w*. Job 32.3
who also do no *w*., but walk in his Ps.119.3
I hate robbery and *w*. Is.61.8
no *w*. was found on his lips Mal.2.6
but this man has done nothing *w*. Lk.23.41
We find nothing *w*. in this man Acts 23.9
But if you do *w*., be afraid Rom.13.4
it does not rejoice at *w*. 1 Cor.13.6
suffering *w*. for their wrongdoing 2 Pet.2.13
WRONGDOER
be not envious of *w*. Ps.37.1
If then I am a *w*., and have Acts 25.11
to execute thy wrath on the *w*. Rom.13.4
the *w*. will be paid back for Col.3.25
or a *w*., or a mischief-maker 1 Pet.4.15
WRONGDOING
but an avenger of their *w*. Ps.99.8
say what *w*. they found when I Acts 24.20
who loved gain from *w*. 2 Pet.2.15
All *w*. is sin, but there is sin 1 Jn.5.17
WROUGHT
Jacob and Israel, 'What has God *w*.!' Num.23.23
the LORD has *w*. deliverance in 1 Sam.11.13
he has *w*. desolations in the earth Ps.46.8
I muse on what thy hands have *w*. Ps.143.5
thou hast *w*. for us all our works Is.26.12
mighty works are *w*. by his hands Mk.6.2
his deeds have been *w*. in God Jn.3.21
what Christ has *w*. through me Rom.15.18

YEAR
three times in the *y*. shall all Ex.23.17
atonement upon its horns once a *y*. Ex.30.10
a lamb a *y*. old for a burnt offering Lev.12.6
you shall hallow the fiftieth *y*. Lev.25.10
bought it until the *y*. of jubilee Lev.25.28
As a servant hired *y*. by *y*. shall Lev.25.53
at the time appointed every *y*. Est.9.27
rejoice among the days of the *y*. Job 3.6
crownest the *y*. with thy bounty Ps.65.11
For a thousand *y*. in thy sight are Ps.90.4
The *y*. of our life are threescore Ps.90.10
the *y*. draw nigh, when you will Ec.12.1
In the *y*. that King Uzziah died Is.6.1
to proclaim the *y*. of the LORD's Is.61.2
my *y*. of redemption has come Is.63.4
offerings, with calves a *y*. old? Mic.6.6
go up *y*. after *y*. to worship Zech.14.16
the acceptable *y*. of the Lord Lk.4.19
priest goes, and he but once a *y*. Heb.9.7

continually offered *y.* after *y.*	Heb.10.1	ZACCHAEUS	
spend a *y.* there and trade	Jas.4.13	Lk.19.2,5,8	
and a thousand *y.* as one day	2 Pet.3.8	ZEAL	
and bound him for a thousand *y.*	Rev.20.2	The *z.* of the LORD will do this	2 Kg.19.31

YES

what you say be simply '*Y.*' or 'No'	Mt.5.37	*z.* for thy house has consumed me	Ps.69.9
ready to say *Y.* and No at once?	2 Cor.1.17	*Z.* for thy house will consume me	Jn.2.17
promises of God find their *Y.*	2 Cor.1.20	they have a *z.* for God, but	Rom.10.2
but let your *y.* be *y.* and your no	Jas.5.12	Never flag in *z.*, be aglow with	Rom.12.11

YESTERDAY

		as to *z.* a persecutor of the church	Phil.3.6
we are but of *y.*, and know nothing	Job 8.9	ZEALOUS	
are but as *y.* when it is past	Ps.90.4	they are all *z.* for the law	Acts 21.20
Y. at the seventh hour the fever	Jn.4.52	being *z.* for God as you all are	Acts 22.3
the same *y.* and today and for ever	Heb.13.8	so extremely *z.* was I for the	Gal.1.14

YIELD

		who are *z.* for good deeds	Tit.2.14
but *y.* yourselves to the LORD	2 Chr.30.8	if you are *z.* for what is right?	1 Pet.3.13
The earth has *y.* its increase	Ps.67.6	the more *z.* to confirm your call	2 Pet.1.10
our land will *y.* its increase	Ps.85.12	be *z.* to be . . . without spot	2 Pet.3.14
a loud voice and *y.* up his spirit	Mt.27.50	so be *z.* and repent	Rev.3.19
Do not *y.* your members to sin	Rom.6.13	ZEBEDEE	
y. your members to righteousness	Rom.6.19	Mt.4.21; 20.20; Mk.1.20; Jn.21.2	
later it *y.* the peaceful fruit of	Heb.12.11	ZECHARIAH	
No more can salt water *y.* fresh	Jas.3.12	(1) king of Israel; begins to reign, 2 Kg.14.29;	
y. its fruit each month	Rev.22.2	killed by Shallum, who succeeds him, 2	

YOKE

		Kg.15.10; (2) father of Abi, Hezekiah's
Your father made our *y.* heavy	1 Kg.12.4	mother, 2 Kg.18.2; (3) prophet, Zech.1.1; (4)
you made your *y.* exceedingly heavy	Is.47.6	father of John the Baptist, Lk.1.5; is promised
I break the *y.* of Nebuchadnezzar	Jer.28.11	a son, Lk.1.13; doubting, is stricken with dumb-
that he bear the *y.* in his youth	Lam.3.27	ness, Lk.1.22; his recovery and song, Lk.1.64,
but I will put Ephraim to the *y.*	Hos.10.11	68–79; (5) others, 2 Chr.26.5; Ezra 8.16; Neh.
Take my *y.* upon you, and learn from	Mt.11.29	11.12; Is.8.2
For my *y.* is easy, and my burden is	Mt.11.30	ZEDEKIAH
I have bought five *y.* of oxen	Lk.14.19	(1) false prophet, 1 Kg.22.11; 2 Chr.18.10,23;
by putting a *y.* upon the neck of	Acts 15.10	(2) another, Jer.29.22; (3) (Mattaniah), king
not submit again to a *y.* of slavery	Gal.5.1	of Judah, 2 Kg.24.17; 25; 2 Chr.36.10–11;

YOUNG

		Jer.37–39; 52
I am *y.* in years, and you are aged	Job 32.6	ZEPHANIAH
The *y.* lions suffer want and hunger	Ps.34.10	(1) priest, 2 Kg.25.18; Jer.29.25; 37.3; (2)
I have been *y.*, and now am old	Ps.37.25	prophet, Zeph.1–3; (3) others, 1 Chr.6.36;
How can a *y.* man keep his way pure?	Ps.119.9	Zech. 6.10, 14
Rejoice, O *y.* man, in your youth	Ec.11.9	ZERUBBABEL
Behold, a *y.* woman shall conceive	Is.7.14	prince of Judah, Ezra 2.2; restores the worship
their *y.* shall lie down together	Is.11.7	of God, Ezra 3.2; Neh.12.47; Hag.1.1,14;
Spare not her *y.* men	Jer.51.3	2.2; Zech.4.6
y. men and maidens, little children	Ezek.9.6	ZION

Does a *y.* lion cry out from his den	Am.3.4	David took the stronghold of *Z.*	2 Sam.5.7
The *y.* man said . . . "All these I	Mt.19.20	the city of David, which is *Z.*	2 Chr.5.2
Y. man, I say to you, arise	Lk.7.14	let Mount *Z.* be glad! Let the	Ps.48.11
at the feet of a *y.* man named Saul	Acts 7.58	Walk about *Z.*, go round about her	Ps.48.12
a *y.* man named Eutychus was	Acts 20.9	Do good to *Z.* in thy good pleasure	Ps.51.18
so train the *y.* women to love	Tit.2.4	in whose heart are the highways to *Z.*	Ps.84.5
y. men, because you are strong	1 Jn.2.14	The LORD is great in *Z.*	Ps.99.2

YOUTH

		For the LORD will build up *Z.*	Ps.102.16
man's heart is evil from his *y.*	Gen.8.21	May all who hate *Z.* be put to shame	Ps.129.5
a man of war from his *y.*	1 Sam.17.33	For the LORD has chosen *Z.*	Ps.132.13
have revered the LORD from my *y.*	1 Kg.18.12	and wept, when we remembered *Z.*	Ps.137.1
Remember not the sins of my *y.*	Ps.25.7	Sing us one of the songs of *Z.*	Ps.137.3
O God, from my *y.* thou hast taught	Ps.71.17	let the sons of *Z.* rejoice in their	Ps.149.2
so that your *y.* is renewed like	Ps.103.5	For out of *Z.* shall go forth the law	Is.2.3
your Creator in . . . your *y.*	Ec.12.1	I am laying in *Z.* for a foundation	Is.28.16
Even *y.* shall faint and be weary	Is.40.30	For the LORD will comfort *Z.*	Is.51.3
that he bear the yoke in his *y.*	Lam. 3.27	and come to *Z.* with singing	Is.51.11
these I have observed from my *y.*	Mk.10.20	awake, put on your strength, O *Z.*	Is.52.1
My manner of life from my *y.*	Acts 26.4	sound of wailing is heard from *Z.*	Jer.9.19
Let no one despise your *y.*	1 Tim.4.12	for Mount *Z.* which lies desolate	Lam.5.18
		the LORD roars from *Z.*, and utters	Jl.3.16

Woe to those who are at ease in Z.	Am.6.1	I am laying in Z. a stone that	Rom.9.33
I am jealous for Z. with great	Zech.8.2	The Deliverer will come from Z.	Rom.11.26
I will brandish your sons, O Z.	Zech.9.13	come to Mount Z. and to the city	Heb.12.22
Tell the daughter of Z., Behold	Mt.21.5	Behold, I am laying in Z. a stone	1 Pet.2.6
Fear not, daughter of Z.	Jn.12.15	on Mount Z. stood the Lamb	Rev.14.1